ANNUAL REVIEW OF SOCIOLOGY

ANNUAL REVIEW OF SOCIOLOGY

VOLUME 16, 1990

W. RICHARD SCOTT, *Editor*
Stanford University

JUDITH BLAKE, *Associate Editor*
University of California, Los Angeles

ANNUAL REVIEWS INC.   4139 EL CAMINO WAY, P.O. BOX 10139,   PALO ALTO, CALIFORNIA 94303-0897

ANNUAL REVIEWS INC.
Palo Alto, California, USA

International Standard Serial Number: 0360–0572
International Standard Book Number: 0–8243–2216-9
Library of Congress Catalog Card Number: 75-648500

⊗   The paper used in this publication meets the minimum requirements of American National Standard for Information Sciences—Permanence of Paper for Printed
Library Materials, ANSI Z39.48-1984.

Typesetting by Kachina Typesetting Inc., Tempe, Arizona; John Olson, President
Typesetting Coordinator, Janis Hoffman

PRINTED AND BOUND IN THE UNITED STATES OF AMERICA

Annual Review of Sociology
Volume 16, 1990

CONTENTS

vi   CONTENTS   (*continued*)

RELATED ARTICLES FROM OTHER *ANNUAL REVIEWS*

From the *Annual Review of Anthropology,* Volume 19 (1990)

Recent Advances in Evolutionary Culture Theory, *W. H. Durham*
Women's Voices: Their Critique of the Anthropology of Japan, *M. Tamanoi*
Functional Analysis in Anthropology and Sociology, *S. N. Eisenstadt*
History, Structure, and Ritual, *J. D. Kelly and M. Kaplan*

From the *Annual Review of Psychology,* Volume 41 (1990)

Invariants of Human Behavior, *H. A. Simon*
Social and Personality Development, *W. A. Collins and M. Gunnar*
Social and Community Intervention, *K. Heller*
Attitudes and Attitude Change, *A. Tesser and D. Shaffer*
Progress in Small Group Research, *J. M. Levine and R. L. Moreland*

From the *Annual Review of Public Health,* Volume 11 (1990)

Geographic Access to Physician Services, *J. P. Newhouse*
Measurement of Health Status in the 1990s, *D. L. Patrick and M. Bergner*

Matilda White Riley

Annu. Rev. Sociol. 1990. 16:1–25

THE INFLUENCE OF SOCIOLOGICAL LIVES: PERSONAL REFLECTIONS

Matilda White Riley

National Institute on Aging, National Institutes of Health Building 31C, Room 5C32, Bethesda, Maryland 20892

KEY WORDS: influence, lives, age, gender, dynamic systems, sociological practice

Abstract

In contrast to the well-established influence of social change on sociological lives, the author develops a theory of the influence exerted *by* the lives and experiences of sociologists on social and intellectual structure and change, both in sociology and in society as a whole. Writing in a semi-autobiographical vein, she uses as examples of this influence fragments from her earlier writings in four areas of current sociological concern: sociological practice, gender, age, and dynamic social systems. These fragments are interwoven with anecdotal accounts of experiences from the lives of well-known sociologists and the author herself, spanning much of the twentieth century. While giving a flavor of her own contributions and also several thwarted attempts, these reflections illustrate how the degree of sociological influence depends on the mesh between the attributes of particular lives and the opportunities afforded at the time by the state of the discipline and of society. Several types of historical structures and changes are identified as either facilitating or hindering the flow of influence, including trends in sociological thought and methods of research, ideologies and values paramount in the discipline, and social and cultural changes in society as a whole.

1

For the future, the question raised is how, in a rapidly changing world, to identify channels for exercising influence on sociology as well as on public policy and professional practice. The concluding hope is that other sociologists may be sensitized to a self-conscious awareness of the special opportunities for influence available in the unique historical era in which their lives unfold.

INTRODUCTION

In the summer of 1949, while my husband and two children were setting up camp in Grand Teton National Park, I sat on a huge boulder writing a grant application. My proposal was to describe and show the relevance for sociology of numerous research designs developed during my years of directing research at the Market Research Company of America. Encouraged by our Chicago colleagues, Clyde Hart and Everett and Helen Hughes, the proposal was designed to influence sociological work by making available from my own life experience examples of the use of methods that were new at that time (as in cross-section surveys, intensive interviewing and observation, panel studies, probability sampling, and small group interactions).

That proposal failed. Yet analysis of the failure is instructive here for exploring the topic of this essay: *the influence exerted through the lives of sociologists on sociology and on society*. The experience illustrates some of the major obstacles that block channels of influence at particular periods of history: in this instance, the difficulties of securing funding (that application was for $5000, a modest sum even in those days); the paucity of vehicles for communicating potentially useful research approaches; the marginal level of sociological interest in methodological advances; and the consequent lag in influence as many of these approaches became the stuff of sociological research only many years later, if at all.

Now, 40 years later, this time on the shores of Maine's Casco Bay, I look back on the implications of this and other personal experiences for the concept under consideration here: the influence of sociological lives. My reminiscences are prompted by the incipient development of such a concept in the introductory "Notes" (1988a) to *Sociological Lives* (Riley 1988b). Those "Notes" examined the experiences of the eight sociologists contributing to that volume. Their essays, though only indirectly focused on the topic, nevertheless suggest numerous ways in which the influence of their lives as sociologists was felt by the discipline. From just these few life histories it becomes clear that the degree of sociological influence depends on the mesh between the attributes of particular lives and the concurrent opportunities afforded by the state of the discipline and of society. That introductory chapter concluded with these thoughts:

Collectively, the essays begin to show how sociologists living at particular moments in history have been influencing social policies, practices, and the shape of social structures; and how they have been influencing the development of sociology, its content and goals, and its intellectual and organizational arrangements. Perhaps the concept of "the influence of sociological lives," like the concept of "sociological autobiography,"[1] may enhance our understanding of the interplay between social structures and human [in this instance sociological] lives. (p. 40)

Intrigued by the potential of such a concept, I want now to pursue it further by adding to the experiences reported in *Sociological Lives* a few experiences and fragmentary writings from my own life and the lives of close associates. My emphasis throughout is not on the well-established influence of social and intellectual structures *on* sociological lives. Rather, the focus is in the other direction of the interplay: on the influence exerted *by* the lives and experiences of sociologists on social and intellectual structure and change in sociology and in society as a whole. The concern with lives in historical context is distinct from evaluation of particular ideas, exegesis of particular works, or particular continuities in social research.

This attempt to learn more from my own life about how influence operates begins with some clues from *Sociological Lives* and then reviews fragments from my earlier writings and associated experiences in four areas of current sociological concern: sociological practice, gender, age, and dynamic social systems. The essay ends with the thought that other sociologists might be sensitized by a self-conscious awareness of the special significance of the unique historical era in which their lives unfold.

AFTERTHOUGHTS ON *SOCIOLOGICAL LIVES*

What, then, is this concept of the influence of sociological lives? Quite inadvertently, the autobiographical essays in *Sociological Lives*[2] raise important questions about how structural changes evolve from the experiences of successive cohorts of individual sociologists, and most particularly from the lives and work of individuals who reach positions of leadership at particular moments in history. For example, how does it happen that the intellectual growth of William Julius Wilson is a powerfully active force in influencing both sociological thought and public policy—rather than merely a passive reflection of structural change and academic controversy? About other sociologists, whether born earlier or later than he, such general questions are

---

[1]As in the opening chapter by Robert K. Merton of the volume on *Sociological Lives*.

[2]*Sociological Lives*, to which frequent reference is made here, is the companion volume to *Social Structures and Human Lives* in the Presidential Series of the American Sociological Association (ASA).

raised as: How does sociological influence operate? What "channels of influence" open or close as social and intellectual structures change? What can block the channels, and how are barriers removed? What attributes of lives serve as sources of influence under particular historical conditions? In short, how do lives of sociologists in successive cohorts mesh with the changing channels of opportunity?

Partial answers to these questions are suggested by the essayists, who represent cohorts from four decades of this century (their birth dates range from 1909 to 1947) and who thus confronted widely differing historical structures and exigencies. Among these answers, *sociotemporal location* emerges as a central force, affecting both the lives of sociologists as sources of influence and the channels that provide access to influence. On the one hand, whether or not a sociologist's work can spark enthusiastic response depends on the historical context. On the other hand, whether or not the intellectual and social climate is open for positive response also depends on the historical context. Over the course of history, the succession of cohorts provides the linkages between the influencer and the influenced, between sociological lives and changes in the discipline and in society.

Sources of Influence

Several essays illustrate how sociologists living under particular sociotemporal conditions can exert influence: through the focus or style of their work, the nature of their experiences, or according to such attributes as gender or race. For example, Rosabeth Kanter, referring to the stormy 1960s, describes the mesh between phases of discontinuity in her unfolding individual career and the changing society; thus she points to changes in her own life encouraging her to seize timely opportunities for influence. Tad Blalock complains that, with few exceptions during the 1950s and 1960s, his mathematical modelling as a form of theorizing was entirely foreign to his sociological contemporaries; thus his work was ahead of its time, producing a lag in its impact on the discipline. By contrast, Bernice Neugarten's career was precisely "on time" for influencing studies in human development at the University of Chicago, though here again there has been a lag in widespread sociological recognition.

Other essays illustrate how influence is affected by such attributes of sociological lives as gender or race, depending upon the attitudes prevalent at the time. Thus, Alice Rossi describes how, during the 1950s, sex discrimination and antinepotism rules greatly reduced the educational and occupational openings for academic women in her cohort—forcing many to lower aspirations of ever becoming influentials, or even to withdraw from the labor force into fulltime motherhood. (Only much later, following the women's movements, did the topic of gender become central to sociological thinking, thus opening channels of influence.) The essays tell little about the undoubtedly significant implications for influence of differing statuses in the world of sociology, because all these authors are similarly active and visible in the field. Nor do the essays provide many clues to the importance of location in the age structure, since none of the authors have yet completed their life course. (Left for future analysts are questions of how age affects the potential for influence of sociologists born recently—like Bill Wilson or Theda Skocpol—or even those, like Bernice Neugarten or myself, who were born much earlier.)

Opportunities and Obstacles

While individual sociologists in successive cohorts are pursuing their careers, the historical milieu is changing, and with it the channels through which their influence may be felt. My "Notes on Influence" suggest various ways in which the opportunities and obstacles encountered at particular moments in a person's life reflect the coexisting exigencies in the discipline and in society:

> Whether or not channels of influence are accessible during the lifetimes of particular sociologists seems to depend on broad social and intellectual trends and structural changes. Changes affecting the flow of influence include those in the state of the art and the organization of research; in the effectiveness of communication; and, perhaps most important, in the goals and interests of the discipline. In sociology, some of these goals and interests seem to derive from trends in thought; others from emergence of immediate social problems, disruptions, or controversies; and still others from ideologies and values paramount at the time. Sometimes adherence to vested ideas and concerns produces outright resistance to new influences. Sometimes influences from sociology diffuse outward to other disciplines or to policies and practices. Moreover, channels blocked at one time may be opened at a later time, producing a "lag" in the cumulation of scientific work (Riley 1988-a:36).

As a starting point, then, for further conceptual exploration here, at least five types of historical structures and changes can operate either to facilitate or to hinder the flow of influence: (a) social and cultural changes in the society as a whole; and trends in (b) sociological thought, (c) methods of sociological research, (d) the organization of sociological research, and (e) ideologies and values related to the discipline. My personal exploration relates to the conjunction between particular efforts in my lifetime and such types of period-specific opportunities or barriers to influence at those particular times. Dates are essential for linking lives to history (especially when only a single cohort—rather than the (preferable) succession of cohorts—is available for identifying the linkages).

To broaden the base beyond my own cohort, I draw freely on the work of the essayists in *Sociological Lives,* of other sociologists whose experiences touch upon my own, and of my significant collaborators and colleagues. In particular, my own recollections cannot be separated from those of my husband, Jack (properly, John W. Riley, Jr.). Our joint lives have been intertwined for nearly 60 years of marriage and colleagueship. As he and I often say, our collaboration as sociologists has spanned a large part of the twentieth century and almost our entire life course: we first published empirically based articles on contraception; then sequentially on children, adolescents, and midlife careers; then on old age and death; and now we plan to turn back to leisure, the topic which, in our earliest and most idealistic years, we had dreamed of being one day "mature" enough to tackle!

SOME AREAS OF POTENTIAL SOCIOLOGICAL INFLUENCE

This pursuit of reminiscences and introspections that might identify and clarify factors opening or blocking channels of influence is a nostalgic affair. It touches the nerve involved in steering between self-blame and self-congratulation. It requires searching through many dusty pages of books, reprints, and unpublished manuscripts. These manuscripts span five decades of my own sociological biography.[3] They are full of surprises (how often, by forgetting, we fail to be influenced by our own earlier efforts!). Yet they provide fertile ground for asking why some seem to have exerted a degree of influence (though often marked by considerable time lag), whereas others have evoked strong resistance or—worse still—no response whatsoever.

Hoping to avoid a particularistic evaluation of certain topics as more or less "significant" than others, I have selected as case examples a few fragments and incidents relevant for each of four areas of sociological concern today: sociological practice, gender, age, and dynamic social systems.[4] Nonetheless, my biases show through. I cannot resist an overarching emphasis on the fourth area, "dynamic social systems" (variously involving "multilevel" or "macro-micro" analysis), especially as it evokes the central goal of improving the mesh between theory and research.

This dual focus (though with reference only to measurement, not to analysis) appears in our work as early as 1954, in *Sociological Studies in*

---

[3]In still an earlier decade, as a junior at Radcliffe, I coauthored a book on *Gliding and Soaring* (1931. P. & M. White. New York: Whittelsey House) which, though scarcely relevant for sociological influence, provided an invaluable introduction to the culture of preparing and publishing a book.

To shorten the "literature cited" for this essay, only immediately relevant works are cited; a full bibliography may be obtained from the author.

[4]This arrangement by substantive areas rather than by chronology reflects the conceptual, as opposed to any autobiographical, focus of this essay; thus the discussion skips back and forth over the course of my life.

Scale Analysis, by Riley, Riley & Toby. Jack introduced the first chapter of that book as follows:

> *[Fragment]* This book attempts to codify, in methodological terms, one aspect of the interplay between theory and research . . . It is the reconstructed story of how a recently contrived research method, scale analysis, was bent to the task of translating vague theory into precise variables.
>
> . . . the study of the single variable is not a simple task . . . On the one hand, many concepts involve the notion, not of an isolated act or attitude, but of *patterns of action,* of the 'uniformities in the sayings and doings of men,' to use Talcott Parsons' phrase. On the other hand, sociological concepts, insofar as they reflect the collective acts or attitudes of the members of a group, imply a *structure among the members* of the group who act in complementary roles with reference to one another. (pp. 5, 8)

Sociological Practice

In the area now called "sociological practice" (or, as Paul Lazarsfeld called it as the theme of his Presidential volume, *The Uses of Sociology,* 1967), the American Sociological Association (ASA) has just launched the new *Sociological Practice Review*—a considerable "lag" indeed from my effort in 1949 to specify for sociologists the relevant "practical" methods of market research.

EARLY EXPERIENCES   These experiences of my early life were part of a persistent effort to link theory with research methods. I was firmly imbued with the sociological perspective even before entering the "practice" of market researcher. (As a wife I then simply accepted whatever occupational opportunities arose.) When I married Jack in 1931 he had just entered the newly formed Harvard Department of Sociology, and we shared the high excitement of discovering the convergence between his studies with Pitirim Sorokin on social change and its meaning, and my studies with Irving Babbitt on the universals in human thought that persist across time and place. Through Jack, I learned the basics of sociology. As the first graduate assistant in the Department, I had the privilege of working with Carl Zimmerman on an analysis of the Le Play studies of family budgets in Europe. This task entailed first translating from many languages and then analyzing the detailed case studies of households in diverse cross-cultural settings, in order to test certain Engelian "laws" (concerning the inelasticity of demand for food, in contrast to other budgetary categories). From this endeavor I derived an early comprehension of the family group as a solidary system of interdependent members.

While not in the forefront of my mind when I joined the Market Research Company of America, this exposure to sociology surely informed the concepts as well as the methods of the numerous and varied studies we designed during the late 1930s and 1940s. Often advised by such experts as Paul Lazarsfeld, W. Edwards Deming,[5] or Raymond Franzen, we gradually solved many practical problems. For example, we used door-to-door interviewers to conduct classical experiments in the household, in order to examine consumption of new products (White & White 1948). We devised national surveys of contraceptive behaviors and attitudes, leading to improved estimates of fertility and to the development of "the pill." We were the first, outside the Federal government, to design and conduct a national probability sample of the United States. We invented a gadget (called the "Chronolog") for obtaining private information from different members of a household. Along the way we were forced to learn from many false starts and mistakes. It was my enthusiasm for communicating to sociologists the practical implementations of these and other methodological tools which prompted my unsuccessful early foray into grantsmanship.

CHANNELS OF INFLUENCE   That this attempt failed in 1949 is not surprising. The incident is one example of abandoning the effort to communicate systematically what I had learned as a sociological practitioner. (Instead, I accepted the first Executive Officership of the then American Sociological Society.) How many such efforts are abandoned and hence never recorded in the literature? (I seem to remember Bob Merton once referring to his files of unfinished projects as "little dead children"—though he now says my memory does not "resonate" with his.)

Further contributing to my failure here was the general resistance at that time to "commercial" research—even though Paul Lazarsfeld, on his first visit to this country as a Rockefeller Fellow in the 1930s, found market research in some respects more advanced than academic research. Jack has never forgotten Sorokin's ire when, as a graduate student asked to design some research on the effectiveness of advertising, Jack came up with a plan drawn from market research. Far more sophisticated than the academic procedures of the day, Jack's plan was scoffed at as "tainted." Only later did the innovative experiences of market research take firm root in sociology, after they had been legitimated through the work of prestigious sociological researchers, and through such organizations as the Bureau of Applied Social Research at Columbia and the National Opinion Research Center at the University of Chicago. Even Hans Zeisel's *Say It With Figures* (first published during World War II, when Hans was my colleague in the Market Research Company of America, and now in its sixth edition, 1985) has perhaps been less influential among his fellow sociologists than among

---

[5]The mathematician who used his methods of quality control, first, to invent area sampling and, more recently, to guide Japanese manufacturers in procedures for which they hold him in the highest esteem.

researchers across the full range of scholarly, professional, and practical affairs.

These experiences also illustrate the outcome of sociological influence for the little-developed midcentury organizational arrangements for funding and conducting sociological research. They supplement the report by William Sewell in *Sociological Lives* of the long lag before his final successes in enlarging the scale, scope, and funding of sociological research and graduate training, both in his own University of Wisconsin and at the national level (see also Sewell 1989).

CONTINUING EFFORTS   Not deterred by my own initial setback, I have made continuing efforts to apply "practical" market research experiences to sociological work. Jack and I reported the market research survey of contraception and published it in an early issue of the *American Sociological Review* (and signed it as Riley & White, 1941—note the use of my "maiden name" even when collaborating with my husband). Though largely atheoretical, the findings startled the demographers who had heretofore assumed that most Catholics used only "natural" contraceptive methods (despite the name Riley, we are not Catholics). That study became the baseline for subsequent series on fertility. This and other experiences with market research based on groups (such as families or companies) led to my long struggle against studies which inappropriately treat groups or societies as mere aggregates of individuals.

Another market research example from these early writings is found in a conceptual chapter in *Sociological Studies in Scale Analysis*. Here we provided for use in sociological measurement an analogue of Durkheim's "organic solidarity" (the changes since 1954 in family buying behaviors are striking):

[*Fragment*]   Lacking any systematic theory, market research has often made use of the group, recognizing it, on a common-sense basis, as an interpersonal, frequently differentiated unit. Conscious use of the group in market research rests . . . upon the obvious fact that the market for many products is made up, not of individuals as such, but of households. In some instances, to be sure, the demand for a product may come from only one member of the family: the housewife, not the whole family, may be the sole user and purchaser of a household cleanser.

In other instances, however, the demand is a composite of the demands of the several family members, as in the case of most food products. Hence, if a new food product is to be tested for market acceptance, usually it is not enough merely to interview the housewife, ask her to taste it or try it, and to report her reactions. When, instead, samples of the product are left in the home for use under normal conditions, it is often the case that the several members have differing reactions: the housewife may like the taste but find it difficult to prepare; another may dislike the product but wish to collect the jars it comes in; another may like it but prefer a substitute which he is more in the habit of eating, and so on. The researcher recognizes it as his task to obtain the synthesis of all such reactions, the net which can be used to predict whether or not this household would purchase this new product if it were put onto the market. The new product researcher has effective operating techniques for just this purpose. After the period of trial use of the product [in which actual consumption by all family members is observed], he offers the housewife her choice of a supply of the new product or a supply of the old one. Her choice is then taken to represent the composite family demand, in the same sense that her purchase at the grocery store reflects not only her wishes but also those of the other family members taken as a whole. (Riley, Riley & Toby 1954, pp. 193–194)

In market research, as in all sociological practice, the channels of influence run in both directions: sociologists use sociological tools in nonacademic settings, just as they also, in turn, bring the results of this work back into sociology. In the 1950s, during my early days as Executive Officer of the ASA, I worked with Donald Young, then President of Russell Sage Foundation, on a series of ASA-Russell Sage Bulletins on Sociology and the Practicing Professions. In another instance, Jack Riley, shifting his career in 1960 from the university to the insurance industry (whose business was viewed as involving the lives, hopes, and problems of *people*), led the way in applying sociological principles to the world of corporate affairs. Today, prestigious sociologists teach in schools of business and other applied areas; in *Sociological Lives,* for example, Rosabeth Kanter's autobiography shows how her sociological influence is exercised through teaching tomorrow's economic and political leaders, working with corporations, and publishing widely read books. Today sociology, though by no means universally accepted, is utilized throughout the business world, just as knowledge and approaches developed in business and industry have become essential to sociology.

OTHER EXAMPLES   In another domain of sociological practice, military research, Jack's experience (but only indirectly my own) illustrates how channels of influence become open or closed with historical changes in values and ideologies. During World War II, while Samuel Stouffer and his colleagues were producing their monumental studies on *The American Soldier,* Jack's studies of French civilian attitudes toward the Allies (e.g. J. Riley 1947) not only provided essential facts to Eisenhower's military headquarters, but also fed directly into the sociological literatures on war and on mass communication. During the Korean war, he again participated in surveys that were useful not only in advising generals in the field, but also in informing scholars about Communist methods of sovietizing populations under their control; *The Reds Take a City,* by J. Riley & Schramm 1951, has been translated into some 15 languages (see also Schramm & J. Riley 1951). The Vietnam war, however, with its contributions to newly emerging values and life-styles, dampened much of the influence of military sociology, with the personal consequence that for many years neither Jack nor I have cited his war studies. With current changes in public attitudes and the recrudescence of sociological analysis of the impact of war on human lives, however, this early work takes on new significance. The recent review by Robin Williams (1989) of *The American Soldier* "several wars later," which dramatizes the impact of "shifts in attention, emphasis, and evaluation," points to renewed interest in "military sociology" after its long separation from "peace studies" (pp. 166, 170; see also Mayer 1988, and Elder & Clipp 1988).

Sociology of Gender

The trends in ideologies and values that have often operated to open or close channels of influence in sociological practice take a different form in research on gender. Here the channels are affected by massive social and cultural changes in society as a whole and also by trends in sociological thought. During the 1950s at Rutgers University, though the changes were already swirling around us, we had little interest in gender. We spent years studying adolescents, focusing on such topics as socialization, interpersonal influence, and intergenerational relationships. But the early findings were frustrating. Why? Because, as we repeatedly said to one another, "They only show that boys differ from girls. And everyone already knows that!" Again, we failed to publish—this time because we expected little sociological response.

THE ERA OF "INNOCENCE"   In the first half of this century, as the auto-biographies in *Sociological Lives* show, gender was scarcely a central concern of sociology, and hence it was not a source of influence. Even Alice Rossi, talking of a time prior to her many influential writings on gender, speaks of her early "innocence" of the invidious position of women. Bernice Neugarten reports *no* instance in which her gender worked to her advantage or her disadvantage in her research career! For myself, my daughter rebukes me for passive acceptance when, in my college years, the publisher of my book on gliding and soaring changed my name to "Mat" because "no one will read a book on that subject written by a girl;" or when, in 1931, I was turned down for a teaching assistantship because, I was told, "as a woman you will not continue a career"! It was only later, as sex discrimination became a social issue, that gender became a major area of sociological inquiry. Thus, Theda Skocpol, representing the most recent cohort in *Sociological Lives,* writes of her plans to "join the many others in our discipline who are already drawing on the travails of changing gender relations to enrich the sociological imagination."

WOMEN'S CHANGING OCCUPATIONAL ROLE   Yet well before the women's movements of the 1960s, the long-term increases in women's participation in the labor force had begun subtly to redirect the course of sociological influence. In line with this change, we finally turned attention to the gender differences observed in the Rutgers research, as reported in a piece on "Woman's Changing Occupational Role: A Research Report" (Riley, Johnson & Boocock, 1963). The research objective here was to discern the factors that dispose some members of the oncoming cohort of young people to favor, and others to frown upon, the norm of women's employment. Beginning with data collected in 1961 from a sample of New Jersey high school students, the study went on to test its predictions through a special analysis of Census data for adult women in the United States as a whole. These predictions were that the economic status of the family, traditionally the major determining factor in whether or not a wife is in the labor force, was giving way to the rising power of education, and to the redefinition of women's paid work as contributing not only to the family income, but also to self-actualization and the "good life." In retrospect, the study is historically interesting for its microlevel contributions to macrolevel changes in a period of social transition, as illustrated in the following excerpt:

> [*Fragment*]   The study reveals the unanticipated finding that the family's economic status (as measured by the father's occupation)—often so powerful a factor in sociological analysis—proves to bear little relationship to the career attitudes of these adolescents.
>
> This surprising finding . . . proves, upon further investigation, to reflect two quite different tendencies in the data. In the lower status families, the mothers are more likely to work. And since acceptance is relatively high among adolescents whose mothers work, many girls from lower status families will expect to work themselves—even for economic reasons. On the other hand, the higher status families are more likely than the lower to provide college or graduate educations for their offspring. And this fits into the emerging tendency for adolescents planning advanced education to want to work for primarily non-economic reasons. Thus the "effect" of father's lower economic status appears to be mediated through the experience of having a mother who works; whereas the "effect" of father's higher economic status seems mediated through education and a good life view. High status and low status families produce similar acceptance, but by quite different paths.
>
> This process among adolescent girls, by which career acceptance becomes relatively independent of an economic base, seems to reflect the situation [as seen in Census data] in the country as a whole. At a given point in time, two factors (among others) appear to exercise marked effects upon the labor force participation of the wife—but in opposite directions. Her participation tends to *increase* as her education rises (reflected in our survey data by the association between planned education and the adolescent girl's disposition to work). Yet, at the same time, her participation tends to *decrease* as her husband's income rises (consistent with the association between mother's working and family status in our sample). Moreover, the better educated women tend to marry the financially more success-ful men. Thus, at this stage of the transition, many women are under the marked crosspressures of high education, which appears to facilitate their working, and high income, which appears to inhibit it.
>
> There are some indications that over time this conflicting influence of husband's income and wife's education may be resolved. Since more and more women are going on to higher education, one might expect the decline to occur in the importance of the economic, rather than the educational, factor. And, indeed, the rather scanty trend data available suggest that . . . the husband's income seems to be having a decreasing effect upon the labor force activity of his wife.

What is the broader meaning of the loosened ties between the woman's occupational role and its traditional economic base? Perhaps, to be the husband-of-the-working-wife . . . may no longer constitute either a stigma or a threat. A job for the individual woman may become an extension of her traditional primary role as wife and mother within the family . . . Thus redefined, the woman's job may come to strengthen both the differentiation and the integration of the roles of husband and wife within the family (Riley, Johnson, & Boocock (1963).

Though timidly stated and now outdated, these observations foreshadowed some of the subsequent changes both in popular thought and in sociology. There were also intriguing findings on socialization for the future: Parents of our respondents, while favoring a career for their daughters, wanted their sons to marry a wife who would stay home and look after household and children! Provocative as such findings were, however, they were ahead of their time. Talcott Parsons, who often brought into our Rutgers research his eminent common sense on concrete issues, made somewhat similar remarks about the changes in women's occupation and education (Parsons & White 1961, p. 120 n.), though the remarks did little to change his image as a "traditionalist" in matters of gender role. The trends in thought had not yet caught up with social changes.

Today, sociology's major focus on gender is exemplified in many ways: e.g. the launching of a new journal on *Gender and Society,* the 1989 address by Beth Hess as President of the Eastern Sociological Society, or the ASA Presidential volume on *Gender and the Life Course* by Alice Rossi (1985). In one of its aspects, my own current work comports with this focus (e.g. as one contributor to the Rossi volume, author of several pieces on older women, and sponsor of a forthcoming volume on *Gender, Health, and Longevity*—Ory & Warner, 1990).

STUDIES OF SEXUAL ATTITUDES AND BEHAVIORS   One other current experience has disturbing implications for sociological influence. Half a century ago (as indicated above) our studies of contraception were successful in developing nonthreatening research approaches that could encourage women respondents to talk freely and in detail about their sexual behavior. Today at the National Institutes of Health, together with other government agencies and with such sociological colleagues as Wendy Baldwin, Edward Laumann, and James Coleman, we have been making elaborate preparations for a cross-sectional survey of health and sexual behavior, with special reference to prevention of AIDS. However, the topic has proven so politically divisive that Federal officials are refusing to fund "a project that would seek on a national scale to inquire in great detail about the most private aspects of people's sex lives" (*Washington Post,* 7/26/89). Even under threat of mortal epidemic, then, ideologies can be politicized to create major obstacles to the flow of sociological influence (cf. Riley, Ory & Zablotsky 1989).

Sociology of Age

If our early work on gender illustrates failures of influence because of intellectual timing and problems of communication, our work on age has also been somewhat ahead of the major trends in the society, in sociological thought, and in both the prevailing styles and the capacities of research methods. Because much of our recent writing documents the development of a sociology of age (e.g. Riley, Foner, & Waring 1988; Riley Huber, & Hess 1988; Riley 1987), the topic needs scant attention here. I shall merely indicate some of the ways in which age is now gradually attracting systematic sociological attention—both positive and negative.

EXPERIENCES OF A DEVELOPING FIELD   One might have expected a sociology of age to develop early. Aging and cohort flow are powerful and universal processes, and the roles and institutions of every society are structured to accommodate people who differ in age. Indeed, many sociologists in previous cohorts had already dealt with isolated aspects of the topic; but the work was not cumulative. What was missing was a model that could integrate these aspects and could embrace the dynamic interplay between individuals who are growing older and sociocultural structures that are changing.

In the early 1970s, we formulated one such model, referring to it as an "age stratification system" (Riley, Johnson & Foner, 1972). In terms of sociological influence, our strategy for specifying and implementing this model, as I now look back on it, should have been more immediately effective than it was, for we involved an entire working group of influential scholars, including such sociologists as Robert Merton, Talcott Parsons, John Clausen, Harriet Zuckerman, Orville Brim, Gerald Platt, and Harris Schrank.

In fact, however, during the subsequent decade, the model seemed to prove useful to only a few sociologists, while it also elicited considerable criticism and a great deal of confusion. Despite our efforts to explicate and simplify, the complexity of a dynamic multilevel system of this kind eludes easy grasp. The discipline appeared unready conceptually and methodologically to handle such complexity, or to deal with concepts like the "asynchrony" between aging processes and social change, or the "structural lag" that occurs in society because few useful or esteemed roles are available for the growing numbers of long-lived older people. Ironically, our efforts to simplify in themselves brought complaints about our parsimonious use of familiar terms and overly elliptical statements.

In the early 1970s, age had not yet become a central focus of sociological concern. It had not generated the social issues that Charles Willie (in his Epilogue to *Sociological Lives*) describes as "an abiding and stimulating force in the careers of many sociologists." Only recently have several social changes begun to unblock the channels of influence. Among these changes are: a sudden awakening to the fact that we now live in an aging society in which most people survive into old age; a new appreciation of the succession of cohorts, most particularly the "baby boom" cohort; and a recent politicized controversy over "intergenerational equity." This controversy, brought to sociological attention by Samuel Preston (1984, 1988), further documents the importance of current ideological issues in opening (and, in other instances, closing) channels for sociological influence.

AGE-BASED INEQUALITIES   Much of the confusion blocking acceptance of the age stratification model has centered on issues of inequality. The confusion arises from use here of the term "stratification," which is often misinterpreted as class stratification. This misinterpretation misses the larger points about age, of which inequality is but one. Anne Foner, co-author of much of my work on age, has attempted to set the record straight by repeatedly demonstrating that age is itself an independent basis for inequality, distinct from social class but interrelated with it (e.g. Foner 1974, 1988).

Foner argues that the dynamics underlying *cohort succession* and *aging* produce age differences in economic status and power *within* social classes, thereby tending to undermine class solidarity. In contemporary America, regardless of class, both young and old are on the average less advantaged than are the middle-aged—in part, because the young and old belong to cohorts with very different experiences and different adaptations. Many members of the cohorts now young have suffered from prolonged periods of unemployment—and are thus likely to feel excluded and alienated from family and community. In contrast, members of cohorts now past age 65, though also disadvantaged, have lived through an era marked by improvement in material welfare—which may help explain their relatively high levels of life satisfaction and their failure to act like other disadvantaged groups.

The processes of aging also affect relationships among older, middle-aged, and younger adults within social classes. Those now of working age have supported government programs that provide pensions and other benefits for the old, expecting that they themselves in turn will receive benefits from these programs when they grow old. Such anticipations of one's own aging may help explain why prolonged or serious age-based conflicts over economic issues have not erupted in the past and do not appear likely in the future (here Foner's estimate departs from Preston's).

Social class, so long a central focus of sociology, is only one of several bases for social inequalities and cleavages (cf. Foner 1979). Moreover, as Sorokin (1968) put it, the several lines of social differentiation are continually changing, so that social class in its modern sense "existed before the eighteenth century only in rudimentary form, and only since then has it grown into one of the most powerful social groups in the Western world" (14:488).

As so often in the past, Sorokin's words may be prophetic: given the contemporary changes in social structures in this country, age, gender, race, and other bases of inequality may well be undermining the overarching power of social class.

AGE AND VALUES   In addition to issues of inequality, other assumptions about basic values are implicit in the sociology of age. Such assumptions, not immediately attuned to current thinking about stratification, are only occasionally brought into question by sociologists. Yet work in the sociology of age—with its encompassing concern with human lives and sociocultural structures—should ultimately recall attention to underlying values, perhaps thereby influencing sociological thought.

One set of questions concerns the value attached to the prevention of disease, a central goal underlying much work in gerontology. The "medical model," with its overemphasis on disease or physical health is currently supported by legislators, lobbyists, and vested pharmaceutical interests, and threatens to override federal funding for research based on broader models of aging (cf Estes & Binney 1989). Sociologists, many of whom tend to reject biological emphases, would undoubtedly agree on the value of maintaining health and effective functioning far into old age. But what about longevity? Do we prize long life in itself, even without those elements of "life satisfaction" that received so much attention in earlier research on aging?—longevity, even without a sense of self-esteem or personal efficacy?

Quite another question concerns the value currently placed, in modern capitalist societies, on achievement—on work, material gain, success (a question recently explored in depth by Amitai Etzioni in *The Moral Dimension*, 1988). Yet changes in achievement values may be needed if large numbers of older individuals increasingly undertake new assignments—paid or voluntary—at lower than their former levels of pay or prestige. Is it likely that new societal values may be forged by current cohorts of older people, as they spend many years in retirement or, alternatively, undertake new careers with small financial reward?

Even though most might agree in principle that good health, combined with adequate income, ought to be an essential floor for the good life of older people, what account should be taken (reverting to W. I. Thomas) of recognition, esteem, the chance for new adventure, love? Perhaps these questions are moot, but is it not possible that a focus on age could redirect sociological inquiry along such lines?

Dynamic Social Systems

Studies of age, because they involve dynamic social systems, also raise the pertinent conceptual and methodological issues running throughout my sociological life. I was strongly influenced during the 1950s by continuing communication with Talcott Parsons, Freed Bales, Edward Shils, and many of their collaborators and students, whose notion of groups as systems composed of interdependent parts began to pervade my own sociological efforts. A "social system (or multi-level) approach" became the hallmark of much of my work, particularly in efforts to link theory and research method. The wide applicability of this approach is documented by its use as the framework for analyzing the broad range of studies examined two-and-a-half decades ago in *Sociological Research* (Riley et al 1963). That Joan Huber chose the "macro-micro" theme for the 1989 meetings of the ASA speaks to the revitalized concern with aspects of a social system approach.

Three examples of this pervasive approach illustrate how the flow of influence can be blocked by countervailing trends in thought and in methods of research.

USE OF THE APPROACH IN RESEARCH   In our early use of scale analysis to study informal groups of adolescents (Riley, Riley & Toby 1954), empirical regularities were observed in the "collective data" which did not appear in the individual data. Buried in our discursive explorations of the meaning of such a finding is the following simplistic example:

> [*Fragment*]   A relevant single case is provided by William Foote Whyte in which Long John's 'friendship with the three top men [Doc, Mike and Danny] gave him a superior standing' in the gang. In Doc's words, 'We give him so much attention that the rest of the fellows have to respect him.' [Or, as restated schematically] The respect of the 'other fellows' (B) for Long John (C) is found to depend upon the fact that the gang leaders, Doc, Mike and Danny (A), like Long John. This is analogous to our statistical data which suggest that whenever one person, B, follows C as a leader, then another person, A, must like C as a friend." (pp. 248–249)

It was in this connection that, as elsewhere in the same book, we applied Durkheim's schema of organic vs mechanical solidarity to analysis of small social systems:

> [*Fragment*]   [The problem] requiring clarification deals with the distinction between a social system, on the one hand, in which the acts of individuals are interdependent, and a mere aggregate of individuals, on the other, who are not "interacting" with reference to the dimension under scrutiny. (p. 189)

After numerous empirical experiments with the data, and sophisticated mathematical support from our colleague, Richard Cohn, we formulated two key elements in a social system approach: (*a*) That the group, not the individual, should be used as the research case, but that (*b*) the contributions of the individual members within the group must be identified (pp. 229, 238). This formulation gradually became clearer in our later writings and was adapted to include analysis of process and change. These two elements proved to be central to the approach, yet extremely difficult to implement in large-scale studies where multiple levels—from individual to group to society—are all intertwined. Indeed, how can the researcher examine changes in a sample of groups, and at the same time keep track of the contributions to those changes from particular members of these groups? Although my most complete discussion of these issues is in *Sociological Research* (Riley et al 1963, Unit 12), other writings are cited here as instructive for the topic of sociological influence.

USE OF THE APPROACH IN INTERPRETATION   In 1963, in an interpretation of "Sorokin's Use of Sociological Measurement," Mary Moore and I explored how a social system approach might be used with large systems where, in contrast to small peer groups or street gangs composed of interdependent individuals, whole societies are viewed as composed of classes as the interdependent parts. I quote at length from this essay (which, incidentally, we had the privilege of discussing with Sorokin himself) because it attempts to spell out the details:

> [*Fragment*]   The sociologist of today often seeks measures which will fit together two types of indicants: those which refer to collective acts or attitudes and their underlying meaning, and those which refer to the actors as parts of the group. Much present confusion over this problem has arisen because one major line of development in recent years has concentrated on measures of the *individual,* thus isolating for exclusive attention the component of actions and attitudes. And when this line of development is carried over to the group, it often leads to treatment of the *group* as an undifferentiated entity which is formally analogous to the individual. Such a "sociologistic" treatment (to borrow Sorokin's term) might classify orchestral performances, first, according to the pattern of their notes (acts) and, second, according to the proportions of the members (actors) who play strings, woodwinds, brasses, or percussion instruments—all without any fitting together of actors and their respective acts, without taking cognizance of the orchestration involved.
>
> Yet these sociologistic measures may fail to match the concept which the sociologist has in mind. He often wishes to represent the group, not as an undifferentiated entity, but as a system of parts . . . Because of growing awareness of such problems, there is an urgent present search for *social system measures*—as distinguished in this sense from sociologistic measures. One solution which has been recently suggested lies in *identifying the actors* in respect to their contributions to the over-all pattern. Such social system measures would indicate *which* members of the orchestra contribute *which* notes to the symphonic pattern . . .
>
> Our re-analysis of Sorokin's research suggests that some portions of it anticipate exactly this kind of solution to the problem. For example, in his appraisal of the economic well-being of countries, he starts out by rating each society as a whole according to its changing prosperity. Then he goes beyond this . . .: he also shows the prosperity ratings of each of the main *classes* within the society. As he says, "even though the country as a whole is on the upward trend, this does not mean, necessarily, that the economic situation of all its classes follows the same trend." Thus he accounts for the over-all trend in terms of

the trends for the various classes (clergy, nobility, etc,). That is, in our formulation, his group measure of prosperity identifies the various parts (classes) within the group with respect to their prosperity, and follows each of the parts through the over-all process. (pp. 217–18).

RESISTANCE TO THE APPROACH   Most instructive for the topic of influence are the extraordinarily extensive and abortive discussions that ensued from what we felt was a relatively innocuous formulation of a social system approach. While sociological theorists of the day were receptive, some leading methodologists, including Samuel Stouffer and Paul Lazarsfeld simply could not accept it. To them, empirical regularities and patterns could be explained only in terms of processing through the minds of *individuals*—although, to be sure, correlated aspects of *groups* could be observed, if not explained. The interdependence between parts and whole eluded them. (There is a parallelism here to Sorokin's "sociologistic" vs "psychologistic" reductionism.) Indeed, Lazarsfeld once confessed privately that he had spent one long night attempting to derive our social system findings for *groups* through random combinations of *individual* data.

Back in 1957, the ideal opportunity arose for countering the resistance to a social system approach. Invited by Lazarsfeld to contribute a chapter to his book on panel analysis, I seized upon a problem he himself had defined, and labored over a long manuscript intended to clarify the approach by playing Hamlet to his Hamlet. His problem as reformulated, as well as my opportunity to confront it, has been described as follows:

[*Fragment*]   . . . Difficulties in relating system levels appeared in the study of friendship process (Lazarsfeld & Merton 1954) in which Lazarsfeld's scheme for panel analysis could not handle Merton's detailed account of the "patterned sequences of interactions." The Lazarsfeld scheme (his well-known 16-fold table), designed to study individuals but here transferred to friendship groups, could show only how many members liked or agreed with others, but not which members. The effect was to reify the group by obscuring any internal "division of labor" whereby individual-level changes in affect or attitude might affect the group-level formation or dissolution of friendships."[6] (Riley 1987, p. 6; see also Riley et al 1963, pp. 562, 728 ff)

That this chapter was never published (but merely delivered at the 1959 ASA meetings) tells us something about how channels of influence can be

---

[6]I remember discussing the problem at length with Bob Merton, whose response was, "I wish you luck! Paul and I communicate every day on many topics, but this is the one topic on which our communication founders." To be sure, Lazarsfeld wrote extensively about group indices, and about group properties as contextual characteristics of individuals. Without belaboring the point (fuller discussion appears in Riley et al 1963, pp. 700–739, and elsewhere), these are *partial* approximations of the system approach, as are sophisticated analyses of the 1950s and 1960s by such sociologists as James Davis, Herbert Menzel, or James Coleman.

blocked. Lazarsfeld once told me that he withheld publication of the entire book because, challenged by our approach, he was trying to subsume it within his own developing methodological framework. Our consequent failure to reach the relevant methodologists is summed up—quite appropriately in a volume in honor of Talcott Parsons—as follows:

> [*Fragment*]   Despite explicit warnings over a decade ago against applying the scheme for individual panel analysis directly to social system models, experts on panel analysis today still claim—entirely disregarding the internal shifts often involved in system change—that "the determinants of organizational change could be analyzed by the same methods that are used in analyzing panels of individuals" (Barton, 1968). Once again the refinements developed for research on individuals require careful scrutiny and many modifications if their benefits are to be transmitted to sociological research on social systems. (Riley & Nelson 1971, pp. 42–43)

In sum, numerous obstacles block continuing research on dynamic social systems composed of identifiable and interdependent parts: These complex systems are difficult to comprehend and even more difficult to translate into empirical operations. In a recent review Robin Williams (1989:160), citing the work of Merton & Kitt (1950), bemoans the 40-year failure to develop their recommended indices "*both* of social structure and of the behavior of individuals situated within that structure." Furthermore, as Paul DiMaggio emphasized at the 1989 ASA meetings, "grand theories" must also incorporate the "meso-level" into their macro-micro analyses, if both social relationships and culturally institutionalized patterns are to be taken properly into account.

Mathematical difficulties have constituted a major obstacle to research on such sweeping theories, especially theories that emphasize the systemic interdependence of lower-level parts and the centrality of process and change. Much of the credit for our own—though elementary—early innovations in research design goes not to the conventional statisticians of the day, but to our mathematical colleagues, especially Richard Cohn, who worked almost daily with the Rutgers research group, and to Frederick Mosteller at Harvard, who often advised us (see, e.g., Riley et al 1954, pp. 720 ff; Cohn et al 1960). Among the few sociologists at that time to comprehend the special mathematical demands was James Coleman. At a Johns Hopkins seminar arranged by Sarane Boocock to discuss the Rutgers work, he differed from his colleagues in envisioning models beyond the conventional regression analyses! Recently, however, powerful mathematical and computer-aided advances are beginning to be applied to issues of social structure and change (as by Coleman, Charles Tilly, and Harrison White, among others), and sociologists are now far better equipped for continuing study of the complex interplay between changing societies and the successive cohorts of interacting and interrelated individuals.

PROBLEMS OF COMMUNICATION

No discussion of channels of influence can end without taking note of the sociologists' efficacy (or lack of it) in communicating their own work. As set forth in *Sociological Lives,* the life of Lewis Coser stands as one model of how sociological influence can be disseminated. Describing his "double career" over the past 35 years as both sociologist and journalist, he shows the benefits of having "cultivated a kind of double vision, a dual set of premises of pure sociological analysis and impure social and moral partisanship." While avoiding the potential role conflict between scientist and partisan, Coser has become a sophisticate in the lessons of scholarly publication. In my own experience, unlike Coser's, few of these lessons have been heeded, and an account of their neglect may serve as warnings to sociologists working today.

For one thing, the placing of scholarly articles affects the attention they attract from sociologists. Several of our writings, such as "Woman's Changing Occupational Role" described above, were not published in mainstream journals, nor included in any standard volume of abstracts. They stand in contrast, for example, to our abstracted piece in the *Public Opinion Quarterly* on "Aging and Cohort Succession: Interpretations and Misinterpretation" (Riley 1973), which has frequently been cited. Many of our other publications were prepared as contributions to edited volumes which, though they often provide useful background, tend to attract specialized or narrow audiences. Still other articles, because they appeared in interdisciplinary publications (such as handbooks of gerontology, or publications of the Institute of Medicine or the American Philosophical Society) predictably were overlooked by sociologists. Although transcending disciplinary boundaries should be a high scientific priority today, it often impedes the cumulation of a unified body of knowledge in a single discipline.

My most important contributions to sociology, I have always felt, are in the two-volume textbook on *Sociological Research* (Riley et al 1963). Though I signed it as the major author, it contains the best thinking of a host of advisors, colleagues, and students. With his characteristic acumen, Robert Merton, as editor, scrutinized and made suggestions on every page. The book was long and widely used in teaching here and abroad. Yet, as with most textbooks, its original scientific contributions are not recognized as such. Had they been separately published in refereed sociological journals, they might have been more often cited and more nearly incorporated into the developing body of sociological thought.

To be sure, the influence exerted by a textbook is invisible. Many sociologists, whose early thinking was shaped by materials read during their student days, later join the ranks of "invisible influentials." These "influentials," whether teachers or practitioners, make use of numerous and often hidden channels that proliferate throughout sociology and society, thereby imbuing students and others with sociological knowledge and perspectives.

Moreover, styles of publishing follow trends of their own that can affect sociological influence, as Edward Nelson and I learned to our dismay when we published *Sociological Observation* (1974) as part of a series sponsored by the ASA. We reprinted 28 pieces of research by leading sociologists, analyzed each piece as a case study, and wrote surrounding text to demonstrate the largely unexploited relevance of methods of observation for examining a wide range of sociological theories. The book, as a collateral text, was expected to be largely self-teaching, and several of its contributors feel it would still be useful today. Yet the entire series was quickly discontinued because the publisher found "little market at that time for books of readings." Thus another effort to strengthen theory and method was aborted.

Quite apart from influence, every author (at least since Shakespeare) hopes to leave behind a rounded body of work. Jack and I have on our agenda for retirement a volume that brings together in one place some of the activities of our intertwined sociological lives. So much we have learned from this review!

NOTES FOR THE FUTURE

In these selected reflections, I am again impressed by the power of sociotemporal location as a significant factor in sociological influence. The lives of sociologists and their consequences are linked to history in diverse ways; and the particular channels opened or closed during their careers, their successes and failures in seizing opportunities and handling obstacles, the responses of their successors—all are affected by the historical era in which their lives are embedded. As one recent example, Charles Carmic's 1989 reassessment of Parsons' *Structure of Social Action* suggests how authors in one cohort, by attacking the assumptions of scholars in earlier cohorts, often impede understanding of their own work by members of the oncoming cohorts who begin with entirely different assumptions. Camic shows how Parsons, in defending sociology against the then-established power of neoclassicism, behaviorism, and the biological sciences, has been judged by many successors as thereby *over*emphasizing the normative slant on subjective attitudes, values, and symbols.

The rudimentary clues to the operation of influence gleaned here from my own autobiography are mere afterthoughts specifying themes drawn from the eight autobiographies in *Sociological Lives*. These clues indicate how any serious study of the influence of sociological lives would be required to go far beyond such reminiscences as mine.

Among the critical lacunae here is the question of age, or location within the life course. What are the links between the ages at which particular individuals are doing their work and the historical eras experienced by their cohorts? Others have studied the influence *on* scientists of early-career experiences, or of the changes in power and esteem occasioned by midcareer advances or by long-term retirement (e.g. Zuckerman & Merton 1972; Messeri 1988). But how do such life events affect the influence exerted *by* sociologists? To answer such questions would require intensive scrutiny of many diverse sociological lives drawn from many different cohorts.

Another obvious omission here concerns the meaning of influence, and its possible measures for use in research. A large body of sociological work is available as background here. This work ranges from Sorokin's use of citations to measure influence; to the early studies of influentials by Paul Lazarsfeld, Robert Merton, and Elihu Katz, among others; to more recent developments in network analysis by such scholars as Edward Laumann, James Coleman, and Ronald Burt. Long ago Jack and I described in detail how the flow of communications involves mutual interchanges between the communicator and the recipient of the message, each influenced by a surrounding network of primary groups, and both encompassed within the same wider society and the same secular trends (J. & M. Riley 1959). Within so complex a system, new and special approaches are needed for tracing the flow of sociological influence.

For the immediate future, however, the question is how, in a rapidly changing world, to identify the appropriate channels of opportunity for exercising sociological influence—both on the development of the discipline and on issues of public policy and professional practice. Perhaps the slight answers suggested in these personal reflections may serve as useful guides.

ACKNOWLEDGMENTS

I am indebted to the many colleagues and friends who took part in these recollected experiences, though none of them is responsible for the reconstructions, which are entirely my own. Helpful comments and suggestions were provided on early and late drafts by my life-long colleague and husband, John W. Riley, Jr.; my life-long editor and friend, Robert K. Merton; my long-time associates, Anne Foner, Beth Hess, Joan Waring, and Dale Dannefer; and my new associate, Katrina Johnson. I also thank Robin Williams, who made thoughtful proposals for reworking my 1988 "Notes on the Influence of Sociological Lives;" Richard Scott, who performed yeoman service as editor of the Annual Review of Sociology; Bernard Barber, W. Edwards Deming, Bernice Neugarten, David Riesman, Charles Tilly, and several other thoughtful readers.

Literature Cited

Barton, A. H. 1968. Organizations: methods of research. In *International Encyclopedia of the Social Sciences*, ed. D. L. Sills, vol. 11:341. New York: Macmillan

Carmic, C. 1989. *Structure* after 50 years: the anatomy of a charter. *Am. J. Sociol.* 95:38–107

Cohn, R., Mosteller, F., Pratt, J. W., Tatsuoka, M. 1960. Maximizing the probability that adjacent order statistics of samples from several populations form overlapping intervals. *Ann. Math. Statistics* 31:1095–1104

DiMaggio, P. 1989. *The micro-macro dilemma in organizational research: implications for role-system theory.* Presented at Meet. Am. Sociol. Assn., 84th, San Francisco

Elder, G. H. Jr., Clipp, E. C. 1988. War experiences and social ties: influences across 40 years in men's lives. In *Social Structures and Human Lives*, ed. M. W. Riley, B. J. Huber, B. B. Hess. Newbury Park: Sage

Estes, C. L., Binney, E. A. 1989. The biomedicalization of aging: dangers and dilemmas. *The Gerontologist.* 29:587–96

Foner, A. 1974. Age stratification and age conflict in political life. *Am. Sociol. Rev.* 39:187–96

Foner, A. 1979. Ascribed and achieved bases of stratification. *Annu. Rev. Sociol.* 5:219–42

Foner, A. 1988. Age inequalities: are they epiphenomena of the class system? In *Social Structures and Human Lives*, ed. M. W. Riley, B. J. Huber, B. B. Hess. Newbury Park: Sage

Hess, B. B. 1989. *Beyond dichotomy: making distinctions and recognizing differences.* Pres. Mtgs. Eastern Sociol. Soc. Baltimore, Maryland

Huber, B. J. 1988. Social structures and human lives: variations on a theme. In *Social Structures & Human Lives*, ed. M. W. Riley, B. J. Huber, B. B. Hess. Newbury Park: Sage

Lazarsfeld, P. F., Sewell, W. H., Wilensky, H. L. eds. 1967. *The Uses of Sociology.* New York: Basic

Lazarsfeld, P. F., Merton, R. K. 1954. Friendship as social process: a substantive and methodological analysis. In *Freedom and Control in Modern Societies*, ed. M. Berger, T. Abel, C. H. Page, pp. 21–54. New York: Van Nostrand

Mayer, K. U. 1988. German survivors of World War II: the impact on the life course of the collective experiences of birth cohorts. In *Social Structures and Human Lives*, ed. M. W. Riley, B. J. Huber, B. B. Hess. Newbury Park: Sage

Merton, R. K. 1988. Some thoughts on the concept of sociological autobiography. In *Sociological Lives*, ed. M. W. Riley. Newbury Park: Sage

Merton, R. K., Kitt, A. S. 1950. Contributions to the theory of reference group behavior. In *Continuities in Social Research: Studies in the Scope and Method of* The American Soldier, ed. R. K. Merton, P. F. Lazarsfeld. Glencoe, Ill: Free Press

Messeri, P. 1988. Age, theory choice, and the complexity of social structure. In *Social Structures and Human Lives*, ed. M. W. Riley, B. J. Huber, B. B. Hess. Newbury Park: Sage

Ory, M. G., Warner, H. R., eds. 1990. *Gender, Health, and Longevity.* New York: Springer. In press

Parsons, T., White, W. 1961. The link between character and society. In *Culture and Social Character: the Work of David Riesman Reviewed*, ed. S. M. Lipset, L. Lowenthal. Glencoe Ill: Free

Preston, S. H. 1984. Children and the elderly: divergent paths for America's dependents. *Demography* 21:435–57

Preston, S. P. 1988. Age-structural influences on public transfers to dependents. In *Social Structures and Human Lives*, ed. M. W. Riley, B. J. Huber, B. B. Hess. Newbury Park: Sage

Riley, J. W. Jr. 1947. Opinion research in liberated Normandy. *Am. Sociol. Rev.* 12:698–703

Riley, J. W. Jr., Riley, M. W. 1959. Mass communication and the social system. In *Sociology Today: Problems and Prospects*, ed. R. K. Merton, L. Broom, L. S. Cottrell, Jr. New York: Basic

Riley, J. W. Jr., Riley, M. W. 1940. The use of various methods of contraception. *Am. Sociol. Rev.* 5:890–903

Riley, J. W. Jr., Schramm, W. 1951. *The Reds Take a City.* New Brunswick: Rutgers Univ. Press

Riley, M. W. 1973. Aging and cohort succession: interpretations and misinterpretations. *Public Opinion Q.* 37:35–49

Riley, M. W. 1987. On the significance of age in sociology. *Am. Sociol. Rev.* 52:1–14

Riley, M. W. 1988a. Notes on the influence of sociological lives. In *Sociological Lives*, ed. M. W. Riley. Newbury Park: Sage

Riley, M. W. ed. 1988b. *Sociological Lives.* Newbury Park: Sage

Riley, M. W., Cohn, R., Toby, J., Riley, J. W. Jr. 1954. Interpersonal orientations in small groups: a consideration of the questionnaire approach. *Am. Sociol. Rev.* 19: 715–24

Riley, M. W., Foner, A., Waring, J. 1988. Sociology of age. In *Handbook of Sociology*, ed. N. Smelser. New York: Sage

Riley, M. W., Huber, B. J., Hess, B. B., eds. 1988. *Social Structures and Human Lives.* Newbury Park: Sage

Riley, M. W., Johnson, M., Boocock, S. S. 1963. Women's changing occupational role. *Am. Behav. Scientist* 6:33–7

Riley, M. W., Johnson, M., Foner, A. 1972. *A Sociology of Age Stratification.* New York: Russell Sage

Riley, M. W., Moore, M. E. 1963. Sorokin's use of sociological measurement. In *Pitirim A. Sorokin in Review,* ed. P. J. Allen. Durham: Duke Univ. Press

Riley, M. W., Nelson, E. E. 1971. Research on stability and change in social systems. In *Stability and Social Change: A Volume in Honor of Talcott Parsons,* ed. B. Barber, A. Inkeles, pp. 407–49. Boston: Little, Brown

Riley, M. W., Nelson, E. E. 1974. *Sociological Observation: A Strategy for New Social Knowledge.* New York: Basic

Riley, M. W., Ory, M. G., Zablotsky, D., eds. 1989. *AIDS in an Aging Society: What We Need to Know.* New York: Springer

Riley, M. W., Riley, J. W. Jr., Cohn, R. M., Moore, M. E., Johnson, M. E., Boocock, S. S., Foner, A. 1963. *Sociological Research.* New York: Harcourt Brace & World

Riley, M. W., Riley, J. W. Jr., Toby, T. 1954. *Sociological Studies in Scale Analysis.* New Brunswick: Rutgers Univ. Press

Rossi, A. S., ed. 1985. *Gender and the Life Course.* New York: Aldine

Schramm, W., Riley, J. W. Jr. 1951. Communications in the sovietized state, as demonstrated in Korea. *Am. Sociol. Rev.* 6:757–86

Sewell, W. H. 1989. Some reflections on the golden age of interdisciplinary social psychology. *Annu. Rev. Sociol.* 15:1–16

Sorokin, P. A. 1968. Social differentiation. In *International Encyclopedia of the Social Sciences,* ed. D. L. Sills, vol. 14. New York: Macmillan

White, P., White, M. 1948. *New Product Development.* New York: Funk & Wagnalls

Williams, R. M. Jr., *The American Soldier:* an assessment, several wars later. *Public Opin. Q.* 53:155–74

Zeisel, H. 1985. *Say It With Figures.* New York: Harper & Row. 6th ed.

Zuckerman, H., Merton, R. K. 1972. Age, aging, and age structure in science. In *A Sociology of Age Stratification: Volume III. Of Aging and Society,* M. W. Riley, M. Johnson, A. Foner. New York: Russell Sage

[1]The US Government has the right to retain a nonexclusive, royalty-free license in and to any copyright covering this paper.

Annu. Rev. Sociol. 1990. 16:27–65

ALTRUISM: A Review of Recent Theory and Research[1]

Jane Allyn Piliavin and Hong-Wen Charng

Department of Sociology, 8128 Social Science Building, University of Wisconsin, Madison, Wisconsin 53706

KEY WORDS: Altruism, helping behavior, philanthropy, public goods

---

Altruism is not . . . an agreeable ornament to social life, but it will forever be its fundamental basis. How can we really dispense with it?

> E. Durkheim, *The Division of Labor in Society.* (1933, p. 228)

"How selfish soever man be supposed, there are evidently some principles in his nature, which interest him in the fortune of others, and render their happiness necessary to him, though he derives nothing from it, except the pleasure of seeing it."

> Adam Smith, *The Theory of Moral Sentiments* (1969, p. 47)

Abstract

The literature on altruism in social psychology, and to a lesser degree in sociology, economics, political behavior and sociobiology since the early 1980's is reviewed. The authors take the position that in all of these areas, there appears to be a "paradigm shift" away from the earlier position that behavior that appears to be altruistic must, under closer scrutiny, be revealed as reflecting egoistic motives. Rather, theory and data now being advanced are more compatible with the view that true altruism—acting with the goal of benefitting another—does exist and is a part of human nature.

[1]The authors would like to thank Gerald Marwell and Irving Piliavin for careful, critical readings of previous drafts of this manuscript and an anonymous reviewer for helpful comments. We would also like to thank numerous librarians, who must remain nameless, for tracking down elusive references, sometimes over the phone at the last minute.

27

0360-0572/90/0815-0027$02.00

Research in social psychology during the 80's had a decreased emphasis on situational determinants of helping. Rather, it has focussed mainly on the following topics: the existence and nature of the altruistic personality, the debate concerning the nature of the motivation underlying helping behavior, and the nature of the process of the development of altruism in children and adults. During this time there has also been considerable theoretical and empirical work on possible biological bases for altruism, and on the evolutionary processes by which these might have developed. Within economics, politics, and sociology, the issues of behavior in social dilemmas, the provision of public goods, private and corporate philanthropy, and voluntarism (including donation of time, money, and physical parts of the self) are discussed.

INTRODUCTION

In spite of these comments from two founders of sociology and economics, for a long time it was intellectually unacceptable to raise the question of whether "true" altruism could exist. Whether one spoke to a biologist, a psychologist, a psychiatrist, a sociologist, an economist, or a political scientist the answer was the same: Anything that *appears* to be motivated by a concern for someone else's needs will, under closer scrutiny, prove to have ulterior selfish motives.

In all of these areas we are now seeing a "paradigm shift."[2] The initial leadership came from sociobiology, systematized in E. O. Wilson's *Sociobiology: A New Synthesis* (1975). Around that same time, Phelps (1975, p. 2), introducing *Altruism, Morality, and Economic Theory,* said, "The range of altruistic behavior . . . is impressive. . . ." By 1982, Margolis stated, "Almost no economist would deny the possibility of altruism in rational choice (p. 12)."[3] In social psychology, it has largely been Batson's experimental work (and Coke 1981; for a review, see Batson 1990) and Hoffman's systematic presentation of his theory of the origins of altruism (1981) that have led to a reconsideration of egoistic models. These American contributions were, however, foreshadowed by work, untranslated, of Reykowski (1979) and Karylowski (1975) in Poland.

---

[2]Margolis notes that "A reasonable indicator of when a paradigm is starting to become an intellectual handicap might be when things that are obvious and obviously important can be seen more easily by a naive observer than by specialists . . ." (1982, p. 71).

[3]Margolis (1982) points out that three economists in the 1950s—Arrow (1963), Buchanan (1954), and Harsanyi (1955)—touched on the possibility of a dual preference structure that would allow for motives other than pure selfishness. Arrow (1975) suggests that there can be three classes of motives for giving: a generalized desire to benefit others, a desire to be the agent by which others benefit, or a sense of obligation, based on social norms or an implicit social contract.

The central point we attempt to make in this review is that the data from sociology, economics, political science, and social psychology are all at least compatible with the position that altruism is part of human nature. People do have "other-regarding sentiments," they do contribute to public goods from which they benefit little, they do sacrifice for their children and even for others to whom they are not related. Recognizing this, a number of other interesting questions can then be raised. Is there evidence for an "altruistic personality," or is altruism largely determined situationally? How are altruistic motivations developed, and what are some mediating dimensions? Are there different kinds of altruism that can be distinguished on the basis of their underlying mechanism? Is there a genetic component to these altruistic tendencies, and if so, how might it affect the development and expression of altruism? What is the extent of public volunteering and charitable giving in our society, and to what extent can we call it altruism? Our emphasis will be mainly on the social psychology and human development literatures, although we also discuss issues in social dilemmas, public goods provision, philanthropy, and voluntarism.[4]

WHAT IS ALTRUISM?

Writers from different disciplines define altruism differently. At one extreme, the sociobiologist Wilson (1975, p. 578) defines altruism as "self-destructive behavior performed for the benefit of others." More generally, sociobiologists call behavior altruistic if it benefits the actor less than the recipient. The economist Margolis (1982, p. 15) says, "What defines altruistic behavior is that the actor could have done better for himself had he chosen to ignore the effect of his choice on others. . . ." Altruists are defined in the social dilemma literature as individuals who give more weight to others' than to their own outcomes in deciding on game strategies (Liebrand 1986). What all of these definitions share is an emphasis on the costs to the altruist; they do not mention motives.

Differences in the definitions of psychologists—who have been unable to agree on a single definition of altruism—involve the relative emphasis on two factors: intentions and the amount of benefit or cost to the actor (Krebs 1987).

[4]We do not attempt a thorough review of recent altruism research in all of these academic areas. A review of the biological literature to 1975 is found in Wilson (1975); there are three relatively recent reviews of the sociobiological approach to human altruism and prosocial behavior in Hoffman (1981), Cunningham (1985–1986), and Krebs (1987). Reviews of the social psychological literature can be found in Staub (1978), Piliavin et al (1981), Rushton (1980), Dovidio (1984), and Dovidio, Piliavin, Goertner, Schroeder, and Clark (forthcoming). Reviews of the "social dilemma" literature have been provided by Dawes (1980), Edney (1980; Dawes & Orbell (1981), Stroebe & Frey (1982), and Messick & Brewer (1983). The political area is reviewed by Rasinski & Tyler (1986).

Bar-Tal (1985–1986) notes that, with few exceptions, most of those who emphasize the motivational aspect of altruism agree that: "altruistic behavior (*a*) must benefit another person, (*b*) must be performed voluntarily, (*c*) must be performed intentionally, (*d*) the benefit must be the goal by itself, and (*e*) must be performed without expecting any external reward" (p. 5).

Sober (1988) points out the essential differences between "evolutionary altruism"—essentially altruism that emphasizes consequences to the actor and the recipient—and what he calls "vernacular altruism" which "has to do with motives . . . with the motive of benefitting others." (p. 76). He points out that in order to have motives, one must have a mind, which is clearly not the case for the lower species to whom evolutionary altruism is usually applied. As sociologists, we have chosen to adopt a largely motive-based definition of altruism as behavior costly to the actor involving other-regarding sentiments; if an act is or appears to be motivated mainly out of a consideration of another's needs rather than one's own, we call it altruistic. The actor need not have *consciously* formulated an intention to benefit the other for an act to qualify, however.[5]

On the Possibility of More Than One Type of Altruism

Several authors (Hill 1984, Vine 1983, Krebs 1987) suggest that there may be at least two kinds of altruism. Although Hill points out that much altruism is in response to perceived social expectations, he adds that "spontaneous acts of real bravery are undertaken without any such conscious aim in view" (p. 24). Vine (1983, p. 8) states, "Our altruistic impulses are likely to be stronger towards kith and kin partly because of this underlying organismic causation, requiring less rational deliberation and self-persuasion, less active cultivation of altruistic dispositions."

Wilson (1976) has referred to "hard core" altruism, "irrational and uni-laterally directed at others . . . relatively unresponsive to reward and punishment . . . likely to have evolved through . . . kin selection" (p. 371).

Simmons et al (1977) point out that the decision to donate a kidney to a relative is in most cases made very quickly, often without any sense of having made a decision at all. In some cases of bystander intervention, individuals also appear to help almost reflexively. Piliavin et al (1981) note that "the same factors that facilitate impulsive helping—clarity, reality, involvement with the victim—have also been demonstrated to be related to greater levels of bystander arousal" (p. 238). Krebs concludes, "Evidence on impulsive help-ing suggests that . . . humans . . . may be genetically disposed to engage in impulsive acts of helping . . . The finding that prior experience with a victim

---

[5]In many cases of extreme heroism, actors have no consciousness of having made a decision to act. We would not wish to exclude such acts from the altruistic category for this reason.

facilitates impulsive helping is consistent with evidence on familiarity in support of the possibility that impulsive helping is an anachronistic anomaly" (1987, p. 113). Hoffman (1981) has suggested two different mechanisms underlying the empathy which precedes helping: a flexible mechanism that is susceptible to developmental influences and a "reflexive" mechanism that is not.

In other words, we may have mechanisms both for "evolutionary altruism" and for "vernacular altruism." The former would be very primitive, leading to impulsive responding in emergencies in which the victim is seen as part of a "we"—the "anachronistic anomaly." The other—probably much more common—would be more complexly developed, although it may have some hereditary components.

IS THERE AN ALTRUISTIC PERSONALITY?

It is undoubtedly futile to search for the altruistic personality, since there are so many different forms altruistic behavior can take. Summary articles reviewing experimental research have generally found inconsistent relationships between personality characteristics and prosocial behavior. A few regularities do occur: people high in self-esteem, high in competence, high in internal locus of control, low in need for approval, and high in moral development appear to be more likely to engage in prosocial behaviors (Staub 1978, Aronoff & Wilson 1984, Piliavin et al 1981, Rushton 1981). Similarly, a 1981 review of the literature on blood donation (Boe & Ponder) reported only that donors have an altruistic approach to life, a desire for self-sacrifice, and a strong need for recognition and prestige. Romer et al (1986) found that those they had classified as altruists helped significantly more than did others, particularly when they were not going to receive compensation, and that "Few selfish persons volunteered to help, regardless of whether they had been offered compensation" (p. 1007).

Oliner & Oliner (1988) found very few personality differences between 231 gentiles who saved Jews in Nazi Europe and 126 nonrescuers matched on age, sex, education, and geographic location during the war. Rescuers did have higher ethical values, beliefs in equity, greater pity or empathy, and were more likely to see all people as equal. Simmons et al (1977)[6] found no differences between those who donated a kidney to a relative and a standardization group on any of the standard scales of the MMPI. Reddy

[6]The most recent presentation of this work is to be found in Simmons, Marine, and Simmons, *The Gift of Life: The Effect of Organ Transplantation on Individual Family and Societal Dynamics*. New Brunswick, NJ: Transaction Books, 1987. The authors only learned of this new edition after this review had gone to press; thus the references in the text remain to the earlier edition.

(1980) found little evidence for relationships between most personality and attitudinal measures and charitable giving; the exception was alienation, which decreased giving. A more fruitful approach might be to look at certain theoretically promising dimensions of personality and see whether they are related in sensible ways to altruistic action.

Moral Norms and Attribution of Responsibility To the Self

In both the Oliner & Oliner study of the rescuers of Jews and in past reviews of the altruism literature, something like "moral values" seems to be implicated in altruism. Schwartz (1970; Schwartz & Howard 1982, 1984) has postulated that helping behavior is affected by personal norms, i.e. feelings of moral obligation to perform or refrain from certain actions. "Thus personal norms are situated, self-based standards for specific behavior generated from internalized values during the process of behavioral decision making" (Schwartz & Howard 1984, p. 234). The personality construct of attribution of responsibility to the self (AR) measures the extent to which individuals are likely to act on personal norms. Schwartz (1970) found that those with strong personal norms regarding bone marrow donation and high scores on attribution of responsibility to the self were significantly more likely to volunteer to join a marrow donor pool.

A study using blood donation as the behavior later found that 34% of individuals high on both AR and personal norms gave blood when solicited, while less than 10% of all others did so (Zuckerman et al 1977). Attribution of responsibility alone was related to willingness to volunteer as a bone marrow donor in a sample of pheresis donors (Briggs et al 1986). And in a study focussed on the impact of perceived community norms on community differences in blood donation, personal norms were the major factor in predicting donations at an individual level (Piliavin & Libby 1986). On the other hand, sometimes people may feel some degree of moral obligation *not* to give help to some individuals, or in some instances groups. Schwartz & Fleishman (1982) found that people with such negative personal norms (i.e. who felt they should *not* help the welfare recipient) help less than people with no norms.

Karylowski (1982) has argued that altruistic helping can be based either on the need to live up to such a moral imperative (endocentric altruism) or on the desire to improve another's condition (exocentric altruism). In the former case, the individual must actually help in order to feel gratification; in the latter, it is enough that the other receives help, regardless of the source of that help. Little research has been done on exocentric altruism (but see Batson 1987, below).

"Free Ridership"

The concept of "free riding" means the tendency to let others pay the costs of public goods that are available to all, such as public TV. When rendered as a personality construct, "free-ridership" is closely related to Schwartz's "attribution of responsibility to the self." In one study that found but few dimensions that differentiated blood donors from nondonors, donors were found to display a lesser "free-rider" tendency (Condie et al 1976). More recently, donors with a lower "free-rider" tendency were found to be more likely to develop a psychological commitment to donation and to continue giving (Piliavin & Callero, in press). Closely related to the question of personal norms and free riding is the issue of "fairness." Marwell & Ames (1981) found that investment of funds in a group exchange (the "altruistic" choice) was related quite strongly ($r = .47$) with reports that the individual was "concerned with fairness" when investing.

Trust and Faith in People

The only way in which kidney donors differed from nondonors in the Simmons et al (1977) research was on a five-item scale of faith in people;[7] 74% of donors but only 43% of nondonors scored high. Research on behavior in experimental social dilemmas has found stable individual differences in the willingness to cooperate—to consider the outcomes of the others in making decisions. Cunha (1985) found that subjects who behaved competitively in a social dilemma situation were very low on a battery of measures of trust obtained earlier, as compared to cooperators, who were both trusting and trustworthy. Kramer et al (1986) also found that "others' lack of reciprocation did not cause cooperators to abandon their own efforts to conserve the collective pool . . . This would seem to support our interpretation that social motives reflect individual values . . . rather than merely strategic concerns." The motivation of one cooperator was clear when she said, "Sure, I would have liked to have made more (money), but not if it meant having to hurt others" (p. 590). Liebrand et al (1986) and Beggan et al (1988) present data that indicate that the meaning of the cooperation-competition dimension is different for cooperators and competitors. Cooperators see it as "good-bad;" competitors see it as "strong-weak."

Risk-Taking

There is some evidence that propensities to take risks may be related specifically to willingness to engage in potentially costly altruistic acts. In a study of 27 gentiles who rescued Jews during World War II, London (1970) concluded that they were characterized by "a spirit of adventurousness." Two studies have found risk-taking among blood donors: a measure of "sensation-seeking" was positively related to willingness to consider blood donation (Farnill & Ball 1982), and frequent donors were more likely to agree that they "would

---

[7]An example item: "Would you say most people are more inclined (1) to help others, or more inclined (2) to look out for themselves?"

try anything once" than non donors (Needham Harper Worldwide 1986). A study of individuals who had been injured by intervening in a crime in progress (Huston et al 1976) found them to be "risk-takers, men on familiar and rather amiable terms with violence . . . much more easily provoked than [a control group] (p. 64)." Wilson & Petruska (1984) found that esteem-oriented subjects (high in self-efficacy, mastery, self-worth) were more likely to initiate helping behavior in a simulated emergency than were safety-oriented subjects (high in need for security, avoidance of anxiety). A group of 20 founders of activist community service organizations were characterized by "Riskiness, not necessarily in the entrepreneurial sense, but rather the readiness to take a chance" (B. Berkowitz 1987, p. 323).

Gender and Gender Role

Piliavin & Unger (1985) reviewed sex and gender differences in the several steps of the psychological process in responding to situations in which help is needed: preattentive processing, arousal, and cost/reward calculations.[8] Evidence for differences in processing comes from Austin (1979), who found that men and women were equally likely to intervene at a high level of harm, but women more likely to intervene at low levels; women seem to have a lower threshold for noticing. In regard to arousal, Hoffman (1977) reviewed 16 studies and found that females had higher scores on the vicarious response to another's expression of affect than did males.[9] Eisenberg et al (1988) found that girls exhibited more facial sympathy and reported more distress than boys. Women report themselves to be more empathic than do men (Eisenberg & Lennon 1983).

Eagly & Crowley (1986) argue that sex differences in helping behavior are derived from social roles occupied by men and women. Women report providing their friends with more personal favors, emotional supports, and counseling about personal problems than men do (Aries & Johnson 1983, Berg 1984, Johnson & Aries 1983). Helping expectations for men are associated with nonroutine and risky actions and protective roles. Using meta-analysis, they found support for social role theory in explaining differences in male and female. Their predictions were confirmed that "men should be more helpful than women to the extent that (a) women perceived helping as more dangerous than men did, (b) an audience witnessed the helping act, and (c) other potential helpers were available." Sex differences in helping behavior may be due to gender-related traits of masculinity and femininity, rather than to sex per se or to gender roles. Results have been extremely inconsistent (see Senneker & Hendrick 1983, Tice & Baumeister 1985, Siem & Spence 1986).

[8]For an elaboration of this model, see Piliavin et al 1981.
[9]He believes this difference to be in part of genetic origin.

Situational Factors in Altruism

The best known situational effect in the literature is the bystander effect, namely, that the knowledge of the presence of others who might help inhibits intervention in an emergency. In an extensive review, Latane et al (1981) found robust evidence of the effect of perceived group size on helping.[10] Striking data not included in these analyses come from Simmons et al (1977). The likelihood of an individual in need of a kidney receiving one from a sibling decreased almost linearly from 51% when there was only one eligible sibling to 0% when there were 10 or 11.

Studies have showed that the bystander effect is caused by diffusion of responsibility (i.e. when an individual believes that there are other bystanders who can offer help, pressure to rescue the victim is reduced), informal social influence (the reactions from other bystanders), and normative social influence (personal beliefs of social evaluations about providing/or not providing help). It is only under very specific circumstances that trigger impulsive helping that the bystander effect does not operate (for a review, see Piliavin et al 1981; and Dovidio 1984).

Other Situational Effects

Although 32% of rescuers of Jews claim to have begun helping Jews on their own initiative, rescuers were more likely to have been asked for help directly than were nonrescuers (Oliner & Oliner 1988). Simmons et al (1977) found that kidney donors were more likely to have been informed *in person* of the need for a donor than were nondonors (80% vs 58%). Studies of those who volunteer time, donate to charity, or give blood indicate strongly that personal request and social pressure are very important reasons for participation (Heshka 1983, Americans . . . 1981, Reddy 1980, Sills 1957, Drake et al 1982), and the commonest reason given for nondonation is not having been asked.

Female victims are likely to receive more help (Eagly & Crowley 1986). Less costly, unambiguous, and highly urgent situations promote helping behaviors (Shotland & Stebbins 1983). Rapoport (1988) found that subjects given a higher level of resources in a social dilemma game—the "rich"—contributed more to the common pool. Poppe & Utens (1986) find that individuals take more from a pool and give less if there are more resources; when resources decrease, they become more altruistic.

---

[10]"We are aware of 4 dozen published or unpublished studies from nearly 3 dozen different laboratories reporting data from over 5000 persons faced with the opportunity to help either alone or in the presence of others. With very few exceptions, individuals faced with a sudden need for action exhibit a markedly reduced likelihood of response if other people actually are, or are believed to be, available" (Latane et al 1981, p. 290).

Person-by-Situation Interactions

Kerber (1984) found that people high in altruism saw helping situations as more rewarding and less costly than did people low in altruism. The same was true for Simmons et al's (1977) kidney donors, as compared to nondonors. Wilson & Petruska (1984) found that the esteem-oriented (high in self-efficacy, mastery, self-worth) subjects were more likely to initiate helping than were safety-oriented (high in need for security, avoidance of anxiety) subjects when interacting with a passive confederate. Esteem-oriented subjects were more likely to be influenced by a high competence confederate, and safety-oriented subjects were more likely to be influenced by a high status confederate.[11] Finally, Deutsch & Lamberti (1986) found differences in the impact of prior social approval on the helping of those low and high in need for approval;[12] "subjects who were high in need for approval were subsequently more likely to help a confederate who had dropped books if they [the subjects] had been socially rewarded than if they had been punished. Subjects low in need for approval were unaffected by the previous social reinforcement" (p. 149).

THE EMPATHY-ALTRUISM HYPOTHESIS

Empirical studies have consistently shown that empathy is causally related to prosocial behavior. For a comprehensive review of this relationship, see Eisenberg & Miller (1987); however, this link does not necessarily demonstrate that the prosocial behavior is altruistically motivated. The arousal vicariously induced by grasping another's situation may produce either sympathy or aversive arousal such as personal distress or sadness, which Batson and his associates (Batson 1987, Batson et al 1983, see also Piliavin et al 1981) argue are distinct emotional states. For empirical evidence supporting the idea that sympathy and personal distress are distinct emotional states, see Batson (1987 review), Fultz et al (1988), Eisenberg et al (1989), Eisenberg et al (1988), Batson et al (1981), Sterling & Gaertner (1984).

Batson et al then test the hypothesis that sympathy evokes altruistic motivation to have the other's need reduced, while personal distress does not;[13] they

---

[11]The high vs. low competence model was manipulated by the confederate who performed excellent vs. poor creative thinking tasks in the experiment. The high vs. low status model was manipulated by the confederate being a first year doctoral student vs. freshmen.

[12]Need for approval was measured by the Marlowe-Crowe social desirability scale.

[13]Consistent with Batson's theorizing, the economist Margolis suggests that ". . . psychic income [feeling better about oneself by behaving in a certain way] . . . does not either explain group-interested motivation or add to it. (p. 68)"

use a paradigm with a 2 (high vs low empathy) by 2 (easy vs difficult escape) design.[14] If high empathy evokes a desire to reduce personal distress, people should help less in a situation that is easy to escape; if empathy evokes a desire to reduce the other's suffering, then there should be no difference in helping between easy and difficult escape situations. Empirical studies have consistently supported the empathy-altruism prediction (Batson et al 1981, Batson et al 1988, Batson et al 1983).

Three egoistic alternatives to the empathy-altruism hypothesis have been proposed. (*a*) "The empathy-specific punishment hypothesis claims that people have learned through prior reinforcement that a special obligation to help—and special guilt and shame for failure to help—are attendant on feeling empathy. As a result, when they feel empathy . . . they are egoistically motivated to avoid these empathy-specific punishments" (Batson et al 1988, p. 58). (*b*) The empathy-specific–rewards hypothesis argues that through prior experiences people learn that special rewards (e.g. praise, honor) are attendant on helping when one feels empathy (Batson 1987, Thompson et al 1980, Meindl & Lerner 1983). According to this hypothesis "individuals feeling a high degree of empathy will be in a more positive mood when they have been the agent of the victim's relief than when they have not. . . . the empathy-altruism hypothesis predicts that individuals feeling a high degree of empathy will be in as positive a mood when the victim's need is relieved by other means as when by their own action" (Batson et al 1988, p. 53). (*c*) The "negative-state relief model" (NSR) proposed by Cialdini and his associates (Baumann et al 1981, Cialdini et al 1987) claims that empathy creates personal sadness that needs to be removed, and that the egoistic desire to manage personal sadness is a primary cause of helping behaviors. However, since empirical studies have failed to find consistent support for any of these three alternative hypotheses (Batson et al 1988, Cialdini et al 1987, Manucia et al 1984, Schaller & Cialdini 1988, Batson et al 1989), we must conclude that there is an altruistic motivation behind prosocial behavior when empathy is aroused.

Using a very similar conceptualization, Weiner's attribution-affect model of helping (1980a, b) holds that another's need, if perceived as beyond the victim's control, leads to empathy[15] and helping; if perceived as controllable, anger and withholding of help result. Considerable support exists for this model as well (Meyer & Mulherin 1980, Reisenzein 1986, Reisenzein et al 1984).

---

[14]In some studies, empathy is measured; in others, it is manipulated by inducing identification or an objective stance towards the victim.

[15]Weiner actually uses the term "sympathy," as does Eisenberg, for the concept referred to as "empathy" by Batson.

Moods and Helping Behavior

Results of research relating negative moods to helping have been inconsistent; sometimes the negative mood has a positive effect on helping behavior, sometimes a negative effect, and sometimes no effect at all, suggesting that moderator variables affect the influence of negative mood on helping behavior. Carlson & Miller (1987) have summarized three theoretical perspectives and have used metaanalysis to test the results of 47 articles. Results supported a focus of attention model and a responsibility/objective self-awareness model, but not the negative state relief model; these results further weaken theoretical approaches to helping based on reward mechanism (i.e. the relief of distress).

In contrast, research has consistently found that a positive mood promotes helpfulness. People in a good mood may perceive things in a more positive way and may increase positive cognitions[16] (Bower 1981, Clark & Teasdale 1985, Forgas et al 1984). As a result, they may provide more help because they perceive a potential helping opportunity more favorably (Clark & Isen 1982, Clark & Waddell 1983). Carlson and his associates (Carlson et al 1988) have reviewed the literature on positive mood and prosocial behavior, covering six distinctive perspectives, and have done a meta-analysis of 34 articles. Results supported what they call the "focus of attention," "social outlook," and "mood maintenance" hypotheses, but not the "objective self-awareness," "concomitance," and "separate process" models. Objective self-awareness appears to augment helpfulness by enhancing the prosocial feelings and perceptions that result from a good mood, but not because people want to avoid the negative affect that may arise from failing to fulfill what they see as a helping obligation. The critical conclusion is that affect is extremely important as a factor in increasing or decreasing helping, and that its effect is influenced by and influences cognitive processes.

DEVELOPMENT OF ALTRUISM

Generosity and other forms of helping behavior have been found to increase with children's age, especially as children near adolescence (Chambers & Ascione 1987; see Staub 1979 for an extensive review). Much research has been addressed to the question of what mediating processes may contribute to this change. As children grow up, their altruism may be increased because of growing empathic sensitivity, greater ability in perspective-taking, broader knowledge of cultural norms, increased social responsibility and competence, or enhanced moral reasoning capabilities.

---

[16]Carlson et al (1988) called this process priming: "A good mood state is hypothesized to function as a cue that temporarily increases the likelihood that positive cognition will be generated in response to a subsequent stimulus. This process, called priming, can set a self-perpetuating cognitive loop of positive thoughts and associations into motion" (p. 211).

Empathy

According to Hoffman's (1981, 1982a, 1984a) proposed developmental model, in the first year of life, a child can not differentiate self and other. Thus, when s/he sees other's distress, a global empathic distress is elicited,[17] and the child is not clear about who is experiencing the distress. Through the end of the first year, the child's helping behavior is still "quasihedonistic," motivated by the need to alleviate its own rather than the other's distress. At 2 or 3 years, the child gains more advanced role-taking skills (the ability to understand others' affective and cognitive states), and his/her helping behaviors are more responsive to other's needs and feelings. The final stage comes when "children can be aroused empathically by information pertinent to someone's feelings even in that person's absence" (1982a, p. 288).

Although research on adults has shown a causal relationship between empathy and helping behavior (see Batson et al 1989), research concerning the same association in children has inconsistent results. However, negative findings (Underwood & Moore 1982, Eisenberg & Miller 1987) may be due to problems with the picture/story procedure, the most common procedure used to assess children's empathy, which has been questioned on both methodological and conceptual grounds (see Eisenberg 1986).[18] When spontaneous facial/gestural responses are used as an indicator, empathy is also only sometimes found in preschool children to be positively associated with helping (Chapman et al 1987, see Eisenberg & Miller 1987). However, Eisenberg et al (1988) argued that the nonsignificant relations may be due to the failure to differentiate between sympathetic reactions and personal distress. They found that sad/concerned expressions (an indicator of sympathy) were positively associated with spontaneous prosocial behaviors; anxious expressions (an indicator of personal distress) were not. Children's self reports were unrelated to facial/gestural expressions and helping behaviors, a result consistent with the view that the nonsignificant relations between empathy and children's helping behaviors may be due to methodological problems.

[17]Hoffman called it "a fusion of unpleasant feelings and of stimuli that come from the infant's own body" (1982a, p. 287).

[18]FASTE (Feshback and Roe Affective Situations Test for Empathy) is the most popular instrument in the picture/story method, which is designed for young, school-age children and consists of 8 stories, depicting emotions of sadness, anger, fear, and happiness. The children are told a brief story with pictures showing, then they are asked to indicate how they feel. Many researchers modify FASTE in their studies.

It is not clear that the short stories induce empathy (Eisenberg-Berg & Lennon 1980); some stories may induce more than one type of emotion, such as fear or anger (Hoffman 1982b); since the children are repeatedly asked how they feel, their answers might be affected by social desirability (Eisenberg & Lennon 1983; Hoffman 1982b); children's answers vary depending on experimenters' sex and children's sex (see Eisenberg & Lennon 1983). Moreover, the children have to be able to label their feeling correctly, and for young children this may be a difficult task (Eisenberg-Berg & Lennon 1980).

Prosocial Moral Reasoning

Children's prosocial moral reasoning changes with age. Studying children's prosocial reasoning about a hypothetical dilemma[19], Eisenberg and her associates (for review, see Eisenberg 1982, 1986) found that during the elementary school years, hedonistic reasoning decreases, while needs-oriented reasoning increases until the age of 7–8 (Eisenberg & Lennon 1983, Eisenberg et al 1984). Stereotypic and approval-oriented concerns increase in the elementary school years, and then decrease in high school (Eisenberg et al 1984, Eisenberg-Berg 1979). Self-reflective, empathically oriented concern was hardly used by elementary school children, but it increased with age into high school. Reasoning about internal values is very infrequent in school age children but is salient in some high school students (Eisenberg et al 1984, Eisenberg-Berg 1979). Research has shown that there are positive associations between moral reasoning and prosocial behaviors. For a complete review, see Eisenberg (1982, 1986).

Self-Attributions of Motivations To Help

Based on studies of children's self-attributions about their own helping behavior, Bar-Tal proposed six phases in the development of helping behavior (Bar-Tal & Raviv 1982), moving from concrete rewards to true altruism as the child develops.[20] Bar-Tal and his associates found that older children are more likely to help without being told or offered rewards: young children reported altruistic motives relatively infrequently, but these increased with age (Bar-Tal & Nissim 1984; Bar-Tal et al 1980). Levin & Bekerman-Greenberg (1980) categorized kindergarten, second, fourth, and sixth grade children's answers, regarding why they did or did not share, into five levels, similar to those used by Bar-Tal. Eisenberg and her associates have also

---

[19]Eisenberg and her associates constructed five levels of prosocial moral reasoning: 1) Hedonistic, self-focus orientation: self concerned not moral concerned. 2) Needs-oriented: concerning other's need even though the other's needs directly conflict with one's own need. 3) Stereotyped orientation: Judgments based on stereotyped images of good or bad persons or on other's approval. 4a) Self-reflective empathic orientation: concern with other's humanness. 4b) Transitional level: Concern for the larger society. 5) Strongly internalized stage: judgment based on internal values, norms, or responsibility.

[20]1)Phase 1: Compliance-Concrete and defined reinforcement. Children help because they are asked to do so and the request is accompanied by concrete rewards or threats of punishment. 2) Phase 2: Compliance. The motivation for help is compliance with authority. Concrete reinforcements are not necessary. 3) Phase 3: Internal initiative–concrete reward. Helping behaviors are voluntary but are motivated by the anticipations for rewards. 4) Phase 4: Normative behavior. Compliance with social demands and social norms. 5) Phase 5: Generalized reciprocity. The belief that reciprocal social contracts (i.e. if they help others when they are in need, others will help them in return) motivates the helping behaviors. 6) Phase 6: Altruistic behavior. Helping behavior is motivated by benefits to another person.

examined children's reasoning about their own naturally occurring helping behaviors (Eisenberg et al 1984).

These authors conclude that preschoolers' and elementary school children's self-report reasoning for helping are predominately pragmatic, empathic, or reward oriented. However, from age 4 to elementary-school years, reward-oriented motives seem to decrease, while other-oriented, altruistic motives, and normative reasons increase. In summary, "it appears that the cognition associated with children's prosocial actions becomes more internal and less related to external gain with development" (Eisenberg 1986, p. 92).

Sensitivity to Social Norms

The increases of helping behaviors may be due to the greater sensitivity to social norms. Cialdini et al (1981) proposed a three-step process for the development of altruism: presocialization, awareness that others value altruistic behaviors, and finally the internalization of altruistic norms. If children are in the second stage, they should donate more when they know the social expectations. Forming et al (1985, study 1) found that second and third graders, but not first graders, increased their donations when an evaluative audience was present. Zarbatany et al (1985) studied first, third, and fifth graders and also found that: "Older children were indeed more generous than their younger counterparts, but only under conditions of at least moderate and detectable adult influence. Where such influence was minimal, fifth graders were no more generous than were younger children" (p. 755). However, some studies have also found that generosity does not increase linearly: second graders (seven-year olds) donated less than either younger or older children (Forming et al 1985, study 1; Forming et al 1983; Grunberg et al 1985).

PROCESSES IN THE DEVELOPMENT OF ALTRUISM

Modeling

According to social learning theory, behaviors can be learned through observation of others, who are referred to as "models" (Bandura 1977). Experimental studies have consistently shown that children display greater generosity when they are exposed to generous models than to selfish models (Lipscomb et al 1982, 1985; also see Rushton 1980). Inconsistent modeling has predictable effects. Lipscomb et al (1985) found that children exposed to a model who behaved inconsistently (once generously, once selfishly) donated less than children exposed to a consistently generous model, but more than children exposed to a consistently selfish model. Studies (Lipscomb et al 1982, 1985) also found that older children—who have presumably internalized social norms—were less affected by the models' behaviors than were kindergarten-age children.

Parents are models for children (for an extensive review on family influences on children's helping behaviors, see Radke-Yarrow & Zahn-Waxler 1986). A study by London (1970) of 27 rescuers of Jews concluded that the rescuers were characterized by "an intense identification with a parental model of moral conduct" (p. 245). Rosenhan (1970) found that "fully committed" civil rights workers differed from those who made only one or two freedom rides mainly in having had a close relationship with a morally committed parent or other person. B. Berkowitz (1987) found that a large proportion of "local heroes"—a group of 20 people who had started grass-roots community organizations—spontaneously mentioned the influence of one or both parents. Almost 60% of a sample of 237 first-time college donors said that someone in their families gave blood, and of that 60%, nearly half stated that the family members gave regularly (Piliavin & Callero, in press). One experimental study has also demonstrated a positive impact of modeling on blood donation decisions among adults (Rushton & Campbell 1977).

Parental Child-Rearing Practices

Hoffman (1984b) pointed out the importance of parental discipline: "It is only in discipline encounters that the child may have the earliest experience of being expected to control his deviant actions for reasons that derive from his own active consideration of these norms" (p. 120). Generalizing from a large body of research, Hoffman concluded that "(1) a moral orientation characterized by independence of external sanctions and by high guilt is associated with the use of inductions . . ., discipline techniques that point up the effects of the child's behavior on others; (2) A moral orientation based on fear of external detection and punishment. . . . is associated with the frequent use of power-assertive discipline . . .; (3) that the occasional use of power assertion to let the child know that the parent feels strongly about a particular act of value, or to control the behavior of a child who is acting in an openly defiant manner . . . may make a positive contribution to moral internalization . . .; (4) there appears to be no relationship between moral internalization and love withdrawal. . . ." (p. 120–21).

Karylowski (1982) points out that "endocentric" and "exocentric" altruism may be developed on the basis of somewhat different child-rearing practices. No consistent relationship between the use of love withdrawal and altruism has been found, although this technique has been consistently associated with the development of other positive moral behaviors. However, he found that mothers of endocentric girls used love withdrawal, persuading a child to apologize, indefinite labeling (e.g. "Good kids act like. . . ."), and pointing out inconsistencies between the child's behavior and some social role.

Marwell (1982) has proposed that we learn to be happy when others are happy and sad when they are sad because of our inherent dependence on those around us, mainly parents. We learn that "When others in our environment are unhappy they tend to punish us, even when we are not the source of their unhappiness." Presumably those who have been more dependent, or more perceptive regarding their dependency, will grow up to be more oriented towards satisfying the needs of others.

Learning by Doing: The Impact of Helping on the Helper

Attribution theory (Heider 1958, Kelley 1967) suggests that if we perceive that we have taken an action ourselves, without external coercion or large reward, we are likely to attribute to ourselves a predisposition toward that action and to be more likely to act in ways consistent with it. Consistent with the theory, people *perceive* themselves to have acted less altruistically if they helped (*a*) after being offered money as an incentive, (*b*) under reciprocity pressures, that is, if the person they helped had previously helped them, or (*c*) if normative expectations to help had been made salient (Batson et al 1978, Thomas & Batson 1981; Thomas et al 1980). One would also expect that those who have helped in the presence of such extrinsic pressures will be less likely to help on another occasion because they are less likely to attribute altruistic motives to themselves. After a review of such research, it was concluded, "These studies suggest that, over time, the use of extrinsic pressure to elicit helping from morally mature adults can backfire" (Batson et al 1987, p. 595).

Lightman (1982) has reported that changes in the motivations reported by blood donors are important both for their initial decision and for their most recent decision. External motivations decreased in importance—company of a friend, persuasion or encouragement by others, there being a blood drive or an emergency, while internal ones—a general desire to help others, a sense of duty, and support for the work of the Red Cross—increased. The author concludes (p. 64), "With the repeated performance of a voluntary act over time, the sense of personal, moral obligation assumed increasing importance as a motivator; a supportive and favourable context in general became much less vital."

In support of this conclusion, a correlational analysis of a longitudinal sample of college donors revealed that the number of donations was significantly related to change in the overall strength of motivation, to decreases in saying that they gave so as not to disappoint others, and to increases in reporting that they were motivated by moral obligation and a sense of responsibility to the community (Piliavin & Callero, in press). The effects were stronger among donors who reported no external justifications (e.g. a blood drive) at their most recent donation.

Role Identities

Some theorists (McCall & Simmons 1978, Stryker 1980, Turner 1978) suggest that commitment to some behaviors can reflect the development of a significant "role-identity," which can become an important dimension of the self. Analyses of a longitudinal sample of adult blood donors found that the two main factors leading to commitment to such a role-identity are repeated donations and the perceived expectations of significant others that one will continue donation (Piliavin & Callero, in press; Callero 1985, 1985–1986; Charng et al 1988). Once developed, this sense of self becomes the primary factor influencing intentions to continue giving blood; intentions and habit were the only significant predictors of continued donation.

The Effect of Having One's Help "Spurned"

Rosen et al (1985–1986, p. 147) propose that "the spurning of . . . altruistic offers has deleterious implications for the mental health and ensuing behavior of those would-be helpers," because rejection has negative implications for the self. The authors cite three correlational studies indicating that client resistance is stressful for professional helpers (Farber 1983), adversely affects their liking for clients (Wills 1978), and may contribute to "burnout" (Pines 1982). Rosen et al (1987) find, based on five studies, that "rejected" subjects had more negative feelings than those whose offer of help was accepted, and the former rated the person in need of help more negatively on one or more scales. Unfortunately, the impact of rejection on the potential helper's altruistic self-concept was not measured.

Being rejected from blood donation also leads to negative mood, to decisions that one is the kind of person who should not give blood, and to lower estimates of the likelihood of return to give again. In five separate samples, temporarily deferred donors are less likely to return; the effect is stronger among early career donors. (Piliavin & Callero 1990; Evans 1981; Piliavin 1987) Thus, it would appear that experiencing rejection *does* affect a would-be-helper's self-image.

IS ALTRUISM INNATE?

If altruism is part of human nature, it may have a genetic component. Before rejecting this notion out of hand, please remember that we have a great deal in common with other animals.[21] Dennis Wrong, in his classic paper, "The

---

[21]For example, According to Britten (1986) we share over 98% of our DNA sequences with the chimpanzee, and over 92% with the old world monkeys.

oversocialized conception of man in modern sociology," reminded us, "In the beginning, there is the body (1961, p. 191)." We share the lower centers of our brains—where the "fight or flight" mechanisms operate—with all other vertebrates (MacLean 1973). Many other social animals engage in clearly altruistic behavior: birds give predator alarms; mother rats endure severe shock to rescue their young; baboons help defend their troops; porpoises buoy up their injured fellows. It is parsimonious to assume that we at least share *tendencies* toward similar actions.

Of course, we no longer believe that the higher mammals—such as human beings—usually act under the control of instincts. Vine (1983) stresses that genetic involvement does not imply that traits must be fixed action patterns, essentially suggesting that a variety of traits related to altruism could underly such acts. And MacDonald states, "Altruism, attachment, and the affective systems generally are environment-expectant systems, i.e. systems in which genes specify not the behavioral phenotype, but the reaction of the organism to the environment . . . there may indeed be a biologically based empathic emotion that gives rise to altruistic behavior. However, the affective responses to the models in one's environment as well as the actions of the models are also important in determining the circumstances under which altruistic behavior actually occurs" (1984, p. 107). Hill (1984) points out that, "It is very unlikely that these "social genes" program for a particular pattern . . . they only permit or facilitate the learning of certain forms of behavior and also the internalization which may accompany the learning during socialization" (p. 23).

Secondly, sociobiologists have now demonstrated mathematically (Boorman & Leavitt 1980) and by means of computer simulations (Morgan 1985) that under certain conditions, there are three separate selection processes that can actually lead to the establishment and perpetuation of "altruist" genes in populations. In *group selection,* an altruistic gene can become established if mating takes place in relatively isolated groups, and whole groups will survive or die based on their genetic composition. An altruist gene that got started in such a small group could very well lead to a better outcome for that group relative to other groups. *Kin selection* occurs if self-sacrificing behavior is more likely to benefit others with whom one shares a high proportion of genes. That is, if the altruist dies but saves many brothers, sisters, and cousins who also carry altruist genes, more altruist genes are perpetuated than if the altruist had lived.

Reciprocity selection operates if the bearers of an altruist gene—whether they are related or not—are more likely to benefit each other by their altruistic behavior than to benefit random others. Reciprocal altruism is a tricky concept, defined initially by Trivers (1971) as involving (*a*) a cost to the altruist, (*b*) a benefit to the recipient, and (*c*) a "significant" delay between the time the recipient receives a benefit and repays the altruist.[22] Because of the "payback" aspect, many authors claim that "reciprocal altruism isn't altruism" (Krebs 1987, Sober 1988).

Morgan (1985) provides a computer simulation of the development of altruism under varying circumstances in a population divided into "clans."[23] The results show that, if clans do not divide into smaller groups as they grow, it is only under reciprocity conditions that an altruistic gene is able to establish itself. However, when clans do split, and interaction is "clannish"—that is, ingroup oriented—the gene can establish itself under any of three circumstances, whether altruists benefit only kin or only other altruists, or extend benefits to everyone. This study thus provides evidence for the operation of all three possible mechanisms of selection.[24] It is clearly possible that altruism could have evolved as a characteristic of our species.

Finally, from what we can infer based on present day hunting and gathering societies, early humans probably lived in rather isolated groups, mainly composed of close kin. This is exactly the circumstance that—according to these analyses—should most facilitate the development of a genetic predisposition to altruism. They were regularly exposed to danger from predators, making the evolution of warning and rescue behaviors adaptive. And the relative randomness of individual success in obtaining food should also have made the development of reciprocity adaptive.

What Might Be the Components of an Inherited Predisposition to Altruism?

The two main processes that presumably underlie the establishment and maintenance of an altruistic gene in the population are kin selection and reciprocity selection. Assuming this, what sorts of characteristics would we expect to be selected for?

---

[22]A critical problem for the evolution of strictly defined reciprocal altruism (RA) is that it is hard to see how a new gene for RA could become established. If the frequency of the gene is very low, its bearer will not be likely to meet other RAers, and will be "giving away" its benefits at costs. Rothstein & Pierotti (1988) suggest that other noncostly forms of social behavior could have evolved first, through the operation of kin selection. A generalization of these behaviors to a "time-lagged" form could then more easily have occurred. Moore (1984) also suggests that RA could get started through sharing of resources under circumstances in which this was not costly, such as meat sharing among primates.

[23]The three experimental variations involve, first, whether or not clans divide when they get large; second, whether interactions are limited to clan members or randomly distributed; finally, whether altruists extend benefits (a) to anybody, (b) only to other altruists, or (c) only to other clan members.

[24]The simulations also demonstrate that in clans containing both altruists and nonaltruists, individual altruists have lower survival and leave fewer descendents. However, the more altruists there are in a clan, the better off the clan members are, on average.

Cognitive Factors in the Evolution of Altruism

THE PROBLEM OF RECOGNITION.   For kin altruism, the potential altruist must be able to recognize (consciously or unconsciously) who its kin are, and for reciprocal altruism, it is critical that individuals bearing the reciprocity gene must be matched with each other. In proposing genetic similarity theory, Rushton et al (1984) suggest that recognition of the fact that the other is genetically similar underlies both types of selection. They present data showing that a wide variety of animals (e.g. quail, ground squirrels, macaques) reared apart can recognize their relatives and that animals (including humans) mate with those more like them chromosomally. They also bring in the social psychological literature on similarity and attraction and ingroup ethnic preferences in support of their thesis.

The economist Margolis (1982) presents an economic model based on evolutionary theory which assumes that each person has two kinds of preferences: group-oriented and self-oriented.[25] In trying to define the "group" in which an individual might have an interest, Margolis notes, "Specifically, we would expect that the cognitive cues that identify group-interest would have evolved from cues that originally developed as means of identifying kin . . . or cues that served to identify individuals with whom a reciprocity relation exists. For we would suppose that group-commitments arise when evolutionary conditions are such . . . that propensities that have their roots in strictly 'selfish gene' motivation are perpetuated beyond the conditions in which they arose" (p. 48). He later adds that "The Darwinian viewpoint suggests that group-loyalty is triggered by perceived similarities . . . group-loyalty is encouraged toward others who look like us, have similar tastes, follow similar customs, speak the same language, and so on" (pp. 128–129).

Studies provide evidence for kin recognition among humans. New mothers are able to identify their newborn infants by sight or by odor. Unrelated individuals were also able to match mothers and infants with above chance accuracy using the same cues (Porter 1987). Glassman et al (1986) make the following assumptions: (a) each person has critical traits in the self that s/he most highly values, (b) the genes that underly these traits are widely disseminated, (c) individuals will use the possessors of these traits—perceived or sensed through "emotional affinities"—as targets of altruistic efforts. For this selection to work, one need only assume a greater than zero accuracy of trait detection.

DETECTING CHEATING.   For reciprocal altruism to develop, there must also be ways of detecting and punishing those who do cheat or of socializing them

---

[25]He assumes that self-oriented preferences include one's immediate family, and claims that this has all along been a common assumption among economists (rather neatly assuming kin selection). The group (of group-oriented preferences) can be defined narrowly (e.g. a friendship group) or broadly (one's nation, the world).

in such a way that they refrain from cheating. Moore (1984) suggests that the ability to learn quickly, and the propensity to learn the right things (e.g. I get punished for behaving selfishly) may really underlie the development of reciprocal altruism. The arguments of Rushton et al (1984) and Glassman et al (1986) also suggest that intelligence—or at least perceptiveness—should be a factor in successful altruistic action. Cunningham (1985–1986) suggests that "Attributional processes which sometimes precede helping, that involve determining whether the misfortune afflicting the beneficiary was externally or internally caused, may have developed to prevent investment in those who create problems for themselves and are poor risks for reciprocation" (p. 56).

Several writers (Vine 1983, Lopreato 1981, Badcock 1986) focus on the possibility that the capacity for self-deception might have developed in connection with reciprocal altruism. Since being a nonaltruist among altruists is the best possible survival strategy, as long as one is not caught, the ability to deceive both others and oneself regarding one's altruism would be adaptive. In a theory of altruism that provides a Freudian dynamic linkage between genes and behavior, Badcock (1986) discusses the role of the defense mechanism of repression in this connection. He cites Trivers (1981) as follows, "cheating must be disguised—increasingly—even to the actor himself" (p. 26). "As mechanisms for spotting deception become more subtle, organisms may be selected to render some facts and motives unconscious, the better to conceal deception. In the broadest sense, the organism is selected to become unconscious of some of its deception, in order not to betray, by signs of self-knowledge, the deceptions being practised" (p. 35). Taylor & McGuire (1988) point out that the theory of reciprocal altruism has had an important influence on "our understanding of cheating and on the evolutionary issues associated with detecting noncooperators." These issues are the same as those dealt with under the rubric of "free riding" in the economics literature.

Emotional Factors in the Evolution of Altruism

Hoffman (1981), Cunningham (1985–1986), and MacDonald (1984) all implicate empathy as the prime candidate for an inherited capacity closely allied with the evolution of altruistic tendencies.[26] In the view of MacLean (1973), the brain structures required for primitive empathy were present early in evolution, making it hard for social beings such as our ancestors to ignore the pain or distress experienced by another.

A wide range of other emotions are suggested as concomitants of the evolution of altruism and as proximal mechanisms by which the altruistic gene might operate. Vine (1983, p. 4) quotes Trivers that reciprocity selection

[26]Hoffman, for example, notes that 1- and 2-day-old infants will cry in response to the sound of another infant's cry.

will tend to favor the evolution of strong emotions, "not only of liking and gratitude, but of hatred and indignation when aid is not reciprocated as expected . . . guilt at failure to reciprocate, and consequent 'reparative altruism' . . . highly elaborated cognitive-affective capacities and dispositions for the moral regulation of social relationships and interactions." Moore (1984) proposes that selection for sharing (which is not costly) could lead to positive emotions also being associated with all forms of helping. "Conscious manipulation of these emotions could then form the basis of a generalized, or societal, reciprocity ethic such as is now found in humans (Trivers 1971) and possibly odontocete cetaceans [whales and porpoises] (Connor & Norris 1982)." Trust is another possible candidate for an important related affective dimension of relevance.

Sociological Concepts in Relationship to the Evolution of Altruism

A number of writers bring in the concept of social norms as ways in which reciprocal altruism, once established, may be enforced (Morgan 1985, Taylor & McGuire 1988). Lopreato notes that social approval, used to reward conformity to norms, is a "sign that we are doing right as well as *a promise of future reward*. This latter property . . . may have facilitated the evolution . . . of the need for approval" (1981, p. 120). Hill (1984) discusses sociocultural and biological evolution in relation to each other. One conclusion is that the desire to attain prestige—a psychological extension of the dominance relations of other animals—may underly some acts of altruism.[27]

Evidence in Support of Sociobiological Hypotheses

Direct evidence for the heritability of altruistic tendencies comes from a study of 1400 adult monozygotic and dizygotic twins by Rushton et al (1986). Heritability estimates of 56%, 68%, and 72% were obtained for the three traits of altruism, empathy, and nurturance; for all three scales, about 50% of the variance was attributable to genetic effects. Similarly, Segal (1984) found striking evidence for greater cooperation between monozygotic than between dizygotic twins in an experimental study. Thirty-two out of 34 (94%) pairs of monozygotic but only 6 out of 13 (46%) dizygotic pairs completed a cooperative experimental puzzle task. On a second task, on which the choice was to work for self or other, monozygotic twins also worked significantly harder than did dizygotics for their co-twins. On the other hand, Simmons et al (1977) found that 86% of parents, but only 47% of siblings, who were eligible agreed to donate a kidney to their relative when asked. Since both parents and

---

[27]Food-sharing in primates is related to their place in dominance hierarchies, and in many cultures (e.g. the Kwakiutl) gift-giving is used to enhance prestige.

siblings share half of their genes, this difference must reflect mechanisms other than genetic ones. Based on extensive research on twins, Plomin (as quoted in Franklin 1989) believes that " 'niceness'—whether a person is more trusting, sympathetic and cooperative . . . is much more influenced by environment—mostly early environment—than by genes" (p. 38).

A number of studies involving role-playing or "as if" methods (Bar-Tal et al 1977, Cunningham 1983, M. R. Cunningham, J. Jegerski, & C. L. Gruder, in preparation) found that closeness of kinship was associated with expectations that help would be given, with resentment were it to be withheld, and with willingness to provide aid. Using anthropological data Essock-Vitale & McGuire (1980) found support for four hypotheses: (*a*) Kin will be given more unreciprocated help than nonkin; (*b*) kin will be given more help than nonkin, with close kin receiving the most help; (*c*) friendships will be reciprocal; and (*d*) large gifts and long-term loans are most likely to come from kin. Following 300 interviews with women, Essock-Vitale & McGuire (1985) found that exchanges (financial, emotional, illness-related, etc) with blood relatives (both giving and receiving) were the most common, and the more important the help, the more likely it was to come from kin.

A sociobiological perspective would predict that we would be more likely to help others perceived as similar or those to whom we felt close kin-like ties. Midlarsky (1985–1986) explored the dimensions of the identification of non-Jewish helpers with potential Jewish victims during the Holocaust, and derived three: political, theological, and socioeconomic. Experimental research has also shown that similarity in attitudes, personality, political opinions, and national identifications between the victim and the potential helper promotes helping behaviors. The effect of similarity in race depends on the situation (for a review, see Dovidio 1984; see also Piliavin et al 1981).

Oliner & Oliner (1988) found that rescuers of Jews had somewhat more information about Jews and closer ties with Jews. Simmons et al (1977) had potential kidney recipients rate their emotional closeness to all possible donors before the choice of a donor was made; recipients felt very close to 63% of the eventual donors but to only 42% of the eventual nondonors. Within sibling donor-recipient pairs, donors were significantly closer in age and were more likely to be of the same sex than were nondonors. Although each of these studies is individually open to methodological criticism or to alternative interpretations, most are at least consistent with the possibility that there are hereditary components to human altruism. The same results could of course also occur through a variety of social-psychological processes, such as normative pressures to favor those who are close friends, kin, and similar.

ALTRUISM AND THE PROVISION OF PUBLIC GOODS

It is within the arena of the provision of public goods that the question of altruism has arisen for economists. As Kim & Walker (1984) put it, "Economic theory . . . makes the . . . prediction: that the free rider problem will cause a group to provide itself with no more than a minimal level of the public good, even when every member of the group could be made better off if the public good were provided at a much greater level" (p. 3). The findings in the area clearly disprove this expectation (Marwell & Ames 1981; see Messick & Brewer 1983 for a review). Although there are clearly individual differences in the extent to which individuals contribute to public goods (see Personality section, above), and although the level of "free riding" is such that the optimal levels of provision of public goods are seldom attained, the "strong version" of the free rider hypothesis is almost never supported (for two exceptions, see Kim & Walker 1984, Isaac et al 1985). Marwell & Ames found support for it only when economists were used as subjects.

Potential Solutions to Social Dilemmas

Messick & Brewer (1983) suggest that there are two classes of solutions to the problems posed by free riding in social dilemmas: individual and structural. Individual solutions depend for their success on changing the attitudes, motivations, perceptions, and eventually the behavior of individuals without altering the essentially voluntary nature of contribution. Structural solutions follow the recommendation of Garrett Hardin (1968), who believed that the only way to change behavior in such situations was through "mutual coercion, mutually agreed upon." Most recent work in social dilemmas has focussed on these issues.

Individual Level Solutions To Social Dilemmas

COMMUNICATION   The most effective alteration in the social dilemma aimed at individual change is allowing communication among the members. Why does this work? (a) Communication allows group members to develop a strategy in which a subset is designated as those who are to contribute (Braver & Wilson 1986, van de Kragt et al 1986). (b) Discussion reveals or helps develop group norms, group identity, and "other-regarding sentiments" (Braver & Wilson 1986, van de Kragt et al 1986, Orbell et al 1988). (c) Communication makes public the intentions of individual others and allows for the development of trust, eliminating the fear of being a "sucker" (Orbell et al 1988). This fear of being taken advantage of if one contributes is, of course, at the heart of the free rider problem.

Other ways of developing a sense of group identity ought also to increase cooperation—or altruism—in social dilemma situations. Kramer & Brewer (1986) report four experiments in which groups of three subjects were led to focus on either a subordinate group identity (e.g. college student) or a superordinate identity (resident of Santa Barbara) when playing a dilemma game, purportedly with another subgroup of three (e.g. elderly Santa Barbara residents). The authors state, "In general, individuals were found to be more likely to exercise cooperative restraint to conserve an endangered resource when a collective level group identity was present" (p. 225).

EFFECT OF INFORMATION   A number of recent studies have explored the effect of information on the development of cooperative behavior in social dilemmas. Allison & Messick (1985) and Powers & Boyle (1983) found positive effects of providing feedback on cooperation; Schroeder et al (1983) found that subjects who were able simply to make comparative appraisals of the actions of others *decreased* in cooperation through a modeling mechanism.

Structural Solutions To Social Dilemmas

Legislation has typically been the route by which "fairness" has been regulated in the marketplace. Baumol (1975) points out that "social responsibility" can't work for corporations, because their job is to make money for their stockholders. His solution is what he calls "meta-voluntarism"—systematic cooperation in the design and implementation of measures that are basically involuntary—rather than the current situation of resisting all regulation.

A few investigators have examined experimentally what circumstances might lead groups to opt for such structural solutions to social dilemmas as electing a leader to make the decisions or privatization of the public good (Messick et al 1983; Samuelson & Messick 1986a, b; Samuelson et al 1984, 1986). These authors looked at both subjects' individual "harvesting"—taking resources from the common pool—and their willingness to vote for structural change. In general, the efficiency of use variable—whether the resource pool is being under-, over-, or optimally used—had an effect on harvesting, with subjects taking more in the underuse condition. Subjects in the overuse conditions also voted overwhelmingly for the structural solution of electing a leader, while those in the underuse and optimal use conditions seldom did. In contrast, the inequity factor—whether there is wide variation in how much different individuals are taking—has different effects in the United States and in the Netherlands. It affects harvesting only in the United States,—the greater the variability, the more individual subjects take from the pool—and affects willingness to vote for structural change only in the Netherlands. It seems, then, that the perception of differences in altruism leads to an individualistic solution, namely, "I'm going to get mine," in a highly individual-oriented country, the United States, and to a collective solution in a more socialist society, the Netherlands.

On the Impossibility of Sharing with Everyone

In a paper entitled "Discriminating altruisms," Garrett Hardin (1982) states the following, "A species composed only of pure altruists is impossible" (p. 164), and "The central characteristic of all forms of altruism is this: *discrimination is a necessary part of a persisting altruism*" (p. 167). By this he means that a propensity for altruism towards any- and everyone could not logically have evolved, because such individuals inevitably lose out in competition with egoists. It is only when there are groups that *reciprocally* benefit each other more than they benefit other people that an altruist tendency can survive. As soon as it becomes universal altruism, however, it is doomed. He points out some of the mechanisms through which his "discriminating altruisms"—selectively helping only certain people and not others—presumably operate: the power of loyalty and the pleasure of serving a cause greater than oneself. These clearly are operating in the social dilemma situations we have just been discussing. When groups are given the opportunity to communicate, free riding diminishes; the reasons involve the development of a sense of group identity, "other-regarding sentiments", trust, and expectations of reciprocity. It is only with complete anonymity, lack of connection with others, and strong economic incentives towards selfishness that classical economic theory can be expected to operate in the real world (Kim & Walker 1984). The rest of the time—given half a chance, in other words—at least "moderate altruism" (Sober 1990) will often appear.

"Altruistic" Voting

What is the evidence regarding the willingness of citizens to tax themselves for the benefit of others? The major theoretical approach to voting behavior has been essentially the same as classical economics (Becker 1976). Rasinski & Rosenbaum state, "this perspective predicts that citizens will be responsive to increased taxation to the extent that this taxation is in their economic self-interest" (1987, p. 991). While no one would suggest that voters completely ignore their own interests, a newer perspective proposes that non-self-interested factors form the basis for political behavior (see Rasinski & Tyler 1986, for a review). These factors include a sense of civic duty (Katosh & Traugott 1982), public-regardingness (Wilson & Banfield 1964), and concerns about justice (Tyler & Caine 1981; Tyler et al 1985). Rasinski & Rosenbaum state (1987, p. 992), "In fact, . . . research suggests that the citizen's sense of public responsibility may completely overcome his or her own self-interest when making decisions about public services and the funding of such services" (Cook 1979, Smith 1982, Wilson & Banfield 1964).

Rasinski & Tyler (1986) found that non-self-interested factors (e.g. concern for the quality of education and sympathy with teachers over low salaries) carried more weight in predicting hypothetical votes for school tax increases in a school district in Illinois than did self-interest (e.g. home ownership or having children in school). "This suggests an unusually unselfish willingness to sacrifice some of one's own gain in order that those crucial to the maintenance of quality schools receive better treatment" (p. 1002). The authors point out the consistency of this finding with prior work showing strong public support for policies that benefit the general social welfare.

The "Third Sector" and the Provision of Public Goods

Weisbrod (1975) has analyzed the participation of the voluntary nonprofit sector in a three-sector economy (the other sectors are public—government—and private) in the provision of public goods. One conclusion based on his work is that "The function of third sector institutions is thus to voice and act on the demands not of the general body but of minorities whose demands differ in kind or in degree from those of the majority . . ." (Douglas 1983, p. 118). Some of the public goods we want are altruistic—that the old, the poor, and the infirm be cared for adequately. "Weisbrod's model suggests that there will be a minority that believe in a higher level of social services than that for which most of their fellow citizens are willing to pay" (p. 149), and that voluntary action is the answer.

Voluntary Organizations and Volunteering

Alexis de Tocqueville (1974, Part 2, p. 485) said, "The Americans make associations to give entertainments, to found seminaries, to build inns, to construct churches, to diffuse books, to send missionaries to the Antipodes . . . Wherever at the head of some new undertaking you see the government in France, or a man of rank in England, in the United States you will be sure to find an association."

What do we know about volunteers? A survey of 1753 individuals, 14 years of age and older (Americans Volunteer 1981), found that among regular volunteers, the 30% who had done two or more hours per week within the last three months, the median number of hours worked per week was 4. Extrapolating this to 30% of perhaps 150 million adults in the United States suggests over 9 billion volunteer hours worked per year, which at minimum wage of $3.25 per hour comes to roughly $30 billion of free work.[28] The three top areas of participation were religion, education, and health.

---

[28]Clotfelter (1985) states, "In 1980 as many as 80 million Americans did some volunteer work, spending the equivalent of about 8 billion hours in such activity. The market value of this time has been estimated to be on the order of $60 billion . . ." (p. 3).

Volunteers generally give "altruistic" reasons for becoming involved, such as feelings of obligation to the community and wanting to help others (Americans Volunteer 1981, Sills 1957, Pearce 1983). However, self-oriented reasons are also very common, such as interest in the activity, perceived benefits to those they know, getting job experience, enhancing social status, or simply having social contacts. Two studies of the elderly (see Chambre 1987) suggest that, for them, self-fulfillment is a more important motivation than altruism.

In a case study of 70 heavily involved "society" women, Daniels (1988) reports their primary motive to be a sense of moral obligation to do something for the community because of their privileged position—rather a sense of "noblesse oblige." "They give generously because they have become affluent . . ." (p. 204). It was also clear, however, that their activities provided prestige, power, and the ability to satisfy ambitions from which these intelligent, college-educated women were otherwise blocked.

Private Philanthropy

By far the commonest form of voluntary action in the United States is the donation of money to charitable causes. In 1982, charitable giving by individuals amounted to $48.69 billion, plus another $5.45 billion in bequests (Clotfelter 1985). The three most popular areas for voluntary work—religion, education, and health—are also the most popular areas for financial contribution (Reddy 1980).[29] Social desirability, wanting recognition, getting ahead in one's career, expectations of respect from significant others, identification with certain groups (e.g. Jews with Israel), positive attitudes to the community are all important motives in addition to altruism. So are positive or negative attitudes towards the particular charity, especially issues of relative administrative costs and the kind of clients served. "In contrast to the negligible effects of . . . do-good motives the motivation to reduce taxes is the most powerful single variable in those studies that have included it (Reddy 1980, p. 391)."

Reddy (1980) reports seven studies between 1957 and 1975 that have found relationships between participation in voluntary associations and giving: the more participation, the more contributions. Americans Volunteer (1981) also found that volunteers are more likely to give money to charity than are nonvolunteers (91% vs 66%).

Helping in Disasters

Dynes & Quarantelli (1980) reviewed a large number of studies on responses to disasters. Generally, rather high proportions of individuals help under

---

[29]Not all charitable giving is altruistic. Donations to the church provide activities to the members; supporting the symphony ensures its continuation for one's own enjoyment.

disaster circumstances. In an Arkansas tornado and the Wilkes-Barre flood, for example, about 25% reported participating in rescue efforts. In Wilkes-Barre, 4.5% of households provided multiple volunteers, supplying almost 20% of all volunteers. They conclude, "The social-organizational view suggests behavior is best explained as being guided by norms embedded in roles" (p. 347).

Blood Donation

In 1988, about 14 million units of blood were donated in the United States. The literature on blood donation has recently been reviewed (Piliavin & Callero in press, Piliavin 1990), and discussions of some aspects are to be found in other sections of this report. By far the most frequent reason given for donation is humanitarian or altruistic, although many donors will admit to "a feeling of self-satisfaction" or even pride (Piliavin & Callero in press). Three studies (Boe 1977, Needham Harper Worldwide 1986, Weisenthal & Emmot 1979) found that the most active donors were more likely to make charitable contributions and to do volunteer work and charitable fundraising than were nondonors.

Posthumous Organ Donation

Signing a donor card that allows one's organs to be used in the event of one's sudden death can be seen as a form of voluntarism. A review of the psychological aspects of organ donation is to be found in Perkins (1987). Shanteau & Harris (1990), who provide the most up to date "sampler" of current research, state, "the shortage of donated organs is not due to lack of knowledge or awareness of the plight of would-be recipients. Instead, the problem arises from factors such as unstated motivations, perceived risks, and unarticulated fears about donation." Parisi & Katz (1986) report that their cluster analysis revealed two dimensions of attitudes toward posthumous donation: the positive one involved belief in the humanitarian benefits of organ donation and feelings of pride experienced by the donor, the negative, fears of body mutilation and of receiving inadequate medical treatment when one's life is at risk.

Conclusions Regarding Voluntarism

Humanitarian, altruistic reasons are often given by people who volunteer time, money, or blood, but these are not the only—or sometimes the main—motivations. It is usually not possible to demonstrate that altruism is truly a cause of voluntarism, since longitudinal, prospective work on volunteers has not been done. Only in the area of blood donation is it clear that those who express more "altruistic" and "community oriented" motives are indeed more likely to continue in the activity than are those who do not (Piliavin & Callero, in press).

Corporate Philanthropy and Social Responsibility

Corporate contributions for charitable and similar purposes were $2.7 billion in 1980 (Frederick 1983), $2.9 billion in 1981, and $3.1 billion in 1982 (Galaskiewicz 1985). On the other hand, "corporations have never approached the limits of giving encouraged by Internal Revenue Service rules, which until 1981 permitted the deduction of such contributions up to 5 percent of pretax income and now allow up to 10 percent of pretax income. The national average for corporations hovers around 1 percent" (p. 149).

Our focus in this review has been on individual motivations for altruism. Thus, to pursue the "corporate actor" in depth would be to go a bit far afield. Is there any evidence for corporate "altruism?" The answer appears to be "no." Fry et al (1982) note that "Existing literature has focused on three rationales for corporate philanthropy: through-the-firm giving [by owners and managers], corporate statesmanship [social responsibility], and profit motivated giving" (p. 94). Their review of past work and their own results suggest little support for either of the first two possibilities. Their conclusion is that "it would seem ill-advised to use philanthropy data to measure altruistic responses of corporations" (p. 105). In agreement with earlier results of Galaskiewicz (1985), Moore & Richardson (1988) conclude that "Peer group pressure has also been an important aspect of encouraging a growing corporate responsiveness to these social issues" (p. 270). "Rationales . . . based on community or morality . . . had [no] effect at all on the level of company giving" (Galaskiewicz 1985, pp. 215–217). Clarkson (1988) analyzes the "corporate responsibility" of 32 corporations in Canada and essentially concludes that giving is good for business.

Our conclusion from the limited literature we have been able to discover on corporate responsibility is that "enlightened self-interest" rather than altruism is what drives socially responsible behavior in this area. Normative pressures can increase social responsibility, largely because such pressures lead corporate officers to perceive that socially responsible behavior is in the corporation's own best interest. Although individual corporate officers may feel empathy or have "group-oriented feelings," corporations obviously do not. The behavior of those corporate officers, acting for the corporation, must be largely determined by the self-interest of the company. If altruism is seen as based on those feelings, then, corporate philanthropy is not and cannot be altruism.

IMPLICATIONS FOR INCREASING ALTRUISM IN SOCIETY

In recent years, Republican administrations have called for "a new voluntarism," most recently expressed in Bush's phrase "a thousand points of light." Concurrently, the "taxpayers' revolt" and the Reagan cutbacks in government support imply that the provision of many services that used to come from the government must and morally ought now to be provided privately. Yet, as more women have gone out to work, the pool of traditional volunteers has begun to dry up—" there is no one to organize the annual town fair, it is nearly impossible to find a mother to organize a Brownie troop . . ." (p. 212, Kaminer 1984). What is the answer?

The altruistic impulse does exist. We have argued in this review that altruism—or at least the willingness to consider others in our overall calculations of our own interests—is natural to the human species. Whether this "naturalness" is encoded in the genes, inculcated through socialization, or based in social norms, we have suggested that the typical person finds a need to participate in cooperative social endeavors that benefit others or the community at large. Terkel writes, "Most of us have jobs that are too small for our spirit. Jobs are not big enough for people . . . most of us are looking for a calling" (p. xxix, 1972). Kaminer says, "Paid work is simply a matter of earning a living. Volunteering is 'doing something you care about.' " (p. 217).

The solution may thus lie in cooperative arrangements among corporations, government, and voluntary action organizations, supported no longer by "stay at home mothers" but by employed men and women. More people will have to contribute, perhaps during lunch breaks, evenings, and weekends. The challenge must be to arouse the altruistic spirit in individuals by using similarity, group identification, "mock kinship," and to use normative pressure against corporations and other institutions in which feelings cannot be aroused, to work together to provide those services no longer available in the public sector.

Literature Cited

Allison, S. T., Messick, D. M. 1985. Effects of experience on performance in a replenishable resource trap. *J. Pers. Soc. Psychol.* 49:943–48

Americans Volunteer. 1981. *Go 80193.* Princeton, NJ: Gallup

Aries, E. J., Johnson, F. L. 1983. Close friendship in adulthood: Conversational content between same-sex friends. *Sex Roles* 9:1183–96

Aronoff, J., Wilson, J. P. 1984. *Personality in the Social Process.* Hillsdale, NY: Erlbaum

Arrow, K. J. 1963. *Social Choice and Individual Values.* New York: Wiley. Rev. Ed.

Arrow, K. 1975. Gifts and exchanges. See Phelps 1975, pp. 13–28

Austin, W. 1979. Sex differences in bystander intervention in a theft. *J. Pers. Soc. Psychol.* 37:2110–30

Badcock, C. R. 1986. *The Problem of Altruism.* Oxford, England: Blackwell

Bandura, A. 1977. *Social Learning Theory.* Englewood Cliffs, NJ: Prentice-Hall

Bar-Tal, D. 1985–1986. Altruistic motivation to help: Definition, utility and operationalization. *Humboldt J. Soc. Relat.* 13:3–14

Bar-Tal, D., Bar-Zohar, Y., Greenberg, M. S., Hermon, M. 1977. Reciprocity behavior in the relationship between donor and recipient and between harm-doer and victim. *Sociometry* 40:293–98

Bar-Tal, D., Nadler, A., Blechman, N. 1980. The relationship between Israeli children's helping behavior and their perception on parents' socialization practices. *J. Soc. Psychol.* 111:159–67

Bar-Tal, D., Nissim, R. 1984. Helping behavior and moral judgment among adolescents. *Br. J. Psychol.* 2:329–36

Bar-Tal, D., Raviv, A. 1982. A cognitive-learning model of helping behavior development: Possible implications and applications. See Eisenberg 1982, pp. 199–218

Batson, C. D. 1990. How social an animal? The human capacity for caring. *Am. Psychol.* In press

Batson, C. D. 1987. Prosocial motivation: Is it ever truly altruistic? *Adv. Exp. Soc. Psychol.* 20:65–122

Batson, C. D., Batson, J. G., Griffitt, C. A., Barrientos, S., Brandt, J. R. et al 1989. Negative-state relief and the empathy-altruism Hypothesis. *J. Pers. Soc. Psychol.* 56:922–33

Batson, C. D., Coke, J. S., Jasnoski, M. L., Hanson, M. 1978. Buying kindness: effect of an extrinsic incentive for helping on perceived altruism. *Pers. Soc. Psychol. Bull.* 4:86–91

Batson, C. D., Coke, J. S. 1981. Empathy: A source of altruistic motivation for helping? In *Altruism and Helping Behavior*, ed. J. P. Rushton, R. M. Sorrentino, pp. 169–88. Hillsdale, NJ: Erlbaum

Batson, C. D., Duncan, B. D., Ackerman, P., Buckley, T., Birch, K. 1981. Is empathic emotion a source of altruistic motivation. *J. Pers. Soc. Psychol.* 40:290–302

Batson, C. D., Dyck, J., Brandt, J. R., Batson, J. G., Powell, A. L., et al. 1988. Five studies testing two new egoistic alternatives to the empathy-altruism Hypothesis. *J. Pers. Soc. Psychol.* 55:52–77

Batson, C. D., Fultz, J., Schoenrade, P. A., Paduano, A. 1987. Critical self-reflection and self-perceived altruism: when self-reward fails. *J. Pers. Soc. Psychol.* 53:594–602

Batson, C. D., O'Quin, K., Fultz, J., Vanderplas, M., Isen, A. 1983. Self-reported distress and empathy and egoistic versus altruistic motivation for helping. *J. Pers. Soc. Psychol.* 45:706–18

Baumann, D. J., Cialdini, R. B., Kenrick, D. T. 1981. Altruism as hedonism: Helping and self-gratification as equivalent responses. *J. Pers. Soc. Psychol.* 40:1039–46

Baumol, W. J. 1975. Business responsibility and economic behavior. See Phelps 1975, pp. 45–56

Becker, G. S. 1976. *The Economic Approach to Human Behavior*. Chicago: Univ. Chicago Press

Beggan, J., Messick, D., Allison, S. 1988. Social values and egocentric bias: Two tests of the might over morality hypothesis. *J. Pers. Soc. Psychol.* 55:606–11

Berg, J. H. 1984. Development of friendship between roommates. *J. Pers. Soc. Psychol.* 46:346–56

Berkowitz, B. 1987. *Local Heroes.* Lexington, Mass: Lexington Books

Boe, G. P. 1977. *A descriptive characterization and comparison of blood donors and non-donors in a community blood program.* (Diss. Abstr. Int.), 1977:3879 College Station, Tex: Texas A&M Univ.

Boe, G. P., Ponder, L. D. 1981. Blood donors and non donors: A review of the research. *Am. J. Med. Technol.* 47:248–53

Boorman, S. A., Levitt, P. R. 1980. *The Genetics of Altruism.* New York: Academic Press

Bower, G. H. 1981. Mood and memory. *Am. Psychol.* 36:129–48

Braver, S. L., Wilson, L. A. 1986. Choices in social dilemmas: Effects of communication within subgroups. *J. Confl. Resolut.* 30:51–62

Briggs, N. C., Piliavin, J. A., Lorentzen, D., Becker, G. A. 1986. On willingness to be a bone marrow donor. *Transfusion* 26:324–30

Britten, R. J. 1986. Rates of DNA sequence evolution differ between taxonomic groups. *Science* 23:1393–98

Buchanan, J. M. 1954. Individual choice in voting and the market. *J. Polit. Econ.* 62:334–43

Callero, P. L. 1985. Role-identity salience. *Soc. Psychol. Q.* 48:203–15

Callero, P. L. 1985–1986. Putting the social in prosocial behavior: An interactionist approach to altruism. *Humbolt J. Soc. Relat.* 13:15–34

Carlson, M., Charlin, V., Miller, N. 1988. Positive mood and helping behavior: A test of six hypotheses. *J. Pers. Soc. Psychol.* 55:211–29

Carlson, M., Miller, N. 1987. Explanation of the relation between negative mood and helping. *Psychol. Bull.* 102:91–108

Chambers, J. H., Ascione, F. R. 1987. The effects of prosocial and aggressive videogames on children's donating and helping. *J. Genet. Psychol.* 148:499–505

Chambre, S. M. 1987. *Good Deeds in Old Age: Volunteering by the New Leisure Class.* Lexington, Mass: Lexington Books

Chapman, M., Zahn-Waxler, C., Cooperman, G., Iannotti, R. 1987. Empathy and responsibility in the motivation of children's helping. *Dev. Psychol.* 23:140–45

Charng, H.-W., Piliavin, J. A., Callero, P. L. 1988. Role-identity and reasoned action in the prediction of repeated behavior. *Soc. Psychol. Q.* 51:303–17

Cialdini, R. B., Baumann, D. J., Kenrick, D. T. 1981. Insights from sadness: A three-step model of the development of altruism as hedonism. *Dev. Rev.* 1:207–23

Cialdini, R. B., Schaller, M., Houlihan, D., Arps, K., Fultz, J., Beaman, A. 1987.

Empathy-based helping: Is it selflessly or selfishly motivated? *J. Pers. Soc. Psychol.* 52:749–58

Clark, D. M., Teasdale, J. D. 1985. Constraints on the effects of mood on memory. *J. Pers. Soc. Psychol.* 48:1595–1608

Clark, M. S., Isen, A. M. 1982. Toward understanding the relationship between feeling states and social behavior. In *Cognitive Social Psychology*, ed. A. Hastorf, 78–108. A. M. Isen. New York: Elsevier

Clark, M. S., Waddell, B. A. 1983. Effects of moods on thoughts about helping, attraction, and information acquisition. *Soc. Psychol. Q.* 46:31–35

Clarkson, M. B. E. 1988. Corporate social performance in Canada, 1976–1986. See Preston 1988, pp. 241–66

Clotfelter, C. T. 1985. *Federal Tax Policy and Charitable Giving.* Chicago: Univ. Chicago Press

Condie, S. J., Warner, W. K., Gillman, D. C. 1976. Getting blood from collective turnips: Volunteer donation in mass blood drives. *J. Appl. Psychol.* 61:290–94

Connor, R. C., Norris, K. S. 1982. Are dolphins reciprocal altruists? *Am. Nat.* 119:358–74

Cook, F. L. 1979. *Who Should Be Helped: Public Support for Social Services.* Beverly Hills: Sage

Crawford, C., Smith, M., Krebs, D., eds. 1987. *Sociobiology and Psychology.* Hillsdale, NJ: Erlbaum

Cunha, D. 1985. *Interpersonal trust as a function of social orientation.* PhD thesis. Univ. Del.

Cunningham, M. R. 1983. *Altruism and attraction from a sociobiological perspective.* Pap. pres. 91st Ann. Meet. Am. Psych. Association, Anaheim, Calif., August

Cunningham, M. R. 1985–1986. Levites and brother's keepers: A sociobiological perspective on prosocial behavior. *Humboldt J. Soc. Relat.* 13:35–67

Cunningham, M. R., Jegerski, J., Gruder, C. L. 1990. Kin selection and reciprocal altruism in humans: Charity begins at home. In preparation

Daniels, A. K. 1988. *Invisible Careers: Women Civic Leaders from the Volunteer World.* Chicago: Univ. Chicago Press

Dawes, R. M. 1980. Social dilemmas. *Am. Psychol. Rev.* 31:169–93

Dawes, R. M., Orbell, J. 1981. Social dilemmas. In *Progress in Applied Social Psychology*, ed. G. M. Stephenson, J. H. Davis, Vol. 1. Chichester: Wiley

Derlega, V. J., Grzelak, J., eds. 1982. *Cooperation and Helping Behavior.* New York: Academic Press

Deutsch, F. M., Lamberti, D. M. 1986. Does social approval increase helping? *Pers. Soc. Psychol. Bull.* 12:149–58

Douglas, J. 1983. *Why Charity? The Case for a Third Sector.* Beverly Hills: Sage

Dovidio, J. F. 1984. Helping behavior and altruism: An empirical and conceptual overview. *Adv. Exp. Soc. Psychol.* 17:361–427

Dovidio, Piliavin, Goertner, Schroeder, and Clavic (forthcoming)

Drake, A. W., Finkelstein, S. N., Sopolsky, H. M. 1982. *The American Blood Supply.* Cambridge, Mass: MIT Press

Durkheim, E. 1933. *The Division of Labor in Society.* New York: Macmillan

Dynes, R. R., Quarantelli, E. L. 1980. Helping behavior in large-scale disasters. In *Participation in Social and Political Activities*, ed. D. H. Smith, J. Macaulay, pp. 339–54. San Francisco: Jossey-Bass

Eagly, A. H., Crowley, M. 1986. Gender and helping behavior: A meta-analysis review of the social psychological literature. *Psychol. Bull.* 100:283–308

Edney, J. J. 1980. The commons problem: Alternative perspectives. *Am. Psychol.* 35:131–50

Eisenberg, N. 1986. *Altruistic Emotion, Cognition, and Behavior.* Hillsdale, NJ: Erlbaum

Eisenberg, N. 1982. The development of reasoning regarding prosocial behavior. In *The Development of Prosocial Behavior*, ed. N. Eisenberg, pp. 49–250. New York: Academic Press

Eisenberg, N., Fabes, R. A., Miller, P. A., Fultz, J., Shell, F., et al. 1989. Relation of sympathy and personal distress to Prosocial behavior: A multimethod study. *J. Pers. Soc. Psychol.* 57:55–66

Eisenberg, N., Lennon, R. 1983. Sex differences in empathy and related capacities. *Psychol. Bull.* 94:100–31

Eisenberg, N., McCreath, H., Ahn, R. 1988. Vicarious emotional responsiveness and prosocial behavior: Their interrelations in young children. *Pers. Soc. Psychol. Bull.* 14:298–311

Eisenberg, N., Miller, P. A. 1987. The relation of empathy to prosocial and related behaviors. *Psychol. Bull.* 101:91–119

Eisenberg, N., Pasternack, J. F., Lennon, R. 1984. *Prosocial Development in Middle Childhood.* Pap. pres. Biennial Meet. Southwest Soc. Res. Hum. Dev. Denver

Eisenberg, N., Pasternack, J. F., Cameron, E. Tryon, K. 1984. The relations of quantity and mode of prosocial behavior to moral cognitions and social style. *Child. Dev.* 55:1479–85

Eisenberg, N., Schaller, M., Fabes, R. A., Bustamante, D., Mathy, R. M., et al. 1988. Differentiation of personal distress and sympathy in children and adults. *J. Pers. Soc. Psychol.* 24:766–75

Eisenberg-Berg, N. 1979a. Development of children's prosocial moral judgement. *Dev. Psychol.* 15:128–37

Eisenberg-Berg, N., Lennon, R. 1980. Altruism and the assessment of empathy in the preschool years. *Child Dev.* 51:552–57

Essock-Vitale, S. M., McGuire, M. T. 1980. Predictions derived from the theories of kin selection and reciprocation assessed by anthropological data. *Ethol. Sociobiol.* 1:233–43

Essock-Vitale, S. M., McGuire, M. T. 1985. Women's lives viewed from an evolutionary perspective. II. Patterns of helping. *Ethol. Sociobiol.* 6:155–73

Evans, D. E. 1981. *Development of intrinsic motivation among first time donors.* PhD Thesis. Univ. Wisc., Madison

Farber, B. A. 1983. Psychotherapists' perceptions of stressful patient behavior. *Prof. Psychol. Res. Pract.* 14:697–705

Farnill, D., Ball, I. L. 1982. Sensation seeking and intention to donate blood. *Psychol. Rep.* 51:126

Forgas, J. P., Bower, F. H., Krantz, S. E. 1984. The influence of mood on perceptions of social interactions. *J. Exp. Soc. Psychol.* 20:497–513

Forming, W. J., Allen, L., Jensen, R. 1985. Altruism, role-taking, and self-awareness: The acquisition of norms governing altruistic behavior. *Child Dev.* 56:1223–28

Forming, W. J., Allen, L., Underwood, B. 1983. Age and generosity reconsidered: Cross-sectional and longitudinal evidence. *Child Dev.* 54:585–93

Franklin, P. 1989. What a child is given. *N.Y. Times Mag.* Sept. 3, 1989, pp. 36–41, 49

Frederick, W. C. 1983. Corporate social responsibility in the Reagan era and beyond. *Calif. Manage. Rev.* 25:145–57

Fry, L. W., Keim, G. D., Meiners, R. E. 1982. Corporate contributions: Altruistic or for-profit? *Acad. Manage. J.* 25:94–106

Fultz, J., Schaller, M., Cialdini, R. B. 1988. Empathy, sadness, and distress: Three related but distinct vicarious affective responses to another's suffering. *Pers. Soc. Psychol. Bull.* 14:312–25

Galaskiewicz, J. 1985. *Social Organization of an Urban Grants Economy: A Study of Business Philanthropy and Nonprofit Organizations.* New York: Academic Press

Glassman, R. B., Packel, E. W., Brown, D. L. 1986. Green beards and kindred spirits: A preliminary mathematical model of altruism toward nonkin who bear similarities to the giver. *Ethol. Sociobiol.* 7:107–15

Grunberg, N. E., Maycock, V. A., Anthony, B. J. 1985. Material altruism in children. *Appl. Basic Soc. Psychol.* 6:1–11

Hardin, G. 1968. The tragedy of the commons. *Science* 162:1243–48

Hardin, G. 1982. Discriminating altruisms. *Zygon* 17:163–86

Harsanyi, J. 1955. Cardinal welfare, individualistic ethics, and interpersonal comparisons of utility. *J. Polit. Econ.* 63:309–21

Heider, F. 1958. *The Psychology of Interpersonal Relations.* New York: Wiley

Heshka, S. 1983. Situational variables affecting participation in voluntary associations. See Smith 1983, pp. 138–47

Hill, J. 1984. Human altruism and sociocultural fitness. *J. Soc. Biol. Struct.* 7:17–35

Hoffman, M. L. 1977. Sex differences in empathy and related behaviors. *Psychol. Bull.* 84:712–20

Hoffman, M. L. 1981. Is altruism part of human nature? *J. Pers. Soc. Psychol.* 40:121–37

Hoffman, M. L. 1982a. Development of Prosocial motivation: Empathy and guilt. See Eisenberg 1982, pp. 281–314

Hoffman, M. L. 1982b. The measurement of empathy. In *Measuring Emotions in Infants and Children*, ed. C. E. Izard, pp. 279–96. Cambridge, UK: Cambridge Univ. Press

Hoffman, M. L. 1984a. Interaction of affect and cognition on empathy. In *Emotions, Cognition, and Behavior*, ed. C. E. Izard, J. Kagan, R. B. Zajonc, Cambridge, UK: Cambridge Univ. Press

Hoffman, M. L. 1984b. Parent discipline, moral internalization, and development of prosocial motivation. In *Development and Maintenance of Prosocial Behavior*, ed. E. Staub, D. Bar-Tal, J. Karylowski, J. Reykowski, pp. 117–37. New York: Plenum

Huston, T. L., Geis, G., Wright, R. 1976. The angry Samaritans. *Psychol. Today* 10:61–64

Isaac, R. M., McCue, K. F., Plott, C. R. 1985. Public goods provision in an experimental environment. *J. Public Econ.* 26:51–74

Johnson, F. L., Aries, E. J. 1983. Conversational patterns among same-sex pairs of late-adolescent close friends. *J. Pers. Soc. Psychol.* 142:225–38

Kaminer, W. 1984. *Women Volunteering.* Garden City, NY: Anchor

Katosh, J. P., Traugott, J. W. 1982. Cost and values in the calculus of voting. *Am. J. Polit. Sci.* 26:361–76

Karylowski, J. 1982. Two types of altruistic behavior: Doing good to feel good or to make the other feel good. See Derlega & Grzelak 1982, pp. 396–419

Karylowski, J. 1975. *Z Badan Nad Mechanizmani Pozytywnych Ustosunkowan Inter personalnych.* Wroclaw, Poland: Ossolineaum

Kelley, H. H. 1967. Attribution theory in social psychology. In *Nebraska Symposium on Motivation,* ed. D. Levine, 14:192–240. Lincoln: Univ. Nebr. Press

Kerber, K. 1984. The perception of nonemergency helping situation, rewards, and the altruistic personality. *J. Pers.* 52:177–87

Kim, O., Walker, M. 1984. The free rider problem: Experimental evidence. *Public Choice* 43:3–24

Kramer, R. M., Brewer, M. B. 1986. Social group identity and the emergence of cooperation in resource conservation dilemmas. See Wilke et al 1986, pp. 205–34

Kramer, R. M., McClintock, C. G., Messick, D. M. 1986. Social values and cooperative response to a simulated resource conservation crisis. *J. Pers.* 54:576–92

Krebs, D. 1987. The challenge of altruism in biology and psychology. See Crawford et al 1987, pp. 81–118

Latane, B., Nida, S., Wilson, D. 1981. The effect of group size on helping behavior. In *Altruism and Helping Behavior,* ed. J. P. Rushton, R. M. Sorrentino, pp. 287–317. Hillsdale, NJ: Erlbaum

Levin, I., Bekerman-Greenberg, R. 1980. Moral judgment and moral behavior in sharing: A developmental analysis. *Genet. Psychol. Monogr.* 101:215–30

Liebrand, W. B. G. 1986. The ubiquity of social values in social dilemmas. See Wilke et al 1986, pp. 113–34

Liebrand, W. B. G., Jansen, R. W. T. L., Rijken, V. M., Suhre, C. J. M. 1986. Might over morality: Social values and the perception of other players in experimental games. *J. Exp. Soc. Psychol.* 22:203–15

Lightman, E. S. 1982. Continuity in social policy behaviours: The case of voluntary blood donorship. *J. Soc. Policy* 10:53–70

Lipscomb, T. J., Larrieu, J. A., McAllister, H. A., Bregman, N. J. 1982. Modeling and children's generosity: A developmental perspective. *Merrill-Palmer Q.* 28:275–82

Lipscomb, T. J., McAllister, H. A., Bregman, N. J. 1985. A developmental inquiry into the effects of multiple models on children's generosity. *Merrill-Palmer Q.* 31:335–44

London, P. 1970. The rescuers: motivational hypotheses about Christians who saved Jews. In *Altruism and Helping Behavior: Social Psychological Studies of Some Antecedents and Consequences,* ed. J. Macaulay, L. Berkowitz, pp. 241–50. New York: Academic Press

Lopreato, J. 1981. Toward a theory of genuine altruism in homo sapiens. *Ethol. Sociobiol.* 2:113–26

MacDonald, K. 1984. An ethological-social learning theory of the development of altruism: Implications for human sociobiology. *Ethol. Sociobiol.* 5:97–109

MacLean, P. D. 1973. *A Triune Concept of the Brain and Behavior.* Toronto, Canada: Univ. Toronto Press

Manucia, G. K., Baumann, D. J., Cialdini, R. B. 1984. Mood influences on helping: Direct effects or side effects? *J. Pers. Soc. Psychol.* 46:357–64

Margolis, H. 1982. *Selfishness, Altruism, and Rationality.* Cambridge: Cambridge Univ. Press

Marwell, G. 1982. Altruism and the problem of collective action. See Derlega & Grzelak 1982, pp. 207–30

Marwell, G., Ames, R. 1981. Economists free ride, does anyone else? Experiments on the provision of public goods, IV. *J. Public Econ.* 15:295–310

McCall, G. J., Simmons, J. L. 1978. *Identities and Interactions.* New York: Free Press

Meindl, J. R., Lerner, M. J. 1983. The heroic motive: Some experimental demonstrations. *J. Exp. Soc. Psychol.* 19:1–20

Messick, D. M., Brewer, M. B. 1983. Solving social dilemmas. A review. In *Review of Personality and Social Psychology,* ed. L. Wheeler, P. Shaver, 4:11–44. Beverly Hills: Sage

Messick, D. M., Wilke, H., Brewer, M. B., Kramer, R. M., Zemke, P. E., Lui, L. 1983. Individual adaptations and structural change as solutions to social dilemmas. *J. Pers. Soc. Psychol.* 44:294–309

Meyer, J. P., Mulherin, A. 1980. From attribution to helping: An analysis of the mediating effects of affect and expectancy. *J. Pers. Soc. Psychol.* 39:201–10

Midlarsky, M. I. 1985–1986. Helping during the Holocaust: The role of political, theological, and socioeconomic identifications. *Humboldt J. Soc. Relat.* 13:85–305

Moore, C., Richardson, J. J. 1988. The politics and practice of corporate responsibility in Great Britain. See Preston 1988, pp. 267–90

Moore, J. 1984. The evolution of reciprocal sharing. *Ethol. Sociobiol.* 5:4–14

Morgan, C. J. 1985. Natural selection for altruism in structured populations. *Ethol. Sociobiol.* 6:211–18

Needham Harper Worldwide. 1986. *A Life Style Profile of Blood Donors.* Unpublished observations

Oliner, S. P., Oliner, P. M. 1988. *The Altruistic Personality: Rescuers of Jews in Nazi Europe.* New York: Free Press

Orbell, J. M., van de Kragt, A. J. C., Dawes, R. M. 1988. Explaining discussion-induced cooperation. *J. Pers. Soc. Psychol.* 54:811–19

Parisi, N., Katz, I. 1986. Attitudes toward posthumous organ donation and commitment to donate. *Health Psychol.* 5:565–80

Pearce, J. L. 1983. Participation in voluntary associations: How membership in a formal organization changes the rewards of participation. See Smith 1983, pp. 148–56

Perkins, K. A. 1987. The shortage of cadaver donor organs for transplantation: Can psychology help? *Am. Psychol.* 42:921–30

Phelps, E. S., ed. 1975. *Altruism, Morality, and Economic Theory*. New York: Sage

Piliavin, J. A. 1987. Temporary deferral and donor return. *Transfusion* 27:199–200

Piliavin, J. A. 1990. Why they 'Give the gift of life to unnamed strangers': A review of research on blood donors since Oswalt (1977). *Transfusion*. In press

Piliavin, J. A., Callero, P. L. 1990. *Giving the Gift of Life to Unnamed Strangers*. Baltimore: Johns Hopkins Univ. Press. In press

Piliavin, J. A., Dovidio, J. F., Gaertner, S. L., Clark, R. D. III. 1981. *Emergency Intervention*. New York: Academic Press

Piliavin, J. A., Libby, D. 1986. Perceived social norms, personal norms, and blood donation: aggregate and individual level analyses. *Humboldt J. Soc. Relat.* 13:159–94

Piliavin, J. A., Unger, R. K. 1985. The helpful but helpless female: Myth or reality? In *Women, Gender, and Social Psychology*, ed. V. O'Leary, R. K. Unger, B. S. Wallston, pp. 149–90. Hillsdale, NJ: Erlbaum

Pines, A. 1982. Helpers' motivation and the burn-out syndrome. In *Basic Processes in Helping Relationships*, ed. T. A. Wills. New York: Academic Press

Poppe, M., Utens, L. 1986. Effects of greed and fear of being gypped in a social dilemma situation with changing pool size. *J. Econ. Psychol.* 7:61–73

Porter, R. H. 1987. Kin recognition: Functions and mediating mechanisms. Crawford et al 1987, pp. 175–204

Powers, R. B., Boyle, W. 1983. Generalization from a commons dilemma game: The effects of a fine option, information, and communication on cooperation and defection. *Simul. Games* 14:253–74

Preston, L. E. 1988. *Research in Corporate Social Performance and Policy*, Vol. 10. Greenwich, Conn: JAI Press

Radke-Yarrow, M., Zahn-Waxler, C. 1986. The role of familial factors in the development of prosocial behavior: Research findings and questions. In *Development of Antisocial and Prosocial Behavior: Research, Theories, and Issues*, ed. D. Olweus, J. Block, M. Radke-Yarrow, pp. 207–33. New York: Academic Press

Rapoport, A. 1988. Provision of step-level public goods: Effect of inequality in resources. *J. Pers. Soc. Psychol.* 54:432–40

Rasinski, K. A., Rosenbaum, S. M. 1987. Predicting citizen support of tax increases for education: A comparison of two social psychological perspectives. *J. Appl. Soc. Psychol.* 17:990–1006

Rasinski, K. A., Tyler, T. R. 1986. Social psychology and political behavior. In *Political Behavior Annual*, ed. S. Long, Vol. 1. Boulder, Colo: Westview

Reddy, R. D. 1980. Individual philanthropy and giving behavior. In *Participation in Social and Political Activities*, ed. D. H. Smith, J. Macaulay, pp. 370–99. San Francisco: Jossey-Bass

Reisenzein, R. 1986. A structural equation analysis of Weiner's attribution-affect model of helping behavior. *J. Pers. Soc. Psychol.* 50:1123–33

Reisenzein, R., Morrow, W., Weiner, B. 1984. *The effects of false sympathy and anger feedback on judgments of help-giving, sentiments, and perceived causality*. Free Univ. Berlin, Federal Republic of Germany. Unpublished ms.

Reykowski, J. 1979. *Motywacja, Postawy Prospoleczne A Osobowosc*. Warszawa: PWN

Romer, D., Gruder, C. L., Lizzadro, T. 1986. A person-situation approach to altruistic behavior. *J. Pers. Soc. Psychol.* 51:1001–12

Rosen, S., Mickler, S. E., Collins, J. E. 1987. Reactions of would-be helpers whose offer of help is spurned. *J. Pers. Soc. Psychol.* 53:288–97

Rosen, S., Mickler, S. E., Spiers, C. 1985–1986. The spurned philanthropist. *Humboldt J. Soc. Relat.* 13:145–58

Rosenhan, D. 1970. The natural socialization of altruistic autonomy. In *Altruism and Helping Behavior: Social Psychological Studies of Some Antecedents and Consequences*, ed. J. Macaulay, L. Berkowitz, pp. 251–68. New York: Academic Press

Rothstein, S. I., Pierotti, R. 1988. Distinctions among reciprocal altruism, kin selection, and cooperation and a model for the initial evolution of beneficent behavior. *Ethol. Sociobiol.* 9:189–209

Rushton, J. P. 1980. *Altruism, Socialization, and Society*. Englewood Cliffs, NJ: Prentice-Hall

Rushton, J. P. 1981. *The altruistic personality*. In *Altruism and Helping Behavior: Social Personality, and Developmental Perspectives*, ed. J. P. Rushton, R. M. Sorrentino, pp. 251–66.

Rushton, J. P., Campbell, A. C. 1977. Modeling, vicarious reinforcement and extroversion and blood donating in adults: immediate and long-term effects. *Eur. J. Soc. Psych.* 7:297–306

Rushton, J. P., Fulker, D. W., Neale, M. C., Nias, D. K. B., Eysenck, H. J. 1986. Altruism and aggression: The heritability of individual differences. *J. Pers. Soc. Psychol.* 50:1192–98

Rushton, J. P., Russell, R. J. H., Wells, P. A. 1984. Genetic similarity theory: Beyond kin selection altruism. *Behav. Genet.* 14:179–93

Samuelson, C. D., Messick, D. M. 1986a. Alternative structural solutions to resource dilemmas. *Organ. Behav. Hum. Decis. Process.* 37:139–55

Samuelson, C. D., Messick, D. M. 1986b. Inequities in access to and use of shared resources in social dilemmas. *J. Pers. Soc. Psychol.* 51:960–67

Samuelson, C. D., Messick, D. M., Rutte, C. G., Wilke, H. 1984. Individual and structural solutions to resource dilemmas in two cultures. *J. Pers. Soc. Psychol.* 47:94–104

Samuelson, C. D., Messick, D. M., Wilke, H. A. M., Rutte, C. G. 1986. See Wilke et al 1986, pp. 29–54

Schaller, M., Cialdini, R. B. 1988. The economics of empathic helping: Support for mood management motive. *J. Exp. Soc. Psychol.* 24:163–81

Schroeder, D. A., Jensen, T. D., Reed, A. J., Sullivan, D. K., Schwab, M. 1983. The actions of others as determinants of behavior in social trap situations. *J. Exp. Soc. Psychol.* 19:522–39

Schwartz, S. H. 1970. Elicitation of moral obligation and self-sacrificing behavior: An experimental study of volunteering to be a bone marrow donor. *J. Pers. Soc. Psychol.* 37:283–93

Schwartz, S. H., Fleishman, J. A. 1982. Effects of negative personal norms on helping behavior. *Pers. Soc. Psychol. Bull.* 8:81–86

Schwartz, S. H., Howard, J. 1982. Helping and cooperation: A self-based motivational model. In *Cooperation and helping behavior: Theories and Research,* ed. V. J. Derlega, J. Grzelak, pp. 328–56. New York: Academic Press

Schwartz, S. H., Howard, J. 1984. Internalized values as motivators of altruism. In *Development and Maintenance of Prosocial Behavior: International Perspectives on Positive Morality,* ed. E. Staub, D. Bar-Tal, J. Karylowski, J. Reykowski, pp. 229–56. New York: Plenum

Segal, N. L. 1984. Cooperation, competition, and altruism within twin sets: A reappraisal. *Ethol. Sociobiol.* 5:163–77

Senneker, P., Hendrick, C. 1983. Androgyny and helping behavior. *J. Pers. Soc. Psychol.* 45:916–25

Shanteau, J., Harris, R. 1990. *Psychological Research on Organ Donation.* Washington, DC: APA Publ. In press

Shotland, R. L., Stebbins, C. A. 1983.

Emergency and cost as determinants of helping behavior and the slow accumulation of social psychological knowledge. *Soc. Psychol. Q.* 46:36–46

Siem, F. M., Spence, J. T. 1986. Gender-related traits and helping behaviors. *J. Pers. Soc. Psychol.* 51:615–21

Sills, D. L. 1957. *The Volunteers.* Glencoe, Ill: Fress Press

Simmons, R. G., Klein, S. D., Simmons, R. L. 1977. *The Gift of Life: The Social and Psychological Impact of Organ Transplantation.* New York: Wiley

Simmons, R. G., Marine, S. K., Simmons, R. L. 1987. *The Gift of Life: The Effect of Organ Transplantation on Individual Family and Societal Dynamics.* New Brunswick, NJ: Transaction

Smith, A. 1969. *The Theory of Moral Sentiments.* Indianapolis: Liberty Classics

Smith, D. H., ed. 1983. *International Perspectives on Voluntary Action Research.* Washington, DC: Univ. Press America

Smith, T. W. 1982. Public support for educational spending: Trends, rankings, and models, 1971–1978. In *Monitoring Educational Outcomes and Public Attitudes,* ed. K. J. Gilmartin, R. J. Rossi, New York: Human Sciences

Sober, E. 1990. What is psychological egoism? *Behaviorism.* In press

Sober, E. 1988. What is evolutionary altruism? *Can. J. Philos.* 14:75–99

Staub, E. 1978. *Positive Social Behavior and Morality,* Vol. 1. New York: Academic Press

Staub, E. 1979. *Positive Social Behavior and Morality: Socialization and Development,* Vol. 2. New York: Academic Press

Sterling, B., Gaertner, S. L. 1984. The attribution of arousal and emergency helping: A bidirectional process. *J. Exp. Soc. Psychol.* 20:286–96

Stroebe, W., Frey, B. S. 1982. Self-interest and collective action: The economics and psychology of public goods. *Br. J. Soc. Psychol.* 23:121–37

Stryker, S. 1980. *Symbolic Interactionism: A Social Structural Version.* Menlo Park: Benjamin/Cummings

Taylor, C. E., McGuire, M. T. 1988. Introduction. Reciprocal altruism: 15 years later. *Ethol. Sociobiol.* 9:67–72

Terkel, S. 1975. *Working.* New York: Avon

Thomas, G. C., Batson, C. D. 1981. Effect of helping under normative pressure on self-perceived altruism. *Soc. Psychol. Q.* 44:127–31

Thomas, G. C., Batson, C. D., Coke, J. S. 1980. Do good Samaritans discourage helpfulness?: Self-perceived altruism after exposure to highly helpful others. *J. Pers. Soc. Psychol.* 40:194–200

Thompson, W., Cowan, C., Rosenhan, D. 1980. Focus of attention mediates the impact of negative affect on altruism. *J. Pers. Soc. Psychol.* 38:291–300

Tice, D. M., Baumeister, R. F. 1985. Masculinity inhibits helping in emergencies: Personality does predict the bystander effect. *J. Pers. Soc. Psychol.* 49:420–28

Tocqueville, A. de. 1974. *Democracy in America.* Transl. H. Reeve. New York: Schocken

Trivers, R. L. 1971. The evolution of reciprocal altruism. *Q. Rev. Biol.* 46:35–37

Trivers, R. L. 1981. Sociobiology and politics. In *Sociobiology and Human Politics,* ed. E. White. Lexington and Toronto:

Turner, R. H. 1978. The role and the person. *Am. J. Sociol.* 84:1–23, 4, 8

Tyler, T. R., Caine, A. 1981. The influence of outcomes and procedures on satisfaction with formal leaders. *J. Pers. Soc. Psychol.* 41:642–55

Tyler, R. R., Rasinski, K. A., McGraw, K. M. 1985. The influence of perceived injustice upon support for the president, political authorities, and government institutions. *J. Appl. Soc. Psychol.* 48:72–78

Underwood, B., Moore, B. 1982. Perspective-taking and altruism. *Psychol. Bull.* 91:143–73

van de Kragt, A. J. C., Dawes, R. M., Orbell, J. M., Braver, S. R., Wilson, L. A. II. 1986. Doing well and doing good as ways of resolving social dilemmas. See Wilke et al 1986, pp. 112–204

Vine, I. 1983. Sociobiology and social psychology—Rivalry or symbiosis? *Br. J. Soc. Psychol.* 22:1–11

Weiner, B. 1980a. A cognitive (attribution)-emotion-action model of motivated behavior: An analysis of judgments of help giving. *J. Pers. Soc. Psychol.* 39:186–200

Weiner, B. 1980b. May I borrow your class notes? An attributional analysis of judgments of help giving in an achievement-related context. *J. Ed. Psychol.* 72:676–81

Weisbrod, B. 1975. Towards a theory of the non-profit sector. See Phelps 1975, pp. 171–96

Weisenthal, D. L., Emmot, S. 1979. Explorations in the social psychology of blood donation. In *Research in Psychology and Medicine,* ed. D. F. Osborne, M. M. Gruneberg, J. R. Eiser, 1979:36–38. New York: Academic Press

Wilke, A. M., Messick, D. M., Rutte, C. G., eds. 1986. *Experimental Social Dilemmas.* Frankfurt am Main: Verlag Peter Lang

Wills, T. A. 1978. Perceptions of clients by professional helpers. *Psychol. Bull.* 85:968–1000

Wilson, E. O. 1975. *Sociobiology: The New Synthesis.* Cambridge, Mass: Harvard Univ. Press

Wilson, E. O. 1976. The war between the words: biological versus social evolution and some related issues: Section 2. Genetic basis of behavior—especially of altruism. *Am. Psychol.* 31:370–71

Wilson, J. P., Petruska, R. 1984. Motivation, model attributes, and prosocial behavior. *J. Pers. Soc. Psychol.* 46:458–68

Wilson, J. Q., Banfield, E. C. 1964. Public-regardingness as a value premise in voting behavior. *Am. Polit. Sci. Rev.* 50:491–505

Wrong, D. 1961. The oversocialized conception of man. *Am. Soc. Rev.* 26:183–93

Zarbatany, L., Hartmann, D. P., Gelfand, D. M. 1985. Why does children's generosity increase with age: Susceptibility to experimenter influence or altruism? *Child Dev.* 56:746–56

Zuckerman, M., Siegelbaum, H., Williams, R. 1977. Predicting helping behavior: Willingness and ascription of responsibility. *J. Appl. Soc. Psychol.* 7:295–99

Annu. Rev. Sociol. 1990. 16:67–86

POVERTY AND OPPORTUNITY STRUCTURE IN RURAL AMERICA

Ann R. Tickamyer

Department of Sociology, University of Kentucky, Lexington, Kentucky 40506–0027

Cynthia M. Duncan

Department of Sociology, University of New Hampshire, Durham, New Hampshire 03824

KEY WORDS: rural poverty, economic restructuring, labor markets, inequality, regional development and underdevelopment

Abstract

Rural areas have a disproportionate share of the US poverty population. Like poor urban communities, the persistence and severity of poverty in rural America can be linked to a limited opportunity structure which is the outcome of both past social and economic development policies and current economic transformation. Many rural communities lack stable employment, opportunities for mobility, investment in the community, and diversity in the economy and other social institutions. They are increasingly socially and spatially isolated and particularly vulnerable to adverse effects from structural economic change. This study reviews research on rural poverty and traces its relationship to its historical roots in social, political, and economic inequality and to current economic restructuring. Relevant sources of information on rural poverty include classic community and regional analyses, studies of rural-urban migration, regional development and underdevelopment, economic restructuring, and labor market analysis.

INTRODUCTION

Political and economic forces in the 1980s have prompted a resurgence of poverty research. Initially, new research efforts emphasized growing poverty

67

in urban areas, especially among predominantly black, inner city ghetto residents (Wilson 1987, Wilson & Aponte 1985). Researchers sought a better understanding of the dynamics of poverty, using the rich data accumulated from panel studies to explore who was poor, for how long, and why. At the microlevel, household structure and labor force attachment emerged as the most fundamental explanatory variables (Bane & Ellwood 1986, Duncan 1984). These findings stimulated further research which included much greater attention to local economic conditions and the social and cultural milieu at the community level.

New research on the dynamics of poverty coincided with the realization that the national economy had undergone permanent, structural change. The global reach of the economy signaled a shift from goods-producing to service-producing industries in advanced industrial nations, and a consequent restructuring of economic opportunities (Levy 1987, Harrison & Bluestone 1988). Some economists argued that a service-based national economy would result in greater inequality as the skilled blue collar jobs that offer occupational and social mobility evaporate, and the occupational structure becomes skewed, with low-skill, low-wage jobs at one end and highly paid professional service jobs at the other (Leigh-Preston 1988, Bluestone & Harrison 1988, Thurow 1987).

These trends have stimulated concern about rural poverty, where restructuring has exacerbated long-term economic distress (Brown & Deavers 1988, Deavers 1989, Duncan & Tickamyer 1988, Levy 1987, Tickamyer & Duncan 1990). Rural America has long had a disproportionate share of the nation's poverty population. Currently communities located outside metropolitan statistical areas have one fifth of the nation's population but one third of the poor. Jobs have been scarce and unstable in most rural communities for decades, and people have responded by combining different kinds of work or by migrating to cities for better employment opportunities. Now that the central cities and rural areas are experiencing a decline in jobs that offer a stable future for those with limited skills and education, scholars and policymakers again recognize the importance of better understanding the poverty population. New studies emphasize the diverse circumstances of the poor, distinguishing between the working poor, who suffer from low wages or underemployment, and the nonworking poor, who are disabled, elderly, or trapped in chronic poverty areas (Auletta 1982, Cottingham & Ellwood 1989, Dunbar 1984, Ellwood 1988, Levitan & Shapiro 1987, Sandefur & Tienda 1988).

This review examines research on rural poverty, tracing its relationship to inequality and economic transformation. We show that despite the lack of a well-defined tradition of rural poverty research, there have been relevant studies embedded in classical regional and community analyses, work on migration, development, and more recently, on economic restructuring and labor market analysis. At micro and macro levels, these studies demonstrate that the structure of work opportunities has prevented poor rural people and communities from escaping poverty. The spatial dimension of limited opportunity has created and perpetuated a social structure that reinforces poverty and underdevelopment.

PAST NEGLECT OF RURAL POVERTY

Preoccupation with urban poverty follows a long tradition in American social science (Wilson & Aponte 1985). In the late nineteenth and early twentieth century, poverty was viewed as one of many social pathologies associated with urbanization, mass immigration, and industrialization, and it drew the attention of both scholars and reformers (Bremmer 1956, Katz 1983, 1986, Patterson 1981, Wilson & Aponte 1985, Wirth 1938). During this period, many rural poor left marginal farms and hard times in more remote areas to join immigrants and other low-income groups in growing urban centers (Byerly 1986, Hareven & Langenbach 1978, Riis 1890).

Others remained poor in rural areas, but rural poverty did not receive the same attention as urban poverty, and until very recently, rural poverty has been the direct focus of only a small number of sociological studies. Baldwin (1968) argues that lack of visibility and widespread belief that all rural residents could prosper in farming obscured rural poverty until the Depression. After some attention from New Deal policymakers, interest again waned. A content analysis of 50 years of *Rural Sociology* from its inception in 1936 showed that articles on poverty declined from a high of 3% in its first decade to virtually nothing by the 1980s (Christenson & Garkovich 1985).

Rural poverty has also been neglected by mainstream and rural sociologists because of uncertainty about the validity of "rural" as a separate analytic category for understanding modern industrial societies (Falk & Gilbert 1985; Gilbert 1982; Newby 1982; Pahl 1968a, 1968b; Stein 1972; Wirth 1938). When urban sociologists discovered family and kin networks thriving in urban neighborhoods (Bott 1957, Gans 1962, 1968, Whyte 1981), the old gemeinschaft/gesellschaft categories appeared to lose their "spatial" dimension. Many urban sociologists regard spatial and ecological variables as descriptive rather than explanatory, and they therefore assume that "rurality" is a matter of degree on a linear rural-urban continuum. They attribute differences between rural and urban communities, and consequently rural and urban poverty, to a residual, almost atavistic, rural culture with little contemporary sociological significance. Conversely, the idea that the rural economy, culture, and lifestyle differ significantly from urban environments often arises from a nostalgic romanticization of agrarian society that ignores rural poverty.

Sociological neglect of rural poverty has left us with an incomplete understanding of poverty in advanced, industrialized, capitalist, and *urbanized* society. The conditions that generate rural poverty in the 1980s and 1990s are more severe and clearly more permanent than in previous decades, but they are not fundamentally new conditions. While growing numbers of working poor and a shortage of jobs offering upward mobility to low-skill workers are contributing to a new crisis in central cities, this lack of opportunity is not new to rural areas. Similarly, the deepening socioeconomic and cultural isolation of urban ghettos described by Wilson (1987) has been the experience of generations of the rural poor, especially in the South, where rigid social stratification has kept them out of the mainstream. Thus, understanding the circumstances of the rural working poor who are trapped by tight labor markets, or probing the chronically dependent poor in remote and isolated areas, can deepen our understanding of the poor in both urban and rural areas.

POOR RURAL PEOPLE AND PLACES

In the 1950s rural poverty was far more severe than urban poverty, with over a third of rural residents in poverty compared to 15% in urban areas and 18% in central cities. The combination of national economic growth and substantial outmigration from depressed areas brought a precipitous drop in rural poverty, and by the late 1960s rural poverty had fallen to 18% (compared to 13% in central cities). During the mid-1970s the poverty rate in rural areas continued to decline to a low of 14% in 1978, but hard economic times in the late 1970s and early 1980s brought new increases in rural poverty, until the rate reached 18% in the mid-1980s. The 1980s saw a significant increase in all poverty rates. By the decade's end the 17% poverty rate in rural America nearly equaled the 19% rate in the central cities. Although there are compositional differences between the rural and urban poor (the rural poor are more likely to be white, elderly, or in two-parent households with at least one worker), those who are most vulnerable in the central cities—blacks, children, and those in female-headed households—are even more likely to be poor if they live in rural areas. Regional differences are also important. Rural poverty has always been most severe and most heavily concentrated in the South, a fact recognized by both New-Deal and War-on-Poverty policymakers. In addition to plaguing the deep South, chronic poverty and underdevelopment have troubled communities in the Ozark and Appalachian mountains, and on American Indian reservations.

By and large, characteristics of the rural poor have been documented over the last decade by researchers associated with the Economic Research Service of the Department of Agriculture (see Brown et al 1988, Davis 1979, Deavers & Hoppe 1990, Ghelfi 1986, Hoppe 1985, Morrissey 1985, Oliveira 1986,

Ross & Morrissey 1987, Ross & Rosenfeld 1988). In addition, the persistence of severe rural poverty even during a national economic recovery has stimulated attention from several leading public policy-oriented organizations, including the Population Reference Bureau (O'Hare 1988), the Center on Budget and Policy Priorities (1989), and the House Select Committee on Children, Youth, and Families (1989). Like their influential predecessors *The Other America* (Harrington 1962) and *The People Left Behind* (President's Commission on Rural Poverty 1966), these reports are aimed at raising public concern and spurring policymakers to action.

Community Studies

Few studies probe the dynamics of rural poverty, and researchers interested in understanding rural poverty in the past must make their own interpretations of classic ethnographic studies and journalistic accounts. Studies for such interpretation were made from the Depression era through to the present time and cover poor rural households in most regions of the country. Earlier studies are densely descriptive, personalized accounts. Although there are exceptions, authors frequently accept popular stereotypes about low-income, non-middle class groups. Taking the potential biases of the writers into account, we find significant differences between poverty in the rural South and poverty in other rural areas. Southern rural poverty among both blacks and whites is rooted in a rigidly stratified political and economic system that perpetuated landlessness and dependency. Elsewhere rural poverty was the result of unstable, seasonal employment or marginal agriculture.

THE DEEP SOUTH AND APPALACHIA   Work about southern poverty through the 1930s includes a number of classic community studies and social histories that describe an entrenched social structure in which lines were clearly drawn between the haves and the have-nots (Agee & Evans 1941, Baldwin 1968, Conrad 1965, Davis et al 1941, Dollard 1957). The combined disdain and paternalism of white elites characterized an oppressive system that blocked opportunities for advancement and encouraged dependent behavior for both white and black laborers and tenants. In the late 1930s, three monographs from the Works Progress Administration provided detailed descriptions of the oppressive nature of Southern rural poverty. For example, Zimmerman & Whetten (1971) found that southern children on relief were much more likely to have dropped out of school than were poor rural children in the north, midwest, and west. Conrad (1965) and Baldwin (1968) show how Southern white farm leaders successfully blocked federal efforts to diversify and democratize the structure of Southern agriculture in the 1930s. Without access to land or education, these rural poor had no way to escape poverty, although both white and black tenants moved from plantation to plantation every couple of years, in search of some better opportunity.

When Stein (1972) compares Davis et al's findings in *Deep South* to community studies in large northern cities, he points out that in the southern communities every institution was focussed on keeping blacks subordinate to whites, whereas in Chicago, even though "officialdom" was controlled by middle and upper class white elites, "they were at least 'formally' dedicated to defending and protecting the individual." The Southern rural poor never had such protection. These community studies report that Southern white elites treated the rural poor like incompetent children, who deserved their low status because they were ignorant and shiftless. Although similar attitudes about the poor are found in all areas (see Steinberg 1981, Lemann 1989), in the South these middle-class prejudices against lower-class behavior were undergirded by a repressive, almost feudal economic system. Each of these early studies describes a system in which the poor were denied basic educational, economic, and political opportunities. The distinct political economy of the plantation-based south left a legacy of rural poverty for those who did not migrate (Billings 1979, 1988; Cobb 1982; Mandel 1978; Wright 1986).

More recent work suggests little has changed. Studies by Marshall and Godwin (1971), the Southern Regional Council's Task Force on Southern Rural Development (1977), and Rungeling et al (1977) document the rural poor's continued lack of job and education opportunities and their dependence upon the entrenched white power structure. Racism and elitism among white administrators undermine welfare programs and corrupt implementation of the meager employment and training programs that exist. Preliminary results from new ethnographic studies of poor households headed by females in the rural South show the same patterns. Dill et al (1988) find racism and lack of political power to be key factors in the perpetuation of rural poverty among black women. Beckley (1988) shows how plantation system dependency is transferred to dependency on the elite-controlled welfare system in small Southern communities.

Appalachian poverty has received almost as much scholarly attention, and certainly as much popular attention, as that of the Deep South. The most influential study is Kentucky lawyer Harry Caudill's *Night Comes to the Cumberlands* (1962), a rambling, undocumented account that feeds stereotypes held about Appalachia since the turn of the century (Walls 1978, Shapiro 1978). Caudill describes Appalachians as ignorant, hopelessly discouraged and fatalistic, their spirits broken by ruthless coal barons. Similar descriptions followed (Ball 1968, Fetterman 1967, Lantz 1971), each suffering from sentimental hyperbole, a deficit of evidence, and an overdependence on culture of poverty theories. However, in the absence of more serious study, many subsequent analysts have treated these works as scholarship (see Duncan 1986).

Some recent works remain strongly influenced by these predecessors while simultaneously offering contradictory accounts (cf Deloria 1984, Auletta 1982). Despite stereotypes about shiftless Appalachians, Auletta's anecdotes actually describe individuals who hate the stigma of living on welfare and long for independence. In an area with few employment opportunities, finding work is even more difficult because they are stigmatized by their families' lack of success.

There are also alternative portraits of persistent poverty in Appalachia that connect the structure of the national and regional political economy to inequality and powerlessness in mountain communities (Billings 1974, Gaventa 1980). Similarly, at the local level authors in Hall & Stack's collection (1982) show how kinship and landholding patterns perpetuate existing social divisions and factional politics, ostracizing poor families. Duncan (1988) found that in coal communities, the few stable jobs available go either to family members or to political supporters, locking out those whose families "never amounted to anything." Studies of noncoal communities portray self-sufficient people who cannot find stable work that frees them from poverty, and consequently many migrate to seek jobs elsewhere (Beaver 1986; Coles 1971a,b; Schwarzweller et al 1971).

COMMUNITY STUDIES IN THE NORTH   In contrast, the high value placed on independence is a recurring theme in ethnographic and community studies in the Northeast. Studies of a New Hampshire dairy farming area (MacLeish & Young 1942) and a Maine fishing community (Hughes et al 1960) portray a relatively unoppressive social structure in which good schools were provided for the children of laborers and hard work sometimes permitted escape from poverty. In the rural farm economy of the 1940s and 1950s, mobility was possible and frequently achieved by individuals who started with very little. While these studies report examples of ethnic and racial prejudice, elitist attitudes were not reinforced by an economic system with no opportunity for improvement as they were in the South.

Fitchen's case study of the rural poor in a declining community in upstate New York (1981) is a contemporary version of these northeastern community studies. Her historical review of the social class structure before farming declined also indicates that hard workers could achieve land ownership and upward mobility. However, the poor she describes in the 1970s face limited economic opportunities. Although they are not trapped by an explicitly oppressive social system as are their southern counterparts, their inability to find and keep stable jobs has become a chronic problem. Their behavior and circumstances resemble that of marginal workers in cities who cannot break out of poverty (cf Liebow 1967, Stack 1974).

The structure of economic opportunity in a given place or time provides the context for the behavior of the rural poor. In a recent study of two poor fishing communities on Maryland's eastern shore, Ellis (1986) describes isolated, almost self-contained island communities in which people work mostly for themselves. Independence is highly valued in this culture, and working for wages, like being illiterate or having an illegitimate child, condemns one to the lowest status on the island.

NATIVE AMERICANS, HISPANICS, AND POOR FARMERS   Although several new ethnographic studies are underway on poverty among Native Americans, Hispanics, and marginal farmers, most previous work consists of either statistical or journalistic descriptions. Exceptions are Snipp & Summers' (1988) analysis of Native Americans using the special Indian Census from 1980, Sandefur & Scott's (1984) comparison of black and American Indian labor force participation, and Palerm's (1988) study of low-income Hispanics in California agricultural communities. In these works, the limited opportunity structure, for both work and acquisition of assets, clearly explains the persistent poverty experienced by these minorities. Montejano's (1987) social history of Mexican-anglo relations along the Texas border, like earlier Southern studies, attributes the chronic rural poverty that plagues that region to rigid class stratification emerging from the structure of the political economy. Those who migrated to cities escaped these constraints and had opportunities for upward mobility.

In every region, the rural poor seek stable, secure support but are handicapped by isolation and limited opportunities. Like the inner city poor described by Wilson (1987), the rural poor have little experience outside their small communities (Duncan & Tickamyer 1988, Williams & Kornblum 1985). Like Liebow's (1967) streetcorner men, they value work and self-sufficiency, but years of disappointment and unsteady work have made them cautious about trying new avenues or venturing out from the world they know and the family on whom they rely. In the South these limitations are compounded by rigid class and race stratification that discourages efforts to become self-sufficient and upwardly mobile.

Migration and the Rural-Urban Poor Linkage

Migration literature is extensive and beyond the scope of this review, but several studies contribute an important dimension to understanding rural poverty because they link patterns of economic success in migration to the industrial structure (Levy 1987; Lieberson 1978, 1980; Long 1974; Long & Heltman 1975; Ritchey 1974). There has been some renewed debate recently about the extent to which rural migrants contribute to urban poverty, and more specifically, the extent to which rural Southern blacks bring lifestyles and culture that perpetuate inner city poverty through dependency and out-of-wedlock births (G. Duncan 1988, Lemann 1986, Wilson 1987). Most scholars insist that these debates about culture and life style are best analyzed in terms of economic opportunity, both past and present.

Generally, past studies indicated that migrants have done better than non-migrants, whether they were white Appalachians, Native Americans, or blacks. But as Levy (1987) points out, success was possible because cities could absorb in-migrants from rural areas when cheap housing and steady manufacturing jobs were available. By the mid-1980s production jobs that offered opportunities for rural migrants were disappearing, especially for poorly educated black men. G. Duncan and his colleagues (1988) see evidence that rural Southern migrants now in their middle ages have not fared so well in the cities, a phenomenon explained by recent analyses of industrial restructuring. The same factors that constrict opportunities in the central cities now contribute to further decline in rural areas, and the emergence of a "new rural poor" (Stinson 1988), making it clear that growing inequality has a spatial as well as social dimension.

SPATIAL ANALYSIS OF ECONOMIC OPPORTUNITY

Spatial analyses of poverty draw from a variety of disciplines and theoretical perspectives, and these have been reviewed extensively elsewhere (Henry 1989, Kale 1986, Rees & Stafford 1986, Snipp & Bloomquist 1989, Summers 1986, Summers & Branch 1984, Weaver 1984, Walton 1987). They are important because they provide the economic underpinnings for understanding rural poverty and form key links between old and new forms of rural poverty. During the postwar period of economic growth and prosperity, many rural areas remained pockets of poverty and deprivation. Reorganization of agriculture, federal farm programs and subsidies, new technology, and the opportunities and costs of international markets and competition reduced employment in the traditional agriculture and resource extraction sectors. At the same time, relocation of mature and footloose industries to rural areas indicated that rural industrialization might bring revitalization to these communities. By the late 1970s, regional economists were analyzing the spatial dimensions of economic development, hoping to learn how to stimulate chronically depressed rural economies.

Initially a laissez-faire model of rural industrial development prevailed. Capital's pursuit of cheap labor would induce firms to locate in rural areas, bringing new jobs, income, and tax revenues, diversifying economies, and reversing the flow of outmigrants and the decline of small communities. Later, national, state, and community intervention policies provided programs to improve rural infrastructure and provide subsidies, tax breaks, and training facilities for relocating firms (Lyson 1989, Summers et al 1976). While these efforts to attract firms to rural areas never constituted a coherent policy, the combination of such initiatives has constituted a defacto industrial policy (Falk & Lyson 1988).

Since new jobs were the outcome of a "filtering down" process in which mature, labor-intensive industries at the bottom of the product cycle reduced labor costs by moving to low-wage, nonunionized areas, the impact on rural poverty was minimal in most areas (Bloomquist 1987, Lonsdale & Seyler et al 1979, Seyler 1979a,b, Thompson 1965). The rural South was particularly vulnerable to this type of development because of its legacy of political and labor repression, and numerous studies document the pitfalls of this strategy in the South (Beaulieu 1988; Cobb 1982, 1984; Falk & Lyson 1988; Horan & Tolbert 1984; Malizia 1978; Molnar 1986; Rosenfeld et al 1985, 1988). Few of the new industries created enough forward and backward linkages to greatly assist local economic growth, and major financial transactions which might boost local development frequently occurred outside the region. In the rare cases where new industries brought higher skilled, better paid jobs, they also imported outside workers who, unlike indigenous residents, had the qualifications necessary for such positions. Subsidies and tax breaks used to lure firms ate into or negated anticipated tax revenues. Finally, since the primary goal of relocation was to reduce labor costs, many rural plants have been quick to remove operations in search of still cheaper labor offshore. The definitive summary of the outcome of rural industrialization suggests that few of the predicted benefits actually were realized (Summers et al 1976).

On the other hand, in the most depressed areas, any job creation may improve community economic viability (Seyler 1979, Summers et al 1976, Summers & Selvik 1979). In rural Appalachia, areas with substantial manufacturing employment have higher quality of life and lower poverty rates even though they may have lower aggregate income than comparable areas with little manufacturing (Tickamyer & Duncan 1984). In the Ozarks, jobs created by new industry were judged beneficial to local residents, reducing poverty status for some residents and permitting the return of outmigrants (Kuehn 1979). In Georgia, industrialization has decreased some forms of income inequality, although it has increased black-white differences (Colclough 1989). Studies of other chronically depressed areas also show mixed results with some places and groups improving while others do not (Seyler 1979, Shaffer 1979). The mixed results suggest that industrial growth is beneficial to communities to the extent it improves the amount and diversity of employment opportunities and the distribution of income across different groups (Duncan 1985). This in turn depends on political and social factors, as well as the economic structure of the region.

The deficiencies of rural industrialization policies prompted a search for alternative models of rural development. Analysts from a variety of theoretical perspectives shared a critical stance toward traditional economic models, demonstrating that economic growth in itself does not necessarily benefit either persons or places. Large-scale economic growth, if it is not well distributed or if it is imbedded in a repressive political economy, may do little to change patterns of persistent poverty of rural areas, as has been found in the Deep South and Appalachia. Rapid growth, resulting in boom/bust cycles may create new problems and new poverty as in western energy boomtowns (Markusen 1980). New jobs, in peripheral industries and the secondary sector may create new forms of working poverty (Duncan & Tickamyer 1988, Tickamyer & Duncan 1990, Shapiro 1989).

Critical analysts looked beyond the inadequacies of growth to locate the origins of regional poverty in the spatial dimensions of the political economy of advanced capitalism. In this view, regional inequality arises from the dynamics of the capital accumulation process itself (Howes & Markusen 1981, Markusen 1985, Weaver 1984). The exploitive nature of capital-labor relations is reflected in the way capital exploits rural areas for natural resources and cheap labor. Movement of industry into remote areas cannot alleviate rural poverty; it creates or exacerbates it, just as movement of capital out of particular regions continues the impoverishment of dependent areas.

RURAL WORK AND POVERTY AFTER RESTRUCTURING

Even as development officials ardently pursued new industries, profound changes in the US economy suggested that critics of this policy were right. In the 1980s, industrialization became an increasingly unlikely remedy for rural poverty as the United States moved from a goods producing economy dominated by mass production techniques and mass markets to a service economy based on new technology aimed at specialized markets in a global setting (Noyelle 1986, 1987).

Economic Restructuring

These changes have reverberated throughout the economy, changing the industrial and occupational mix, the organization and technologies of production, and the distribution of jobs and income. Analysts vary on whether they emphasize the negative impacts of deindustrialization such as rising unemployment, income inequality, deskilled and degraded labor, declining union membership, and blue collar employment (Bluestone & Harrison 1982, Harrison & Bluestone 1988) or the positive opportunities offered by restructuring, including innovative technologies and management techniques, improved productivity and efficiency, and the growth of professional and paraprofessional occupations (Piore & Sabel 1984, Reich 1983). All agree, however, that the dislocations resulting from these changes not only have created immediate hardship for numerous persons and places, but also will have long-term effects on the social and spatial organization of economic life.

Initial attention to the spatial dimension of restructuring focussed on the internationalization of the division of labor, the declining significance of national boundaries, and the presence of regional disparities and competition. However, the aftermath of the recessions of the early 1980s made it increasingly apparent that there was an important urban and rural dimension as well. While many urban areas had renewed growth in income and employment and a significant drop in poverty rates, unemployment remained high in rural areas, and there was little reduction in poverty through the end of the decade (Deavers 1989). Less diverse rural economies have been hard hit by restructuring and slow to recover. Workers displaced from agriculture, manufacturing, and resource extraction became newly poor (or poorer), augmenting already large poverty rolls (O'Hare 1988).

It should be no surprise that rural areas have fared badly. Restructuring has meant a shift from the resource extraction and low-wage manufacturing industries, which make up the backbone of most rural economies, toward service industries that depend on agglomeration in urban economies. Long-term decline of employment in the agriculture, mining, and timber sectors coincided with the rapid decline in mature manufacturing (Bloomquist 1988, McGranahan 1988, Singelmann 1978, Tienda 1986). Industries located in rural areas are particularly vulnerable to foreign competition and unfavorable exchange rates, and as employees of peripheral industries, workers have little protection. Although there has been considerable service sector growth in rural areas, jobs are disproportionately located in low-wage consumer and personal services which have limited development potential (Deavers 1988, McGranahan 1988, Miller & Bluestone 1988). More desirable producer services generally prefer urban locations.

In sum, structural changes in the 1980s have intensified chronic economic instability in rural areas where industries have always been volatile, unstable, and vulnerable to cyclical trends. Markets in resource industries and low-wage manufacturing change according to endlessly varying conditions of production, including weather conditions, labor relations, and the effect of international relations on trade. Rural workers in resource industries expect booms and busts in their local economies, and most families working in the agriculture, mining or timber industry can recount ups and downs experienced by each generation. During the 1960s and 1970s, manufacturing provided some stability for rural workers, but this ended with the upheavals created by restructuring. Substantial numbers of "new poor" joined the chronically poor in remote, depressed areas. These "new poor" made it clear that rural poverty would persist as long as there were few job opportunities, and existing employment was unstable and poorly paid.

Labor Market Analysis

The changes in employment which accompanied restructuring have prompted attention to the characteristics of labor markets. New work on rural labor markets has had to overcome an urban bias, partly because most economic development theories emphasize the centrality of urban markets even for rural areas, and partly because data collection problems limit availability of rural labor market data (Tickamyer 1988). Recently, however, there has been expanded interest in rural labor markets, including new techniques for studying how they operate (see Falk & Lyson 1989).

Most recent labor market research investigates the social division of labor and the organization of the workplace with relatively little attention to labor market ecology (Snipp & Bloomquist 1989). However, just as variations in economic structure and development entail a spatial dimension, the concept of a labor market implies that the wage-labor exchange takes place in a particular locale. With the exception of those few privileged workers who enter national labor markets, this locale is circumscribed by residence. To understand the way labor markets structure opportunity, it is necessary to provide geographic delineation of a labor market area (Horan & Tolbert 1984; Tickamyer & Bokemeier 1988, 1989; Tolbert & Killian 1987).

Researchers concerned with spatial components of labor markets generally take one of two approaches. Either they use existing administrative boundaries as the primary unit of analysis for labor market studies, or they aggregate over the characteristics of the primary unit to locate individuals in certain types of areas. In the first approach, counties, metropolitan statistical areas, or even states are used as the units, and researchers examine differences in their characteristics such as size, population structure, industrial employment and diversity. A number of recent studies analyze variation in rural poverty and economic structure at the county level (Colclough 1988, Reif 1987, Tickamyer & Tickamyer 1988, Tomaskovic-Devey 1987). They find significant variation in aggregate income and poverty levels by type of rural economy, with resource-based economies consistently showing the worst performance. The second approach begins with individuals in a particular locale and then treats characteristics of these areas such as unemployment rates and type of industrial employment either as controls or as structural level influences on individual outcomes in multilevel models (Horan & Tolbert 1984). Most research in this tradition remains oriented toward urban areas. However, new studies using Census journey-to-work data permit examination of rural local labor market areas (Killian & Hady 1988, Tolbert 1989, Tolbert & Killian 1987). Multilevel models confirm that rural resource-based economies have a negative impact on individual poverty levels, earnings, and income (Tickamyer & Bokemeier 1988, 1989).

Studies of rural labor markets parallel current urban poverty research on the ecology of opportunity (Wilson 1987). For rural areas, labor markets provide the link between the economic outcomes for individuals, families, and households and the macro-level operation of the economy described by the application of theories of uneven development at regional, national, and international levels. It is becoming clear that the socioeconomic characteristics of communities have an impact on the economic success of residents regardless of their own socioeconomic background. Location in social space affects economic opportunity and life chances of persons in that locale, providing the parameters for aspirations and opportunities.

Regional and local labor market research confirms that rural poverty is not simply the result of lack of economic growth or the lack of income and employment, but it is also the result of inequality in the distribution of income, jobs, and resources within communities as well as regions (Bluestone & Harrison 1982, Leigh-Preston 1988). The type of employment available can generate patterns of inequality and poverty (Reif 1987, Tomaskovic-Devey 1987). Rural areas are dominated by low wage employment in agriculture, service, and manufacturing sectors. Where relatively high wage employment exists, such as in mining and other resource extraction, these industries tend to be highly volatile, leading to great instability in employment even though jobs may command high pay when they exist (Tickamyer & Duncan 1984). Many other jobs are part-time and seasonal such as in agriculture and construction, making underemployment a chronic condition for the "working poor" (Lichter 1988, 1989, Tickamyer & Duncan 1990). While some farm families combine off-farm employment with farm labor to raise income, many are still unable to earn enough to escape poverty (Lyson 1986, Molnar 1986, Thompson et al 1986).

Minorities and women are especially vulnerable to job insecurity and limited opportunities. For example, counties with a large black population were more likely to suffer plant and employment losses in the decade between 1970 and 1980 (Colclough 1988). Large gaps between white and black workers in rural areas persist in all economic sectors (Cho & Ogunwole 1989). Southern rural blacks are particularly vulnerable to underemployment with rates 39% higher than for urban blacks in the same region (Lichter 1989). Women have much more limited employment opportunities, much flatter earnings curves, and higher poverty rates in rural counties and labor market areas dominated by agriculture and mining (Tickamyer & Bokemeier 1988, Tickamyer & Tickamyer 1988). Recent studies suggest that the scarcity of work and the inadequacy of wages are becoming even more serious for young people. Poverty for young rural adults increased at double the rate for older workers between 1979 and 1986 (O'Hare 1988).

People respond to the depressed state of rural labor markets in a variety of ways. Outmigration has increased, and those remaining often work intermittently in odd jobs, bartering goods and services in the informal sector to piece together a living from miscellaneous sources (C. M. Duncan 1988, Beckley 1988, Sherman 1988). A growing trend toward informalization of the labor market has been observed in rural as well as urban areas, with an increase in industrial homework, low wages, and sweatshop conditions (Portes et al 1989, Davidson 1989).

Finally, these problems are exacerbated even further when the welfare system parallels labor market opportunities. Persons who are privileged in the labor market also fare better when they are unemployed. For example, a dual system of social welfare programs mirrors the segmented labor markets in which women typically work (Folbre 1984). Because women frequently are not employed in the formal labor force, have part-time and intermittent employment, or have jobs in peripheral industries and in secondary occupational labor markets, they are often not eligibile for entitlements such as unemployment compensation, but must rely on a secondary welfare system where coverage is stigmatized, uncertain, and variable from place to place. These disadvantages are common to many rural workers for whom lack of opportunity in the labor market extends to inadequate protection by the "safety net" of social welfare programs.

CONCLUSION

Rural poverty has always been linked to the limited opportunity structure in rural communities. These limits are both a legacy of past social and economic development policies and practices and of current restructuring. There is too little work, and the lack of diversity in the economy extends to social and political institutions, creating a highly stratified and unequal social structure.

Like poor urban communities, poor rural areas lack stable employment, opportunities for mobility, diversity of social structure, and investment in community. Instead, these poor communities are becoming more isolated economically and socially. If the trend toward greater polarization on the national economy continues, there is a real danger that even those rural communities that had stable and diverse social and economic structures will face decline. In 1988 we wrote of the need for more community studies and longitudinal research to explore the dynamics of poverty, labor markets and political structures in rural America. While some progress is being made, this review demonstrates that greater research effort is needed.

ACKNOWLEDGMENTS

Both authors contributed equally to this article. We would like to acknowledge the support of the Ford Foundation and the Rural Economic Policy Program of the Aspen Institute. Thanks to Dwight Billings for a critical reading and Melissa Forsyth, Beth Jacobsen, and Betty Witham for research and technical assistance.

Literature Cited

Agee, J., Evans, W. 1941. *Let Us Now Praise Famous Men*. Boston: Houghton Mifflin

Auletta, K. 1982. *The Underclass*. New York: Random House

Baldwin, S. 1968. *Poverty and Politics: The Rise and Decline of the Farm Security Administration*. Chapel Hill: Univ. North Carolina Press

Ball, R. A. 1968. A poverty case: the analgesic subculture of the southern Appalachians. *Am. Sociol. Rev.* 33:885–94

Bane, M. J., Ellwood, D. T. 1986. Slipping into and out of poverty: the dynamics of spells. *J. Hum. Resources* 21:1–23

Beaulieu, L. J., ed. 1988. *The Rural South in Crisis*. Boulder/London: Westview

Beaver, P. D. 1986. *Rural Community in the Appalachian South*. Lexington, Ky: Univ. Press Kentucky

Beckley, G. 1988. *Dependency and Self-Reliance in Rural Mississippi*. Presented at Aspen Institute Rural Poverty Conf. Wye, Maryland

Billings, D. B. 1974. Culture and poverty in Appalachia. *Social Forces* 53(2):315–31

Billings, D. B. 1979. *Planters and the Making of a "New South."* Chapel Hill: Univ. North Carolina Press

Billings, D. B. 1988. The rural south in crisis: a historical perspective. See Beaulieu 1988, pp. 13–29

Billings, D. B., Blee, K., Swanson, L. 1986. Culture, family, and community in pre-industrial Appalachia. *Appalachian J.* 13(2):154–70

Bloomquist, L. E. 1987. Performance of the rural manufacturing sector. See Brown et al 1988, pp. 49–76

Bluestone, B., Harrison, B. 1982. *The Deindustrialization of America: Plant Closings, Community Abandonment, and the Dismantling of Basic Industry*. New York: Basic

Bott, E. 1957. *Family and Social Network*. London: Tavistock

Bremner, R. H. 1956. *From the Depths*. New York: New York Univ. Press

Brown, D., Deavers, K. 1988. Rural change and the rural economic agenda for the 1980s. See Brown et al 1988, pp. 1–28

Brown, D. L., Reid, J. N., Bluestone, H., McGranahan, D., Mazie, S. M. eds. 1988. *Rural Economic Development in the 1980's: Prospects for the Future*, Rural Dev. Res. Rep. No. 69. Washington, DC: U.S. Dept. Agric. Econ. Res. Serv.

Byerly, V. 1986. *Hard Times Cotton Mill Girls*. Ithaca, NY: Cornell Univ. ILR Press

Caudill, H. 1962. *Night Comes to the Cumberlands: Biography of a Depressed Region*. Boston: Little Brown

Center on Budget and Policy Priorities. 1989. *Poverty in Rural America: A National Overview*. Washington, DC

Cho, W. K., Ogunwole, S. 1989. Black workers in southern rural labor markets. See Falk & Lyson 1989, pp. 189–206

Christenson, J., Garkovich, L. 1985. Fifty years of *Rural Sociology:* status, trends and impressions. *Rural Sociol.* 50(4):503–22

Cobb, J. 1982. *The Selling of the South: The Southern Crusade for Industrial Development, 1936–1980*. Baton Rouge: Louisiana State Univ. Press

Cobb, J. 1984. *Industrialization and Southern Society: 1877–1984*. Lexington, Ky: Univ. Press Kentucky

Colclough, Glenna. 1988. Uneven development and racial composition in the deep South. *Rural Sociol.* 53:73–86

Colclough, G. 1989. Industrialization, labor markets and income inequality among Georgia counties: 1970–1980. See Falk & Lyson 1989, pp. 207–22

Coles, R. 1971a. *Migrants, Sharecroppers, Mountaineers: Volume II of Children in Crisis*. Boston: Little, Brown

Coles, R. 1971b. *The South Goes North: Volume III of Children in Crisis*. Boston: Little, Brown

Conrad, D. E. 1965. *The Forgotten Farmers: Story of Sharecroppers in the New Deal*. Urbana, Ill: Univ. Ill. Press

Cottingham, P. H., Ellwood, D. T., eds. 1989. *Welfare Policy for the 1990s*. Cambridge, MA: Harvard Univ. Press

Davidson, O. G. 1989. Rural sweatshops: doing home work down on the farm. *Nation*, July 17:87–90

Davis, A., Gardner, B. B., Gardner, M. R. 1941. *Deep South: A Social Anthropological Study of Caste and Class*. Chicago: Univ. Chicago Press

Davis, T. F. 1979. *Persistent Low-Income Counties in Nonmetro America*. Washington, DC: US Dept. Agric. Econ. Res. Serv. Rep. No. 12

Deavers, K. 1988. Choosing a rural policy for the 1980's and '90's. See Brown et al, 1988, pp. 377–95

Deavers, K. 1989. Rural America: lagging growth and high poverty . . . do we care? *Choices* (2):4–7

Deavers, K., Hoppe, R. A. 1990. Policy options for the rural poor in the 1990s: the past is prologue. In *Rural Policy for the 1990s*, ed. J. Christenson, C. Flora. In press

Deloria, V. Jr. 1984. Land and natural resources. See Dunbar 1984, pp. 152–90

Dill, B. T., Timberlake, M., Williams, B. 1988. *Racism and Politics in Depressed,*

Rural Southern Communities. Presented at Aspen Inst. Rural Poverty Conf., Wye, Md.

Dollard, J. 1957. Caste and Class in a Southern Town. New York: Doubleday, 3rd ed.

Dunbar, L. ed. 1984. Minority Report: What Has Happened to Blacks, Hispanics, American Indians, and Other Minorities in the Eighties. New York: Pantheon

Duncan, C. M. 1985. Capital and the state in regional economic development. PhD thesis. Univ. Kentucky, Lexington

Duncan, C. M. 1986. Myths and realities of Appalachian poverty. In Proc. 1986 Conf. on Appalachia, ed. R. Eller, pp. 25–32. Lexington: Appalachian Ctr. Univ. Kentucky

Duncan, C. M. 1988. Poverty, Work, and Social Change in the Appalachian Coal Fields. Pres. Ann. Meet. Am. Sociol. Assoc., Atlanta

Duncan, C., Tickamyer, A. 1988. Poverty research and policy for rural America. Am. Sociol. 19(3):243–259

Duncan, G. 1984. Years of Poverty, Years of Plenty: The Changing Economic Fortunes of American Workers and Families. Ann Arbor: Inst. Soc. Res.

Duncan, G. 1988. The Persistence of Urban Poverty and Its Demographic and Behavioral Correlates. Ann Arbor: Survey Research Center

Ellis, C. 1986. Fisher Folk: Two Communities on Chesapeake Bay. Lexington, Ky: Univ. Press Kentucky

Ellwood, D. 1988. Poor Support: Poverty in the American Family. New York: Basic

Falk, W. W., Gilbert, J. 1985. Bringing rural sociology back in. Rural Sociol. 50(4):561–77

Falk, W. W., Lyson, T. A. 1988. High Tech, Low Tech, No Tech: Recent Industrial and Occupational Change in the South. Albany: State Univ. New York Press

Falk, W. W., Lyson, T. A., eds. 1989. Research in Rural Sociology and Development Vol. 4. Greenwich, Conn: JAI

Fetterman, J. 1967. Stinking Creek. New York: E. P. Dutton

Fitchen, J. 1981. Poverty in Rural America: A Case Study. Boulder, Colo: Westview

Folbre, N. 1984. The pauperization of motherhood: patriarchy and public policy in the U.S. Rev. Radical Polit. Econ. 16:72–88

Gans, H. 1962. The Urban Villagers. New York: Macmillan

Gans, H. 1968. Urbanism and suburbanism as ways of life. See Pahl 1968a, pp. 95–118

Gaventa, J. 1980. Power and Powerlessness: Quiescence and Rebellion in an Appalachian Valley. Urbana: Univ. Ill. Press

Ghelfi, L. 1986. Poverty among Black Families in the Nonmetro South. Washington, DC: US Dept. Agric. Econ. Res. Serv. Rep. No. 62

Gilbert, J. 1982. Rural theory: the grounding of rural sociology. Rural Sociol. 47(4):609–33

Hall, R. L., Stack, C. B., eds. 1982. Holding on to the Land and the Lord: Kinship, Ritual, Land Tenure, and Social Policy in the Rural South. Athens: Univ. Georgia Press

Hareven, T. K., Langenbach, R. 1978. Amoskeag: Life and Work in an American Factory-City. New York: Pantheon

Harrington, M. 1962. The Other America. New York: Macmillan

Harrison, B., Bluestone, B. 1988. The Great U-Turn: Corporate Restructuring and the Polarizing of America. New York: Basic

Henry, M. S. 1989. Some economic perspectives on rural labor markets. See Falk & Lyson, 1989, pp. 29–54

Hoppe, R. A. 1985. Economic Structure and Change in Persistently Low-Income Nonmetro Counties. Washington, DC: US Dept. Agric. Econ. Res. Serv. Rep. No. 50

Horan, P. M., Tolbert, C. 1984. The Organization of Work in Rural and Urban Labor Markets. Boulder/London: Westview

Howes, C., Markusen, A. 1981. Poverty: a regional political economy perspective. In Nonmetropolitan America in Transition, ed. A. H. Hawley, S. M. Mazie, pp. 437–63. Chapel Hill: Univ. North Carolina Press

Hughes, C. C., Tremblay, M., Rapoport, R. N., Leighton, A. H. 1960. People of Cove and Woodlot: Communities from the Viewpoint of Social Psychiatry. New York: Basic

Kale, S. 1986. Stability, growth, and adaptability to economic and social change in rural labor markets. See Killian et al 1986, pp. 125–54

Katz, M. B. 1983. Poverty and Policy in American History. New York: Academic

Katz, M. B. 1986. In the Shadow of the Poorhouse: A Social History of Welfare in America. New York: Basic

Killian, M. S., Hady, T. F. 1988. The economic performance of rural labor markets. See Brown et al 1988, pp. 181–200

Killian, M. S., Bloomquist, L. E., Pendleton, S., McGranahan, D. A., eds. 1986. Symposium on Rural Labor Markets Research Issues, Staff Report No. AGES860721. Washington, DC: US Dept. Agric. Econ. Res. Serv.

Kuehn, J. A. 1979. Nonmetropolitan industrialization and migration: an overview with special emphasis on the Ozark region. See Lonsdale & Seyler 1979, pp. 137–48

Lantz, H. R. 1971. People of Coal Town. Carbondale: Southern Ill. Univ. Press. 2nd ed.

Leigh-Preston, N. 1988. The Nation's Changing *Earnings Distribution from 1967 to 1986: What Has Happened to the Middle?* Berkeley: Inst. Urban and Regional Dev., Work. pap. No. 491

Lemann, N. 1986. The origins of the underclass. *Atlantic Monthly* June:31–55, July:54–68

Lemann, N. 1989. Up and out: the underclass is not new, and not hopeless. *Washington Post National Weekly Edition,* May 29:25–26

Levitan, S., Shapiro, I. 1987. *Working But Poor: America's Contradiction.* Baltimore: Johns Hopkins Univ. Press

Levy, Frank, 1987. *Dollars and Dreams: The Changing American Income Distribution.* New York: Russell Sage

Lichter, D. 1988. Race and underemployment: black employment hardship in the rural south. See Beaulieu 1988, pp. 181–97

Lichter, D. 1989. Race, employment hardship, and inequality in the American nonmetropolitan South. *Am. Sociol. Rev.* 54(3):436–46

Lichter, D., Constanzo, J. A. 1986. Nonmetropolitan underemployment and labor-force composition. *Rural Sociol.* 52:(3):329–44

Lieberson, S. 1978. A reconsideration of the income differences found between migrants and northern-born blacks. *Am. J. Sociol.* 83:940–66

Lieberson, S. *A Piece of the Pie: Blacks and White Immigrants Since 1880.* Los Angeles: Univ. Calif. Press

Liebow, E. 1967. *Tally's Corner: A Study of Streetcorner Men.* Boston: Little, Brown

Long, L. H. 1974. Poverty status and receipt of welfare among migrants and nonmigrants in large cities. *Am. Sociol. Rev.* 39:46–56

Long, L. H., Heltman, L. R. 1975. Migration and income differences between black and white men in the North. *Am. J. Sociol.* 80:1391–1409

Lonsdale, R. E., Seyler, H. L., eds. 1979. *Nonmetropolitan Industrialization.* Washington, DC: V. H. Winston

Lyson, T. 1986. Entry into farming: implications of a dual agricultural structure. See Molnar 1986, pp. 155–76

Lyson, T. 1989. *Two Sides to the Sunbelt: the Growing Divergence between the Rural and Urban South.* New York: Praeger.

MacLeish, K., Young, K. 1942. *Culture of a Contemporary Rural Community: Landaff, New Hampshire.* Rural Life Studies 3. Washington, DC: U.S. Dept. Agric. Bur. Agric. Econ.

Malizia, E. 1978. Organizing to overcome uneven development: the case of the U.S. South. *Rev. Radical Pol. Econ.* 10: 87–94

Mandel, J. R. 1978. *The Roots of Black Poverty: The Southern Plantation Economy*

After the Civil War. Durham, NC: Duke Univ. Press

Markusen, A. 1980. The political economy of rural development: the case of western U.S. boomtowns. In *The Rural Sociology of the Advanced Societies: Critical Perspectives,* ed. F. H. Buttel, H. Newby, pp. 405–32. Montclair, NJ: Allenheld, Osmun & Co.

Markusen, A. 1985. *Profit Cycles, Oligopoly, and Regional Development.* Cambridge: MIT Press

Marshall, R., Godwin, L. 1971. *Cooperatives and Rural Poverty in the South.* Baltimore: Johns Hopkins Univ. Press

McGranahan, D. A. 1988. Rural workers in the national economy. See Brown et al 1988, pp. 29–47

Miller, J. P., Bluestone, H. 1988. Prospects for service sector employment growth in nonmetro America. See Brown et al 1988, pp. 135–57

Molnar, J., ed. 1986. *Agricultural Change.* Boulder/London: Westview

Montejano, D. 1987. *Anglos and Mexicans in the Making of Texas, 1836–1986.* Austin: Univ. Texas Press

Morrissey, E. 1985. *Characteristics of Poverty in Nonmetro Counties.* Washington, DC: U.S. Dept. Agric. Econ. Res. Serv. Rep. No. 52

Newby, H. 1983. The sociology of agriculture: toward a new rural sociology. *Annu. Rev. Sociol.* 9:67–81

Noyelle, T. J. 1987. *Beyond Industrial Dualism: Market and Job Segmentations in the New Economy.* Boulder/London: Westview

Noyelle, T. J. 1986. Economic transformation. *Ann. Am. Acad. Polit. Soc. Sci.* 488 (Nov.):9–17

O'Hare, W. 1988. *The Rise of Poverty in Rural America.* Washington, DC: Popul. Ref. Bur.

Oliveira, V. J. 1986. *Distribution of Rural Employment Growth by Race: A Case Study.* Washington, DC: US Dept. Agric. Econ. Res. Serv. Rep. No. 54

Pahl, R. E., ed. 1968a. *Readings in Urban Sociology.* Oxford: Pergamon

Pahl, R. E., 1968b. The rural-urban continuum. See Pahl 1968a, pp. 263–305

Palerm, J. V. 1988. *The New Poor in Rural America: Chicano-Mexican Communities and Agribusiness in Rural California.* Pres. Aspen Inst. Rural Poverty Meet., Wye, Md.

Patterson, J. T. 1981. *America's Struggle Against Poverty 1900–1980.* Cambridge/London: Harvard Univ. Press

Piore, M. J., Sabel, C. F. 1984. *The Second Industrial Divide.* New York: Basic

Portes, A., Castells, M., Benton, A., eds. 1989. *The Informal Economy.* Baltimore: Johns Hopkins Univ. Press

President's National Advisory Commission on

Rural Poverty. 1968. *The People Left Behind: The Rural Poor*. Washington, DC

Rees, J., Stafford, H. A. 1986. Theories of regional growth and industrial location: their relevance for understanding high-technology complexes. In *Technology, Regions, and Policy*, ed. J. Rees, pp. 23–50. New Jersey: Rowman & Littlefield

Riech, R. B. 1983. *The Next American Frontier*. New York: Times Book

Reif, L. L. 1987. Farm structure, industry structure, and socioeconomic conditions in the United States. *Rural Sociol.* 52(4):462–82

Riis, J. A. 1890. *How the Other Half Lives: Studies Among the Tenements of New York*. New York: Scribner's

Ritchey, P. N. 1974. Urban poverty and rural to urban migration. *Rural Sociol.* 39:13–27

Rosenfeld, S. A., Bergman, E., Rubin, S. 1985. *After the Factories: Changing Employment Patterns in the Rural South*. Research Triangle Park, NC: Southern Growth Policies Board

Rosenfeld, S., Bergman, E., Rubin, S. 1988. *Charting Growth in the Rural South: A Review of After the Factories*. Research Triangle Park, NC: Southern Growth Policies Board

Ross, P. J., Morrissey, E. S. 1987. Two types of rural poor need different kinds of help. *Rural Dev. Perspect.* Oct:7–10

Ross, P. J., Rosenfeld, S. A. 1988. Human resource policies and economic development. See Brown et al 1988, pp. 333–57

Rungeling, B., Smith, L. H., Briggs, V. M. Jr., Adams, J. F. 1977. *Employment, Income, and Welfare in the Rural South*. New York: Praeger

Sandefur, G., Scott, W. 1984. *A Sociological Analysis of White, Black, and American Indian Male Labor Force Activities*. Madison, Wis: Inst. Res. Poverty Discussion Pap.

Sandefur, G. D., Tienda, M. 1988. *Divided Opportunities: Minorities, Poverty, and Social Policy*. New York: Plenum

Schwarzweller, H. K., Brown, J. S., Mangalam, J. J. 1971. *Mountain Families in Transition: A Case Study of Appalachian Migration*. University Park, Penn: Penn. State Univ. Press

Seyler, H. L. 1979a. Contemporary research emphases in the United States. See Summers & Selvik 1979, pp. 43–58

Seyler, H. L. 1979b. Industrialization and household income levels in nonmetropolitan areas. See Lonsdale & Seyler 1979, pp. 149–60

Shaffer, R. E. 1979. The general economic impact of industrial growth on the private sector of nonmetropolitan communities. See Lonsdale & Seyler 1979, pp. 103–18

Shapiro, H. D. 1978. *Appalachia on Our Mind: The Southern Mountains and Mountaineers in American Consciousness, 1870–1920*. Chapel Hill: Univ. North Carolina Press

Shapiro, I. 1989. *Laboring for Less: Working but Poor in Rural America*. Washington, DC: Ctr. Budget Policy Priorities

Sherman, R. 1988. *A Study of Traditonal and Informal Sector Micro-Enterprise Activity and Its Impact on the Pine Ridge Indian Reservation Economy*. Washington, DC: Aspen Inst.

Singelmann, J. 1978. *From Agriculture to Services: The Transformation of Industrial Employment*. Beverly Hills, Calif: Sage

Snipp, C. M., Bloomquist, L. 1989. Sociology and labor market structure: a selective overview. See Falk & Lyson 1989, pp. 1–28

Snipp, M., Summers, G. 1988. *Poverty and American Indians*. Pres. Aspen Inst. Rural Poverty Meet., Wye, Md.

Southern Regional Council Task force on Southern Rural Development. 1977. *Increasing the Options*. Atlanta: Southern Regional Council

Stack, C. 1974. *All Our Kin*. New York: Harper & Row

Stein, M. 1972. *The Eclipse of Community*. Princeton, NJ: Princeton Univ. Press

Steinberg, S. 1981. *The Ethnic Myth: Race, Ethnicity, and Class in America*. New York: Atheneum

Stinson, T. F. 1988. *Helping people in place*. Pap. pres. Congressional Record, Oct. 14: S16238–40

Summers, G. F. 1986. Rural community development. *Annu. Rev. Sociol.* 12:347–71

Summers, G. F., Branch, K. 1984. Economic development and community social change. *Annu. Rev. Sociol.* 10:141–66

Summers, G. F., Selvik, A., eds. 1979. *Nonmetropolitan Industrial Growth and Community Change*. Lexington, Mass: Lexington

Summers, G. F., Evans, S. D., Clemente, F., Beck, E. M., Minkoff, J., 1976. *Industrial Invasion of Nonmetropolitan America*. New York: Praeger

Thompson, A., Yeboah, A. O., Evans, S. H. 1986. Determinants of poverty among farm operators in North Carolina. See Molnar 1986, pp. 177–99

Thompson, W. R. 1965. *A Preface to Urban Economics*. Baltimore: Johns Hopkins Univ. Press

Thurow, L. C. 1987. A surge in inequality. *Sci. Am.* 256(5):30

Tickamyer, A. 1988. *The Working Poor in Rural Labor Markets*. Pres. Aspen Inst. Rural Poverty Meet., Wye, Md.

Tickamyer, A., Bokemeier, J. 1988. Sex

differences in labor market experiences. *Rural Sociol.* 53(2):166–89

Tickamyer, A., Bokemeier, J. 1989. Individual and structural explanations of nonmetropolitan women and men's labor force experiences. See Falk & Lyson 1989, pp. 153–170

Tickamyer, A., Duncan, C. 1984. Economic activity and the quality of life in eastern Kentucky. *Growth Change* 15:43–51

Tickamyer, A., Duncan, C. 1990. Work and poverty in rural America. In *Rural Policy for the 1990s,* ed. J. Christenson, C. Flora. Boulder/London: Westview. In press

Tickamyer A., Tickamyer, C. 1988. Gender and poverty in central Appalachia. *Soc. Sci. Q.* 69(4):874–91

Tienda, M. 1986. Industrial restructuring in metropolitan and nonmetropolitan labor markets: Implications for equity and efficiency. See Killian et al 1986, pp. 33–70

Tolbert, C. M. 1989. Labor market areas in stratification research: concepts, definitions, and issues. See Falk & Lyson 1989, ppl 81–98

Tolbert, C., Killian, M. 1987. *Labor Market Areas for the United States.* Staff Rep. No. AGES870721. Washington, DC: US Dept. Agric. Econ. Res. Serv.

Tomaskovic-Devey, D. 1987. Labor markets, industrial structure, and poverty: a theoretical discussion and empirical example. *Rural Sociol.* 52(1):56–74

US Congress, House Select Committee on Children, Youth, and Families. 1989. *Working Families at the Margins: The Uncertain Future of America's Small Towns.* Washington, DC:USGPO

Walls, D. S. 1978. *Central Appalachia in advanced capitalism: its coal industry structure and coal operator associations.* Phd thesis. Univ. Kentucky, Lexington

Walton, J. 1987. Theory and research on industrialization. *Annu. Rev. Sociol.* 13:89–108

Weaver, C. 1984. *Regional Development and the Local Community: Planning, Politics and Social Context.* Chichester/New York: Wiley

Whyte, W. F. 1981. *Street Corner Society: The Social Structure of An Italian Slum.* Chicago: Univ. Chicago Press. 3rd ed.

Williams, T., Kornblum, W. 1985. *Growing Up Poor.* Lexington, Mass: Heath

Wilson, W. J. 1987. *The Truly Disadvantaged.* Chicago: Univ. Chicago Press

Wilson, W. J., Aponte, R. 1985. Urban poverty. *Annu. Rev. Sociol.* 11:231–58

Wirth, L. 1938. Urbanism as a way of life. *Am. J. Sociol.* 44(1):1–24

Wright, G. 1986. *Old South, New South: Revolutions in the Southern Economy Since the Civil War.* New York: Basic

Zimmerman, C. C., Whetten, N. L. 1971. Rural families on relief. In *Poverty U.S.A.: Rural Poor in the Great Depression.* Works Progress Admin., Reprint. New York: Arno

Annu. Rev. Sociol. 1990. 16:87–110

ROLE CHANGE

Ralph H. Turner

Department of Sociology, University of California, Los Angeles, California 90024

KEY WORDS: role, social change, occupational change, gender role change

Abstract

Selected recent research dealing with change in a variety of roles is reviewed in order to formulate general principles governing role change. Studies of quasichange reveal conditions leading to the abortion of potential role change. Studies of occupational, family, and gender role change reveal the sources of impetus to role change and the conditions facilitating and impeding the implementation of change. A tentative general model for role change is suggested on the basis of the evidence reviewed.

INTRODUCTION

Much has been written over the last half century about changes in gender roles, family roles, occupational roles, and others, but few efforts have been made to develop generalized theories of role change. This review attempts to make explicit the more general principles of role change implicit in a representative set of recent studies of change in specific roles.

Before we examine particular studies, we must be clear about the meaning of *role* and *role change*. A *social role* is a comprehensive pattern of behavior and attitudes, constituting a strategy for coping with a recurrent set of situations, which is socially identified—more or less clearly—as an entity. A social role is played recognizably by different individuals, and supplies a major basis for identifying and placing persons in a group, organization, or society (Turner 1968, p. 552). It can be thought of as consisting of rights and duties, or of expected behavior, provided these terms are interpreted broadly.[1] Social roles are of four types: *basic roles,* like gender and age roles, that are

87

0360-0572/90/0815-0087$02.00

grounded in society at large rather than particular organizations; *structural status roles,* like occupational, family, and recreational roles that are attached to position, office, or status in particular organizational settings; *functional group roles,* like the "mediator" and "devil's advocate," which are not formally designated or attached to particular group positions or offices, but are recognized items in the cultural repertoire; and *value roles,* like the hero, traitor, criminal, and saint, which embody the implementation or the negation of some recognized value or value complex. Because no sociological literature was found that dealt with changes in the latter two types of roles, this review deals exclusively with basic roles and structural status roles.

Role change can be defined as a change in the shared conception and execution of typical role performance and role boundaries. Role change must be distinguished from *role transition* or *reallocation,* the movement of individuals out of one role and into another. Role change must also be distinguished from normal variability, as each incumbent develops a uniquely individual version of a particular role within generally accepted boundaries (Thornton & Nardi 1975), and as the role is implemented in relation to varying *alter role* behavior and in varying situations. Role change is different from deviance, which is behavior interpreted as outside the role boundaries rather than as a new way of playing the role, or a new role.

Roles can change in several ways. A new role can be created or an established role can be dissolved; a role can change quantitatively, either by the addition or subtraction of duties or rights or by a gain or loss of power or prestige (role expansion or contraction); and a role can change qualitatively by a change in the relative salience of its component elements, by substitution of elements, or by reinterpretation of its meaning. Since a role always bears a functional or representational relationship to one or more other roles, change in one role always means change in a system of roles, e.g. the teacher role cannot change without complementary change in the student role; women's role cannot change without complementary change in the men's role.

Role change has not been a major topic in any of the leading comprehensive treatments of role theory (Rocheblave-Spenle 1962, Banton 1965, Biddle & Thomas 1966, Biddle 1979, Heise 1981, Zurcher 1983), though there are abundant implications for role change in the standard discussions of role strain and role conflict. The prevailing tendency has been to take roles as givens, and to deal principally with execution and adaptation to roles by their in-

---

[1]This definition of role is more inclusive than some, stressing the *gestalt* character of the role rather than its attachment to a particular status. The rationale for this conception is explained in Turner, 1962 and 1985.

cumbents. Two studies are major exceptions. Eisenstadt et al (1967) used case studies of change in seven different work roles in Israel to develop a theory and hypotheses about role change in general. They stressed the distinctive causes for change in the technical, normative, and cognitive components of roles. They then described a two-stage process of *role recrystallization* beginning with a strain in the role system following initial change in some of its components, followed by a chain reaction of adjustment to strain on different role levels. Lipman-Blumen (1973) developed a theory of role change on the premise that crisis in a social system provides the most favorable condition for rapid and widespread role transformation. Crisis conditions precipitate *dedifferentiation,* as roles assimilate elements from other roles, followed by *reconfiguration* in a different pattern as the crisis subsides.

Others who have treated generalized role change include Bernard (1976), who suggested three models for role change—Lipman-Blumen's *crisis* model, Allport's *J-curve,* and *diffusion* theory. According to Allport's *J-curve,* there is always some degree of individual deviance from any social norm; when that individual deviance reaches some tipping point (e.g. 50% nonconforming), the role changes. According to *diffusion* theory, role change begins with a few innovators, followed by more early acceptors, and then an early majority and a late majority, and finally the few laggards, after which diffusion reaches a plateau when no more people change to the new role conception. In applying her analysis to women, Bernard proposed that, regardless of the model chosen, two things had to happen before women could see their low status as discriminatory: "A critical mass of potential innovators had to be reached and their consciousness had somehow or other to be raised" (p. 219). In a more limited statement, Turner (1970) proposed that role change is most likely "when precipitating conditions operate on a role system that is in a state of *unstable equilibrium* . . . when either sentiment [emotionally invested role conceptions] or reciprocity [functional interdependence] alone is maintaining the system" (p. 205). Guttentag & Secord (1983, p. 156) observed that "adult roles are shaped, maintained, or changed through what can be thought of as two relatively independent sources: the social exchanges of the role partners, and the task demands that bear on those roles." In developing a microsociological theory of role differentiation, Turner & Colomy (1988) attributed role change to disfunctionality, unacceptable representationality, and impaired tenability of roles. A role is disfunctional when its execution no longer appears to have the intended effect (functionality is similar to task demands); it is unacceptable representationally when the image and sentiment evoked by the role are unfavorable; it is untenable when the costs of performing the role seem to outweigh the benefits in the eyes of the role incumbent (tenability is similar to partners' social exchanges).

In reviewing relevant literature, I begin with examples of quasi-change, which reveal the impetus for change in the absence of conditions necessary to complete the process. Next I examine studies of change in occupational roles, where the process is clearest and completion of the change is most often institutionally formalized. Changes in family roles are less clear and less institutionalized and typically combine structural status role change with basic role change. I look at the most nebulous changes, in basic roles, in conjunction with family roles. Since a basic role is enacted principally in conjunction with some other type of role, changes have mostly to do with changing compatibility between a basic role and another type of role (e.g. can a woman be an airline pilot?) and with personal style.

For a framework within which to view the various studies, I assume that the crucial process in role stability is *accommodation* (not usually consensus), which involves variable combinations of internalized belief (role conceptions), effectiveness, coercion, and absence of apparent alternatives. When an accommodation is threatened by destabilizing conditions, one outcome can be the creation or intensification in role-system incumbents of an *impetus* to change the roles. The impetus may or may not lead to role change, depending upon whether conditions are favorable for *implementing* the change. The change cycle is complete when a new accommodation is reached on the basis of a reorganized system of roles. Accommodation is always relative rather than absolute, as are stability and change, so that the periods of restabilization at the end of a change cycle differ only in degree of volatility from the periods of change. Our task in this review is to identify some of the conditions under which destabilization results in a strong impetus to change the roles, and the conditions that facilitate implementation of the change.

INCOMPLETE ROLE CHANGE

Zurcher (1983) presented a series of case studies of situations in which role incumbents improvised roles that deviated from their official roles, systematically and on a sustained basis. The common cause in most of these cases was role-related challenge to incumbent self-conceptions, particularly when the role setting denied incumbents sufficient personal autonomy. For example, male student hashers in college sorority houses adopted a variety of practices to offset the demeaning nature of the role, naval reservists during their annual drill periods found ways to achieve balance in their temporary role, and naval recruits learned to play the sailor role in boot camp without allowing it to dominate their self-conceptions. The result in most cases was the development of an informal version of the role, either at variance from, or in elaboration of, the formal role version. Role incumbents were satisfied to carry on in this fashion, while legitimate role definers and enforcers either ignored or resigned themselves to the pattern of petty deviance. Thus, accommodations were reached without requiring role change.

In her account of changing department store roles, Benson (1986, p. 228) describes the saleswomen's *work culture:*

> the ideology and practice with which workers stake out a relatively autonomous sphere of action on the job. . . . More than simply reactive, work culture embodies workers' own definition of a good day's work, their own sense of satisfying and useful labor. While condemning oppressive aspects of the job, it also celebrates the skill it demands and the rewards it brings.

While informal roles (including work culture) do not constitute role change because the formal role definitions are maintained, they highlight *insufficient fit between role and person*—especially insufficient autonomy—as an impetus to role change. While achieving role tenability looms largest for the hashers and sailors, the work culture also brings functional and representational improvement for saleswomen. Critical for our analysis is the observation that development of a stable informal role serves as a mechanism that can abort potential role change.

Challenging the "vacancy assumption"—that organizational role incumbents are fitted into pre-defined jobs—Miner (1987, Miner & Estler 1985) investigated the creation of *idiosyncratic jobs* in formal organizations. An idiosyncratic job is a set of rights and duties specially designed to fit the interests and capabilities of a particular incumbent. It can be developed around an existing employee *(evolved job)* or be designed for an organizational recruit *(opportunistic hire)*. While all role relationships are subject to some negotiation, these are instances in which negotiation is carried to the point of creating a new position rather than simply adapting an existing one.

Creating idiosyncratic roles is another way to forestall a more general pattern of role change, or it can be the first step to role change when the idiosyncratic role becomes a model. In a six-year study of nonacademic positions in a research university, Miner (1987, p. 344) found that "Somewhere between 7 and 12 percent of all jobs new to their departments were created through the idiosyncratic job process. . . ." Over a span of six years, 16% of the idiosyncratic jobs had multiple incumbents (Miner & Lehner 1988), suggesting that the negotiation of an idiosyncratic role can be an initial step in the establishment of a new role.

Miner hypothesized that idiosyncratic jobs are the result of benign opportunism on the part of managers in situations of ambiguity and uncertainty. More specifically, she found that change in size and mission ambiguity were correlated with both kinds of idiosyncratic jobs, while resource uncertainty was correlated with evolved jobs but not with opportunistic hires.

Zurcher, Benson, and Miner all take the absence of fit between person and role as the underlying dynamic in quasi or completed role change. However, for Zurcher and Benson the initiative is with role incumbents, and for Miner the initiative can be with legitimate role definers (managers in this case) or incumbents. Lacking either the initiative or the collaboration of legitimate role definers, Zurcher's and Benson's subjects fall short of actually changing their roles. So long as the role-person misfit is an isolated instance, the idiosyncratic role cannot be a step toward a role change.

Also working from the assumption of a misfit between role and incumbent, Turner (1979–1980) suggested a principle of *substitutability* between role differentiation and role allocation. From the point of view of either the incumbent or management, a lack of fit between the interests and abilities of role incumbents and the requirements of a role can be resolved either by role reallocation—reassigning personnel—or role redifferentiation—redefining the role. Reallocation of personnel within roles is, thus, another step that can abort potential role change.

What, then, determines whether reallocation of personnel or role change will occur? Turner advances three propositions for empirical test. First, role change is more likely when the focal role system is relatively independent of other role systems, while reallocation is more likely when the focal role system is strongly interdependent with roles in other systems, as in the interdependence of work and family roles. Second, role change is more likely when incumbents are strongly tied to the focal role system, and less likely when incumbents have only weak ties to particular systems, making reallocation an easy solution to the lack of fit. Third, role change is more likely when incumbents in the system import strongly differing degrees of power from outside the system, and less likely when they import relatively little or equal power from outside.

OCCUPATIONAL ROLE CHANGE

A major body of research into occupational change deals with processes of professionalization and deprofessionalization. Traditional treatments distinguished professional from nonprofessional occupational roles in terms of exclusive expertise, based on extended education, adherence to strict ethical codes, service orientation, commitment to a view of the profession as a calling, and a publicly acknowledged right to autonomy in carrying out duties. Recent analyses place less emphasis on these socially positive features and stress power as a primary criterion. In a typical example, Rothman (1984, p. 185) defines professions as "occupational groups able to exercise a monopoly over the provision of expert services while enjoying relative freedom from external intervention and direction (autonomy)." "Professional authority and right to monopoly are strongly legitimated by a well rooted 'mythology of professionalism' which proclaims the altruism, ethical scrupulousness, and neutrality of expertise which these occupations are reputed to offer" (Esland 1980, p. 213).

Professionalization

Treating professionalization as a continuum, Khoury (1980) applied Gutman scaling to a sample of all occupations to determine whether professions develop by a uniform series of stages. Since no ordering of events met scalability criteria, he concluded that there was no uniform process for professional development. However, he found some support for an order suggested by Wilensky, from establishment of training schools, to founding of professional associations, to political agitation to gain the support of law, to adoption of a formal code of ethics.

Taking the power to establish and maintain boundaries around its task domain as the key, Kronus (1976) examined the struggle over task boundaries between physicians and pharmacists in Britain and the United States, during three centuries. From 1617 to the early 1800s in Britain, the pharmacist role evolved from merely compounding drugs to serving as a general practitioner of medicine. The process began with role expansion by pharmacists, partly in response to demand from clients without access to high-status physicians. Physician-initiated political action to prohibit the practice of medicine by pharmacists backfired because of strong client support for pharmacists. With legal sanction, pharmacists then instituted training for general medical practice. Pharmacists effectively resisted a challenge from chemists who also sought to practice medicine, on the grounds that chemists lacked the necessary formal training. Pharmacists were similarly able to practice medicine in the United States, in spite of more restrictive legislation, initially because there were so few trained physicians and later because Jacksonian populism swept away all proprietary legislation. However, the late nineteenth and early twentieth centuries saw an explosion of technical knowledge, which was then used by physicians to secure the legal monopoly of medical practice that they now command in both countries.

In explaining the augmented power vested in the physician's role in late nineteenth and early twentieth century America, Starr (1982) also credits the expansion of technical knowledge, but emphasizes increased cohesion within the profession and a more generalized public acceptance of professional authority as, "in a sense, America's cultural revolution" (p. 17). "At a time when traditional certainties were breaking down, professional authority offered a means of sorting out different conceptions of human needs and the nature and meaning of events" (p. 19). Starr's emphasis on the rise (and later decline) of professional authority in general is echoed in Abbott's (1988) view that individual professions are part of a system of professions, such that what happens to one affects all.

In Kronus' analysis, the impetus for enlarging role boundaries came from role incumbents and was strategically implemented by the establishment of training facilities and other timely maneuvers. But success also depended upon mobilized client support, upon having neither too few nor too many role practitioners, on the availability of differentiating technical knowledge and skills, and on historical cultural shifts which made one role's claims more credible than another's.

The changing role of China's "barefoot doctors" provides another instructive case (Rosenthal & Greiner 1982). The role was created by government fiat in 1965, partly to answer an unmet need for medical care in rural areas, and partly for more political reasons. Barefoot doctors were originally chosen by their neighbors; they gave only part time to their medical and public health duties, received only work points and no wages, and received minimal training. Recently, steps have been taken to augment the training, to subject them to greater control by the medical profession, to emphasize their clinical tasks more than public health responsibilities, to pay wages, and possibly to transform them into full-time medical workers. We know less about the impetus for these changes than we do for British and American pharmacy and medicine. However, the impetus for creation and for subsequent upgrading of the role appears to have come from external legitimate role definers rather than role incumbents. Perceived client needs were important for both creation and upgrading, though we do not know whether clients were mobilized to speak for themselves or not.

Paralleling the upgrading of barefoot doctors was the effort of American department store managers at the beginning of the twentieth century to transform and upgrade the "shopgirl" role into a "saleswoman" role through a concerted program of training and supervision, so they might sell more effectively to increasingly sophisticated shoppers (Benson 1986).

Role expansion for registered nurses has been facilitated by a shortage of primary care physicians; by federal government concern to fill the gap in medical services available for the poor and middle income population; by the physician's assistant movement, which had relatively limited success but demonstrated that parts of the physician's previously exclusive role could be performed by less medically trained personnel; and by the women's movement (Bullough 1976).

Deprofessionalization

More has been written about *deprofessionalization* than professionalization recently. "*De*professionalization is defined as a loss to professional occupations of their unique qualities, particularly their monopoly over knowledge, public belief in their service ethos, and expectations of work autonomy and authority over the client" (Haug 1973). Haug & Sussman (1969) reminded students that, contrary to the assumption of autonomy and control over their work, most professionals were, by then, employed in bureaucracies. This organizational setting added the authority of administrator of bureaucratic rules to the independent professional's authority over the client, but also limited his/her professional autonomy. However, at the same time, clients were increasingly rejecting both grounds for professional authority. This was partly because the same pattern of bureaucratization brought clients together over extended periods of time, facilitating the development of collective behavior. These developments are documented especially with respect to medicine (Reeder 1972, Starr 1982), higher education, law (Rothman 1984), and social welfare (Simon 1983, Fabricant 1985).

The impetus for deprofessionalization comes from changes in other roles in the professional's role set[2], such as client and manager, but also indirectly from the effects of impersonal social structural processes. Conditions commonly mentioned as favorable to deprofessionalization include computerization of knowledge and rising levels of general education, which threaten the professional's monopoly of knowledge; bureaucratic employment; the rise of consumer movements and demands for public accountability, which undermine both autonomy and control over the client and call into question belief in the professional's altruism toward the client; and resurgence of populist themes stressing the superiority of experience over formal education. Reeder (1972) explains changes in the physician-patient relationship on the basis of (a) reorientation of medical care away from treatment toward prevention, concerning which clients feel less sense of urgency; (b) bureaucratization of medical services making for standardized patterns of experience, attitudes, and values; and (c) growth of a general consumer movement.

Rothman (1984), writing about law, stresses that the effects of increasing role specialization and greater heterogeneity among role incumbents weaken the group solidarity that is essential to the pursuit of professional status. As well, encroachments occur from allied professions aggressively claiming the right to perform tasks previously monopolized by lawyers. If law is embattled, the profession of social work "has ceded to the professions of law and management both its ideological custody of the welfare system and its preeminent role in its administration" (Simon 1983, p. 1199). In addition, Simon details the cultural development of a system of legal doctrine that impairs the social worker's discretion and authority, and notes

---

[2]Merton (1957) defines the role set as "that complement of role relationships which persons have by virtue of occupying a particular social status" (p. 110). I am using the term here strictly to refer to the set of *alter* roles whose incumbents hold and communicate expectations concerning conduct of the focal role.

a political change as social work's traditional labor constituency increasingly assumed an adversarial attitude toward the benefactors of social progams.

Writing about American medicine, Ritzer & Walczak (1986) suggest that revelations of professional abuse and the profitability of malpractice suits to the legal profession weaken the physician's role. But they contend that a society-wide trend toward formal rationalization as an organizational principle is most crucial. "What this means, at the most basic level, is that medicine may be losing some of its commitment to larger values (e.g. the welfare of the patient above all else) under pressure of the demand of formal rationality (e.g. efficiency or cost effectiveness above all else)" (p. 50).

Haug & Lavin (1983) find, in both state and nationwide surveys, that consumerist attitudes on the part of clients are not necessarily translated into action in the physician-client encounter. Young people are more likely to hold challenging attitudes toward physician authority, but knowledgeability about health, possession of health problems, and discontent with prior health care count most in translation of such attitudes into behavior. They identify the sources of patient consumerism as: a general rise in public expectations concerning rights and duties, general antiauthority trends in society, generally higher education levels, use of paraprofessionals (demonstrating that medicine is not so mysterious after all), increased public belief in the efficacy of self-care, rising doubts about medical ethics, and doubts about the effectiveness with which physicians police each other.

Not all sociologists concur in the diagnosis of the causes of widespread deprofessionalization. Friedson (1984) concludes that the influence of consumer movements has declined since the 1960s and early 1970s, that professional monopolies remain largely intact, that advancement in professionals' technical knowledge outpaces the public's general education advances, that computerized knowledge does not diminish professional discretion and skill in its use, that self-employment is not a requisite for exercise of professional discretion, and that control over professionals, while more formalized and hierarchical than before, remains in the hands of professionals. He acknowledges that the variables stressed by other writers have had important effects on the nature of professional roles, but denies that these effects constitute deprofessionalization.

These discussions of professionalism deal principally with quantitative role change, i.e. the enhancement or loss of privilege, power, and prestige. At the microsociological level, the focus is on role tenability (the balance of benefits to costs to the incumbent), rather than functionality. Both advocates and critics of the deprofessionalization thesis would probably agree that role enhancement or loss occurs with changes in the ability of role incumbents to differentiate the tasks they perform from tasks performed in other roles, to gain support through services to incumbents of one or more other roles in their role sets, to secure legitimation for the role, and to overcome competition from incumbents of allied roles. These conditions are in turn affected by several variables. First are changes in the characteristics and collective action of the focal role incumbents, especially as they affect solidarity within the role and relations within the role set. Second are changes in the nature and distinctiveness of tasks in the role, brought about by such macrochanges as advances in science and computerization of knowledge. Third are changes in organizational setting and legitimate role definers. And fourth are broad cultural currents, such as Jacksonian populism and the more recent ascendency of formal rationality.

Professionalization as Qualitative Change

While today we think of professionalization as enhancing the benefits and standing of a role, at earlier times it was often the culmination of a qualitative change which may or may not have been experienced as improvement by the incumbents. Fox (1982) described the transformation of the scientist in nineteenth century France from "a notable with distinction in the eyes of an admiring nonspecialist public" to a professional whose audience was mostly others in the same specialty. The change came as many scientists fought to create a more intellectually rewarding role, against the political establishment and fellow scientists who experienced high tenability in the traditional role. Advancement of knowledge, increasing numbers of scientists, and the example of the more professional role of the scientist in neighboring Germany contributed to dissatisfaction with the earlier role.

McWilliams (1985) described the transformation, during the first half of the twentieth century, of British probation workers from "missionaries" pleading for mercy for convicted criminals, to trained professionals who attempted to make scientific diagnoses. Here the impetus for change came from officials seeking more useful advice in making probation decisions, and from probation workers who took the practice of medicine and social welfare as prototype roles.

In one of the finest recent studies of role change, Scott (1978) traced the transformation, between 1750 and 1850, of New England clergy from public officers to professionals. In mid-eighteenth century New England, the pastor was chosen and supported by all residents of the community, normally served a single parish for life, and had as his principal responsibility the maintenance of communal order. Religious discipline and social discipline were one. But nationhood and the emergence of political parties destroyed the communalism on which the pastor's authority was based, and subsequent pastoral partisanship rendered his pronouncements and his adjudication of personal disputes controversial rather than authoritative. By 1815, the "clergy had abandoned public office to the electoral culture" (p. 34) and evolved a new strategy for implementing their traditional goal of maintaining public order. The new evangelical conception of social order placed more weight on internal control than external control of individual conduct, and was aimed at resuscitating moral opinion as a force in the community. The new conception called for active recruitment and for educational societies and colleges to train the new clergy. Expansion of the clergy and divorcement from communal power centers meant that new recruits were most often poor young men, rather than scions of leading families, with little sense of themselves as members of a social or cultural elite. During the 1830s and 1840s abolitionism polarized the pastorate and religious congregations, made pastoral tenure temporary and conditional on satisfying the congregation, and threatened the stability and effectiveness of the religious institutional structure. By 1850 a campaign to protect individual churches from disruptive external influences and to render the pastor role once again tenable and effective led to abandonment of the traditional goal of preserving public order and the more recent goal of establishing a moral community. The church became almost exclusively a devotional center, and the pastor was judged by the quality of his preaching and by how well he served the personal and spiritual needs of the congregation. Pastors still articulated a body of Christian social doctrine but were primarily "physicians of the soul." At the same time, the clergy had become: "a coherent, self-conscious occupational body, organized and defined by a set of institutions which were outside lay or public control, which controlled the special learning needed to become a clergyman, and which possessed the power to determine who could enter the clerical ranks" (pp. 154–55).

In this study we see clearly the larger social structural bases for role stability and change and the extended process of developing a workable new role. The traditional role was anchored in both the church and the environing community. When the mode of community organization changed, the pastor was deprived of his traditional functions in the community. Since the effectiveness of his role in the church was largely dependent upon the functional and representational characteristics of his community role, the role also lost its function within the church. There followed a period in which pastors sought to regain the lost community functions by role modifications, which, however, not only were counterproductive in the community but also further undermined the pastors' ability to function within the church. During this period of disestablishment the role became less tenable, so the church had to depend upon recruiting new incumbents from less powerful segments of society, whose personal styles fitted a more restricted role definition. The role might have ceased to exist, except for a religious constituency demanding service and the incumbents' collective efforts to establish the organizational bases for a profession.

Recapitulation: The Impetus to Role Change

At this point, let me briefly summarize the variety of sources for role change already encountered (leaving aside temporarily the conditions affecting implementation). The initial *impetus* to change may come from (A) widespread misfit between role and person with respect to functionality, tenability, or the representational character of the role. The misfit may result from (a-1) change in the attitudes, abilities, or resources of recruits, or from (a-2) systematic change in the attitudes, abilities, or resources of persons who are already incumbents, as in a role that fosters continuing education. The impetus may come from (B) prior change in the role of a significant *alter*. The *alter* may be (b-1) a collaborator role in the division of labor, (b-2) a competitor role experiencing role expansion or contraction, or (b-3) a client role, making different demands than before. The impetus may come from (C) change in the environing social structure, leading to (c-1) change in the need or demand for services rendered or potentially rendered by the role or (c-2) change in the availability of resources and social support for performance of the role. There may be (D) change in cultural values, as they apply to the role and to its various goals and functions. One, or more often several, of these conditions appear to have caused the initial destabilization that created an impetus to role change in the studies already reviewed.

Cultural Change and Occupational Role Change

Change in cultural values as an important source of the impetus to change merits further attention on the basis of several studies of changes in religious occupations (Blomjous 1969, Bocock 1970, Holifield 1977, Mohler 1970, Towler 1970, Wessels 1973). Bocock (1970) reports that Anglican clergy had come to be evaluated more on the basis of their work with the poor and the sick than on the basis of their traditionally more essential liturgical performance. Catholic priests in American inner cities had shifted their role emphasis from expressive to instrumental orientation and their priorities from preacher and priest functions toward prophetic and pastoral role functions (Stewart 1969). The favored leadership style throughout the church changed from authoritarian to facilitative (Hoge 1987). These changes are generally attributed to the secularization of society and to the fact that the modern laity no longer feel themselves at the mercy of the supernatural, but rather, as masters of their environments (Blomjous 1969), though they may also have been partly a temporary consequence of the 1960s cultural upheaval. Holifield (1977) argues that the conception of an ideal minister has changed, over a longer time perspective, to correspond with society's more general "heroic ideal", from the early nineteenth century learned and refined gentleman, to the man of power characterized by forcefulness, vision, control, and command, to the early twentieth century exponent of the social gospel, to the efficient and well-organized administrative expert, and finally to the well-credentialled specialist and technician.

Similar changes in the nun's role have been reported, for the same cultural reasons, but the changes have been more extensive (Brown 1972, Wills 1972, Ebaugh 1977, Weaver 1985). The influence of the women's movement and difficulties in recruiting and holding women to the nun role have contributed substantially to the greater militancy and flexibility of the nun role in comparison with the priest role. Because of historic blurring of the traditional distinction between sacred and secular [cultural change], nuns are no longer extolled for choosing a superior way of life; this affected the representationality and tenability of the role. And the very education that church leaders encouraged opened new vistas to nuns, leading to their radicalization. The obstacles to implementing role change are weaker for nuns than priests because their work is not so closely supervised, they are more remote from central church authority in the chain of command, much that they do is not widely visible, and they work as groups rather than as individuals so it is harder to hold them accountable. In addition, nuns live and work as communitarians and are therefore more easily mobilized for collective action (Wills 1972).

Also changing, as part of the religious role system and in some respects leading the change, has been the Catholic layperson role. Hoge (1981) speaks of "a great reversal, in which the ghetto Catholicism of the immigrant era was replaced by a middle-class Catholicism that embraced American culture" (p. 25). Role incumbent change through assimilation into American culture caused a shift away from traditionally expected docility toward acceptance of selectivity regarding beliefs and exercises as appropriate for Catholic laity.

RECAPITULATION: IMPLEMENTATION OF ROLE CHANGE

A provisional list of conditions for *implementing* a new pattern of roles is intended to complement the prior list of conditions fostering an *impetus* to change. Variables can be stated from the focal role point of view: what conditions foster a positive outcome, whether in accomplishing or resisting change? The following generally applicable conditions have been suggested in the studies reviewed thus far: (*a*) Structural autonomy of the focal role, in contrast to integration into an organization such as a bureaucracy; (*b*) unity, resources, and mobilization of the focal role's incumbents; (*c*) mobilized client demand, support, and trust; (*d*) cultural credibility of the proposed new pattern of roles, including compatibility with the values of contemporary social movements; and (*e*) institutional, including legal, support. If the impetus to change involves or affects encroachment of one role on what is conceived as the territory of another role, the process of change becomes competitive. Then the following conditions also come into play: (*f*) antic-

costs of the encroachment to the encroached upon, affecting the amount of resistance to be met; (*g*) unity, resources, and mobilization of incumbents of the encroached upon role; (*h*) scarcity and monopolizability of role-relevant skills; (*i*) the support structures, such as special schools and training programs, developed for each of the roles in contention.

AGE ROLES: FAMILY AND BASIC

It is difficult to examine structural status role change in the family apart from change in basic roles because age and sex are the fundamental organizing principles in families. Consequently, many or even most family role changes may be by-products of more generalized age and gender role changes. Well-documented changes in grandparent roles in western nations illustrate this linkage:

> Grandparenthood today is evolving into a different role. The pattern is based on intermittent contact, informality, and playfulness. Instead of being concerned primarily with socializing, teaching, or transmitting values and family heritage to their grandchildren, today's grandparents are likely to emphasize having fun with their grandchildren and being companions rather than authority figures. (Nahemow 1985, p. 190)

Surveyed grandparents said that being a material or financial resource person was the best expression of grandparenthood, and they wished to be viewed (representation) as a "fun person" (Crawford 1981). The change is chiefly the result of lowered average age at marriage and smaller and more closely spaced families, so that more people become grandparents in their 40s and 50s (Crawford 1981). But it also reflects a change in the basic role of the elderly to a more active style, because of improved longevity, health, and financial independence, and the segregation of many of the elderly into age-homogeneous settings where heightened interaction can speed up the process of subcultural redefinition (Perkinson 1980). It might be added that the traditional socialization function was deemphasized when it became a source of intrafamilial conflict because of generational differences in life-style. At the same time, the responsibilities of grandparents in case of death or divorce of the parents have not been clarified (Johnson 1983). Thus we see the impetus to change in the misfit between role and person, brought on by demographic changes and reinforced by cultural change; further impetus is provided by the discovery of a new role formulation generally rewarding to all three generations; but this is still incomplete.

In an insightful historical study, Zelizer (1987) examined changes in the American child role from the eighteenth century to the present. She notes that children in eighteenth century rural America were economically valuable as working members of the family but were not sentimentalized. Opportunities for child labor outside the home increased children's economic value for working class families in the nineteenth century. But child labor laws and compulsory education had nullified their economic value for all classes by the 1930s. Paradoxically, their sentimental value increased as their household contributions decreased, until today children have become simultaneously economically worthless and expensive. "Properly loved children, regardless of social class, belonged in a domesticated, nonproductive world of lessons, games, and token money" (p. 12).

Zelizer notes that "children were removed from the market between 1870 and 1930 in large part because it had become more economical and efficient to educate them than to hire them" (p. 112). This change reflected "profound changes in the economic, occupational, and family structures" (p. 11). But it "was also part of a cultural process of 'sacrilization' of children's lives. The term sacrilization is used in the sense of objects being invested with sentimental or religious meaning" (p. 11). Sacrilization of children was an aspect of a broader cultural movement including a more sensitive response to all death and perhaps other humanitarian tendencies. No explanation is offered for this broad cultural movement.

Zelizer raised the question whether, by the 1980s, this form of child role had become a luxury society could ill afford, thus presaging further role change. And Garbarino (1986) noted a shift away from the child-centered life-styles of the first half of the twentieth century toward a more adult-oriented agenda, provoked by monetarization of the household and mothers working, while fathers still limited their participation in child rearing. One might say that the changes forced on parental roles by the "priceless child" role were neither functional nor tenable for the parents, and as their roles change, profound but as yet unfocused changes are occurring once again in the child role.

Also based on historical research, Hareven (1977a) noted that our present distinct separation between age roles is a recent phenomenon. "Under the demographic conditions of the nineteenth century, higher mortality and higher fertility, functions within the family were less specifically tied to age, and members of different age groups were consequently not so completely segregated by the tasks they were required to fulfill" (p. 62). In addition to demographic changes, "the decline in instrumental family relationships and the related emergence of privatism as the major ideological base of the family in society have tended to reinforce role segregation along age and sex lines" (p. 68). If age and perhaps sex roles have become more rigid, this observation would contradict a more general principle, announced by Ruth Hartley (1970), that highly generalized roles like gender and age tend to break down as social organization becomes more complex, making for flexibility and diffuseness of basic roles.

GENDER ROLE CHANGE: FAMILY AND BASIC

The abundantly reported evidence for change in women's roles both in the family and in other settings need not be repeated here (Lipman-Blumen & Tickamyer 1975, Miller & Garrison 1982, Laslett & Brenner 1989). Chafetz (1984) offers a general model for explaining women's traditionally disadvantaged role, in which technological, demographic, and environmental variables affect the organization of work, which in turn affects family structure, which is the proximate cause for the shape of women's role. Recently women's opportunities outside the family and options within the family have multiplied, and cultural role conceptions have been adjusted. Historical research has shown that the now eroding pattern of husband as exclusive breadwinner with wife limited to domestic duties was only a temporary aberration from the typical pattern of full participation by both husband and wife in economic production. The critical change brought on by industrialization was separation between the locus of economic production and the home, leading to a sharper division of economic and domestic responsibilities between husband and wife roles (Ridley 1968, Hareven 1977b, Pleck 1983, Davis 1984). More recent changes appear to have been brought on by the need for the wife's income in the effort to meet contemporary rising living standards, by earlier completion of child-rearing, and dissipation of the neighborhood as a locus for meaningful activity. Education expanded women's horizons and made the distinction between men's and women's capabilities less credible. But regardless of these influences, Davis (1984) points to a fundamental structural weakness in the exclusively male breadwinner system. When women have no control over the forces affecting their lives and men find life-long responsibility for sole support of the family a heavy burden, the system could not operate without strong normative controls, which collapsed with the demographic and social changes accompanying advanced industrialism. Heer & Grossbard-Schechtman (1981) offer a more specific explanation for some of the changes. They propose that the marriage squeeze (shortage of eligible males) and the contraceptive revolution combined to reduce the "compensation" men were required to give women either for wifely and maternal duties or for sexual companionship without procreative intent. Guttentag & Secord (1983) propose a general theory of the effect of the sex ratio on the relative dependency and power in dyadic relations, which effect is then reflected in the constitution of male and female roles. Whicker (1986) stresses the importance of birth control, but in a more positive sense than Heer and Grossbard-Schechtman, as giving freedom to women.

The nature of the instigations to role change, as briefly summarized, fit easily into the framework already suggested. It is the incomplete and uncertain stabilization of a new pattern of gender roles, both within and outside of the family, that can shed more light on the dynamics of role change. While paternal role change is attributed largely to changes in women's roles (Lamb 1979), Pleck (1977) also attributes a growing feeling of restriction in the traditional role to many men. Nevertheless, men's gender role conceptions have changed less than those of women (Eversoll 1979). Female employment does not necessarily lead to more egalitarian lifestyles (Szinovacz 1977), and while husbands today are performing an increasing proportion of the couple's total family work, "husbands increase their absolute level of work little, if at all, when their wives are employed" (Pleck 1983, p. 267). While many husbands share some of the childcare responsibilities, an effort made necessary by the daytime absence of the working mother from the home (Rotundo 1985), few men are equal partners in parenting (Gerson 1985).

Obstacles to Gender Role Change

Resistance to gender role change comes from both women and men. Using five sample surveys from 1964 to 1974, Mason et al (1976) found that level of education and being employed were the two most important personal variables for predicting liberal gender role attitudes in women, with the husband's educational level also contributing to egalitarian attitudes. Gerson (1985) found a deepening division over gender roles between traditionally and nontraditionally oriented women, with the former finding it in their interest to preserve traditional arrangements and beliefs.

However, the most significant resistance probably comes from men. Although most men share a belief in equal opportunity in the abstract, Goode (1981) describes a generalized perspective, through which superordinates see their positions and their subordinates, that explains much male resistance. For example, superordinates do not observe subordinates' behavior, including talents and accomplishments, as carefully as subordinates do superordinates' behavior; superordinates take social structure for granted and therefore assume their superior accomplishments are a result of inborn superiority. They are more aware of their burdens and responsibilities than of their unearned advantages, and view even small losses of deference, advantages, or opportunities as major threats. Since any given cohort of men know they did not create the system, they reject the charge that they conspired to dominate women. Goode concludes with an opinion, that "a loss of centrality, a decline in the extent to which they are the center of attention," is the shift that troubles men most. Indeed, as Benson (1968) has shown, a series of conditions, beginning with industrialization and the breadwinner's separation from the home, and continuing with women's increasing opportunities to work, and egalitarian ideologies fostered in the second World War have considerably weakened the father's authority in the family.

The problems in shifting from traditional to egalitarian gender roles are clearest in the case of parenting. Among intact middle-class families in which the husband was the primary caregiver, most men said that the arrangement impeded their own career advancement (Radin 1982), although this finding would probably apply less to non-upwardly-mobile working-class men. Several investigators found that men who assumed major child-rearing responsibilities were subject to criticism, ridicule, and negative pressures from friends, associates, employers, and sometimes even their wives (Lewis 1981, Pleck et al 1986, Hanson 1985), though Radin (1982) found no such pressures in her university-community sample. In addition, Pleck et al (1986) attribute male reluctance to modelling after their fathers, to social attitudes, and to lack of specific parenting skills.

Sharing parenting responsibilities is a particularly sensitive matter for women. Gerson (1985) noted that most women in her sample found it difficult to make fathers equal partners in childrearing. Radin (1982) found, in a sample of middle-class families, that the greatest regret for women who relinquished primary caregiving responsibilities to the husband, was the loss of personal closeness to their own children. At a more tangible level, so long as women's pay is usually less than men's, few families can afford to substitute the wife's earning for the husband's, in order to facilitate his fuller participation in childrearing (Gerson 1985).

If these several obstacles to gender role change are inverted, they can be related to the facilitating conditions suggested by the literature on occupational role change. Structural autonomy and insulation from supervision find a counterpart in the observation that collapse of the normative control system allowed a latent impetus to change to become manifest. Unity and mobilization of role incumbents are matched in the crucial part played by the women's movement. Also the chilling effect on role change of the deep divisions between women with traditional and nontraditional role conceptions is the negative of unity and mobilization. Mobilized client demand is manifest in the opening up of jobs for women, particularly with expansion of the service sector where women employees are especially sought after. Cultural credibility of a new role pattern is reflected in the views of men and women, and it is clear that the change is uneven in this respect. Cultural credibility is also manifested in the need for consistency between family roles and basic roles, which becomes an obstacle when basic roles change less easily than family roles. Institutional support involves legislative and judicial successes and failures. An important variable that was overlooked in the occupational change review must be added to the list, namely, the costs of changing to an alternative role pattern. The dilution of the successful mother's special relationship with her children appears to be an inhibiting cost, as is giving up the freedom from economic responsibility for those women whose marriages have given them that luxury.

Gender role change involves encroachment on alter roles, because of the close interdependency of men's and women's roles, especially within the family. Hence the perceived costs of encroachment to incumbents of the encroached upon role are important. Here may be the principal source of male resistance to a fully egalitarian role pattern. Men have not been mobilized to defend their turf in the way that women have, but a more subtle mobilization takes place through the predominantly male dominated organizational structure of modern society. Women's increased education and employment experience contribute to the impetus toward change, but also are crucial in helping to reduce the scarcity and monopolizability of skills that would otherwise block role change. Although this review has not touched on them, such support structures as consciousness-raising groups, hot lines, and women's studies programs have undoubtedly been important change facilitators.

TOWARD A GENERALIZED MODEL FOR ROLE CHANGE

Because of space limitations, conditions specifically conducive to the emergence of new roles and the abandonment of old ones have not been explored. Neither has the considerable literature on role change in other cultures. We have also touched only briefly and unsystematically on the *process* of role change. However, the preceding discussion can be summarized as a provisional model for role change, presented in diagramatic form in Figure 1. The impetus toward role change can be set in motion by a change in the cultural value assigned to the focal role or to its various goals and functions, a social structural change that modifies the demand for role-relevant services or affects the availability of resources or social support for performance of the role, or a demographic or technological change that modifies relevant personal characteristics of role incumbents or potential incumbents, the number of potential recruits, or the consequences of role conformity or nonconformity. These initiating changes may affect the focal role indirectly through modifying the supporting network, as with the New England Protestant ministers, indirectly through modifying a close alter role, as with a changed women's role forcing balancing changes in men's roles, or directly through creating a role-person misfit in the focal role. Under some circumstances a misfit between role and person is resolved by reallocation without role change, as when no-longer subservient workers in an authoritarian firm are replaced when a factory is moved to a region where potential workers are impoverished and have not been unionized. A unique role-person misfit can also be resolved without role change by negotiating an idiosyncratic role, though if the lack of fit becomes more widespread, the idiosyncratic role can become the model for a new role pattern. The impetus toward role

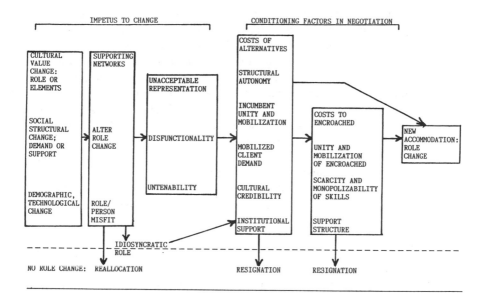

Figure 1 Model for role change

change is completed if the effect of these changes on the focal role is either to render the representational character of the role unacceptable, or to make the role disfunctional or untenable.

Whether the impetus will lead to successful negotiation of a new role pattern depends upon several conditioning factors. These factors include (*a*) whether there appears to be a realistically achievable alternative role pattern whose benefit/cost ratio is more favorable than the old pattern; (*b*) the extent of structural autonomy of the role setting, the extent of freedom from close observation, or the weakening of normative controls over role performance; (*c*) the extent to which role incumbents are unified in their desire for role change and mobilized to promote change; (*d*) the extent to which there is mobilized "client" demand for the services this role provides or would provide under a new pattern; (*e*) the cultural credibility of the potential new role pattern; and (*f*) success in gaining institutional support for the new pattern, including in many cases legal and judicial action. Not all of these conditioning factors will be relevant for all kinds of potential role change, but if the total effect of the relevant conditions is negative or insufficiently positive, the response from the focal role will be resignation rather than role change. If the role changes envisioned involve encroachment on the rights or duties of other roles, a potentially competitive situation is created, and several more conditioning factors come into play. These include the costs to incumbents of the encroached upon role, which influence the likelihood of mobilized opposition to change; the unity and mobilization of incumbents of an encroached upon role; the scarcity and monopolizability of skills necessary for the execution of the focal role; and the success of focal role incumbents in creating effective support structures. Again, if the balance of these conditions is insufficiently favorable, resignation rather than role change is the result.

If conditions are favorable, the outcome is role change. The restructuring and stability are, however, relative rather than absolute. Sufficient acknowledgement of the new pattern and accommodation to it make it the new basis on which people interact. The accommodation is seldom consensus. It is usually a mixture of accepting the bad with the good, seeing no other feasible way to arrange things, and some consensus, with only faintly visible coercion in the background because of the unequal power of parties to the accommodation.

ACKNOWLEDGMENTS

I have benefitted from James Benton's and Linda VanLeuven's assistance in searching recent literature, and from helpful criticisms and suggestions from Richard Scott and two anonymous reviewers.

Literature Cited

Abbott, A. 1988. *The System of Professions: An Essay on the Division of Expert Labor.* Chicago: Univ. Chicago Press

Banton, M. 1965. *Roles: An Introduction to the Study of Social Relations.* New York: Basic Books

Benson, L. 1968. *Fatherhood: A Sociological Perspective.* New York: Random House

Benson, S. P. 1986. *Counter Cultures: Saleswomen, Managers, and Customers in American Department Stores, 1890–1940.* Urbana: Univ. Illinois Press

Bernard, J. 1976. Change and stability in sex-role norms and behavior. *J. Soc. Issues* 32:207–23

Biddle, B. J. 1979. *Role Theory: Expectations, Identities, and Behaviors.* New York: Academic Press

Biddle, B. J., Thomas, E. J., eds. 1966. *Role Theory: Concepts and Research.* New York: Wiley

Blomjous, J. J. 1969. *Priesthood in Crisis.* Milwaukee: Bruce

Bocock, R. J. 1970. The Role of the Anglican clergyman. *Social Compass* 17:533–44

Brown, M. B. 1972. Where have all the Sisters Gone? *U.S. Catholic* 37(Feb.):6–13

Bullough, B. 1976. Influences on role expansion. *Am. J. Nursing* 76:1496–81

Chafetz, J. S. 1984. *Sex and Advantage: A Comparative, Macro-Structural Theory of Sex Stratification.* Totowa, NJ: Rowman & Allanheld

Crawford, M. 1981. Not disengaged: Grandparents in literature and reality, An empirical study in role satisfaction. *The Sociol. Rev.* 29:499–519

Davis, K. 1984. Wives and work: The sex role revolution and its consequences. *Popul. Dev. Rev.* 10:397–417

Ebaugh, H. R. F. 1977. *Out of the Cloister: A Study of Organizational Dilemmas.* Austin: Univ. Tex. Press

Eisenstadt, S. N., Weintraub, D., Toren, N. 1967. *Analysis of Processes of Role Change.* Jerusalem: Israel Univ. Press

Esland, G. 1980. Professions and professionalism. In *The Politics of Work and Occupations,* ed. G. Esland and G. Salaman, pp. 213–50. Toronto: Univ. Toronto Press

Eversoll, D. 1979. The changing father role: Implications for parent education programs for today's youth. *Adolescence* 14:535–44

Fabricant, M. 1985. The industrialization of social work practice. *Soc. Work* 30:389–95

Fox, R. 1982. The scientist and his public in nineteenth-century France. *Soc. Sci. Inform.* 21:697–718

Freidson, E. 1984. The changing nature of

professional control. *Annu. Rev. Sociol.* 10:1–20

Garbarino, J. 1986. Can American families afford the luxury of childhood? *Child Welfare* 65:119–28

Gerson, K. 1985. *Hard Choices: How Women Decide about Work and Motherhood.* Berkeley: Univ. Calif. Press

Goode, W. J. 1981. Why men resist. In *Rethinking the Family: Some Feminist Questions,* ed. B. Thorne, M. Yalom, pp. 131–50. New York: Longmans

Guttentag, M., Secord, P. F. 1983. *Too Many Women? The Sex Ratio Question.* Beverly Hills: Sage

Hanson, S. 1985. Fatherhood: contextual variations. *Am. Behav. Sci.* 29:55–77

Hareven, T. K. 1977a. Family time and historical time. *Daedalus* 106(Spring):57–70

Hareven, T. K. 1977b. The family and gender roles in historical perspective. In *Women and Men: Changing Roles, Relationships, and Perceptions,* ed. L. A. Cater, A. F. Scott, W. Martyna, pp. 93–118. New York: Praeger

Hartley, R. E. 1970. American core culture: changes and continuities. In *Sex Roles in Changing Society,* ed. G. H. Seward, R. C. Williamson, pp. 126–49. New York: Random House

Haug, M. R. 1973. Deprofessionalization: An alternative hypothesis for the future. *Sociol. Rev. Monogr. 20: Professionalization and Social Change,* ed. P. Halmos, pp. 195–211

Haug, M. R., Lavin, B. 1983. *Consumerism in Medicine: Challenging Physician Authority.* Beverly Hills: Sage

Haug, M. R., Sussman, M. B. 1969. Professional autonomy and the revolt of the client. *Soc. Prob.* 17:153–61

Heer, D. M., Grossbard-Schechtman, A. 1981. The impact of the female marriage squeeze and the contraceptive revolution on sex roles and the women's liberation movement in the United States, 1960 to 1975. *J. Marriage Fam.* 43:49–65

Heise, J. 1981. Social roles. In *Social Psychology: Sociological Perspectives,* eds. M. Rosenberg, R. H. Turner, pp. 94–129. New York: Basic Books

Hoge, D. R. 1981. *Converts, Dropouts, Returnees: A Study of Religous Change among Catholics.* New York: Pilgrim

Hoge, D. R. 1987. *The Future of Catholic Leadership: Responses to the Priest Shortage.* Kansas City, Mo: Sheed & Ward

Holifield, E. B. 1977. The hero and the minister in American culture. *Theology Today* 33:370–79

Johnson, C. L. 1983. A cultural analysis of the grandmother. *Res. Aging* 5:547–67

Khoury, R. M. 1980. Is there a process of

occupational professionalization? *Int. Behav. Sci.* 12:39–60

Kronus, C. L. 1987. The evolution of occupational power: an historical study of task boundaries between physicians and pharmacists. *Sociol. Work Occup.* 3:3–37

Lamb, M. 1979. Paternal influences and the father's role: A personal perspective. *Am. Psychol.* 34:938–43

Laslett, B., Brenner, J. 1989. Gender and social reproduction: historical perspectives. *Annu. Rev. Sociol.* 15:381–404

Lewis, R. A. 1981. Men's liberation and the men's movement: implications for counsellors. *Personnel Guidance J.* 60:256–59

Lipman-Blumen, J. 1973. Role de-differentiation as a system response to crisis: occupational and political roles of women. *Sociol. Inq.* 13:105–29

Lipman-Blumen, J., Tikamyer, A. R. 1975. Sex roles in transition: a ten-year perspective. *Annu. Rev. Sociol.* 1:297–337

Mason, K. O., Czajka, J. L., Arber, S. 1976. Change in United States women's sex-role attitudes, 1964–1974. *Am. Sociol. Rev.* 41:573–96

McWilliams, W. 1985. The mission transformed: professionalization of probation between the wars. *Howard J. Crim. Justice* 24:257–74

Merton, R. K. 1957. The role set. *Br. J. Sociol.* 8:106–20

Miller, J., Garrison, H. H. 1982. Sex roles: the division of labor at home and in the workplace. *Annu. Rev. Sociol.* 8:237–62

Miner, A. S. 1987. Idiosyncratic jobs in formalized organizations. *Admin. Sci. Q.* 32:327–51

Miner, A. S., Estler, S. E. 1985. Accrual mobility: job mobility in higher education through responsibility accrual. *J. Higher Educ.* 56:121–43

Miner, A. S., Lehner, C. 1988. *The ecology of jobs: idiosyncratic jobs as a source of organizational routines.* Unpublished paper.

Mohler, J. S. 1970. *The Origin and Evolution of the Priesthood.* Staten Island: Alba House

Nahemow, N. 1985. The changing nature of grandparenthood. *Med. Aspects Hum. Sexuality* 19(April):175–190

Perkinson, M. A. 1980. Alternate roles for the elderly: an example from a midwestern retirement community. *Hum. Organ.* 39:219–26

Pleck, J. H. 1977. The work-family role system. *Soc. Prob.* 24:417–27

Pleck, J. H. 1983. Husband's paid work and family roles: current research issues. In *Research on the Interweave of Social Roles,* ed. H. Z. Lopata and J. H. Pleck, III:251–333. Greenwich, Conn.: JAI

Pleck, J, Lamb, M. E., Levine, J. A. 1986.

Facilitating future change in men's family roles. In *Men's Changing Roles in the Family*, ed. R. A. Lewis, M. B. Sussman, pp. 11–16. New York: Haworth

Radin, N. 1982. Primary caregiving and role-sharing fathers. In *Nontraditional Families: Parenting and Child Development*, ed. M. Lamb, pp. 173–204. Hillsdale, NJ: Lawrence Erlbaum

Reeder, L. G. 1972. The patient-client as consumer: some observations on the changing professional-client relationship. *J. Health Soc. Behav.* 13:406–12

Ridley, J. C. 1968. Demographic change and the roles and status of women. *Ann. Am. Acad. Polit. Soc. Sci.* 375:15–25

Ritzer, G., Walczak, D. 1986. The changing nature of American medicine. *J. Am. Culture* 9:43–51

Rocheblave-Spenle, A-M. 1962. *La Notion de Role en Psychologie Sociale*. Paris: Presses Univ. France

Rosenthal, M. M., Greiner, J. R. 1982. The barefoot doctors of China: from political creation to professionalization. *Hum. Organ.* 41:330–41

Rothman, R. A. 1984. Deprofessionalization: the case of law in America. *Work Occup.* 11:183–206

Rotundo, E. A. 1985. American fatherhood: A historical perspective. *Am. Behav. Sci.* 29:7–23

Scott, D. M. 1978. *From Office to Profession: The New England Ministry, 1750–1850*. Philadelphia: Univ. Penn. Press

Simon, W. H. 1983. Legality, bureaucracy, and class in the welfare system, *Yale Law Rev.* 92:1198–1269

Starr, P. 1982. *The Social Transformation of American Medicine*. New York: Basic

Stewart, J. H. 1969. The changing role of the Catholic priest and his ministry in an inner city context: a study in role change. *Sociol. Anal.* 30:81–90

Szinovacz, M. E. 1977. Role allocation, family structure, and female employment. *J. Marriage Fam.* 39:781–91

Thornton, R., Nardi, P. M. 1975. The dynamics of role acquisition. *Am. J. Sociol.* 80:870–85

Towler, R. 1970. The role of the clergy. In *The Christian Priesthood*, ed. N. Lash and J. Rhymer, pp. 165–96. London: Darton, Longman, & Todd

Turner, R. H. 1962. Role-taking: process versus conformity. In *Human Behavior and Social Processes*, ed. A. Rose, pp. 20–40. Boston: Houghton-Mifflin

Turner, R. H. 1968. Role: sociological aspects. In *International Encyclopedia of the Social Sciences*, 13:552–57. New York: Macmillan & Free Press

Turner, R. H. 1970. *Family Interaction*. New York: Wiley

Turner, R. H. 1979–1980. Strategy for developing an integrated role theory. *Humboldt J. Soc. Relat.* 7:123–39

Turner, R. H. 1985. Unanswered questions in the convergence between structuralist and interactionist role theories. In *Perspectives on Micro-Sociological Theory*, ed. H. J. Helle, pp. 22–36. London & Beverly Hills: Sage

Turner, R. H., Colomy, P. 1988. Role differentiation: orienting principles. In *Advances in Group Processes*, ed. E. J. Lawler, B. Markovsky, 5:1–27. Greenwich, Conn.: JAI

Weaver, M. J. 1985. *New Catholic Women: A Contemporary Challenge to Traditional Religious Authority*. San Francisco: Harper & Row

Wessels, Cletus. 1973. Ministry: yesterday, today, and tomorrow. *Am. Ecclesiastical Rev.* 167:264–74

Whicker, M. L., Kronenfeld, J. J. 1986. *Sex Role Changes: Technology, Politics, and Policy*. New York: Praeger

Wills, G. 1972. The liberated New York nuns. *New York:* 5:37–42

Zelizer, V. A. 1987. *Pricing the Priceless Child: The Changing Social Value of Children*. New York: Basic

Zurcher, L. A. 1983. *Social Roles: Conformity, Conflict, and Creativity*. Beverly Hills: Sage

Annu. Rev. Sociol. 1990. 16:111–35

ETHNICITY AND ENTREPRENEURSHIP

Howard E. Aldrich

Department of Sociology, University of North Carolina, Chapel Hill, North Carolina 27599

Roger Waldinger

Department of Sociology, The City College, City University of New York, New York 10031, and Graduate School, City University of New York, New York 10036

KEY WORDS: ethnic stratification, entrepreneur, opportunity structure, immigrant, small business

Abstract

We examine various approaches to explaining ethnic enterprise, using a framework based on three dimensions: an ethnic group's access to opportunities, the characteristics of a group, and emergent strategies. A common theme pervades research on ethnic business: Ethnic groups adapt to the resources made available by their environments, which vary substantially across societies and over time. Four issues emerge as requiring greater attention: the reciprocal relation between ethnicity and entrepreneurship, more careful use of ethnic labels and categories in research, a need for more multigroup, comparative research, and more process-oriented research designs.

INTRODUCTION

The growth of new ethnic populations in Europe since 1945 as well as new waves of immigrants to the United States after the 1965 reform of immigration laws has made ethnic enterprise a topic of international concern. The new ethnic populations are growing at a time of restructuring in western econo-

111

0360-0672/90/0815-0111$02.00

mies, and large numbers of immigrant and ethnic minorities find themselves caught in the conjuncture of changing conditions. Members of some groups have entered business ownership in numbers disproportionate to their group's size, whereas others have shunned entrepreneurial activities.

In this chapter, we present a general framework within which the contributions of various approaches to explaining ethnic enterprise can be understood. The framework we propose is based on ethnic groups' access to opportunities, group characteristics, and emergent strategies, all of which are embedded within changing historical conditions. Within this framework, we review the concepts and research findings of the past several decades.

Focus of Our Review

"Ethnic" is an adjective that refers to differences between categories of people (Petersen 1980). When "ethnic" is linked to "group," it implies that members have some awareness of group membership and a common origin and culture, or that others think of them as having these attributes (Yinger 1985). We assume that what is "ethnic" about ethnic enterprise may be no more than a set of connections and regular patterns of interaction among people sharing common national background or migratory experiences. We emphasize the subcultural dimension of ethnicity—the social structures through which members of an ethnic group are attached to one another and the ways in which those social structures are used.

Entrepreneurship, in the classic sense, is the combining of resources in novel ways so as to create something of value. Much of the recent management literature on entrepreneurship focuses on business foundings, but the term has been expanded in the past few decades and used to encompass nearly all stages in the life cycle of businesses (Bird 1989). The entrepreneurial dimensions of *innovation* and *risk* are particularly salient when we examine ethnic businesses. Rather than breaking new ground in products, process, or administrative form, most businesses simply replicate and reproduce old forms. Simple reproduction is especially likely in the retail and services sector, where most ethnic enterprises are founded. Risks, however, are high for most businesses, regardless of whether they are innovative (Aldrich & Auster 1986). Liabilities of newness and smallness affect all businesses, ethnic or not.

Many writers have suggested making a distinction between entrepreneurs and owner/managers on the basis of either innovativeness or risk, but few have done a convincing job. Neither economists (Baumol 1968:66) nor sociologists (Wilken 1979:60) have been able to operationalize this distinction so that "entrepreneurs" are clearly differentiated from "owners" or even the self-employed. Therefore, in our review we follow the lead set by anthropologists and define entrepreneurs operationally as owners and operators of business enterprises (Greenfield et al 1979). This definition includes self-employed persons who employ family labor as well as those who employ outsiders.

Our review is based on the observation that some ethnic groups, particularly among first and second generation immigrants, have higher rates of business formation and ownership than do others. The historical record shows considerable disparities in self-employment among the various European ethnic groups in the United States; business participation rates are no less varied among contemporary immigrants in the United States and Europe today. To the extent that higher levels of entrepreneurship cannot be explained solely by the personal characteristics of owners, then we must turn to social structural and cultural conditions for an explanation.

Limitations of Current Research

What empirical research is available on which to build sound, cross-national, historically valid generalizations? Ideally, we would like information on multiple groups, spanning long periods, and from many different societies. Such information should include individual, group, and social context characteristics, with explicit attention paid to replicating and building on previous research.

In practice, information on ethnic enterprise comes from three sources: government censuses, survey research, and field studies. Using government census data is complicated because of political sensitivities over "ethnic origin" questions in government-sponsored information acquisition. Major controversy has erupted, for example, in Great Britain and West Germany in the past decade over whether such questions should be included, and if so, in what form. In the United States, unlike other industrialized nations, the government has maintained a *Survey of Minority and Women-Owned Businesses,* conducted every five years for the past two decades. That source is limited because the sociological definition of "ethnic business"—a business whose proprietor has a distinctive group attachment by virtue of self-definition or ascription by others—is more encompassing than the official definition of "minorities," which includes only black, Hispanic, Asian, and Native American groups.

The decennial Census of Population has been a fertile source of data on this wider range of ethnic entrepreneurial groups (Light & Sanchez 1987), especially with the addition of the ancestry item to the 1980 Census (Fratoe 1986, Lieberson & Waters 1988). However, the US Census has a major drawback—by law, the Census Bureau is forbidden to ask questions about religion. Thus, there are no official statistics about religio-ethnic groups—Jews, Muslims, and so forth—that are significant for the understanding of ethnic business. The Canadian census, which asks questions about religion and ethnic status, is a richer source, although it is rarely exploited for this purpose.

With these limitations in mind, many researchers have turned to community surveys and intensive case studies for in-depth information on specific groups. Investigators studying lengthy historical periods are forced to rely on incomplete and inconsistent information, or to draw dynamic inferences from cross-sectional surveys which include multiple generations of a group (Bonacich & Modell 1980). Survey research has provided valuable information, but as in other areas of sociology, the individual becomes de facto the unit of analysis, and the social context for behavior is lost.

A FRAMEWORK FOR UNDERSTANDING ETHNIC ENTREPRENEURSHIP

Our framework for understanding ethnic business development is built on three interactive components: opportunity structures, group characteristics, and strategies (Waldinger et al 1990). *Opportunity structures* consist of market conditions which may favor products or services oriented to co-ethnics, and situations in which a wider, non-ethnic market is served. Opportunity structures also include the ease with which access to business opportunities is obtained, and access is highly dependent on the level of interethnic competition and state policies. *Group characteristics* include predisposing factors such as selective migration, culture, and aspiration levels. They also include the possibilities of resource mobilization, and ethnic social networks, general organizing capacity, and government policies that constrain or facilitate resource acquisition. Ethnic *strategies* emerge from the interaction of opportunities and group characteristics, as ethnic groups adapt to their environments.

Opportunity Structures

The structure and allocation of opportunities open to potential ethnic business owners have been shaped by historically contingent circumstances. Groups can only work with the resources made available to them by their environments, and the structure of opportunities is constantly changing in modern industrial societies. Market conditions may favor only businesses serving an ethnic community's needs, in which case entrepreneurial opportunities are limited. Or, market conditions may favor smaller enterprises serving non-ethnic populations, in which case opportunities are much greater. Even if market conditions are favorable, immigrant minorities must gain access to businesses, and non-ethnic group members often control such access. Political factors may impede, or less frequently, enhance, the workings of business markets.

MARKET CONDITIONS   As the world economic system has evolved, opportunity structures have changed and immigrant ethnic groups have found themselves facing very different market conditions. Markets in some business sectors have opened, whereas others have closed. In almost all markets, small businesses—once thought headed for inexorable decline—have shown remarkable resiliency and continue to attract new owners. Many immigrants and their children have turned to small business enterprise, some in new ethnic enclaves and others in businesses serving a wider market.

Ethnic consumer products   For a business to arise, there must be some demand for the services it offers. The "protected market hypothesis" (Light 1972) posits that the initial market for ethnic entrepreneurs typically arises within the ethnic community itself. If ethnic communities have special sets of needs and preferences that are best served by those who share those needs and know them intimately, then ethnic entrepreneurs have an advantage. Servicing these special ethnic consumer needs involves a direct connection with the immigrants' homeland and knowledge of tastes and buying preferences—qualities unlikely to be shared by larger, native-owned competitors (Aldrich et al 1985).

Immigrants also have special problems caused by the strains of settlement and assimilation and aggravated by their distance from governmental mechanisms of service delivery. Consequently, the business of specializing in the problems of immigrant adjustment is another early avenue of economic activity. Ethnic consumer tastes provide a protected market position, in part because the members of the community may have a cultural preference for dealing with co-ethnics, and in part because the costs of learning the specific wants and tastes of the immigrant groups discourage native firms from doing so, especially at an early stage when the community is small and not readily visible to outsiders.

Ethnic residential concentration has provided a strong consumer core for many ethnic entrepreneurs, especially for immigrant groups in the early decades of their settlement in their host country. Patterns of chain migration and majority group discrimination lead to the build-up of ethnic residential areas, presenting ethnic entrepreneurs with a captive market, thus adding a second meaning to the phrase "protected market" (Aldrich et al 1985). The initial clustering of migrants in cities has often led to long-term concentrations, facilitating recruitment networks for ethnic suppliers and workers.

If ethnic businesses remain limited to the ethnic market, their potential for growth is sharply circumscribed (Aldrich et al 1983, Mohl 1985). The obstacle to growth is the ethnic market itself, which can support only a restricted number of businesses because it is quantitatively small and because the ethnic population is often too impoverished to generate buying power sufficient to fuel growth. Moreover, the environment confronting the ethnic entrepreneur is severe: Because exclusion from job opportunities leads many immigrants to seek out business opportunities, business conditions in the ethnic market tend toward proliferation of small units, intense competition, and a high failure rate, with the surviving businesses generating scanty returns for their owners.

However, under some conditions, ethnic markets may serve as an export platform from which ethnic firms may expand. One case in point is the experience of Cuban refugees in Miami, Florida (Portes 1987). The early refugees converged on a depressed area in the central city, where housing costs were low and low-rent vacant space was available. As the refugee population grew, and the customer base expanded, retail businesses proliferated (Mohl 1985). The availability of a near-by, low-cost labor force, linked together through informal networks, enabled Cuban entrepreneurs to branch out into other industries, such as garments and construction, where they secured a non-ethnic clientele. Once in place, these "export industries" served as a base for additional expansion of the ethnic economy: the export industries generated a surplus that trickled down to merchants serving the local, specialized needs of the Cuban communities. The export industries also enabled ethnic entrepreneurs to diversify, by moving backward or forward into related industries. The vibrant Cuban ethnic economy has turned Miami into a center for investments from Latin America as well as an entrepot for trade with that area, and Cuban entrepreneurs have been able to move into more sophisticated and higher profit fields (Levine 1985).

This example notwithstanding, we note that the growth potential of immigrant business hinges on its access to customers beyond the ethnic community. The crucial question, then, concerns the types of economic environments that might support neophyte immigrant entrepreneurs.

Non-ethnic markets   The structure of industry—number of businesses, capital and technological requirements—is a powerful constraint on the creation of new businesses. New firms are unlikely to arise in industries characterized by extensive scale economies and high entry costs. However, most western economies contain niches where techniques of mass production or mass distribution do *not* prevail. Researchers have identified four circumstances under which small ethnic enterprises can grow in the open market: underserved or abandoned markets, markets characterized by low economies of scale, markets with unstable or uncertain demand, and markets for exotic goods.

One such niche consists of *markets that are underserved* by the large, mass-marketing organizations. In the United States and some Western European nations, immigrants are heavily concentrated in the core areas of urban centers that are both ill-suited to the technological and organizational conditions of large enterprise *and* favorable to small enterprises. In Paris, London, New York, and Los Angeles, the core urban market is increasingly abandoned by the large food retailers, leaving a substantial consumer base for small local immigrant vendors.

Markets where *economies of scale* are low are another fertile field for immigrant business. In the absence of capital-intensive, high-volume competitors, small immigrant shopkeepers in urban cores can successfully pursue a strategy of self-exploitation. As Ma Mung & Guillon (1986) observed, the immigrant-owned neighborhood shops of Paris offer the same products as their French counterparts, but provide different services: longer hours, year-round operation, easily available credit, and sales of very small quantities.

A niche for immigrant firms also arises in markets affected by *instability or uncertainty*. When demand falls into stable and unstable portions, and the two components can be separated from one another, industries may be segmented into noncompeting branches (Piore 1980): one branch is dominated by larger firms, handling staple products; a second, composed of small-scale firms, caters to the unpredictable and/or fluctuating portion of demand. Immigrant garment firms—a ubiquitous presence in many of the major immigrant-receiving cities in the west—thrive on the availability of short-run products that larger firms cannot handle effectively (Morokvasic et al 1990).

A final niche in the general market arises where the demand for *exotic goods* among the native population allows immigrants to convert both the contents and symbols of ethnicity into profit-making commodities. Selling exotic goods and services offers a fruitful path of business expansion because immigrants have a special product that only they can supply or present in conditions that are seemingly authentic (Palmer 1984). Not only do immigrants lack competitors in "exotic markets," but they can also offer their products at relatively low prices and thereby capture a clientele priced out of the businesses run by native entrepreneurs (Ma Mung & Guillon 1986).

Market conditions, then, may be supportive of ethnic businesses either because ethnic owners enjoy a protected market position or because the environment is supportive of any neophyte capitalist willing to take higher than normal risks (abandoned markets, low economies of scale, and unstable demand). In this latter sense, ethnic owners truly are entrepreneurs, as they assume high risks under uncertain conditions.

ACCESS TO OWNERSHIP   Given the existence of markets, potential ethnic entrepreneurs still need access to ownership positions. Two conditions affecting access have been identified: (*a*) the level of interethnic competition for jobs and businesses; and (*b*) state policies, which have varied considerably among traditional, colonial, nation-building, and modern nation states.

Interethnic competition for vacancies   The likelihood of entering a supportive business niche is greatly affected by the level and nature of interethnic
competition for jobs and business opportunities. Competition may be direct,
in which case immigrants or ethnic minorities are likely to lose access to
desirable markets, or it may be mediated through processes of residential and
occupational succession, in which case vacancies open up in a predictable and
patterned way.

Research has found two outcomes of direct interethnic competition over
business opportunities: (*a*) when the competition is high, ethnic groups
concentrate in a limited range of industries, and (*b*) at very high levels of
competition, a group may be forced out of more lucrative activities, and either
squeezed into interstitial lines or pushed out of business altogether.

Two natural experiments, one involving Japanese and the other Chinese,
document the power of interethnic competition and state policies. First,
severe competition with whites in Canada in the late nineteenth and early
twentieth centuries led to the almost complete exclusion of Japanese from
major social institutions (Makabe 1981). For example, when the Canadian
government took away their right to vote, they lost access to the professions.
In Brazil early in this century, the lack of notable interethnic competition
meant that discrimination and exclusion movements did not materialize, and
the Japanese successfully entered a number of industries. Aided by the
Japanese government's friendly relations with Brazil, the Japanese developed
important social and financial skills. Second, consider the contrasting experience of the Chinese, originating from the same province, who settled in Lima,
Peru, and New York City in the early twentieth century. According to Wong
(1978), the level of discrimination was much higher in the United States than
Peru. For example, the US Chinese Exclusion Act of 1882 was not repealed
until 1943, and US miscegenation laws were not overturned by the Supreme
Court until 1967. By contrast, Peru placed few barriers in the way of Chinese
immigration and had no miscegenation laws, facilitating a very high in-
termarriage rate. Unlike the New York Chinese, who were heavily concentrated in a few industries in Chinatown, the Chinese in Lima were involved in a wide range of businesses. The associational structure of the
Chinese community in Peru was weak because it was not forced to contend
with the same level of interethnic competition as its counterparts in New
York, where ethnic identity was a salient issue for immigrants.

These contrasts draw attention to the relationship between context and
group responses. In general, economic exclusion strengthens group cohesion,
thereby increasing the density of ethnic networks, and in turn, increasing
access to group resources. Similarly, labor market disadvantage affects pre-
dispositions toward business opportunities. These issues are further developed
when we discuss group characteristics.

Interethnic competition may not only determine the range of accessible economic activities, but may also lead to expulsion or displacement from more valued niches. In these instances, dominant group members may follow strategies of social closure to reduce minorities' access to business or labor markets (Parkin 1979). Because ethnic monopolies are costly to some component of the dominant group population—whether employers, workers, or customers—recourse to state intervention is often sought.

Chinese immigrants to California in the nineteenth century encountered fierce competition from whites. In California, after the decline of mining in the late 1860s, Chinese workers went back to the cities, where they tried to enter the construction, manufacturing, and other better paying sectors. "Prompted by the leaders of the nascent unions and by political demagogues, white workers undertook a virulent and eventually successful campaign to drive 'the coolies' out. . . ." leaving the Chinese the laundry business and precious little else (Ong 1981:100).

The impact of competition was more severe on blacks than on Chinese in the United States (Lieberson 1980). Black businesses grew slowly after the abolition of slavery, initially developing in such lines as catering, tailoring, and barbering, following the patterns established prior to 1863. These businesses were mainly the province of a small mulatto elite who depended on connections to a white clientele. By the late 1800s, increased desire among whites for both physical and social distance from blacks, combined with greater competition from immigrants, pushed blacks out of their traditional trades and back into serving mostly black customers (Aldrich 1973).

Theories of *residential segregation and succession* point to forces *reducing* interethnic competition for business vacancies, although we recognize that segregation itself reflects a dominant group's success in insulating itself from a minority group. At the neighborhood level, replacement opportunities for immigrant owners selling to their co-ethnic neighbors emerge as a result of ecological succession. As the native group in a residential area no longer replaces itself, native entrepreneurs seek business opportunities outside the local area. Given a naturally high rate of failure among all small businesses, the absence of members from the older established group willing to open new firms in "changed" neighborhoods creates vacancies for potential immigrant business owners (Aldrich & Reiss 1976, Aldrich et al 1989).

Finally, we note that the classic pattern of *occupational succession,* observed in other areas of the labor market, also affects access to opportunities for ethnic entrepreneurs. In the general economy, the petite bourgeoisie often does not reproduce itself, but rather survives through the recruitment of owners from lower social classes (Bechhofer & Elliot 1981). To some extent, it is the very marginality of the small business position that discourages heirs from taking up their parents' modest enterprises (Berteaux & Berteaux-Wiame 1981).

In the central cities of the United States, where small business has been concentrated among European immigrants and their descendants, the changing social structure of Italian, Jewish, and other European ancestry groups has further diminished the allure of petty enterprise. As these native groups have faltered in their recruitment to small business, their share of the small business sector has inevitably declined, in part because of the high death rate to which all small businesses are prone. The exodus of Jewish or Italian petty merchants has provided replacement opportunities for Korean, Chinese, or Arab businessowners, who depend almost entirely on a non-ethnic clientele (Kim 1981).

Currently, indirect competition appears to characterize the relationship between immigrant entrepreneurs and members of dominant ethnic groups in most industrial societies. While occupational succession leads immigrants to move into positions vacated by whites, those same businesses are often coveted by members of nondominant ethnic groups. Thus, in the United States, interethnic competition among nondominant ethnic groups is an increasingly common phenomenon, as in black-Korean conflict (Kim 1987, Light & Bonacich 1988).

State policies   Elite sponsorship of middleman minorities is a characteristic of traditional, state-building, and colonial situations. The roles of Greeks and Armenians in the Ottoman Empire, and German and Jewish capitalists in tsarist Russia (Armstrong 1976), exemplify the traditional and state-building contexts: in these instances, middleman minorities were valued for their skills, and for their network of family and personal relations, which facilitated long-distance communications and transactions and thereby increased access to capital. In Southeast Asia and Africa, similar conditions led to the growth of Indian and Chinese trading networks (Curtin 1984), whose role was later transformed and enlarged by the integration of these areas into the European world economy (Yambert 1981).

Sociological accounts often emphasize that sponsoring elites benefit from the vulnerability of middleman minorities (Stone 1985), but middleman minorities are not necessarily easily dispatched. Though made in a Third World context, the argument that "business rivals are a prerequisite for business rivalries" (Horowitz 1985:116) holds for Europe as well: middleman minorities have hung on where they retain sufficient value to the dominant elite, where indigenous challengers are relatively few in number, and where the extraterritorial dimension of the middleman diaspora does not pose a political threat.

When these conditions no longer hold, the mobilization of lower strata of the dominant ethnic group upsets the alliance between middleman and dominant groups, especially under conditions of late and uneven modernization (Armstrong 1976). Thus, state sponsorship of middleman minorities has often been succeeded by policies designed to replace middlemen by indigenous capitalists. The interwar years in Europe saw numerous such cases, as when Polish government policies in the 1930s worked to benefit Poles at the expense of all other minorities (Goldscheider & Zuckerman 1984). Similar actions have been taken by newly independent states in the Third World.

Analytically, the concept of middleman minorities does not fit modern, multiethnic nation states, as the greater separation—or perhaps the more subtle and indirect linkages—of political and economic power in the United States and other capitalist countries limits the possibility of direct elite sponsorship (Jain 1988, Kashima 1982). Nonetheless, there is a close *descriptive* parallel between the classic middleman minorities and those contemporary ethnic groups—Koreans in the United States, East Indians in Britain, Moroccans in France—whose businesses are principally dependent on commercial transactions with out-group members. As noted, these latter opportunities arise as the consequence of occupational succession, and recent research has not provided evidence that these new immigrant entrepreneurs have significantly benefitted from elite sponsorship. Consequently, we propose the term "pseudo-middleman minorities" to distinguish contemporary ethnic groups that specialize in trade from the classic middleman of earlier periods.

Presently, the main impact of government policies on ethnic entrepreneurship in North America, Australia, and western Europe is *indirect,* derivative of broader immigration and labor market policies. A basic distinction can be made between countries in which labor recruitment was the dominant factor in immigration policy and countries in which other objectives—population growth, family reunification—have had higher priority. In the first instance, immigrants are subject to a high level of labor market control, which hinders rather than encourages immigrant entrepreneurship (Blaschke et al 1990). In Germany, for example, immigrant workers cannot open a business until they have obtained a residence permit, which they may only receive after more than eight years of labor migrant status in the country. By comparison, immigration countries, like the United States, place virtually no formal barriers to immigrant geographical or economic mobility and thereby increase the potential immigrant business start-up rate.

All western societies also maintain policies that implicitly *impede* ethnic business development. Policies that regulate business and labor markets, through licensing and apprenticeship requirements, health standards, minimum wage laws and the like, raise the costs of entry and operation for small firms—ethnic or not. The impact of these policies is most severe in countries like Germany and the Netherlands, where the small business sector continues to bear the imprint of its traditional artisanal, or guild-like past. In other countries, such as the United States, restraints on commercial competition are weak and apprenticeship requirements lax, with the result that ethnic entrepreneurs can more easily move into supportive markets.

Less significant than these indirect policy effects are those programs designed to provide economic assistance to immigrants and ethnic minorities. In the United States, minority businesses were ignored by the federal government until the 1960s, when "black capitalism" emerged in response to the black protest movement. Minority set-aside programs were introduced into government contracting procedures, and special minority enterprise investment programs were created. The amount of money allocated was never very large, but the effort was a significant symbol of minority business's importance in American society. Programs assisting Cuban and Indo-Chinese refugees have also provided financial and other forms of help for prospective business owners. However, the long-term economic significance of these various programs was small, and little concrete evidence of their consequences could be found in the 1980s.

Group Characteristics

Opportunity structures provide the niches and routes of access for potential entrepreneurs, but that is only half the picture. Group characteristics are emphasized by researchers concerned with why particular ethnic groups are disproportionately concentrated in ethnic enterprises (Portes 1987). We have identified two dimensions of group characteristics: predisposing factors and resource mobilization.

PREDISPOSING FACTORS   By predisposing factors we mean the skills and goals that individuals and groups bring with them to an opportunity. Hirschman (1982) argued that an ethnic group's socioeconomic achievements are partly a function of the human capital of individuals and the sociocultural orientation—motives, ambitions—derived from group membership. Selective migration has been particularly important for US ethnic groups, and favorable sociocultural orientations are often a reaction to conditions encountered in a new situation.

Selective migration   The selective nature of migration directs our attention to the human capital immigrants bring to their host societies. For example, the initial Cuban migration to the United States was highly selective, as middle and upper-middle class Cubans—many with substantial education, business experience, and capital—fled Castro's policies (Perez 1986). Similarly, in the post-1965 migration stream, the majority of Koreans worked in white collar or professional jobs before migrating to the United States (Min 1988). Before we invoke group-level explanations, human capital theorists suggest we control for individual-level endowments.

Frazier (1949) emphasized the importance of prior buying and selling experience for immigrants entering business. His argument focused on the negative consequences that *lack* of such experience had on black Americans, whereas most subsequent writers have focused on groups which have benefitted from prior business experiences. Capital, connections, and specific business skills expedited the rapid emergence of a Chinese subeconomy in Paris, following the arrival of Chinese refugees from Vietnam in the mid 1970s (Guillon & Taboada-Leonetti 1986). Senegalese traders have penetrated European and American cities in spite of lacking co-ethnic clients, higher education, and occupational training, because they could draw on prior business experience (Salem 1981).

Whether experience in the art of trading and selling is a *necessary* condition for business success is difficult to determine. Writers have often emphasized the prior business experience of turn-of-the-century Jewish immigrants to Western Europe and the United States. However, Jewish emigration from the Pale of Settlement was highly selective, and artisans, not business owners or traders, were the most likely to leave Russia. Merchants and dealers accounted for one third of the gainfully employed Jews in Russia, but only 6% of the immigrants in 1899–1910 were merchants or dealers (Rubinow [1905] 1975). The case of Greek immigrants is even more striking, as they have been a presence in urban restaurants in the United States since the early twentieth century (Fairchild 1911) though they apparently originated predominantly in fishing villages and rural areas (Herman 1979).

Some immigrant group members have not been able to turn their previous education and experience into positions comparable to those they held prior to migrating, because they had language problems or lacked proper credentials. These persons, finding their way into well-paying white collar work blocked, have sometimes turned to entrepreneurship (Min 1988).

Settlement characteristics   Settlement characteristics, of which group size and residential concentration are perhaps the most important, influence business development trajectories in a complicated way. Two business patterns have already been noted: the local ethnic market, arising as a consequence of residential clustering, and mainly dominated by retail and service businesses catering to a coethnic clientele; and the pseudo-middleman minority situation, in which geographically dispersed, ethnic businesses service an out-group clientele. A third pattern is the "ethnic enclave" (following the terminology coined by Portes). Though the enclave bears a resemblance to the local ethnic market in its spatial concentration and in the patronage it receives from nearby co-ethnic shoppers, it differs in two respects. First, the enclave's industrial structure is diversified beyond the "local economy" industries characteristic of a local ethnic market. Second, the enclave's industries are also linked to the general, nonethnic market (Portes & Bach 1985). Thus, population size and concentrations are necessary and sufficient conditions of local markets, but not of ethnic enclaves.

The turn-of-the-century Jewish immigrant community on Manhattan's Lower East Side—with its incredible concentration of retail and manufacturing firms in many business lines—presents the ethnic enclave in its classic form (Rischin 1962). Modern-day versions include the Chinatowns of New York (Wong 1987) and San Francisco (Godfrey 1988), as well as the Cuban subeconomy in Miami, which contains the single largest agglomeration of ethnic firms enumerated in 1982 (US Dept. of Commerce 1982).

The typology outlined above is, of course, an abstraction; in practice, multiple and overlapping patterns are likely. In Los Angeles, for example, Koreatown seems to fulfill the conditions of an ethnic enclave. However, the majority of Korean business owners in Los Angeles are in a pseudo-middleman minority situation, as the customer base needed to support the 21% self-employment rate of Koreans cannot be found in a Korean clientele alone (Light & Bonacich 1988:164). San Francisco's Chinatown can be classified as an enclave, but the emerging satellite Chinatowns in Richmond and Sunset best fit the description of a local ethnic market, and the many Chinese restaurants and laundry businesses fall into the pseudo-middleman minority category (Godfrey 1988:103–104). These patterns might be conceptualized as comprising stages in a developmental sequence (Waldinger et al 1990, Chapter 4). The very first Korean merchants to set up stores in emerging Hispanic immigrant neighborhoods in New York, for example, were veterans of an earlier Korean migration to Latin America (Kim 1981). As the Korean population in New York grew over the course of the 1970s and 1980s, it gradually provided the customer base for a dynamic, diversified local ethnic market (Kim 1987). By contrast, the Jewish ethnic enclave of the Lower East Side lasted for barely a generation. By the 1920s, with the decline of the Jewish working class, petty Jewish entrepreneurs increasingly sold to non-Jewish clients or employed a gentile labor force, producing a pseudo-middleman minority situation.

The interaction between such predisposing factors as settlement characteristics and opportunity structures emerges with particular salience when we examine intragroup differences in business activity. Though the Jewish Lower East Side exemplifies the ethnic enclave, self-employment rates for Russian Jewish immigrants were actually much higher outside New York. At the turn of the century, high self-employment rates for Russian Jews were positively correlated with small Jewish populations and low garment industry employment (Perlman 1983). Indeed, in small cities and towns, Russian Jewish migrants were almost entirely dependent on commercial transactions with outsiders, thereby reproducing the traditional patterns of Eastern Europe

(Morawska 1988). Thus, in large ethnic concentrations, intense competition from co-ethnics for an inherently limited number of small business opportunities imposes a significant ceiling effect, notwithstanding other group traits that provide a strong inclination toward business ownership.

Culture and aspiration levels   Many researchers believe that some ethnic traditions contain economically useful practices. Others, however, warn that culture is fluid and adapts to changing circumstances: "An analysis that views cultural attributes as unchanging . . . cannot explain the differential socio-economic achievement of Chinese and Japanese Americans prior to and after World War II nor account for the differences between Asian Americans and other ethnic and minority groups" (Nee & Wong 1985; 287). Strictly cultural arguments also omit structural conditions that give rise to, and reinforce, attitudes favorable to economic achievement.

Attention to context highlights the fluidity of economic orientations and their responsiveness to changing conditions. Immigrant workers often begin as temporary workers in small businesses, seeking jobs that provide opportunities to work long hours and accumulate savings. Once their plans for return are postponed or abandoned, immigrants may have acquired skills which represent "sunk capital," and therefore provide an incentive to start up as self-employed (Bailey 1987). Native workers, not having "sunk capital," are far less likely to acquire entrepreneurial skills in businesses like restaurants or garments where the relative returns to investment in human capital are low. Immigrants will also be more satisfied than native-born workers with low profits from small business because of wage differences between their origin and destination countries (Light 1984).

The classic model of *middleman minorities,* as refined by Bonacich (1973) and others, includes three traits characterizing a group's cultural patterns: first, a sojourner orientation to their host country; second, distinctive social and cultural characteristics that promote solidary communities; and third, distinctive economic traits, including concentration in entrepreneurial roles, a tendency to keep capital liquid, and a preference for kin and co-ethnic labor (O'Brien & Fugita 1982).

The middleman minority model is subject to criticism on several counts. First, the model is ahistorical, ascribing traits that are abstracted from the social and economic structures in which either the classic- or the pseudo-middleman minorities have been found. For example, Jain (1988) showed that British colonialism had much to do with the preference of Indian traders for liquidity, because British imperial policy did not allow South Asians to own land for agricultural purposes; by necessity they concentrated on trade and commercial activities. Second, the argument that immigrants who move as sojourners will opt for business over employment, as the better way of rapidly accumulating portable investement capital, is vulnerable on both logical and empirical grounds. Setting up a business is a more risky endeavor than working for someone else. When faced with the alternative of safely banking a nest egg to be returned back home, or investing in a business whose chance for success is always open to doubt, a prudent sojourner is likely to keep on working for someone else. Indeed, Ward's (1987) study of south Asians in Britain showed that they only resort to business in those cities where the available jobs are relatively poorly paid, preferring employment over business in high wage areas. Other research found that a sojourning orientation made no difference in the business operations of Asians in Britain (Aldrich 1977, Aldrich et al 1983), and that Korean pseudo-middleman minority store owners in New York were far less likely to be sojourners than their Hispanic counterparts who sold to an entirely co-ethnic clientele (Waldinger 1989). Third, the model's emphasis on distinctive economic traits, such as a preference for hiring co-ethnic workers or maintaining small firms when market conditions would allow for expansion, is based on the assumption that middleman minorities are not "modern capitalists in orientation" (Bonacich & Modell 1980:32). However, the empirical evidence speaks strongly to the contrary; for example, German Jewish department stores employed non-Jewish women in the inter-war period (Gross 1975), and Korean garment factory owners currently recruit Hispanic workers in New York and Los Angeles (Min 1989).

These specific criticisms also direct our attention to a broader observation: for every study that emphasizes an ethnic group's culture as a key factor in its economic achievements in business, another exists that emphasizes the often radical cultural changes occurring over a few generations. Separating the effects of the cultural values with which a group arrives in a host society from effects of the values generated by its post-migration experiences is extremely difficult. Clearly, some ethnic groups have high rates of entrepreneurship which persist over several generations. But as Steinberg (1981) has argued, structural factors limit the capacity of ethnic communities to preserve and pass on "traditional" ethnic customs and values. We remain skeptical of an over-socialized conception of an ethnic group's cultural heritage, apart from the social structure and institutions it constructs within the context of the larger society. Thus, we emphasize resource mobilization over cultural factors in our review.

RESOURCE MOBILIZATION   Founding and running a business, no matter how small, is a demanding task, and only a fraction of those who start are ultimately successful. The basic resources needed—labor and capital—are no different for ethnic entrepreneurs than others. Personalistic and familistic ties are part of business operation in all capitalist societies (Zimmer &

Aldrich 1987). Bechhofer & Elliot (1981) also noted that the general features of the petty bourgeoisie are much the same everywhere, particularly dependence on family labor and the use of hired labor as an extension, rather than a replacement, of the owner's labor.

Class versus ethnic resources   Light (1984) distinguished between "class" and "ethnic" resources in an attempt to separate the purely ethnic from the generic process of resource mobilization. Increased attention to class resources separate from ethnic resources was provoked, in part, by the emergence of middle-class entrepreneurs among recent immigrants, such as Cubans and Koreans. Light defined class resources as private property in the means of production and distribution, human capital, money to invest, and bourgeois values, attitudes, knowledge, and skills transmitted intergenerationally. Ethnic resources, in Light's model, are any and all features of their ethnic group that potential owners can use, such as cultural endowments, reactive solidarity, and sojourning orientation. In practice, few researchers have held to this distinction, but in theory, the distinction is critical, as it emphasizes the strong continuity between studies of small business in general and ethnic enterprise in particular.

We would expect *viable* business enterprises to look very much alike, regardless of ownership. Theories of ethnic businesses posit that such enterprises differ from others because of the social structure within which resources are mobilized. Researchers have focused on ethnic resource mobilization as a collective, rather than purely individual, activity, as ethnic entrepreneurs draw on family, kin, and co-ethnic relations for labor and capital. Because so many researchers have not compared their findings to non-ethnic business operations, they have tended to overstate the uniquely "ethnic" component in resource mobilization.

Ethnic social structures: social networks and organizing capacity   Ethnic social structures consist of the networks of kinship and friendship around which ethnic communities are arranged, and the interlacing of these networks with positions in the economy (jobs), in space (housing), and in society (institutions). Breton's (1964) concept of *institutional completeness* captures the spirit of much research on ethnic business, as it refers to the relative number of formal organizations in an ethnic community and the resulting complexity of relations between co-ethnics. We focus on the role of ethnic institutions in raising capital, recruiting labor, and dealing with suppliers and customers.

Information about permits, laws, management practices, reliable suppliers, and promising business lines is typically obtained through owners' personal networks and via various indirect ties that are specifically linked to their ethnic communities. The structure of such networks differs, depending upon the characteristics of the group. Some groups have very hierarchically organized families and a clear sense of family loyalty and obligation, whereas others have more diffusely organized families. Ritualized occasions and large-scale ceremonies also provide opportunities for acquiring information, and some groups have specialized associations and media which disseminate information. When co-ethnics supply such information, the consequence is often a piling up or concentration by an ethnic group within a limited number of industries. Newcomers finding employment among co-ethnics in these immigrant small business industries automatically gain access to contacts, opportunities to learn on the job, and role models. They therefore enjoy a higher probability of subsequent advancement to ownership than do their counterparts who work in larger firms among members of the dominant ethnic group.

Rotating credit associations are commonly used in many ethnic groups to raise capital (Ardener 1964). Light (1972) argued that traditional rotating credit associations among the Japanese and Chinese enabled locality-based groups to capitalize small businesses, whereas US blacks lacked such institutions and were thus at a disadvantage. Ethnic credit associations are based on levels of ethical accountability and frugality (Woodrum 1981) and have been found in a variety of guises among immigrants to the United States. Such associations were particularly important for groups that were discriminated against by regular financial institutions (Gerber 1982).

Rotating credit associations are important, but three research findings suggest their significance may have been overstated. First, entrepreneurs are often highly innovative in their search for capital, and ethnic owners have created many vehicles for raising capital other than rotating credit associations (Russell 1984). Second, some groups have many active rotating credit associations but do not use them to fund businesses (Bonnett 1981). Third, recent research has found that the great majority of ethnic owners fund their businesses from their own personal savings, with some money from their families (Min 1988).

Families, in addition to providing capital, are often the core workforce for small businesses. Thus, immigrants who arrive in a country with their families intact, or who can quickly reconstitute the family through subsequent migration, have an advantage over those who cannot. Similarly, ethnic groups with larger families, with high participation rates by family members, and with norms stressing collective achievement have some advantage over others.

Some research indicates that a strong family structure is not sufficient, nor perhaps even necessary, for ethnic entrepreneurs' success. In her study of

Mexican-American and Anglo-American families in three Southern California cities, Keefe (1984) found evidence of a strong extended family structure among the Mexican-American families, but no indication such strength was channelled into business activities. Chan & Cheung (1985) found that most Chinese businesses in Toronto either had *no* employees or no family members as employees. Zimmer & Aldrich (1987), in their research on South Asian and white shopkeepers in three English cities, found little difference between the two groups in their use of family labor.

Recent theoretical writings on ethnicity have stressed the advantages of ethnic over other forms of social organization (Glazer & Moynihan 1975, Olzak 1983), and some research on ethnic business supports this idea. Considerable attention has been paid to vertical and horizontal interfirm linkages that appear to reduce transaction costs and lower intraethnic competition (Wilson & Martin 1982). In contrast to the historical record (Light 1972), research on contemporary immigrant groups provides little evidence of price or entry regulation, vertical integration, or other joint monopolistic activities. Research on Korean retailers in the United States (Min 1988) does show that backward linkages to co-ethnic suppliers can be advantageous: transactions are made in the native language; co-ethnic wholesalers are more flexible on credit; and they carry the type of merchandise that appeals to Korean merchants' customers. However, in spite of these advantages, most Korean merchants make equal use of Korean and non-Korean suppliers. The common inability of ethnic trade associations to control competition between co-ethnics is additional evidence of the weakness of cultural constraints in the face of economic opportunities (Bailey 1987:55).

Ethnic institutions, such as churches and voluntary associations, are often supported by ethnic entrepreneurs for business reasons as well as a sense of in-group loyalty. For example, among Poles and Slavs, fraternal, mutual benefit societies sponsored by the Catholic Church have often contributed indirectly to ethnic businesses (Cummings 1980). Bonacich & Modell (1980) noted that the Nisei who had social bonds to their ethnic group in a variety of informal and formal contexts were more likely to participate in the ethnic economy, and vice versa. Boswell (1986:364) argued that "Chinese merchants subsidized traditional Chinese cultural and clan activities in part to maintain their trade monopoly."

As Bonacich (1973) observed, in-group solidarity is often a reaction to hostility from the host society. For example, Chicano used car dealers in the American Southwest are limited in their ability to cultivate interpersonal relations with people who could give them access to better automobiles because of white dealers' hostilities and ethnic stereotyping. Consequently, Chicano dealers "cannot accumulate sufficient capital to increase their credit floor plan and thus trade in the high volume that would make them competitive with white dealers" (Valdez 1984:236). Instead, they sell to co-ethnics in the barrio who need credit.

Available evidence certainly indicates that many ethnic groups have a level of institutional completeness and internal solidarity that gives some of their members an advantage in mobilizing resources. The resources themselves are generic to the business founding and survival process, but models of ethnic entrepreneurship have probably exaggerated the unique advantage of certain groups because few studies are truly comparative—examining in detail both ethnic and non-ethnic businesses. The conditions facilitating resource mobilization are historically contingent, heavily dependent upon individual initiative, and subject to manipulation by dominant groups.

Ethnic Strategies

Strategies emerge from the interaction of opportunity structures and group characteristics, as ethnic entrepreneurs adapt to the resources available to them, building on the characteristics of their groups (Boissevain et al 1990, Boissevain & Grotenbreg 1986). Our use of the term "strategies" to characterize ethnic entrepreneurs' actions is in the same spirit as Hamilton's (1985:408) use of the term to explain patterns of temporary migration: strategy is a "technical term meaning the positioning of oneself to others in order to accomplish one's goals. Whereas one's reasons for action may be subjective and strictly personal, one's strategy is shaped by social circumstances . . . the strategy becomes social insofar as individuals recognize the actual or possible influence of others, their values and actions, upon their own goals."

Ethnic business owners commonly confront a number of problems in founding and operating their businesses, in addition to those we have already reviewed: acquiring the *training and skills* needed to run a small business; recruiting and managing efficient, honest, and cheap *workers;* managing relations with *customers* and *suppliers;* surviving strenuous business *competition;* and protecting themselves from *political attacks*.

Training and skills are typically acquired on the job, often while the potential owner is an employee in a co-ethnic or family member's business. Ties within the ethnic economy widen workers' contacts, increasing the probability of their moving up through a variety of jobs and firms in which skills are acquired (Portes & Bach 1985, Waldinger 1986). Family and co-ethnic labor is critical to most small ethnic businesses. Such labor is largely unpaid, and kin and co-ethnics work long hours in the service of their employers. Ethnic entrepreneurs manipulate family and co-ethnic perseverance and loyalty to their own advantage, but they also incur obligations in doing so.

Customers and clients play a central role in owners' strategies, as building a loyal following is a way of off-setting the high level of uncertainty facing small ethnic businesses. Some owners provide special services, extend credit, and go out of their way to deliver individual services to customers. Often, however, providing special services to one's co-ethnics causes trouble for owners, who then are faced with special pleading to take lower profits for their efforts (Aldrich et al 1983).

The intense competition generated in the niches occupied by ethnic businesses is dealt with in at least four ways: (*a*) through self-exploitation; (*b*) expanding the business by moving forward or backward in the chain of production, or by opening other shops (Werbner 1984); (*c*) founding and supporting ethnic trading associations (Light & Bonacich 1988); and (*d*) cementing alliances to other families through marriage (Sway 1988). Finally, ethnic entrepreneurs often need protection from government officials, as well as from rival owners outside their ethnic community. Government is dealt with by ethnic owners in much the same way that non-ethnic owners always have: bribery, paying penalties, searching for loopholes, and organizing protests.

Ethnic strategies, then, reflect both the opportunity structure within which ethnic businesses operate *and* the particular characteristics of the owner's group. Accordingly, ethnic strategies may be thought of as at the *center* of our framework, emphasizing their emergent character. The strategies adopted by the various ethnic groups in capitalistic societies around the world are remarkably similar.

CONCLUSIONS

We have used a framework based on three interactive components— opportunity structures, group characteristics, and strategies—to review recent scholarship on ethnic business development. Of necessity, we cast a wide net in our search for relevant research, as contributions have been made by investigators in many disciplines and from a variety of approaches. A common theme pervades most of this work: ethnic groups adapt to the resources made available by their environments, which vary substantially across societies and over time.

Among the many issues deserving greater attention, we include the following: the reciprocal relation between ethnicity and entrepreneurship, more careful use of ethnic labels, the need for more multiple group, comparative research, and the need for more process-oriented research designs. First, ethnicity, defined as self-identification with a particular ethnic group, or a label applied by outsiders, is neither primordial nor imported prior to contact with a host society. Instead, ethnicity is a possible outcome of the patterns by which intra- and inter- group interactions are structured. The emergence of ethnic communities and networks may generate an infrastructure and resources for ethnic businesses *before* a sense of group awareness develops. In turn, an ethnic business niche may give rise to, or strengthen, group consciousness. Ethnic boundaries, as social constructions, are inherently fluid.

Second, much of the research on ethnic businesses fits Yinger's (1985:158) description of other research in the field of ethnic studies, as it is based on the "single fact of an ethnic (or state-origin) label, with little attention to the salience of the label, to the strength of identification with the ethnic group compared with other identities, or to the distinction between country of origin and ethnicity." Reliance on census data collected for other purposes is the culprit in most cases, and one remedy would be more studies specifically designed to measure multiple indicators of a person's ethnic identification, as well as involvement in entrepreneurship.

Third, as Miyamoto (1986) pointed out, we need more rigorous, detailed comparative data on multiple groups, studied over the same period, with comparable information collected on each group. Currently, studies using census data often include multiple groups, but as the census collects little information on entrepreneurial activities, and practically nothing on ethnic processes, they have limited utility for examining most questions of interest. The modal study using survey or field work data includes only one group, with only implicit comparisons made to others.

Fourth, almost no studies of ethnic enterprise have examined *performance* over time, and so we have little understanding of the contribution ethnic group structures and strategies make to entrepreneurial success. More dynamic research designs, such as panel studies, are clearly needed.

Acknowledgments

Order of authorship is alphabetical, as this has truly been a collaborative effort. Comments from Melanie Archer, Judith Blau, Pyong Gap Min, David Torres, W. Richard Scott, Catherine Zimmer, and two anonymous reviewers helped us revise the manuscript. We thank Greg Floyd and Jane Scott for their bibliographic help, and Sharon Byrd and Deborah Tilley for preparing the final manuscript. Howard Aldrich's work on this article was facilitated by a grant from the Institute for Research in Social Science, University of North Carolina, Chapel Hill. Roger Waldinger's work on this article was made possible, in part, by a fellowship from the Robert F. Wagner, Sr., Institute on Urban Public Policy, Graduate Center, City University of New York.

Literature Cited

Aldrich, H. E. 1973. Employment effects of white-owned businesses in the black ghetto. *Am. J. Sociol.* 78:1403–26

Aldrich, H. E. 1977. *Testing the middleman minority model of Asian entrepreneurial behavior: Preliminary results from Wandsworth, England.* Pap. pres. Ann. Meet. Am. Sociol. Assoc., Chicago

Aldrich, H. E., Cater, J., Jones, T., McEvoy, D. 1983. From periphery to peripheral: The South Asian petite bourgeoisie in England. In *Research in the Sociology of Work,* Vol. 2, ed. I. H. Simpson and R. Simpson, pp. 1–32. Greenwich, Conn: JAI

Aldrich, H. E., Reiss, A. J. Jr. 1976. Continuities in the study of ecological succession: Changes in the race composition of neighborhoods and their businesses. *Am. J. Sociol.* 81:846–66

Aldrich, H. E., Cater, J., Jones, T., McEvoy, D., Velleman, P. 1985. Ethnic residential concentration and the protected market hypothesis. *Soc. Forc.* 63:996–1009

Aldrich, H. E., Zimmer, C., McEvoy, D. 1989. Continuities in the study of ecological succession: Asian business in three English cities. *Soc. Forc.* 67:920–44

Aldrich, H. E., Auster, E. R. 1986. Even dwarfs started small: liabilities of age and size and their strategic implications. In *Research in Organizational Behavior,* vol. 8, ed. B. M. Staw and L. L. Cummings, pp. 165–98. Greenwich, Conn: JAI

Ardener, S. A. 1964. The comparative study of rotating credit associations. *J. R. Anthropol. Inst.* 94:201–9

Armstrong, J. A. 1976. Mobilized and proletarian diasporas. *Am. Polit. Sci. Rev.* 9:393–408

Bailey, T. 1987. *Immigrant and Native Workers: Contrasts and Competition.* Boulder, Colo: Westview

Baron, S., 1975. *The Economic History of the Jews.* New York: Schocken

Baumol, W. J. 1968. Entrepreneurship in economic theory. *Am. Econ. Rev.* 58:64–71

Bechhofer, F., Elliot, B. eds. 1981. *The Petite Bourgeoisie: Comparative Studies of the Uneasy Stratum.* London: Macmillan

Bertaux, D., Berteaux-Wiame, I. 1981. Artisanal bakery in France: How it lives and why it survives. In *The Petite Bourgeoisie. Comparative Studies of an Uneasy Stratum,* ed. F. Bechhofer and B. Elliot, pp. 155–81. London: MacMillan

Bird, B. J. 1989. *Entrepreneurial Behavior.* Glenview, Ill: Scott, Foresman

Blaschke, J., Boissevain, J., Grotenbreg, H.,

Joseph, I., Morokvasic, M., Ward, R. 1990. European trends in ethnic business. See Waldinger et al 1990

Boissevain, J., Blaschke, J., Grotenbreg, H., Joseph, I., Light, I., Sway, M., Waldinger, R., Ward, R., Werbner, P. 1990. Ethnic entrepreneurs and ethnic strategies. See Waldinger et al 1990

Boissevain, J., Grotenbreg. 1986. Culture, structure and ethnic enterprise: the Surinamese of Amsterdam. *Ethnic Racial Stud.* 9(1):1–23

Bonacich, E. 1973. A theory of middleman minorities. *Am. Sociol. Rev.* 38:583–94

Bonacich, E., Modell, J. 1980. *The Economic Basis of Ethnic Solidarity in the Japanese American Community.* Berkeley: Univ. Calif. Press

Bonnett, A. W. 1981. Structured adaptation of black migrants from the Caribbean: An examination of an indigeneous banking system in Brooklyn. *Phylon* 42:346–55

Boswell, T. E. 1986. A split labor market analysis of discrimination against Chinese immigrants, 1850–1882. *Am. Sociol. Rev.* 51:352–71

Breton, R. 1964. Institutional completeness of ethnic communities and the personal relations of immigrants. *Am. J. Sociol.* 70:193–205

Chan, J., Cheung, Y. W. 1985. Ethnic resources and business enterprise: A study of Chinese businesses in Toronto. *Hum. Organ.* 44:142–54

Cummings, S. 1980. *Self-Help in Urban America: Patterns of Minority Economic Development.* Port Washington, NY: Kennikat Press

Curtin, Philip. 1984. *Cross-Cultural Trade in World History.* Cambridge: Cambridge Univ. Press

Fairchild, H. S. 1911. *Greek Immigration to the United States.* New Haven: Yale

Fratoe, F. 1986. A sociological analysis of minority business. *Rev. Black Polit. Econ.* 15:5–30

Frazier, E. F. 1949. *The Negro in America.* New York: Macmillan

Gerber, D. 1982. Cutting out Shylock: Elite anti-semitism and the quest for moral order in the mid-nineteenth century American market place. *J. Am. Hist.* 9:615–37

Glazer, N., Moynihan, D. P. eds. 1975. *Ethnicity.* Cambridge, Mass: Harvard

Godfrey, B. J. 1988. *Neighborhoods in Transition: The Making of San Francisco's Ethnic and Nonconformist Communities.* Berkeley: Univ. Calif. Press

Goldscheider, C., Zuckerman, A. 1984. *The*

Transformation of the Jews. Chicago: Univ. Chicago Press

Greenfield, S. M., Strickon, A., Aubey, R. T. 1979. *Entrepreneurs in Cultural Context*. Albuquerque: Univ. N. Mex. Press

Gross, N. 1975. *The Economic History of the Jews*. New York: Schocken

Guillon, M., Taboada-Leonetti, I. 1986. *Le Triangle de Choisy: Un Quartier Chinois a Paris*. Paris: Ciemi L'Harmattan

Hamilton, G. 1985. Temporary migration and the institutionalization of strategy. *Int. J. Intercultural Relat*. 9:405–25

Herman, H. 1979. Dishwashers and proprietors: Macedonians in Toronto's restaurant trade. In *Ethnicity at Work*, ed. S. Wallman, pp. 71–92. London: Macmillan

Hirschman, C. 1982. Immigrants and minorities: Old questions for new directions in research. *Int. Migrat. Rev*. 16:474–90

Horowitz, D. 1985. *Ethnic Conflict*. Berkeley: Univ. Calif. Press

Jain, P. C. 1988. Towards class analysis of race-relations-overseas Indians in colonial Post-colonial societies. *Econ. Polit. Weekly* 23:95–103

Kashima, T. 1982. Book review of Bonacich and Modell. *Am. Hist. Rev*. 87:1476

Keefe, S. E. 1984. Real and ideal extended familism among Mexican-Americans and Anglo-Americans: On the meaning of 'close' family ties. *Hum. Organ*. 43:65–70

Kim, I. 1981. *The New Urban Immigrants: The Korean Community in New York*. Princeton: Princeton Univ. Press

Kim, I. 1987. The Koreans: small business in an urban frontier. In *New Immigrants in New York City*, ed. N. Foner, pp. 219–42. New York: Columbia Univ. Press

Levine, B. B. 1985. The capital of Latin America. *Wilson Q*. 9:47–69

Lieberson, S. 1980. *A Piece of the Pie*. Berkeley: Univ. Calif. Press

Lieberson, S., Waters, M. 1988. *From Many Strands: Ethnic and Racial Groups in Contemporary America*. New York: Russell Sage

Light, I. 1972. *Ethnic Enterprise in America*. Berkeley: Univ. Calif. Press

Light, I., Sanchez, A. 1987. Immigrant entrepreneurs in 272 SMSAs. *Sociol. Perspect*. 30:373–99

Light, I. 1984. Immigrant and ethnic enterprise in North America. *Ethnic Racial Stud*. 7:195–216

Light, I., Bonacich, E. 1988. *Immigrant Entrepreneurs*. Berkeley: Univ. Calif. Press

Makabe, T. 1981. The theory of the split market labor market: A comparison of the Japanese experience in Brazil and Canada. *Soc. Forc*. 59:786–809

Ma Mung, E., Guillon, M. 1986. Les commercants etrangers dans l'agglomeration Parisienne. *Rev. Europeene des Migrations Int*. 2:105–34

Min, P. G. 1988. *Ethnic Business Enterprise: Korean Small Business in Atlanta*. New York: CMS

Min, P. G. 1989. *Some positive functions of ethnic business for an immigrant community: Korean immigrants in Los Angeles*. Final report submitted to the National Science Foundation, Washington, DC

Miyamoto, S. F. 1986. Book review of Ward and Jenkins. *Contemp. Sociol*. 15:142–43

Mohl, R. 1985. An ethnic 'boiling pot': Cubans and Haitians in Miami. *J. Ethnic Stud*. 13:51–74

Morawska, E. 1988. A Replica of the 'old-country' relationship in the ethnic niche: Eastern European Jews and Gentiles in small-town western Pennsylvania. *Am. Jewish Hist*. 77:87–105

Morokvasic, M., Waldinger, R., Phizacklea, A. 1990. Business on the ragged edge: immigrant and minority business in the garment industries of Paris, London, and New York. See Waldinger et al 1990

Nee, V., Wong, H. Y. 1985. Asian American socioeconomic achievement. *Sociol. Perspect*. 28:281–306

O'Brien, D. J., Fugita, S. S. 1982. Middleman minority concept: Its explanatory value in the case of the Japanese in California agriculture. *Pac. Sociol. Rev*. 25:185–204

Olzak, S. 1983. Contemporary ethnic mobilization. *Annu. Rev. Sociol*. 9:355–74

Ong, P. 1981. An ethnic trade: The Chinese laundries in early California. *J. Ethnic Stud*. 8:95–113

Palmer, R. 1984. The rise of the Britalian culture entrepreneur. In *Ethnic Communities in Business*, ed. Robin Ward and Richard Jenkins, pp. 89–104. Cambridge: Cambridge Univ. Press

Parkin, F. 1979. *Marxism: A Bourgeois Critique*. New York: Columbia

Perlman, J. 1983. Beyond New York: The occupations of Russian Jewish immigrants in Providence, R.I., and other small Jewish Communities, 1900–1915. *Am. Jewish Hist.*, 72:369–94

Perez, L. 1986. Immigrant economic adjustment and family organization: The Cuban success story reexamined. *Int. Migrat. Rev*. 20:4–20

Petersen, W. 1980. Concepts of ethnicity. In *Harvard Encyclopedia of American Ethnic Groups*, ed. S. Thernstrom, pp. 234–42. Cambridge, Mass: Harvard

Piore, M. J. 1980. The technological foundations of dualism and discontinuity. In *Dualism and Discontinuity in Industrial Society*, ed. S. Berger and M. J. Piore, pp. 55–81. Cambridge: Cambridge Univ. Press

Portes, A., Bach, R. 1985. *Latin Journey.* Berkeley: Univ. Calif. Press

Portes, A. 1987. The social origins of the Cuban enclave economy of Miami. *Sociol. Perspect.* 30:340–72

Rischin, M. 1962. *The Promised City.* Cambridge, Mass: Harvard

Rubinow, I. 1975 [1905] *The Condition of the Jews in Russia.* New York: Arno

Russell, R. 1984. The role of culture and ethnicity in the degeneration of Democratic firms. *Econ. Indust. Dem.* 5:73–96

Salem, G. 1981. De la brousse senegalaise au Boul' Mich: le systeme commercial mouride en France. *Les Cahiers d'etudes africaines* 81–83:267–88

Steinberg, S. 1981. *The Ethnic Myth: Race, Ethnicity, and Class in America.* New York: Atheneum

Stone, J. 1985. *Ethnic Conflict in Contemporary Society.* Cambridge: Harvard Univ. Press

Sway, M. 1988. *Familiar Strangers: Gypsy Life in America.* Urbana Ill.: Univ. Ill. Press

United States Department of Commerce. 1982. *Survey of Minority and Women-Owned Businesses.* Washington, DC: US Govt. Printing Off.

Valdez, A. 1984. Chicano used car dealers: A social world in microcosm. *Urban Life* 13:229–46

Waldinger, R. 1986. *Through the Eye of the Needle: Immigrants and Enterprise in New York's Garment Trades.* New York: New York Univ. Press

Waldinger, R. 1989. Structural opportunity or ethnic advantage: immigrant business development in New York. *Int. Mig. Rev.* 23:48 72

Waldinger, R., Aldrich, H. E., Ward, R.

1990. *Immigrant Entrepreneurs: Immigrant and Ethnic Business in Western Industrial Societies.* Beverly Hills, CA: Sage

Ward, R. 1987. Small retailers in inner urban areas. In *Business Strategy and Retailing,* ed. Gerry Johnson, pp. 275–87. New York: Wiley

Werbner, P. 1984. Business on trust. Pakistani entrepreneurship in the Manchester garment industry. In *Ethnic Communities in Business: Strategies for Economic Survival,* ed. Robin Ward and Richard Jenkins, pp. 166–88. Cambridge: Cambridge Univ. Press

Wilken, P. 1979. *Entrepreneurship: A Comparative Historical Study.* Norwood, NJ: Ablex

Wilson, K., Martin, W. A. 1982. Ethnic enclaves. A comparison of Cuban and Black economies in Miami. *Am. J. Sociol.* 88: 135–60

Wong, B. 1978. A comparative study of the assimilation of the Chinese in New York City and Lima, Peru. *Comp. Stud. Soc. Hist.* 20:335–58

Wong, B. 1987. The Chinese: New immigrants in New York's Chinatown. In *New Immigrants in New York,* ed. N. Foner, pp. 243–72. New York: Columbia Univ. Press

Woodrum, E. 1981. An assessment of Japanese American assimilation, pluralism, and subordination. *Am. J. Sociol.* 87:157–69

Yambert, K. 1981. Alien traders and ruling elites: the overseas Chinese in Southeast Asia and the Indians in East Africa. *Ethnic Groups* 3:173–98

Yinger, J. M. 1985. Ethnicity. *Annu. Rev. Sociol.* 11:151–80

Zimmer, C., Aldrich, H. 1987. Resource mobilization through ethnic networks: Kin ship and friendship ties of shopkeepers in England. *Sociol. Perspect.* 30:422–55

Annu. Rev. Sociol. 1990. 16:137–59

THE SOCIOLOGY OF NONPROFIT ORGANIZATIONS AND SECTORS

Paul J. DiMaggio

Department of Sociology, Yale University, New Haven, Connecticut, 06520

Helmut K. Anheier

Department of Sociology, Rutgers University, New Brunswick, New Jersey 08903

KEY WORDS: organizations, nonprofit, voluntary sector, institutions

Abstract

Interest in and research on nonprofit organizations and sectors have developed rapidly in recent years. Much of this work by sociologists has focussed on particular subsectors rather than on nonprofits as a class. This review attempts to extract from a large and varied literature a distinctively sociological perspective on nonprofits, which it contrasts to influential work in economics. Two questions—"Why (and where) are there nonprofit organizations" and "What difference does nonprofitness make?"—are addressed at the levels of organization, industry, and firm. Three central conclusions, each with research implications, emerge from this review: (*a*) The origins and behavior of nonprofit organizations reflect institutional factors and state policies as well as the social-choice processes and utility functions emphasized by economists. (*b*) Understanding the origins of nonprofit sectors and behavioral differences between nonprofits and for-profit or government organizations requires an industry-level ecological perspective. (*c*) "Nonprofitness" has no single transhistorical or transnational meaning; nonprofit-sector functions, origins, and behavior reflect specific legal definitions, cultural inheritances, and state policies in different national societies.

137

0360-0572/90/0815-0137$02.00

INTRODUCTION

The past two decades have witnessed a groundswell of interest in nonprofit organizations (NPOs) and nonprofit sectors (NPSs). For social scientists, the origin and behavior of sectors that stand outside market and state are tantalizing puzzles. The curiosity of US scholars has been piqued by rapid post-war nonprofit sector growth: By 1984 charitable nonprofit organizations (including foundations and churches) generated 5.6% of national income and 9.5% of employment (paid and volunteer) (Hodgkinson & Weitzman 1986). Increased regulation has accompanied growth, stimulating sector-level political mobilization by NPOs formerly organized only at the level of their own industries. Such efforts have supported research and conferences, improved the quality of aggregate data, and encouraged scholars to think in sectoral terms. Policy interest in NPOs, reflected in social-science research activity, has also emerged in Europe and the Third World (James 1989).

Yet sociologists have made little effort to develop systematic approaches to NPOs and NPSs per se; most research focusses on particular industries in which nonprofit organizations are prominent. This review develops a sociological perspective on the nonprofit form, emphasizing comparison among NPOs in different industries and societies. Thus we draw very selectively on voluminous specialized literatures (e.g. on health, the arts, voluntary associations, social services, community organizations, churches, social movement organizations), and we emphasize research focussing on "non-profitness" per se, including work in other disciplines.

For the United States, unless otherwise specified, "nonprofit organizations" are those falling under section 501(c)3 of the Internal Revenue Code (a category including most nonprofit hospitals, cultural organizations, traditional charities, foundations, schools, daycare centers and foundations, among others), or the smaller, related 501(c)4 category (civic leagues and social welfare organizations, which are denied tax-deductible contributions but which may engage in some political or commercial activities from which (c)3s are barred); these do *not* include such mutual-benefit associations as labor unions, workers or consumers cooperatives, veterans organizations, or political parties, which the law treats separately. 501(c)3s and 4s are subject to the nondistribution constraint (which proscribes distributing net income as dividends or above-market remuneration); they must serve one of several broadly defined collective purposes; and they receive certain tax advantages (Simon 1987). In discussing nonprofit sectors *outside* the United States, we vary terminology according to national legal and political traditions.

THE ISSUES

Two problems are fundamental. First, *origin:* why do nonprofit organizations exist? This question concerns the intersectoral division of labor: the distribution of functions among for-profits (FPs), NPOs, and public agencies. Given the apparent disadvantages of NPOs with respect to incentives (compared to for-profits) and revenue generation (compared to government), why are there so many of them? Second, there is the issue of organizational *behavior*. To what extent, and why, do NPOs' performance, structures, service and client mix, strategies, and human-resource policies differ from those of other forms? We may pose each problem at three levels of analysis: (*a*) organization, (*b*) industry and (*c*) nation-state (with the understanding that structural features at any level will influence processes at lower levels). Cross-classifying problems and levels yields six questions, which structure this review:

Origins 1:   Why are some organizations nonprofit, and others for profit, and still others public?

Origins 2:   What explains differences among industries in the division of labor among NP, government, and FP forms?

Origins 3:   How can one explain cross-national variation in the definition, prevalence, and role of the nonprofit form?

Behavior 1: Within industries, what if any behavioral differences exist between NPOs and FPs or government agencies.

Behavior 2: What, if any, differences in the structure and performance of industries are associated with the division of labor among public, FP and NP enterprises?

Behavior 3: What, if any, are the implications for national societies of the prevalence and distribution of NPOs?

WHY ARE THERE NONPROFIT ORGANIZATIONS?

Organization Level

One can predict the legal form of most organizations if one knows the industry and nation-state in which they operate. Residual variation (and NPOs) are encapsulated in a relatively small, albeit important, set of industries where two or more forms are well represented: in the United States, hospitals, daycare, museums, universities, home health care, social services, broadcasting, and a few others.

Many such industries comprise well-defined niches (commercial television and public broadcasting). Given an account of activities and official goals, one can identify legal form with almost complete accuracy. In some (hospitals, daycare), NP and FP forms compete within the same niche, a situation likely to be unstable. In a few cases (local arts agencies, which include NP, public, and hybrid specimens), form is weakly related to niche but competition is minimal. Few studies explore why entrepreneurs select particular legal forms when they have a choice, or why some organizations change form.

Factors suggested in the literature include founder dispositions [e.g. religious values, profit-mindedness, risk averseness, or altruism (James & Rose-Ackerman 1986)], access to capital markets (Hollingsworth & Hollingsworth 1987), and eligibility rules for government aid (DiMaggio 1987).

Industry Level: The Division of Labor Among Forms

ECONOMIC THEORY   Economists have done much on this topic (Hansmann 1987, Rose-Ackerman 1986). According to Hansmann, the nondistribution constraint renders nonprofit organizations more likely than for profit organizations to use consumers' and donors' dollars reliably for service provision: directly, because monitoring and enforcement make profiteering risky; and indirectly, because entrepreneurs preoccupied with profits apply their talents elsewhere. Thus to predict which industries will be NP-dominated we must ask: When do consumers require the assurance the nondistribution constraint provides? The answer: When they cannot make informed choices because (*a*) donors buy services for unknown third parties (overseas charities), (*b*) known beneficiaries are seen as unreliable witnesses to service quality (daycare centers, mental hospitals), (*c*) pooled donations cannot be tracked to specific services (political advocacy), or (*d*) services are so complex that ultimate consumers cannot evaluate their quality and so important that low quality poses unacceptable risk (medical care) (Hansmann 1980). Weisbrod (1988) suggests that NPOs emerge for these reasons in particular sectors of industries: e.g. providing high-quality services with special attributes that are hard to detect, or serving low-education consumers with insufficient access to product information. Hansmann (1981) offers a separate explanation, emphasizing voluntary price discrimination through donations, for the few industries (e.g. theatres, universities) in which services are consumed by purchasers who *are* able to assess their quality.

Weisbrod (1988) employs public-choice ideas to explain the relative prevalence of NPOs and government in providing collective goods (those from the benefits of which free riders cannot be excluded). Government, which supplies such goods at levels demanded by the median voter, is preferred when demand is homogeneous because it can tax away the free-rider problem. When demand is heterogeneous, citizens who want more or different goods than the state provides form NPOs to supplement public provision. As wealth rises, demand for collective goods increases, causing government to replace NP providers. With still greater wealth, substitution of private for public goods (e.g. bottled spring water for good municipal water works) leads to declining state provision (Weisbrod 1977).

Such ingenious arguments go far to explain which industries are likely to have NPSs. But their capacity to explain variation in NP activity within industries over time and space is limited. First they neglect supply-side factors, especially social cohesion among potential beneficiaries or entrepreneurs (Ben-Ner & Van Hoomissen 1989), that influence the capacity of NPOs to respond to demand. Second they view states as competing providers rather than (as is often the case) financiers or consumers of NP services. Third, they neglect such institutional factors as state policy, organizing norms, ideology and religion.

HISTORICAL PERSPECTIVE   In historical perspective, US NPOs appear less a single form than a kind of cuckoo's nest occupied by different kinds of entrepreneurs for different purposes. Three entities—status groups, professions, and the state—have been particularly active.

Status groups   US NPOs were differentiated from for-profit firms over the course of the nineteenth century (Hall 1982). In the late 1800s, impetus for the formation of NPOs came from emerging upper classes eager to control unruly urban environments and to define social boundaries. The charitable and cultural enterprises of the Gilded Age performed such new public functions as social welfare and aesthetic improvement in ways the market could not support and the polity might not tolerate (McCarthy 1982, Story 1980).

Urban elites remain prominent in NPO governance, largely as members of boards of trustees and volunteer committees. Evidence suggests that such activities promote and maintain upper-class solidarity and permit elites to monitor and control NP policies (Salzman & Domhoff 1983, Ostrander 1987, Daniels 1988). The character of elite influence may be changing, however. Local upper-class patrons and trustees are losing influence in many fields due to declining dependence on donations, increased support from government, and managerial professionalization. Greater demand for trustees as the number of NPOs has risen renders some boards more heterogeneous than in the past. Most important, the central role in elite participation has moved from local upper classes to corporate managers, who are recruited on the basis not of kin but of company affiliation (Useem 1984). Although demographically similar to traditional trustees, many are "corporate rationalizers" (Alford 1975), impatient with communal governance styles and supportive of managerial reform (DiMaggio 1991). And direct company giving has become more generous and systematic (Useem 1987, Galaskiewicz 1985). Attracting prestigious trustees and corporate support sustains NPOs' legitimacy and revenues (Zald 1967, Provan 1980).

Other status groups (workers, ethnic and religious communities) form NPOs. [The number of churches strongly predicts intercounty variation in the NP share of employment in four New York state multiform industries (Ben-Ner & Van Hoomissen 1989)]. Although lacking definitive data, we suspect that such NPOs are often less stable, less likely to incorporate, and less likely to claim community-wide missions than those created by the wealthy. Many status-based NPOs (including those attached to upper classes) resemble bureaucracies less than formal structures draped around the ongoing life of densely connected networks, geared to producing "goods" (solidarity, self-esteem, distinction, work experience, opportunities for association) external to formal missions (Rothschild-Whitt 1979, Milofsky 1987). [For economic models of NPOs emphasizing status groups, see Ben-Ner 1986, Hansmann 1986; see also reviews of specialized literatures on social movement organizations (Jenkins 1987) and voluntarism (Van Til 1988).]

Professionals   During the Progressive Era the organizing impulse shifted from local upper classes to nationally mobilizing professionals. Majone (1984) notes a similarity between the justifying ideologies of professions and of NPOs: service ethos, autonomy from market values, and exercise of expertise on behalf of the common good. Although some professionals (lawyers, accountants) found the FP form suited to their needs, most turned to NPOs. In hospitals, universities, and social-service agencies, by the 1920s professionals employed by NPOs dominated national discourse and organization, while sharing local authority with upper-class trustees (Perrow 1963, Starr 1982).

Professionals retain much influence in many NPOs. Hospitals vie for doctors, who bring prestige and patients; some economists view NP hospitals as, in effect, physicians' cooperatives (Pauly & Redisch 1973). But scholars agree that medical authority has declined due to supply factors, regulatory and competitive pressures, and changes in administrative rules and structures (Gray 1990, Starr 1982). Declines are also noted in the organizational power of social workers (Kramer 1987), professors (Freidson 1986), and curators (Peterson 1986).

Nonetheless, in most fields nonprofit organizations remain more conducive than for-profits to professional autonomy by virtue of their charters, which mirror professional ideologies; governance systems, which often include professional participation; and revenue structures, which empower professionals with access to private donors—doctors, curators—or funding agencies—academics. Moreover, the declining influence of particular professions often reflects increased competition for organizational authority—Scott (1983) reports that hospitals employ workers in up to 200 professions—and the gravitation of power in many NPOs from service to technobureaucratic professions (Larson 1977). The persistent elective affinity between NPOs and professionals is reflected in the greater propensity of NPO-employed than of other professionals to espouse "new class" social and political views (Brint 1987, Macy 1988).

The state   By 1960 the engine of voluntarism had shifted again, this time, ironically, to the state, with the growth of "third-party government", that is, state delegation of functions by grant or contract to NPOs (Salamon 1981). Far from competing over a fixed set of functions, the US domestic state and NPS grew in tandem, the former expanding domains of public responsibility and financing programs the latter implemented. By 1975, government had replaced private donors as the largest source of NPO revenues.

Although early work noted increased interdependence between public and NP sectors (Smith 1975, Kramer 1981), Reagan administration domestic budget cuts provided stimulus to and a laboratory setting for research. Studies have documented the financial dependence of NPOs on the state (Salamon & Abrahamson 1982), investigated effects of federal cutbacks (Altheide 1988, Wolch 1990, reviewed in Salamon 1987) and proposed theoretical accounts (Kramer 1987, Gronbjerg 1987).

INSTITUTIONS   An historical perspective brings into focus explanatory factors that play little role in economic models (which in turn possess an elegance that more historically attentive explanations lack). Specifically, the prevalence of NPOs within industries is related to three aspects of institutional structure.

Key decisions   Pivotal decisions by organizational entrepreneurs are institutionalized in models that raise the cost of new forms while making it inexpensive to adhere to tradition (Stinchcombe 1965, DiMaggio & Powell 1983). Mechanisms reproducing existing forms include interorganizational networks seeking state restraint of entry by new kinds of providers; scale economies in organizing due to availability of models and experienced participants (Marrett 1980, Wievel & Hunter 1985); and consumer expectations resistant to change. Thus, initial choices of form, which may be subject to large stochastic elements, exert long-term effects.

Public policy   Comparing US states, Hansmann (1985) reports significant relationships between tax policy and the NP proportion of schools and nursing homes. Econometric studies summarized by Jencks (1987) reveal the influence of tax rates on private donations. Within industries, narrow decisions are consequential: the Supreme Court's *Thor* ruling on inventory depreciation made NP publishers more attractive to authors who want to keep their books in print, benefitting university presses that had experienced severe competitive pressures (Powell 1985). Medicare cost-plus reimbursement encouraged FP entry in the hospital field; the switch to Diagnosis Related Groups (DRGs) slowed the pace (Gray 1990). Weisbrod (1988) demonstrates varied effects of different forms of government financing on public donations to NPOs. Hunter

(1981) describes how expanded federal responsibility led community advocates to shift from neighborhood organizing to national federations.

Climates of opinion   Perceptions of the trustworthiness of forms (rather than measurable differences) shape decisions of consumers and policy makers (Hansmann 1987). Certain goods are seen as inappropriate for market exchange or requiring special protection from corruption by the profit motive (Titmuss 1971, Hansmann 1989), and definitions of "public goods" and "community needs" vary over time (Gronbjerg 1986).

ECOLOGY   The arguments reviewed have been implicitly ecological: they portray for-profit, nonprofit, and public forms as competing or cooperating within industries, the success of each determined by material and ideological environments. It follows that an ecological approach (McPherson 1983, Hannan & Freeman 1989) is well suited to test theories about the intersectoral division of labor. One must transform such arguments from hypotheses about proportions of activity (in which form they have thus far been tested) into propositions about change over time in birth and death rates of NP, FP, and public firms and transition rates from one form to another. Although such rates *may* move in tandem (e.g. the same factors may simultaneously generate high death and low birth rates for NPOs and low death and high birth rates for FPs) it is likely that different factors influence different rates and that no one theory of industry composition will suffice. Some recent studies take an ecological approach to populations consisting predominantly or exclusively of NPOs, including human-service agencies (Singh et al 1990), minority organizations (Minkoff 1988), trade associations (Aldrich et al 1989), hospitals (Alexander & Amburgey 1987), and art museums (Blau 1989). But none has designed population models to test explanations of the kind reviewed here.

Explaining Cross-National Variation

Theories of NPO prevalence originated in work on the United States. NPOs outside the United States and comparative issues have just recently begun to receive attention (James 1987b, 1989, Anheier 1990, Anheier & Seibel 1990). Key issues are summarized below under six headings.

ORGANIZATIONAL AND SECTORAL EQUIVALENCE   Few countries use the term "nonprofit sector." Nonetheless, comparative researchers assume implicitly, that the French *économie sociale* (Forsé 1984), the United Kingdom's *voluntary sector* (Knapp et al 1990, Ware 1989), the German *gemeinnützige Organisationen* (Anheier 1988), and the US *nonprofit sector* share many central features. Comparativists face difficulty in establishing cross-national equivalence, however. Rosas (1984) reports that NPOs like the Red

Cross, for example, receive different treatment in different nations. Hood & Schuppert (1988) demonstrate cross-national differences in regulatory and tax treatment of semipublic NPOs (including such hybrids as quasi-nongovernmental organizations—QUANGOs). Such difficulties reflect variation in principles of definition and classification, ranging from France's *étatist* tradition, which discourages intermediate corporate forms between citizen and state (Archambault 1990), to the incorporation of such organizations in the fabric of consociational democracies in the Netherlands (Lijphart 1984), Austria (Katzenstein 1984), and Belgium (Billiet 1984).

Differences in legal tradition further confound comparison. In Roman law countries, the nondistribution constraint is less central to distinguishing NP from FP enterprise than is an organization's professed mission, a difference based on civil-law notions of "ideal" vs "commercial," and "private law" vs "public law," associations. The resulting classification of organizations as public, commercial, or noncommercial ("ideal") yields sectors not readily comparable to those in common law nations. Service-providing "commercial" NPOs enter commercial GNP accounts, even if they do not distribute profits; NPOs almost entirely financed by the state are included in public GNP (Venanzoni 1981). The role of organized religion, ranging from voluntary congregations to state churches, further complicates the search for sectoral equivalence. In West Germany, for instance, churches enjoy far-reaching internal regulatory autonomy under ecclesiastical law, which is constitutionally equivalent to secular law, and church and secular foundations form parallel universes. Available public statistics on German foundations refer to the 5,000 secular foundations only, rendering 40,000 Catholic and 15,000 Protestant foundations almost invisible in official accounts (Anheier 1988).

HETEROGENEITY   Following Weisbrod, James (1987b) argues that society's religious, ethnic, and ideological heterogeneity generates differentiated demand for collective goods and stocks of religious entrepreneurs. James finds substantial, if qualified, support for this position in research on cross-national variation in the size and scope of NP primary and secondary education. Heterogeneity alone is insufficient to generate effective demand if different groups are markedly unequal in political power, however. The extent to which religion, ethnicity, and language are correlated with one another and with social status (Blau 1977) should condition the effect of social heterogeneity on NPSs.

VALUE RATIONALITY   NPOs are often based on strong ideological, especially religious, orientations: value-rational rather than means-rational, in Weber's terms. Cross-national variation in such values and in religious traditions influences the size and form of NPSs: in the only cross-national quantitative analysis, James & Levin (1986) found religious factors significant predictors of the proportionate role of private schools.

HISTORICAL CONTINGENCIES   Because NPOs adapt less quickly to environmental change than do FPs (which are subject to market discipline) or government agencies (which are politically accountable), NPSs incorporate and preserve responses to historical political and social conflicts. Anheier (1988) suggests that the present legal, organizational, and political profile of the German NPS more clearly reflects the structure of German society between 1900 and 1933 than it does that of contemporary Germany.

INTERSECTORAL RELATIONS   Variations in relations between nonprofit organizations and state and corporate sectors also influence cross-national variation in NPO prevalence and role. For example, US corporations make substantial donations to certain NP subsectors, a practice far less common in most of Europe. The structure of state/NP relations is also crucial: e.g. whether NPOs are subject to fragmented centralization coordinated through grants (Scott & Meyer 1990) or are integrated into corporatist systems of interest mediation and conflict accommodation (Lijphart 1984).

POLITY STRUCTURE   National societies develop distinctive political traditions and institutional models that are imprinted in national dispositions toward organizing (Jepperson & Meyer 1990). Definitions of public and private, and the division of labor between public and private sectors, are neither stable nor formalized, but rather tend to shift over time (Kramer 1981). Bauer (1987) contends that NPSs' political orientations reflect the regulatory regimes under which they operate. Many Roman law nations, especially the more centralized, have *state-oriented* NPSs, with NPOs more similar to state agencies than to FPs, and sectoral cultures that emphasize service provision over volunteering. By contrast Common law countries have *market-oriented* NPSs with the opposite characteristics. The social democracies are a special case; their decommodification of goods and services and redefinition of services as "entitlements" militate toward larger states and smaller NPSs (Esping-Anderson 1988).

Cross-national research underscores the limits of economic explanation and the centrality of institutional factors. Microeconomic approaches cannot explain cross-national variation in the size and composition of NPSs because they take account of neither religious nor political factors (James 1987b). In such political orders as the Dutch *verzuiling,* French *étatisme,* Germany's *Subsidiarität,* either the state or religious entrepreneurs allied with political elites developed the NP form. Models that posit instrumentally rational actors and an umpire state without influence on sectoral boundaries or institutional choice are ill equipped to deal with such cases.

BEHAVIORAL EFFECTS OF NONPROFITNESS

Organization Level

Research has centered on hospitals (Gray 1986, 1990) and schools (Levy 1986b, James & Levin 1986, James 1987a), with comparisons by organizational form in structure, services provided, clients served, and various measures of performance.

EFFICIENCY   Contrary to orthodox economic theory, research on hospitals reports that NPOs are less expensive (in per-diem patient cost) and thus ostensibly more efficient than FPs; by contrast, nursing-home studies find that FPs are cheaper (Gray 1990, Marmor et al 1987). There are many reasons to question if such studies really tap efficiency (Steinberg 1987, Gray 1990). Weisbrod (1988) dismisses comparative efficiency research as systematically biased by failure to take into account subtle differences in output mix and clientele.

SERVICE AND CLIENT MIX   Research on hospitals demonstrates that NPOs have lower prices and offer slightly more unprofitable services and care to nonpaying patients than do FPs (though not as much as publics), but care quality (as measured) is not systematically influenced by form (Gray 1986, 1990; Marmor et al 1987). Several studies report NP nursing homes superior to FP in care-quality measures (Gray 1986). Weisbrod suggests that FPs attend to easily observable aspects of quality (which may influence revenues), but economize (and are thus inferior to NPs) on less visible quality aspects: he and Schlesinger (1986) interpret findings that FP nursing homes have fewer code violations but more customer complaints than do secular NPOs as supporting this view. (Church-owned NPOs have fewer than either.) Private schools have lower student-teacher ratios than public, a sign of either higher quality or lower productivity (Levy 1987). Coleman et al (1982) found that comparable students learn somewhat more in NP than in public schools, although effects differ by student type and between Catholic and other NPOs. Institutional context is critical: NP hospitals accepting federal Hill-Burton construction funds were obliged to provide services to the indigent; by contrast, reliance of NP hospitals on bond issues for capital places a premium on minimizing financial risk (Gray 1990).

HUMAN RESOURCES   Each of two contrary hypotheses receives some support. (Possible heterogeneity of samples and unmeasured sources of variation dictate caution in interpretation). *Rent theories* reason that NPOs use tax savings to pay higher wages than FP competitors. Most hospital studies find wages higher in NPOs than in FPs (Steinberg 1987); a New York study found NP wages higher in most industries, though FP wages were catching up (Ben-Ner & Van Hoomissen 1989). *Recruitment theories* hold that NPO employees are willing to work for less because their values differ systematically from those of employees of FP firms: Religious nursing homes pay lower wages than FPs (or secular NPOs) (Borjas et al 1983); teachers forego much income to teach in NP rather than public schools (Chambers 1984). Using sophisticated estimation methods, Preston (1985, 1988) reports that NP employees value job quality more and wages less than FP staff.

Four studies of colleges and universities have explored the relationship between form and inequality. Tolbert found the ratio of female to male faculty members higher in NP than in public institutions (even controlling for female student-body share), but discovered no systematic relationship between form and gender inequality in salary (1982, 1986). Two studies (Pfeffer & Davis-Blake 1987, Pfeffer & Langton 1988) report significantly higher levels of overall salary inequality in NP than in public institutions.

STRUCTURE   Structural differences among forms reflect differences in institutional systems or environments that vary among industries (Scott & Meyer 1988). Public schools, for example, are much more likely than NPOs to be part of complex hierarchal systems; FP hospitals are more likely than NPOs to belong to large chains. Such variation has consequences at the organizational level: Public schools are structurally more complex, less coherent, and more intensely administered than NPOs (Scott & Meyer 1988). Research on structural differences in similar environments tends to report weaker effects. NP hospitals have larger and more diverse boards than do FPs (Fennell & Alexander 1987); anecdotal accounts suggest that NP board meetings are more contentious than those of FPs, and NP trustees more likely than FP directors to try to influence staff and administrators directly (Middleton 1987).

STRATEGY   NPOs are believed to respond less readily than FPs to market changes, owing to different goals and less access to capital (Hansmann 1987, Steinberg 1987). California NP hospitals, for example, were slower than FPs or publics to adopt a wide range of technical innovations over a 20-year span (Zucker & Taka 1987). Economists posit that NPOs are less prone to maximize net earnings or market share than FPs; what they *do* maximize is debated (Hansmann 1987, DiMaggio 1987). NPs are larger than FPs in most industries, perhaps evidence of relative generalism (Ben-Ner & Van Hoomissen 1989). Results of several studies suggest that NPOs are less central than FPs and publics in interorganizational exchange networks (Galaskiewicz

1979, Knoke & Rogers 1979, Knoke & Wood 1981); whether this reflects the NPOs' desire for autonomy or their unattractiveness as partners (Kramer 1987) is uncertain. NPOs pursue cartelization strategies that (because they aim at donors rather than consumers) are defined as cooperation rather than restraint of trade: united fund-raising bodies are prominent vehicles (Seeley et al 1957, Polivy 1982). Again, ecological factors appear more important than generic differences.

COMMENT   The research literature is vast and inconclusive. An exhaustive review [much less discussion of public/FP differences (Bozeman 1987)] is beyond this chapter's scope. When so much research yields such ambiguous findings, one must ask if the questions are posed correctly. We suggest that the quest for generalizable differences among NPOs, proprietaries, and public agencies is problematic for several reasons.

Heterogeneity   Variation *within* populations defined by legal form may swamp variation between them. Public museums, for example, include municipal, state, and federal variants (most but not all of which are quasi-NPOs rather than line agencies) and branches of state universities. Differences in several kinds of services are greater among these subtypes than between NPOs or publics as a whole (DiMaggio & Romo 1984). NP hospitals include chains and independents; some NP hospitals have FP subsidiaries; some NPOs arc managed by FPs (Gray 1990). Heterogeneity is also produced by variation among NPOs in resource-dependence patterns, e.g. extent of reliance on private donations (and whether these arc from a few big donors or many small ones), sale of services (and whether sales are to consumers or third parties), and government assistance [and the mechanisms—grant, contract, vouchers—through which such support is tendered (Kramer 1981, Salamon 1987)]. Studies that distinguish between religious and secular NPOs often find systematic differences between them.

Unclear boundaries   Lines between public, NP, and FP enterprise are often unclear: indeed "publicness" is better viewed as a continuous variable than as a category (Starr & Immergut 1987, Levy 1987). Is a NP hospital run by a FP management company as "nonprofit" as one that is not? Are NPOs funded through closely monitored contracts as "private" as those receiving categorical entitlements with only superficial financial monitoring? When regulation is both detailed and uniform across provider types, behavioral correlates of form are likely to be weak.

Compositional effects   Most important, differences in the behavior of NP and other firms in the same industry often flow from industry composition.

Cross-national research makes this especially apparent: Geiger (1986) and Levy (1986a) report dramatic variation in the niches occupied by NP and FP higher education in different societies. In industries with significant direct provision by government, NPOs tend to specialize by service and clientele, and measurable differences between NP and FP providers are modest. When the state delegates service provision to NPOs, they are more heavily regulated, provide a wider range of services to a broader clientele, and differ more sharply from FPs.

A corollary is that it is hazardous to extract policy implications even from well-designed comparative performance studies. Take, for example, the superior achievement of students in NP schools (Coleman et al 1982). As Murnane (1986) has argued, policy changes enabling more students to attend private schools would likely alter aspects of the niches (student-body composition, regulatory environment) publics and privates occupy, thus altering the conditions responsible for the findings on which such recommendations are based. Reviewing research on comparative performance of NP and FP hospitals and nursing homes, Gray (1990) warns that we cannot assume that processes generating differences and similarities will persist far into the future.

Goals and constituencies If generic NP/FP differences exist, they may derive from the greater number and abstractness of the former's goals and their more complex and varied constituencies. Multiple, ambiguous goals and environmental heterogeneity yield complex administrative structures (Scott & Meyer 1990), difficulty in evaluation (Kanter & Summers 1987), internal conflict and demanding publics (Zolberg 1986), concern with legitimacy (Gronbjerg 1986), weak external boundaries (Middleton 1987), and frequent goal displacement (Sills 1957, Powell & Friedkin 1987). Whether such differences, which vary by field with regulatory policy, influence the kinds of measures upon which research has focussed is unclear. Given available evidence, one can conclude only that legal form *does* make a difference, but the difference it makes depends on the institutional and ecological structures of the industry in question.

Industry Level

In most industries, routines, programs, goals, public accounts, and structures are subject to both competitive and institutional isomorphic pressures (Hannan & Freeman 1989, DiMaggio & Powell 1983). Such pressures presumably dampen such behavioral consequences of legal form as might otherwise exist. Competition among FP and NP health-care providers, for example, is said to make the latter more socially responsible and the former more efficient than they would otherwise be (Gray 1991). Hollingsworth & Hollingsworth (1987) report declining differences on a range of structural and performance variables of NP, FP, and public hospitals between 1935 and 1979. Competition among NP and public universities yield advantages to those in each form that adopt fundraising structures pioneered by the other (Tolbert 1985).

Thus form-related differences might emerge more strongly in comparisons among industries with differing compositions in one society, or between the same industries in different places. The first approach, however, is likely to confound differences stemming from dominant forms with those caused by task environment and technology. The second risks confusing the effects of form with correlated variation in state structure and social organization. Nonetheless, the possibility that the division of labor among forms within an industry influences all firms in similar ways merits pursuit, perhaps through qualitative and quantitative historical studies of industries during periods of change.

Societal Level

NPSs are often described as sources of diversity and innovation. They contribute to pluralism by creating centers of influence outside the state and provide vehicles through which disenfranchised groups may organize. They enlarge the menu of models among which policy makers may choose when experimenting locally with solutions to social ills (Douglas 1983, 1987; Simon 1978).

Other authors portray NPSs as reflecting elite interests (Arnove 1980, Cookson & Persell 1985, Stanfield 1984). Collins (1987) suggests that because of tax advantages accruing to donations, charity represents a form of regressive redistribution in which the rich exchange donations for entry into prestigious charitable activities; this entry in turn enhances and legitimates their social status (Ostrander 1984).

Each of these images can be amply illustrated: social movement organizations, progressive foundations, some religious schools and human-rights organizations boost diversity; boarding schools, business-supported policy research centers, and some arts organizations may reproduce patterns of inequality. (Many NPOs sustain diversity *and* privilege.) What is less clear is whether such varied activities have any *net* effect on societies, what the effect is, and how it varies cross-nationally.

Streeck & Schmitter (1985) argue that interest-mediating organizations (a category that overlaps NPOs) produce, as well as reflect, differentiated tastes and values. But the relationship between interest mediation and diversity depends on state and polity structures. Whereas in pluralist systems NPOs may enhance diversity, in corporatist systems they may develop "welfare cartels" or "supply oligopolies" of social services (Heinze & Olk 1981). Thus, under corporatism, structures meant to accommodate social conflicts and to integrate society also exercise domination and control. By contrast, in the consociational democracies of the Netherlands and Belgium, NPOs provide institutional infrastructure to segmented and potentially antagonistic publics.

In corporatist *and* consociational democracies, NPO self-governance enables the state to delegate sensitive issues to specialized agencies outside the political center. Seibel (1989) describes the NPS's "mellow weakness" as a politically attractive but ineffectual safety-valve, to which the state offloads insoluble problems (e.g. the alleviation of poverty) that would otherwise threaten its legitimacy. Estes & Alford (1990) contend that service to the state has made US NPOs more bureaucratic and, at times, more market-oriented than they would otherwise be, thus undermining their legitimacy. At the other extreme, delegating public tasks to NPOs or QUANGOs (quasi-autonomous nongovernmental organizations) may result in the emergence of policy-making circuits that compete with government (Billiet 1984).

NPOs are active in politically sensitive policy areas in liberal polities, too (Jenkins & Eckert 1986, Laumann & Knoke 1988). Meyer (1987) views NPOs as rationalizers in societies (like the United States) with weak or weakened state centers: The often-latent political functions of voluntary associations become manifest in institutionalized negotiations of organizational status groups, in which NPOs, public agencies, QUANGOs, and firms are major actors. Several political theorists warn that dense networks of private associations may contribute to the paralysis of social and political action (Lowi 1969, Olson 1982).

A variant of this theme can be found in the work of European scholars who discuss NPOs under such rubrics as "the crisis of the welfare state" (Offe 1985). In order to maintain stability and legitimacy, so the argument goes, the Keynesian welfare state delegates more and more functions to private and semipublic organizations. The state, its sovereignty over specialized constituencies reduced, then faces "steering problems" and is unable to govern. Thus, whereas Tocqueville viewed voluntary associations as indicators of the robustness of liberal democracy, such theorists see in their proliferation a sign of legitimation crisis.

Research on the role of NPOs in nonwestern societies offers support for the "diversity" argument. Fruhling (1989, 1987) describes the role of NP human-rights organizations as vehicles for opposition to Latin American authoritarian regimes and their capacity to maintain networks that are mobilized during transitions to democracy. A large literature focusses on the role of Third-World "nongovernmental" organizations in social and economic development (Anheier 1987, Smith 1990).

Little research exists on NPSs in Eastern European nations, and fundamental differences in national-account statistics prevent comparison with the west. Such sectors have emerged throughout the region, however. Marschall (1990) describes the renaissance of the Hungarian NPS; Grosfeld & Smolar (1988) report on the growth of a Polish NPS, located not between state and economy but between a Communist-party–controlled sector and a relatively underdeveloped civil society represented by the Catholic church and the Solidarity movement. Like other Eastern European countries, the Soviet Union has introduced "association laws" in order to increase the number and scope of nonstate, NP entities.

COMMENT   NPSs are seen as protectors of both pluralism and privilege, sites of democracy and control, sources of innovation and paralysis, instruments of and competitors to states. Such arguments must be formulated more rigorously for systematic cross-national research to assess their merits. We hazard only two generalizations. First, the extent to which such roles are played depends on the manner in which NPSs are constituted in particular societies and on their relationships to other sectors. Second, NPSs are unlikely to exert strong causal effects on features of states and polities. Elites may use NPOs to further their interests but usually have more effective vehicles, e.g. laws permitting the private mobilization of dynastic capital for public purposes seem more likely to stem from than to cause upper-class power.

CONCLUSIONS

Developing a sociological theory of NPOs is difficult not just because these sectors are internally diverse, but because the nonprofit label is culturally loaded, often evoking ideological reactions. Some critics view NPOs as instruments of capital; others scorn them for evading the laws of the marketplace. For the most part, however, sociology remains a liberal discipline, and the NPS is often seen as the locus of values—voluntarism, pluralism, altruism, participation—that liberals hold dear. If academics are the prototype of the "new class," NPOs (including the universities in which they work) are prototypical newclass institutions. No wonder many scholars have been too quick to apply complimentary but misleading adjectives ("voluntary," "independent," "private") to this complex and heterogeneous region of the organizational universe (Alexander 1987).

We hope the reader will take three lessons from this review, each of which militates away from broad generalization:

1. The origins and behavior of NPOs reflect not just incentive structures and utility functions, which economists emphasize, but also institutional structures and state policies.

2. Research on NPOs can profit from an ecological approach, both con-

ceptually (viewing differences among forms as reflecting the division of labor among them) and methodologically.

3. Modern NPSs are constituted as adjuncts to, or in opposition to, states; "nonprofitness" has little consistent transnational or transhistorical meaning.

Many resources are available: Balkanized literatures on specific industries and organizational data sets with neglected measures of legal form are two of the most important. Although we are skeptical about the plausibility of any *general* "theory of nonprofit organizations," we are optimistic about sociology's potential for developing a more sophisticated and more empirically informed understanding of the origins and behavior of NPOs.

ACKNOWLEDGMENTS

We gratefully acknowledge the support of Yale's Program on Non-Profit Organizations for related research, and helpful comments from Chip Clarke, Dick Scott, and two anonymous reviewers. Presentations on which this review is based in part received useful comment and criticism in seminars at Yale's Institution for Social and Policy Studies/Program on Non-Profit Organizations, Independent Sector's Research Forums, the Indiana University Center on Philanthropy, and Princeton University conferences organized by Robert Wuthnow and supported by the Lilly Endowment.

Literature Cited

Aldrich, H., Staber, U., Zimmer, C., Beggs, J. 1989. *Minimalism and mortality: Patterns of disbandings among American trade associations in the 20th century*. Ms. Univ. N. Carolina

Alexander, J. A., Amburgey, T. L. 1987. The dynamics of change in the American hospital industry: Transformation or selection? *Med. Care Rev.* 44:279–321

Alexander, J. C. 1987. The social requisites for altruism and voluntarism: Some notes on what makes a sector independent. *Sociol. Theory* 5:165–71

Alford, R. R. 1975. *Health Care Politics: Ideological and Interest-Group Barriers to Reform*. Chicago: Univ. Chicago Press

Altheide, D. L. 1988. Mediating cutbacks in human services: A case study in the negotiated order. *Sociol. Q.* 29:339–55

Anheier, H. K. 1987. Indigenous voluntary associations, nonprofits and development in Africa. See Powell 1987, pp. 416–33

Anheier, H. K. 1988. *The third sector in West Germany*. Pres. Symp. on Religion and the Independent Sector. Princeton Univ., Princeton, NJ

Anheier, H. K. 1990. Themes in international research on the nonprofit sector. *The Non-*

profit and Voluntary Sector Q. 19: Forthcoming.

Anheier, H. K., Seibel, W., eds. 1990. *The Third Sector: Comparative Studies of Nonprofit Organizations*. New York: DeGruyter

Archambault, E. 1990. Decentralization and the nonprofit sector in France. In *The Third Sector: Comparative Studies of Nonprofit Organizations*, ed. H. K. Anheier, W. Seibel. New York: DeGruyter

Arnove, R. S. ed. 1980. *Philanthropy and Cultural Imperialism: Foundations at Home and Abroad*. Bloomington: Indiana Univ. Press

Bauer, R. 1987. Intermediäre Hilfesysteme personenbezogener Dienstleistungen in zehn Ländern. In *Verbandliche Wohlfahrtspflege im internationalen Vergleich*, ed. R. Bauer, A. Thränhardt, pp. 9–30. Opladen: Westdeutscher Verlag

Ben-Ner, A. 1986. Non-Profit Organizations: Why do they exist in market economies? In *The Economics of Nonprofit Institutions: Studies in Structure and Policy*, ed. S. Rose-Ackerman, pp. 94–113. New York: Oxford Univ. Press

Ben-Ner, A., Van Hoomissen, T. 1989. The relative size of the nonprofit sector in the mixed economy: Theory and estimation. Ms. Univ. Minn., Minneapolis

Billiet, J. 1984. On Belgian pillerization: Changing patterns. *Acta Politica* 19:117–28

Blau, J. 1989. The disjunctive history of U.S. museums, 1869–1959. Ms. Univ., N. Carolina, Chapel Hill

Blau, P. M. 1977. *Inequality and Heterogeneity: A Primitive Theory of Social Structure.* New York: Free

Borjas, G. J., Frech, H., Ginsburg, P. B. 1983. Property rights and wages: The case of nursing homes. *J. Human Res.* 17:231–46

Bozeman, B. 1987. *All Organizations are Public: Bridging Public and Private Organization Theory.* San Francisco: Jossey-Bass

Brint, S. 1987. The occupational class identifications of professionals: Evidence from cluster analysis. *Res. Soc. Strat. Mobility* 6:35–57

Chambers, J. G. 1984. Patterns of compensation of public and private school teachers. Stanford Univ., Proj. Rep. No. 84-A18, Inst. Res. Educ. Finance Govern.

Coleman, J., Kilgore, S., Hoffer, T. 1982. *High School Achievement: Public, Catholic and Private Schools Compared.* New York: Basic.

Collins, R. 1987. The independent sector: Altruism and culture as social products. Pres. Conf. on the Sociol. of Independent Sector, Princeton Univ. NJ

Cookson, P., Persell, C. H. 1985. *Preparing for Power: America's Elite Boarding Schools.* New York: Basic

Daniels, A. K. 1988. *Invisible Careers: Women Civic Leaders from the Volunteer World.* Chicago: Univ. Chicago Press

DiMaggio, P. J. 1987. Nonprofit organizations in the production and distribution of culture. See Powell 1987, pp. 195–220

DiMaggio, P. J. 1991. Social structure, institutions and cultural goods: The case of the U.S. In *Social Theory and Emerging Issues in a Changing Society,* ed. J. Coleman, P. Bourdieu. Forthcoming

DiMaggio, P. J., Powell, W. W. 1983. The iron cage revisited: Institutional isomorphism and collective rationality in organizational fields. *Am. Sociol. Rev.* 82:147–60

DiMaggio, P. J., Romo, F. P. 1984. The determinants of humanities educational programming in U.S. art and history museums. Rep. Natl. Endowment for the Humanities, Off. Planning Policy Assess.

Douglas, J. 1983. *Why Charity? The Case for the Third Sector.* Beverly Hills: Sage

Douglas, J. 1987. Political theories of nonprofit organization. See Powell 1987, pp. 43–54

Esping-Anderson, G. 1988. *Politics against Markets: The Social Democratic Road to Power.* Princeton, NJ: Princeton Univ. Press

Estes, C. L., Alford R. R. 1990. Systemic crisis and the nonprofit sector: Toward a political economy of the nonprofit service health and social services sector. *Theory & Society.* Forthcoming

Fennell, M. L., Alexander, J. A. 1987. Organizational boundary spanning in institutionalized environments. *Acad. Manage. J.* 30:456–76

Forsé, M. 1984. Le création d'associations: Un indicateur de changement social. *Observations et Diagnostics Economiques* 6:125–45

Freidson, E. 1986. *Professional Powers: A Study of the Institutionalization of Formal Knowledge.* Chicago: Univ. Chicago Press

Fruhling, H. 1987. Non-governmental human rights organizations and redemocratization in Brazil. Yale Prog. Non-Profit Organ. Work. Pap. No. 124

Fruhling, H. 1989. Nonprofit organizations as opposition to authoritarian rule: The case of human rights organizations in Chile. In *The Nonprofit Sector in International Perspective: Studies in Comparative Culture and Policy,* ed. E. James, pp. 358–76. New York: Oxford Univ. Press

Galaskiewicz, J. 1979. *Exchange Networks and Community Politics.* Beverly Hills: Sage

Galaskiewicz, J. 1985. *Social Organization of an Urban Grants Economy: A Study of Business Philanthropy and Nonprofit Organizations.* Orlando: Academic Press

Geiger, R. 1986. *Private Sectors in Higher Education: Structure, Function and Change in Eight Countries.* Ann Arbor: Univ. Michigan Press

Gray, B. H., ed. 1986. *For-Profit Enterprise in Health Care.* Washington: National Acad. Press

Gray, B. H. 1990. *Profit, Corporate Change and Accountability in American Health.* Rep. Submitted 20th Century Fund

Gronbjerg, K. A. 1986. Communities and nonprofit organizations: Interlocking ecological systems. Pap. pres. ann. meet. Am. Sociol. Assoc.

Gronbjerg, K. A. 1987. Patterns of institutional relations in the welfare state: Public mandates and the nonprofit sector. *J. Voluntary Action Res.* 16:64–80

Grosfeld, I., Smolar, A. 1988. The independent sector in Poland: Between omnipresent state and weak market. Presented at Symp. on Religious and the Independent Sector. Princeton Univ., NJ

Hall, P. D. 1982. *The Organization of American Culture, 1700–1900: Institutions, Elites, and the Origins of American*

Nationality. New York: New York Univ. Press

Hannan, M., J. Freeman. 1989. *Organizational Ecology*. Cambridge: Harvard Univ. Press

Hansmann, H. 1980. The role of nonprofit enterprise. *Yale Law J.* 89:835–901

Hansmann, H. 1981. Nonprofit enterprise in the performing arts. *Bell J. Econ.* 12:341–61

Hansmann, H. 1985. The effect of tax exemption and other factors on competition between nonprofit and for-profit enterprise. Yale Prog. on Non-Profit Organ. Work. Pap. No. 65

Hansmann, H. 1986. Status organizations. *J. Law, Econ., Organ.* 2:119–30

Hansmann, H. 1987. Economic theories of nonprofit organization. See Powell 1987, pp. 27–42

Hansmann, H. 1989. The economics and ethics of markets for human organs. *J. Health Policy, Politics Law*. Forthcoming

Heinze, R., Olk, T. 1981. Die Wohlfahrtsverbände im System sozialer Dienstleistungspoduktion: Zur Entstehung und Struktur der bundesrepublikanischen Verbändewohlfahrt. *Kölner Zeitschr. für Soziol Sozialpsychol.* 33:94–114

Hodgkinson, V., Weitzman, M. 1986. *Dimensions of the Independent Sector*. Washington: Ind. Sector

Hollingsworth, R., Hollingsworth, M. E. 1987. *Controversy about American Hospitals: Funding, Ownership and Performance*. Washington: Am. Enterprise Inst.

Hood, C., Schuppert G., eds. 1988. *Delivering Public Services in Western Europe: Sharing Western European Experience of Para-Government Organization*. London: Sage

Hunter, A. 1981. The neighborhood movement as communal class politics. Ms. Northwestern Univ.

James, E. 1987a. The public/private division of responsibility for education: An international comparison. *Econ. Educ. Rev.* 6:1–14

James, E. 1987b. The nonprofit sector in comparative perspective. See Powell 1987, pp. 397–415

James, E., ed. 1989. *Nonprofit Organizations in International Perspective: Studies in Comparative Culture and Policy*. New York: Oxford Univ. Press

James, E., Rose-Ackerman, S. 1986. *The Nonprofit Enterprise in Market Economies*. London: Harwood Acad. Publishers.

James, T., Levin, H. M. 1986. *Comparing Public and Private Schools*. London: Falmer

Jencks, C. 1987. Who gives to what? See Powell 1987, pp. 321–39

Jenkins, J. C., Eckert, C. M. 1986. Channeling black insurgency: Elite patronage and professional social movement organizations in the development of the black civil-rights movement. *Am. Sociol. Rev.* 51:812–29

Jenkins, J. C. 1987. Nonprofit organizations and policy advocacy. See Powell 1987, pp. 289–318. New Haven: Yale Univ. Press

Jepperson, R., Meyer, J. W. 1990. The public order and the construction of formal organizations. In *The New Institutionalism in Organization Theory*, ed. W. W. Powell & P. J. DiMaggio. Chicago: Univ. Chicago Press. Forthcoming.

Kanter, R. M., Summers, D. V. 1987. Doing well while doing good: Dilemmas of performance measurement in nonprofit organizations and the need for a multiple constituency approach. See Powell 1987, pp. 154–66

Katzenstein, P. 1984. *Corporatism and Change: Austria, Switzerland and the Politics of Industry*. Ithaca: Cornell Univ. Press

Knapp, M., Robertson, E., Thomason, C. 1990. Public money, voluntary action: Whose welfare? In *The Third Sector: Comparative Studies of Nonprofit Organizations*, ed. H. K. Anheier, W. Seibel. New York: DeGruyter

Knoke, D., Rogers, D. L. 1979. A block model analysis of interorganizational relations. *Sociol. Soc. Res.* 64:28–50

Knoke, D., Wood, J. B. 1981. *Organized for Action: Commitment in Voluntary Associations*. New Brunswick: Rutgers Univ. Press

Kramer, R. M. 1981. *Voluntary Agencies in the Welfare State*. Berkeley: Univ. Calif. Press

Kramer, R. M. 1987. Voluntary agencies and personal social services. See Powell 1987, pp. 240–57

Larson, M. S. 1977. *The Rise of Professionalism: A Sociological Analysis*. Berkeley: Univ. California Press

Laumann, E. O., Knoke, D. 1988. *The Organizational State*. Madison: Univ. Wisconsin Press

Levy, D. C. 1986a. *Higher Education and the State in Latin America: Private Challenges to Public Dominance*. Chicago: Univ. Chicago Press

Levy, D. C., ed. 1986b. *Private Education: Studies in Choice and Public Policy*. New York: Oxford Univ. Press.

Levy, D. C. 1987. A comparison of private and public educational organizations. See Powell 1987, pp. 258–76

Lijphart, A. 1984. *Democracies: Patterns of Majoritarian and Consensus Government in 21 Countries*. New Haven: Yale Univ. Press

Lowi, T. J. 1969. *The End of Liberalism: Ideology, Politics and the Crisis of Public Authority*. New York: Norton

Macy, M. 1988. New-class dissent among social-cultural specialists: The effects of occupational self-direction and location in the public sector. *Sociol. Forum* 3:325–56

Majone, G. 1984. Professionalism and nonprofit organizations. *J. Health Policy, Politics and Law* 8:639–59

Marmor, T. R., Schlesinger, M., Smithey, R. 1987. Nonprofit organizations and health care. See Powell 1987, pp. 221–39

Marrett, C.B. 1980. Influences on the rise of new organizations: The formation of women's medical societies. *Admin. Sci. Q.* 25:185–99

Marschall, M. 1990. The nonprofit sector in a centrally planned economy. In *The Third Sector: Comparative Studies of Nonprofit Organizations,* ed. H. K. Anheier, W. Seibel. New York: DeGruyter

McCarthy, K. 1982. *Noblesse Oblige: Charity and Cultural Philanthropy in Chicago, 1849–1929.* Chicago: Univ. Chicago Press

McPherson, J. M. 1983. An ecology of affiliation. *Am. Sociol. R.* 48:519–32

Meyer, J. W. 1987. The independent sector: Tocquevillian centralization. Pres. Symp. on Sociol. Ind. Sector. Princeton Univ., NJ

Meyer, J. W., Scott, W. R. 1983. *Organizational Environments: Ritual and Rationality.* Beverly Hills: Sage

Middleton, M. 1987. Nonprofit boards of directors: Beyond the governance function. In *The Nonprofit Sector: A Research Handbook,* ed. W. W. Powell, pp. 141–53. New Haven: Yale Univ. Press

Milofsky, C. 1987. Neighborhood based organizations: A market analogy. See Powell 1987, pp. 277–95

Minkoff, D. 1988. From service provision to institutional advocacy: The shifting legitimacy of organizational forms, 1955–78. Pres. at 1989 Annu. Meet. Am. Sociol. Assoc.

Murnane, R. J. 1986. Comparisons of private and public schools: The critical role of regulations. In *Private Education: Studies in Choice and Public Policy,* ed. D. Levy, pp. 138–52. New York: Oxford Univ. Press

Offe, C. 1985. *Disorganized Capitalism.* Cambridge: MIT Press

Olson, M. 1982. *The Rise and Decline of Nations: Economic Growth, Stagflation, and Social Rigidities.* New Haven: Yale Univ. Press

Ostrander, S. A. 1984. *Women of the Upper Class.* Philadelphia: Temple Univ. Press

Ostrander, S. A. 1987. Elite domination in private social agencies: How it happens and how it is challenged. In *Power Elites and Organizations,* ed. G. W. Domhoff, T. R. Dye, pp. 85–102. Newbury Park: Sage

Pauly, M. P., Redisch, M. R. 1973. The not-for-profit hospital as a physician's cooperative. *Am. Econ. Rev.* 63:87–99

Perrow, C. 1963. Goals and power structures: A historical case study. In *The Hospital in Modern Society,* ed. E. Friedson, pp. 112–46. New York: Macmillan.

Peterson, R. A. 1986. From impressario to arts administrator: Formal accountability in nonprofit cultural organizations. In *Nonprofit Enterprise in the Arts: Studies in Mission and Constraint,* ed. P. J. DiMaggio, pp. 161–83. New York: Oxford Univ. Press

Pfeffer, J., Davis-Blake, A. 1987. *Determinants of salary inequality in organizations.* Ms. Stanford Univ., Calif.

Pfeffer, J., Langton, N. 1988. Wage inequality and the organization of work: The case of academic departments. *Admin. Sci. Q.* 33:588–606

Polivy, D. K. 1982. A study of the admissions policies and practices of eight local United Way organizations. Yale Program on Nonprofit Organ. Work. Pap. No. 62 New Haven

Powell, W. W. 1985. *Getting into Print: The Decision-Making Process in Scholarly Publishing.* Chicago: Univ. of Chicago Press.

Powell, W. W. ed. 1987. *The Nonprofit Sector: A Research Handbook.* New Haven: Yale Univ. Press

Powell, W. W., Friedkin, R. J. 1987. Organizational change in nonprofit organizations. See Powell 1987, pp. 180–94

Preston, A. 1985. Women in the white collar non-profit sector: The best option or the only option? Yale Prog. Non-Profit Organ. Work. Pap. No. 101

Preston, A. 1988. The effects of property rights on labor costs of nonprofit firms: An application to the day care industry. *J. Industrial Econ.* 36:337–50

Provan, K. C. 1980. Board power and organizational effectiveness among human service agencies. *Acad. Manage. J.* 23:221–36

Rosas, A. 1984. Notes on the legal status of national Red Cross Societies. In *Studies and Essays on International Humanitarian Law and Red Cross Principles,* ed. C. Swinarski, pp. 954–73. Geneva: Nijhoff

Rose-Ackerman, S., ed. 1986. *The Economics of Nonprofit Institutions: Studies in Structure and Policy.* New York: Oxford Univ. Press

Rothschild-Whitt, J. The collectivist organization. *Am. Sociol. R.* 44:509–28

Salamon, L. M. 1981. Rethinking public management: Third-party government and the changing forms of public action. *Public Policy* 29:255–75

Salamon, L. M. 1987. Partners in public service: The scope and theory of government-nonprofit relations. See Powell 1987, pp. 99–117

Salamon, L. M., Abrahamson, A. J. 1982. *The Federal Budget and the Nonprofit Sector.* Washington: Urban Inst. Press

Salzman, H., Domhoff, G. W. 1983. Nonprofit organizations and the corporate community. *Soc. Sci. Hist.* 7:205–16

Scott, W. R. 1983. Health care organizations in the 1980s: The convergence of public and professional control systems. In *Organizational Environments: Ritual and Rationality,* ed. J. W. Meyer, W. R. Scott, pp. 99–127. Beverly Hills: Sage

Scott, W. R., Meyer, J. W. 1988. Environmental linkages and organizational complexity: Public and private schools. In *Comparing Public and Private Schools: Vol. 1, Institutions and Organizations,* ed. T. James, H. M, Levin., pp. 128–160. New York: Falmer

Scott, W. R., Meyer, J. W. 1990. The organization of societal sectors: Propositions and early evidence. In *The New Institutionalism in Organization Theory,* ed. W. W. Powell and P. J. DiMaggio. Chicago: Univ. Chicago Press. Forthcoming

Seeley, J. R., Junker, B. R., James, R. W. 1957. *Community Chest.* Toronto: Univ. Toronto Press

Seibel, W. 1989. The function of mellow weakness: Nonprofit organizations as problem nonsolvers in Germany. In *The Nonprofit Sector in International Perspective: Studies in Comparative Culture and Policy,* ed. E. James., p. 177–92. New York: Oxford Univ. Press.

Sills, D. L. 1957. *The Volunteers: Means and Ends in a National Organization.* Glencoe: Free

Simon, J. G. 1978. Charity and dynasty under the federal tax system. *Probate Lawyer* 5:1–92

Simon, J. G. 1987. The tax treatment of nonprofit organizations: A review of federal and state policies. See Powell 1987, pp. 67–98

Singh, J., Tucker, D., Meinhard, A. 1990. Institutional change and ecological dynamics. In *The New Institutionalism in Organizational Theory,* ed. W. W. Powell, P. J. DiMaggio. Chicago: Univ. of Chicago Press. Forthcoming.

Smith, B. 1990. *More than Altruism: The Politics of Private Foreign Aid.* Princeton, NJ: Princeton Univ. Press

Smith, B. L. R. ed. 1975. *The New Political Economy: The Public Use of the Private Sector.* New York: Wiley

Stanfield, J. S. 1984. *Philanthropy and Jim Crow in American Social Science.* Westport: Greenwood

Starr, P. 1982. *The Social Transformation of American Medicine.* New York: Basic

Starr, P., Immergut, E. 1987. Health care and the boundaries of politics. In *The Changing Boundaries of the Political,* ed. C. Maier, pp. XXX–XX. New York: Cambridge Univ. Press

Steinberg, R. 1987. Nonprofit organizations and the market. See Powell 1987, pp. 118–38

Stinchcombe, A. J. 1965. Organizations and social structure. In *Handbook of Organizations,* ed. J. G. March, pp. 142–93. Chicago: Rand McNally

Story, R. 1980. *The Forging of an Aristocracy: Harvard and Boston's Upper Class, 1800–1870.* Middletown, Conn.: Wesleyan Univ. Press

Streek, W., Schmitter, P. C. 1985. *Private Interest Government: Beyond Market and State.* Beverly Hills: Sage

Titmuss, R. 1971. *The Gift Relationship: From Human Blood to Social Policy.* New York: Vintage

Tolbert, P. S. 1982. *Sources of organizational demography: Faculty sex ratios in colleges and universities.* Ms. Cornell Univ., Ithaca

Tolbert, P. S. 1985. Resource dependence and institutional environments: Sources of administrative structure in institutions of higher education. *Admin. Sci. Q.* 30:1–13

Tolbert, P. S. 1986. Organizations and inequality: Sources of earnings differences among male and female faculty. *Sociol. Educ.* 59:227–36

Useem, M. 1984. *The Inner Circle: Business and Politics in the U.S. and U.K.* New York: Oxford Univ. Press

Useem, M. 1987. Corporate philanthropy. See Powell 1987, pp. 340–59

Van Til, J. 1988. *Mapping the Third Sector: Voluntarism in a Changing Social Economy.* New York: Foundation Ctr.

Venanzoni, G. 1981. *Private Non-Profit Institutions Serving Households.* Final Rep. to Statist. Off. Eur. Commun., Luxembourg

Ware, A. 1989. *Between Profit and State: Intermediate Organizations in Britain and the United States.* Cambridge: Polity

Weisbrod, B. A. 1975. Toward a theory of the voluntary non-profit sector in a three sector economy. In *Altruism, Morality and Economic Theory,* ed. E. Phelps, pp. 171–96. New York: Russell Sage

Weisbrod, B. A. 1977. *The Voluntary Nonprofit Sector: An Economic Analysis.* Lexington: Heath

Weisbrod, B. A. 1988. *The Nonprofit Economy.* Cambridge: Harvard Univ. Press

Weisbrod, B. A., Schlesinger, M. 1986. Public, private, nonprofit ownership and the response to asymmetric information: The case of nursing homes. In *The Economics of Nonprofit Institutions: Studies in Structure* and Policy, ed. S. Rose-Ackerman, pp. 133–51

Wievel, W., Hunter, A. 1985. The interorganizational network as a resource: A comparative case study on organizational genesis. Admin. Sci. Q. 30:482–96

Wolch, J. R. 1990. The Shadow State: Government and the Voluntary Sector in Transition. New York: Foundation Ctr.

Zald, M. N. 1967. Urban differentiation, characteristics of boards of directors and organizational effectiveness. Am. J. Sociol. 73: 261–71

Zolberg, V. L. 1986. Tensions of mission in American art museums. In Nonprofit Enterprise in the Arts: Studies in Mission and Constraint, ed. P. J. DiMaggio, pp. 184–198. New York: Oxford Univ. Press

Zucker, L. G., Taka, P. L. 1987. Modeling institutional and task environment change: Period and cohort effects on innovation in hospital organizations, 1959–1979. Pap. pres. NSF/ASA conference on institutional theory, Center for Advanced Study in the Behav. Sci. Stanford, Calif.

Annu. Rev. Sociol. 1990. 16:161–95
Copyright © 1990 by Annual Reviews Inc. All rights reserved

THEORY AND RESEARCH IN ORGANIZATIONAL ECOLOGY

Jitendra V. Singh

Joseph Wharton Term Associate Professor of Management, Department of Management, The Wharton School, 2020 Steinberg Hall-Dietrich Hall, University of Pennsylvania, Philadelphia, PA 19104

Charles J. Lumsden

Medical Research Council Career Scientist and Associate Professor, Department of Medicine, 7313 Medical Science Building, University of Toronto, Toronto, Ontario M5S 1A8 Canada

KEY WORDS: organizational ecology, organization evolution, organizational change, organizational theory; foundings and mortality of organizations

Abstract

Major theory and research in organizational ecology are reviewed, with an emphasis on the organization and population levels of analysis and processes of organizational foundings, mortality, and change. The main approach to organizational foundings examines the roles of density dependence and population dynamics. Six approaches to studying organizational mortality are fitness set theory, liability of newness, density dependence, resource partitioning, liability of smallness, and the effects of founding conditions. Research on organizational change is just beginning to appear in the literature. The convergence between ecological and institutional research is discussed, especially the role of legitimacy in population dynamics, and the effects of institutional variables on vital rates. Some key criticisms of organizational ecology are addressed, and some suggestions for future research are proposed.

161

INTRODUCTION

Organizational ecology focuses on the study of organizational diversity. Its key concerns are to investigate how social conditions influence (*a*) the rates of creation of new organizational forms and new organizations, (*b*) the rates of demise of organizational forms and organizations, and (*c*) the rates of change in organizational forms. The emphasis is on the evolutionary dynamics of processes influencing organizational diversity. And, in contrast to the predominance of adaptation in the study of organizations, organization ecology investigates the role of selection processes.

Although differences exist among individual researchers, one significant premise underlies thinking in organizational ecology. Under specific conditions, processes of change in organizational populations parallel processes of change in biotic populations. This similarity invites investigation of population biology ideas and models to see how they illuminate organizational processes of interest. Often, though, this is misunderstood by critics as the use of biological theory to explain organizational change or the use of biological metaphors to study organizations.

In its classical form, the principal tenet of organizational ecology can be stated succinctly: once founded, organizations are subject to strong inertial pressures, and alterations in organizational populations are largely due to demographic processes of organizational foundings (births) and dissolutions (deaths). Most research in organizational ecology has dealt either with tests of the selectionist tenet or with demographic processes in organizational populations.

Although the first substantive discussion of a selectionist approach to organization-environment relations appeared in the *Annual Review of Sociology* over a decade ago (Aldrich & Pfeffer 1976), the only comprehensive review of organizational ecology to appear here was more recent (Carroll 1984a). Following Hannan & Freeman (1977:933–34), Carroll distinguished between three different levels of analysis in organizational ecology: the organizational level, the population level, and the community level. These three levels of analysis are characterized respectively by developmental, selection, and macroevolutionary approaches to study evolution. Carroll's review comprehensively placed the development of organizational ecology in a broader theoretical perspective, tracing its intellectual roots to human ecology (Hawley 1950, 1968), and building links with disparate fields like urban sociology and business policy.

Since this first review, when the first few empirical studies in organizational ecology had just begun to appear, research in organizational ecology has blossomed. Some of the recent events that symbolized the coming of age of organizational ecology are the publication of a key text, *Organizational*

Ecology (Hannan & Freeman 1989), and two collections: *Ecological Models of Organization* (Carroll 1988), and *Organizational Evolution: New Directions* (Singh 1990).

Because research in organizational ecology now constitutes a large body of work, our review is limited primarily to work that has appeared since Carroll (1984) and to the organization and population levels of analysis.

In this review, consistent with Hannan & Freeman (1989:7), we argue that the evolution of populations of organizational forms can best be studied by examining how social and environmental conditions influence the rates at which new organizations are created, the rates at which existing organizations die out, and the rates at which organizations change forms. The next three sections of the paper review the current literature on foundings, disbandings, and changes in organizational forms. The fourth section reviews the growing convergence between ecological and institutional research. The fifth section reviews and evaluates some of the main criticisms that have been leveled against organizational ecology research. The final section concludes with some significant unanswered questions and some speculations about what new directions may usefully be pursued.

ORGANIZATIONAL FOUNDINGS

Compared with the extensive literature on organizational mortality, there are fewer studies of organizational foundings in the ecological literature. As Delacroix & Carroll (1983) suggest, this may be due in part to the conceptual and methodological peculiarities of studying foundings. Since there is no organization prior to founding, the population or environment itself needs to be treated as the level of analysis. Another difficulty concerns determining the specific point when a founding occurred and distinguishing between all organizing attempts and those that successfully culminate in an operating organization. Researchers usually do not treat organizing attempts as foundings, preferring to focus instead on creation of an operating entity that acquires inputs and provides outputs (Delacroix & Carroll 1983) or its formal incorporation (Tucker, Singh, & Meinhard, 1990), although some theoretical treatment of emerging organizations does exist (Katz & Gartner 1988). Most of the recent literature on organizational foundings has concentrated on density dependence and population dynamics explanations of foundings. This section reviews the underlying theory and empirical evidence.

Density Dependence and Population Dynamics

Delacroix & Carroll (1983) argued that the cyclical patterns of organizational foundings over time that are typically observed may be explained by the effects of prior organizational foundings and failures on the availability of resources. Thus, the disbanding of an existing organization may create free-floating resources which could be reassembled into new organizations. An upper limit exists to this positive effect of prior failures on current foundings, however, since an even larger number of deaths would signal an environment noxious to potential entrepreneurs, which would thereby discourage foundings. This effect would lead to a curvilinear relationship between current foundings and prior failures. Similarly, the effect of prior foundings should also be curvilinear. At first, prior foundings would encourage potential entrepreneurs to create new organizations by signalling a fertile niche. But as the number of foundings increases further, this imitation process would lead to so many foundings that competition for resources would discourage further foundings.

Hannan's (1986) synthesis of institutional and ecological ideas also dealt with density dependence of organizational founding rates. The early range of density legitimates the organizational form itself and helps increase the founding rate. But as density increases further, the legitimacy process begins to be dominated by the competitive process, and this decreases the founding rate. Like its influence on mortality rate, density has a nonmonotonic effect on founding rate, except that the effect is first positive and then negative. And this model can be extended to include competition between populations of organizational forms, by modeling cross-population density effects (Hannan & Freeman 1988a).

We think the evidence in support of the hypothesized nonmonotonic pattern of density dependence of foundings is strong (see Table 1), particularly from studies designed specifically to test the model (Carroll & Swaminathan 1989a, Hannan & Freeman 1987). Of course, it is important to model density and population dynamics arguments together, because it seems that population dynamics effects are related to both density dynamics and changes in density levels (Tucker et al 1988:151). When the two are modeled together there is some evidence that population dynamics effects may be weaker than density dependence effects. It would be useful to study the generalizability of these results and to explore the causes for population differences, if any are observed.

ORGANIZATIONAL MORTALITY

We have identified at least six different themes in how ecologists have approached the study of mortality—fitness set theory, the liability of newness, density dependence and population dynamics, resource partitioning theory, the liability of smallness, and the impact of founding conditions on organizational mortality. This section reviews both theoretical arguments and empirical evidence for each of these approaches.

Fitness Set Theory

In an influential paper in which they persuasively argued the case for a selection approach to organizations, Hannan & Freeman (1977) suggested two broad starting points. The first was competition theory, which would specify the process of optimization by which forms become isomorphic with their environments. The second was niche-width theory, which specified whether, and under what conditions, specialist or generalist strategies provided organizations with an evolutionary advantage. In carrying out an empirical test of these niche-width arguments, Freeman & Hannan (1983) also elaborated and refined the theory. Building on work by Levins (1968) in bioecology, Freeman & Hannan focussed on two features of environmental variations—*levels of environmental variability* and *grain*. Whereas variability refers to the variance in environmental fluctuations about their mean, grain refers to the *patchiness* of these variations, with many small periodic variations being *fine grained* and a few large periodic variations being *coarse grained*. Levels of variability and grain could vary independently of each other. The predictions based on niche-width theory (for concave fitness sets, in which typical environmental fluctuations are large relative to the tolerances of organizations for these fluctuations) were that in fine-grained environments, the specialist strategy would be favored, i.e. specialist organizations would have a lower mortality rate regardless of the level of environmental variability because they would ride out brief tough times. And in the case of coarse-grained environments, a specialist strategy would be favored for low levels of environmental variability, but a generalist strategy would be favored for high levels of variability (Freeman & Hannan 1983:1126–29).[1] In contrast, received organization theory predicts that generalism is favored only for high levels of environmental variability, since diversified organizations spread out their risk.

This question, though interesting and important, has not been researched enough (see Table 2 for summarized empirical evidence). Although the available data are in agreement with fitness set theory predictions, particularly the Freeman & Hannan (1983) study designed specifically to test these ideas,

---

[1]Herriott (1987) commented that in the case of high temporal variability and coarse grain (and a concave fitness set), the prediction of fitness set theory should be a polymorphic population which is generalist, but is composed of specialist forms. In their reply, Freeman & Hannan (1987b) pointed out that restaurants, contrasted with, say, multinational conglomerates, are simpler organizations in which polymorphism is unlikely, so, generalists prevail over specialists under these conditions.

Table 1 Organizational foundings

Approach	Population	Key[a] Variable(s)	Concordance	Reference
Density dependence and population dynamics	Argentine newspapers, 1800–1900	Births, deaths	+ +[1,2]	Delacroix & Carroll (1983)
	Irish newspapers, 1800–1925	same as above	+ +[2,3]	Carroll & Huo (1986)
	Local newspaper industry, 125 year period	same as above	+[3,4,5]	
	Metro Toronto VSSOs, 1970–82	Births, deaths, institutional changes	+ +[6]	Tucker et al. (1988); Singh, Tucker & Meinhard (1990)
	same as above	same as above (separate analysis for specialists and generalists)	+ +[7]	Tucker, Singh & Meinhard (1990)
	US national labor unions, 1836–1985	Population density	+ +[8]	Hannan (1986)
	same as above	Population density, births	+[9] (industrial unions) + +[9] (craft unions)	Hannan & Freeman (1987)
	California wineries, 1941–84	Births	+ +[10]	Delacroix & Solt (1988)
	9 19th/20th century newspaper populations	Population density, births, deaths	+ + (6 pop.)[11] + (3 pop.)	Carroll & Hannan (1989)
	US brewing industry, 1633–1988	Population density, births, deaths	+ +[12, 13]	Carroll & Swaminathan (1989a)
	US and German breweries,	Population density, births	+ + German + US[14]	Carroll et al (1989)

US semiconductor companies, 1947–84	Population density, entries	+	Hannan & Freeman (1989)
PA telephone firms, 1877–1933	Population density, population mass	–[15]	Barnett & Amburgey (1989)
Worker cooperatives in Atlantic Canada, 1940–1987	Population density, births, deaths	+[16]	Staber (1989a)

[1] Quadratic effects of prior births were insignificant in some models, but in the right direction.
[2] Quadratic effects of prior births or deaths were insignificant in some models, but in the right direction.
[3] Periods of political turmoil significantly increased newspaper foundings.
[4] Predicted curvilinear effects of prior failures not found, quadratic effect of prior births not significant in some models.
[5] Stronger effects of institutional environment on foundings than task environment effects.
[6] Significant independent effects of population dynamics and institutional changes; some evidence that institutional changes significantly altered population dynamics.
[7] Population dynamics, institutional changes and their interaction influence specialist foundings more strongly than generalist foundings.
[8] Results for industrial union foundings marginally significant; density of industrial unions depresses foundings of craft unions, but not vice versa.
[9] More complex models than Hannan (1986) estimated that controlled for prior density and births.
[10] Density dependence and population dynamics not estimated, strong effects of prior foundings.
[11] Political turmoil raises foundings; population dynamics effect of prior foundings, failures do not appear stable.
[12] Quadratic effect of density not significant but in right direction in more complex models.
[13] Curvilinear effects of failures significant and in wrong direction, effects of foundings in right direction in complex models.
[14] Curvilinear effects of foundings not significant, and in wrong direction for US breweries.
[15] Curvilinear effects of density in predicted directions when modeled alone; become significant but in wrong directions when mass modeled together.
[16] Predicted curvilinear effects of births and deaths for worker cooperatives but not for consumer or marketing cooperatives; predicted density dependence for consumer and marketing cooperatives, but wrong direction for worker cooperatives.

[a] KEY: + refers to statistical significance, agreement with theory; + refers to right direction, non-significant; – refers to wrong direction, non-significant; – refers to statistical significance, disagreement with theory

more studies are needed that explicitly contrast predictions from received organization theory and fitness set theory in other populations. The question of organizational polymorphs needs particular attention.

Liability of Newness

In the investigation of regularities that underlie patterns of organizational mortality, an influential and productive issue has been the liability of newness, the propensity of young or new organizations to have higher failure rates. Stinchcombe (1965) argued that this happens for several reasons, some internal to the organization and others external. Young organizations and the individuals in them have to learn new roles as social actors. A significant amount of time and effort has to be expended to coordinate these new roles for the individual actors and in their mutual socialization. And in dealing with external clients, customers and other relevant actors, new organizations are forced to compete with existing organizations that have well-established client groups who are familiar with the organization. The failure to attract business away from an established competitor is one of the key factors contributing to failure of a new organization.

A complementary treatment of the liability of newness comes from Hannan & Freeman's (1984) elaboration of their earlier theoretical statement (Hannan & Freeman 1977). They argued that in modern societies organizational forms that have high levels of reliability and accountability are favored by selection processes. Reliability and accountability of organizational forms require that the organizational structure be highly reproducible. Due both to processes of internal learning, coordination, and socialization within the organization and to external legitimation and development of webs of exchange, the reproducibility of organization structure increases with age. Because greater reproducibility of structure also leads to greater inertia, however, organizations become increasingly inert with age. And since selection processes favor organizations with inert structures, organizational mortality rates decrease with age—the liability of newness.

Even though the burden of the evidence supports the liability of newness (see Table 2), we think two issues bear further examination. One—it seems clear from several studies that explicitly modeling covariates can alter patterns of age dependence. Methodologically, one alternative explanation to age dependence of mortality is population heterogeneity (Tuma & Hannan 1984, Freeman et al 1983, Carroll 1983), and the findings may simply reflect this—although Hannan (1988a) estimated models containing effects of unobserved heterogeneity and still found negative age dependence. Age can also be seen as a surrogate for multiple underlying constructs that vary with age; for example, specific survival related competencies or external institutional support. Thus, there is a need to model relevant covariates explicitly in multiple populations and to examine the cumulative results of such studies. Two—it also appears that population differences exist in age dependence patterns. It is important to ask what factors distinguish populations with monotone and nonmonotone age dependence patterns. The Levinthal & Fichman (1988) work (which is also a special case of unobservable heterogeneity) shows how endowments can lead to nonmonotone age dependence patterns.

Resource Partitioning Theory

Compared with Hannan & Freeman's theory of the dynamics of niche width (Hannan & Freeman 1977, Freeman & Hannan 1983) in which they drew upon insights from fitness set theory, Carroll (1985) proposed a model for the dynamics of niche width which applies to markets characterized by strong economies of scale. He asked whether it is better for an organization to be a specialist or a generalist, given a high market concentration in the environment.

In a geographically dispersed market, with high, concentrated demand in the core, and heterogeneous pockets of demand in the periphery, each organization attempts to capture the center of the market. This is true when there are only a few organizations; but as the number of organizations increases, large, powerful generalists push other organizations from the center of the market. When generalists become numerous, some are pushed to the periphery, and outcompete specialists for resources, based on their size. Thus, when the number of generalists in the market increases in a dispersed market, the life chances of specialists deteriorate vis-á-vis generalists. But when a few generalists dominate the core of the resource space—i.e. the concentration of generalists is high—specialists can thrive on the periphery and outcompete generalists. The process by which this happens is called resource partitioning, because it makes specialists and generalists appear to operate in distinct resource spaces. Resource partitioning predicts that when concentration in the generalist mass market is high, the mortality rate of generalists increases and the mortality rate of specialists decreases. The evidence seems to support resource partitioning ideas (see Table 2). However, their generalizability and competing theoretical views need further examination. For example, illuminating the relationship between fitness set theory and resource partitioning and their relative contributions to mortality can bring about a better understanding of form-environment relations.

Liability of Smallness

Related to the discussion above of the liability of newness, another important stream of research has addressed how organizational size may systematically influence mortality rates. In their discussion of selection and inertia in organizational populations, Hannan & Freeman suggested that the level of structural

Table 2 Organizational mortality

Approach	Population	Key[a] variable(s)	Concordance	Reference
Fitness set theory	Restaurants in 18 California cities, 1974–1977	Variability, grain, form	+ + coarse-grained + fine-grained	Freeman & Hannan (1983)
	US semiconductor firms, 1948–1984	same as above	+ + coarse-grained — fine-grained, low variability + fine-grained, high variability	Freeman & Hannan (1987a; 1989)
Liability of newness	Argentine newspapers, 1800–1900	age	+ +	Carroll & Delacroix (1982)
	Irish newspapers, 1800–1975	same as above	+ +	Carroll (1983)
	52 data sets on retail, manufacturing and other enterprises	same as above	+ +	Carroll (1983)
	US national labor unions, 1800–1980	same as above	+ +[1,2]	Freeman, Carroll & Hannan (1983)
	7 US metro newspapers, 1800–1975	same as above	+ +[1,2]	same as above
	US semiconductor firms, 1957–1979	same as above	+ +[1,2]	same as above
	Restaurants in 18 California cities, 1974–1977	same as above	+ +	Freeman & Hannan (1983)
	Metro Toronto voluntary service organizations (VSSOs) 1970–1982	same as above	+[3]	Singh, Tucker & House (1986)
	Local newspaper industry, 125 year period	same as above	+ +	Carroll & Huo (1986)
	All Finnish newspapers, 1771–1963	same as above	+ +	Amburgey, Lehtisalo & Kelly (1988)
	US national labor unions, 1836–1985	same as above	+ +[4]	Hannan (1988a)

SE Iowa telephone companies, 1900–1917	same as above	+/−[5]	Barnett & Carroll (1987)
US state bar associations, 1870–1920	same as above	+[6]	Halliday, Powell & Granfors (1987)
California wine industry, 1940–1985	same as above	+[5]	Delacroix, Swaminathan & Solt (1989)
Finance units in 3 US cities, 1890–1975	same as above	−[6]	Meyer, Stevenson & Webster (1985)
Business interest associations, 1936–1983	same as above	−[7]	Aldrich & Staber (1983)
Metro Toronto VSSOs, 1970–1982	same as above	−[7]	Tucker, Singh & House (1984)
Knights of Labor local assemblies, 1869–1900	same as above	−[7]	Carroll & Huo (1985; 1988)
Dyadic auditor-client attachments, 1973–1986	same as above	−−[7]	Levinthal & Fichman (1988)
Worker cooperatives in Atlantic Canada, 1940–1987	same as above	−[7]	Staber (1989b)
Child care organizations in Metro Toronto, 1971–1987	same as above	−−[7]	Baum (1989a)

[1] Initial size at founding controlled.
[2] Death rates did not appear to reflect only the (potentially confounding) factor of historical variations in mortality rates.
[3] Modeling external legitimacy covariates explicitly made age dependence of mortality rate insignificant.
[4] Disbanding, absorption and merger showed strong, monotonic, negative age dependence.
[5] More complex models in which other variables modeled explicitly.
[6] Negative age dependence disappeared after controlling for other covariates.
[7] Age dependence of mortality rates showed significant non-monotonic patterns.

[a] KEY: + + refers to statistical significance, agreement with theory; + refers to right direction, non-significant; − refers to wrong direction, non-significant; −− refers to statistical significance, disagreement with theory

Table 2 (*Continued*)

Approach	Population	Key variable(s)	Concordance	Reference
Resource partitioning	Newspapers in 7 US metro areas, 1800–1975	Conc. of circulation, specialism/generalism	+[1]	Carroll (1985)
	Music recording industry	Conc. of advertising, specialism/generalism	+	Carroll (1987)
	US microbreweries and brew pubs, 1975–1988	Founding and mortality rates, market conc.	+ +[2]	Carroll & Swaminathan (1989b)
Liability of smallness	7 US metro newspaper populations, 1800–1975	Log membership at founding	–[3]	Freeman, Carroll & Hannan (1983)
	US labor unions, 1800–1980	Log circulation at founding	+ +	*same as above*
	Metro-Toronto VSSOs, 1970–1982	Size of board at founding	+ +[4]	Singh, Tucker & House (1986)
	California restaurants, 1974–1977	Log sales	+ +	Freeman & Hannan (1983)
	US semiconductor firms, 1946–1984	Numbers of employees	+	Freeman (1989)
	US national labor unions, 1836–1935	Log size	–[5]	Hannan (1988a)
	SE Iowa telephone companies, 1900–1917	Log number of telephones	+ +	Barnett & Carroll (1987)
	California wineries, 1940–85	Storage capacity	+ +	Delacroix, Swaminathan & Solt (1989)
	SE Iowa telephone firms, 1900–1917	Log number of telephones	+	Barnett (1989)
	PA telephone firms, 1877–1934		+	
	US state bar associations, 1870–1930	Number of workers	+ +	Halliday, Powell & Granfors (1987)

Founding conditions			
Argentine newspapers, 1800–1900	Creation during peak or trough years of business cycle	– – Argentine[6]	Carroll & Delacroix (1982)
Irish newspapers, 1800–1975		+ Irish	
same as above	Creation during politically turbulent years	+ + Argentine	same as above
	same as above	+ Irish	
Local US newspaper industry, 125 year period	same as above	+ +	Carroll & Huo (1986)
US national labor unions, 1836–1985	Population density at founding	+[7]	Carroll & Hannan (forthcoming)
Argentine newspapers, 1800–1900	same as above	+ + Argentine[7]	same as above
Irish newspapers, 1800–1970	same as above	+ Irish	same as above
San Francisco region newspapers, 1840–1975	some as above	+[7]	same as above
US breweries, 1633–1988	same as above	+ +[7]	same as above
Metro Toronto VSSOs, 1970–1982	Population density at founding	+ +[8]	Tucker, Singh & Meinhard (1989)
same as above	Form	+ +[8]	same as above
same as above	Concentration	+ +[8]	same as above
same as above	Institutional change	+ +[8]	same as above

[1] Not all coefficients significant; population size of local environment controlled.
[2] Founding rates increased and mortality rates decreased as market concentration rose.
[3] Large member of missing cases.
[4] At VSSO founding, board members are the only people available to do the organization's work.
[5] Larger unions had a higher mortality rate, contrary to Freeman, Carroll & Hannan (1983).
[6] Being created in a peak year raised mortality.
[7] Liability of scarcity and tight niche packing, the latter marginalizing newcomers, makes density at founding positively correlated with mortality.
[8] Time varying environmental conditions—concentration, density and favorable and unfavorable institutional change—were controlled for in complex models.

KEY: + + refers to statistical significance, agreement with theory; + refers to right direction, non-significant; – refers to wrong direction, non-significant; – – refers to statistical significance, disagreement with theory

Table 2 (*Continued*)

Approach	Population	Key variable(s)	Concordance	Reference
	US trade associations, 1900–1983	Population density at founding	+	Aldrich et al (forthcoming)
	same as above	Number of predecessors	+ +	same as above
	same as above	Founded through mergers	+ +	same as above
Density dependence and population dynamics	US national labor unions, 1836–1985	Population density	+ +	Hannan (1986) Hannan & Freeman (1988b)[1]
	US semiconductor firms, 1946–1984	same as above	+ +	Freeman (1989)
	9 19th/20th century newspaper populations	same as above	+ + (3 pop.) + (3 pop.) − (3 pop.)	Carroll & Hannan (1989)
	US brewing industry, 1633–1988	same as above	+ +[2]	Carroll & Swaminathan (1989a)
	Metro Toronto VSSOs, 1970–1982	same as above	−[3]	Singh, Tucker & Meinhard (forthcoming); Tucker et al. (1988)
	SE Iowa telephone firms, 1900–1917	same as above	−[3]	Barnett & Carroll (1987)

PA telephone firms, 1877–1934 SE Iowa telephone firms, 1900–1930	same as above	—[4]	Barnett (1989)
PA telephone firms, 1877–1933	Population density, population mass	—[5]	Barnett & Amburgey (1989)
US and German breweries, 1900–1982	Population density	+ +US — —German	Carroll et al. (1989)
Bavarian breweries, 1900–1981	National and state level population density	—	Swaminathan & Wiedenmayer (1989)
California wineries, 1940–1985	Population density	—[6]	Delacroix, Swaminathan & Solt (1989)
Cement industry, 1886–1982 Glass container industry, 1899–1984 Window glass industry, 1890–1934 Minicomputer industry, 1964–1980	Population density, major technological changes	+[7]	Anderson (1988)

[1] Model controlled for age, features of national, political and social environments.
[2] Model controlled for linear effects of prior foundings and failures.
[3] Mortality rate increased at low densities, decreased at higher densities.
[4] Density showed competitive effects when only the linear term was modeled; quadratic term not significant for Iowa, significant for Pennsylvania.
[5] Predicted curvilinear effects when density modeled alone; when curvilinear density and mass dependence modeled together, no effects significant, but in expected directions; when only mass and density effects modeled, density has only competitive effects.
[6] Effects of density sensitive to model specification. Some evidence of lateral migration of firms to neighboring niche to escape overcrowding.
[7] Linear effects of density were modeled alone and were competitive; era of ferment following technological change increased mortality.

KEY: + + refers to statistical significance, agreement with theory; + refers to right direction, non-significant; – – refers to wrong direction, non-significant; – – refers to statistical significance, disagreement with theory

inertia increases with size (1984, p. 158). According to Hannan & Freeman, since selection processes in modern societies are such that they favor organizations with greater structural inertia (i.e. inert organizations have lower mortality rates) larger organizations must have lower mortality rates. This propensity of smaller organizations to have higher mortality rates is known as the liability of smallness (Aldrich & Auster 1986, Freeman et al 1983).

Aldrich & Auster (1986) have suggested some of the reasons underlying the liability of smallness. Smaller organizations have several disadvantages, compared with large organizations. They have greater difficulty in raising capital. Tax laws, in particular the favorable tax treatment of capital gains, create incentives for small-firm owners to sell out to large firms, whose borrowed funds for acquisition purposes have tax-deductible interest. Governmental regulations have more impact on small organizations as they attempt to deal with city, county, state, and federal levels of government. Finally, in competing with large organizations for labor input, small organizations are at a major disadvantage, since they cannot offer the long-term stability and internal labor markets that large organizations are thought to have.

Although the liability of smallness is an important substantive question in its own right, another significant reason it has been pursued is one related to the liability of newness. Most new organizations tend to be small. If small organizations have higher death rates, as the liability of smallness suggests, liabilities of newness and smallness are confounded and need to be separated out. Thus, many studies of liability of newness also focus on the liability of smallness.

With few exceptions, there seems to be strong empirical support for the liability of smallness (see Table 2). Extending the findings to other populations and formulating more complex models should help to establish the results more firmly.

Founding Conditions

Although the impact of founding conditions, whether organizational or environmental, on mortality rate has usually not been treated as a separate topic for investigation—often it is appended to discussion of liability of newness—we think it has sufficient theoretical importance to warrant separate treatment. The key theoretical concern dates back to a paper by Stinchcombe (1965). In an influential paper that investigated links between organizations and social structure, Stinchcombe proposed a relationship between the historical time at which an organization is created and the social structure in existence at the time. Some of the features of the social environment at the time of founding influence (or *imprint*) the organizational processes that subsequently get institutionalized and then resist alteration. Thus, some of the features acquired at founding are carried by organizations throughout their life cycles. A systematic exploration of the impact of these conditions at founding informs this broader theoretical concern.

Tucker et al (1989) suggested another important reason to study the influence of founding conditions on mortality. Selection processes are known to operate on variations that exist in populations of organizations (Aldrich 1979, Aldrich & Pfeffer 1976, Campbell 1969, McKelvey & Aldrich 1983). One way to reinterpret, for example, evidence on the liability of newness, or on organizational form-environment fit, is that both provide variations in populations of organizations; some of these enhance life chances, whereas others do not. Thus, individual organizations in a population differ from one another both by organizational age and by fit between form and environment. One important implication of imprinting arguments is that the behavior of contemporary organizations continues to be influenced by differences in founding conditions, and these differences are another way in which organizations differ from each other. In other words, differences in founding conditions and their impact on mortality rates are another way in which selection processes operate in organizational populations.

Carroll & Hannan (1990) have suggested that density at founding may increase the mortality rate for at least two reasons. First, a liability of scarcity; intense competition at founding means new organizations face stronger selection pressures. Surviving organizations cannot devote necessary resources to formalizing structures and routines and this makes them inferior competitors at every age. Second, tight niche packing occurs because when density is high, new entrants find themselves pushed to the margins of the resource space, since they can't compete directly with established organizations. As they adapt to the thinner resources at the margins, they also get committed to persisting there, which results in higher mortality.

The evidence strongly suggests that variations in founding conditions are systematically related to mortality rates, even after accounting for, in some studies, age dependence and environmental conditions (see Table 2). Some issues useful to explore further are processes of imprinting in organizations and the question of whether founding conditions affect organizational foundings and mortality in similar or different ways.

Density Dependence and Population Dynamics

Hannan (1986) synthesized ideas from the institutional approach to organizations (Meyer & Rowan 1977, Meyer & Scott 1983, DiMaggio & Powell 1983) and organizational ecology (Hannan & Freeman 1977) in a novel modeling framework to study how organizational mortality and founding rates are related to density, the number of organizations in the population. Underlying the usual Lotka-Volterra model of population growth from bioecology is the assumption that mortality rate increases approximately linearly with population size. In incorporating sociological mechanisms into models of population growth, Hannan argued that population density captures both legitimation and competitive forces. In the early stages of the development of a new organizational form, growth in numbers legitimates the organizational form itself, thereby decreasing the mortality rate. But as density continues to increase, competitive pressures overwhelm the legitimation effects, increasing mortality rates. Thus, mortality rate is related nonmonotonically to density, decreasing initially and then rising again as density continues to increase. This model can also easily be extended to include competition between populations by asking whether the mortality rate of one population increases as the density of the other population increases through explicitly modeling cross-population density effects. These arguments were presented in a more formalized manner by Hannan & Freeman (1988a).

The evidence in favor of the Hannan (1986) model of density dependence is strong (see Table 2), particularly the Hannan & Freeman (1988b) labor union study and the Carroll & Swaminathan (1989a) brewery study, both designed specifically to test the model. But we think the discrepant findings need to be considered further.

One weakness of density-dependence arguments has been that, implicitly, each organization in the population is assumed to have an equivalent impact on mortality rates, although some studies do control for total population size. In contrast to density-dependence arguments which relate density to mortality rate, mass dependence arguments (a plausible alternative view) use a measure of population mass, the density with each organization weighted by its size (for example, Barnett & Amburgey 1990). Thus, larger organizations exert more influence on the population in this model. However, the findings for density from such models are very sensitive to the details of the model specification (Barnett & Amburgey 1990), suggesting that the covariates needed for robust description of mass versus density dependence are not yet fully understood.

Carroll & Hannan (1989), in an attempt to reconcile the differences in results that various studies have turned up, suggest that the studies that don't provide consistent evidence do not have data on the complete history of the population, especially including the early period. Excluding this early period in the history is particularly problematic for the facilitative legitimacy effect in the density dependence model which occurs early on. Thus, the Tucker et al (1988) study which examines a population of voluntary social service organizations during 1970–1982, and the Delacroix et al (1989) study, which lacks data on the California wine industry during the post-Prohibition years, 1934–1939, are both potentially subject to this problem.

The Carroll & Hannan conjecture may not explain all the inconsistent results for density dependence of mortality rates. Two caveats come to mind. One is that studies of the telephone organization populations (Barnett & Carroll 1987, Barnett 1989, Barnett & Amburgey 1990) do appear to have some data on the early history of the population, yet do not display the early legitimacy-enhancing, mortality-reducing effects of density. Instead, the effects are competitive. But it may still be argued that data for the earliest post-Bell patent period are unavailable here, except for Barnett (1989). The second caveat is that, although this explanation accounts for why the negative linear effect of density on mortality rate may not be as predicted, it does not explain why the quadratic effect (density squared) also goes against predictions of the model (Tucker et al 1988, Carroll et al 1989). We think the Carroll & Hannan explanation may be partly true, but it does not explain all of the results. An alternative possibility is that there may be systematic differences across populations in patterns of density dependence of mortality areas. For example, in some populations legitimacy may have a nonmonotonic relationship with density, first increasing and then decreasing. It also seems to be the case that such models produce density results that are rather sensitive to model specification (Barnett & Amburgey 1990).

ORGANIZATIONAL CHANGE

In this section we review the theoretical arguments and empirical evidence that deal with questions of change in *individual* organizational forms. As we had pointed out above, change in populations of organizational forms, the central focus of organizational ecology, needs to be studied by the systematic examination of mortality rates of organizations, founding rates of organizations, and rates of organizational change (Hannan & Freeman 1989:7). The previous two sections of this paper demonstrated that compared with the extensive literature on organizational mortality, few studies have dealt with foundings. Even less work has been done on rates of organizational change or transformation (Aldrich & Marsden 1988:377). Most ecological thinking maintains that the larger part of population change occurs through the population level demographic processes of organizational founding and mortality, and change in individual organizations contributes considerably less to population change (Hannan & Freeman 1977, 1984).

We think there are at least three key reasons for this inattention to organizational change. First, ecological theorists have argued persuasively that, due to both internal structural arrangements and external environmental constraints, organizations are subject to strong inertial pressures which severely inhibit organizational capacities to change (Hannan & Freeman 1977:930–33).

This has been argued to be particularly true of core organizational features such as the stated goals, forms of authority, core technology, and marketing strategy of the organization (Hannan & Freeman 1984:156). Second, ecological theorists argue for an explicit focus on populations of organizations (Hannan & Freeman 1977, 1989, Staber & Aldrich 1989). As such, organizational level phenomena are of only secondary interest. Third, empirical, ecological studies tend to rely on data gathered from historical archives over long periods of time. Even if the theory were to accommodate a specific interest in organizational change, internal organizational data may typically be difficult to obtain. However, despite all of the above, there exist both theoretical and empirical approaches to this question of organizational change.

Inertia and Rates of Organizational Change

Hannan & Freeman (1984), building upon their earlier argument (1977), hypothesized that some kinds of organizational changes occur frequently in organizations, and sometimes these may even be radical changes (1984, p. 149). But the nature of selection processes is such that organizations with inert features are more likely to survive (p. 155). And as they age, they become progressively more inert (p. 157).

Aldrich & Auster (1986:168–70) argued for a *liability of aging* in older organizations, a process that severely limits the possibility of organizational transformation, and that arises from a combination of internal and external factors. This liability of aging manifests itself in the reduced propensity of older organizations to undergo changes or transformations. Among the internal factors, vested interests harden with age, because power distributions get institutionalized, and organizations become more internally homogeneous which lowers their sensitivity to external changes and, thereby, their propensities to change. The main external reason is that older organizations get embedded in their surroundings and develop exchange relationships that curtail their autonomy and ability to change.

Singh, Tucker & Meinhard (1988) point out one difficulty with the liability of aging argument, that it does not distinguish between change processes and their consequences for mortality. Instead, Singh et al developed a rigidity-of-aging thesis, based in the literature, which specified that rates of change in organizational features decline as organizations age. Whether this rigidity of aging poses a liability for organizations is a separate question and is probably best addressed separately. But in addition to this rigidity-of-aging view, they also developed a competing theoretical view, the fluidity-of-aging thesis, which specified that rates of change in organizational features increase as organizations age. Whereas the rigidity-of-aging view is generally consistent with ecological views of structural inertia (Hannan & Freeman 1984) and related to the liability of aging (Aldrich & Auster 1986), the fluidity of aging is based on a view of boundedly rational organizational decisionmakers attempting to adapt to constantly changing, uncertain environments. They tested these competing theoretical models of how rates of change in organizational features vary with organizational age, using data from a population of voluntary social service organizations. Initial results seemed to indicate that for all organizational features studied, rates of change monotonically increased with age, after controlling for organizational form and size of board of directors at founding, and institutional environmental conditions and population density over time. This suggested strong support for the fluidity-of-aging thesis. However, when the time since the last change was also modeled explicitly—because the longer this period, the greater the probability of a change occurring—the results changed substantially. These results seemed more consistent with the position that for changes in core features (e.g. sponsor), rates of change declined with age, and for changes in peripheral features (e.g. structure, chief executive), rates of change increased with age. Thus, the rigidity-of-aging thesis appeared to hold true for core features, but the fluidity-of-aging thesis seemed most descriptive of peripheral features of organization.

In other relevant studies, the evidence has been mixed. In an analysis of strategic domain changes in a cohort of daycare centers, Baum (1989b) did not find support for the rigidity-of-aging thesis. Instead, the rates of strategic change first reached a maximum during an adolescent phase, then declined, reached a peak during an obsolescent phase, and declined again. Ginsberg & Buchholtz (1989) studied conversion from nonprofit to for-profit status by health maintenance organizations (HMOs) following a radical environmental shift. Their results showed that older HMOs took longer to convert than younger ones, which was consistent with the rigidity-of-aging thesis. Kelly & Amburgey (1989) found that in the US airline industry, rates of change in core features, such as business level changes to specialism or generalism, and corporate level changes to generalism, all declined with age. This lent support to the thesis of Singh, Tucker & Meinhard's (1988) concerning the rigidity of aging. In a study of changes in strategy by semiconductor companies Boeker (1987) found that the difference between initial strategy and current strategy increased significantly with age, which was generally consistent with the fluidity-of-aging thesis. And Amburgey & Kelly (1985), in a study of transformations in a population of US business periodicals, found that rates of change in features studied all declined with age.

We think this question is rather underinvestigated, given its importance. There is some contradictory evidence, but some evidence also suggests that the distinction between core and peripheral features (Hannan & Freeman 1984, Scott 1987b) is useful to the study of rates of change in organizations.

Thus, rates of change in core features may decrease with age, and rates of change in peripheral features may increase with age. It is important, first of all, to see if these findings generalize to other populations. A broader theoretical issue is to specify more clearly the role that inertia plays in organizational change and, following Hannan & Freeman (1984), to explicate how inertial forces apply respectively to core and peripheral features of organization.

CONVERGENCE OF ECOLOGICAL AND INSTITUTIONAL RESEARCH

During recent years, organizational ecology and the institutional approach to organization (DiMaggio & Powell 1983, Meyer & Rowan 1977, Meyer & Scott 1983, Scott 1987a, Zucker 1987) have been two of the more actively researched areas. Whereas they were initially seen as separate theoretical views, a significant recent trend suggests convergence of these ideas, which may be viewed as an exciting research development in organization theory. In this section, we review aspects of this convergence.

In relating ecological and institutional theories of organization, two questions can be raised. One, how do changes in the institutional environment influence ecological dynamics. Two, how do ecological dynamics culminate in institutional change. We think there has been a greater convergence of ecological and institutional ideas around the first question (but see Hannan 1988b for a discussion of how ecological dynamics more generally influence social change). Two important ways in which this convergence has occurred are in the effects of institutional variables on vital rates in organizational populations, and the role of legitimacy in population dynamics.

Effects of Institutional Variables on Vital Rates

The general approach adopted is examining the effects of exogenous institutional variables on founding, disbanding, and change rates in organizations (see, for example, Singh, Tucker and Meinhard, forthcoming).[2] Carroll & Huo (1986) distinguished between the effects of task and institutional environmental variables on foundings and failures in a local newspaper industry. They found that task environmental variables related to customers, competitors, suppliers, and regulatory groups influenced newspaper performance (as measured by circulation) more than foundings and failures. On the other hand, institutional variables, especially political turmoil, influenced foundings and failures significantly, but not newspaper performance.

Tucker et al (1988) asked whether changes in the institutional environment significantly altered the ecological dynamics of founding and mortality in a

[2]Hannan & Freeman (1989; Chapter 3) also devote considerable attention to the interaction of competitive and institutional processes in creating and eroding boundaries between organizational populations.

population of voluntary social service organizations. Singh, Tucker & Meinhard (forthcoming), in a study of broader scope, dealt more elaborately with issues of multicollinearity and autocorrelation in the earlier study and also examined the effects of institutional changes on rates of organizational change. The results showed strong evidence for the independent influence of ecological dynamics (curvilinear effects of prior foundings and failures) and institutional changes (favorable and unfavorable programs and policies of the state) on current foundings and mortality. And results also showed strongly that both favorable and unfavorable institutional changes significantly raised rates of change in organizational features. This idea, while central to institutional theory (Meyer & Rowan 1977) had, to the best of our knowledge, not been studied empirically earlier.

Tucker, Singh, & Meinhard (1990) further studied whether the interactive effects of institutional changes and ecological dynamics on voluntary organization foundings described above also held for subpopulations of specialists and generalists. Consistent with expectations, the results showed that the founding patterns of specialist and generalist organizations were significantly different. For specialist foundings, the curvilinear effects of lagged foundings, disbandings, and density, and the effects of institutional changes were all significant, but they were insignificant for generalist foundings. Further, although institutional changes altered the density dynamics of specialist foundings, there was no effect on generalist foundings. Thus, the interactive effects of ecological and institutional variables may vary by organizational form.

In a different vein, Barnett & Carroll (1989) have examined competitive patterns among different organizational forms in the early American telephone industry (1902–1942), and different institutional environments created by legal constraints and how these shaped the competitive patterns. The results showed that, consistent with their expectations, there were more telephone companies in states that had greater internal local political differentiation, an indicator of institutional (political) constraint. With regard to regulatory changes, the evidence was that state-level interconnection laws intensified the symbiotic relationship between large and small telephone companies. The other regulatory change, the Kingsbury Commitment, fundamentally changed the relationship between large and small companies from a symbiotic to a competitive one. Thus, particularistic constraints intended to reduce competition from a dominant organization led to an unintended increase in competition among other organizations.

Legitimacy and Population Dynamics

In addition to how institutional variables, particularly those related to the role of the state, influence founding, disbanding, and change in organizations, another significant convergence between ecological and institutional ideas concerns legitimacy and the role it plays in population change. Because we have already reviewed above some of the relevant literature, we deal with it briefly here.

Legitimacy features in population dynamics through how external institutional support reduces selection pressures on organizations. This idea is, of course, central to institutional theory (Meyer & Rowan 1977, Meyer & Scott 1983) because the isomorphism of an organization with the institutional environment enhances legitimacy and so provides greater access to resources, which reduces mortality rates. In organizational ecology one of the important reasons young organizations have a liability of newness is that they lack external legitimacy and institutional support (Hannan & Freeman 1984). Acquisition of external legitimacy and institutional support significantly reduced the death rate in a population of voluntary organizations (Singh, Tucker & House 1986).

The other argument which puts legitimacy at the core of organizational ecology is the density dependence of founding and mortality rates, reviewed in greater detail above (Hannan 1986, Hannan & Freeman 1987, 1988b). In the early range of density, it is argued that the growth in numbers of organizations legitimates the organizational form itself, decreasing the mortality rate and increasing the founding rate. Although some studies do not demonstrate the common pattern of results, these ideas are strongly supported by data from multiple, diverse organizational populations.

SOME CRITICISMS OF ORGANIZATIONAL ECOLOGY

Organizational ecology has attracted its share of critical attention (see, for example, Astley 1985, Perrow 1985, Young 1988), and some of the criticisms are currently being actively debated (Freeman & Hannan 1989, Brittain & Wholey 1989, Young 1989). The main criticisms relate to the supposedly deterministic nature of ecological ideas, the lack of attention to adaptation and change, the nature of the key constructs and the units of study, the nature of the organizational populations studied, and the divergence between theoretical constructs and their measures, particularly in the density-dependence arguments.

Strategy researchers in particular (see Bourgeois 1984) have been vocal about the seeming determinism of organizational ecology. We think there are enough variations on this theme to warrant separating out the main arguments. Three stand out, their interpretations depending on what is meant by determinism. The most commonly shared belief is that ecological thinking is deterministic, as opposed to voluntaristic, and that managerial agency and free will are denied in this approach (Astley & Van de Ven 1983). Another related interpretation of the criticism is that ecological ideas are monocausal and make the case for a new form of environmental determinism. A third interpretation is that the arguments are deterministic in that they are nonprobabilistic and, given low levels of fitness to environmental conditions, suggest the inevitability of organizations being selected out.

Organizational ecology is not deterministic in any of these senses. Hannan & Freeman acknowledged that leaders of organizations formulate strategies and help organizations adapt (1977, p. 930). In fact, they consider the environment as consisting mainly of other organizations, so environmental effects reflect, in part, the effects of actions of other organizations. However, their main interest lay in a selectionist approach which emphasized the population level of analysis instead of the adaptation of single organizations. There is little disagreement between approaches to strategic change in organizations initiated by managerial actions and selection ideas—they are simply at different levels of analysis (Burgelman & Singh 1989). Even though some empirical studies are focused more narrowly, most ecological research takes the view that selection in organizational populations is multicausal, not monocausal. For example, selection pressures, and, hence, mortality rates, are highest for young organizations. But, in addition to the effects of age, the economic and political conditions at founding (Carroll & Delacroix 1982), the acquisition of external legitimacy (Singh, Tucker & House, 1986), and initial organizational size also influence mortality rates (Freeman et al 1983). Ecological ideas are, moreover, probabilistic as opposed to deterministic. Since the instantaneous transition rates (of founding, disbanding, or change) are the object of study, even an organization with relatively low fit with environmental conditions has some probability, though admittedly small, of surviving for a long time. If anything, pre-ecological organizational research has tended to take the deterministic view of organizational evolution (for example, the contingency theory of the 1960s and 1970s), and ecological research has attended more to its probabilistic and dynamic nature. The criticism of ecological ideas as deterministic is simply wrong.

A second related criticism is that ecological thinking is not sufficiently attentive to organizational change and adaptation (Astley & Van de Ven 1983, Fombrum 1988, Perrow 1986, Young 1988). There is validity to this criticism, although the current provisos need refining. Their genesis dates back to Hannan & Freeman (1977). Hannan & Freeman (1977) noted that a full treatment of organization-environment relations covers both adaptation and selection, and that they are complementary processes (p. 930). They chose to focus on selection, arguing that selection rather than adaptation would explain change in organizational populations. But, as long since noted, change in organization per se is quite another matter.

Indeed, on this question of organizational change, some other early theorizing focused directly on organizational transformations (Aldrich & Pfeffer

1976, Aldrich 1979, Aldrich & Auster 1986, McKelvey & Aldrich 1983). In a revision and extension of their earlier arguments, Hannan & Freeman (1984) tried to deal substantively with organizational change. They acknowledged that organizations do make changes, sometimes even radical changes, but that inert organizations were favored by selection processes. In their core features, organizations become progressively more inert as a consequence of selection processes.

Clearly, however, some prominent views in organizational ecology maintain that the primary manner in which populations of organizations change over time is through differential foundings and disbandings of organizational forms (Carroll 1987, 1988:2, Hannan & Freeman 1989). This view follows from the assumption that inertial pressures severely constrain the extent to which organizations can change forms. Interest in populations as the unit of analysis need not necessarily preclude attention to organizational change. It is at the population level that the selectionist tenet is empirically testable. Recent empirical evidence indicates that organizational changes are systematically related to organizational mortality (e.g. Carroll 1984b, Singh, House & Tucker, 1986). Consequently, improved treatments of organizational populations will have to address foundings, disbandings, and change in organizational forms. Thus, for example, researchers have been engaged in some empirical studies examining rates of change in organizations (Kelly & Amburgey 1989, Singh et al 1988).

Another critical argument relates to the nature of the units being studied and some key constructs of the theory. For instance, Young (1988) has argued that concepts such as organizational birth and death are problematic. Only a facile argument would claim that these problems are specifically related to organizational ecology. We think it less useful to search for definitions of birth and death that are workable in all contexts, since none may exist. More to the point is examining whether births and deaths have been defined and measured reasonably in specific settings. For example, one way to define these events is to tie them to the notion of an organization as a legal entity—a substantively meaningful step, because legal entity status means an organization is legally liable and can incur legal obligations. We are inclined to dismiss Young's global claim that the lack of concepts generalizable to all contexts is a fatal flaw in ecological thinking.

A fourth criticism heard frequently is that organizational ecologists study only trivial organizations, not the giant corporations that have tremendous economic impact (Astley & Van de Van 1983:254; Perrow 1986:211). The larger and more powerful organizations are able to exert more influence on their environments and, the critique goes, are not subject to selection pressures in the same way that small, numerous organizations are (Scott 1987b). Although some ecological studies have focused on small organizations (e.g.

Freeman & Hannan 1983), several have addressed a much broader range of size. Thus, both large and small organizations have been included in the populations studied (for example, Hannan & Freeman 1988, Carroll 1987, Freeman et al 1983). Moreover, large organizations are not immune to selection pressures, although the time spans needed to study them may be longer. Even the Fortune 500 is a very mobile group. In the last five years well over 100 departures have occurred from this prestigious group, mainly through acquisitions, mergers, leveraged buyouts or declines in size (Fortune 1989). However, in the mix of adaptation and selection processes that influence organizational evolution, the relative role of selection is probably less profound for these large organizations.

The final criticism we address here relates specifically to the density dependence of founding and mortality rates of organizations (Hannan 1986, Hannan & Freeman 1987, 1988b, Carroll & Hannan 1989a). An early objection to density-dependence ideas was that the simple count of the number of organizations contained in the density measure assumes an equal competitive impact of each organization. Although this may be useful in a bioecological context, since the assumption is roughly true there, in organizational populations it seems likely that larger organizations have a stronger competitive impact. This is an important criticism and has been addressed by Barnett & Amburgey (1990) in a recent study of the density dependence of founding and mortality rates in the early telephone industry. Population mass dependence of founding and mortality rate, in which each organization is weighted by its size, was explored as an alternative to density dependence. When mass and density dependence were modeled simultaneously, the predicted nonmonotonic density dependence patterns were not obtained. This alternative approach holds promise and provides one of the most plausible alternatives, one that may establish the density dependence findings more firmly.

In a recent interchange (Carroll & Hannan 1989a, b, Zucker 1989), Zucker has argued that density dependence ideas are problematic because the underlying processes of legitimation and competition are, in fact, not studied directly even though they are central to the theory. Instead, models of density dependence are tested. This is problematic because the link between legitimacy and density has not been demonstrated. In their reply to Zucker, Carroll & Hannan (1989b) argue that their indirect use of legitimacy is quite consistent with how institutional theorists themselves have treated it, and that they do not think it is necessary to observe legitimation directly.

The most critical aspect of Zucker's point is that the gradual rise of legitimacy in relation to density in the early range of density may not be appropriate, and that reduced legitimacy, rather than increased competition, may account for increasing mortality in the late range of density (e.g. the fur industry in the Netherlands). Zucker's argument may inappropriately be interpreted as disproving Carroll & Hannan. But we think the more crucial issue concerns alternative interpretations of their empirical findings. Thus, in the semiconductor industry, it may be argued that the early range of density reflects more the learning and copying of technological skills and is probably indistinguishable from legitimacy. A fruitful way in which to pursue this debate is to devise alternative interpretations of the current findings, and test the competing hypotheses with new data. A key question that deserves investigation is whether legitimacy rises monotonically in the early years of an organizational form.

A currently unresolved aspect of density-dependence ideas concerns studies which give the predicted results for organizational foundings but show discrepant findings for mortality (Barnett 1989, Carroll et al 1989, Tucker et al 1988, Delacroix & Solt 1988, Delacroix et al 1989). As discussed above, the discrepant mortality findings may result because data on the early history of the population are not available. If that is so, the question is, how are the supportive results for foundings to be interpreted, since they too are based on data from these incomplete observation windows. A reconciliation of these findings is currently an open question in need of further explanation.[3]

FUTURE DIRECTIONS

As an intellectual enterprise, organizational ecology has been fruitful in recent years. Yet some important unanswered questions remain, a few of which we address below (see also Hannan & Freeman 1989:336–41 for a related discussion).

Community ecology, the study of the evolution of patterns of community structure, promises to be an important domain in the future. An organizational community is a collective of interacting organizational populations. Hitherto, community ecology has been insufficiently researched by ecologists, as a consequence of which critical questions dealing with the emergence and disappearance of organizational forms have not been addressed (Astley 1985, Carroll 1984a). Recently, though, there is a trend toward more work on community level problems. Barnett & Carroll (1987) studied mutualism and competition between organizations in the early telephone industry and showed that mutualism existed between individual organizations, while communities of organizations showed indirect evidence of competition. This supported the view that environment can be studied by examining the interdependencies between organizations. Beard & Dess (1988) proposed two ways of operationalizing and applying the community ecology concept, using input-output analysis. One way is to define the niche of each organizational species in terms of other species and directly interacting environmental elements. The

[3]This argument is based on a personal discussion with Paul DiMaggio who pointed this out.

other is to model the resource dependence of an organizational species using a Leontief input-output model. Staber (1989c) studied interdependencies between populations of worker, marketing, and consumer cooperatives in Atlantic Canada. Whereas results showed mutualism between and within the worker and marketing cooperative populations, consumer cooperatives showed competition within the population but commensalistic relations with worker and marketing cooperatives. McPherson (1990) has developed an ecological model of community organization based on how organizations compete for members. This model emphasizes the crucial role of social networks in processes of recruitment and generates hypotheses about stability and change in niches, and growth, decline, origin, and death of voluntary groups.

The question of organizational speciation, the creation of basically new forms of organization, is also fundamental and open, although some work has been done on niche formation in the wine industry (Delacroix & Solt 1988) and on the emergence of new industries (Van de Ven & Garud 1987). We think that entrepreneurship plays a key role in creating new organizational forms, each of which spawns a population of similar forms as imitators rush in to copy the innovation. These new populations become members of the community of organizational populations. Certain consequences of their appearance are therefore ecological in nature, but the mechanism of speciation and its community dynamics goes well beyond the usual boundaries of ecological analysis. Recently, we have shown (Lumsden & Singh, 1990) that one may begin to model such speciation steps in a manner that relates entrepreneurial thinking to the large-scale structure of the organizational community. The results of such models begin to quantify the rates and time courses of organizational speciation without drawing heavily on analogies to biological speciation. Although the initial results are promising, critical discussion of the species concept in organizational theory has just begun.

Speciation is a particularly dramatic instance of micro events (entrepreneurship) altering macroscopic structure (the appearance of a new organizational form, with subsequent alterations in community dynamics, and the evolution of other populations). It is not, however, an isolated instance: Heretofore, organizational ecology has been concerned mainly with populations (and how their vital rates create demographic change) and, to a lesser extent, the community; the internal workings of individual organizations are of secondary significance. Organization theorists point out that it is necessary to focus on intraorganizational evolution, and relate these patterns of behavior and decision to organizational demography (Burgelman & Singh 1988). Although the critical issue of organizational adaptation and change has been a hotly debated rationale for incorporating micro analyses into organizational ecology (Astley & Van de Ven 1983, Perrow 1986, Young 1988), the recent evidence that intraorganizational change alters mortality per se (Carroll 1984b, Singh et al 1986) suggests that it may not be appropriate to ignore internal organizational change in ecological models.

Organizations, of course, are not simply hierarchical systems in which individual acts of choice and behavior determine population dynamics. People constitute, and are acted upon by, organizations and interactions among organizations. Their understanding of, beliefs about, and attitudes toward organizations help shape the decisions from which the organizations themselves take form. Systems of this type, in which underlying constituents comprise and react to the overall organization, are termed *heterarchies* (Hofstadter 1979). They are hierarchical forms with feedback. An outstanding problem is to incorporate heterarchical thinking into organizational ecology, allowing inferences about individual behavior to be deductively related to the demographic measures of population change (and vice versa). Similar interests in evolutionary biology have led recently to the introduction of modeling methods to do just this—i.e. expose the reciprocal contact between individual and community to quantitative analysis (Lumsden & Wilson 1981, Findlay & Lumsden 1988). This approach, called gene-culture theory, provides tools and a pertinent metaphor through which organizational ecology can begin to synthesize individual and demographic thinking into one system.

In biological heterarchies (gene-culture populations) of any complexity, there is no fixed environment. Other populations, communities, or assemblages of propagating genes change in response to changes in the population we are observing. Under the organizing influence of natural selection, an adaptive response in one population may result in adaptive counter-responses in others. This is coadaptation, a consequence of the evolutionary relationship between the populations linked together in biotic ecosystems. In the place of immutable, exogenous conditions, an evolving population experiences a complex array of other populations that react to it (Roughgarden 1979, Grene 1983).

In some ways, we think, communities of organizational populations are similar. Particularly in the case of powerful organizations (Perrow 1986) that are agents for change and are central within their societies, the appropriate ecological metaphor is coevolution, in which the demography (and evolution) of multiple populations is considered simultaneously through coupled, generally nonlinear, demographic equations. Intriguingly, the biological literature on coevolution and coadaptation has been growing rapidly over the past decade and now provides a rich selection of models (Roughgarden 1979, Feldman 1989). In the spirit of earlier developments in organizational ecology, we think it would be useful to examine how such models can improve our understanding of organizational evolution.

A final direction that holds considerable promise is more critical examination of the nature of organizational evolution. For biological organisms, evolution is fundamentally genealogical and based ultimately on the propagation of genes, and for a few species, social learning along lines of descent. Organizations do not replicate in this manner. Organizational evolution begins with the appearance of a new form, the product of entrepreneurial thought, and ends with the extinction of the last members of the population that imitation creates around the founding member. It makes sense to speak of organizational founding and failure, together with selection, adaptation, learning, populations, and communities. It is less sensible to seek analogues of genes and genealogies when in fact there may be none close to what exists in the biological world.

The latter is a problem only if one expects organizational ecology to resemble, in its generalizations as an evolutionary science, evolutionary biology itself. But the alternative is more interesting and, in view of what we have said thus far, more plausible. Although the evolution of organizational populations parallels that of biotic entities in some ways, in others it is strikingly different. There is speciation without genealogy, and a preponderance of Lamarckian (social learning) rather than Mendelian inheritance (Nelson & Winter 1982, Winter 1990). Evolution, however, is a meaningful, even essential, concept through which change in populations of organizations is to be understood. The details of these new steps in the future development of organizational ecology provide organization theorists with fundamental challenges.

ACKNOWLEDGMENTS

This paper has benefitted greatly from discussions and comments on an earlier draft by Howard Aldrich, Bill Barnett, Glenn Carroll, John Freeman, Mike Hannan, Jim March, Marshall Meyer, and Dick Scott. Discussions with Paul DiMaggio, Charles Perrow, Mary Ann Glynn, and Steve Mezias during a seminar at the School of Organization and Management, Yale University, are also gratefully acknowledged. The responsibility for all errors of omission or commission is solely ours. Without the unflagging cooperation, enthusiasm, and editorial assistance of John Rutter, this paper would not have been done on time, and we owe a debt of gratitude to him.

Literature Cited

Aldrich, H. E. 1979. *Organizations and Environments*. Englewood Cliffs, NJ: Prentice Hall

Aldrich, H. E., Auster, E. R. 1986. Even dwarfs started small: Liabilities of age and size and their strategic implications. In *Research in Organizational Behavior*, vol. 8, ed. B. M. Staw, L. L. Cummings, pp. 165–198. Greenwich, Conn: JAI

Aldrich, H. E., Marsden, P. V. 1988. Environments and organizations. In *Handbook of Sociology*, ed. N. Smelser, pp. 361–392. Newbury Park, Calif: Sage

Aldrich, H. E., Pfeffer, J. 1976. Environments of organizations. *Annu. Rev. Sociol.* 2:79–105

Aldrich, H. E., Staber, U. 1983. *The organization of business interest associations*. Unpublished ms. Sociology, Univ. N. Carolina, Chapel Hill

Aldrich, H. E., Staber, U., Zimmer, C., Beggs, J. 1990. Minimalism and mortality:

Patterns of disbandings among American trade associations in the 20th century. In *Organizational Evolution: New Directions,* ed. J. V. Singh. Newbury Park, Calif: Sage

Amburgey, T. L., Kelly, D. 1985. Adaptation and selection in organizational populations: A competing risks model. Pres. 45th Acad. Manage. Ann. Meet., San Diego, Calif.

Amburgey, T. L., Lehtisalo, M., Kelly, D. 1988. Suppression and failure in the political press: Government control, party affiliation, and organizational life chances. In *Ecological Models of Organization,* ed. G. R. Carroll, pp. 153–73. Cambridge, Mass: Ballinger

Anderson, P. 1988. The population dynamics of Schumpeterian competition. In Acad. Manage. Best Papers Proc.:150–54. Anaheim, CA: Acad. Manage.

Astley, W. G. 1985. The two ecologies: Population and community perspectives on organizational evolution. *Admin. Sci. Q.* 30(2):224–41

Astley, W. G., Van de Ven, A. H. 1983. Central perspectives and debates in organization theory. *Admin. Sci. Q.* 28(2):245–73

Barnett, W. P. 1989. The organizational ecology of a technological system. Unpublished ms. Grad. School Bus., Univ. Wisc. Madison

Barnett, W. P., Amburgey, T. L. 1990. Do larger organizations generate stronger competition? In *Organizational Evolution: New Directions,* ed. J. V. Singh. Newbury Park, Calif: Sage

Barnett, W. P., Carroll, G. R. 1987. Competition and mutualism among early telephone companies. *Admin. Sci. Q.* 32(3):400–421

Barnett, W. P., Carroll, G. R. 1989. How institutional constraints shaped and changed competition in the early American telephone industry: An ecological analysis. Unpublished ms. Grad. School Bus. Univ. Wisc., Madison

Baum, J. A. C. 1989a. Liabilities of newness, adolescence and obsolescence: Exploring age dependence in organizational mortality. Work. pap. Stern School Bus., New York Univ.

Baum, J. A. C. 1989b. Organizational change, inertia and mortality: Toward an adaptation-selection approach to organizational evolution. Work. pap. Stern School Bus., New York Univ.

Beard, D. W., Dess, G. G. 1988. Modeling organizational species' interdependence in an organizational community: An input-output approach. *Acad. Mgmt. Rev.* 13(3):362–73

Boeker, W. 1987. The permanence of organizational strategy. Unpubl. ms. Grad. School Bus. Columbia Univ. New York

Bourgeois, L. J. III. 1984. Strategic management and determinism. *Acad. Mgmt. Rev.* 9(4):586–96

Brittain, J. W., Freeman, J. 1980. Organizational proliferation and density dependent selection. In *The Organizational Life Cycle,* ed. J. R. Kimberly, R. H. Miles, pp. 291–338. San Francisco: Jossey Bass

Brittain, J. W., Wholey, D. R., 1989. Assessing organizational ecology as sociological theory: Comment on Young. *Am. J. Soc.* 95:439–444

Burgelman, R. A., Singh, J. V. 1989. Strategy and organization: An evolutionary approach. Work. Pap. 89–04, Reginald H. Jones Ctr. Manage. Policy, Strat., Organ. Wharton School. Univ. Penn.

Campbell, D. T. 1969. Variation, selection, and retention in sociocultural systems. *Gen. Syst.* 16:69–85

Carroll, G. R. 1983. A stochastic model of organizational mortality: Review and reanalysis. *Soc. Sci. Res.* 12:303–29

Carroll, G. R. 1984a. Organizational Ecology. *Annu. Rev. of Sociol.* 10:71–93

Carroll, G. R. 1984b. Dynamics of publisher succession in newspaper organizations. *Admin. Sci. Q.* 29(1):93–113

Carroll, G. R. 1985. Concentration and specialization: Dynamics of niche width in populations of organizations. *Am. J. Sociol.* 90:1262–83

Carroll, G. R. 1987. *Publish and Perish: The Organizational Ecology of Newspaper Industries.* Greenwich, Conn: JAI

Carroll, G. R. ed. 1988. *Ecological Models of Organization.* Cambridge, Mass: Ballinger

Carroll, G. R., Delacroix, J. 1982. Organizational mortality in the newspaper industries of Argentina and Ireland: An ecological approach. *Admin. Sci. Q.* 27:169–98

Carroll, G. R., Delacroix, J., Goodstein, J. 1988. The political environments or organizations: An ecological view. In *Research in Organizational Behavior,* vol. 10, ed. B. M. Staw, L. L. Cummings, pp. 359–92. Greenwich, Conn: JAI

Carroll, G. R., Hannan, M. T. 1989a. Density dependence in the evolution of populations of newspaper organizations. *Am. Sociol. Rev.* 54:524–41

Carroll, G. R., Hannan, M. T. 1989b. On using institutional theory in studying organizational populations. *Am. Sociol. Rev.* 54:545–48

Carroll, G. R., Hannan, M. T. 1990. Density delay in the evolution of organizational populations: A model and five empirical tests. In *Organizational Evolution: New Directions,* ed. J. V. Singh. Newbury Park, Calif: Sage

Carroll, G. R., Huo, Y. P. 1985. Losing by winning: The paradox of electoral success by organized labor parties in the Knights of Labor era. Unpublished ms. Ctr. Res. Manage. Univ. Calif., Berkeley

Carroll, G. R., Huo, Y. P. 1986. Organizational task and institutional environments in ecological perspective: Findings from the local newspaper industry. *Am. J. Sociol.* 91:838–73

Carroll, G. R., Huo, Y. P. 1988. Organizational and electoral paradoxes of the Knights of Labor. In *Ecological Models of Organization,* ed. G. R. Carroll, pp. 175–93. Cambridge, Mass: Ballinger

Carroll, G. R., Preisendoerfer, P., Swaminathan, A., Wiedenmayer, G. 1989. Brewery and braurei: The comparative organizational ecology of American and German brewing industries. Work. app. OBIR-34, Ctr. Res. Manage. Univ. Calif. Berkeley

Carroll, G. R., Swaminathan, A. 1989a. Density dependent organizational evolution in the American brewing industry from 1633 to 1988. Techn. Rep. OBIR-35. Ctr. Res. Manage. Univ. Calif. Berkeley

Carroll, G. R., Swaminathan, A. 1989b. The organizational ecology of strategy groups in the American brewing industry from 1975 to 1988. Tech. Rep OBIR-36, Ctr. Res. Manage. Univ. Calif. Berkeley

Delacroix, J., Carroll, G. R. 1983. Organizational foundings: An ecological study of the newspaper industries of Argentina and Ireland. *Admin. Sci. Q.* 28:274–91

Delacroix, J., Solt, M. E. 1988. Niche formation and foundings in the California wine industry, 1941–84. In *Ecological Models of Organizations,* ed. G. R. Carroll. Cambridge, Mass: Ballinger

Delacroix, J., Swaminathan, A., Solt, M. E. 1989. Density dependence versus population dynamics: An ecological study of failings in the California wine industry. *Am. Sociol. Rev.,* 54:245–62

DiMaggio, P. J., Powell, W. W. 1983. The iron cage revisited: Institutional isomorphism and collective rationality in organizational fields. *Am. Sociol. Rev.* 48:147–60

Feldman, M. W. ed. 1989. *Mathematical Evolutionary Theory.* Princeton, NJ: Princeton Univ. Press

Findlay, C. S., Lumsden, C. J. 1988. *The Creative Mind.* London: Academic

Fombrum, C. J. 1988. Crafting and institutionally informed ecology of organizations. In *Ecological Models of Organizations,* ed. G. R. Carroll, pp. 223–39. Cambridge, Mass: Ballinger

Fortune. 1989. A new era of rapid rise and ruin. April 24, 1989, pp. 77–88

Freeman, J. 1989. Ecological analysis of semiconductor firm mortality. In *Organizational Evolution: New Directions,* ed. J. V. Singh. Newbury Park, Calif: Sage

Freeman, J., Hannan, M. T. 1983. Niche width and the dynamics of organizational populations. *Am. J. Sociol.* 88:116–45

Freeman, J., Hannan, M. T. 1987a. Specialist strategies and organizational mortality in the U.S. semiconductor industry. Pres. 47th Acad. Manage. Annu. Meet. New Orleans, Louisiana

Freeman, J., Hannan, M. T. 1987b. The ecology of restaurants revisited. *Am. J. Sociol.* 92:1214–20

Freeman, J., Hannan, M. T. 1989. Setting the record straight on organizational ecology: Rebuttal to Young. *Am. J. Sociol.* 95:425–39

Freeman, J., Carroll, G. R., Hannan, M. T. 1983. The liability of newness: Age dependence in organizational death rates. *Am. Sociol. Rev.* 48:692–710

Ginsberg, A., Buchholtz, A. 1989. Reshaping organizational identity: Converting from nonprofit to for-profit status. Work. pap. Stern School Bus. New York Univ.

Grene, M. ed. 1983. *Dimensions of Darwinism: Themes and Counterthemes in Twentieth-Century Evolutionary Theory.* Cambridge, Mass: Cambridge Univ. Press

Halliday, T. C., Powell, M. J., Granfors, M. W. 1987. Minimalist organizations: Vital events in state bar associations, 1870–1930. *Am. Sociol. Rev.* 52:456–71

Hannan, M. T. 1986. A model of competitive and institutional processes in organizational ecology. Techn. Rep. 86–13. Dep. Sociol. Cornell Univ.

Hannan, M. T. 1988a. Age dependence in the mortality of national labor unions: Comparisons of parametric models. *J. Math. Sciol.* 14:1–30

Hannan, M. T. 1988b. Organizational population dynamics and social change. *Eur. Sociol. Rev.* 4(2):95–109

Hannan, M. T., Freeman, J. 1977. The population ecology of organizations. *Am. J. Sociol.* 82:929–64

Hannan, M. T., Freeman, J. 1984. Structural inertia and organizational change. *Am. Sociol. Rev.* 49:149–64

Hannan, M. T., Freeman, J. 1987. The ecology of organizational founding: American labor unions, 1836–1985. *Am. J. Sociol.* 92:910–43

Hannan, M. T., Freeman, J. 1988a. Density dependence in the growth of organizational populations. In *Ecological Models of Organizations,* ed. G. R. Carroll, pp. 7–31. Cambridge, Mass: Ballinger

Hannan, M. T., Freeman, J. 1988b. The ecology of organizational mortality: American labor unions, 1836–1985. *Am. J. Sociol.* 94:25–52

Hannan, M. T., Freeman, J. 1989. *Organizational Ecology*. Cambridge, Mass: Harvard Univ. Press

Hawley, A. 1950. *Human Ecology*. New York: Roland

Hawley, A. 1968. Human ecology. In *International Encyclopedia of the Social Sciences*. New York: MacMillan

Herriott, S. R. 1987. Fitness set theory in population ecology of organizations: Comment on Hannan and Freeman. *Am. J. Sociol.* 92:1210–13

Hofstadter, D.R. 1979. *Gödel, Escher, Bach: An Eternal Golden Braid*. New York: Basic

Katz, J., Gartner, W. B. 1988. Properties of emerging organizations. *Acad. Mgmt. Rev.* 13:429–41

Kelly, D., Amburgey, T. A. 1989. Airline dynamics: Strategic change and structural inertia. *Work. pap. Grad. School of Business*, Univ. Wisc. Madison

Levins, R. 1968. *Evolution in Changing Environments*. Princeton, NJ: Princeton Univ. Press

Levinthal, D. A., Fichman, M. 1988. Dynamics of interorganizational attachments: Auditor-client relationships. *Admin. Sci. Q.* 33:345–69

Lumsden, C. J., Singh, J. V. 1990. The dynamics of organizational speciation. In *Organizational Evolution: New Directions*, ed. J. V. Singh. Newbury Park, Calif: Sage

Lumsden, C. J., Wilson, E. O. 1981. *Genes, Mind, Culture: The Coevolutionary Process*. Cambridge, Mass: Harvard Univ. Press

McKelvey, B., Aldrich, H. E. 1983. Populations, natural selection and applied organizational science. *Admin. Sci. Q.* 28:101–28

McPherson, M. 1990. Evolution in communities of voluntary organizations. In *Organizational Evolution: New Directions,* ed. J. V. Singh. Newbury Park, CA: Sage

Meyer, J. W., Rowan, B. 1977. Institutional organizations: Formal structure as myth and ceremony. *Am. J. Sociol.* 83:340–63

Meyer, J. W., Scott, W. R. 1983. *Organizational Environments: Ritual and Rationality*. Beverly Hills, Calif: Sage

Meyer, M. W., Stevenson, W., Webster, S. 1985. *Limits to Bureaucratic Growth*. New York: de Gruyter

Nelson, R. R., Winter, S. G. 1982. *An Evolutionary Theory of Economic Change*. Cambridge, Mass: Harvard Univ. Press

Perrow, C. 1986. *Complex Organizations: A Critical Essay*. New York: Random. 3rd ed.

Roughgarden, J. 1979. *Theory of Population Genetics and Evolutionary Ecology*. New York: MacMillan

Scott, W. R. 1987a. The adolescence of institutional theory. *Admin. Sci. Q.* 32:493–511

Scott, W. R. 1987b. *Organizations: Rational, Natural and Open Systems*. Englewood Cliffs, NJ: Prentice-Hall. 2nd ed.

Singh, J. V. ed. 1990. *Organizational Evolution: New Directions*. Newbury Park, Calif: Sage

Singh, J. V., House, R. J., Tucker, D. J. 1986. Organizational change and organizational mortality. *Admin. Sci. Q.* 31:587–611

Singh, J. V., Tucker, D. J., House, R. J. 1986. Organizational legitimacy and the liability of newness. *Admin. Sci. Q.* 31: 171–93

Singh, J. V., Tucker, D. J., Meinhard, A. G. 1988. Are voluntary organizations structurally inert? Exploring an assumption in organizational ecology. Pres. Acad. Manage. Annu. Meet. Anaheim, Calif.

Singh, J. V., Tucker, D. J., Meinhard, A. G. Forthcoming. Institutional change and ecological dynamics. In *The New Institutionalism in Organizational Analysis*, ed. W. W. Powell, P. J. DiMaggio. Chicago, Ill: Univ. Chicago Press

Staber, U. 1989a. Organizational foundings in the cooperative sector of Atlantic Canada: An ecological perspective. *Organ. Stud.* 10:381–403

Staber, U. 1989b. Age-dependence and historical effects on the failure rates of worker cooperatives: An event history analysis. *Econ. Ind. Democracy* 10:59–80

Staber, U. 1989c. Mutualism and competition: Patterns of organizational interdependence in the cooperative sector. Work. pap. Faculty Admin. Univ. New Brunswick, Canada

Staber, U., Aldrich, H. E. 1989. Organizational transformation and trends in U.S. employment relations. *Ind. Re. J.* 110:18

Stinchcombe, A. L. 1965. Organizations and social structure. In *Handbook of Organizations*, ed. J. G. March, pp. 153–93. Chicago, Ill: Rand McNally

Swaminathan, A., Wiedenmayer, G. 1989. Does the pattern of density dependence in organizational mortality rates vary across levels of analysis? Evidence from the German brewing industry. Work. pap. Grad. School Bus. Univ. Calif., Berkeley

Tucker, D. J., Singh, J. V., House, R. J. 1984. The liability of newness in voluntary social service organizations. Pres. Am. Sociol. Assoc. Annu. Meet. San Antonio, Texas

Tucker, D. J., Singh, J. V., Meinhard, A. G. 1989. Founding conditions, environmental selection and organizational mortality. Work. pap., School Soc. Work, McMaster Univ.

Tucker, D. J., Singh, J. V., Meinhard, A. G. 1990. Organizational form, population dynamics and institutional change: A study of founding patterns of voluntary organizations. *Acad. Manage. J.* 33:151–78

Tucker, D. J., Singh, J. V., Meinhard, A. G., House, R. J. 1988. Ecological and institutional sources of change in organizational populations. In *Ecological Models of Organizations,* ed. G. R. Carroll, pp. 127–51 Cambridge, Mass: Ballinger

Tuma, N. B., Hannan, M. T. 1984. *Social Dynamics: Models and Methods.* New York: Academic

Van de Ven, A. H., Garud, R. 1987. A framework for understanding the emergence of new organizations. In *Research in Technological Innovation, Management and Policy,* Vol. 4, ed. R. S. Rosenbloom, R. A. Burgelman. Greenwich, Conn: JAI

Winter, S. G. 1990. Survival, selection and inheritance in evolutionary theories of organization. In *Organizational Evolution: New Directions,* ed. J. V. Singh. Newbury Park, Calif: Sage

Young, R. C. 1988. Is population ecology a useful paradigm for the study of organizations? *Am. J. Sociol.* 94(1):1–24

Young, R. C. 1989. Reply to Freeman and Hannan and Brittain and Wholey. *Am. J. Soc.* 95:445–446

Zucker, L. G. 1987. Institutional theories of organization. *Am. Sociol. Rev.* 13:443–64

Zucker, L. G. 1989. Combining institutional theory and population ecology: No legitimacy, no history. *Am. Sociol. Rev.* 54:542–45

Annu. Rev. Sociol. 1990. 16:197–220

CHILDREN'S PEER CULTURES

William A. Corsaro and Donna Eder

Department of Sociology, Indiana University, Bloomington, Indiana 47405

KEY WORDS: children, socialization, peers, culture, adolescents

INTRODUCTION

The Importance of Peer Culture in Theories of Child Development and Socialization

Despite its long history as an important concept in sociological theory, there have been few studies of children's peer culture. By peer culture, we mean a stable set of activities or routines, artifacts, values, and concerns that children produce and share in interaction with peers. Most research on peer culture has focused on adolescent peer values, interests, and identities (Coleman 1961, Cusick 1972, Simmons & Blyth 1987). Recently, however, detailed ethnographic studies have been made of interactive processes within the peer culture of preschool and elementary school children (Berentzen 1984, Corsaro 1985, Davies 1982, Fine 1987, Goodwin 1989, Mandell 1986, Rizzo 1989, Thorne 1986), as well as of preadolescents and adolescents (Eder 1985, Everhart 1983, Lesko 1988, Willis 1981, Wulff 1988). In this chapter we examine these and other studies: (*a*) to describe activities, routines, values, and concerns within the peer cultures of children from the preschool years through adolescence; (*b*) to identify specific themes and changes in children's peer cultures and how these are related to demands from the adult world; and (*c*) to develop the theoretical implications of the research for an interpretive theory of childhood socialization.

Before turning to these issues, we will first consider the place of peer

0360-0572/90/0815-0197$02.00

culture in various theories of child development and socialization. Our purpose is to identify the individualistic bias of most theories and to stress the importance of peer culture for the development of an interpretive theory of childhood socialization.

BEHAVIORIST THEORIES   Until the mid-1960s most theories of child development were behaviorist, with an emphasis on modeling and reinforcement as the key mechanisms in human learning. Given the power of adults and their control over valued cultural resources, it is not surprising that behaviorists stress the importance of adult inputs to children. Children are relegated to a passive role, and socialization is seen as a unilateral process with children shaped and molded by adults. Thus, research from this perspective often involves attempts to discover and measure consistencies and variations in adult socialization practices. The peer group plays a minor role in the socialization process initially; but with growing autonomy from adults in adolescence, the peer group can become an important source of reinforcement.

Overall, the behaviorist approach places little emphasis on social interaction and culture. Its individualistic basis and emphasis on simplistic processes (imitation and reinforcement) to explain complex phenomenon has come under criticism in recent years. In fact, some behaviorists (see Bandura 1986) have recently incorporated cognitive elements into their theories of learning and development. One result of the questioning of the narrowness of the behaviorist position has been a definite trend toward the acceptance of a constructivist approach in developmental psychology.

CONSTRUCTIVIST THEORIES   Best represented in the cognitive developmental theory of Piaget (1950, 1968), the constructivist approach stresses the child's active role, arguing that children interpret, organize, and use information from the environment and, in the process, acquire adult skills and knowledge. Several important developments have accompanied the general acceptance of the constructivist position. First, numerous scholars have extended Piaget's work on intellectual development to the study of social cognition, suggesting that children often interact with others in response to disequilibria (Damon 1977, Turiel 1983, Youniss 1980). The increasing concern with children's social cognition has led to numerous studies of children's social relations and friendships. In fact, some constructivist theorists (Youniss 1980) now argue that peers may be as important as adults for children's acquisition of social skills and knowledge.

Although these developments are clearly in the right direction, the constructivist approach like behaviorism still relies on what Harré (1986) terms "the doctrine of individualism." For example, understanding of children's interactions remains at an interpersonal level. Interpersonal alignments (e.g. adult-child versus peer) are compared and contrasted to show how they differentially affect individual development. But how interpersonal relations reflect cultural systems, or how children, through their participation in communicative events, become part of and in turn collectively reproduce these cultural patterns is not seriously considered.

This adherence to individualism is also seen in the overwhelming concern with the endpoint of development. For example, work on social cognition focuses on identifying stages in the abstract conception of friendship. Children's conceptions are elicited through clinical interviews, and their underdeveloped conceptions are compared to those of competent adults (Damon 1977, Youniss 1980). Yet, constructivists fail to study what it is like to be or have a friend in children's social worlds or how developing conceptions of friendship get embedded in peer culture.

INTERPRETIVE THEORIES   One important outcome of the acceptance of the constructivist approach in developmental psychology has been the recent translation and interpretation of the theoretical work of the Soviet psychologist, Vygotsky (Vygotsky 1978, Wertsch 1986). Vygotsky's views extend the constructivist emphasis on children's activities beyond acknowledging that they are interactive events to emphasizing that such events are basic to producing and maintaining cultural systems. Although Vygotsky provided a foundation for a more culturally oriented view of socialization, much of his research focused on individual development.

Vygotsky's views have, however, influenced a number of scholars who argue that theories of socialization must break free from the individualistic doctrine that sees social development solely as the private internalization of adult skills and knowledge (Bruner 1986, Cicourel 1974, Corsaro 1988, Valsiner 1987, Wertsch 1989). These theorists offer an interpretive approach which maintains that childhood socialization is a collective process that occurs in a public rather than a private realm. In this view, it is "not just that the child must make his knowledge his own, but that he must make it his own in a community of those who share his sense of belonging to a culture" (Bruner 1986:127). The approach is essentially interpretive, stressing that children discover a world endowed with meaning and help to shape and share in their own developmental experiences through their participation in everyday cultural routines (Corsaro & Rizzo 1988, Schieffelin & Ochs 1986).

Although the degree of children's participation in such routines is affected by cultural values and increases with age and experience, the interpretive view calls into question the linear model of socialization that sees childhood only as a period of apprenticeship that prepares children for competent membership in adult society. The interpretive approach views development as reproductive rather than linear. From this perspective, children enter into a social nexus and, by interacting and negotiating with others, establish understandings that become fundamental social knowledge on which they continually build. Thus, the interpretive model refines the notion of stages by viewing development as a productive-reproductive process of increasing density and a reorganization of knowledge that changes with children's developing cognitive and language abilities and with changes in their social worlds.

A major change in children's worlds is their movement outside the family. By interacting with playmates in organized play groups and nursery schools, children produce the first in a series of peer cultures in which childhood knowledge and practices are gradually transformed into the knowledge and skills necessary to participate in the adult world. A major aim of the interpretive approach is the documentation of peer cultures and the development of a better understanding of their crucial role in childhood socialization.

Peer Cultures as Autonomous and Creative Social Systems

Children's participation in cultural routines is an essential element of the socialization process. In adult-child interaction, children are often exposed to social knowledge they do not fully grasp. However, because of the predictable participant structure of cultural routines, interaction normally continues in an orderly fashion, and ambiguities are often left to be pursued over the course of children's interactive experiences. A frequent pattern involves children's exposure to social knowledge and communicative demands in everyday activities with adults which raise confusions, uncertainties, fears and conflicts that are later reproduced and readdressed in the activities and routines making up peer culture (Corsaro 1985).

However, the production of peer culture is a matter neither of simple imitation nor of direct appropriation of the adult world. Children creatively appropriate information from the adult world to produce their own unique peer cultures. Such appropriation is creative in that it both extends or elaborates peer culture (transforms information from the adult world to meet the concerns of the peer world) and simultaneously contributes to the reproduction of the adult culture. Thus, children's peer cultures have an autonomy and irreducibility (Willis 1981) that make them worthy of documentation and study in their own right.

We refer to this process of creative appropriation as *interpretive reproduction* in line with Giddens' notion of the duality of social structure. In his theory of structuration Giddens argues that "the structural properties of social systems are both medium and outcome of the practices they recursively organize" (1984:25). It is in this sense that the interpretive approach differs from other reproductive theories of socialization and education (Bowles & Gintis 1976, Bourdieu & Passeron 1977). These theories have focused primarily on access to cultural resources and differential treatment by teachers which leads to socialization and education outcomes in line with the prevailing class system. In this deterministic view the "actually varied, complex, and creative field of human consciousness, culture, and capacity is reduced to the dry abstraction of structural determination" (Willis 1981:204).

In contrast, in the interpretive view structure is seen as both constraining and enabling. The process is interpretive in the sense that children do not merely individually internalize the external adult culture. Rather children become a part of adult culture and contribute to its reproduction through their negotiations with adults and their creative production of a series of peer cultures with other children.

A major task for socialization theorists is the identification of the central elements of peer cultures throughout childhood and adolescence. Once identified these elements can then be analyzed in terms of their meaning, their organizational significance within peer culture, and for their contribution to the reproduction of the adult world. We now turn to a review of studies that have begun to address these issues.

PEER CULTURE IN EARLY CHILDHOOD

The Social Worlds of Young Children

Although children's sense of belonging to a peer culture is supported and extended in a wide range of social-ecological settings, the direct study of peer interaction is relatively recent, with most studies confined to a single setting (usually the school classroom or playground). There have, however, been a few studies in the home, neighborhood, and community.

Research on the sharing and transmission of peer culture through interaction with siblings or playmates in the home setting is rare. The pioneering research by Dunn (1988, also see Schutze et al 1986) on the sibling relationship provides some clues to how the wider peer culture is first introduced to young children by older siblings. Recent cross-cultural research on language socialization is useful in estimating the role of siblings (Eisenberg 1986, Miller 1986).

In addition to interaction with siblings, young children normally have extended contact with same age peers in the home. Although such interactive experiences vary across cultural, social class, and ethnic groups, for most children these interactions involve fairly brief periods of play with one or two other children under close parental supervision. Mueller (1972) has documented how object-centered contacts (cooperative play with toys) serve as a basis for the emergence of social interchange during the second year. With further language development these interchanges are expanded to shared routines among toddlers who have a history of interaction and may serve as the beginnings of friendship and a peer culture (Budwig et al 1986, Vandell & Mueller 1980).

Studies of peer play and culture in the neighborhood and community are more numerous. While Heath's (1983) impressive study of language, life, and work in communities and classrooms documents young children's introduction to peer culture in neighborhoods in small town and rural settings, Goodwin's (1989) ethnography of elementary school children sheds light on children's production of peer culture on the streets of Philadelphia. A growing number of studies look at peer interaction and culture in the neighborhood and playground outside the United States. The classic descriptions of children's folklore by Opie & Opie (1959, 1969) and Gomme (1964) generated interest in children's social worlds in Europe. Recently we have seen a movement toward more analytic work on children's cultures with important research by Berentzen (1989) on Norwegian children's peer culture in the home and neighborhood, and Katriel's (1985; 1987) studies of peer routines in the everyday life of Israeli children.

With a majority of young children now attending child care and early education programs in most industrial societies, there is increasing concern about the effects of such experiences on children's lives. As a result, we have seen several studies of children's play and culture in preschool settings (Berentzen 1984, Corsaro 1985, 1988, Corsaro & Rizzo 1988, Mandell 1986). Finally, there have been additional studies of elementary school children's peer culture in the classroom and playground (Best 1983, Davies 1982, Hanna 1988, Rizzo 1989, Sluckin 1981, Thorne 1986).

Overall, recent research has identified specific processes, routines, concerns, and values in children's cultures. The studies suggest that peer culture emerges, develops, and is maintained and refined across the various social settings making up children's worlds. We now turn to a review of these findings and an interpretation of their importance for peer culture.

Social Relations and Peer Concerns

Although a wide range of features of the peer culture of young children have been identified, two central themes consistently appear: children make persistent attempts to *gain control* of their lives and to *share* that control with each other. In the preschool years there is an overriding concern with social participation and with challenging and gaining control over adult authority. Once children move into elementary school such challenging of adult authority persists, but there is also a gradual movement toward social differentiation within the peer group. This differentiation is marked by negotiations and conflicts as children attempt to gain control over the attitudes and behaviors of peers.

SHARING AND FRIENDSHIP   A consistent finding in studies of young children's peer interaction is that solitary play is rare and that children expend considerable time and energy in establishing and maintaining peer contacts (Corsaro 1985, Rizzo 1989, Rubin et al 1976). Gaining access to play groups, maintaining joint action, and making friends are complex processes for young children. Gaining access is particularly difficult in preschool settings since young children tend to protect shared space, objects, and ongoing play itself from the intrusions of others. Corsaro (1985) argues that this tendency is directly related to the fragility of peer interaction, the multiple possibilities of disruption in most preschool settings, and the children's desire to maintain control over shared activities. Several studies (Corsaro 1979, Dodge et al 1983, Forbes et al 1982) have documented the complex "access strategies" children develop in their persistent attempts to overcome resistance to entry bids. These strategies reflect children's acquisition of essential social skills for entry into and participation in peer culture.

Having gained access to play groups, children discover that it is in the course of shared play that the meaning of the concepts of *friend* and *peer* arise. For example, Corsaro (1981) found that nursery school children use their developing conception of friendship to build solidarity and mutual trust, often marking the importance of shared activity with the phrase "We're friends, right?" On the other hand, while friendship serves these specific integrative functions for nursery school children, Corsaro noted few examples of enduring friendships based on the recognition of personal characteristics of playmates. However, this finding does not deny that such friendships may exist among preschool children in the home and neighborhood. Clearly there is a need for studies of children's friendships in such settings.

Rizzo (1989) reports that first grade children appeared to have an internalized concept of friendship which served multiple functions in peer relations. Specifically, Rizzo found that first grade children "attempted to determine the existence of friendship by comparing the internal concept with specific features of interactions with frequent playmates, to act in accordance with this concept when with their friends, and to object when their friends failed to live up to their expectations" (Rizzo 1989:105). Rizzo argues further that disputes resulting from such objects not only helped the children obtain a better understanding of what they could expect from each other as friends, but also brought about intrapersonal reflection resulting in the children's development of unique insight into their own actions and roles as friends (see Davies 1982 and Goodwin 1982a for similar findings regarding disputes and friendship).

Several studies have identified routines that stress communal sharing in peer culture: Goodwin's (1985) study of negotiations during the game of "jump rope"; Mishler (1979) on "trading and bargaining" of six year olds at lunchtime in elementary school; and Katriel's (1987) analysis of ritualized sharing among Israeli children. Although the identification of such routines is central in studies of peer culture, we only have space to discuss Katriel's study in some detail.

The sharing routine Katriel identified *(xibùdim)* usually occurred on the way home from school:

> A group of five children approaches the *falafel* [snack or treat] stand. One exclaims "I'm buying." Another counters, *"Bexibùdim! Bexibùdim!"* in a melodious chant. He gets a *falafel* portion, holds it in his hands, and all take a bite in turn, with a gay clamor. After the third one has eaten, the buyer mutters, *"Hey, beraxmanut"* (with pity) and offers it to the last child. He then eats his falafel, walking along with his friends. (Katriel 1987:309)

As the example illustrates, the routine has a definite structure: (*a*) *opening* or announcement of an intention to buy a treat by a particular child; (*b*) *acknowledgment* by other children usually involving the exclamation *"Bexibùdim! bexibùdim!"* uttered in a melodious chant; (*c*) the *purchase* of the treat by the proposer; (*d*) the *offering* and sharing of the treat, with each accompanying child taking a small bite; and (*e*) the optional *recycling* of a second round of sharing. As we can see from the example, the sharing routine involves delicate negotiation in that, as Katriel has noted, the bite size has to be regulated so that everybody gets a share with about half of the treat left for the owner (e.g. the owner's request for pity before offering the last bite, in the example). This and other aspects of the routine support Katriel's insightful interpretation of the routine as a "symbolic sacrifice in which one's self-interest and primordial greed are controlled and subordinated to an idea of sociality shaped by particular cultural values, such as equality and generalized reciprocity" (1987:318).

CONTROL AND AUTONOMY   Children's attempts to challenge adult authority and gain control over their lives are a major aspect of peer culture from the earliest years. For example, Dunn (1988) reports a major increase in amusement at forbidden acts between 14 and 24 months in children she studied in home settings. Laughing at such misdeeds was also often shared with older siblings as a challenge to parental authority. Once children enter child care and education settings, they quickly develop a strong group identity (Corsaro 1985, Rubin 1980) that is strengthened by challenging and even mocking teachers and other adult caretakers (Best 1983, Corsaro 1985, Davies 1982). Additionally, children produce a wide set of innovative routines and practices that indirectly challenge and circumvent adult authority (Berentzen 1989, Corsaro 1990, Davies 1982, Hanna 1988, Nasaw 1985).

Corsaro (1985, 1990), in line with Goffman (1961), has referred to such routines as secondary adjustments. A frequent secondary adjustment involves the use of subterfuge. For example in both the United States and Italy there was a rule that prohibited (or severely restricted) the bringing of toys or other personal objects from home to nursery school. Such objects were attractive to other children because they were different from the everyday materials in the school. As a result, the teachers were constantly settling disputes about sharing the personal objects. Therefore, the rule specified that such objects should not be brought to school, and if they were, they must be stored in one's locker until the end of the day. In both the American and Italian schools that Corsaro studied, the children attempted to evade this rule by bringing small personal objects that they could easily conceal in their pockets. Particular favorites were toy animals, Matchbox cars, sweets, and chewing gum. Sweets were a preferred choice because the child and peers could share the forbidden objects and then go on to consume the evidence, often with teachers close at hand.

The teachers often overlook these violations because the nature of the secondary adjustments often eliminates the organizational need to enforce the rule. The children share and play with smuggled personal objects surreptitiously to avoid detection by the teachers. If the children always played with personal objects in this fashion, there would be no conflict and hence no need for the rule. Thus, "in an indirect way the secondary adjustment endorses the organizational need for the rule" (Corsaro 1990:23).

Finally, children attempt to gain control over fears, confusions, and curiosities from the adult world through their participation in numerous play routines, rituals, and games (Corsaro 1985, Garvey 1984, Goodwin 1985, 1988, Gottman 1986). Corsaro (1988, Corsaro & Heise 1989) has identified the structure and meaning of one such play routine in the peer culture of American and Italian children. The routine ("approach-avoidance") involves the identification of a threatening agent or monster, the careful approach, and the escape from the monster after an attack ensues.

The routine has two key features. First, the threatened children have a great deal of control because they initiate and recycle the routine through their approach, and they have a reliable means of escape (home base) in the avoidance phase. Second, in the production of the routine the children share in the building tension, excitement of the threat, and relief and joy of the escape. Overall, approach-avoidance demonstrates how children cope with real fears by incorporating them into peer routines they produce and control. Several cross-cultural studies of children's play (Schwartzman 1978, Barlow 1985) report variants of the approach-avoidance routine, suggesting that the routine may be a universal feature of peer culture.

CONFLICT AND SOCIAL DIFFERENTIATION   While social participation and friendship are central elements of peer culture, there is a clear pattern of increased differentiation and conflict in peer relations throughout childhood. The first sign of social differentiation is increasing gender separation. Gender segregation begins in preschool (Berentzen 1984) and becomes so dramatic in elementary school that "it is meaningful to speak of separate girls' and boys' worlds" (Thorne 1986:167). Studies of these separate worlds show that boys interact in larger groups (Lever 1976), engage in more aggressive and competitive play (Best 1983, Goodwin 1980ab), and frequently organize their activities and relations around organized sports (Fine 1987, Lever 1976, Thorne & Luria 1986).

Thorne, however, argues that much of the research tends to exaggerate difference, and that the studies "ignore similarities, with little theoretical effort to integrate findings of both similarity and difference: (1986:170). She (1986, 1989; Thorne & Luria 1986) offers a social contextual approach that stresses variation in cross-gender contacts or "borderwork," travelling in the world of the other sex (e.g. "tomboys"), and situations of easeful cross-gender interaction. Thorne's work along with recent research by Goodwin (1980ab, 1985, 1989) and Hughes (1988) challenges many earlier findings regarding the lack of conflict and competition in girls' interactions and the simple structure of girls' peer play.

This recent research on conflict in girls' peer interaction reflects a growing interest in the role of conflict in children's friendships and peer culture (Shantz 1987, Shantz & Hobart 1989). Studies of conflict in peer culture challenge the assumption that such behavior is inherently disruptive and disorderly, demonstrating that conflicts and disputes provide children with a rich arena for the development of language, interpersonal and social organization skills and knowledge (Goodwin & Goodwin 1988).

Although preschool children frequently quarrel over possession of play materials and entry into play groups, they are also capable of highly complex arguments and debates regarding the nature of fantasy play and claims or opinions about their social and physical worlds (Corsaro & Rizzo 1988, 1990, Eisenberg & Garvey 1981, Genishi & Di Paolo 1982, Pontecorvo & Orsolini 1989). Research on peer conflict among elementary school children clearly shows how disputes are a basic means for constructing social order, cultivating, testing, and maintaining friendships, and developing and displaying social identity (Boggs 1978, Davies 1982, Fine 1987, Goodwin 1980ab, 1982a, Goodwin & Goodwin 1988, Katriel 1985, Maynard 1985, Rizzo 1989).

An especially impressive example of research on children's dispute routines is Goodwin's (1980a) analysis of gossip disputes among black female preadolescents. Unlike the direct competitive disputes of males (Goodwin 1982a, Labov 1972), black females frequently engage in gossip disputes during which absent parties are evaluated. The airing of such grievances frequently culminates in he-said-she-said confrontions in which one girl (A) challenges another girl (B) about what B told a third girl (C) about A.

Goodwin's analysis specifies the complex linguistic embedding structures that the children use in such confrontations to order a field of events, negotiate identities, and to construct social order. The gossip routine is important because it is inappropriate to insult, command, or accuse others openly in the girls' peer culture. Thus, the he-said-she-said routine provides "an event through which complaints about others may be aired and character may be generated" (Goodwin 1980a:688).

Overall, this review indicates the existence of a rich peer culture among young children. From the first years of life, children collectively produce innovative peer cultures that play a central role in the socialization process. The review also demonstrates the importance of studying socialization experiences from the children's perspective by directly entering their everyday worlds.

PEER CULTURE IN ADOLESCENCE

Peer Relations

Studies of adolescent culture in school settings consistently report that being with friends is the most salient aspect of school life for most students (Cusick 1972, Everhart 1983, Willis 1981). This is largely because friendship groups provide students with the opportunities to engage in interactions that provide the basis of their culture. Through these interactions youth develop their own interpretations of significant meanings while they produce humorous and other playful routines which become central to their microcultures (Everhart 1983, Willis 1981, Fine 1987, Wulff 1988).

During adolescence, best friendships are also increasingly valued as a source of mutual intimacy. Many adolescents report that their best friendships are characterized by acceptance, understanding, self-disclosure, and mutual advice. Close friendships provide adolescents with an important opportunity for developing greater self-knowledge through a process of mutual reflection. In contrast, parents are perceived as being less accepting and more likely to act as experts or authorities. Since these factors are likely to impede the process of mutual reflection, adolescents tend to discuss their problems, feelings, fears, and doubts with best friends rather than parents (Youniss & Smollar 1985).

The importance of mutual intimacy and openness in friendship increases during adolescence, often replacing the importance of friendship choices based on popularity (Youniss & Smollar 1985). Loyalty and commitment also become more salient in later adolescence, often replacing the importance of shared activities (Bigelow & LaGaipa 1980). Finally, older adolescents tend to be more similar in terms of attitudes toward school, college plans, and achievement than are younger adolescents (Epstein 1983). This greater similarity is assumed to be the result both of more selectivity in choosing friends and of peer influence.

There is also considerable diversity in the experience and basis of friendship for females and males. As in early childhood, female friendship groups tend to be closely knit and egalitarian, while male friendship groups tend to be loosely knit with clear status hierarchies (Karweit & Hansell 1983). For example, Youniss & Smollar (1985) found that female friends are more likely to engage in intimate disclosure, sharing their problems, feelings, fears, and doubts with their close friends. However, while males are less likely to engage in intimate disclosure, 40% of the close male friendships in their study did involve a high degree of mutual intimacy. For other males, shared activities continue to be an important basis for friendship throughout adolescence. These findings indicate that while gender and developmental differences are important in the experience of friendship, there is also considerable diversity within gender groups as well as within groups of adolescents of the same age.

Finally, there are important differences in the experience of friendship by social class. In an ethnographic study of high school students, Eckert (1988) found that students from middle-class backgrounds, and especially those who were members of elite groups, were more likely to base their friendships on interests and activities, often switching their friendships as their interests change. In contrast, students from working-class backgrounds placed more emphasis on loyalty and stability, with friendships determining their involvement in activities instead of vice versa. Lesko (1988) reports similar findings from her ethnographic study of a Catholic high school. Girls who were members of the elite group tended to value social and academic competition and were less loyal to their friends than were girls in other groups.

These findings point to the importance of peer status in adolescence. As students move into middle or junior high schools, they are suddenly confronted with a much larger group of same age peers. This allows for the possibility of more cliques forming as well as for a hierarchy of cliques to be established. If certain students have more positive visibility they are likely to form the core of the elite group since in this type of environment, status is often based on "being known" by your peers (Eder 1985).

Adolescents are most likely to gain positive visibility through participation in extracurricular activities, especially those like male athletics that draw large groups of spectators (Gordon 1957, Coleman 1961, Cusick 1973, Karweit 1983, Eder & Parker 1987). These activities also tend to give positive visibility to female cheerleaders (Eder 1985, Eder & Parker 1987). Status hierarchies are often unidimensional in early adolescence, with limited avenues for peer status for both males and females. This may be due in part to the fact that middle school and junior high schools tend to offer fewer extracurricular activities but may also reflect a greater concern with school-wide popularity at this age. In high school, several elite groups may be based on different types of activities (Larkin 1979), with participation in multiple activities often leading to higher status (Karweit 1983).

On the other end of the continuum, several studies have focused on rejected children; these studies find that children who are disliked by their peers in early childhood continue to be disliked in adolescence (Coie & Dodge 1983, Coie et al 1988). These psychologists attribute such persistent rejection to poor social skills and aggressive behavior on the part of the rejected children. However, another study, focused on "bullies" and "whipping boys," found that bullies tended to initiate the most fights and that "whipping boys," who tended to be disliked by peers, were more often the targets of aggression (Olweus 1978). Olweus believes that a variety of social processes contribute to the persistence of these patterns, including social contagion or the tendency for other peers to imitate the aggressive "bullies." Using an ethnographic approach, Evans & Eder (1989) also found that isolates in middle school tend to be the targets of aggression and that the persistence of the rejection is due in part to attempts by other students to distinguish themselves from those students they perceive to be deviant. The processes which contribute to low peer status and peer rejection need further investigation since rejected students are often not members of peer groups and thus are not exposed to important aspects of peer culture.

Peer Concerns

While the main concerns of the peer culture of students from middle-class backgrounds are closely tied to visible school activities and to the dynamics for obtaining peer status, peer concerns of working-class students often represent a rejection of academic concerns and the social values of the elite group. Also, to the extent that concern with peer status decreases in later adolescence, it is often accompanied by increased diversity in peer subcultures.

One of the early studies of adolescent culture found white middle-class males to be primarily concerned with athletic skills, dating, sexual prowess, and drinking prowess (Schwartz & Merton 1966). More recent studies report a continued interest in athletic and other extracurricular activities through which middle-class males receive status from peers as well as some control over school resources including use of space and time (Eckert 1988). Some athletic events, such as football, continue to promote a concern with toughness and aggression even among middle and upper middle class males (Kessler et al 1985, Eder & Parker 1987). Other recent studies have found a trend toward greater diversity within white middle-class males, leading to the development of numerous microcultures with distinct interests and concerns (Kinney 1989).

The avenues for peer status for white middle-class girls are based less on achievement. In early adolescence, middle-class females gain status through activities such as cheerleading and through friendships with popular girls (Eder 1985). This contributes to a greater focus on social skills and a greater concern with being well liked (Rosenberg & Simmons 1975). By high school, there is again more diversity among white middle-class girls. Girls in more elite groups are concerned with being "in everything," and they see the ideal student as someone with lots of involvements (Lesko 1988). Other middle-class girls, described as "mellows" or "normals," place a stronger emphasis on friendship and are often more concerned with family and nonschool activities (Lesko 1988, Kinney 1989).

Working-class males tend to have much less control over school resources, thus a major concern within their subcultures is seeking more control over their lives through defiance of rules, authority, and academic work (Willis 1981, Everhart 1983). Their peer cultures also focus on fighting, insult exchanges, and other forms of humor since these are activities over which they have more control and which are viewed as masculine (Kessler et al 1985, Willis 1981). Other studies have examined working-class students in the "burnout" subculture (Eckert 1988, Lesko 1988) where there is an open pursuit of pleasure through drinking, smoking, and "bumming" around.

Studies of black working-class and lower-class males have reported similar findings. The main concerns of the street peer groups in inner-city neighborhoods were toughness, trouble, excitement, autonomy, and cleverness. Status among these males was determined primarily by courage and skill in physical fighting, experience in deviant behavior, and skills in various verbal activities such as ritual insulting, story-telling, and joke-telling (Labov 1972). A study of working-class blacks in a junior high school found that they perceived themselves and were perceived by others to be tough, aggressive rule breakers, unconcerned with school (Schofield 1982). MacLeod (1987), however, found that while white lower-class males were concerned with fighting ability, quick wit, and group solidarity, black males were more concerned with athletic ability and male-female interaction. He also found that black males were more involved in school activities, especially athletic activities, and had higher career aspirations than did white males.

White working-class females are also often likely to view themselves as "non-conformists" and "trouble-makers" within the school environment. However, they are more likely than males to engage in less visible forms of deviance during class such as reading magazines, passing notes, and day-dreaming (Griffin 1985; Wulff 1988). Those who join "burnout" peer cultures openly pursue pleasure and are explicit about their sexuality, with some females emphasizing sensuality in their appearance (Lesko 1988). At the same time, in these groups there is less concern with "being nice" and more directness in interaction styles than is found among many middle-class females (Goodwin 1982, Lesko 1988).

Some studies have found considerable ethnic diversity in the concerns of working-class females. While white females are often concerned with romance and marriage as a source of status, black and Asian females are more critical of romance myths and less concerned with getting a boyfriend (McRobbie 1978, Griffin 1985). However, a study of an interracial group of working-class females in Britain (Wulff 1988) found that these girls had many similar concerns and were primarily interested in "growing up," which meant having more responsibility as well as having romantic and sexual relationships. They were also concerned with excitement and heightened pleasure as well as with ethnicity and expressions of ethnicity. Because these girls had frequent opportunities to interact through the youth club, they were developing perspectives on ethnicity that differed from those of their parents and were also developing concerns and perspectives that crossed ethnic boundaries.

Interactive Processes and Language Activities

Ethnographers and sociolinguists have recently begun to pay more attention to the processes by which adolescent peer cultures are created. Willis (1981), for example, found that informal group interaction and humor are essential elements for creating and maintaining a counter-culture. His work demonstrates how everyday activities are critical for establishing a shared interpretation on what it means to be working-class males.

Wulff (1988) has argued that microcultures often have considerable diversity, including individuals with different ideas, interests, and perspectives. She views culture as something *distributed* among people in a group, with some individuals reflecting certain meanings more strongly through their personalities than do others. For example, the most popular girl in the club embodied the shared value of maturity.

> As long as Doreen remained a member of the club, she was its most popular member, the girl whom the greatest number of the others would describe as a friend. She was more of a young woman than the others: tall, beautiful, often with a sophisticated hair style. She could also tell stories about love dramas at parties for older teenagers. At the same time, her maturity distanced her slightly from the rest of the girls, but this only increased their admiration for her. (Wulff 1988, p. 75)

Certain localities and events can also manifest the meanings of the subculture. Thus, a subculture is created through shared significant events, recurrent or unique experiences in certain localities, and the appearance and behaviors of certain individuals.

Another approach to understanding the creation of subcultures is to examine the language activities that provide the basis for informal group life. As in research on younger children, the concern is to identify the resources and skills needed to build the interaction. Such construction often involves adolescents incorporating their own unique contributions and modifications to aspects of adult culture. Language activities are crucial for culture production since it is through language that shared interpretations develop. Some of the activities in which adolescents routinely engage include insulting, teasing, story-telling, and gossip.

Although most research on insulting has involved black male adolescents (Labov 1972, Kochman 1983, Goodwin 1982a), recent studies have looked at such speech events among white males and black and white working-class females (Everhart 1983, Goodwin 1982a). Studies of ritual insulting among males have shown how being able to interpret insults as playful and responding with more clever or elaborate insults are essential skills for successful participation in certain male subcultures. Males who lack these skills are more likely to become targets of serious ridicule or physical attacks as the conflict escalates (Labov 1972, Everhart 1983). On the other hand, by responding playfully to insults, a sense of solidarity based on shared interpretation is developed (Everhart 1983). At the same time, since this activity is often competitive in nature it also provides males with a way to establish and reinforce status hierarchies (Labov 1972, Goodwin 1982a).

Another form of group humor that has been studied recently is playful teasing. Here again, interpreting teasing remarks as playful and responding in a playful manner are essential skills (Fine 1984, Eder 1990). If someone failed to respond in a playful manner when being teased, other group members might encourage them to not take the teasing comments seriously as in this example from a group of seventh grade girls:

Nancy was there today and they were teasing her about putting catsup on her food and also about how short her pants were. (They are her mother's pants and are two inches too short.) Also, when she was gone, Betty wrote in Nancy's book and Nancy was really angry with her when she came back. Most of the girls in the group were looking at Nancy and laughing; they kept saying, "Laugh." They wanted her to laugh and not be angry, or be able to be kidded. (Eder 1990, p. 8)

On the other hand, some adolescents were able to turn a potentially serious insult into a teasing remark by responding playfully, as in this example:

They were kidding Sylvia for awhile about her name and various things. Then at one point Rita said, "Sylvia's showing off her bra with her white tee-shirt," referring to the fact that you could see her bra through her tee shirt. Sylvia wasn't insulted or hurt. Instead she lifted up her shirt and said, "When I show off my bra, I'll do it like this!" (Eder 1990, p. 24).

Finally, teasing is more loosely structured than ritual insulting, allowing for collaborative participation which can build solidarity among the "teasers" as well as the targets. While there is a loose structure and familiarity to teasing routines, they also allow novel responses given their playful, humorous nature.

Storytelling is also a common activity among adolescents, taking a variety of forms including fight stories and collaborative narratives. Since stories are based on past experiences, full participation depends on shared experiences among group members. In fact, the greater the prior shared knowledge, the more likely group members will be able to interpret the story accurately. Shuman (1986) found that the females who had the most knowledge about a fight were entitled to tell fight stories, and only those who were close friends were allowed to hear certain fight stories such as those involving family disputes. Other studies have found that storytelling is used among males to demonstrate cleverness and the importance of certain events (Labov 1972, Goodwin 1982a). Finally, storytelling in peer culture is often collaborative (Goodwin 1982b, Eder 1988) with collaboration serving both to strengthen group ties and to allow for the development of shared perceptions and orientations.

Although gossip is a common activity among adolescents, it has not been adequately studied. In a study of younger adolescents, Eder & Enke (1988) found that gossip was an important means for transmitting gender concerns regarding appearance and conceited behavior. Male gossip, on the other hand, occurred less frequently and focused primarily on the athletic achievements and physical abilities of other males. There was a strong emphasis on consensus within groups making it difficult for members to express counter viewpoints unless they spoke up immediately. However, on certain topics such as romance there was less consensus, since here gossip was a means for developing new group norms. Parker & Gottman (1989) also found that gossip was primarily used for group solidarity in early adolescence, but that in later adolescence, gossip provided an entry into the psychological exploration of the self. In another study of older adolescent females, Fine (1986) found that gossip was used primarily to clarify moral concerns and values. The females Fine studied were concerned with reaching consensus, and they minimized potential conflict by expressing counter views in ways that allowed their views to be easily modified.

These studies of speech activities suggest that some activities are more predominant in some subcultures than are others, and that the functions that certain speech activities serve within a given subculture may change over time. Many of the studies show how speech activities serve to make meanings and interpretations visible to others, thus making shared meanings possible. Through detailed study of activities such as these, we can better understand the role which adolescents play in defining and shaping their own peer cultures.

CENTRAL THEMES IN PEER CULTURE FROM EARLY CHILDHOOD THROUGH ADOLESCENCE

A major feature of the socialization process is children's production of and participation in a series of peer cultures in which childhood knowledge and practices are gradually transformed into the knowledge and skills necessary to participate in the adult world. Although there have been no longitudinal studies documenting children's transition from one peer culture to another, the previous review of recent studies allows us to identify specific patterns and themes of peer cultures throughout childhood and adolescence.

One central theme in peer culture is the importance of *sharing* and *social participation*. In the preschool and early elementary school years children immensely enjoy simply doing things together (Corsaro 1985, Parker & Gottman 1989). However, generating shared meaning and coordinating play are difficult tasks for young children. Thus, children spend a great deal of time creating and protecting basic activities and routines in their peer culture (Corsaro 1985). Although these routines reflect a range of concerns in the peer culture, they most importantly provide young children with a sense of excitement and emotional security.

In preadolescence and adolescence, children easily generate and sustain peer activities. However, they have now collectively produced a set of stratified groups, and issues of acceptance, popularity, and group solidarity become paramount. The primarily nonverbal play routines of early childhood are gradually replaced by verbal activities (Labov 1972, Goodwin 1982, Fine 1987). Gossip is a central activity since it reaffirms peer group membership and reveals basic values and beliefs of group members (Eder & Enke 1988, Parker & Gottman 1989).

A second central theme of peer culture involves children's attempts *to deal with confusions, concerns, fears, and conflicts* in their daily lives. Although some of these disturbances are generated within the peer culture itself, they often arise from children's experiences in the adult world. Young children are frequently warned of dangers by caretakers and more indirectly through their exposures to movies and fairy tales. Children, in turn, frequently incorporate a wide range of fears and dangers (from threatening agents such as monsters and witches to dangerous events like fires, floods, and becoming lost) into their peer culture. By engaging in shared fantasy play (Corsaro 1985, Gottman 1986) and producing games, routines, and rituals (Corsaro 1988, Schwartzman 1978) children more firmly grasp and deal with social representations of evil and the unknown in the security of the peer culture.

For older children, the peer group (especially same-sex friendship groups) provides a secure base for making sense of and dealing with new demands regarding personal relations, sexuality, and identity development (Fine 1981, Parker & Gottman 1989). Everyday activities in preadolescent and adolescent culture enable peers to negotiate and explore a wide range of norms regarding: personal appearance and the presentation of self, friendship processes, heterosexual relations, and personal aspirations and achievement. Through activities like gossip, teasing and insult routines, collaborative story-telling, and humor (Eder 1988, 1989, Eder & Enke 1988, Fine 1984, 1987, Goodwin 1982a,b, Labov 1972, Lesko 1988, Wulff 1988), adolescents indirectly explore developing norms and expectations without the risk of direct confrontation and embarrassment.

A final theme in peer culture is children's *resistance to and challenging of adult rules and authority*. Children challenge adult rules in the family from the first years of life (Dunn 1988, Miller 1986). Such activity becomes more widespread and sophisticated when children discover their common interests in day care settings and nursery schools. In such settings children cooperatively produce a wide set of practices in which they both mock and evade adult authority. In fact, many of these "secondary adjustments" to adult rules are more complex (structurally and interactively) than the rules themselves (Corsaro 1985, 1989).

Although older children continue to resist adult authority, early childhood and preadolescent cultures are characterized by a focus on interpersonal relations and differences among peers. However, with greater freedom and autonomy on the one hand and lack of full adult status on the other, resistance of adult authority reemerges as an important feature of adolescent peer culture (Griffin 1985, Wulff 1988). In fact, several studies of working-class males have documented the existence and significance of well-developed "counter cultures" for adolescent socialization and education (Everhart 1983, Willis 1981). Overall, it is clear that the resistance of adult rules and authority provides children with a sense of control and autonomy, and for this reason such resistance may be a universal feature of peer culture.

While recent studies have allowed us to identify the above patterns, there are still substantial gaps in our knowledge of children's peer cultures. First, although the number of studies of routines and language activities in peer culture has increased, a clear need exists for more research of this type. Routines and language activities are of crucial importance because it is through such activities that peer culture is produced and maintained. Second, most of the studies to date have identified features of peer culture in educational settings or other formal organizations like clubs or athletic teams. More work is needed in informal settings like the home, neighborhood, and playground as well as in businesses that cater to youth (fast food restaurants, shopping malls, cinemas, video game salons, etc). In some of these environments such as neighborhood settings, adolescents are less likely to be segregated by gender, and they tend to engage in a wider variety of activities. Thus, peer interaction in these settings is important for exposing adolescents to a greater diversity of peer cultures and interactive styles (Goodwin 1989). We also need to know much more about children's peer relations in the work place. Some of the best work on peer culture in work settings is the historical analysis by Nasaw (1985) on American urban children at the turn of the century and by Berggreen (1988) on Norwegian children. Both of these studies show how children's work and play often coexisted and how peer culture was tied to the requirements and the economic rewards of labor. Recent studies by Solberg (1988) on Norwegian children's work in the home, by Gullestad (1988) on young girls' interactions while "walking" and caring for infants in Oslo, and by Hundeide (1988) comparing the social worlds of Norwegian and Asian children nicely demonstrate the importance of work in the peer culture of young children. Studies such as these not only increase our knowledge of features of peer culture, they also provide the kind of comparative data necessary to document cultural diffusion (Fine 1987).

Although there have been several ethnographic studies of particular peer groups over several months or even years, no longitudinal studies chart children's transitions from one peer culture to another. A clear need exists for such studies of children as they move from preschool settings to elementary school, from elementary school to junior high, from junior high to high school, and finally from high school to college or full-time employment. Finally, historical and cross-cultural work on children's peer cultures is lacking. Such studies are necessary for discovering universal features of peer culture and for documenting how elements of the world of children and adults interact over time and across diverse cultural groups.

A great deal of theoretical development and research on peer relations and friendships has occurred recently in developmental psychology (Berndt & Ladd 1989, Gottman & Parker 1986, Mueller & Cooper 1986). Most of this work is in line with what we earlier referred to as the constructivist approach to socialization. Overall, this research has greatly increased our knowledge of children's peer relations and social development. In fact, some studies have reported findings and interpretations very much in line with the general trends in peer culture we outlined above (Gottman & Mettetal 1986, Parker & Gottman 1989). However, the focus of these studies is on individual development. Social structure and culture are seen as "social-ecological niches" that embody demands to which individual children must adapt (Parker & Gottman 1989).

As we argued earlier, sociological approaches to socialization must break free from this individualistic emphasis. Social structure and culture are not merely static niches or environments, they are public and collective processes of negotiation and interpretative apprehension (Cicourel 1974, Geertz 1973, Rosaldo 1984). From this interpretive perspective, socialization is not only a matter of adaptation and internalization, but also a process of appropriation, reinvention, and reproduction. Central to this view of socialization is the appreciation of the importance of communal activity—children's negotiating, sharing, and joint culture creating with adults and peers (Bruner 1986, Vygotsky 1978). Although recent work on both adult-child and peer interaction from this interpretive perspective has greatly increased our understanding in this area, much work remains to be done.

Literature Cited

Asher, S. R., Gottman, J., eds. 1981. *The Development of Children's Friendships*. New York: Cambridge Univ. Press

Bandura, 1986. *Social Foundations of Thought and Action: A Social Cognitive Theory*. Englewood Cliffs, NJ: Prentice-Hall

Barlow, K. 1985. *Play and learning in a Sepik society*. Presented at Ann. Meet. Am. Anthropol. Assoc. 84th, Washington, DC

Berentzen, S. 1984. *Children Constructing Their Social World*. Bergen Stud. Soc. Anthropol. No. 36. Bergen, Norway: Univ. Bergen

Berentzen, S. ed. 1989. *Ethnographic Approaches to Children's Worlds and Peer Cultures*. Trondheim Norway: Norwegian Ctr. Child Res.

Berentzen, S. 1989. The interactional contexts of children's peer group activities. See Berentzen 1989, pp. 9–43

Berggreen, B. 1988. Infantilization of children as an historical process. In *Proc. Conf. Growing Into a Modern World*, vol. 2, ed. K. Ekberg, P. Mjaavatn, pp. 829–42. Trondheim, Norway: Norwegian Ctr. Child Res.

Berndt, T., Ladd, G. eds. 1989. *Peer Relationships in Child Development*. New York: Wiley

Best, R. 1983. *We've All Got Scars*. Bloomington: Ind. Univ. Press

Bigelow, B. J., LaGaipa, J. 1980. The development of friendship values and choice. In *Friendship and Social Relations in Children*, ed. H. C. Foot, A. J. Chapman, J. Smith, pp. 15–44. New York: Wiley

Boggs, S. 1978. The development of verbal disputing in part-Hawaiian children. *Lang. Soc.* 7:325–44

Bourdieu, P., Passeron, J. 1977. *Reproduction*. Beverly Hills, Calif: Sage

Bowles, S., Gintis, H. 1976. *Schooling in Capitalist America*. New York: Basic

Bruner, J. 1986. *Actual Minds, Possible Worlds*. Cambridge, Mass: Harvard Univ. Press

Budwig, N., Strage, A., Bamberg, M. 1986. The construction of joint activities with an age-mate: The transition from caregiver-child to peer play. See Cook-Gumperz et al 1986, pp. 83–108

Cicourel, A. V. 1974. *Cognitive Sociology*. New York: Free

Coie, J. D., Dodge, K. A., Kupersmidt, J. 1988. Peer group behavior and social status. In *The Rejected Child*, ed. S. Asher, J. Coie, 1988. New York: Cambridge Univ. Press

Coie, J. D., Dodge, K. A. 1983. Continuities and changes in children's social status: A five-year longitudinal study. *Merrill-Pal.* 29:261–82

Coleman, J. 1961. *The Adolescent Society*. New York: Free

Cook-Gumperz, J., Corsaro, W. A., Streeck, J. eds. 1986. *Children's Worlds and Children's Language*. Berlin: Mouton

Corsaro, W. A. 1979. "We're friends, right?": Children's use of access rituals in a nursery school. *Lang. Soc.* 8:315–36

Corsaro, W. A. 1981. Friendship in the nursery school: Social organization in a peer environment. See Asher & Gottman 1981, pp. 207–41

Corsaro, W. A. 1985. *Friendship and Peer Culture in the Early Years*. Norwood, NJ: Ablex

Corsaro, W. A. 1988. Routines in the peer culture of American and Italian nursery school children. *Social Educ.* 61:1–14

Corsaro, W. A. 1990. The underlife of the nursery school: Young children's social representations of adult rules. In *Social Representations and the Development of Knowledge*, ed. B. Lloyd, G. Duveen, pp. 11–26. Cambridge: Cambridge Univ. Press

Corsaro, W. A., Rizzo, T. A. 1988. *Discussione* and friendship: Socialization processes in the peer culture of Italian nursery school children. *Am. Sociol. Rev.* 53:879–94

Corsaro, W. A., Rizzo, T. A. 1990. Disputes in the peer culture of American and Italian nursery school children. In *Conflict Talk*, ed. A. D. Grimshaw, pp. 21–66, Cambridge: Cambridge Univ. Press

Corsaro, W. A., Heise, D. R. 1989. Event structure models from ethnographic data. *Sociological Methodology*, In press

Cusick, P. 1973. *Inside High School*. New York: Holt, Rinehart & Winston

Damon, W. 1977. *The Social World of the Child*. San Francisco: Jossey-Bass

Davies, B. 1982. *Life in the Classroom and Playground: The Accounts of Primary School Children*. London: Routledge

Dodge, K., Schlundt, D., Schocken, I., De-Lugach, J. 1983. Social competence and children's sociometric status: The role of peer group entry strategies. *Merrill-Pal.* 29:309–36

Dunn, J. 1988. *The Beginnings of Social Understanding*. Oxford: Basil Blackwell

Eckert, P. 1988. Adolescent social structure and the spread of linguistic change. *Lang. Soc.* 17:183–208

Eder, D. 1985. The cycle of popularity: Interpersonal relations among female adolescents. *Sociol. Educ.* 58:154–65

Eder, D. 1988. Building cohesion through collaborative narration. *Soc. Psych. Q.* 51:-225–35

Eder, D. 1990. The role of teasing in adolescent peer culture. In *Sociological Studies of Child Development*, Vol. 4. ed., S Cahill. Greenwich, Ct: JAI. In press

Eder, D., Enke, J. 1988. *Gossip as a means for transmitting and developing social structure*. Pres. Am. Sociol. Assoc. Meet. Atlanta, Georgia

Eder, D., Parker, S. 1987. The cultural production and reproduction of gender: The effect of extracurricular activities on peer group culture. *Sociol. Educ.* 60:200–213

Eisenberg, A. 1986. Teasing: Verbal play in two Mexicano homes. See Schieffelin & Ochs 1986, pp. 182–97

Eisenberg, A., Garvey, C. 1981. Children's use of verbal strategies in resolving conflicts. *Discourse Processes* 4:149–70

Ekberg, K., Mjaavatn, P. E., eds. 1988. *Proc. Conf. Growing Into a Modern World*, Vols. 1, 2, & 3, Trondheim, Norway, 1987 Trondheim: Norwegian Centre

Epstein, J. 1983. Examining theories of adolescent friendships. See Epstein & Karweit 1983, pp. 39–62

Epstein, J. L., Karweit, N., eds. 1983. *Friends in School: Patterns of Selection and Influence in Secondary Schools*. New York: Academic

Evans, C., Eder, D. 1989. *"No exit": Processes of social isolation in the middle school*. Pres. Am. Sociol. Assoc. Meet. San Francisco, Calif.

Everhart, R. 1983. *Reading, Writing and Resistance: Adolescence and Labor in a Junior High School*. Boston: Routledge

Fine, G. A. 1981. Friends, impression management, and preadolescent behavior. See Asher & Gottman 1981, pp. 29–52

Fine, G. A. 1984. Humorous interaction and the social construction of meaning: Making sense in a jocular vein. In *Studies in Symbolic Interaction*, vol 4, ed. N. Denzin, 83–101. Greenwich, Conn: JAI

Fine, G. A. 1986. The social organization of adolescent gossip: The rhetoric of moral evaluation. See Cook-Gumperz, Corsaro, & Streeck pp. 405–23

Fine, G. A. 1987. *With the Boys: Little League Baseball and Preadolescent Culture*. Chicago: Univ. Chicago Press

Forbes, D., Katz, M., Paul, B., Lubin, D. 1982. Children's plans for joining play: An analysis of structure and function. In *Children's Planning Strategies*, ed. D. Forbes, M. Greenberg, pp. 61–79. San Francisco: Jossey-Bass

Garvey, C. 1984. *Children's Talk*. Cambridge, Mass: Harvard Univ. Press

Geertz, C. 1973. *The Interpretation of Cultures*. New York: Basic

Genishi, C., Di Paolo, M. 1982. Learning through argument in a preschool. In *Communicating in the Classroom*, ed. L. C. Wilkinson, pp. 49–68. New York: Academic

Giddens, A. 1984. *The Constitution of Society*. Oxford, England: Polity

Goffman, E. 1961. *Asylums*. Garden City, NY: Anchor

Gomme, A. 1964. *The Traditional Games of England, Scotland, and Ireland*. 2 vol. New York: Dover

Goodwin, M. H. 1980a. "He-said-she-said": Formal cultural procedures for the construction of a gossip dispute activity. *Am. Ethnol.* 7:674–95

Goodwin, M. H. 1980b. Directive/response speech sequences in girls' and boys' task activities. In *Women and Language in Literature and Society*, ed. S. McConnell-Ginet, R. Borker, N. Furman, pp. 157–73. New York: Prager

Goodwin, M. H. 1982a. Processes of dispute management among urban Black children. *Am. Ethnol.* 9:76–96

Goodwin, M. H. 1982b. "Instigating": Story telling as a social process. *Am. Ethnol.* 9:799–819

Goodwin, M. H. 1985. The serious side of jump rope: Conversational practices and social organization in the frame of play. *J. Am. Folklore* 98:315–30

Goodwin, M. H. 1989. *Language as Social Process: Conversational Practices in Urban Black Children*. Bloomington: Ind. Univ. Press

Goodwin, M. H., Goodwin, C. 1988. Children's arguing. In *Language, Gender, and Sex in a Comparative Perspective*, ed. S. Phillips, S. Steele, C. Tanz, pp. 200–248. New York: Cambridge Univ. Press

Gordon, C. W. 1957. *The Social System of the High School: A Study in the Sociology of Adolescence*. Glencoe, Ill: Free Press

Gottman, J. 1986. The world of coordinated play: Same-and cross-sex friendship in young children. See Gottman & Parker, 1986, pp. 139–91

Gottman, J., Mettetal, G. 1986. Speculations about social and affective development: Friendship and acquaintanceship through adolescence. See Gottman & Parker, 1986, pp. 192–240

Gottman, J., Parker, J., eds. 1986. *Conversations of Friends: Speculations on Affective Development*. New York: Cambridge Univ. Press

Griffin, C. 1985. *Typical Girls?: Young Women From School to the Job Market*. London: Routledge

Gullestad, M. 1988. Children's care for children. See Ekberg & Mjaavatn 1988, vol. 3, pp. 1205–17

Hanna, J. L. 1988. *Disruptive School Behavior: Class, Race and Culture*. New York: Holmes & Meier

Harré, R. 1986. The step to social constructionism. In *Children of Social Worlds: Development in a Social Context*, ed. M. P. Richards, P. Light, pp. 287–96. Cambridge, Mass.: Harvard Univ. Press

Heath, S. B. 1983. *Ways with Words: Language, Life, and Work in Communities and Classrooms*. New York: Cambridge Univ. Press

Hughes, L. A. 1988. "But that's not *really* mean": Competing in a cooperative mode. *Sex Roles.* 19:669–687

Hundeide, K. 1988. Contrasting lifeworlds: Slum children and Oslo middleclass children's world views. See Ekberg & Mjaavatn 1988, vol. 2, pp. 646–58

Karweit, N. 1983. Extracurricular activities and friendship selection. See Epstein & Karweit 1983, pp. 131–140

Karweit, N., Hansell, S. 1983. Sex differences in adolescent relationships: Friendship and status. See Epstein & Karweit 1983, pp. 115–130

Katriel, T. 1985. *Brogez:* Ritual and strategy in Israeli children's conflicts. *Lang. Soc.* 14:467–90

Katriel, T. 1987. *"Bexibùdim!"*: Ritualized sharing among Israeli children. *Lang. Soc.* 16:305–20

Kessler, S., Ashenden, D., Connell, R., Dowsett, G. 1985. Gender relations in secondary schooling. *Sociol. Educ.* 58:34–47

Kinney, D. 1989. *Dweebs, headbangers, and trendies: Adolescent identity formation and change within socio-cultural contexts*. PhD thesis. Ind. Univ., Bloomington

Kochman, T. 1983. The boundary between play and nonplay in black verbal dueling. *Lang. Soc.* 12:329–37

Labov, W. 1972. *Language in the Inner City: Studies in the Black English Vernacular*. Philadelphia: Univ. Penn. Press

Larkin, R. 1979. *Suburban Youth in Cultural Crisis*. New York: Oxford

Lesko, N. 1988. *Symbolizing Society: Stories, Rites and Structure in Catholic High School*. Philadelphia: Falmer

Lever, J. 1976. Sex differences in the games children play. *Soc. Probl.* 23:478–87

MacLeod, J. 1987. *Ain't No Makin' It: Leveled Aspirations in a Low-Income Neighborhood*. Boulder, Colo: Westview

Mandell, N. 1986. Peer interaction in day care settings: Implications for social cognition. In *Sociological Studies of Child Development*, ed. P. A. Adler and P. Adler, vol. 1, pp. 55–79, Greenwich, Conn: JAI

Maynard, D. 1985. On the functions of social conflict among children. *Am. Sociol. Rev.* 50:207–23

McRobbie, A. 1978. Working class girls and the culture of femininity. In *Women Take Issue*, ed. Women's Studies Group: Ctr. Contemp. Cult. Stud., Univ. Birmingham, pp. 96–108. London: Hutchinson

Miller, P. 1986. Teasing as language socialization and verbal play in a white working-class community. See Schieffelin & Ochs 1986, 199–212

Mishler, E. 1979. "Won't you trade cookies with the popcorn?": The talk of trades among six-year-olds. In *Language, Children, and Society: The Effects of Social Factors on Children's Learning to Communicate*, ed. O. Garnica, M. King, pp. 221–36. Elmsford, NY: Pergamon

Mueller, E. 1972. The maintenance of verbal

exchanges between young children. *Child Dev.* 43:930–38

Mueller, E., Cooper, C., eds. 1986. *Process and Outcome in Peer Relationships.* New York: Academic

Nasaw, D. 1985. *Children of the City.* Garden City, NY: Anchor

Olweus, D. 1978. *Aggression in the Schools: Bullies and Whipping Boys.* London: Wiley

Opie, I., Opie, P. 1959. *The Lore and Language of School Children.* Oxford: Oxford Univ. Press

Opie, I., Opie, P. 1969. *Children's Games in Street and Playground.* Oxford: Oxford Univ. Press

Parker, J., Gottman, J. 1989. Social and emotional development in a relational context: Friendship interaction from early childhood to adolescence. See Brendt & Ladd 1989, pp. 95–132

Piaget, J. 1950. *The Psychology of Intelligence.* London: Routledge

Piaget, J. 1968. *Six Psychological Studies.* New York: Vintage

Pontecorvo, C., Orsolini, M. 1989. Discussing and explaining a story at school. *Discourse Processes.* In press

Rizzo, T. A. 1989. *Friendship Development Among Children in School.* Norwood, NJ: Ablex

Rosaldo, M. 1984. Toward an anthropology of self and feeling. In *Culture Theory: Essays on Mind, Self, and Emotion,* ed. R. Schweder, R. LeVine, pp. 137–58. Cambridge: Cambridge Univ. Press

Rosenberg, F., Simmons, R. 1975. Sex differences in the self-concept in adolescence. *Sex Roles* 1:147–59

Rubin, K., Maioni, T., Hornung, M. 1976. Free play behaviors in middle- and lower-class preschoolers: Parten and Piaget revisited. *Child Dev.* 47:414–19

Rubin, Z. 1980. *Children's Friendships.* Cambridge, Mass: Harvard Univ. Press

Schieffelin, B. 1986. Teasing and shaming in Kaluli children's interactions. See Schieffelin & Ochs 1986, pp. 165–181

Schofield, J. 1982. *Black and White in School.* New York: Praeger

Schutze, Y., Kreppner, K., Paulsen, S. 1986. The social construction of the sibling relationship. See Cook-Gumperz et al 1986, pp. 129–46

Schwartz, G., Merton, D. 1967. The language of adolescence: An anthropological approach to the youth culture. *Am. J. Sociol.* 72:453–68

Schwartzman, H. 1978. *Transformations: The Anthropology of Children's Play.* New York: Plenum

Shantz, C. 1987. Conflicts among children. *Child Dev.* 58:283–205

Shantz, C., Hobart, C. 1989. Social conflict and development: Peers and siblings. See Brendt & Ladd 1989, pp. 71–94

Shuman, A. 1986. *Storytelling Rights.* Cambridge: Cambridge Univ. Press

Simmons, R., Blyth, D. 1987. *Moving Into Adolescence: The Impact of Pubertal Change and School Context,* New York: Aldine

Sluckin, A. 1981. *Growing Up in the Playground.* London: Routledge

Solberg, A. 1988. The working life of children. See Ekberg & Mjaavatn 1988, vol. 2, pp. 1069–82

Thorne, B. 1986. Girls and boys together . . . but mostly apart: Gender arrangements in elementary school. In *Relationships and Development,* ed. W. Hartup, Z. Rubin, pp. 167–84. Hillsdale, NJ: Erlbaum

Thorne, B. 1989. Crossing the gender divide: What "tomboys" can teach us about processes of gender separation among children. See Berentzen et al 1989, 139–73. In press

Thorne, B., Luria, Z. 1986. Sexuality and gender in children's daily worlds. *Soc. Probl.* 33:176–89

Turiel, E. 1983. *The Development of Social Knowledge.* New York: Cambridge Univ. Press

Valsiner, J. 1987. *Culture and the Development of Children's Action.* New York: Wiley

Vandell, D. L., Mueller, E. 1980. Peer play and friendships during the first two years. In *Friendship and Childhood Relations,* ed. H. C. Foot, A. J. Chapman, J. R. Smith, 181–208. New York: Wiley

Vygotsky, L. S. 1978. *Mind in Society.* Cambridge, Mass.: Harvard Univ. Press

Wertsch, J. ed. 1986. *Culture, Communication, and Cognition: Vygotskian Perspectives.* New York: Cambridge Univ. Press

Wertsch, J. 1989. A sociocultural approach to mind. In *Child Development Today and Tomorrow,* ed. W. Damon, 14–33. San Francisco: Jossey-Bass

Willis, P. 1981. *Learning to Labour: How Working Class Kids Get Working Class Jobs.* New York: Columbia Univ. Press

Wulff, H. 1988. *Twenty Girls: Growing Up, Ethnicity and Excitement in a South London Microculture.* Stockholm Stud. Soc. Anthropol., No. 21. Stockholm, Sweden: Univ. Stockholm

Youniss, J. 1980. *Parents and Peers in Social Development: A Sullivan-Piaget Perspective.* Chicago: Univ. Chicago Press

Youniss, J., Smollar, J. 1985. *Adolescent Relations with Mothers Fathers and Friends.* Chicago: Univ. Chicago Press

Annu. Rev. Sociol. 1990. 16:221–40
Copyright © 1990 by Annual Reviews Inc. All rights reserved

THEORIES AND METHODS OF TELEPHONE SURVEYS

Robert M. Groves

University of Michigan, Survey Research Center, 426 Thompson Street, Ann Arbor, Michigan 48109

KEY WORDS: telephone survey methods, telephone survey theories, telephone survey errors

Abstract

This discussion of the theories and methods of telephone surveys begins by considering the theories relevant to understanding mode effects. It analyzes theories related to coverage error, psychological theories of compliance and persuasion relevant to nonresponse error, sociological theories relevant to nonresponse error, and cognitive and social psychological theories relevant to measurement error.

The second part of the chapter discusses results from methodological studies and deals with four kinds of error: coverage error, sampling error, nonresponse error, and measurement error.

The third section of the chapter deals with computer-assisted data collection. The chapter concludes with a summary and a short anticipation of the future in telephone survey studies.

INTRODUCTION

A common method of data collection within sociology is survey research, using samples of persons contacted by interviewers who ask prescribed questions of respondents and record their answers. Following the data collection the researcher usually codes answers into numerically labelled categories and with the aid of statistical software performs quantitative analysis of the data to test theoretical assertions.

221

0360-0572/90/0815-0221$02.00

To most sociologists survey research is a method or tool, whose end is a greater understanding of sociological principles. There are, however, a set of design and analytic concepts that impact the quality and cost of survey data. These theoretical roots of the survey method are found in statistics (e.g. for sample selection and estimation procedures), in psychology (e.g. for interviewing methods and respondent answering strategies), and in sociology (e.g. for the reaction of different social groups to the method). For that reason, any "theory of the survey" must draw on several disciplines to be usefully descriptive of the performance of the method (see Groves 1988). The purpose of a survey theory is to anticipate the behavior of persons involved in the measurement (interviewers, respondents, others) in reaction to different design features of the survey (topic of measurement, question structure, interviewing style, etc). The dependent variables of the theory are therefore both quality and cost characteristics of the data collected by the survey. For example, a theory of surveys would be able to predict the level of measurement error and cost of data collection for an open question versus a closed question format for a particular indicator of an underlying concept. It is in this context that we discuss the use of telephone surveys, a version of a survey whereby the interviewer administers the questionnaire to the sample person on the telephone.

The decision to use the telephone as a communication medium for the collection of survey data is only one of hundreds of choices that the researcher must make when mounting a survey effort. These decisions include the choice of the target population to study, the choice of a sampling frame from which to select the sample, the selection technique for the sample, the indicators of underlying concepts of interest, the question wording, structure, and order, the training of interviewers, the mode of coding or processing the data, and so on. Each of these can affect the cost and error structure of the resulting research. However, choice of the telephone mode often has implications for sampling frame and design, centralization of interviewers, use of advance letters, supervisory procedures, etc.

In most countries of the world, commercial survey researchers seem to begin to use telephone surveys before governmental or academic researchers do. (This probably occurs because of the commercial researchers' emphasis on populations with larger discretionary income.) In the United States, Scandinavia, and a few other countries, telephone surveys have, at this writing, become the dominant mode of data collection. This is a large change from the practices of 20 to 30 years ago. Clearly, increasing coverage of the population by telephones, cheaper long distance communication, the development of efficient sampling techniques, and computer-assisted telephone interviewing (CATI) systems have spurred this change. Telephone surveys are more compatible than face-to-face surveys with the increasing number of calls needed to contact sample households, since the effort and cost of another dialing are far smaller than for a trip to visit the household. The ubiquity of telephone surveys has even led to concern about "oversurveying" of the population (Goyder 1987).

This paper addresses the unique properties of telephone surveys that can affect the errors and costs of data collected by the method. It begins by reviewing concepts of human attitudes and behavior that are related to the cost and error structure of telephone survey data (Section 2); it then reviews the empirical results of evaluations of telephone data collection relative to alternative modes (Section 3); it discusses the impact of computer assistance in the data collection process (Section 4); and ends with some speculations about the future of the method (Section 5).

This paper does not address the rationale for choosing the survey method versus alternative means of collecting information about humans (e.g. laboratory experiments, participant observation, ethnography, interaction analysis). This chapter also does not address the use of telephone surveys for studies of organizations or other groups of persons; it concentrates on the use of the method to interview persons in studies of individual attitudes or behaviors. Finally it focuses on initial contact by telephone and not the use of the method in panel surveys.

THEORIES RELEVANT TO UNDERSTANDING MODE EFFECTS

Theories Relevant to Coverage Error

The invention of the telephone enlarged the social group with which one has frequent oral communication. The early history of the telephone suggests that it was found most valuable initially by businesses as a substitute for the telegraph (Aronson 1977). Initial social uses of the home telephone were limited to the wealthy. Public pay telephones spread the technology to larger groups.

The introduction of the telephone to different countries appears to have depended on the role of government policy in telecommunications. Countries with strong central governments which decide to achieve near universal telephone coverage of the country tend to have higher rates of coverage of the population by telephones. In a review of telephone coverage in different countries, Trewin & Lee (1988) show that the highest density is in Scandinavia; over 97% of the population is reachable by telephone (compared to the 92% in the United States). Throughout the world, managers of telephone companies have made investment decisions based on the relative cost of providing telephone service. Building transmission lines in sparsely settled rural areas is relatively expensive (in costs per person served), and these areas are typically the last to be served.

In areas where telephone service is available, it is likely that there are some "rational choice" aspects to telephone subscription. In all countries some fee is required for telephone installation and continued service. The burden of those fees is probably judged relative to discretionary income available to the households. Thus, poorer households may disproportionately lack telephones.

Similarly, the perceived value of the telephone must lie in the benefit of discretionary oral communication with the larger world. Households with larger social networks engage in more frequent contact with the outside world. Persons without such networks are unlikely to value the service to the same degree. For this reason larger households might disproportionately have telephones. We would expect that societies in which residential mobility is common (where networks are more geographically dispersed) would tend to have higher coverage than others. Similarly, to the extent that telecommunication is a substitute for travel to another location, those areas with poorer transportation services would value telecommunication more highly.

These observations suggest that the kind of telephone communication judged appropriate may vary across groups, because the use of the medium is socially valued and defined. For example, people in Britain commonly assert that their telephone conversations are shorter than face-to-face conversations, more often devoted to business purposes, and often used to schedule a face-to-face meeting. In this sense, they are auxiliary, supplementary to face-to-face meetings. This led to the belief that telephone surveys would have high nonresponse rates in Britain (Sykes & Collins 1988).

There is little information on the strength and ubiquity of these norms across cultures. The reaction to a request for a telephone interview may, however, evoke these norms. The norms themselves may be related to how telephone service spread in a particular society—whether it was initially a medium of business communication, a method for contact with geographically remote network members, or both. Further these norms need not be static; they should be able to be changed over time, as relative prices of telecommunication and face-to-face communication vary and the density of the telephone network increases. These may produce cohort differences in telephone usage patterns.

In summary, since the coverage of the household population by telephones affects the error properties of estimates from telephone surveys, the decision to subscribe to telephone service is important to understand. Given the history of the development of telephone systems, it appears that cost of service is evaluated by households relative to the considered importance of oral communication with others distant from the home. Households with relevant others physically at a distance assess the cost differently than do those without such networks. Groups placing great value on face-to-face communication may tend to discount the benefits of the telephone. All of the benefits of the service are also judged relative to the cost of local and long distance telephone calls, and of the cost and speed of transportation and mail service.

Psychological Theories of Compliance and Persuasion Relevant to Nonresponse Error

The discussion above has identified several concepts relevant to the quality of responses obtained in telephone interviews. Other literatures discuss the likelihood of a person accepting a request for a telephone interview. The social psychology of compliance and altruism has outlined a set of concepts that appear to act as influences on cooperation with a request from a stranger (Cialdini 1984). The concept of "reciprocation" is similar to the basic tenets of social exchange theory whereby interaction would be preferred with actors who have previously provided some benefit to the subject. As Dillman (1978) has noted, there are a variety of survey design features that have been used to evoke the reciprocation influence (e.g. advance letters, incentives, personalized requests). With random digit dialing only the telephone number is known by the researcher, and hence the survey request most often is preceded by no other contact with the sample person. This suggests lower response rates on the telephone compared to face-to-face surveys.

A large set of studies demonstrated that "authority" characteristics of the requester aid in obtaining compliance to a request. "Authority" in this context involves sanctions for the request from legitimate agencies of power within the society. The authority of the survey agency is typically communicated by advance letters, identification badges worn by interviewers, written literature given by the interviewer, oral presentations by the interviewer, and descriptions of the survey in the general media. Again with random digit dialing only the oral presentation by the interviewer is routinely possible.

Petty & Cacioppo (1986) describe a theory of attitude change that appears to have relevance to telephone survey requests. Using their terminology we note that the decision to accept or reject a survey request can arise either from deep cognitive processing of the arguments provided by the interviewer or from "peripheral" cues. The amount of elaboration of the arguments for participating in the survey is a function of motivation to engage in that activity, viewed as exogenous to the theory. Peripheral cues can lead to acceptance or rejection of the survey request, as can central route processing.

The theory offers an explanation for some of the failures to increase response rates in telephone survey experiments. Refusals in telephone surveys often occur before any arguments for participating can be presented by the interviewer. A set of peripheral cues appear to be used by sample persons to precipitate their refusal. One notion is that the person is cued to label the call as a sales call or a polling effort of no consequence. Given likely negative attitudes about such contacts, a refusal follows. Under this view, no set of arguments that the interviewer might have prepared can overcome the power of the negative peripheral cues. The success of refusal conversion efforts on some of these cases may attest to the negation of the cue for a sales call (since failed sales calls rarely are followed by another attempt).

Sociological Theories Relevant to Telephone Survey Nonresponse Error

Goyder (1987) has presented the most complete review of sociological concepts relevant to survey nonresponse. He places large emphasis on the influence of marginality to the society and describes how, viewing surveys as information gathering tools of the dominant group, those at its fringes would disproportionately opt out. This fringe group may lie disproportionately among the nontelephone household population. Missing this group would imply higher response rates in telephone surveys than in face-to-face surveys.

Counteracting those possible benefits of telephone noncoverage on telephone survey response rates is the fact that telephone surveys threaten the privacy of the household, perhaps more forcibly than do face-to-face surveys. Communication theorists have commented on the compulsion to answer a ringing telephone simply because the caller cannot be identified without answering it (in contrast to most face-to-face situations). Thus, many phone answerers hearing the introductory words of the interviewer immediately infer that an unsolicited request will follow.

Goyder also invokes social exchange theory concepts to describe how attention to the sample person's needs and desires in the survey design may lead to greater participation in the survey. Goyder (as Dillman above) cites repeated callbacks, not as repeated invasions of privacy, but as means of communicating the importance of the sample person to the research (a perceived benefit) that might stimulate complementary reactions, as a reciprocal gesture.

Communication Theories Relevant to Measurement Error

Some psychological properties of the telephone medium have been repeatedly observed by communication theorists. First, the telephone mode is labelled as restricted in its "channel capacity" (Williams 1977). That is, a smaller set of messages can be communicated in the medium than in face-to-face communication. The absence of communication based on visual stimuli is the obvious root source of these limitations, but the effect of these limitations on the behavior of actors is of theoretical interest.

The reduced channel capacity affects a set of affective adjuncts to cognitive components in judgments. That is, when persons are asked to use information communicated in the audio-only medium to make a judgment (Reid 1977), they express less confidence in their judgment than under similar circumstances in a face-to-face setting. This implies a set of nonverbal cues that are components of judgments necessarily absent in telephone communication.

Despite this there do not seem to be impediments to completing jointly defined tasks on the telephone. Short et al (1976) found no increased errors in the quality of communication of verbal material in the audio-only condition. These experiments also examined the quality of collaborative work *after* the decision to cooperate has been taken. Because of their use of volunteer subjects, they did not examine the relative ability to persuade others to comply with requests using the telephone.

The audio medium entails greater "social distance" between actors than is true in face-to-face encounters (de Leeuw & van der Zouwen 1988). This dimension has been related to hypotheses about the role of social desirability on survey errors (Colombotos 1965, de Leeuw & van der Zouwen 1988). It is thought that the avoidance of revealing characteristics believed to be negative would be heightened in the physical presence of another, reduced somewhat in telephone communication, and reduced still further in self-administered forms. However, this logic seems incomplete. The reduction of influences related to social desirability must first rely on the "credibility" of the confidentiality guarantee of the researcher. That is, once the respondent believes that his answers will not be later revealed to others, those effects will be eliminated. This credibility, often a judgment with a large affective base, may be more difficult to make in a telephone interview. Hence, with the establishment of credibility the quality of threat on the telephone is reduced moreso than in face-to-face communication. Without it, the "physically removed" interviewer may produce greater total threat to the respondent.

The concept of social distance may produce other differences between the two modes of data collection. Face-to-face conversations in surveys most often take place in the respondents' homes. The respondents thus must invite the interviewer into their home, and a large set of social norms may be evoked as the interviewer becomes a quasi-guest. It is not unusual for interviewers to be asked if they would like tea or coffee or some other drink, to be asked where they would like to sit, etc. In contrast, the telephone interviewer remains outside the social boundaries of the home; the guest script is not evoked in most telephone conversations. Unless their behavior is grossly inappropriate, guests to a home are rarely invited to leave. Without such normative constraint, telephone conversations are more easily terminated.

A frequent judgment by communication researchers is that the audio channel is less effective, relative to the face-to-face channel, in communicating psychological states of speakers. Actors have reduced abilities to communicate affect and in turn to evaluate each others' subjective states (Ekman 1965; Mehrabian 1968). Face-to-face encounters include nonverbal communication of the failure to comprehend (e.g. a look of puzzlement), failure to agree with a speaker (e.g. head nodding), or boredom (e.g. eye focus on objects irrelevant to the communication).

The audio channel also strips from the speakers knowledge of some socially valued characteristics of each other—dress, grooming style, and physical features. The only socially valued physical features that can be communicated are those related to speech acts. That is, when racial group membership is revealed by speech style, then one would expect that all the judgments and behavioral influences of the actors flowing from that knowledge would operate. Similarly, voice characteristics often communicate the sex and age of the speaker. There is a rich literature on the effects of race and gender of interviewer on survey responses (e.g. Schuman & Converse 1971; Groves & Fultz 1985).

RESULTS FROM METHODOLOGICAL STUDIES

All surveys are subject to a variety of errors—noncoverage, nonresponse, sampling, and a variety of measurement errors: those arising from interviewers, respondents, and questionnaires. This section reviews the current state of empirical reasearch on these error sources in telephone surveys.

Coverage Error

In the United States about 92 to 93% of all households have a telephone (Thornberry & Massey 1988). This percentage has remained fairly constant during the 1980s, with only a small loss of coverage occurring after the divestiture of ATT in the early 1980s. The causes of noncoverage related to profit goals of the industry are certainly reflected in the data. Compared to urban households rural nonfarm households have lower coverage by telephone (90%); rural areas in the West are particularly poorly covered (82.5%). This no doubt reflects the relatively large costs of introducing the telecommunications hardware in low density rural locales. Of all major regions in the United States, the South has the lowest coverage (89.6% of all households).

Some of the evidence of rational choice influences on the decision to subscribe to telephone service are also supported in the empirical data. One indirect indicator of the richness of social networks is the number of persons in the household. Households containing only one person have lower proportions of telephone subscription than do others.

By far the most powerful empirical correlates of telephone subscription in most analyses are income-related (Groves & Kahn 1979, Thornberry &

Massey 1988). When household income is transformed into a measure of relative poverty status (by adjusting income by number of persons in the household), 96.3% of those households above poverty status have a telephone, and only 72.6% of those below the poverty threshold are covered. This is a better measure of discretionary income available to the household than is total family income.

In a multivariate analysis, Thornberry & Massey find that family income, age, and education are the most important correlates of nontelephone status. Elderly persons and highly educated persons have higher coverage rates than do other groups. Elderly persons of all race and education groups have higher coverage. There are three possible reasons for this: (a) social networks of the elderly value that ability to check on their status without a face-to-face visit, (b) the elderly person values the ability to seek assistance quickly in emergencies, and (c) the telephone substitutes for burdensome travel to conduct business.

Noncoverage *error* is a function of the rate of nontelephone households and the difference between the telephone and nontelephone households. For example, with a linear statistic (like a mean from a simple random sample) the mean based on telephone cases can be expressed as

$$\bar{Y}_{tel} = \bar{Y}_{total} + \left(\frac{N_{NT}}{N}\right)(\bar{Y}_{tel} - \bar{Y}_{nontel}),$$

where $\bar{Y}_{total}$, mean for the total population; N_{nt}, number of persons without telephones in the population; N, total number of persons in the population; $\bar{Y}_{tel}$, mean for the persons with telephones; $\bar{Y}_{nontel}$, mean for the persons without telephones.

Thus, even if large portions of a population do not have a telephone, no coverage error might result if, on the survey variables, they resemble those with telephones. Conversely, if those persons without telephones are very different from those with telephones, large coverage errors can result despite the fact that only a small portion of the population does not have telephones. For analytic statistics (like a regression coefficient) noncoverage can affect estimates if those without telephones have distinctive covariance properties between the independent and dependent variables (see Heckman 1979).

The nontelephone population is demonstrably different from others on large numbers of variables commonly of interest to sociologists. Those living in nontelephone households are found to be in bed because of illness more often than are those with telephone; those without experience some limitation in the daily activities because of chronic health conditions; they make fewer doctor visits, are less often covered by medical insurance, and exhibit poorer knowledge about preventive health measures (Thornberry & Massey 1988), are disproportionately victimized by crimes (McGowan 1982), and disproportionately unemployed (Steel & Boal 1988). Basically, these survey variables are all correlates of the income measures found to be highly correlated with telephone status.

COVERAGE PROPERTIES OF DIFFERENT FRAMES   Although the estimates above give an indication of the level of telephone ownership among those persons living in housing units in the United States, it may not reflect the proportions actually covered in a telephone survey. That coverage rate is dependent on the chosen sampling frame, the materials listing telephone numbers eligible for sampling. Telephone numbers in the United States have three parts, a three-digit area code, a three-digit prefix, and a four-digit suffix. US area codes number over 100 and are geographically defined units, for the most part not crossing state lines. Prefixes themselves do not define geographical units, but they are limited geographically. "Exchanges" are geographical areas in which all households are served by the same set of prefixes. There are about 17,000 exchanges, but 35,000 prefixes. Exchanges do not follow local government, census unit, or any other mapping system. Sparsely settled exchanges (in rural areas) have one prefix for all customers. Densely populated exchanges can have hundreds of prefixes. Each prefix can serve up to 10,000 customers (having suffixes 0000–9999).

Sampling frames for telephone surveys cover different portions of this population. There are three alternative sampling frames (a) telephone directories, (b) computerized files based on directories, and (c) area code–prefix frames available from Bell Communications Research. With over 1500 different telephone companies in the United States, there is little standardization in the coverage properties of telephone directories. Most are published once a year; some are published twice a year. For a national sample, gathering the printed books is not feasible; for a local study it can be desirable. The coverage properties of printed books are not well known. Instead, our knowledge about directory listings is based on the second frame above, computerized files constructed by entering information from telephone directories. These suffer from a lag in data entry after publication but resemble the directory frame.

Based on these computerized directories, it is estimated that about 63% of all telephone households appear on the frame nationally (Lepkowski et al 1989). The computerized frames have duplicate listings of numbers under two different names; they tend to omit numbers whose listings do not have a mailing address (Tucker 1989); they have a small set of numbers that are business numbers. Noncoverage by directories is much higher in urban areas than rural areas, among movers versus the nonmobile, and among the poor versus other groups (Piekarski 1989; Lepkowski et al 1989). However, among the numbers on the frame, over 85% are working household numbers.

The third frame, lists of area code–prefix combinations, theoretically covers all possible telephone numbers. At any given moment they also contain new prefixes assigned but not yet activated and some area code–prefix combinations which no longer are in service. Since the frame contains only the first six digits of a telephone number, sampling from the frame requires the generation of the last four digits in some fashion. If all the four digit numbers (from 0000 to 9999) were appended to the area code–prefix combinations, about 22 to 25% of them would be working household numbers. Since there is no information source to tell the researcher which ones are household numbers and which are not, some contact attempts must be conducted. This makes this frame expensive during data collection relative to the other two.

IMPLICATIONS FOR PRACTICE   Researchers in sociology often become expert in one method of data collection and fail to address its strengths and weaknesses for different problems they examine. This can be fatal for telephone surveys. For descriptive purposes a telephone survey of welfare recipients could be very misleading because of the large portion of the target population omitted. Similar problems would exist for telephone surveys of victimization, voter turnout, investment decisions, etc. Telephone surveys in rural or inner-city poor areas are likely to have larger coverage errors than in other areas.

In general there is no easy way to estimate the proportion of any given population accessible by telephone. For local areas, the decennial census data are available. The researcher faced with the choice of survey mode might obtain a public use tape from the National Health Interview Survey (the data source used by Thornberry and Massey 1988) to investigate whether the target population is well covered by telephones. Although it could not be used to measure the coverage rate for small geographical areas, it can be used to learn coverage characteristics of areas like the one to be studied (e.g. towns of 10,000 to 15,000 population).

One result of such an investigation may be that the likely errors from noncoverage are too great to be risked. If so, a personal interview survey or mailed questionnaire (if a good address frame were available) might be in order. There have been some investigations that mix modes of data collection in a single survey. For example, a telephone sample survey might be conducted among those in the target population who have telephones, and a supplementary area probability sample with face-to-face interviewing might be conducted simultaneously to extend coverage of the survey to those without telephones. Dillman & Tarnai (1988), Groves & Lepkowski (1985), Lepkowski & Groves (1986), and Sirken & Casady (1988) investigate desirable design features of such "dual frame, mixed mode" surveys. In addition to

extending coverage to the nontelephone population, these designs also provide comparisons of results from telephone and face-to-face interviewing
among those with telephones. This can be a valuable source of information on
measurement and nonresponse error properties of the modes.

Sampling Error

The survey error most commonly measured is sampling error, because probability samples (which give all members of the population a known nonzero
chance of selection) permit the researcher to estimate sampling variability of
statistics, given the sample design. Sampling error arises because not all
members of the population are measured in the survey *and* members have
different values on the survey variables across the population. Sampling error
is a function of the probabilities of selection assigned to different numbers,
stratification of the frame, and clustering properties of the design (Kalton
1983). Different sample designs are often used for the different sampling
frames described above. Lepkowski (1988) offers a comprehensive review of
sample designs in telephone surveys, and interested readers are referred to
that work.

In addition to the basic level of variation in the characteristic of interest,
sampling error is sometimes affected by the residential clustering of persons
who have similar values on the survey variable. This occurs whenever clusters
of persons are selected into the sample together. Cluster samples tend to have
higher standard errors than do simple element samples because people within
the same cluster resemble one another. This influence on sampling variance is
present in many telephone samples which use banks of 100 consecutive
numbers as sample clusters (see e.g. Waksberg 1978). The level of clustering
effects within telephone exchanges, however, appears to be smaller than that
in residential clusters of area probability samples often used in face-to-face
surveys (Groves 1978). Sampling error is also affected by techiques used to
select individual respondents from among household members in a sample
unit. In this feature telephone surveys are not distinct from face-to-face
surveys in their properties.

Nonresponse Error

A result obtained in many experimental comparisons of face-to-face and
telephone interviewing is a lower level of cooperation obtained on the telephone. Telephone methods are easily used to increase the number of calls on
sample cases, and the proportion of sample cases that are not contacted can
easily be made lower than comparable proportions in a face-to-face survey.
However, the willingness of sample persons to accept a telephone request for

an interview is consistently lower (Hochstim 1967, Groves & Kahn 1979, Cannell et al 1987, Collins et al 1988, Sebold 1988). Refusals on telephone surveys are likely to be obtained very quickly after the telephone is answered. Oksenberg & Cannell (1988) report that large proportions of refusals took place in the first minute of interaction. It seems clear that such decisions are being made on a set of cues peripheral to the interviewer's message.

The lowered response rates are consistent with expressions of reduced communication of affect in audio communication. When survey respondents are asked to indicate a preference for mode of data collection between face-to-face, telephone, and mail modes, they tend to prefer the face-to-face mode or the mail mode rather than the telephone mode (although the tendency is itself affected by the mode in which the question is asked) (Groves 1989). The face-to-face mode is preferred because of the personal contact with the interviewer; the telephone mode because it is convenient; the mail mode because the respondents are free to schedule the completion of the question- naire themselves.

In the United States lowered response rates on the telephone are particularly likely among the elderly. For example, Cannell et al (1987) find a 57% response rate among those 65 or older relative to an overall 80% response. Elderly persons also disproportionately refuse face-to-face surveys, but the differences are more dramatic on the telephone. Interestingly, Collins et al. (1988) fail to find this effect in Great Britain. Although face-to-face surveys continue to show much larger nonresponse rates in urban areas than in other areas, the telephone mode appears to show diminished differences on this score (Groves & Kahn 1979). This appears to be related not to some norma- tive difference but rather to the ability of the telephone survey to gain access to locked apartment buildings in urban areas. There may also be some reduced effect of fear of crime with the telephone medium.

Some telephone interviewer characteristics are related to their nonresponse rates. Groves & Fultz (1985) find that more experienced telephone interview- ers obtain more cooperation from sample persons. Oksenberg & Cannell (1988) hypothesized that certain voice characteristics of the interviewers may produce different compliance rates. In an intensive study of tape recorded introductory comments by telephone interviewers they find that those who spoke rapidly, loudly, with a standard American pronunciation, and with falling intonation on key words early in the introduction, obtained higher cooperation.

There is evidence that authority principles apply to the compliance decision in telephone surveys. Advance letters can be used to increase response rates in some situations (Dillman et al 1976, Traugott et al 1987). Response rates among those households with unlisted numbers are clearly lower than those of other groups (Lepkowski et al 1989). These are persons who may have already made a decision regarding contact with strangers by the telephone medium.

On the other hand, many survey organizations place additional telephone calls to refusal cases, and conversion of 20–40% of these is a common outcome. The success is judged to be a result both of contacting another, more cooperative household member and the transiency of refusals when the same person is contacted again. Another interpretation is that the callback is an indirect communication of the importance of the sample person to the survey, which evokes reciprocating influences.

Since repeated callbacks on sample cases are relatively easy, the level of contact with sample cases is generally quite high. The exception to this is for homes with answering machines, which act as filters between the interviewer and the sample household. About 25% of households are estimated to have answering machines, and in urban areas the proportion is much higher (Tuckel & Feinberg 1989).

Measurement Error

With regard to measurement error it has been documented that the quantity of response is reduced on open questions (Groves 1978, Sykes & Collins 1988); this is often attributed to the faster pace of telephone interviews. Several studies have found a 10–20% shorter length of response for the same set of questions (Groves & Kahn 1979, Sykes & Collins 1988, Körmendi 1988). In several experiments measuring the interviewer component of variation in the data, Groves & Magilavy (1986) and Tucker (1983) show interviewer variance estimates that are relatively lower than comparable estimates from face-to-face interviewing. These results come from centralized telephone interviewing facilities, which place the interviewers under constant supervision and allow interviewers to overhear and exchange interviewing techniques and styles.

Mixed results are reported on whether telephone interviews are subject to diminished social desirability effects on sensitive questions. Some early studies show minor positive effects on reporting of alcohol consumption (Hochstim 1967), but negative ones in overreporting of voting (Groves & Kahn 1979). More recently there are findings from Britain on reporting of alcohol consumption (Sykes and Collins 1988) and income (Körmendi 1988); neither of these show differences larger than those expected by sampling error.

Several studies found higher missing data rates in telephone surveys than in comparable face-to-face surveys (Kormendi 1988; Jordan 1980). Groves & Kahn (1979) report similar findings but note that the differences disappear with tighter control over interviewer behavior and feedback from coders to interviewers regarding item completion. It appears that some of the measured differences may be a result of an organization's inexperience with the mode of data collection.

In de Leeuw and van der Zouwen's (1988) meta-analysis of 31 mode comparison studies involving the telephone, they conclude that differences between modes of data collection are declining over time. That is, early studies show larger effects than do more recent studies. This may imply that the evolution of telephone survey methods has changed their performance relative to other modes of data collection.

Some research attention has focused on questions that involve visual aids in the face-to-face setting (e.g. a graphical display of a scale, a card with many income response categories); these require some adaptation in the telephone setting. A common alteration is the use of an unfolding scale or a two-step procedure (Miller 1984). For example, Miller changes a seven point satisfied-dissatisfied scale using a response card to a four question set, each involving three response categories:

> Now, thinking about your *health and physical condition in general,* would you say you are *satisfied, dissatisfied, or somewhere in the middle?*
> (IF SATISFIED) How satisfied are you with your health and physical condition—completely satisfied, mostly, or somewhat?
> (IF IN THE MIDDLE) If you had to choose, would you say you are closer to being *satisfied,* or *dissatisfied* with your health and physical condition or are you *right in the middle?*
> (IF DISSATISFIED) How dissatisfied are you with your health and physical condition—completely dissatisfied, mostly, or somewhat?

This form of the question was compared to a single question which asked the respondent to give a number from 1 to 7, corresponding to the same response categories. Miller found that the one step method yielded more "right in the middle" responses and somewhat higher intercorrelations, and slightly less missing data. Locander & Burton (1976) and Monsees & Massey (1979) examine a similar question structure for the measurement of income and find answers sensitive to the starting point of the initial questions. Groves & Kahn (1979) note in an examination of a 101 point scale that some mode differences arise because the labelling of scale points with response cards draws visual attention of the respondent. When the same scale is presented (without visual aids on the telephone) as a 101 point dimension, with only the end points and the middle point defined, a very different response distribution results. They infer this is not a pure property of the medium, but a property of the question structure.

COMPUTER-ASSISTED DATA COLLECTION

Computer-assisted telephone interviewing (CATI) employs interactive computing systems to assist interviewers and their supervisors in performing the basic data collection tasks of telephone interview surveys. Survey questions are presented on the screens of computer monitors, the interviewer reads the questions to the respondent and enters the responses via keyboard. Current CATI systems have automated the sampling process of telephone surveys, the scheduling of dialings on sample numbers, the assignment of cases to interviewers, tailoring of question wording to respondents' individual circumstances, editing checks on data entered in response to questions, monitoring of interviews by supervisory staff, recordkeeping for the administration of the surveys, and the preparing of computer data bases suitable for statistical analysis (Nicholls & Groves 1986).

At this writing there have been several studies of CATI's impact on survey costs and errors (Coulter 1985, Groves & Mathiowetz 1984, House 1984, Harlow et al 1985, Catlin & Ingram 1988). These have shown reduced rates of item missing data (the effect of software control over routing through the questionnaire), lower frequencies of interviewer comments, some evidence of lower interviewer variance, more minutes required to complete an interview, but higher productivity because of reduced editing and record keeping burdens. Most experimental comparisons have utilized CATI questionnaires which are simple translations of the paper version of the questionnaire. Larger differences between the two methods appear when changes to the CATI questionnaire are made to enhance checks of consistencies between responses to two different questions (House 1984).

CATI systems have extended the control over interviewer behavior to enforce question wording, probing procedures, and routing through the questionnaire. The systems were initially expected to reduce costs of a telephone survey because of more efficient call scheduling and the elimination of a separate data entry step. There is evidence that call-scheduling algorithms can improve efficiency (Kulka & Weeks 1988), but the technology also requires extensive planning and testing prior to the survey production (House & Nicholls 1988).

Both interviewers and respondents typically show no adverse reaction to CATI. It is largely invisible to the respondent and the ubiquity of computerized data entry in the United States suggests that most respondents have already had similar experiences. There is some documentation that older interviewers learn the rudiments of CATI interviewing at a slower pace than younger interviewers, but no documentation on error effects related to this phenomenon (Groves & Nicholls 1986).

SUMMARY

One way to summarize the status of telephone survey methodology is to review its major known strengths and weaknesses, focusing on coverage error, nonresponse error, sampling error, and measurement error properties. Coverage error in the telephone surveys arises principally from households without telephones. Rational choice models are attractive in predicting telephone subscription, using cost of the service compared to the perceived benefits of oral communication with distant others. Thus, telephone surveys estimating statistics that are correlated with the household income status, size, urban status, and age of household members suffer from greater coverage biases. US telephone coverage rates, now about 92%, appear to have been rising slowly over the past decade.

Principles from the social psychology of compliance and persuasion are applicable to survey nonresponse. Household telephone survey nonresponse rates are generally lower than those of comparable face-to-face surveys, principally because of higher refusal rates. This fact has led researchers to keep telephone interviews as short as possible.

Reduced effects of sample clustering improve the sampling error properties of telephone surveys. It is clear that more efficient sample designs are possible on telephone surveys than most face-to-face household surveys. The method has a great attraction on this score.

The measurement error picture is complex. The faster pace of telephone interviews (a result of pressures to avoid refusals) had led to truncated responses to open questions. There is related speculation of more superficial cognitive processing for closed questions, but only scattered support. Despite logical hypotheses of reduced effects of social desirability in the telephone mode, the empirical results are mixed. One hypothesis is that the increased "social distance" in a telephone communication is counteracted by reduced credibility of interviewers' pledges of legitimacy and confidentiality of the survey effort. The adaptation of questions using visual aids in a face-to-face survey to the telephone mode generally has produced only small differences, except with the use of cards with large numbers of labelled response alternatives. Finally, the reduced channel capacity of the audio-only medium strips away some of the nonverbal sources of measurement error (e.g. effects of interviewer appearance and gestures). Measures of interviewer variance in centralized telephone survey facilities indicate increased uniformity of results across interviewers. This is believed to be a result also of on-going monitoring and supervision of interviewers and the informal exchange of interviewing techniques among interviewers working in close proximity.

THE FUTURE

I shall not violate the norm of engaging in a little futurism in this review paper, if only to assure my embarrassment in looking at this chapter a decade from now. One likely characteristic of the future is the increase in telecommunications in all spheres of life. This includes the nearly complete coverage of the household population by telephones. Conversely, it is also likely that technological developments that constrain access to subscribers may increase. These include the telephone answering machines noted above, but also features of the telephone system which permit the subscriber to limit access to him to a set of chosen persons. These place in the hands of the respondent measures to control access that exceed those available in face-to-face encounters.

As response rates in social surveys continue to decline, the cost of mounting survey research increases both due to extra efforts to contact a busy population and efforts to persuade the reluctant to cooperate. Telephone surveys are attractive to reduce costs of data collection. Unfortunately, telephone survey response rates appear to be affected by the same societal influences as other survey modes, and response rates will likely decline for this medium as well. Nonresponse is particularly damaging to surveys because it eats away the unique power of the methodology relative to other options—the ability to draw inferences to large complex populations based on a sample of individuals. Attempts to reduce nonresponse are likely to become less effective over time. Instead, the researchers must reorient their efforts toward identifying the causes of nonresponse in order to develop better ways of drawing inference from surveys subject to missing data.

The future with regard to measurement error in telephone surveys is less clear. Centralized telephone interviewing appears to have successfully decreased interviewer variability, and empirical data on compliance with training guidelines show that more constant stimuli are being delivered to respondents. This, however, is beginning to call into question the utility of the stimulus-response model of measurement error. That is, the assumption that measurement errors are reduced by assuring constant wording of questions is balanced by the fear that robot-like delivery of questions can produce errors of its own sort. Some rethinking regarding the restrictions on interviewer behavior may occur, moving the methodology toward more normal conversation precepts.

The limitation of the telephone medium to audio information only may be eliminated, although one needs to be skeptical about such predictions. When this possibility arises, a wider variety of question forms will be available for use.

The social role of the telephone appears to be affected by pricing decisions, with some lag for their effects to be felt. Younger persons in several societies appear to use the telephone for longer, more casual discussions than the older cohorts. If prices of long distance communication decline, higher use is expected and more common calls from strangers might be expected. The results that show larger response error problems among elderly respondents thus may change over time. The hypothesis that the effect is due to cohort experiences with the use of the telephone will clearly be tested.

ACKNOWLEDGMENT

The author expresses his appreciation to Statistika Centralbyrån of Sweden for use of its facilities during the writing of this paper.

Literature Cited

Aronson, S. H. 1977. Bell's electrical toy: what's the use? The sociology of early telephone usage, In *The Social Impact of the Telephone*, ed. I. de Sola Pool, pp. 15–39. Cambridge: MIT Press

Cannell, C. F., Groves, R. M., Magilavy, L., Mathiowetz, N., Miller, P. 1987. *An experimental comparison of telephone and personal health surveys*, Washington: Natl Ctr. Health Statist.

Catlin, G., Ingram, S. 1988. The effects of CATI on costs and data quality: A comparison of CATI and paper methods in centralized interviewing. In *Telephone Survey Methodology*, ed. R. M. Groves, P. B Biemer, L. E. Lyberg, J. T. Massey, W. L. Nicholls, and J. Waksberg, pp. 437–51. New York: Wiley

Cialdini, R. B. 1984. *Influence: The New Psychology of Modern Persuasion*, New York: Quill

Collins, M., Sykes, W., Wilson, P., Blackshaw, N. 1988. Nonresponse: The UK experience. See Groves et al 1988, pp. 213–32

Colombotos, J. 1965. The effects of personal vs. telephone interviews on socially acceptable responses. *Public Opin. Q.* 29:457–8

Coulter, R. 1985. A comparison of CATI and non-CATI on a Nebraska hog survey. Statist. Rep. Serv. U.S. Dep. Agric. Washington, DC: USGPO

de Leeuw, E., van der Zouwen, J. 1988. Data quality in telephone and face to face surveys: A comparative meta-analysis. See Groves et al 1988, pp. 283–300

Dillman, D. A. 1978. *Mail and Telephone Surveys*. New York: Wiley.

Dillman, D. A., Gallegos, J. G., Frey, J. H. 1976. Reducing refusals rates for telephone interviews. *Public Opin. Q.* 40:66–78

Dillman, D. A., Tarnai, J. 1988. Administrative issues in mixed mode surveys. See Groves et al. 1988, pp. 509–28

Goyder, J. 1987. *The Silent Minority: Nonrespondents on Sample Surveys*. Boulder: Westview

Groves, R. M. 1978. On the mode of administering a questionnaire and response to open-ended items. *Soc. Sci. Res.* 7:257–71

Groves, R. M. 1978. An empirical comparison of two telephone sample designs. *J. Marketing Res.* 15:622–31

Groves, R. M. 1988. Research on Survey Data Quality, *Public Opinion Quarterly*, 51, Part 2:S156–S172

Groves, R. M. 1989. *Survey Errors and Survey Costs*, New York: Wiley

Groves, R. M., Fultz, N. H. 1985. Gender effects among telephone interviewers in a survey of economic attitudes. *Sociol. Methods Res.* 14:31–52

Groves, R. M., Kahn, R. L. 1979. *Surveys By Telephone*. New York: Wiley

Groves, R. M., Lepkowski, J. M. 1985. Dual frame, mixed mode designs. *J. Official Statist.* 1:263–86

Groves, R. M., Mathiowetz, N. A. 1984. Computer assisted telephone interviewing: effects on interviewers and respondents. *Public Opin. Q* 48:356–69

Groves, R. M., Nicholls, W. L. II. 1986. The status of computer assisted telephone interviewing: Part II—data quality issues. *J. Official Statist.* 2:117–34

Harlow, B. L., Rosenthal, J. F., Ziegler, R. G. 1985. A comparison of computer-assisted and hard copy telephone interviewing. *Am. J. Epidemiol.* 122:335–40

Heckman, J. J. 1979. Sample selection bias as a specification error. *Econometrica* 47:153–61

Hochstim, J. R. 1967. A critical comparison of three strategies of collecting data from households. *J. Am. Statist. Assoc.* 62:976–89

House, C. C. 1984. Computer-assisted telephone interviewing on cattle multiple frame survey. Statist. Rep. Serv., US Dep. Agric. Washington, DC: USGPO

House, C. C., Nicholls, W. L. II. 1988. Questionnaire design for CATI: design objectives and methods. See Groves et al. 1988, pp. 421–36

Jordan, L. A., Marcus, A. C., Reeder, L. G. 1980. Response styles in telephone and household interviewing: A field experiment. *Public Opin. Q.* 44:210–22

Kalton, G. 1983. *An Introduction to Survey Sampling,* Beverly Hills: Sage

Körmendi, E. 1988. The quality of income information in telephone and face to face surveys. See Groves et al 1988, pp. 341–55

Lepkowski, J. M., 1988. Telephone sampling methods in the United States. See Groves et al 1988, pp. 73–98

Lepkowski, J. M., Groves, R. M. 1986. A mean squared error model for dual frame, mixed mode survey design. *J. Am. Statist. Assoc.* 81:930–37

Lepkowski, J. M., Groves, R. M., Parsley, T. 1989. Adjustments for omission of unlisted numbers in telephone surveys. Pres. 1989 meet. Am. Assoc. for Public Opin. Res.

Locander, W. B., Burton, J. P. 1976. The effect of question form on gathering income data by telephone. *J. Market. Res.* 13:189–92

McGowan, H. 1982. Telephone ownership in the National Crime Survey, US Bur. Census. Unpublished memorandum

Miller, P. V. 1984. Alternative question forms for attitude scale questions in telephone interviews. *Public Opin. Q.* 48:766–78

Monsees, M. L., Massey, J. T. 1979. Adapting procedures for collecting demographic data in a personal interview to a telephone interview. *Proc. Section on Survey Res. Meth. Am. Statist. Assoc.* pp. 130–35

Nicholls, W. L. II, Groves, R. M. 1986. The status of computer assisted telephone interviewing: Part I—introduction and impact on cost and timeliness of survey data. *J. Official Statist.* 2:93–115

Oksenberg, L., Cannell, C. F. 1988. Effects of interviewer vocal characteristics on nonresponse. See Groves et al 1988, pp. 257–71

Petty, R. E., Cacioppo, J. T. 1986. *Communication and Persuasion: Central and Peripheral Routes to Attitude Change.* New York: Springer-Verlag

Piekarski, L. B. 1989. Choosing between directory listed and random digit sampling in light of new demographic findings. Pres. 1989 meet. Am. Assoc. Public Opin. Res., May 19

Reid, A. A. L. 1977. Comparing telephone with face-to-face contact. *The Social Impact of the Telephone,* ed. I. de Sola Pool, pp. 387–414. Cambridge: MIT Press

Sebold, J. 1988. Survey period length, unanswered numbers, and nonresponse in telephone surveys. See Groves et al. 1988, pp. 247–56

Short, J., Williams, E., Christie, B. 1976. *The Social Psychology of Telecommunications.* London: Wiley

Sirken, M. G., Casady, R. J. 1988. Sampling variance and nonresponse rates in dual frame, mixed mode surveys. See Groves et al 1988, pp. 175–89

Steel, D., Boal, P. 1988. Accessibility by telephone in Australia: implications for telephone surveys. *J. Official Statist.* 4:285–98

Sykes, W., Collins, M. 1988. Effects of mode of interview: experiments in the UK. See Groves et al 1988, pp. 301–20

Thornberry, O. T., Massey, J. T. 1988. Trends in United States telephone coverage across time and subgroups. See Groves et al 1988, pp. 25–50

Trewin, D., Lee, G. 1988. International comparisons of telephone coverage. See Groves et al 1988, pp. 9–24

Tuckel, P. S., Feinberg, B. M. 1989. The telephone answering machine poses many questions for telephone survey researchers. Pres. 1989 Meet. Am. Assoc. Public Opin. Res.

Tucker, C. 1989. Characteristics of commercial residential telephone lists and dual-frame designs. *Proc. Survey Res. Meth. Section, Am. Statist. Assoc., 1989.* Forthcoming

Waksberg, J. 1978. Sampling methods for random digit dialing, *J. Am. Statist. Assoc.* 73:40–46

Williams, E. 1977. Experimental comparisons of face-to-face and mediated communication: A review, *Psychol. Bull.* 84:963–76

Annu. Rev. Sociol. 1990. 16:241–62

CONCEPTS OF THE LIFE CYCLE:
Their History, Meanings, and Uses in the Social Sciences

Angela M. O'Rand and *Margaret L. Krecker*

Department of Sociology, Duke University, Durham, North Carolina 27706

KEY WORDS: life cycle, life course, aging, family life cycle, organizational life cycle

Abstract

Life cycle is among the most widely used concepts in the social sciences. It may be invoked merely to denote temporality. It may be applied metaphorically or heuristically to initiate an analysis. Or it may comprise the core assumptions of a research program in developmental processes. Strictly defined, life cycle refers to maturational and generational processes in natural populations. Alternative conceptions of life cycle, like *life span* and *life course,* do not share the same intrinsic reference to generation or reproduction that transcends the single lifetime of the individual. Still these concepts are often used interchangeably. The history, meanings, and uses of these concepts across anthropology, psychology, economics, and sociology are reviewed. Three areas of modern sociology—individual aging, family life cycle, and organizational life cycle—are examined specifically in their treatment of life-cycle concepts. Finally, the implications of alternative usages for the study of populations as opposed to individuals and for the study of stability as opposed to change are considered.

INTRODUCTION

Life cycle is among the most widely used concepts in the social sciences. However, the meanings and uses of the concept are diverse and occasionally matters of considerable dispute (Elder 1978a, Featherman 1983, Murphy

241

1987). Strictly defined, the concept is used to represent maturational and generational processes driven by mechanisms of reproduction in natural populations. Often, though, the concept is invoked to denote temporality in a general sense; in this usage, the terms *life cycle, life span,* and *life course* are frequently treated as identical. More often the concept is applied metaphorically or heuristically to initiate analyses of developmental or maturational phenomena across social domains from individuals to organizations.

The variety of meanings and uses is indicative of the concept's wide appeal as a framework for the study of development. It reflects the multiple roles of some concepts in theory construction. However, it also suggests the possibility of imprecise definitions and applications in the social sciences that may create difficulties in the study of development and change.

This review considers the meanings and uses of the concept of life cycle in several disciplinary specialties. After briefly reviewing the evolutionary foundations of the concept in its strictest definition, we examine alternative usages across several social science specialties—in anthropology, economics, psychology, and sociology. Then, we present a focused analysis of the current uses of life cycle in three problem domains of sociology: individual aging, family life cycle, and the organizational life cycle. This examination yields several observations regarding the utility of the life-cycle concepts for different research agendas.

CONCEPTS OF THE LIFE CYCLE ACROSS THE SOCIAL SCIENCES

Despite the goals of conceptual specificity and precision held by the social and natural sciences alike, scientific discourse also seeks what Adams has referred to as *linguistic economy,* or the use of key terms "so natural, fundamental and simple" within the context of a science that they are "used without formal definition" to denote generally very complex phenomena (Adams 1979:243). In the history of biology, concepts such as evolution, heredity, and gene pool have been used in this manner (Adams 1979, Coleman 1971, Gould 1977). In the social sciences, as many or more examples abound, including the concept of life cycle. Moreover, many of these social science concepts, like life cycle, are borrowed from other sciences and used metaphorically to simplify complex social phenomena by invoking familiar schema in scientific thought. As such, key concepts come to be shared in scientific culture both as scientific constructs and as cultural viewpoints broadly understood in Western thought.

Most social science conceptions of life cycle are related to nineteenth century ideas in three areas: in biology, to the relationship between individual development and the historical progression of species (Coleman 1971, Mayr 1982); in social philosophy, to the origins and evolution of family forms and kinship systems from primitive promiscuity to patriarchal monogamy (Leibo-witz 1969), and in early developmental psychology, to human ontogenetic development from conception to death (Reinert 1979, Baltes 1979). Many of these views became reconciled in the Darwinian framework of natural selection (Kohn 1980), which continues to influence the social sciences directly.

The principle model of life cycle that predominated at the end of the nineteenth century referred to the unilinear series of changes (transformations) in form undergone by organisms in their development over time from early stages to equivalent stages in a succeeding generation (Coleman 1971). The irreducible properties of the life cycle, therefore, were successive forms (stages), irreversible development (maturation), and the reproduction of form (generation). These elements of life cycle defined the bases of time and variation over the life span. With Darwin's theory of natural selection, the life-cycle notion was linked to the origin and extinction of species, thus resolving some longstanding debates in biology over the arguable parallelism between individual development and the development of the species (Cole-man 1971, Mayr 1982, Gould 1977). In short, the idea of the life cycle emerged at the end of the century as a complex notion incorporating earlier ideas at the organismic or individual level about inheritance and development and at the species or population level about adaptation, survival, and extinc-tion.

It is no longer a matter of dispute among social historians that Darwin's theory was informed by the social theories of Malthus, Paley, and others (Kohn 1980). These theories emphasized population processes and, indeed, they are credited with converting Darwin to "population thinking" (Mayr 1982). His population thinking was anchored in the core ideas that competi-tion occurs among individuals rather than species and that the variation and reproduction of forms is the central feature of life. Accordingly, the idea of life cycle, as constituted by the notions of stages, maturation, and generation, implies a population process of intergenerational sequences.

In social anthropology, up until the 1960s, the idea of life cycle was strictly defined. Ethnographies of kinship and domestic cycles (Fortes 1949, Goody 1971) and of age-set and generation-group societies (Foner & Kertzer 1978, Kertzer & Keith 1984, Kertzer & Schaie 1989) applied the idea in all respects, and particularly in East African cultures. In this work, the process of social reproduction was defined in terms of "physical continuity and replacement" in the transmission of social capital from one generation to another (Fortes 1971:1–2). Family, kin, or household as the primary unit of study facilitated the focus on reproduction and cross-generation transfer.

This life-cycle approach at the family level had been avoided in social anthropology before the 1940s as a result of the debates over social evolution that predated Darwinian theory by over a century (Leibowitz 1969). Before

1859, the widely held hierarchical notion of social evolution viewed mankind as having progressed from simple to complex technological social systems, with the latter usually classified as successive family or kinship systems based primarily on patterns of sexuality, reproduction, and childrearing. Primitive promiscuity, communal marriage, polygamy, gynecocracy, monogamy—these family forms and others and their evolutionary status characterized the predominant approach to social evolution. But Darwinism stimulated cultural doctrines of racial and sexual superiority that discouraged, if not preempted, further evolutionary analyses of the "family" by anthropology until alternative approaches to social evolution based on ideas other than sexual reproduction (e.g. transactional exchange) emerged nearly a century later (Leibowitz 1969, Fortes 1949, Kertzer & Keith 1984). Social reproduction resurrected the life-cycle notion as a metaphor for intergenerational maintenance, replenishment and exchange.

The more psychologically oriented anthropology which focused on the socialization and psychological development of the individual did not apply the same notion of life cycle. Rather than the domestic cycle, the individual life history or biography—the life span or life course—provided the frame of reference. American anthropologists, like Kroeber and Kluckhohn in their studies of American Indians, sought out data on the "passages" of individuals' lives (Langness & Frank 1981). As such, they examined stages and maturation. But the focus on individual life spans or life courses ignored sexual and social reproduction and intergenerational cycle.

Alternative Conceptions: Life Span and Life Course

The alternative life-cycle conceptions do not contain all three elements of a strict definition—stages, maturation, and generation. Life span refers to the maximum life potential of the average individual. The idea of maturation as duration between beginning (birth) and ending (death) is central to the life-span alternative which lacks intrinsic reference to either stages or generation. Life course, on the other hand, implies the timing and sequencing of stages or phases in the process of maturation, but without intrinsic reference to generation. Life course is also an individual level construct, although it is linked with social processes in the family, the economy, and the polity (Elder 1978a, b, 1987, Hareven & Plakans 1987, Vinovskis 1977, 1988). The life-course perspective is further discussed in the section on individual aging which follows.

Life-Cycle Concepts Across the Social Sciences

The scientific heritage of nineteenth-century evolutionary theories and life-cycle concepts is apparent in the other social sciences. Notions of life cycle in both individual and population terms abound, but the uses of these ideas are frequently inconsistent. A major dimension along which usages are arrayed is the relative emphasis on development as a population-driven process on the one hand or as an ontogenetic, or otherwise deterministic, sequence of forms on the other. These usages are based on different assumptions and/or heuristic treatments of time and variation in the course of development. As such they are conceptualized variously in terms of stages or transitions, maturation, and/or generation.

Life-cycle conceptions of stage, maturation, and/or generation treated as core assumptions in a research program operate differently than do life-cycle frameworks used as heuristic devices, metaphors, or "naive models" (Lakatos 1978). As a metaphor or "naive model," the life cycle serves as an initial framework for observation. However, when the life-cycle concept comprises fundamental assumptions regarding time and variation, it is not viewed as problematic, but as a priori. For example, Erikson's classical eight-stage model of psychosocial crises in the life cycle draws explicitly from evolutionary theory (1963) and assumes the "ontogenesis . . . of an inescapable and intrinsic order of strivings" (Erikson 1968:292) from infancy to old age. His stage-model is conventionally viewed as a strict application of the life-cycle concept. It does not test the life-cycle model, but rather assumes its existence. Yet, Erikson's classic construction does not account for reproduction or generation at the population level. His idea of generativity does not substitute for cyclical reproduction.

Levinson's (1978) "seasons of a man's life" similarly draws upon the assumption of time as an age-related sequence of stages presenting the individual with developmental tasks. Again, however, the social (population) task of generation is omitted. In these psychosocial stage theories, also called normative-crisis models (Clausen 1986), time is defined by developmental stages and variation refers to individuals' relatively (un)successful passages through the earlier predetermined stages.

In economics, similar life-cycle assumptions are sometimes made explicit. In his discourse on "how we live," Fuchs treats the life cycle as the "constant of human existence" in which a "succession of difficult decisions" punctuates the course of modern life (Fuchs 1983:6, 76). His untested assumptions are "protected" (i.e. not directly tested) by analyses that examine life stage–specific propositions about the investment in human capital ("a time to sow—adults 25–44") and/or consumption from human capital ("a time to reap—adults 45–64") over the putative economic life cycle.

In the modern social sciences, however, a priori assumptions about time and variation often are more implicit than explicit in the program. In some research programs, life cycle is mentioned "in passing" to connote a general sense of temporality or direction not clearly specified in the assumptions and not directly tested. Concepts in neoclassical theory in modern economics like "consumption function" and "permanent income" (Friedman 1957), "life-cycle earnings" (Weiss 1986), and "human capital" (Becker 1964, Schultz 1963) are examples of this pattern of use.

An illuminating analysis of the tacit treatment of life cycle in the human capital research program is provided by Blaug (1980). This research program was announced in 1962 in a supplement volume of the *Journal of Political Economy* titled "Investment in Human Beings" and was more fully introduced within two years by Theodore Schultz (1963) and Gary Becker (1964). Blaug argues that the hard core of the human capital program takes the distribution or variation of individuals' "tastes" and "abilities" as given and assumes further that individuals' behaviors (choices) in the present are directly correlated with their futures (particularly their future labor market values, usually measured as alternative returns for present education, work, health, etc). Here, the implicit life cycle is best conceptualized as *life span,* that is, as a smooth but inevitable trajectory of value necessarily linking present (age-related) behavior to future (age-related) returns from the individual's perspective.

Other programs in economics are revising the life-cycle basis of microeconomic theory without abandoning the idea. In these programs, the life-cycle process is defined in stronger ways, that is, metaphorically as "naive models," to test explicit hypotheses regarding time and variation that yield testable models of the life cycle itself. Winston's (1982, 1988) time-specific analysis of the economic activities of firms, households, and markets is an example. He argues that time is treated too casually by economic analysis; time is a "simple unidirectional linear flow, exogenous to the economic actors" (Winston 1982:13). Time orders events sequentially in an analytical sense, and because of its irreversibility, it shapes economic actors' perspectives of events as past, present, and future. Here a life-course conception of life cycle is being applied, with the timing of events within the individual's time perspective defining time and the forms of variation.

Winston's basic assumption is that people live and act in *perspective time,* time experienced as events ordered as past, present, or future. Perspective time, and particularly the present, "is the inescapable context of all actual social behavior" where actors "must make decisions Now, and they do so without the capacity to control the pace of events or to recreate the past, without knowing the events that lie in the future" (1988:33–34). Thus, uncertainty, bounded rationality, surprise, search, and discovery become subjects of testable hypotheses using naive models of reality like assortative mating and spot markets (e.g. in sociology, see England & Farkas 1986) that are akin to the traditional evolutionary life-cycle model coming from biology. However, they are testable in perspective time, as individuals experience normative events in time such as schooling, marriage, and retirement about which actors have relatively more information. The timing of these events is thus treated explicitly.

Winston's revisionism is more extensive than this review has space to consider thoroughly. But the purpose in introducing his project is to illustrate that the programmatic role of a concept such as life cycle is subject to change within developing research programs and that the process of theory development contributes to the diversity in usages within, as well as across, the social sciences. Winston's model does not have the same deterministic assumptions regarding the form, timing, and directionality of the life cycle found in some other neoclassical formulations (see Fuchs 1983), nor does it invoke implicit life-span trajectories like those projected in life-cycle earnings models. His approach tests explicit models of time and variation. He uses life cycle as an individual level concept. His "perspective time" actually fits the life-course conception better than the life-cycle conception.

Other developing social science research programs display the same diversity in explicit or implicit assumptions and naive models related to time and variation over the life spans of social actors at several levels of analysis—the individual, the family, and the organization. Life-span developmental psychology in the research programs of Baltes, Schaie, Brim and their colleagues (e.g. Baltes & Brim 1979; see Featherman 1983 for a review), emergent human development theories in sociology (Featherman & Lerner 1985, Featherman 1986), status attainment models (e.g. Featherman & Hauser 1978), life-course models of age stratification (e.g. Riley 1987, Riley et al 1982) and the timing of life events (e.g. Hogan 1978, Marini 1984), family development theories (e.g. Hareven 1978a, b, Grebenik et al 1989), population ecology models of organizations (e.g. Stinchcombe 1965, Aldrich 1979, Carroll 1984), and demographic models of life cycles and population characteristics (e.g. Coale 1972, Preston 1982)—these research programs invoke different conceptualizations of the life cycle with varying attachments to strong evolutionary assumptions of sequential stages or population processes and wide-ranging applications of metaphors and models.

The following section reviews the usages and developments of the concept in some of these areas as they pertain to three problem domains of concern in sociology—individual aging, family life cycle, and organizational growth and decline processes.

LIFE CYCLE IN THREE PROBLEM AREAS OF SOCIOLOGY

Issues of time and variation are at the core of all sociological analysis. Across specific research programs these two problematics take on specific conceptual forms, including the life cycle per se (Murphy 1987), generation (Eisenstadt 1956), cohort (Ryder 1965, Hareven 1978b), age strata (Riley 1987), growth and decline processes of organizations (Freeman 1982, Whetten 1987), among many others. Strict definitions of life cycle have constituted the core assumptions of several research programs in sociology—e.g. the Chicago School (Park & Burgess 1921), Hawley's human ecology program (1950), and the natural history of organizations (Haire 1959, Greiner 1972). Alternatively, other life-cycle conceptions have inspired model-testing in other research programs—e.g. developmental contextualism in life-span theory (Featherman & Lerner 1985), Boulding's reconstruction of economics (1950), and the population ecology of organizations (Hannan & Freeman 1977, Whetten 1987)—even though the term *life cycle* per se may be applied to the phenomenon under study.

Because of space limitations only three problem areas of sociology are selected to illustrate the history, meanings, and uses of life cycle in sociology. These three research areas are of special interest since they have undergone shifts in their life-cyle conceptualizations that have influenced the treatment of time and variation. Notable shifts in their respective life-cycle conceptions illustrate developments of these research programs that include (*a*) the explicit rejection of assumptions regarding inevitable and predetermined sequences of forms (i.e. life stages, family structures) in the study of individual aging and family development; (*b*) the explicit assumption that development is a process that in fact extends beyond the life spans of individuals (i.e. across generations) in the study of families; and (*c*) the adoption of strong assumptions regarding the historical interplay between individual (organizational) development and social (population) change actually akin to the original formulation of the life-cycle concept across studies of individual, family, and organizational change.

Individual Aging

The field of aging is an intellectual descendent of the longstanding traditions concerned with problems of growth, maturation, senescence, and death of individuals (Tanner 1981, Reinert 1979). Indeed, the terms *aging* and *life cycle* have often been treated as synonymous in this field (Kertzer & Keith 1984). It is instructive to note that in the recently published *Encyclopedia of Aging* which attempts a comprehensive, though telegraphic, overview of the "state of the art," space is not assigned to review the life-cycle concept per se. Instead, it is cross-referenced with the three-page review of life course (Kastenbaum 1987:388–391). Although the life-course section begins by acknowledging that life cycle, life span, and life course are nearly equivalent terms (note: life-span is allocated two pages of its own in the same volume; see Fries 1987:401–402), the content of the review clearly affirms the ascendance of life course as the "new wave" program for studying aging as a dynamic and heterogeneous phenomenon.

This position represents a consensus in the research community (Featherman 1986, Riley 1987, Campbell & O'Rand 1988). Research on aging has undergone a series of problem shifts in the recent 20-year period, moving toward comparative research with a growing emphasis on heterogeneity in the timing and on variation of the population-level and individual-level determinants of the aging process in individuals (Elder 1975). Developing theories of the organization of the life course attempt to reconcile ideas regarding the structural embeddedness of the aging process of individuals with those addressing the historic interplay of aggregate patterns of individual behavior and social change (O'Rand 1990). Specific hypotheses derived from these programs are serious attempts at theory-building. Indeed, in the emergent social theories of aging the overall shift is away from stage- or age-specific theories or idiographic accounts and toward evolutionary and structural theories of human development linking life cycle and population in the contexts of historical change (Birren & Bengtson 1988, Riley 1987).

An interest in cohorts as categories linking population processes with individual life cycles has existed for over two decades (Ryder 1965, Waring 1975, Riley et al 1982, Hareven 1978a, b, Easterlin 1980, Uhlenberg 1988). The idea here is that the relative structural compositions (e.g. size, sex ratio) and the historical experiences of successive birth cohorts moving through time have causal implications for the life courses of individuals. Easterlin's hypothesis of birth and fortune (1980) asks whether the fertility rates of succeeding cohorts are functions of their own numbers and the opportunity structures accessible to them for personal development (e.g. occupational mobility, childbearing/rearing, etc). Thus, the baby-boom generation's cohort-specific life cycle, including a lower fertility rate for example, is accounted for by a population process rather than by ontogenetically determined life-cycle stages. Of course, the implicit assumption of most cohort frameworks is one of homogeneity within cohorts, thus constraining the analysis of variation in individual development (Dannefer 1988).

A second example is Featherman's (1986) project to study individual development as a population process. Featherman argues that "individuals may *manifest* development, but that a *causal* understanding of why individuals develop or tend to manifest only certain ranges and patterns of age-related change must be based on a population level of analysis" (1986:101). Development is distinguished from other types of change as "duration dependent," i.e. as a function of time-in-state (Featherman & Lerner 1985).

Hypotheses generated by Featherman's thesis pertain to variations in time-dependent change or human development across time and across individuals. The program methodology is comprised of observational and analytical strategies that permit the study of "time paths" of behaviors or attributes and the "statistical commonalities" in time-related change of these paths. Time-related changes can be indexed as duration dependence (the rate of change from a state or the "waiting time" to leave a state), age-graded transitions (the age-related movement into and out of states), and event transitions (event-related changes in states). Both normative and nonnormative life-course events are examined as states variously linked through time in individuals' lives. The effect of time in these states (duration dependence) is presumed to be basic to human development. Recent developments in dynamic methods provide the formal-analytic tools for modeling these temporal processes (see Tuma & Hannan 1984, Campbell & O'Rand 1988). Time-, age-, and event-graded individual development is also conceived as historically embedded, yielding the telegraphic characterization of this approach as "developmental contextualism" (Featherman & Lerner 1985).

An example of research consistent with the assumptions of Featherman's program is Duncan's (1988) panel study of age-related and event-related risks for poverty, using data from the Panel Study of Income Dynamics between 1969 and 1979. Duncan challenges the validity of the conventional life-cycle earnings model, i.e. the smooth profile of rising family income in early adulthood periods and falling income at later stages derived from conventional neoclassical assumptions underlying human capital theories. He finds family income to be highly volatile across the life-spans of individuals, with episodes of pervasive income loss tied in complex ways to demographic status (age and gender) and life events (divorce, widowhood, unemployment).

Thus, the emphasis on development as a continuous, population-driven and historically situated process leads to questions regarding the variability and determinants of the timing and ordering of life events. Historical studies (e.g. Hareven 1978a, Uhlenberg 1988), demographic models (e.g. Preston 1982, Oppenheimer 1988), and longitudinal analyses of transitions in modern life (Hogan 1978, Marini 1984, Henretta & O'Rand 1989) have clearly established that selected life cycle stages can be reversible, repeatable, and only loosely coupled with biological and chronological age over the individual life-span and across historical time.

Demographers have clearly established that individual variations in the age-schedule of life events are functions of demographic (Preston 1982) and historical change (Easterlin 1980, Elder 1981). For example, the prevalence and the temporal characteristics of remarriage over time are tied to historical cohorts and to shifting demographic pressures (Uhlenberg 1989), not to immutable family life cycles. Similarly, the timing and ordering of early life events related to major life domains such as education, marriage, and work lead to heterogeneous outcomes later in the life course and thus produce heterogeneity even within cohorts. The transition to adulthood, for example, is age-, event- and duration-dependent, and in turn constrains the shape and time-trajectory of the remaining life courses of individuals, i.e. their midlives (Hogan 1978, Marini 1984) and their late life statuses (Henretta & O'Rand 1989). Thus, "pathways" rather than "stages" are the empirically valid metaphors of the life course (Hogan & Astone 1986), although most research restricts itself to particular transitions representing circumscribed portions of the total life course (e.g. transition to adulthood, retirement, widowhood).

Heterogeneity in life-course transitions is also shaped by the synchronization and conjunction of multiple life events which are always constrained by varying conditions of uncertainty or opportunity. Oppenheimer's theory of marriage timing (1988), for example, ties marriage timing to the transition-to-work. Since work roles are crucial to socioeconomic prospects which, in turn, operate to constrain the assortative mating process, marriage timing is constrained by the transition to work. The conditions of the latter are highly uncertain, both in terms of more instantaneous issues of work role encumbency and commitment and regarding long-term careers. The complexity of the marriage process increases even more when men and women both face problems in the synchronization of both transitions.

Research programs on aging adopt a variety of approaches to the life-cycle problem and have undergone shifts in emphasis toward process and heterogeneity and away from stages and assumptions regarding their internal homogeneity. Although the causal framework of research on aging differs in significant ways from the general evolutionary model of the life cycle inherited from the past, it nevertheless shares a persistent concern in linking individuals to populations.

Family Life Cycle

Scholars of the family trace family life-cycle models within cultures to the turn of the century (see Rountree 1902, especially), but view the postwar period as a significant period of conceptual change, indeed, one of conceptual revolution. There is no shortage of reviews of the demise of the traditional family life-cycle concept (e.g. Elder 1978b, Hiss & Mattesich 1979, Juster & Vinovskis 1987, Murphy 1987, Grebenik et al 1989). That concept in its strongest form denoted a sequence of a priori stages in the family's progression from marriage to widowhood. The stage model, which found perhaps its most fervent advocacy in the work of Edith Duvall (see Murphy 1987), not only based time and variation on the cyclical age-related processes of formation, extension, contraction, and dissolution, it also had only one kind of family in mind—the nuclear family in midtwentieth century western (American) culture, consisting of a married couple with children. The family life-cycle model assumed a particular family type and indexed its development as changes in the size and composition of the unit over time, with the strong assumptions that all members of a cohort married and that no marriage ended without children, in divorce, or in premature death. It omitted considerations of generation or reproduction, in spite of its emphasis on stages of parenthood.

There is also little dispute that the life-course approach with its emphases on heterogeneity of timing, sequencing, and synchronization had the major impact on this conceptual shift (Juster & Vinovskis 1987). The approach to timing of the classical model was established in Glick's demographic study titled "Family Life Cycle" (1947), which identified seven major events in the cycle and calculated age norms of their occurrence. Thus, stage-specific central tendencies became normative benchmarks in the model. Life-course approaches, alternatively, have developed more dynamic heuristics to capture the patterns and causes of temporal pathways through life domains such as the family (Featherman 1986, Hogan & Astone 1986).

The emphasis on the nuclear family not only limited analysis to a family type, it also tended to focus exclusively on its earlier phases, i.e. formation (marriage) and extension (childbearing/rearing) patterns (Grebenik et al 1989). Thus, the timing and sequencing of later family events were largely preempted by the narrow focus. This bias in the family life-cycle literature was revealed most effectively by the new family history which emerged in the 1960s in the works of Goode, Tilly, Aries, Demos, and several others (Elder 1978a, Hareven 1978a). Examinations of family life from the colonial period forward, for example, did not fit with the life-cycle model; variable patterns of marriage timing, childbearing, and remarriage in different historical contexts presented anomalies for the conventional model. In addition, the availability of materials on the entire life courses of individuals provided insights into the increasing heterogeneity among individuals over the life course which demonstrated the life-cycle model's limited capacity to account for variation (Hareven 1978b).

Simultaneously, life-course research had already begun to address the issue of changing gender roles that, by definition, challenged the traditional model (Rossi 1980). Women's increasing participation in the workplace and men's variable work-career patterns coupled with trends toward delayed marriage and lower lifetime fertility were leading to a reconstruction of views regarding men's and women's life courses (e.g. Farber 1961, Wilensky 1960, 1961, Oppenheimer 1974). Farber's formal theory of the family as a set of mutually contingent careers was an early recognition of the inflexibility of the traditional model and the need for an analytical framework to test hypotheses regarding the interplay between individual life courses and the family's life course (Farber 1961). The two decades following Farber's work would give rise to the life-course model described in the earlier section on aging, with its emphases on cohorts, transitions, and issues of temporality regarding timing, order, sequence, and synchronization.

The family research tradition has turned to the explicit treatment of time. Questions pertaining to the interdependence of family time and individual life time within the context of historical time are being raised by what is now referred to as "family development theory" (Hill & Mattessich 1979). This research program has emerged out of the life-cycle tradition in direct response to life-course analysis. Its concerns parallel the life-course problem of the relationship of individual development to population or social change.

The strategy in this program is to account for the variance in family organization over time that is attributable to developmental processes in the family itself and to contextual changes in its environment, respectively. The cohort strategy is the heuristic for this analysis. Comparisons are made between aggregates of families which come into existence during selected time intervals. Inter- and intra-cohort variations become the indexes of developmental versus contextual change, and their interdependence can be determined (Hill & Mattessich 1979).

The family development perspective has moved from a non-intergenerational model of the *family life cycle* to a focus on family processes, a shift in its research agenda which parallels that in the field of aging. New assumptions regarding time and variation have raised new questions. Many of these questions are plausibly raised by the life-course emphasis on individual development and its contingent features. What factors predict the timing of marriage and childbearing? In turn, how do the timing of marriage and childbearing bear upon subsequent transitions in family and work? How does the expanding longevity of the life course influence the duration and sequencing of family events? These questions pertain to family processes *but* in the context of individual life courses.

On the other hand, questions pertaining to variations in intergenerational patterns of exchange within lineage families may present a set of puzzles that the individual life-course perspective cannot usurp or account for (Bengtson et al 1985, Bengtson & Robertson 1985). The "multigenerational family" as a unit of analysis defines time differently from the nuclear family life cycle and from the individual life course (Knipscheer 1988). Long-term trends in the extension of longevity have "verticalized" the family, introducing more generations per family (Bengtson et al 1985) even as the fertility rate has declined. Vertical relations across generations are superseding relations within generations in their relevance for distinguishing family from other social relations over the individual life-span and beyond it (Uhlenberg 1980).

In short, family research has undergone very dramatic changes in theory and method in the recent period. Life-course research has, in some ways, appropriated and redefined many empirical problems relegated historically to the family area. The family life-cycle program has moved toward different questions pertaining to family development processes and, lately, to specific considerations of multigenerational family processes. The traditional life cycle assumptions regarding stage and maturation have been rejected; new programs of research with different assumptions are emerging to replace the older view and to complement related programs like life-course analysis.

Organizational Life Cycle

The research program in modern organizational ecology was initiated in the early work of Freeman & Hannan (1975, Hannan & Freeman 1977) and in Howard Aldrich's exposition of social evolutionary models (Aldrich 1979, Campbell 1969). Its intellectual and historical roots, however, lie in Amos Hawley's human ecology model (1950), plant ecology (Adams 1935), and the Chicago School. Indeed, early research by Park and particularly by Park's students both anticipates more recent ecological-evolutionary approaches in organizational sociology and reflects a similar differentiation of so-called "rational selection" and "natural history" or "natural selection" models (Burns 1980).

Population ecologists adapted bioecological models to study processes of organizational change. These processes are redefined at the level of organizational populations rather than the adaptive or maturational processes of individual organizations. Individual organizations are important primarily as a source of variation from which external (environmental) mechanisms select those organizations that are best suited to, or "fit," the resource space. Consequently, a population of organizations demonstrates increasing "fit" or "isomorphism" with respect to its environment over time (Hannan & Freeman 1977, Aldrich 1979). Understanding the patterns of births and deaths (net mortality) which give rise to various organizational (population) forms is a major goal of this research program.

In spite of the term "organizational ecology" or "population ecology," research programs are active at all levels of analysis—the individual organization, the population of organizations, and the organizational community comprised of interdependent populations (Carroll 1984). These programs share a common substantive dimension—the adoption of life cycle as an analogy or theory-building device to characterize the passage of time and the structural changes in organizations or populations of organizations as processes of growth and decline (Kimberly 1980a, Freeman 1982). Views about the source of variation are similarly tied to the level of analysis adopted and the particular way in which life cycle is used.

Exactly *how* the concept is used varies substantially within this specialty area. It is not used systematically in the ideal typical form of parallel processes of reproduction and maturation at the population- and individual-levels, but clear deviations such as those that are represented by the concepts of life span or life course are equally rare. Instead, fields of study within organizational ecology extract different components from a life-cycle model to account for the phenomenon of organizational change.

Studies of individual organizations adopt an implicit and untested use of life cycle as a core assumption and show a remarkable similarity to the literature on human development. As such, their primary concern lies with the structural development or maturation of organizations although they presume that these are embedded in the reproduction of organizational forms at the population level. An early model proposed by Greiner (1972), for example, is reminiscent of Erikson's stage model of human (psychosocial) development. This model asserts that organizational growth occurs in five distinguishable phases characterized by periods of relative calm ("evolutionary periods") followed by substantial turmoil ("revolutionary periods"). Each of the latter periods is characterized by a particular problem or crisis (e.g. a crisis of leadership, a crisis of control, etc) that management must resolve before organizational development can proceed to the next stage. Other models of organizational life cycles differ on the specific mechanisms determining development but share a linear, unidirectional view of progressive movement and often make strong developmental (ontogenetic) assumptions (Cafferata 1982, see Quinn & Cameron 1983 for a review). The timing of such crises becomes an important research issue in more recent models that incorporate environmental disequilibrium, technological discontinuities, and "reversible" movement or even stagnation (e.g. Tushman & Romanelli 1985). But, the idea that organizational development is an individual-level process of maturational unfolding remains a central feature of these theoretical discussions.

Empirical studies at the organizational level usually adopt, at least implicitly, some such model, but tend to assume rather than test the occurrence of sequential structural changes. As such, explanations frequently rest on the assumption that change over the history of an organization is a manifestation of a similar population-level process (e.g. Langton 1984); or, similarly, that the extraction of one particular period of development (e.g. founding and early growth) is embedded in a longer-term process of maturation (e.g. Kimberly 1980b). Finally, studies of organizational decline and death—which have received much less attention than early development and births—continue to struggle with the deterministic assumptions that underlie stage models of development and try to distinguish processes of organizational decline from so-called "later life" or "aging" of organizations (Whetten 1987, Weitzel & Jonsson 1989). Here, organizational studies are trying to develop alternative explanations that retain the concept of life cycle as a way to characterize the temporal process of growth and decline while rejecting the prominence of *age-related* stages of development (and decline) implied by strict adherence to a life-cycle model.

Life cycle is invoked as a metaphor to test life-cycle processes in population-level studies of organizational mortality and/or foundings. Drawing on recent developments in dynamic analysis (Tuma & Hannan 1984), researchers develop formal statistical models of underlying stochastic processes generating differential rates of mortality (e.g. Freeman et al 1983). Here, the links between processes of growth and decline at the individual (organization) and population levels are elaborated in model parameters that identify and extract separate components of the mortality process. The often hypothesized "liability of newness" (Stinchcombe 1965) experienced by new organizations is decomposed into three components—the rate of "infant mortality," the asymptotic rate of mortality that applies to organizations surviving initial age-dependent mortality, and the speed at which the rate approaches the asymptotic level (e.g. Freeman et al 1983). The "liability of newness" has been demonstrated consistently across various populations, and its explanation typically involves some appeal to an organizational life cycle with the assumption of corresponding population and (individual) organizational processes that accompany this idea.

Both the population-dynamics model of Carroll & Delacroix (1982) and the density-dependence model of Hannan & Freeman (1987) appeal to processes across levels of analysis to account for organizational foundings and deaths. For example, in Delacroix & Carroll's study (1983) of foundings of newspaper organizations in Ireland and Argentina, prior foundings and prior deaths have curvilinear effects on current and future foundings because of material processes (e.g. newly available resources due to a death, creation of a market due to new foundings) and/or subjective evaluations by potential entrepreneurs. Conversely, a very high level of previous deaths or foundings is indicative of a "noxious" or saturated environment. Their study of organizational mortality rates in these same populations (Carroll & Delacroix 1982) also appeals to population-organization links. An analysis of cohort dependence tests the hypothesis that the life chances of individual newspapers will be greater in later cohorts due to the greater maturity of the industry as a whole. The crux of the explanation for the cohort-dependent mortality rates in Argentina but not Ireland lies in (*a*) a time-span of data for Ireland that is incomplete and lacks information on the industry's earliest history or "infancy;" and (*b*) Ireland's closer ties with England which had an established ("mature") newspaper industry. In short, the critical component of the explanation lies in the appeal to an older and hence more mature population (industry) and its influence on the deaths of individual organizations.

Explanations of these phenomena place demands on only the broadest outlines of the idea of life cycle. In 1952, Penrose (1952:805) pointed out that the tendency to invoke a life-cycle analogy in the theory of the firm injected far more assumptions and implications into an explanation than were necessary to account for the fact that "all firms had some sort of a beginning, a period of existence and, if now extinct, an end." Similarly, researchers in organizational ecology avail themselves of "life cycle" as a ready term and explanation, but they focus on the occurrence of events (births and deaths), specifically (and almost exclusively) their occurrence during the early years of an organizational population. They have expressed relatively little interest in the timing and/or sequencing of structural transformations over the life course of an organizational population, the maturational phases that characterize organizations and differentiate populations of organizations, or the variety of hypotheses logically generated and interrelated by a full-fledged and systematic adoption of a life-cycle model.

Notably, this loose adaptation of the concept provides a ready source of variation that can be easily accounted for with reference to a life-cycle trajectory. Not unlike early research on aging, the existence of variation in studies of individual organizations is associated with movement through a series of structural transformations or successive forms in response to environmental exigencies, managerial prowess, or both (e.g. Kimberly 1980b, Langton 1984). Variation plays a more apparent role for population studies; indeed, Hannan & Freeman (1977) spawned this research program by raising questions about the diversity of organizational structures in society.

Yet, despite the key role of variation in population ecology models, its source seems to be of little concern. The population ecology model is "indifferent to the ultimate source of variation, as planned and unplanned variation both provide raw material from which selection can be made" (Aldrich 1979:28). However, since organizations are constrained by strong inertial pressures, the immediate source of variation is always known; organizational births or foundings introduce "raw material" into an existing population of organizations and are then subject to the same environmental selection as their predecessors. In the case of new organizations introduced into, and replicating the form of, an existing population, these selection processes and the resulting organizational form are accounted for by appealing to the maturational "clocks" at the populational level which may either enhance or inhibit the life chances of the individual organization. Alternatively, new organizations which also initiate new forms have the liabilities of newness and "infancy" in the maturational processes, corresponding to the larger social system (Hannan & Freeman 1987). Notably, however, most research focuses on the former type—new examples of existing forms (Hawley 1981, Astley 1985). As such, variation and its potential influence on organizational structures in society is always constrained by time as it is parameterized in a life cycle model (but see Brittain & Freeman 1980; Delacroix et al 1989).

Life cycle operates in a variety of ways in organizational sociology, but, particularly within the most active program of population ecology, in ways that may be at odds with the program's stated goals. Life cycle and the maturational or growth processes it invokes become an economical way (recall Adams 1979) to characterize the passage of time, but it simultaneously raises the salience of orderly processes and logical similarities among individuals (population units) while masking the potential heterogeneity or volatility accompanying this process. The constraints of this metaphorical use of life cycle can be seen in light of recommendations by friendly critics to reconsider and expand the role of variation (e.g. Hawley 1981, Astley 1985) and of recent challenges by competing research programs such as institutional theories (Zucker 1987). Despite recent dialogues between these two schools of thought (e.g. Carroll & Hannan 1989 and the accompanying comment by Zucker), efforts at synthesis reveal the power, and hence the attractiveness, of a heuristic use of life cycle which can readily extract and incorporate components of the competing program and recast it at a single (population) level of analysis without challenging the fundamental assumptions implied by a stricter definition of the concept.

CONCLUSIONS

The meanings and uses of life cycle across the social sciences are varied and widespread. But the problems and prospects attached to their uses are remarkably similar. The level of analysis, conceptualization of time, and sources of variation pose common constraints on the use of life-cycle concepts across the social sciences. Life cycle, most precisely defined, requires explicit treatment of stages (phases), maturation (development), and generation (reproduction). This basic conceptualization provides an "ideal type" of developmental process from which its alternatives diverge.

The life-span alternative tends to represent the duration of the individual's lifetime over which maturation is presumed to occur. Except for events of birth or death, the life span represents an undifferentiated conception of the lifetime. Life course, on the other hand, is distinguished by its focus on the content, timing, and sequencing of phases or events constituting the developmental pathways of individuals. These alternative conceptions do not account for reproduction or generation.

These distinctions are not universally recognized across the social sciences. The concepts are used interchangeably and often invoked only for purposes of linguistic economy, i.e. to denote a sense of temporality in the life of an individual or a collectivity. Yet, the implications of these different conceptualizations are considerable. A careful study of the traditional life-cycle concept reveals its specific relevance to populations rather than individuals, since it involves reproduction and generation. Alternatively, life span and life course are more relevant to the examination of individual lives, although both conceptions have come to be tied to or embedded within population-level frameworks. The life-course conception, particularly, has become associated with age stratification theory which explicitly links individual aging with population change. Thus, the life-course concept has implications for the examination of social change.

However, the strict life-cycle conception is more relevant for the examination of social order and equilibrium processes than for the study of change. The requisite notion of reproduction which defines the "cyclical" component of the traditional concept places limits on the analysis of heterogeneity and change. The demise of the naive use of the traditional family life cycle concept has been traced to this specific limitation.

This dichotomy in the conception of time has been noted by Gould (1987) to express the persistent tension in Western thought between "time's cycle" and "time's arrow." The former accounts for the immanence of cyclical constraints in the process of social order, the latter for linear progression through time in the process of change. These underlying concepts of time, when ignored or confused, can limit the precision of our understanding of development and misspecify the phenomenon under study.

Finally, despite the prescriptive tone with which this study is concluding, it is illuminating to discover the universal appeal of shared concepts in the sciences. The call for an "orthodox" metatheoretical usage of the concept across the social sciences does not dispose of the observation that heuristic uses of the life-cycle idea, even those violating the assumptions of the traditional conception, have been productive in some specialties. It has worked well as a "naive model" for the developing program in the population ecology of organizations. It has been testable in this usage. It is nevertheless the case that some research programs themselves are inconsistent in their declarations of usage and it is here that greater precision is required.

ACKNOWLEDGMENTS

The authors appreciate the assistance of Glen H. Elder, Jr., Ida Harper Simpson, E. Roy Weintraub, Mac O'Barr, and two anonymous reviewers in the preparation of this review.

Literature Cited

Adams, C. C. 1935. The relation of human ecology to general ecology. *Ecology* XVI:316–35

Adams, M. B. 1979. From 'gene fund' to 'gene pool:' On the evolution of evolutionary language. *Stud. Hist. Bio.* 3:241–83

Aldrich, H. 1979. *Organizations and Environments.* Englewood Cliffs, NJ: Prentice-Hall

Astley, W. G. 1985. The two ecologies: Population and community perspectives on organizational evolution. *Admin. Sci. Q.* 30:224–41

Baltes, P. B. 1979. Life-span developmental psychology: Some converging observations on history and theory. See Baltes & Brim 1979, pp. 256–81

Baltes, P. B., Brim, O. G., Jr., eds. 1979. *Life Span Development and Behavior,* Vol. 2. New York: Academic

Becker, G. S. 1975 [1964]. *Human Capital.* New York: Columbia Univ. Press. 2nd ed.

Bengtson, V. L., Cutler, N. E., Mangen, D. J., Marshall, V. W. 1985. Generations, cohorts, and relations between age groups. In *Handbook of Aging and the Social Sciences,* ed. R. H. Binstock, E. Shanas, pp. 303–34. New York: Van Nostrand Reinhold

Bengtson, V. L., Robertson, J. F., eds. 1985. *Grandparenthood.* Beverly Hills: Sage

Birren, J. E., Bengtson, V. L., eds. 1988. *Emergent Theories of Aging.* New York: Springer

Blaug, M. 1980. *The Methodology of Economics.* Cambridge: Cambridge Univ. Press

Boulding, K. E. 1950. *A Reconstruction of Economics.* New York: Wiley

Brittain, J. W., Freeman, J. H. 1980. Organizational proliferation and density dependent selection. See Kimberly & Miles 1980, pp. 291–338

Burns, L. R. 1980. The Chicago School and the study of organization-environment relations. *J. Hist. Beh. Sci.* 16:342–58

Cafferata, G. L. 1982. The building of democratic organizations: An embryological metaphor. *Admin. Sci. Q.* 27:280–303

Campbell, D. T. 1969. Variation and selective retention in socio-cultural evolution. *Gen. Syst.* 14:69–85

Campbell, R. T., O'Rand, A. M. 1988. Settings and sequences: The heuristics of aging research. See Birren & Bengtson 1988, pp. 58–79

Carroll, G. R. 1984. Organizational ecology. *Annu. Rev. Sociol.* 10:71–93

Carroll, G. R., Delacroix, J. 1982. Organizational mortality in the newspaper industries of Argentina and Ireland: An ecological approach. *Admin. Sci. Q.* 27:169–98

Carroll, G. R., Hannan, M. T. 1989. Density dependence in the evolution of populations of newspaper organizations. *Am. Sociol. Rev.* 54:524–41

Clausen, J. 1986. *The Life Course: A Sociological Perspective.* Englewood Cliffs, NJ: Prentice-Hall

Coale, A. J. 1972. *The Growth and Structure of Human Populations.* Princeton: Princeton Univ. Press

Coleman, W. 1971. *Biology in the Nineteenth Century: Problems of Form, Function, and Transformation.* Cambridge: Cambridge Univ. Press

Dannefer, D. 1988. What's in a name? An account of the neglect of variability in the study of aging. See Birren & Bengtson 1988, pp. 356–84

Delacroix, J., Carroll, G. R. 1983. Organizational foundings: An ecological study of the newspaper industries of Argentina and Ireland. *Admin. Sci. Q.* 28:274–91

Delacroix, J., Swaminathan, A., Solt, M. E. 1989. Density dependence versus population dynamics: An ecological study of failings in the California wine industry. *Am. Sociol. Rev.* 54:245–62

Duncan, G. J. 1988. The volatility of family income over the life course. In *Life-Span Development and Behavior,* ed. P. B. Baltes, D. L. Featherman, R. M. Lerner, 9:317–58. Hillsdale, NJ: Erlbaum

Easterlin, R. 1980. *Birth and Fortune: The Impact of Numbers on Personal Affairs.* New York: Basic

Eisenstadt, S. N. 1956. *Generation to Generation.* Glencoe: Free

Elder, G. H. Jr. 1975. Age differentiation and the life course. *Annu. Rev. Sociol.* 1: 165–90

Elder, G. H. Jr. 1978a. Approaches to social change and the family. *Am. J. Sociol.* 84:S1–38

Elder, G. H. Jr. 1978b. Family history and the life course. See Hareven 1978a, pp. 17–64

Elder, G. H. Jr. 1981. History and the family: the discovery of complexity. *J. Marriage Fam.* 43:489–519

Elder, G. H. Jr. 1987. Families and lives: Some development in life-course studies. See Hareven & Plakans 1987, pp. 179–200

England, P., Farkas, G. 1986. *Households, Employment, and Gender: A Social, Economic, and Demographic View.* New York: Aldine

Erikson, E. H. 1963. *Childhood and Society.* New York: Norton. 2nd ed.

Erikson, E. H. 1968. Life cycle. In *International Encyclopedia of the Social Sciences,* ed. D. L. Sills, 9:286–92. New York: Macmillan & Free Press

Farber, B. 1961. The family as a set of mutually contingent careers. In *Household Decision Making,* ed. N. Foote, pp. 276–97. New York: New York Univ. Press

Featherman, D. L. 1983. The life-span perspective in social science research. In *Life-Span Development and Behavior,* ed. P. B. Baltes, O. G. Brim, Jr., 5:1–49. New York: Academic

Featherman, D. L. 1986. Biography, society and history: Individual development as a population process. In *Human Development and the Life Course: Multidisciplinary Perspectives,* ed. A. B. Sorensen, F. Weinert, L. Sherrod, pp. 99–149. Hillsdale, NJ: Erlbaum

Featherman, D. L., Hauser, R. M. 1978. *Opportunity and Change.* New York: Academic

Featherman, D. L., Lerner, R. M. 1985. Ontogenesis and sociogenesis: Problem for theory and research about development and socialization over the lifespan. *Am. Sociol. Rev.* 50:659–76

Foner, A., Kertzer, D. I. 1978. Transitions over the life course: Lessons from age-set societies. *Am. J. Soc.* 83:1081–104

Fortes, M. 1949. *The Web of Kinship Among the Tallensi.* London: Oxford Univ. Press

Fortes, M. 1971. Introduction. See Goody 1971, pp. 1–14

Freeman, J. 1982. Organizational life cycles and natural selection processes. In *Research in Organizational Behavior,* ed. B. M. Staw, L. L. Cummings, 4:1–32. Greenwich, Conn.: JAI

Freeman, J., Carroll, G. R., Hannan, M. T. 1983. The liability of newness: Age dependence in organizational death rates. *Am. Sociol. Rev.* 48:692–710

Freeman, J., Hannan, M. T. 1975. Growth and decline processes in organizations. *Am. Sociol. Rev.* 40:215–28

Friedman, M. 1957. *The Theory of the Consumption Function.* New York: Princeton Univ. Press

Fries, J. 1987. Life-Span. In *The Encyclopedia of Aging,* ed. G. L. Maddox, pp. 401–2. New York: Springer

Fuchs, V. R. 1983. *How We Live.* Cambridge: Harvard Univ. Press

Glick, P. 1947. The family cycle. *Am. Sociol. Rev.* 14:164–74

Goody, J., ed. 1971. *The Developmental Cy-*

cle in Domestic Groups. Cambridge: Cambridge Univ. Press

Gould, S. J. 1977. *Ontogeny and Phylogeny*. Cambridge, Mass: Belknap

Gould, S. J. 1987. *Time's Arrow, Time's Cycle*. Cambridge: Harvard Univ. Press

Grebenik, E., Hohn, C., Mackensen, R. 1989. *Later Phases of the Family Cycle: Demographic Aspects*. Oxford: Clarendon

Greiner, L. E. 1972. Evolution and revolution as organizations grow. *Harv. Bus. Rev.* 50:37–46

Haire, M. 1959. Biological models and empirical histories of the growth of organizations. In *Modern Organization Theory*, ed. M. Haire, pp. 272–306. New York: Wiley

Hannan, M. T., Freeman, J. 1977. The population ecology of organizations. *Am. J. Sociol.* 82:929–64

Hannan, M. T., Freeman, J. 1987. The ecology of organizational founding: American labor unions, 1836–1985. *Am. J. Sociol.* 92:910–43

Hareven, T. K. 1978a. *Transitions: The Family and the Life Course in Historical Perspective*. New York: Academic

Hareven, T. K. 1978b. Cycles, courses, and cohorts: Reflections on theoretical and methodological approaches to the historical study of family development. *J. Soc. Hist.* 23:97–109

Hareven, T. K., Plakans, A., eds. 1987. *Family History at the Crossroads*. Princeton, NJ: Princeton Univ. Press

Hawley, A. H. 1950. *Human Ecology: A Theory of Community Structure*. New York: Free

Hawley, A. H. 1981. Human ecology: persistence and change. *Am. Behav. Sc.* 24:423–44

Henretta, J. C., O'Rand, A. M. 1989. *Retirement of dual-worker couples: Early division of labor and late-life work exit*. Pap. prcs. Ann. Meet. Am. Sociol. Assoc. San Francisco

Hill, R., Mattesich, P. 1979. Family development theory and life-span development. See Baltes & Brim 1979, pp. 162–204

Hogan, D. P. 1978. The variable order of events in the life course. *Am. Sociol. Rev.* 43:573–86

Hogan, D. P., Astone, N. M. 1986. The transition to adulthood. *Annu. Rev. Sociol.* 12:109–30

Juster, S. M., Vinovskis, M. A. 1987. Changing perspectives on the American family in the past. *Annu. Rev. Sociol.* 13:193–216

Kastenbaum, R. 1987. Life-Course. In *The Encyclopedia of Aging*, ed. G. L. Maddox, pp. 388–90. New York: Springer

Kertzer, D. I., Keith, J., eds. 1984. *Age and Anthropological Theory*. Ithaca: Cornell Univ. Press

Kertzer, D. I., Schaie, K. W., eds. 1989. *Age Structuring in Comparative Perspective*. Hillsdale, NJ: Erlbaum

Kimberly, J. R. 1980a. The life cycle analogy and the study of organizations: Introduction. See Kimberly & Miles 1980, pp. 1–14

Kimberly, J. R. 1980b. Initiation, innovation, and institutionalization in the creation process. See Kimberly & Miles 1980, pp. 18–43

Kimberly, J. R., Miles, R. H., eds. 1980. *The Organizational Life Cycle*. San Francisco: Jossey-Bass

Knipscheer, C. P. M. 1988. Temporal embeddedness and aging within the multigenerational family: The case of grandparenting. See Birren & Bengtson 1988, pp. 426–46

Kohn, D. 1980. Theories to work by: Rejected theories, reproduction, and Darwin's path to natural selection. *Stud. Hist. Bio.* 4:67–198

Lakatos, I. 1978. *The Methodology of Scientific Research Programmes*. Philosophical Papers, Vol. 1, ed. J. Worrall & G. Currie. Cambridge: Cambridge Univ. Press

Langness, L. L., Frank, G. 1981. *Lives: An Anthropological Approach to Biography*. Novato, Calif: Chandler & Sharp

Langton, J. 1984. The ecological theory of bureaucracy: The case of Josiah Wedgwood and the British pottery industry. *Admin. Sci. Q.* 29:330–54

Leibowitz, L. 1969. Dilemma for social evolution: The impact of Darwin. *J. Theor. Biol.* 25:255–75

Levinson, D. 1978. *Seasons of a Man's Life*. New York: Knopf. 363 pp.

Marini, M. M. 1984. The order of events in the transition to adulthood. *Sociol. Educ.* 57:63–84

Mayr, R. 1982. *The Growth of Biological Thought: Diversity, Evolution, and Inheritance*. Cambridge, Mass: Belknap

Murphy, M. 1987. Measuring the family life cycle: Concepts, data and methods. In *Rethinking the Life Cycle*, ed. A. Bryman, B. Bytheway, P. Allatt, T. Kiel, pp. 30–50. London: Macmillan

Oppenheimer, V. K. 1974. The life cycle squeeze: The interaction of men's occupational and family life cycles. *Demography* 11:227–45

Oppenheimer, V. K. 1988. A theory of marriage timing. *Am. J. Sociol.* 94:563–91

O'Rand, A. M. 1990. Stratification and the life course. In *Handbook of Aging and the Social Sciences*, ed. R. H. Binstock, L. K. George, pp. 130–48. New York: Academic Press

Park, R. E., Burgess, E. W. 1921. *An Introduction to the Science of Sociology*. Chicago: Univ. Chicago

Penrose, E. T. 1952. Biological analogies in the theory of the firm. *Am. Econ. Rev.* 42:804–19

Preston, S. H. 1982. Relations between individual life cycles and population characteristics. *Am. Sociol. Rev.* 47:253–64

Quinn, R. E., Cameron, K. 1983. Organizational life cycles and shifting criteria of effectiveness: Some preliminary evidence. *Manage. Sci.* 29:33–51

Reinert, G. 1979. Prolegomena to a history of life-span development. See Baltes & Brim 1979, pp. 205–55

Riley, M. W. 1987. On the significance of age in sociology. *Am. Sociol. Rev.* 52:1–14

Riley, M. W., Abeles, R., Teitelbaum, M., eds. 1982. *Aging From Birth to Death: Vol. II Sociotemporal Perspectives.* AAAS Selected Symposium. Boulder, Colo: Westview

Rossi, A. S. 1980. Life span theories and women's lives. *Signs* 6:4–32

Rountree, B. S. 1902. *Poverty: A Study of Town Life.* London: Macmillan

Ryder, N. B. 1965. The cohort as a concept in the study of social change. *Am. Sociol. Rev.* 30:843–61

Schultz, T. W. 1963. *The Economic Value of Education.* New York: Columbia Univ. Press

Stinchcombe, A. 1965. Social structure and organizations. In *Handbook of Organizations,* ed. J. G. March, pp. 142–93. Chicago: Rand McNally

Tanner, J. M. 1981. *A History of the Study of Human Growth.* Cambridge: Cambridge Univ. Press

Tuma, N. B., Hannan, M. T. 1984. *Social Dynamics: Models and Methods.* Orlando, Fla: Academic

Tushman, M. L., Romanelli, E. 1985. Organizational evolution: A metamorphosis model of convergence and reorientation. In *Research in Organizational Behavior,* ed. L. L. Cummings, B. M. Staw, pp. 171–222. Greenwich, Conn: JAI

Uhlenberg, P. 1980. Death and the family. *J. Fam. Hist.* 4:313–20

Uhlenberg, P. 1988. Aging and the societal significance of cohorts. See Birren & Bengtson 1988, pp. 405–25

Uhlenberg, P. 1989. Remarriage: A life-cycle perspective. See Grebenik, Hohn & Mackensen 1989, pp. 66–82

Vinovskis, M. 1977. From household size to the life course. *Am. Behav. Sci.* 21:263–87

Vinovskis, M. 1988. The historian and the life course: Reflections on recent approaches to the study of American family life in the past. In *Life-Span Development and Behavior,* ed. P. B. Baltes, D. L. Featherman, R. M. Lerner, 8:33–59. Hillsdale, NJ: Erlbaum

Waring, J. M. 1975. Social replenishment and social change: The problem of disordered cohort flow. *Am. Behav. Sci.* 19:237–56

Weiss, Y. 1986. The determination of life cycle earnings: A survey. In *Handbook of Labor Economics,* vol I, ed. O. Ashenfelter, R. Layard. Amsterdam: Elsevier

Weitzel, W., Jonsson, E. 1989. Decline in organizations: A literature integration and extension. *Admin. Sci. Q.* 34:91–109

Whetten, D. A. 1987. Organizational growth and decline processes. *Annu. Rev. Sociol.* 13:335–58

Wilensky, H. L. 1960. Work, careers, and social integration. *Int. Soc. Sci.* XII:543–60

Wilensky, H. L. 1961. Orderly careers and social participation: The impact of work history on social integration in the middle mass. *Am. Sociol. Rev.* 26:521–39

Winston, G. C. 1982. *The Timing of Economic Activities: Firms, Households, and Markets in Time-Specific Analysis.* Cambridge: Cambridge Univ. Press

Winston, G. C. 1988. Three problems with the treatment of time in economics: Perspectives, repetitiveness, and time units. In *The Boundaries of Economics,* eds. G. C. Winston, R. F. Teichgraeber III, pp. 30–52. Cambridge: Cambridge Univ. Press

Zucker, L. G. 1987. Institutional theories of organizations. *Annu. Rev. Sociol.* 13:443–64

Annu. Rev. Sociol. 1990. 16:263–99

MARKET AND NETWORK THEORIES OF THE TRANSITION FROM HIGH SCHOOL TO WORK: Their Application to Industrialized Societies

James E. Rosenbaum

Center for Urban Affairs and Policy Research, Northwestern University, 2040 Sheridan Road, Evanston Illinois 60208

Takehiko Kariya

National Institute of Multimedia Education, Chiba, Japan

Rick Settersten

School of Education and Social Policy, Northwestern University, 2003 Sheridan Road, Evanston Illinois 60208

Tony Maier

School of Education and Social Policy, Northwestern University, 2003 Sheridan Road, Evanston Illinois 60208

KEY WORDS: high school-work transition, work entry, network theory, youth labor market, and segmented markets

---

Abstract

The transition from high school to work creates serious problems for American youths and employers. Since single theories have difficulty conceptualizing the reasons for these problems, this paper reviews four theories that elucidate aspects: segmented labor market theory, human capital theory,

263

0360-0572/90/0815-0263$02.00

signaling theory, and network theory. In addition, this review contrasts the American transition system with the transition systems in Japan, West Germany, and the United Kingdom to reveal practices and theoretical issues which are neither salient nor well studied in the American literature. We extend signaling theory to examine youths' use of signals, employers' use of dubious signals (e.g. age) while ignoring promising ones (e.g. grades), and signals which are efficient in the short-term but not in the long-term. We extend network theory to include both personal contacts and institutional linkages. We note the ways poor signals may affect youths' plans and motivation and make them unresponsive to market demands, and the ways institutional networks may affect schooling and work-entry in the United States. Implications for theory, policy, and future research are also considered.

INTRODUCTION

The transition from high school to work is a serious problem. Many high school graduates spend their first years after school unemployed or job hopping, with consequent loss of training and productivity. The youth unemployment rate is two to three times the rate for adult men, and the rate for black youth is about twice that of white youth. Moreover, even youth with jobs are two to three times more likely to be unemployed a year later than are adults (Rytina 1983, p. 5). Why do youth have difficulty getting and keeping jobs?

The problem is hard to conceptualize because it involves many complexities. The school-work transition links three different parties (youth, schools, and employers), and problems can arise from shortcomings in one or more parties, from problems of information flow between them, or from problems in their relationships. Do schools offer the wrong preparation or too little help finding jobs? Do youth fail to learn skills, or do they have faulty job search or work behavior? Do employers avoid considering youth for good jobs, or do they give them a fair chance and find them lacking? Sorting out causal mechanisms is difficult. Moreover, school curricula and employers' needs are continually changing, but there is little coordination among them. Conceptual clarity is needed about these complex phenomena.

This chapter reviews four theories that can help clarify these issues. Although not designed to account for this transition, each theory offers a coherent explanation of youths' work-entry problems. This article reviews the strengths and weaknesses of each for explaining the school-work transition.

We often speak of the youth labor market as if work-entry operated like a market. The problem to be explained is why this market fails to reach an equilibrium where all youth find jobs. The four theories reviewed here offer different explanations for why this does not happen. *Segmented theory* says that employers are unresponsive to youths' skills for many jobs, although the theory is vague about why employers ignore youths' skills and how they confine them in poor jobs. *Human capital theory* accepts market theory and blames youths' problems on their own deficiencies, although it doesn't explain why youth allow their deficiencies to persist or why employers create poor incentives for youth to increase their human capital. Third, *signaling theory* says that employers are unresponsive because of the economic costs of getting good information about youth, but it ignores noneconomic constraints on information. Fourth, building upon market and signaling theories, *network theory* considers the social conditions that make information effective. Information is more likely to be communicated, trusted, and effective if it is embedded in a social network, so some work-entry problems arise because youth do not have ties to employers.

This review extends these theories in two respects. First, while signaling theory is usually only applied to employers' use of signals, we use this theory to explain how youth use signals to set their goals and to infer the payoffs for their efforts. We also examine how poor information makes youth unresponsive to their market situation.

Second, this review also introduces a new perspective on network theory. While most research stresses personal networks, we also describe institutional networks, their responsiveness to market forces, and the factors making them responsive. Institutional networks between high schools and employers occur in the United States, but they are neither salient nor well-studied. Therefore, we review how such networks operate in other nations where they are more salient (Japan, West Germany and the United Kingdom), and how they aid youths' work-entry by improving signals to employers and incentives for youth.

This review focuses mostly on the transition from high school to work. Transitions from other levels of education are important, and some similarities apply across various levels. However, the differences are too great to be covered adequately in this short review.

Segmented Labor Market Theory

Segmented labor market theory contends that labor markets are highly stratified: primary labor market jobs offer high wages, good working conditions, job security, and advancement chances, while secondary labor market jobs lack these attributes. This theory also contends that the secondary sector does not reward workers' skills, so the skills of employees and applicants do not lead to better jobs or wages (Althauser & Kalleberg 1981, Osterman 1980, Sørensen 1977). The theory further specifies that women, minorities, and noncollege youth are confined to the secondary sector, and once employed in this sector, it is hard to escape.

The theory contends that the segmented nature of the labor market helps employers control workers and perpetuates a system of credentialism and inequality (Baron 1984, Cain 1976, Carline et al 1985, Collins 1975, 1979, Kanter 1977, Raffe 1981, Spenner et al 1982). For example, Kanter (1977, p. 48) argues that "homosocial reproduction" occurs in organizations to "carefully guard power and privilege for those who fit in, for those they see as 'their kind.' " Collins (1979) also discusses the use of credentials and social background to ensure "normative control" in the organization. These notions suggest that the real goal served by a segmented market is not to find individuals with better skills, but rather to keep social advancement in the hands of those who have such power.

Extending the notion of social control, one version of segmented labor market theory offers hypotheses about the school criteria employers use for hiring. Extending the work of Kohn & Schooler (1983), Bowles & Gintis (1976) propose that although college graduates are hired based on their ability to be self-directed, noncollege youth are hired based on their rule-following behaviors: effort, deportment, attendance, and punctuality. Bowles & Gintis further propose a correspondence between the social relations in schools and work: that schools evaluate students on criteria similar to employers' hiring criteria. However, this hypothesis was not supported in several empirical tests (Jencks et al 1979, p. 255, Olneck & Bills 1980, Bills 1983, Kariya & Rosenbaum 1988, Rosenbaum & Kariya 1989).

Research supports several aspects of segmented theory: the clustering of job attributes, employers' disregard of applicants' school performance in hiring into secondary labor market jobs, and the diminished career chances of minorities, females, and youth (Bills 1983, Borus et al 1984, Brown 1982, Collins 1979, Crain 1984, Heimer 1985, Johnson & Backman 1973, Meyer 1977, Ornstein 1976, Rosenbaum 1984, Rosenthal & Hearn 1982, Spenner et al 1982).

However, segmented labor market theory has some serious shortcomings. First, while segmented labor market theory asserts that youth cannot get good jobs (Dunlop 1957, Doeringer & Piore 1971, Gordon 1971, Hodson & Kaufman 1982), it does not explain how youth are confined to segments (Granovetter 1981). Moreover, the degree of confinement is exaggerated. While research finds some barriers between labor markets, it also finds extensive evidence of mobility from secondary into primary labor market jobs, particularly for youth (Parcel 1987, p. 38). Evidently, the barriers are semipermeable, and the theory cannot explain exceptions or why they happen.

Second, the theory does not explain why youth are treated differently or how the selection process changes as youth become adults. The theory identifies youth as one of the groups, along with women and blacks, that are relegated to worse jobs. However, unlike other statuses, "youth" changes with time. While segmented theory indicates that people get better jobs after they become adults, it doesn't explain why or how this happens. Youth are assigned to secondary jobs which offer no advancement, but somehow they advance as they age and become adults (Andrisani 1973, 1976; D'Amico & Brown 1982). The theory does not explain how growing older allows them to gain access to better jobs from jobs that offer no advancement.

Third, by focusing only on the employer side of the transition, the theory says very little about individuals. The theory lists which kinds of people are assigned to which jobs, but it doesn't say much about why these groups were chosen, how they respond, how they could alter these assignments, or why and how often exceptions occur. Indeed, segmented theories sometimes argue that confinement occurs because workers lack stable work habits, which is an anomalous contention for a structural theory and which predicts more confinement than actually exists, as noted above (Granovetter 1981).

Finally, since segmented labor market theory ignores the use of information, it does not fully explain employers' choice of selection criteria. If employers received good information about employee productivity, would they ignore it and continue using age, sex, and race? Nor does the theory's stress on social control and noncognitive selection criteria fit with employers' complaints about the poor literacy skills of their workforce and the billion dollars a year they spend on basic skills education for their workers (Eurich 1985).

No theory can explain everything. Although this theory explains why youth, minorities, and women get poor jobs, it exaggerates confinement, and it is particularly weak at explaining exceptions or alternative selection criteria, because of its one-sided focus on the structure of employment We next turn to a theory with the opposite focus, a one-sided focus on individuals.

Human Capital Theory

Human capital theory contends that youths' work-entry problems arise from deficiencies in youth. This theory contends that individuals' abilities and skills are their productive capability—their "human capital." Human capital is analogous to the physical capital (e.g. machinery) in factories: people invest (effort, tuition, etc) to improve their stock of capital and their probable returns in wages.

Human capital theory is based on the market model, which assumes that people compete in free markets and that more valuable people are paid more. Unlike network theory (considered later), market models are critical of institutional linkages between schools and employers, fearing that preferential relations between employers and certain schools would limit competition, reduce employee quality, and raise labor costs. Without such links, employers must rely on pure market forces, and applicants' value alone would determine their selection.

Human capital theory suggests that work-entry problems arise because youth are defective. Taking this view, numerous reports have identified the poor academic skills of American youth as the cause of youth work-entry problems (NCEE 1983, NAS 1984, CED 1985, NAEP 1985).

Yet three aspects of work-entry problems suggest that human capital is not the whole problem. First, the development of human capital in schools (school achievement) is partly determined by effort, which is strongly affected by external incentives. Second, while employers complain about youths' poor human capital, they do not use selection criteria that would help them select applicants with better human capital. Third, although work-entry problems are so pervasive in the United States that they seem intrinsic to youth, Japan eliminated such problems by reforms that improved information flow between schools and employers.

1. *School achievement is partly determined by effort, which is strongly affected by external incentives.*

While human capital theory blames poor school achievement on poor ability or poor instruction, effort and discipline are also critical influences and are important problems in schools. In every Gallup poll over the past 19 years, parents have identified discipline as one of the top problems facing public schools (Gallup 1988). More intensive studies reach similar conclusions (Goodlad 1984). Students' low effort is manifest in a variety of ways: absenteeism, class cutting, tardiness, disruptive behavior, verbal abuse, failure to do homework, and drug or alcohol abuse (Meyer et al 1971, Birman & Natriello 1978, Hollingsworth et al 1984, Cusick 1983, DiPrete et al 1981, Chobot & Garibaldi 1982, DeLeonibus 1978, Thompson & Stanard 1975, Sedlak et al 1986).

These behaviors seriously detract from the development of youths' human capital, but human capital theory cannot explain them. They are less influenced by ability and training than by effort. Effort is affected by many factors, but one important determinant is the incentive structure in schools. Incentives are critical influences on effort, as is widely recognized by psychologists, sociologists, and economists. Since incentives are easier to change than ability or personality, human capital may be most effectively improved by changing the incentive structure of schools.

This conceptual distinction can be seen in practical terms. Policies based on human capital theory have called for longer school days, longer school years, and increased standards. However, if effort is the problem, then such policies would be inadequate. Like pushing on string, increased hours and demands will be ineffective if students do not exert effort. Reforms that require students to spend more hours in school cannot compel them to exert effort and may only increase school drop-outs (McPartland & McDill 1977). Human capital theory is not sufficient to understand these problems.

2. *Despite their complaints about basic skills, employers do not use grades or test scores in hiring*

National panels (NCEE 1983 CED 1985) indicate that employers want applicants to have greater human capital, particularly basic skills in reading, writing, and math. However, employers do not take the actions implied by their stated concerns about basic skills. Grades and test scores have little effect on which youth get jobs, better jobs, or higher wages. Using national survey data (NLS72), Griffin et al (1981) found that aptitude, class rank, and other school information have small and often insignificant effects on employment and job attainments of high school graduates who directly enter the workforce.

Using the same data, Meyer & Wise (1982, p. 312) found that class rank in school had insignificant effects on wage rates two years after graduation (1974) and only barely significant effects four years after graduation (1976). Willis & Rosen (1979) found that a one standard deviation increase in math and reading scores of high school graduates lowered the first job's wage by 3.5%. Bishop (1987) found that although basic achievement raises productivity, it has relatively small effects on youths' wages. Analyzing seniors in the "High School and Beyond" (HSB) survey in the United States and in a corresponding Japanese HSB survey, Kariya & Rosenbaum (1988) found that although grades have small effect on youths' getting white-collar and skilled jobs in the United States, grades have large effects in Japan.

It is puzzling that grades and test scores do not influence hiring. Human capital theory implies that employers would give better jobs and higher pay to youths with better grades, because such youth will be more productive. Indeed, research finds that youth with better high school grades are more productive workers at the outset and that they generally receive higher wages after five to ten years of working (Bishop 1987, 1989). Human capital theory does not explain why grades and test scores do not influence hiring decisions.

3. *The pervasiveness of work-entry problems makes them seem inherent in youths' human capital, but Japan eliminated such problems by reforms.*

Work-entry problems are so pervasive in the United States that they seem intrinsic in youths' human capital. Only half (49.4%) of American noncollege graduates have actually obtained jobs by graduation, and many do not get jobs until three to six months later (Nolfi 1978:53). In contrast, these problems are largely absent in Japan. Of high-school graduates not attending college, virtually all Japanese students (99.5%) start working immediately after graduation (Ministry of Labor 1982).

Of course, it is possible that American youth delay work entry to find more appropriate jobs. However, an American high school graduate's first few jobs are usually dead-end jobs, which offer low pay, little training, and no advancement opportunity. Indeed, most American youth who get jobs right after graduation (58.3%) are only continuing the same part-time jobs they had in high school (Nolfi 1978, p. 53). Compared with Japanese youth, American youth have a higher turnover rate when they first leave school (under age 20) and in later years (age 20–24), both in periods of rapid and slow economic growth (Rosenbaum & Kariya 1989). Moreover, of high school graduates who changed jobs within two years after graduation, 15% of American youths were fired or laid off (NCES 1982), compared to only 3.2% of their Japanese counterparts (Nihon Seishounen Kenyuujo [NSK] 1984).[1]

In contrast, these youth work-entry problems are largely absent in Japan, so they are not inherent in youths' human capital. Indeed, Japan had similar work-entry problems earlier in this century that only ended with policy reforms. While these reforms involved numerous changes, they included improved information transfer between schools and employers which are described later (Inoue 1986, Rosenbaum & Kariya 1989). It appears that youths' work-entry problems may not be due to inherent deficiencies in youths' human capital, but they may be reduced by improved information flow.

In sum, while human capital theory is a plausible explanation of youth work-entry problems, it neglects important issues. Each is related to problems of information. 1. Youths' poor school efforts suggest that they do not get information about incentives to work in school. 2. Employers' disregard of grades and tests suggests that poor information about human capital, rather than poor human capital itself, may account for employers' difficulty getting good workers. 3. Work-entry problems are not due to inherent deficiencies in youths' human capital. Japan eliminated work-entry problems by reforms which improved information flow between schools and employers.

Signaling Theory

While human capital theory does not recognize the practical costs of obtaining information or limits on its availability and usefulness, these are the central

---

[1]This difference in the experiences of high school graduates in the United States and Japan is not due to greater selectivity in Japan. Indeed, a higher proportion of youth graduate high school in Japan (about 95%) than in the United States (about 87%), and the enrollment rate in colleges and post-secondary schools is virtually the same in Japan (55%) and the United States (58%) (US Dep. of Education 1987, p. 47). Indeed, if as human capital theory assumes, low-achieving youth have more work-entry problems, American high school graduation is more selective because of its higher drop-out rate, and it excludes a greater proportion of problem youth than does Japan. If drop-outs had been considered in the above analyses, the United States would have even greater work-entry problems while Japan's rate would only increase slightly.

concerns of signaling theory. How do employers discern human capital? How do they choose which signals to use to select appropriate applicants? Signaling theory describes the economics of these questions. Because of the importance of these questions for the school-work transition, where information is problematic, we devote considerable space to reviewing signaling theory.

"Information is a valuable resource: knowledge *is* power" (Stigler 1961, p. 213). Labor market decisions are an example of Stigler's insight. When making hiring decisions, employers find any information about job applicants' abilities a valuable resource. Yet obtaining information about applicants' true abilities is costly, so employers often hire employees based on available "signals": limited information about job applicants (e.g. Arrow 1973, Spence 1974, Stigler 1961). Therefore, instead of fully assessing applicants' "human capital," employers interpret the information that they can easily obtain—age, sex, race, school prestige, educational credentials, etc—and apply what they have learned from past experience to infer the "conditional probability of competence" of an individual (Blaug 1976, p. 846).

Signaling theory considers the economic aspects of signals. Information has costs, and the central dilemma in many decisions is how to get adequate information at low cost. Signaling theory explains why easily measured indicators like educational credentials have such great influence. Employers can often get better information by giving more realistic and more expensive tests, but they may not do so if they decide that increased information is not worth the cost (Spence 1974).

However, signaling theory does not discuss or predict which signals employers really use, which signals will have the biggest impact on hiring decisions, or whether the same signals are used equally to screen all applicants. Signaling theory also ignores the information process and the structure of the market itself; that is, signaling theory does not consider how information is gathered, coordinated, transmitted, and finally evaluated. As Arrow (1973, p. 144) notes, it is "hard to define the process by which a signal gets to be recognized as such and how the receiver learns to discriminate among them." In addition, signaling theory fails "to distinguish signals from the underlying attributes about which one is really concerned" (Spence 1974, p. 105).

Signaling theory relies on market mechanisms. Market outcomes are the vehicle to transmit information, and markets do not effectively communicate subtle information about applicants. Employers receive only crude signals to differentiate job applicants (age, sex, race, and education are the most common) which they interpret based on their past experiences by a process Thurow (1975) calls "statistical discrimination." Markets provide even worse information to applicants about employers' preferences: the results of employers' hiring decisions as they appear in the "market." Signaling theory ignores the fact that the market is not a good instrument for communicating detailed information about hiring criteria or job candidates.

Signaling theory also ignores normative constraints on signaling use. Are some kinds of signals considered "fair" and others "unfair"? Are some types of signals trusted more than others? Is this normative system explicit or implicit? How do employers deal with conflicting norms about signals, e.g. when informal stereotypes about classes of people conflict with laws against discrimination? For instance, although the use of age, sex, and race as signals is illegal, these signals have traditionally been influential in hiring decisions. Similarly, the use of educational signals is "legally permitted and generally approved" (Blaug 1985, p. 22), while preferences among different colleges are more ambiguous normatively, but used in practice (Rosenbaum, 1984). Finally, if employers violate norms, what sanctions exist and under what circumstances are they exercised? Signaling theory ignores these questions.

According to signaling theory, individual employers decide which signals are important. If each employer makes these choices in isolation without any normative consensus guiding their choices, as market theories assume, then how can youth get a coherent view of the full array of preferences? Moreover, if employers act in isolation from school staff, then how are employers' needs communicated to schools and to students? Such "one-sided" decisions would not necessarily become usable information to schools or youth. Employers interacting with other employers or with school staff, rather than acting in isolation, would create and encourage more meaningful signals.

Despite these limitations, signaling theory helps to frame relevant conceptual issues in the school-work transition: (*a*) What skills do employers want to have signals about? (*b*) Does young age itself serve as a negative signal to employers? (*c*) Which school-generated signals do employers use? (*d*) Do youth use signals in deciding their job preparation? We consider each of these questions.

1. *What skills do employers want from youth labor?*

Before considering what signals employers choose, we must know what personal attributes they want to select. Contrary to popular assumptions, research finds that when selecting noncollege-bound youth, most employers are not looking for labor with specific vocational or occupational skills and training (Blaug 1985, Hamilton 1986, Newitt 1987, Wilms 1984). Instead, employers want employees with essential reading, writing, and mathematics skills (see also CED 1985, NCEE 1983), who can "follow the rules", work hard, and be punctual and reliable in attendance.

Blaug (1985) concludes that the "vast bulk of jobs in an industrial economy involve competences that are acquired on the job in a few weeks and require, not a given stock of knowledge . . . [about a specific vocational area], but the capacity to learn by doing" (p. 20). Employers are looking for applicants equipped with the essential basic skills who demonstrate a potential for training.

2. *Do employers consider young age as a negative signal?*

The pervasiveness of youth work-entry problems suggests that employers may consider young age, per se, as a negative signal. Age is an important influence on life events in many societies. In traditional societies, normative expectations create the basis for age stratification, defining the social roles associated with an age category (Riley & Waring 1976, Neugarten & Hagestad 1976).

In modern society, norms about age stratification are often defined by institutional practices. Schools define the ages of entry and exit into the various levels of education, and these norms have become more uniform in recent years (Kaestle & Vinovskis 1978). In turn, the various levels of school—elementary, junior high, senior high—affect norms about individual behavior, while isolating students from other age groups (Coleman 1974). Work places, though less age segregated than schools, often impose strong age norms on employees' careers (Lawrence 1987, Rosenbaum 1984). Apprentice programs for craft positions often select people within certain narrow age limits (Hogan & Astone 1986, p. 115). Some of these practices are determined by the state (Mayer & Muller 1986), i.e. compulsory school attendance laws and minimum age of employment (Modell et al 1976, Coleman et al 1974). These norms may also be changed by historical events like depressions (Elder 1980) and the size of birth cohorts (Ryder 1965, Riley et al 1972). Thus, age norms are not necessarily rational or consciously decided.

In contrast, economic signaling theory considers age to be an economically rational selection criterion. When employers do not hire new high school graduates into the primary labor market (jobs offering training, advancements, job security, and better wages), economists say this occurs because employers think recent graduates are too young and too unreliable. "Well established firms with a sizeable investment in plant and equipment . . . prefer to hire men twenty five to thirty years of age, who are married and ready to settle down, after they have so to speak, sowed their industrial wild oats in other plants" (Lester 1954, p. 53). Other studies also find that younger workers are hired by smaller firms, construction firms, and firms hiring many clerical workers, while older workers are preferred by manufacturing firms with skilled blue-collar jobs (Malm 1954, Hill & Nixon 1984). A study of 35 Massachusetts firms found that primary labor market firms "generally prefer not to hire young men just out of high school" (Osterman 1980, p. 26). These preferences are sometimes company policies. Several Fortune 100 corporations have policies against hiring applicants under age 25 for full-time jobs

(Hamilton 1987, Rosenbaum 1989). Employers turn to the "less desirable younger workers" only when "the more preferred workers are in short supply" (Nardone 1987, p. 40).

Hamilton (1986, p. 240) suggests that "employers consider young people— especially males under the age of 22—to be inherently irresponsible and thus poor risks for positions that require responsibility and entail an investment in training." Employers may avoid hiring youth because they want employees who are likely to stay in the firm, and age is seen as an indicator of stability. The avoidance of young employees is due not to a lack of skills, which employers feel they can provide, but to employers' inferences about youths' propensity to stay with the firm (Osterman 1980).

As signalling theory indicates, employers choose selection criteria that involve easily obtained information that helps them get better employees. Age is information easily obtained and may predict stability, responsibility, and other aspects of productivity; so it seems to be a useful signal.

But is youth an accurate signal of poor productivity? Remarkably, signaling theorists do not investigate the validity of signals. They assume employers do that. Signaling theory relies on a functionalist inference: if employers use a signal, they must have a good reason to do so. Of course, this may not be true. Selections can be irrational or unsupported by empirical evidence.

Despite many stereotypes about youths' unstable productivity, turnover, and attendance, and unstable attachment to the labor force, the body of empirical work addressing these questions demonstrates mixed and ambiguous findings regarding age-related differences in productivity, turnover, attendance, commitment, and attachment. The general finding of this research is that youth is not a useful signal of productivity (Rhodes 1983, Waldman & Avolio 1986).

Less noted by signaling theorists are questions about the long-term effects of selection practices. First, early selections may have long-term effects on careers. Screening mechanisms used early in a career may continue to shape the individual's entire career trajectory, especially within internal labor markets (Blaug 1976, 1985, Granick 1973, Rosenbaum 1984, Holsinger & Fernandez 1987). Information based on early signals can become incorporated into firms' career systems and indirectly affect later career outcomes.

Second, even if young age accurately signals poor productivity, its use could hurt the productivity of the entire next generation of workers. If employers offer high school graduates only unskilled jobs that do not use basic skills and are not rewarding, then high school students will see no incentives to acquire basic skills or work habits. Then, even if employers offer good jobs to 25-year olds with basic skills, this delayed incentive seven years after graduation may come too late to motivate high school students.

While employers can get more mature workers by hiring 25 year olds, they cannot avoid getting the products of this poor incentive system. The long-term inefficiency of these signaling practices is not considered by the signaling paradigm.

In addition, by waiting until applicants reach age 25, employers will have more difficulty assessing basic skills. This may explain why grades (earned seven years earlier) do not affect hiring for better jobs, since this information is pretty old by the time employers hire 25 year olds.

Although existing research doesn't settle the question whether employers avoid giving youth good jobs because of irrational norms or rational signals, research indicates that age is a poor signal of productivity. The use of such a weak signal also raises questions about why other signals are not used.

3. *Which school-generated signals do employers use?*

Although youth entering the work force have little work experience, they have many years of school experience to signal their ability, academic skills, and work habits. Why do employers use a weak signal such as age rather than more promising signals, such as those conveyed by school performance?

Credentials   One aspect of high schools which clearly affects employment prospects is the diploma (Jencks et al 1979). Over 87% of American youth obtained diplomas in 1988. The diploma is a prerequisite for a decent job and even for less desirable low-skill jobs in many developed and less developed nations (Dore 1976). However, it is not clear why diplomas affect hiring decisions. Does the diploma improve job prospects because it signals greater skills, or it is merely a credential—a symbol of status which signals little about achievement? Researchers are split on this issue, with economists generally taking the former position (Spence 1974) and sociologists the latter (Collins 1971, Kamens 1977, Meyer 1977, Meyer & Rowan 1977). Little evidence is available to resolve the issue.

However, besides credentials, schools also create signals by evaluations and classifications. Schools grade students in courses and rank and differentiate courses by ability and curricular grouping. How do employers respond to this type of information?

Ability and curricular tracks   Schools attach so much importance to ability and curricular tracks that we might expect employers to use them as signals. High schools create tracks to influence students' future paths and the preparation they are to receive. College track aims to prepare youth for college, vocational tracks aim to prepare youth for specific occupational careers, and general track aims to offer general preparation for both. Within curriculum tracks, high ability groups present more demanding curricula than lower ability groups. Indeed, research has shown that ability and curriculum tracks strongly affect students' college plans and admissions (Alexander et al 1978, Heyns 1974, Rosenbaum 1976, 1978, 1980a).

However, the benefits of noncollege tracks are less clear. The general track is the largest noncollege track. It seems to be a residual category which promises very little to students. While college tracks and vocational tracks promise preparation for specific goals, the general track is more vaguely defined. In some schools, general tracks make vague promises of preparation for "further education," or basic skills for work, without offering any specific preparation (Oakes 1985, Rosenbaum 1976, Sedlak et al 1986).

Even where schools are committed to preparing youth for jobs, they are not necessarily effective. Vocational tracks promise clear goals, but they often deliver less than promised. The evidence on the benefits of vocational tracks is mixed. Some studies find no difference between vocational and general track graduates in job level, salaries, or work performance (Kaufman & Schaefer 1967, Garbin 1970, Grasso 1972, Oakes 1985, p. 152). Other studies find that vocational programs give some advantage to students in obtaining a high-status job and in raising wages, if the job is related to one's training (Hotchkiss & Dorsten 1987, Meyer 1982). Moreover, there is great variability in the quality and effectiveness of programs both across and within schools. While vocational tracks are the one area where schools might be expected to connect schools and jobs, research gives an uncertain picture about whether vocational tracks improve job success.

Grades   As noted, employers do not use grades or test scores for hiring (Kariya & Rosenbaum 1988). These school evaluations would provide very inexpensive signals of youths' work habits and their skills in reading, writing, and math—the personal qualities that employers say they need.

Why don't grades and test scores influence the jobs students get? Partly it may be because schools do not try to influence youths' jobs. High schools have traditionally stressed college preparation (Labaree 1989), and while their mission has broadened over this century (Trow 1961), the stress on college is still evident in many school practices. College preparatory classes get better teachers, new textbooks, better science laboratories, and more special programs (Rosenbaum 1978, 1980a, Oakes 1985). Teachers and guidance counselors allocate more time to helping college-bound students (Heyns 1974). While counselors build rapport with college recruiters and help them select appropriate students, they rarely contact employers to help them select students (Borman & Hopkins 1987). Thus, while high schools help most students who apply to college, fewer than 10% of high school seniors entering work report that their high school helped them get their job (NCES 1983).

Another reason grades do not affect jobs is that some schools do not send transcripts to employers. Bishop (1989) notes the experience of Nationwide

Insurance Company which sent applicant-signed transcript requests to 1200 high schools and received only 93 responses.

However, schools should not bear sole responsibility for this failure. Employers tend to be well represented on school boards, and schools usually respond when employers are unhappy with a specific aspect of schools (Useem & Useem 1974). If many employers wanted transcripts or wanted schools to help in job placements, schools would probably respond to their requests. We must wonder whether many employers care about getting transcripts, and whether employers would use grades if they had them.

Research suggests that employers choose not to use grades. A national survey of 1900 personnel officers found that few considered grades important for hiring high school graduates (Crain 1984). A strong personal impression in an interview and a recommendation from a manager were rated "very important" by 76% and 56% of personnel officers, while grades and tests were so rated by only 18% and 12%. In a 1970 survey of employers in ten major entry or near-entry occupations in New York and St. Louis, Diamond (1970) also found that less than half used tests even for the most demanding jobs, and the main hiring criteria for these jobs were impressions in an interview. David Bills found that none of the employers he interviewed were concerned with grades (personal communication, May 27, 1988). Employers rarely obtained school transcripts, and most employers did not even request them. One employer actually refused to consider applicants with high grades because of a belief that these individuals would lack social skills. Even when school experience was considered, it wasn't necessarily academic. A bank personnel officer reported that he sought people with social skills, so that extracurricular activities were more important than grades. Crain and Bills both found that employers care about grades more for college graduates than for high school graduates.

It is not that employers do not want the skills that grades are supposed to signify. Employer complaints about youths' work habits and reading, writing, and math skills indicate that these skills are important to them. However, in informal discussions, employers report that course titles, abbreviations, and grades on school transcripts are hard to interpret (Rosenbaum 1989). Course titles are often designed to attract students' interest, so it is hard to know what skills a course teaches (does "Literature of Self-Exploration" teach reading competence?). Grades are also difficult to interpret. Courses are graded on a curve, but it is not always clear whether the norm is the school, a particular track, or a single classroom. Nor is it clear how much achievement a grade indicates. The difficulty of interpreting and comparing transcripts probably deters many employers from using them.

Employers also do not trust grades and references. Employers do not trust reference letters which applicants may have access to and may even contest with lawsuits. Employers also doubt that grades and test scores indicate the kinds of skills needed in jobs. Many employers report that they did better at work than at school, so their own experience tells them that school grades do not predict work success. They think of grades and test scores as narrow academic indicators. Like Americans generally, they mistrust tests (Jencks & Crouse 1982). These problems of interpretation and trust help to explain employers' reluctance to use grades, tests, and references as signals.

Signaling theory ignores some important factors which affect employers' choice of signals. The cost and predictiveness of signals are not the only determinants of which signals are used. Signals must also be understood and trusted. Signaling theory does not help us know under what conditions information is meaningful and trusted by recipients.

4. *Do youth use signals in deciding their job preparation?*

Although signaling theory focuses on employers' use of signals to select employees, it ignores the other half of the labor market transaction: the ways youth use signals to set their goals and to infer the payoffs to their training and effort (Granovetter 1985, p. 481). Signaling theory ignores the way youth gather information and make decisions about their employment opportunities, even though poor information could make youth unresponsive to their market situation and could reduce their efforts and training.

How do young people find and choose jobs? Most young persons in the United States find jobs "through friends and relatives and through the direct application to employers" (Meyer & Wise 1984, p. 123; also Granovetter 1974); and the state "plays little role in placement of youths or . . . adults into jobs" (Layard 1982, p. 500; Osterman 1988).

Many young people searching for jobs do not know how to fill out applications or how to dress for job interviews, and they lack personal contacts (Rees, 1986). Many youths do not have enough information about jobs or about worklife in general (West & Newton 1983); and school counselors seldom provide such assistance for noncollege-bound youths (Dunham 1980, Rosenbaum 1989). Blaug (1985, p. 26) suggests that youth need to know the "techniques of interviewing and presentation of biographical information."

Youth from low-income or minority backgrounds lack these kinds of information more than others. Young people from higher status backgrounds have better information about employment opportunities (Parnes & Kohen 1975, p. 44), clearer understanding of the workplace and job requirements (Haaken & Korschgen 1988, Kohn 1977), and greater access to "personal contacts" for jobs and "capital to make a start toward independent enterprise" (Kett 1977, p. 152).[2]

---

[2]Of course, other barriers to employment may also operate, including lack of transportation; discrimination on the basis of age, sex, and race; and insufficient training or experience (Hills & Reubens 1983).

Perhaps work-bound youths' most important choices are deciding how much and what kinds of training to get to prepare themselves for work. They must use signals from the labor market to make these decisions. Signals tell youth what they can gain from working hard in school, what courses they should take, or whether they are better off spending their time in after-school jobs or having fun. These signals are likely to be important determinants of youths' school effort, and consequently of how much they learn in school.

Although young children usually believe teachers' claims that good grades will help their future careers, by junior and senior high school, work-bound students are less swayed by grades as incentives and are less susceptible to the statements of school counselors and teachers who spend little time helping them (Heyns 1974).

Moreover, they can see for themselves that grades do not affect labor market outcomes by observing the experiences of their older peers. The above evidence on the way in which employers ignore grades suggests a strong pattern that youth could not miss seeing.

Certainly, work-bound students' behaviors imply that they realize that grades do not matter. Although there is little systematic research on students' perceptions, many studies report that work-bound students do not take grades seriously, except to get the minimum grades needed for a diploma (Cicourel & Kitsuse 1963, Oakes 1985, Rosenbaum 1976, Sedlak et al 1986). As a student reported, "I'm just here to get the diploma, waiting until they give me the diploma" (Rosenbaum 1976). A teacher reported a similar view, "These kids do not want to learn. You can't teach them anything. They are just sitting in these seats until they get their working paper—a diploma." As a result, students do not work in school, and teachers know they cannot make them work (Sedlak et al 1986).[3]

The experience of college-bound students illustrates that signals can have greater impact on youth under other circumstances. Since grades and tracks affect college admissions, college-bound students see incentives to work hard in school, while work-bound students do not. Obviously, there are other differences between these two groups, so this may not be the entire explanation; the different incentive structure cannot be ignored, however.

Thus, work-bound students shift from accepting the general statements of

[3]Not surprisingly, these practices have counterparts in students' behaviors. In the general track, the program which does not even pretend to offer specific preparation for jobs, students are particularly disengaged. The general track tends to have more than its share of effort and discipline problems. Combs & Cooley (1968) found that nearly three quarters of high school dropouts were in the general track at the time they left school. Kelly (1974) found that, even after controlling for sex and social class, noncollege track students are more likely to report drinking alcohol, smoking cigarettes, skipping school, stealing, vandalizing, and gang fighting (see also Rosenbaum 1980, Stinchcombe 1964, Polk & Schafer 1972, Oakes 1985). Of course, it is hard to separate the effects of weak incentives from selection effects which put people into this track.

teachers to observing the experiences of their older peers. Meanwhile, school staff seem to be making less effort to inform and guide their choices than those of college-bound students. As a result, work-bound youth increasingly disregard grades as signals of the kinds of jobs they can get. However, it is not clear that any signals are substituted, so work-bound youth are increasingly deprived of signals to help them decide in what areas to gain training and how hard to work.

Problems in Signaling Theory

Market theory and human capital theory assume that information is sent, that incentives operate, that individuals acquire the right training to fit employers' needs. But without dependable information, markets cannot work effectively. Signaling theory specifies some determinants of the availability and use of information.

However, signaling theory does not explain why employers ignore the signals they get from schools and why schools do not give youth incentives to work in school. These findings are particularly baffling because grades are reasonably good signals of employees' productivity. Although grades have little influence on jobs or wages right after high school, they strongly correlate with productivity at job entry, and they predict wage rates for employees five to ten years later (Bishop 1987, 1989).

While signaling theory focuses on the economic value of information, it cannot explain whether signals are communicated, accepted, trusted, and used. Schools do not try to influence jobs, to make their evaluations important to employers, or even to explain their tracks, course titles, or grades to employers. Similarly, employers rarely contact schools to solicit their evaluations of students or to tell them what kinds of youth they seek to employ. As a result, employers do not understand or trust schools' rankings, and they do not use tracks and grades as signals—despite their stated need for employees with better academic skills.

Evidently, features of the social context affect whether signals are trusted and used by employers and youths. The next section considers some conditions that may affect these features of signals.

Network Theory

While the market model contends that linkages between schools and employers interfere with the efficiency of markets, other models suggest that such linkages can improve market processes. The new institutional economics considers the efficiencies of institutional relationships (Lazear 1979, Rosen 1982, Williamson 1975). Sociological models go even further in contending that markets often "depend on the nature of personal relations and the network of relations between and within firms" (Granovetter 1985, p. 502). Many examples illustrate the point: exchanges among diamond brokers (Ben-Porath 1980), corporations (Useem 1979), salesmen and purchasing agents (Macaulay 1963, p. 63), contractors and subcontractors (Eccles 1981, p. 339), and job applicants and employers (Granovetter 1974). Unlike the market model, this view posits that institutional linkages could increase efficiency and strengthen the relationships between achievement and jobs by increasing information and trust (Stinchcombe 1985, Zucker 1986).

While signaling theory assumes that information is trusted, this is not always the case, as discussed above. Economic actors may be "opportunistic, . . . and agents who are skilled at dissembling realize transactional advantages" (Williamson 1975, p. 255). Giving inflated recommendations is one way to dump a disliked subordinate on a rival employer.

Network theory describes some ways that information is given meaning and trust in transactions, and how information is transmitted not only via market results but also through social networks. Despite the potential rewards for deception, trust arises because transactions are embedded in "personal relations and structures (or 'networks') . . . generating trust and discouraging malfeasance . . . People prefer to deal with individuals of known reputation, or, even better, with individuals they have dealt with before, so social relations . . . are mainly responsible for the production of trust in economic life" (Granovetter 1985, pp. 490–91). For example, purchasing agents know salesmen personally, and disputes are settled in discussions, without legal recourse. "You do not read legalistic contract clauses at each other if you ever want to do business again" (Macaulay 1963, p. 61). Thus, trust arises because transactions occur in networks of personal relationships.

While previous research and theory has stressed personal networks, Rosenbaum & Kariya (1989) indicate that similar issues apply to institutional linkages, which arise from regular patterns of interactions. Trust develops in long-term interdependent role-relationships, and new occupants of these roles will make sacrifices (investments) to maintain the history of trust. For instance, the relationship between a salesman and purchasing agent is likely to be maintained even when a new person takes one of those jobs. Admittedly, the relationship is problematic at first, but the new role occupant has strong incentives to maintain the existing relationship because of the trust, dependability, and "good will" that has been built.

The transition between high school and work illustrates how mistrust creates inefficiencies in markets. High schools and employers are interdependent: Employers depend on schools to supply trained workers, and schools depend on employers to hire their graduates. However, this interdependence has not jelled in the United States, as noted earlier. Employers avoid relying on schools by ignoring grades and by hiring adults over age 25 for good jobs, while teachers doubt that employers care about education, so they deemphasize education for work-bound students (Useem 1986). Mutual mistrust has prevented the fruition of this interdependence between schools and work.

Information by itself is not enough to make a market operate, so this market failure cannot be explained by signaling theory. Understanding and trust are important in evaluating signals. They are not properties of signals, per se, but of the context in which signaling takes place. Markets need ways to guarantee that information is understood and trusted.

One way to increase understanding and trust of signals is to embed them in the context of ongoing social or institutional relationships. Trust arises in social interactions, and social norms give meaning and dependability to exchanges (Granovetter 1985). These contextual features offer performance guarantees that would not emerge from simple market mechanisms.

One problem with these labor market theories is that they are based on observations in the United States. American labor markets generally follow the market model: the ideal market relation is assumed to be between individual job applicants and employers, with schools having no role in the transaction. Schools are not supposed to be involved in helping youth get jobs, and employers are supposed to wait for youth to apply for jobs (Timpane 1984). Youth must navigate the school-work transition themselves.

Therefore, while the United States provides good examples of market processes, institutional linkages between high schools and employers are less common and less studied. American social scientists take this system and its outcomes for granted, so theories about institutional linkages have not been applied to the school-work transition. Would the high school–to-work transition create fewer problems if high schools had direct links with employers, as network theory suggests, or would it create greater inefficiencies as market theory suggests? Studying alternative systems may increase our understanding of market and network systems.

Social Networks Linking High Schools and Employers: Japan

Japan has strong linkages between high schools and employers, so it illustrates the issues raised by network theory, particularly the ways networks act to generate understanding and trust. Despite similarities in the educational systems in Japan and the United States (cf Footnote 1), Japan's work-entry system is in striking contrast to the US market system.

In Japan, many firms have long-term arrangements in which they authorize certain high schools to nominate students to fill their job openings. Schools influence a student's job search, and most youth find their first job without entering the labor market (cf Rosenbaum & Kariya 1989). Hiring occurs in three stages. First, employers offer jobs to a high school. Second, teachers nominate and rank students for these jobs. Third, employers interview nominees and make final selections. The third stage, which is the entire hiring process in the United States, is only part of the process in Japan, for employers hire most nominated students.

First, employers distribute job offers to high schools, offering more and better jobs to higher-ranked schools. Employers prefer to recruit from the same high schools continually so they know what to expect from the schools' graduates (Hida 1982, Iwanaga 1984). These links impose obligations on both schools and employers to satisfy one another. Schools must select students who satisfy employers if they are to keep on receiving their job allocations in the future. Employers must continue hiring a school's graduates to continue having a stable source of employees of dependable quality.

Second, schools nominate students for particular jobs. Early in their senior year, students choose among jobs offered to the school. Homeroom teachers advise them and let them apply for the school's nomination if their choice is appropriate. A committee of teachers nominates and ranks youth for jobs. This system is clearly not a market. Employers cannot choose among all interested students, only those nominated by school staff, and students cannot apply to an employer without the school's nomination. Thus, students compete for jobs before they enter the labor market.

Japanese employers expect schools to nominate the highest achieving students for their best jobs. Like American employers, Japanese employers want youth with good work habits and good basic skills. They do not expect vocational skills, which they feel are easily acquired at work. Grades are the main determinant of school nominations and youths' first jobs in Japan; grades have much stronger influence on jobs in Japan than in the United States (Kariya & Rosenbaum 1988).

The market model implies that such linkages might create favoritism and cronyism, reducing the influence of achievement. Our study of Japan finds the opposite. Grades have *stronger* influence on students' chances of getting good jobs from employers linked to the school than from unlinked ones (Rosenbaum & Kariya 1989). Rather than lowering requirements, linked firms hold youth to even more stringent achievement requirements.

Schools' selectivity is reinforced by an implicit threat of sanctions. If schools fail to send qualified workers, employers stop giving job offers to them in subsequent years. While the actual frequency of such sanctions is not known, teachers perceive the loss of jobs as real risks, and they feel compelled to recommend qualified students to maintain relations with contract employers.

Just as American teachers would be, many Japanese teachers are uncomfortable relying heavily on grades and limiting nominees to the number employers request. However, in a survey of 1408 work-bound high schools, job placement teachers report they stress grades in selecting the assigned number of students because they do not want to endanger their relations with an employer.[4]

Similarly, Japanese employers are uncomfortable relinquishing their control over hiring, and they interview applicants to make sure they are suitable. However, they feel constrained to accept schools' nominations whenever possible. Several employers mentioned cases where they hired students they ordinarily would not have selected because they did not want to hurt their relationships with the schools (Rosenbaum & Kariya 1989). These undesired hirings are the price employers pay to get the benefits of linkages.

The third stage, employers' hiring decision, shows how much control employers relinquish. In a study of a random sample of 964 graduates from seven work-bound high schools, employers hired over 81% of nominees on their first job application, and 85% of nominees for their second job (Rosenbaum & Kariya 1989). Fewer than 3% of all students had to apply to three or more employers. Since some students apply to nonlinked employers or apply with weak rankings by schools, linked schools' influence is probably even stronger than these numbers imply.

Employers' most remarkable concession to maintaining linkages is their hiring in periods of recession. In these periods, employers still try to maintain their hiring relationships with linkage schools, even if they do not need new workers. Although they may reduce the numbers they recruit from linkage schools, they still try to maintain their linkages by hiring some graduates from these schools. Of course, in these periods, they stop recruiting from nonlinked schools entirely (Amano et al 1982).

The Japanese system also has disadvantages. It is criticized for relying too heavily on grades and for excluding other pertinent criteria. Doubts are also raised about how relevant grades are to the job selections for which they are used.

Despite these disadvantages, Japan's system has several advantages: schools—which have extensive information about students and jobs—make the first selections. As a result, employers get better achieving students for their more demanding jobs, and students know how the system works, and they see clear incentives to work in school (cf Rosenbaum & Kariya 1989).

Japan's system illustrates the ways that institutional networks can create useful and trusted information. Employer misunderstanding or mistrust of school rankings, which is a risk of ordinary market relations, is reduced by institutional networks which assure that information is dependable and which provide institutional penalties for bad information.

---

[4]The same constraint would apply if teachers were tempted to favor students from influential families. In fact, such bias rarely if ever occurs. Social background has very little influence on entry jobs. Employer contracts provide strong institutional controls to keep selections meritocratic (Rosenbaum & Kariya 1989). Incidentally, Japanese high schools do not have distinct guidance counselors. College and job placements are handled by teachers.

It might be noted that institutional linkages do not exist in the same sense between Japanese universities and employers. As a result, the same employers who trust high schools to nominate employees do not extend this privilege to university officials. Instead, employers make these selections themselves (cf Cummings 1980, Cummings et al 1979, 1986).

West Germany and Britain

The West German system is one of the most effective in Europe and is another example of relying on "institutional" linkages for the school-work transition. It "offers a comprehensive list of services, organizes the transition from the national government down, [supervises schools' efforts] to initiate and carry out activities without outside supervision, uses bridging agencies that strongly involve the labor market authorities, and integrates youth services with those for adults" (Reubens 1974, cf also Hamilton 1989). It provides clear incentives for students, since students with better educational backgrounds (i.e. higher-ranked education diplomas and/or academic achievements) get into better vocational schools, get apprenticeships in better occupations, and ultimately get better jobs.

It also provides clear linkages between school and work. German schools provide explicit vocational preparation; 88% of work-bound students receive a recognized vocational qualification, and few fall between the cracks (Osterman 1988, p. 114). Moreover, in contrast with the uncertain preparation of the general and vocational tracks in the United States, employers trust vocational graduates to have a dependably high level of skills, and youths' first jobs tend to be related to their preparation. The German Federal Employment Office also enhances the linkage by providing vocational services to schools and individual counseling to those leaving school, of whom 60–80% participate (Arnow et al 1968, p. 142). Employers also contribute to the linkage. "Employers have social obligations to fulfill by training apprentices," and the federal government can levy a payroll tax if a firm fails to provide its share of apprenticeships (Hamilton 1987, p. 322). The German apprentice system enables youth "to move directly into primary-labor-market careers at a time when their counterparts in the U.S. . . . begin a period of low-skill and low-paid work" (Hamilton 1987, p. 314).

In the West German system, school-employer linkages are weaker than in Japan, but stronger than in the United States. German apprenticeships are influenced by educational attainments, i.e. educational levels, school types, educational certificates, and academic achievements (Heinz 1986). In addition, after regular school ends, the "dual system" combines apprenticeships and part-time vocational education through age 18. However, secondary schools are not necessarily involved in placing graduates into apprenticeships, and part-time vocational school achievement does not affect post-apprenticeship jobs (Cantor 1989). Although schools are becoming more involved in placement in recent years, the main role of guidance and placement has been played by public employment offices (Cantor 1989). In the 1981–1982 school year, 60% of prospective graduates came to the public employment service, and two thirds of apprenticeship places were filled by this service. Thus, while educational achievement affects placement into apprenticeships and while schools' influence has increased in recent years, the allocation process relies more on cooperation among government agencies, employers, and trade unions than on schools (Cantor 1989).

On the other hand, West Germany has stronger linkages between school and work than does the United States. Instead of wandering around in the labor market after graduation, many graduates move directly into primary jobs as apprentices. This process is maintained by institutional agreements among states, employers, and trade unions, although females and foreign youth (mostly Turkish) are less likely to get such positions (Herget 1986).

Examinations also create an institutional incentive for learning in this system. At the end of apprenticeship, an examination is given which measures occupational competence, and it affects a student's next job (Cantor 1989).

West Germany also shows how institutional linkages help employers and youth get good information about each other. During the apprenticeship, employers can obtain information about their trainees' job competence in face-to-face situations. Based on this information and the apprenticeship examination, employers make their hiring decisions with considerable confidence about job applicants' productivity. On the other hand, apprenticeships teach youth what job competence is needed for a job and what job conditions prevail. Apprenticeships provide an institutional arrangement that provides relevant information to employers and youth.

Thus, unlike the Japanese system in which schools and employers are directly linked, the West German system creates new institutions to bridge the gap. Government employment offices, which have linkages with schools, employers, and unions, provide counseling and placement. Apprenticeships and examinations also provide institutional linkages which facilitate information flow.

Britain, like the United States, previously had a very loose transition from secondary school to work based on market mechanisms. Facing serious youth employment problems, including high unemployment and turnover, Britain has been moving toward a system similar to the one in West Germany (Raffe 1981). After thorough study of European practices, Britain began new policies that offer part-time vocational training to work-bound youth. In the Youth Opportunities Program (begun in 1978) and its replacement Youth Training Scheme (begun in 1983), Colleges of Further Education have been established to provide part-time vocational education to unemployed youth who left school (Cantor 1989). Some educational programs are combined with apprenticeships like those in West Germany. These recent policy changes indicate that Britain has shifted from free market approaches toward institutional linkages.

British researchers credit the value of such linkages not only to training but also to the smoother flow of information through institutional linkages. The Youth Opportunities Program serves "a screening function . . . by providing prospective employers with a criterion for selection that is complementary or even alternative to educational credentials, and by giving employers a cheap way to gain direct information about potential recruits" (Raffe 1981, p. 219). By this interpretation, Britain has changed its work-entry practices because institutional linkages convey information better than market mechanisms do.

Institutional Networks in the United States

Although we have noted that institutional linkages are less common and less salient in the United States than in some other countries, we expect such linkages may arise in certain circumstances in the United States. For instance, in small towns, a few employers and schools may interact regularly every year, which might lead to linkages. Unfortunately, we know of no systematic evidence to indicate where and to what extent such linkages exist or how they operate.

Linkages are also more likely to occur in private schools, which do not raise concerns about using public resources for the private interests of employers. Post-secondary vocational and technical schools sometimes have linkages with employers. These schools strive to satisfy employers, since their students are primarily concerned about jobs. Few studies have examined these schools, and no study has examined their linkages with employers, so we rely on a report from a single school (Rosenbaum 1989). This school reports that major employers help the school identify job requirements, requisite skills, and a curriculum for teaching these skills. An extensive placement department develops links with new employers. Quality control is also important. The school gives subject area exams every year to assess each department. Counselors recommend students with better grades for the best employers and best jobs. This private vocational school's links with employers are very similar to the high-school-to-employer links in Japan.

Similar linkages may also occur in American higher education. Some colleges regularly recruit the same number of students from certain high schools every year, while not recruiting from other high schools of comparable quality. Guidance counselors in these high schools know the college recruiters, and these relationships may resemble those in Japan. Similarly, some MBA programs regularly send the same number of graduates to certain major employers every year. The two institutions may have close interdependencies: MBA programs seek to improve their graduates' success in getting jobs, while employers seek to list employees' prestigeous degrees (Burke 1984). Grades also affect which MBA students get the best jobs (Burke 1984), just as grades affect college graduates' jobs (Crain 1984). These are often long-standing relationships, and schools and employers may make investments (sacrifices) to maintain these relationships.

Some recent educational reforms in the United States have similarities to Japanese linkages, although none are as strong. A number of reformers have proposed "partnerships" between schools and employers (Seeley 1984, Timpane 1984), and several public school systems have sought to foster such linkages (including Atlanta and Chicago). Accounts of "industry-school partnerships" indicate that businesses offer instructional resources, but the accounts are not clear about whether programs offer job assurances, authorize schools to nominate students, or rely strongly on grades (Spring 1986).

The Boston Compact is one of the few examples of American public high schools trying to make direct hiring linkages between high schools and employers. In 1982, local businesses promised to increase youth employment if the Boston Public Schools improved student achievement, attendance, and graduation rates. Employers have increased jobs for Boston's high school graduates, but the schools have not done so well at improving student attendance or achievement (Farrar & Cipollone 1988).

Although certainly a step in the right direction, the Boston Compact may have failed to have a significant impact on students because, while it gives *schools* incentives to improve average achievement, it does not give *students* incentives to improve their achievement, as the Japanese system does. The fact that even the Boston Compact, which seeks to link hiring with school-wide achievement, does not link hiring with students' grades indicates how reluctant Americans are to make these linkages.

However, a few Boston high schools and employers, acting on their own, informally agreed to use grades, teacher evaluations, and attendance to determine who gets highly prized jobs (white-collar jobs with better pay, better training, advancement, and job security; cf Rosenbaum 1989). These informal arrangements suggest that Japanese linkages are a viable option for American public schools.

There are no studies of the effects of these informal linkages on Boston's students. However, it is evident that these efforts fall short of the Japanese model. These informal linkages apply to only a few schools and are known by only a few juniors and seniors, and even fewer young students. Unlike the Japanese system, the Compact had little way to motivate elementary and junior high students. By the time students became aware of the Compact in high school, they may have felt they were too far behind the schools' achievement standards to catch up.

Unlike Japan which creates incentives all the way through the school system, the Boston Compact has done little to show high school students, much less younger students, that grades matter. The Boston Compact is an effort in the direction of increasing linkages, but it is only a weak approximation.

Despite the several examples listed in this section, what is most remarkable is the virtual absence of studies of linkage practices in the United States. We have no empirical evidence of the incidence of linkages at any level of education or in any type of school. Moreover, we also lack detailed case studies of such linkages and how they work, so little is known about how much long-term investing in linkages occurs in the United States, what forms it takes, or how much it interferes with labor-market processes. In light of the great policy interest in school-employer partnerships, this absence of research is particularly striking.

Implications of Network Theory

Because network theory is a new theory, we have stressed its strengths. We have extended this new theory beyond personal networks to include institutional networks, and we have described some examples from other countries and from higher education in the United States.

This is not to say that network theory is superior to the other three. Segmented labor market theory explains market outcomes when the labor market is unresponsive to individuals. Human capital theory describes individuals' investments in themselves under conditions where they have information about valued market incentives. Signaling theory explains employers' hiring decisions when they have access to inexpensive, trusted information. However, when information is not available or trusted, the latter two theories are less applicable.

Network theory is less parsimonious and less elegant than these theories because it broadens our focus. It raises questions about how information becomes available and trusted through personal and institutional relationships. When these matters are not at issue, network theory is unnecessary. But the theory contends that these matters are often at issue and must be considered.

Network theory can explain some aspects of the school-to-work transition that are not easily explained by other theories. It explains why US employers do not use grades in hiring, but Japanese employers do; why young age is a negative signal in the United States, but not in Japan; why work-bound youth have few incentives for schoolwork in the United States, but not in Japan.

Network theory also shows a large gap in our knowledge of how employers choose signals (Spence 1974). Signaling theory explains why selection criteria are chosen, but not which attributes are used. Educational certificates are nearly universal signals, but other criteria (grades, school tracks, or ages) are not necessarily used as signals. Their use depends on institutional decisions or social beliefs about ability, and perhaps on the relative influence of schools on selections (Rosenbaum 1980a, 1986). The fact that high school grades are important in Japan, but not in the United States, suggests that the selection of signals is not a simple function of technology or capitalism. Apparently, capitalist societies can differ considerably on the selection criteria used, and they may be affected by features of institutional networks.

Institutional networks are an important extension of network theory. Economic models rarely consider how schools and employers invest in stable relationships to maintain their labor supply/demand, although Williamson's (1981) "transaction-specific investments" suggest the possibility of such investments. Moreover, economic models usually assume that schools are not involved in the hiring transaction, and although this assumption is often true in the United States, it has prevented the development of models that are applicable to institutional linkages. Moreover, this assumption has delayed recognition that some American schools do have linkages with employers, which have been ignored in American research.

Institutional networks also extend the analysis of markets beyond temporary market conditions. A Japanese teacher posed the issue clearly, "Getting jobs is only a one-time experience for individual students, but it is repeated year after year for schools." Schools seek dependable *future* demand for students, and employers seek dependable *future* supply of employees. Employers accept most school nominees and hire when they do not need new employees, and these actions are viewed as *investments* in the continuity of their future labor supply. Schools' strict adherence to standards hurts their job placement records in some years, but it is also an investment in their relationships with employers. Though inefficient in the short run, these practices are seen as investments with long-run benefits. When such linkages exist, schools can influence hiring, labor market competition can occur while youth are still in school, and schools' preselections can facilitate employers' hiring decisions.

Institutional networks also extend signaling theory. In Japan, linkages make grades trusted selection criteria, giving employers good indications of youths' human capital, and notifying youth of their relative positions in the "labor queue" (Thurow 1975). They help youth to anticipate their probable career options, to interpret how they are doing, and to increase their efforts or lower their plans accordingly. This delegated job selection also reinforces schools' control over students, and it may also avert motivation crises for students precluded from higher education, since grades are still important in attaining jobs. The continuing incentive to work for good grades may keep students working harder and increasing their basic skills.

In contrast, America's lack of linkages creates serious signaling failures. American employers do not understand or trust information from schools, and students do not get signals about their career options and how they are doing. As a result, employers do not know how to select youth with the best human capital, and so they rely on discriminatory criteria or avoid youth entirely, while youth do not know whether to invest in their human capital. Since school performance has little payoff for jobs, such poor articulation may reduce youths' school motivation (Stinchcombe 1964). Bullock (1972) also finds that American work-bound youth lack motivation to study hard, since they think these efforts are rarely rewarded in the labor market. Thus, the absence of networks between schools and employers may interfere with American youth acquiring marketable skills (Kariya & Rosenbaum 1987, Kariya 1988).

As in any comparison of different societies, one cannot be certain about causality. Fallows (1989) argues that cultural differences contribute to the different outcomes in Japan: Japanese people strive for effort for its own sake, while Americans exert effort for the sake of the rewards it brings. While it is possible that Japanese students might work hard even if incentives were absent, we cannot know that. In fact, Japanese networks provide strong incentives, so the decision whether to work without incentives does not arise. In contrast, American high schools offer no incentives to work-bound students, even though Americans are clearly motivated by material incentives, not effort for its own sake. Fallows' cultural interpretation is untestable and unnecessary: Japanese students get incentives whether they need them or not, while American work-bound students do not get incentives although they clearly need them. Regardless of whether there are cultural differences, they are not needed to explain these outcomes.

Network theory also raises practical issues of great policy importance. As Kurt Lewin said, there is nothing as practical as a good theory. Theories help us have a coherent view of social processes and see problems in our practices. Thus, since human capital and signaling theories are the basis for many current policies, faults in the theories would lead to unanticipated and undesired outcomes. Network theory has identified faulty assumptions in these theories which could explain employer avoidance of youth, youth motivation and discipline problems, schools' lack of authority, the failures of educational reforms that only increase instructional hours. These outcomes are not predicted by human capital or signaling theories. Segmented labor market theory predicts them, but it does not adequately explain them. Network theory is a useful extension because it explains these phenomena, and it suggests possible policy efforts that might successfully address these problems.

Future Research Directions

Although the four theories reviewed here are useful in identifying mechanisms underlying the school-work transition, this review has found important gaps in our knowledge. Many fruitful lines of research are suggested.

Our review of segmented labor market theory indicates that we do not understand how and to what extent employers confine employees within the secondary segment. Research must examine how jobs and occupations limit entry (cf Rosenbaum 1984).

Segmented theory also contends that secondary jobs are unresponsive to market forces, but it does not explain how employers fill these jobs if they do not offer greater rewards during a labor shortage. Do employers make such jobs more attractive, and if not, how do they recruit employees? If they do, which rewards do they increase, and which are unchanged? This theory accurately describes employers' disregard of individual skills, but it does not explain why.

Human capital theory posits deficiencies in individuals due to their lack of self-investments, but it does not explain why individuals do not invest in themselves during a labor shortage when the market presumably offers incentives for such investments. Do youth fail to get appropriate training because of institutional barriers (i.e. poor schools) or because they do not see incentives to learn? Research must study students' perceptions to understand why they do not behave as the theory predicts.

Signaling theory provides a plausible explanation of youths' failure to make self-investments, but research has not considered how youths use signals. Presumably economic considerations affect which signals youths use, but little is known about this. Studies of employers' and youths' perceptions of the availability, costs, and usefulness of information may explain how they respond to signals.

Social networks strongly affect which signals are trusted, but little is known about the incidence and operation of institutional linkages between schools and employers. For instance, how often and in what circumstances do schools help employers get job applicants? We speculated that many schools may have some linkages, particularly for influential employers, for students in specialized vocational programs, and in small towns. However, these are conjectures, and no evidence is available. We described an example of the process in one postsecondary vocational school, and on-going research by V. Mills at Northwestern University is extending this analysis. But more work is needed about the incidence and operation of linkages for such schools.

Even in western Europe, where linkages are more salient than in the United States, linkages have not been studied as far as we can tell. The accounts we have seen implicitly assume that systems work according to policy. Yet institutions often operate differently than official policies, so research is warranted.

Studies are needed to examine how institutions deal with linkages in the United States, and in Europe. What hiring criteria do youths, counselors, and employers expect to be used in linkages, and what criteria are actually used? What mechanisms ensure compliance with expectations, and what penalties result from noncompliance? Do counselors ever abuse their influence by recommending inappropriate students? Do employers ever abuse their influence by forcing schools to change their curriculum toward narrow job skills? Are employers more interested in noncognitive behaviors like obedience, as Bowles & Gintis (1976) imply, or are employers mostly concerned with basic literacy, as they say in public reports?

We also need studies of the perceptions of organizational actors to examine how institutional and personal networks affect the communication and use of information. Do counselors understand or trust information about job openings from some employers more than others? Do employers trust information about job applicants from some schools more than others? Are youth aware of linkages, and if so, does this affect their perceptions of incentives for school performance and their respect for teacher authority, as we have supposed? We know little about perceptions of information, how networks affect these perceptions, and how perceptions affect the use of information.

Economists have long had a monopoly on the study of markets, and the absence of competing paradigms has resulted in many phenomena being ignored. Economic studies of markets rarely consider the social perceptions and uses of information, the social networks that convey information and give it legitimacy, and the institutional arrangements that permit long-term investments in human capital. These topics indicate areas where sociologists can introduce competing theories and research. Surely economists would not dispute the value of increased competition in this marketplace of ideas.

Literature Cited

Alexander, K. L., Cook, M., McDill, E. L. 1978. Curriculum tracking and educational stratification. *Am. Sociol. Rev.* 43(1):7–66

Althauser, R. P., Kalleberg, A. L. 1981. Firms, occupations, and the structure of labor markets: A conceptual analysis. In *Sociological Perspectives on Labor Markets*, ed. I. Berg. pp. 119–52. New York: Academic

Amano, Ikuo, et al. 1982. *Koto Gakko no Shinro Bunka to Sono Kiteiyouin* (Selection Functions of High Schools and Their Determinants) Paper submitted to Toyota Foundation

Amano, Ikuo, et al. 1984. Koto Gakko no Shokugyo Shido to Seito no Shinro Keisei (1) [Vocational Guidance and Students' Career in High School (1)]. *Bull. Dept. Educ. Tokyo Univ.*: 23

Andrisani, P. J. 1973. *An empirical analysis of the dual labor market theory.* Unpublished thesis. The Ohio State Univ. Columbus

Andrisani, P. J. 1976. *Discrimination, segmentation, and upward mobility: a longitudinal approach to the dual labor market theory.* Pres. Joint Meet. Am. Econ. Assoc. and Econometric Soc., Atlantic City

Arnow, S. 1968. *The Transition from School to Work*. Princeton, NJ: Woodrow Wilson Sch.

Arrow, K. J. 1973. Information and economic behavior. In *Collected Papers of Kenneth J. Arrow*, 1984, Volume 4, Chapter 11. Cambridge, Mass: Belknap

Baron, J. N. 1984. Organizational perspectives on stratification. *Annu. Rev. Sociol.* 10:37–69

Ben-Porath, Y. 1980. The F-connection: Families, friends and firms in the organization of exchange. *Popul. Dev. Rev.* 6(1):1–30

Bills, D. 1983. Social reproduction and the Bowles-Gintis thesis of a correspondence between school and work settings. In *Research in Sociology of Education and Socialization*, ed. A. C. Kerckhoff, Vol. 4, pp. 185–210. Greenwich: JAI

Bills, D. 1986. *Educational credentials and hiring decisions: What employers look for in entry-level employees*. Unpubl. paper. Univ. Iowa, Iowa City

Binstock, J. 1970. *Survival in the American college industry*. PhD thesis. Brandeis Univ., Waltham, Mass.

Birman, B. F., Natriello, G. 1978. Perspectives in absenteeism in high school. *J. Res. Dev. Educ.* 11:29–38

Bishop, J. 1987. *Information externalities and the social payoff to academic achievement*. Work. pap. No. 8706. Cornell Univ. Cent. Advanced Hum. Resource Stud.

Bishop, J. 1988. *Why high school students learn so little and what can be done about it*. Work. pap. No. 88-01, Cornell Univ. Ithaca, NY: NY State Sch. Indust. Labor Relat.

Bishop, J. 1989. Why the apathy in American high schools? *Educ. Res.* 18(1):6–10

Blaug, M. 1976. The empirical status of human capital theory: A slightly jaundiced survey. *J. Econ. Lit.* 14(3):827–55

Blaug, M. 1985. Where are we now in the economics of education? *Econ. Educ. Rev.* 4(1):17–28

Borman, K. M., Hopkins, M. C. 1987. Leaving school for work. In *Research in the Sociology of Education and Socialization*, ed. A. C. Kerckhoff, pp. 131–59. Greenwich, Conn: JAI

Borus, M. E., et al. 1984. *Youth and the Labor Market*. Kalamazoo, Mich: W. E. Upjohn Inst.

Bowles, S., Gintis, H. 1976. *Schooling Capitalist in America*. New York: Basic

Brown, C. 1982. Dead end jobs and youth unemployment. In *The Youth Labor Market Problem*, ed. R. Freeman, D. Wise. Chicago: Univ. Chicago Press

Bullock, P. 1972. *Aspiration vs. Opportunity:*

"Career" in the Inner City, Inst. Labor and Indust. Relat. Univ. Mich.

Burke, M. A. 1984. *Becoming a MBA*. PhD Thesis, Northwestern Univ. Evanston, Ill.

Cain, G. G. 1976. The challenge of segmented labor market theories to orthodox theory: A survey. *J. Econ. Lit.* 14(4):1215–57

Callahan, R. 1962. *Education and the Cult of Efficiency*. Chicago: Univ. Chicago Press

Cantor, L. 1989. *Vocational Education and Training in the Developed World: Comparative Study*. New York: Routledge

Carline, D., Pissarides, A. A., Siebert, W. S., Sloane, P. J. 1985. *Labour Economics*. New York: Longman

Chobot, R. B., Garibaldi, A. 1982. In-school alternatives to suspension: A description of ten school district programs. *Urban Rev.* 14:317–36

Cicourel, A. V., Kitsuse, J. I. 1963. *The Educational Decision-Makers*. Indianapolis: Bobbs Merrill

Coleman, J. 1974. *Youth: Transition to Adulthood*. Chicago: Univ. Chicago Press

Collins, R. 1979. *The Credential Society*. New York: Academic

Collins, R. 1975. *Conflict Sociology: Toward an Explanatory Science*. New York: Academic

CED (Committee for Economic Development). 1985. *Investing in Our Children: Business and the Public Schools*. New York: CED

Clark, B. 1960. The 'cooling out' function in higher education. *Am. J. Sociol.* 65:569–76

Clark, B. 1985. The high school and the universities: What went wrong in America. *Phi Delta Kappan* 66:391–97, 472–75

Combs, J., Cooley, W. W. 1968. Dropouts: In high school and after school. *Am. Educ. Res. J.* 5:343–63

Crain, R. 1984. *The quality of American high school graduates: What personnel officers say and do*. Unpubl. pap. Johns Hopkins University. Baltimore, Md.

Cummings, W. 1980. *Education and Equality in Japan*. Princeton: Princeton Univ. Press

Cummings, W. K., Amano, I., Kitamura, K. eds. 1979. *Changes in the Japanese University: A Comparative Perspective*. New York: Praeger

Cummings, W. K., Beauchamp, E. R., Ichikawa, S., Kobayashi, V., Ushiogi, M. 1986. *Educational Policies in Crisis*. New York: Praeger

Cusick, P. A. 1983. *Inside High School: The Student's World*. New York: Longman

D'Amico, R., Brown, T. 1982. Patterns of labor mobility in a dual economy: the case of semi-skilled and unskilled workers. *Soc. Sci. Res.* 11:153–75

DeLeonibus, N. 1978. Absenteeism: The perpetual problem. *Practitioner* 5:13

Diamond, D. E. 1970. *Industry Hiring Requirement and the Employment of Disadvantaged Groups.* NY Univ. Sch. Commerce

DiPrete, T. A., Muller, C., Shaeffer, N. 1981. *Discipline and Order in American High Schools.* Chicago: Natl. Opinion Res. Cent.

Dore, R. 1976. *The Diploma Disease.* Berkeley: Univ. Calif. Press

Doeringer, P., Piore, M. 1971. *Internal Labor Markets and Manpower Analysis.* Lexington, Mass: Lexington

Dunham, D. B. 1980. *The American experience in the transition from vocational schools to work.* Pres. Int. Symp. Problems of Transition from Technical and Vocational Schools to Work. Berlin. ERIC ED186725

Dunlop, J. T. 1957. The task of contemporary wage theory. In *New Concepts in Wage Discrimination,* ed. G. W. Taylor, F. C. Pierson, pp. 117–39. New York: McGraw Hill

Eccles, R. 1981. The quasi-firm in the construction industry. *J. Econ. Behav. Organ.* 2:335–57

Edwards, R. C. 1979. *Contested Terrain, The Transformation of the Workplace in America.* New York: Basic

Elder, G. H. Jr. 1980. Adolescence in historical perspective. In *Handbook of Adolescent Psychology.* New York: Wiley

Eurich, N. P. 1985. *Corporate Classrooms: The Learning Business.* Princeton, N.J.: Carnegie Found. Advancement of Teaching

Fallows, J. 1989. *More Like Us.* Boston: Houghton Mifflin

Farrar, E., Cipollone, A. 1988. *The business community and school reform: The Boston compact at five years.* Unpubl. pap. March State Univ. of NY, Buffalo

Fujita, H. *Education and status attainment in modern Japan.* PhD thesis. Stanford Univ. Stanford, Calif.

Fujita, H. 1979. Shakaiteki Chiikeiseikatei niokeru Kyouiku no Yakuwari (Roles of Education in Processes of Social Status Attainment). In *Nihon no Kaisou Kozo* (Social Stratification in Japan), ed. T. Kenichi, pp. 329–61. Tokyo: Univ. Tokyo Press

Furukawa, Y. 1986. Shuushoku Kettei e muketeno Shidou no Pointo (Points for Vocational Guidance for Deciding Job Plans). *Shiro J.* 291:2–5

Gallup, A. 1988. The Gallup poll of public attitudes to public schools. Phi Delta Kappan 70(1):34–46

Garbin, A. P., et al. 1970. *Worker Adjustment Problems of Youth in Transition from High School to Work.* Columbus: Cent. Vocational Educ. Ohio State Univ. Columbus, Ohio

Goodlad, J. I. 1984. *A Place Called School.* New York: McGraw-Hill

Gordon, D. M. ed. 1971. *Problems in Political Economy: An Urban Perspective,* Lexington, Mass: D. C. Heath

Granick, D. 1973. Differences in educational selectivity and managerial behavior in large companies: France and Britain. *Compar. Educ. Rev.* October:350–361

Granovetter, M. 1974. *Getting a Job.* Cambridge: Harvard Univ. Press

Granovetter, M. 1981. Toward a sociological theory of income differences. In *Sociological Perspectives on Labor Markets,* ed. I. Berg, pp. 11–48. New York: Academic

Granovetter, M. 1985. Economic action and social structure: The problem of embeddedness. *Am. J. Sociol.* 91:481–510

Grasso, J. T. 1972. *The contributions of vocational education, training and work experience to the early career achievements of young men.* PhD Thesis. Ohio State Univ. Columbus, Ohio

Griffin, J. L. et al. 1981. Determinants of early labor market entry and attainment: A study of labor market segmentation. *Sociol. Educ.* 54:206–21

Haaken, J., Korschgen, J. 1988. Adolescents and conceptions of social relations in the workplace. *Adolescence* 23(89):1–14

Hamilton, S. F. 1986. Excellence and the transition from school to work. *Phi Delta Kappan,* November:239–42

Hamilton, S. F. 1987. Apprenticeship as a transition to adulthood in West Germany. *Am. J. Educ.* February:314–45

Hamilton, S. F. 1989. *Apprenticeship for Adults.* New York: Free

Heimer, C. A. 1985. Organizational and individual control of career development in engineering project work. In *Organization Theory and Project Management,* ed. A. L. Stinchcombe, C. A. Heimer, pp. 257–295. Bergen: Norwegian Univ. Press

Heinz, W. R. 1986. *The transition from school to work in crisis: Coping with threatening unemployment.* Pap. pres. AERA Ann. Meet., San Francisco

Herget, H. 1986. *The transition of young people into employment after completion of apprenticeship in the 'dual system.'* Pap. pres. Meet. Int. Experts in Vocational Educ. Training, Bonn, March 7

Heyns, B. 1974. Selection and stratification within schools. *Am. J. Sociol.* 79:1434–51

Hida, D. 1982. Nihon no Koukousei to Shuushoku (Japanese High School Students and Entry into the Labor Force). In *Koukousei* (High School Students), ed. H. Iwaki and H. Mimizuka, *Gendai no Esupuri No. 195.* Tokyo: Shibundou

Hill, R. B., Nixon, R. 1984. *Youth Employment in American Industry*. New Brunswick, NJ: Transaction

Hills, S. M., Reubens, B. G. 1983. Youth employment in the United States. In *Youth at Work: An International Survey*, ed. B. Reubens, pp. 269–319. Totowa, NJ: Rowman & Allanheld Publishers

Hodson, R., Kaufman, R. L. 1982. Economic dualism: A critical review. *Am. Sociol. Rev.* 47:727–39

Hogan, D. P., Astone, N. M. 1986. The transition to adulthood. *Ann. Rev. Sociol.* 12:109–30

Hollingsworth, E., Lufler, H., Clune, W. 1984. *School Discipline*. New York: Praeger

Holsinger, D. B., Fernandez, R. M. 1987. School to work transition profiles. *Sociol. Soc. Res.* 71(3):211–20

Hotchkiss, L., Dorsten, L. E. 1987. Curriculum effects on early post-high school outcomes. In *Research in the Sociology of Education and Socialization*, ed. A. Kerckhoff, pp. 191–219. Greenwich, Conn: JAI. 7th ed.

Hotchkiss, L., Kang, S., Biship, J. 1984. *High School Preparation for Employment*. Columbus, Oh: Nat. Cent. Res. Vocational Educ.

Inoue, K. 1986. Manpower and Development in Japan: A study of the Japanese education and training system. In *Finding Work: Cross-National Perspectives on Employment and Training*, ed. R. Rist, pp. 195–218. London: Falmer

Iwanaga, M. 1984. Jakunen Rodo Shijo no Soshikika to Gakko (The organization of the youth labor market and school). *J. Educ. Sociol.* (Tokyo) 38

Jencks, C., Bartlett, S., Corcoran, M., Crouse, Eaglesfield, J., et al. 1979. *Who Gets Ahead?* New York: Basic

Jencks, C., Crouse, J. 1982. Aptitude vs. achievement: Should we replace the SAT? *Public Interest* 33:21–35

Johnson, J., Backman, J. G. 1973. *The Transition from High School to Work*. Inst. Soc. Res. Ann Arbor: Univ. Mich.

Kaestle, C., Vinovskis, M. A. 1978. From fireside to factory: School entry and school learning in nineteenth-century Massachusetts. In *Transitions: The Family and the Life Course in Historical Perspective*. ed. T. K. Hareven. New York: Academic

Kamens, D. 1977. Organizational and institutional socialization in education. In *Research in Sociology of Education and Socialization*, ed. A. C. Kerckhoff, 4, pp. 116–26. Greenwich, Conn: JAI

Kanter, R. M. 1977. *Men and Women of the Corporation*. New York: Basic

Karabel, J. 1972. Community colleges and social stratification. *Harvard Educ. Rev.* 42:521–62

Kariya, T. 1985. Koutou Gakkou no Kaisou Kouzou to Kyouiku Senbatsu (The Mechanism of Educational Selection through the Hierarchical Structure of Japanese High Schools). *Koutou Kyouiku Kenkyu Kiyou* 4:11–28

Kariya, T. 1986. Tozasareta Skouraizou (Closed Images of the Future). *Kyouiku Shakaigaku Kenkyu* 41:95–109

Kariya, T. 1988. *Institutional networks between schools and employers and delegated occupational selection to schools: A sociological study of the transition from high school to work in Japan*. PhD thesis. Dep. Sociol. Northwestern Univ.

Kariya, T., Rosenbaum, J. E. 1987. Self-selection in Japanese junior high schools. *Sociol. Educ.* 60(3):168–80

Kariya, T., Rosenbaum, J. E. 1988. *Selection criteria in the high school-to-work transition: Results from the High School and Beyond surveys in the US and Japan*. Pres. Ann. Meet. Am. Sociol. Assoc. Chicago (August)

Kaufman, J. K., Schaefer, W. 1967. *The Role of the Secondary School; in the Preparation of Youth for Employment*. University Park, Penn: Inst. Res. Hum. Resources, Penn. State Univ.

Kelly, D. H. 1974. Track position and delinquent involvement. *Sociol. Soc. Res.* 58:380–6

Kett, J. F. 1977. *Rites of Passage: Adolescence in America, 1790 to the Present*. New York: Basic

Kohn, M. 1977. *Class and Conformity: A Study in Values*. Chicago, Ill: Univ. Chicago Press

Kohn, M., Schooler, C. 1983. *Work and Personality*. Norwood, NJ: Ablex

Labaree, D. 1986. Curriculum, credentials and the middle class. *Soc. Educ.* 59:42–57

Lawrence, B. S. 1987. An organizational theory of age effects. In *Research in the Sociology of Organizations*, ed. S. Bacharach, N. DiTomaso. Greenwich, Conn: JAI

Layard, R. 1982. Youth unemployment in Britain and the United States compared. In *The Youth Labor Market Problem*, ed. R. B. Freeman, D. A. Wise, pp. 400–541. Chicago: Univ. Chicago Press

Lazear, E. 1979. Why is there mandatory retirement? *J. Polit. Econ.* 87(6):1261–84

Lester, R. A. 1954. *Hiring Practices and Labor Competition*. Princeton, NJ: Indust. Relat. Section, Princeton Univ.

Macaulay, S. 1963. Non-contractual relations in business: A preliminary study. *Am. Sociol. Rev.* 28(1):55–67

Malm, T. F. 1954. Recruiting patterns and the functioning of labor markets. *Indust. Labor Relat. Rev.* 7(4):507–25

McPartland, J. M., McDill, E. L. 1977. *Violence in Schools*. Lexington, Mass: Heath Lexington

Mayer, K. U., Muller, W. 1986. The state and the structure of the life course. In *Human Development and the Life Course,* ed. A.B. Sorensen, F. E. Weinert, L. R. Sherrod. Hillsdale, NJ: Erlbaum

Meyer, J. Chase-Dunn, C., Inverarity, J. 1971. *The Expansion of the Autonomy of Youth: Responses of the Secondary School to the Problems of Order in the 1960's.* Stanford, Calif: Dept. Sociol., Stanford University Unpublished ms

Meyer, J. 1977. The effects of education as an institution. *Am. J. Sociol.* 83:55–77

Meyer, J., Rowan, B. 1977. Institutional organizations: Formal structure as myth and ceremony. *Am. J. Sociol.* 83:341–63

Meyer, P. 1972. *Schooling and the reproduction of the social division of labor*. Unpub honors thesis. Harvard Univ.

Meyer, R. 1982. An economic analysis of high school vocational education. In *The Federal Role in Vocational Education,* Special Report #39, Nat. Com. Employment Policy. Washington, DC: US Govt. Printing Off.

Meyer, R. H., Wise, D. A. 1982. High school preparation and early labor force experience. In *The Youth Labor Market Problem,* ed. R. B. Freeman, D. A. Wise, pp. 277–347. Chicago: Univ. Chicago Press

Meyer, R. H., Wise, D. A. 1984. The transition from school to work: The experiences of blacks and whites. *Res. Labor Econ.* Vol. 6, pp. 123–76. Greenwich, Conn: JAI

Ministry of Labor. 1981–1983. *Shokugyou Antei Gyoumu Toukei* (Statistics on Employment Stability). Tokyo

Modell, J., Furstenberg, F., Jr., Hershberg, T. 1976. Social change and transitions to adulthood in historical perspective. *J. Family Hist.* 1:7–31

Nardone, T. 1987. Decline in youth population does not lead to lower jobless rates. *Monthly Labor Rev.* Research Summaries, June, 37–41

National Center for Educational Statistics. 1983. *High School and Beyond: 1980 Senior Cohort First Follow-up (1982): Data File User's Manual*. Chicago: Natl. Opinion Res. Cent.

National Commission on Excellence in Education. 1983. *A Nation At Risk*. Washington, DC: USGPO

National Academy of Sciences (NAS). 1984. *High Schools and the Changing Workplace: The Employers' View*. Washington, DC: Natl. Acad. Press.

National Assessment of Educational Progress (NAEP). 1985. *The Reading Report Card*. Princeton, NJ: Educ. Testing Serv.

National Longitudinal Study. 1978. Data File Users Manual. Washington, DC: NCES

Neubauser, A. 1986. Industry/education partnerships: Meeting the needs of the 1980's. In *Becoming a Worker,* ed. K. M. Borman, J. Reisman, pp. 260–74. Norwood, NJ: Ablex

Neugarten, B. L., Hagestad, G. O. 1976. Age and the life course. In *Handbook of Aging and the Social Sciences,* ed. R. H. Binstock, E. Shanas, pp. 35–55. New York: Van Nostrand Reinhold. 1st ed.

Newitt, J. 1987. Will the baby bust work? *Am. Demograph.* September, 33–35:1–63

Nihon Seishounen Kenkyuujo. 1981. *Koukousei Shourai Chousa* (Research on Future Careers of High School Students). Tokyo.

———. 1984. *Gakkoukyouiku to Sono Kouka* (Education and Its Effects). Tokyo

Nolfi, G. J., Fuller, W., Corazzini, A., Epstein, W., Freeman, R. et al. 1978. *Experiences of Recent High School Graduates*. Lexington, Mass: Lexington

Oakes, J. 1985. *Keeping Track*. New Haven, Conn: Yale Univ. Press

Ohhashi, Y. 1981. Rodo Shijo no Nichibei Hikaku (A Comparison of Labor Market in Japan and US). *Gendai Keizai,* Summer, 43

Olneck, M. R., Bills, D. B. 1980. What makes Sammy run? A empirical assessment of the Bowles-Gintis correspondence. *Am. J. Educ.* (November):27–61

Ornstein, M. 1976. *Entry into the American Labor Force*. New York: Academic

Osterman, P. 1980. *Getting Starting: The Youth Labor Market*. Cambridge, Mass: MIT Press

Ostermann, P. 1988. *Employment Futures*. New York: Oxford Univ. Press

Parcel, T. 1987. Theories of the labor market and the employment of youth, ed. A. Kerckhoff. Res. Sociol. Educ. Socialization, vol. 7, pp. 29–55. Greenwood, CT: JAI

Parnes, H. S., Kohen, A. I. 1975. Occupational information and labor market status: The case of young men. *J. Hum. Resourc.* 10(1):44–55

Polk, K., Schafer, W. E. eds. 1972. *Schools and Delinquency*. Englewood Cliffs, NJ: Prentice-Hall

Prime Minister's Office (Youth Bureau). 1978. *Soshikide Hataraku Seishounen no Ishiki*. Report on Youths' Attitudes and Opinions toward Employment in Japan) Tokyo

Raffe, D. 1981. Education, employment and the Youth Opportunities Programme: Some sociological perspectives. *Oxford Rev. Educ.* 7(3):211–222

Rees, A. 1986. An essay on youth joblessness. *J. Econ. Lit.* 24:613–28

Reubens, B. G. 1974. Foreign and American experiences with the youth transition. In *From School to Work,* ed. E. Ginzberg. Washington, DC: Nat. Com. Manpower Policy

Rhodes, S. R. 1983. Age-related differences in work attitudes and behavior: A review and conceptual analysis. *Psychol. Bull.* 93(2):328–67

Riley, M. W., Johnson, M., Foner, A. 1972. *Aging and Society,* Vol. 3: *A Sociology of Age Stratification.* New York: Sage

Riley, M. W., Waring, J. 1976. Age and aging. In *Contemporary Social Problems,* ed. R. K. Merton, R. Nisbet New York: Harcourt, Brace & Jovanovich. 4th ed.

Rosen, S. 1982. Authority, control and the distribution of earnings. *Bell Jour. of Economics,* 13(2):311–23

Rosenbaum, J. E. 1976. *Making Inequality.* New York: Wiley

Rosenbaum, J. E. 1978. The structure of opportunity in school. *Soc. Forc.* 57:236–56

Rosenbaum, J. E. 1980a. Social implications of educational grouping. In *Annual Review of Research in Education,* ed. D. C. Berliner, pp. 361–404. Am. Educ. Res. Assoc.

Rosenbaum, J. E. 1980b. Track misperceptions and frustrated college plans: An analysis of the effects of tracks and track perceptions in the National Longitudinal Survey. *Sociol. Educ.* 53(April):74–88

Rosenbaum, J. E. 1984. *Career Mobility in a Corporate Hierarchy.* New York: Academic

Rosenbaum, J. E. 1986. Institutional career structures and the social construction of ability. In *Handbook of Theory and Research for the Sociology of Education,* ed. G. Richardson, pp. 139–171. Westport, Conn: Greenwood

Rosenbaum, J. E. 1989. *Empowering schools and teachers: A new link to jobs for the non-college bound.* Rep. to US Dep. Labor, Com. on Workforce Quality and Labor Market Efficiency

Rosenbaum, J. E., Kariya, T. 1989. From high school to work: Market and institutional mechanisms in Japan. *Am. J. Sociol.* (May), 94(6):1334–65

Rosenthal, R., Hearn, J. 1982. Sex differences in the significance of economic resources for choosing and attending a college. In *The Undergraduate Women,* ed. P. Perun, pp. 127–57. Lexington, Mass: Lexington

Ryder, N. B. 1965. The cohort as a concept in the study of social change. *Am. Sociol. Rev.* 30:843–61

Rytina, N. 1983. Occupational changes and tenure, 1981. *Job Tenure and Occupational Change,* 1981. Bull. 2161. pp. 4–34. Washington, DC: US Dep. Labor

Sedlak, M. W., Wheeler, C. W., Pullin, D. C., Cusick, P. A. 1986. *Selling Students Short.* New York: Teachers Coll. Press

Seeley, D. S. 1984. Educational partnership and the dilemmas of school reform. *Phi Delta Kappan,* 65(6):383–88

Seiyama, K., Noguchi, Y. 1984. Koukoushingaku niokeru Gakkougai Kyouikutoushi no Kouka (The Extra-School Investment and Opportunity of Entering Higher Ranking High School). *Kyouiku Shakaigaku Kenkyu* 39:113–26

Shokugyou Kenkyuujo (National Institute of Vocational Research). 1981. *Jigyousho no Saiyousennkou nikansuru Chousa* (A Report of Survey of Recruitment and Selection By Firms). Tokyo

Smith, G. M. 1967. *Personality correlates of academic performance in three dissimilar populations.* Proc. 77th Ann. Conv., Am. Psychol. Assoc.

Sørensen, A. 1977. The structure of inequality and the process of attainment. *Am. Sociol. Rev.* 42(6):965–78

Spence, A. M. 1974. *Market Signalling: Information Transfer in Hiring and Related Processes.* Cambridge, Mass: Harvard Univ. Press

Spenner, K., Otto, L. B., Call, V. 1982. *Career Lines and Careers.* Lexington, Mass: Lexington

Spring, J. 1986. Business and the schools: The new partnerships. In *Becoming a Worker,* ed. K. M. Borman, J. Reisman, pp. 244–59. Norwood, NJ: Ablex

Stigler, G. J. 1961. The economics of information. *J. Polit. Econ.* 69:213–25

Stinchcombe, A. L. 1964. *Rebellion in a High School.* Chicago: Quadrangle

Stinchcombe, A. L. 1985. Contracts as hierarchical documents. In *Organization Theory and Project Management,* ed. A. L. Stinchcombe, C. A. Heimer, pp. 121–70. Bergen: Norwegian Univ. Press

Thompson, S., Stanard, D. 1975. Student attendance and absenteeism. *The Practitioner* 1:1–12

Thurow, L. 1975. *Generating Inequality.* New York: Basic

Timpane, M. 1984. Business has rediscovered the public schools. *Phi Delta Kappan* 65(6):389–92

Tominaga, K. 1979. Shakaikaisou to Shakaiidou no Suuseibunseki (Analyses for Changes in Social Stratification and Social Mobility). In *Nihon no Kaisou Kozo* (Social

Stratification in Japan), ed. T. Kenichi. Tokyo: Univ. Tokyo Press

Trow, M. 1961. The second transformation of American secondary education. *Int. J. Compar. Sociol.* 2:144–65

U.S. Department of Education. 1987. *Japanese Education Today.* Washington, DC: USGPO

Useem, M. 1979. The social organization of the American business elite and participation of corporation directors in the governance of American institutions. *Am. Sociol. Rev.* 44:553–72

Useem, E. L. 1986. *Low Tech Education in a High Tech World.* New York: Free Press

Useem, E. L., Useem, L. 1974. *The Education Establishment.* Englewood Cliffs, NJ: Prentice-Hall

Waldman, D. A., Avolio, B. J. 1986. A meta-analysis of age differences in job performance. *J. Appl. Psychol.* 71(1):33–38

West, M., Newton, P. 1983. *The Transition From School to Work.* New York: Nichols

Williamson, O. 1975. *Markets and Hierarchies.* New York: Free Press

Williamson, O. 1981. The economics of organization: The transaction-cost approach. *Am. J. Sociol.* 87(November):548–77

Willis, R., Rosen, S. 1979. Education and self-selection. *J. Polit. Econ.* 87:527–36

Wilms, W. W. 1984. Vocational education and job success: The employer's view. *Phi Delta Kappan* (January):347–50

Zenkoku Koutougakkou Shinroshidou Kyougikai (National Conference of High School Career Guidance). 1986. *Shuushokumondai nikansuru Ankeitochousa* (A Questionnaire Survey for Recruitment Problems). Tokyo

Zucker, L. G. 1986. Production of trust: Institutional sources of economic structure, 1980–1920. In *Research in Organizational Behavior,* ed. B. M. Staw, L. L. Cummings, pp. 53–112. Greenwich, Conn: JAI. 8th ed.

Zucker, L. G., Rosenstein, C. 1981. Taxonomies of institutional structure: Dual economy reconsidered. *Am. Sociol. Rev.* 46:869–84

Annu. Rev. Sociol. 1990. 16:301–27
Copyright © 1990 by Annual Reviews Inc. All rights reserved

DEINSTITUTIONALIZATION: An Appraisal of Reform

David Mechanic

Institute for Health, Health Care Policy and Aging Research, Rutgers University, New Brunswick, New Jersey 08903

David A. Rochefort

Political Science Department, Northeastern University, Boston, Massachusetts 02115

KEY WORDS: mental illness, deinstitutionalization, community mental health, mental hospitals, social psychiatry

Abstract

The number of inpatients in US public mental hospitals declined from 559,000 in 1955 to approximately 110,000 at present. Reductions resulted from release or transfer of long-term inpatients and from entrance barriers to new admissions. The timing and pace of deinstitutionalization substantially varied by state, but three quarters of the national reduction followed the expansion of welfare programs in the middle 1960s. The establishment of community care alternatives was highly inadequate, leaving many severely and persistently mentally ill people without essential services. Problems of care were exacerbated by the contraction of welfare programs in the 1980s, which resulted in serious neglect and homelessness. Plagued by underfinancing and fragmentation of care, new strategies in developing mental health care systems include capitation, case-management approaches, and the development of strong local mental health authorities.

INTRODUCTION

President John F. Kennedy first described his proposal for a national community mental health program in a special message to Congress on February 5,

301

1963. It was subsequently enacted as the Community Mental Health Centers (CMHC) Act of 1963. In his message Kennedy set a quantitative target for this effort: a reduction by 50% or more of the number of patients then under custodial care, within ten or twenty years (Kennedy 1963). In reality, the process of "deinstitutionalization" proceeded even more quickly and more extensively than that. By 1975, the number of patients in state and county mental hospitals had declined by 62% from the time of the President's message (65% from the peak of 559,000 in 1955). Falling further still over the next decade, the institutional census contracted to 110,000 in 1985 (NIMH 1989) despite growth in the US population and irrespective of the increasing number of mental hospital admissions over much of this period.

Rare, indeed, is it in social policymaking for measured accomplishments to outdistance stated goals. Almost as unusual is the degree of fervid enthusiasm—among mental health professionals, advocates, public officials, and members of the general public—that surrounded initiation of the community mental health movement, of which patient relocation was an essential strategy (Rochefort 1984). For many, the proposed redirection in mental health care represented both scientific and humanitarian progress, a major "psychiatric revolution" to sweep away a dark age of institutional confinement (Grob 1987b). Cameron (1978) has described this mind-set as a new ideological consensus which functioned to provide the political energy and commitment necessary to move away from the existing system of hospital-centered care and its entrenched interests.

After some 35 years of programmatic experience, however, reactions to deinstitutionalization today are much less positive. Another ideological consensus may be emerging, one that identifies deinstitutionalization as one of the era's most stunning public policy failures. Critics underscore, especially, the incomplete development and inadequate performance of the supportive services that were meant to accompany patient discharge and patient diversion activities (see, eg, Dear & Wolch 1987, *Newsweek* 1986, Torrey 1988). Some judge it time to return to a state hospital-based mental health system (Gralnick 1985). Emblematic of these currents is a recent letter to the editor of the *New York Times* by Democratic Senator Daniel Moynihan of New York *(New York Times* May 22, 1989). Pointing to the growing numbers of deranged homeless persons and to the undersupply of community-based mental health care in New York City, Moynihan mused that President Kennedy might have set down his pen before signing the CMHC Act had he been able to foresee such outcomes.

The current controversy and large body of accumulated data make the time opportune for appraising the record of deinstitutionalization in the United States. Seeking to provide a comprehensive overview of its causes, nature, and consequences, this chapter addresses several questions pertinent to this sociological phenomenon. What sociohistorical forces—before, coincident with, and after Kennedy's community mental health legislation—gave rise to and facilitated the practice of deinstitutionalization? How far has deinstitutionalization progressed, and at what rates over time and for different geographical areas? What have been the effects of deinstitutionalization on patients and on the general society? We conclude by discussing the challenges of deinstitutionalization as a policy direction of the modern American welfare state.

ROOTS OF REFORM

Deinstitutionalization offers a compelling case study of the complexities of modern social policymaking. Justly recognized as a major innovation in both the philosophy and the practice of mental health services delivery, the program evolved over decades and came to stand, for a brief while at least, as a high priority agenda item at the highest level of government. Throughout, many influences were operative, including changing ideas and attitudes about the nature of mental illness and its treatment, biomedical advances, social research, professional currents, legal activism, and the emergence of a powerful political coalition in support of the mental health reform movement. Just as important, however, the deinstitutionalization experience also illustrates the manner in which forces and events belonging to different policy fields can interact to produce far-reaching, if often unplanned, outcomes.

Sources of Deinstitutionalization

An early impetus to deinstitutionalization derived from World War II and the changing ideologies and experiences associated with it. The environmental and egalitarian notions that developed during this period were related to the horrors of Nazism (Grob 1987b), and these fostered a strong conception of environmental determinism. The experience of psychiatrists during the war in dealing with neuropsychiatric problems during combat promoted a preventive ideology and the translation of military psychiatric techniques to civilian practice. Moreover, the rejection of large numbers of men for the armed services for psychiatric reasons, and the increasing fiscal strain on state mental hospitals with growing patient populations, focussed interest on a broader mental health strategy and a preventive ideology (Mechanic 1989).

Already by the 1950s, some mental institutions were changing administrative practices and beginning a modest process of deinstitutionalization (Bockoven 1972, Scull 1984). A major impetus came through the introduction of the phenothiazines in the middle 1950s that allowed large institutions to modify administrative policies and to reduce coercive restraints. The new drugs helped control patients' most disturbing psychotic symptoms and gave hospital staff and families confidence in the potential of less coercive care and hopes of greater predictability of patients' behavior. At about the same time, the National Institute of Mental Health was developing a research and action agenda based on a belief in prevention and the social malleability of mental disorder. With NIMH encouragement, research was undertaken in large hospitals documenting the deleterious effects of hospitalization on patients' functioning, motives, and attitudes (Goffman 1961, Belknap 1956), and such results supported the growing community mental health rhetoric. For the most part, however, the ideology was based on premises that were either un-documented or false (Mechanic 1989). But the mental health rhetoric had a life of its own and served as the basis for federal policy (Grob 1987a).

It is generally assumed that deinstitutionalization began with a vengeance during the middle 1950s with the introduction of new drugs. As we document later, the timing varied substantially by state, and deinstitutionalization was limited in the early years. During the period 1955 to 1965, public hospital populations decreased by only 1.75% a year on average (Gronfein 1985a). While hospitals were now more ready to return patients to community set-tings, they often had no place to send them and no basis for their support in the community.

Deinstitutionalization accelerated in the late 1960s and 1970s with the growth of the welfare state and with the reinforcement of an egalitarian, noncoercive ethic. By the late 1960s, lawyers socialized in the civil rights battles of the decade turned their attention to the rights of the mentally ill with an attack on civil commitment (Ennis 1972, Miller 1976), and the develop-ment of a legal theory supporting patient rights and the least restrictive alternative (Brooks 1974). With changing state statutes, it became in-creasingly difficult to commit patients to mental hospitals. The growth of welfare enabled the large-scale reduction of public mental hospital pop-ulations and provided large economic incentives to state governments to do so. Thus, it became easier to leave mental hospitals and more difficult to be committed.

Influence of Federal Policy

For one hundred years, since the growth of public mental hospitals in the early and mid-1800s, mental health policy in the United States was the domain of the states. With a series of national legislative enactments following World War II that helped foster community mental health and deinstitutionalization practices, the federal government became the prime agent of innovation and reform in public mental health care. It was to continue to play this role for some 35 years, until intergovernmental changes of the first Reagan adminis-tration reestablished the states' primacy in the design and control of local mental health services.

In addition to creating the National Institute of Mental Health, the National Mental Health Act of 1946 provided funding for the development of pilot community care programs in the states and for the training of mental health professionals. Congress created the Joint Commission on Mental Illness and Health in 1955. Studies conducted under its auspices documented the far-reaching problems of mental health care in the United States, and the commission's final report articulated the case for wholesale system reform, including a redefined role for state mental hospitals as smaller, more intensive treatment sites.

Rounding out these unprecedented legislative activities in mental health was the Kennedy administration's Community Mental Health Centers Act, which sponsored the creation of a new type of community-based facility providing inpatient, outpatient, emergency, and partial hospitalization services, as well as consultation and education to other community organizations. By 1980, more than 700 CMHCs had been funded under the program, or roughly half of the 1500 centers projected as needed for nationwide coverage (Foly & Sharfstein 1983). Other shortcomings of the program included a general lack of coordination between CMHCs and local state hospitals, and a tendency among many centers to underserve the severely and chronically mentally ill (Dowell & Ciarlo 1989). CMHCs thus constituted more of a parallel to existing state care systems than a complementary network of services, yet the program did expand the alternatives to traditional institutions while promoting the community care ideology.

Beginning in 1966, and extending to the late 1970s, federal social welfare programs rapidly expanded. Medicare and Medicaid, introduced in 1966, stimulated an enormous expansion of nursing home beds and provided an alternative for many elderly mentally ill and demented patients. Medicaid assumed the costs of care for patients moved from state institutions to nursing homes. Since states paid no more than half of Medicaid costs, they had strong incentives to shift patients to nursing homes where the federal government would share the costs. In addition, the expansion of disability insurance made it much easier to return patients to family and board-and-care settings with sufficient income to contribute to their support. During this period there was also expanded public housing that provided housing opportunities directly, or indirectly, by adding to low-income housing stock. Thus, the expansion of the welfare state contributed to a stronger economic and residential base for deinstitutionalization. The depopulation of public mental hospitals accelerated, with patient populations decreasing an average of about 8.6% a year between 1965 and 1975 (Gronfein 1985a).

Contending Theoretical Explanations of Deinstitutionalization

Varying theoretical interpretations of deinstitutionalization arise from alternative conceptions of the role of the state in democratic capitalist society, from the degree of credibility given to the self-described objectives of key public actors, and from the phase of the policymaking process described.

One major approach analyzes the landmark community mental health legislation of the early 1960s, recognizing this as the occasion when deinstitutionalization became official national policy. This perspective emphasizes the idealistic and intellectual underpinnings of the community mental health movement, focussing on forces operative in the emergence, formulation, and approval of this legislative agenda. A spirit of melioration is seen as a driving force in the era's politics across a spectrum of issues from civil rights, to health care, to the Peace Corps. The pivotal concept of community was itself an infectious one, influential not only in mental health care but also in the design of contemporary antipoverty measures. Scholarly works highlight the part played by a coalition of reformist officials, liberal politicians, and mental health activists in moving community mental health legislation through the decision-making process (Foley 1975, Connery et al 1968). More detailed background analysis relates this elite action to a historical context of shifting social understandings of the problem of mental illness and its treatment (Rochefort 1984).

A second school of thought looks beyond these auspicious beginnings of deinstitutionalization to some of its worst consequences, including inadequate follow-up services for discharged patients and large-scale transfers to such settings as nursing and boarding homes. In line with a neo-Marxist view of the state, this perspective views deinstitutionalization as a movement concerned less with patient welfare than with easing the growing public fiscal strain of institutional care. Deinstitutionalization thus represents a new style of community-based social control made possible by the advent of modern federal income maintenance and health insurance programs (Scull 1984). Brown (1985) also describes the development of a new medical-industrial complex under which public funds sustain the operation and profits of proprietary facilities.

Some reconciliation between these divergent characterizations is possible by recognizing deinstitutionalization as a disjointed, nonlinear process in which there has been "loose coupling" of policies and results (Gronfein 1985a). Kiesler & Sibulkin (1987) portray this discrepancy in terms of a distinction between de jure and de facto mental health policy, the former being the prescriptions of enacted law, while the latter is "the net outcome of overall practices, whether the outcome is intended or not." Other authors similarly describe deinstitutionalization less in terms of the rational unfolding of an overarching plan than as a hastily conceived, poorly managed undertaking whose thrust has altered over time and across the levels of government that became involved (Mechanic 1989, Lerman 1985, Rochefort 1987). Thus, inadvertence as well as design must be weighted in a complete account of the deinstitutionalization movement (Gronfein 1985a).

DEINSTITUTIONALIZATION TRENDS

Deinstitutionalization has been the "single most important issue" of concern for those in the mental health sphere for the past three decades (Rich 1986). An empirical examination of changes in the role played by public hospitals is central to understanding this process. In addition to an overall pattern of systemic transformation, the data reveal important variations in how this movement developed over time and at the state and local levels. Moreover, far from stimulating the phase-out of all types of institutional care, de-institutionalization practices within state and county mental hospitals actually are associated with the rise of a variety of nontraditional institutions that have acquired an increasingly significant role in the custody and care of the mentally ill.

The National Scene

The most dramatic—and most commonly cited—statistic used to describe the course of deinstitutionalization in the United States is the year-end count of resident patients in state and county mental hospitals. From their initial appearance during the 1800s until the midtwentieth century, these facilities underwent tremendous growth. From the start of the 1930s to 1955 alone, inpatient totals swelled from 332,000 to 559,000 (US Bureau of the Census 1975, p. 84, Table B 423-427). This latter date marks the unofficial onset of deinstitutionalization, followed as it was by consistent annual census declines that only now may be abating (see Table 1). Total resident patients at the end of 1986 numbered 109,939, an 81% reduction from 31 years earlier (NIMH 1989).

A second measure of hospital activity, and one that portrays the de-institutionalization phenomenon in less drastic terms, is inpatient episodes.

Table 1 Resident patients, inpatient episodes, and admissions, state and county mental hospitals, 1950 to 1985

Year	Year end resident patients	Inpatient episodes	Admissions
1950	512,501		152,286
1955	558,922	818,832	178,003
1960	535,540		234,791
1965	475,202	804,926	316,664
1970	337,619		384,511
1975	193,436	598,993	376,156
1980	132,164		b
1985	109,939	459,374[a]	b

Source: NIMH (1989); Morrissey (1989, pp. 318–319, Table 13-2).
[a] Figure cited is based on 1983
[b] After 1975, NIMH stopped reporting admissions and began reporting patient additions.

Cumulated over all facilities in the nation, this statistic takes account of resident census at the year's beginning plus admissions, readmissions, and returns from leave during the reporting year. Total inpatient care episodes for state and county mental hospitals fluctuated in the neighborhood of 800,000 from 1955 to 1965. Thereafter, it fell steadily, reaching a level of 459,000 in 1983, or 44% below the 1955 number of 819,000. Compared to changes in the inpatient census, then, the number of inpatient episodes in public mental hospitals dropped much less precipitously and not until a decade after the resident patients' decline had gotten underway. The reason for the discrepancy in these two trend lines is that admissions to state and county mental hospitals—one of the principal components in the episodes calculation—continued to increase throughout the 1950s, 1960s, and early 1970s, offsetting until 1965 the simultaneous census reductions (Kiesler & Sibulkin 1987, Witkin et al 1987).

At the same time that other operational measures have fallen, the period of time most inpatients spend within state and mental hospitals has also shortened. Average length of stay went from 421 days in 1969 to 143 days in 1982 (Kiesler & Sibulkin 1987). Median length of stay, a better measure of typical hospital stays since its value is less sensitive to the inclusion of a comparatively small number of long-term inpatients, declined as well—from about 41 days in 1970 to 23 days in 1980 (Manderscheid et al 1985).

Despite a general diminution in their service responsibilities, state and county mental hospitals have remained relatively stable in number over recent decades. In 1986, there were 286 such institutions in the United States, 11 more than in 1955. Between the two points in time, the highest count occurred in 1973, at 334 hospitals (NIMH 1989). On the other hand, the size of these public facilities assessed in terms of average number of inpatient beds has dropped sharply, from 1311 in 1970 to 467 in 1984. Considered in conjunction with the nation's population growth during this same period, the change is noteworthy. Beds per 100,000 civilian population went from 207.4 in 1970 to 56.1 in 1984 (Witkin et al 1987).

The Uneven Pace of Deinstitutionalization

Longitudinal analysis shows that deinstitutionalization did not occur at a steady rate (see, e.g., Gronfein 1985a, Lerman 1982, 1985). Inpatient declines during the late 1950s and first half of the 1960s were modest, especially compared to those that followed in the late 1960s and 1970s (see Figure 1). Broken into a series of five-year intervals, the data show an aggregate decrease of only 4.2% for 1955–1960, and 11.3% for 1960–1965. By contrast, the cumulative decreases for 1965–1970, 1970–1975, and 1975–1980 were 29.0%, 42.7%, and 31.7%, respectively (calculated from NIMH 1989). Of the total census reduction of approximately 449,000 that took place

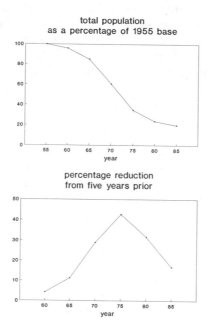

Figure 1   Resident patients in state and county mental hospitals: total population as a percentage of 1955 base and percentage reduction from five years prior

between 1955 and 1985, more than three quarters occurred in the period 1965–1980.

The major impact on deinstitutionalization of the federal health insurance and income maintenance programs that were established or expanded in the late 1960s and early 1970s has already been noted. The above data further underscore the importance of these programs. Community mental health ideologies and even the availability of powerful tranquilizing drugs prior to 1965 failed on their own to drastically alter longstanding patterns of care. Only when these new ideas and treatments were joined by the financing of residential alternatives did the system respond on a large scale (Mechanic 1989).

Noting this unevenness in the historical development of deinstitutionalization, Morrissey (1982, 1989) describes two fundamentally different phases. The "benign" phase which occurred between 1956 and 1965 consisted chiefly of "opening the back doors" of the state institutions to place new admissions and less impaired long-term residents in alternative settings. Many hospital treatment programs were also revitalized in this period. Following this was a "radical" phase from 1966 to 1975, which saw the "closing of the front doors" of these facilities. At a time when many states were experiencing economic hard times, hasty downsizing of residential populations and institutional capacity through patient diversions in addition to massive discharges provided a way of avoiding the expensive hospital improvement programs that new court and regulatory requirements often demanded. Community mental health and patient rights activists joined in support of this development.

Change at the Subnational Level

Corresponding to the lack of uniformity in deinstitutionalization over time is the striking variation among states. Table 2 provides information on the rates of public hospital depopulation across the states for two selected periods, 1967–1973 and 1973–1983. In both instances, values are widely dispersed— no single census reduction category contains as many as half of all states, and the difference between the highest- and lowest-ranking states in the later time-frame exceeds 100 points (signifying that even in this, the heyday of deinstitutionalization, some states experienced a countertrend of hospital inpatient increases). Focussing on the 1956–1965 and the 1966–1975 periods, Gronfein (1985b) found the degree of interstate heterogeneity in de-institutionalization to be greater during the earlier period. Rich (1986) similarly identifies several distinctive configurations for the pace and timing of state hospital inpatient declines in 18 states between 1950 and 1978.

Such variability is consistent with the idiosyncratic nature of individual state mental health systems, which developed for most of their histories free from the standardizing influence of a national mental health policy. A number of factors helped to shape differential state responses to the deinstitutionalization movement, including the starting condition of each state system in the

Table 2 Percentage reduction in year-end resident patients by state groupings, 1967 to 1973 and 1973 to 1983

Percentage reduction	Number of States	
	1967–1973	1973–1983
0% or negative	0	3
1–20%	5	2
21–40%	22	11
41–60%	19	24
61–80%	5	10
81–100%	0	1
Mean reduction	38.8%	46.3%
Range	62.4	119.5
Standard deviation	15.1	23.2
Coefficient of variation	.39	.50

Source: Calculated from Taube (1975, p. 15, Table 4) and Greene et al (1986, p. 15, Table 3). Includes District of Columbia

late 1950s (e.g. the number of state hospitals and the size and composition of their populations); the relative strength of the political base of public mental institutions within the state; the fiscal structure of state mental health services, especially cost-sharing arrangements between state and community entities; the vigor and efficacy of the indigenous community mental health coalition, including its civil libertarian contingent; and the amount of economic strain faced by a given state with the stagflation of the 1970s (Morrissey 1982). Unfortunately, there are few detailed qualitative studies of individual state care systems in this period, making it difficult to trace the relative impacts of such determining features.

Federal influence was strong but indirect. Empirical analysis confirms a significant positive correlation between state hospital inpatient declines and states' involvement in the Medicaid program, particularly in regard to Medicaid payments to nursing homes (Gronfein 1985a). In contrast, neither the introduction of psychotropic drugs in the late 1950s and early 1960s nor CMHC activity in the 1970s—two of the most commonly cited causes of deinstitutionalization—were found to be statistically related to deinstitutionalization trends (Gronfein 1985a,b, 1986b).

Rise of Nontraditional Institutions

With state and county mental hospitals progressively depopulating, other institutional providers gained importance as locations for the treatment and/or residence of mentally ill persons. Private mental hospitals, admittedly a small component, increased 80% in inpatient episodes over the course of the 1970s (Kiesler & Sibulkin 1987). Most dramatic has been the change in service activity of general hospitals. Many established new special psychiatric units, and others admitted mental patients to beds in medical and surgical units. Between 1965 and 1980 there was a six-fold increase in psychiatric inpatient episodes in general hospitals without psychiatric units (Kiesler & Sibulkin 1987). The general hospital has become the leading provider of acute inpatient psychiatric care.

Many elderly mentally ill were transferred from state hospitals in the 1960s and 1970s. Nursing homes continue to receive many chronically mentally ill aged (together with a very much smaller inflow of nonelderly mentally ill) directly from the community and from short-term hospitals. Of the approximately 1.5 million patients currently in nursing homes in the United States, the proportion having a serious psychiatric disorder or dementias may be somewhere between 30 and 75%, depending on how mental disorder is defined (Linn & Stein 1989). And in the community setting, a host of nontraditional institutions have appeared in the form of board-and-care homes, halfway houses, supervised apartments, and other residential facilities. Together these now provide living arrangements for perhaps as many as 300,000–400,000 chronically mentally ill persons (Segal & Kotler 1989).

Deinstitutionalization and Other Problem Populations

Over the past few decades deinstitutionalization has emerged as a principal theme of policy and practice in several other human service areas as well, including developmental disability, physical disability, and corrections (De-Jong 1979, Lerman 1982, 1985, Scull, 1984). Dimensions of this movement are reflected in such measures as a decline in the rate of institutionalization in state mental retardation facilities (from 97.7 per 100,000 in 1965 to 46.8 per 100,000 in 1985) (US Bureau of the Census 1987), reduced use of public training schools for delinquents (whose rate of institutionalization dropped from 98 to 69 per 100,000 youths over 1970–1977) (Lerman 1985), and the increasing percentage of releases on parole from state prisons in the 1960s and 1970s (attaining a level as high as 70%) (Sykes 1978). More recently, supervised home release has increasingly been used for prisoners.

Several key parallels can be drawn between developments within these other deinstitutionalizing areas and mental health (DeJong 1979, Sykes 1978, Lerman 1982, 1985, Rothman 1980, Scheerenberger 1983, Scull 1984, Tyor & Bell 1984). As a frequent scenario, the deinstitutionalization impulse emanated from a combination of sources—ideological, judicial and economic. In part, there was intellectual cross fertilization from mental health to these other fields, but each field also gave birth to its own concepts. Typically, court orders insisted on improved institutional conditions, and availability of increased federal funding for new services also shaped alternatives. Growth of nontraditional institutional forms (halfway houses, foster homes, group homes, treatment centers, etc) developed in all sectors. And in every case, deinstitutionalization eventually stimulated public debate over the method and impacts of program implementation. But important differences exist between these other human service systems and mental health. No other area experienced the scope of deinstitutionalization characteristic of the mental health sector. Institutional-noninstitutional patterns within these respective systems also vary. Whereas new service modalities in mental health developed mostly parallel to traditional institutions and as an alternative, in mental retardation many new residential care facilities are physically a part of the state institution (Lerman 1985). Similarly, expanded community programs in criminal justice, unlike mental health, operate in tandem with a sharply increasing institutional population and a movement to construct additional prison facilities (Scull 1984, *New York Times* May 17, 1987).

Deinstitutionalization in Perspective

Deinstitutionalization arose from complex interacting social forces, was implemented with startling rapidity, and is now beset by political and professional controversy. Such circumstances are conducive to misperception and misunderstanding. Clearly, state and county mental hospitals no longer occupy the preeminent position they once did within the US mental health system. By the same token, however, one should not neglect the significant place that these institutions maintain in contemporary mental health services. By a wide margin, state hospitals remain the foremost provider of total inpatient days of psychiatric care (Kiesler & Sibulkin 1987), and they care for many of the most difficult, troubled, and violent patients. These institutions also continue to house a sizable number of long-term patients—according to one estimate, nearly 20% of their patient population at any point in time have been hospitalized for 20 years or more (Morrissey 1989). State hospitals are reported to absorb nearly two thirds of the expenditures of state mental health agencies (Lutterman et al 1987), although these figures may be exaggerated by the way such data are collected—hospital outreach and community care programs are reported as part of hospital expenditures, and not as a contribution of community care.

Extraordinary growth in the mental health sector as a whole coincided with the deinstitutionalization movement, and it is perhaps this conjunction of historical occurrences that induces premature reports of the death of the public mental hospital. Patient care episodes in specialty mental health organizations, for example, rose from 1.7 million in 1955 to 6.9 million in 1983. An important change from inpatient to outpatient care underlay this increase: In 1955, the distribution of episodes favored inpatient care by a 3.42 : 1 ratio; in 1983, the ratio was 2.69 : 1 in favor of outpatient care (Morrissey 1989, pp. 318–319, Table 13–2; see also Thompson et al 1982). Klerman (1982) estimated a sixfold increase in the population's use of mental health services over this period. With more persons being treated for mental illness, the probability of a typical patient having contact with state and county mental hospitals has been much lowered (Morrissey 1989). Most patients now being treated by community agencies and alternative institutional facilities would not have been in public mental health systems in prior decades. This overall growth of the mental health sector has played a major part in the transformation of the role of state and county mental hospitals (Kiesler & Sibulkin 1987). It has increasingly become the system of last resort for the uninsured, the treatment resistant, and those who are most difficult to relocate to other settings.

The growth of health insurance covering mental health benefits, concurrent with deinstitutionalization, helped transform mental health care. The most significant single change was the development of the general community hospital as the major site for acute psychiatric inpatient care. Many general hospitals developed specialized psychiatric units, and by 1987, the general hospital accounted for some 1.8 million admissions a year of patients with primary diagnoses of psychiatric illness (National Center for Health Statistics 1988). Medicaid became a major source of payment for inpatient psychiatric care in general hospitals for many chronic patients, contributing to a pattern of episodic hospital care characterized by short lengths of stay with little community follow-up (Mechanic 1989).

As care for the most severely mentally ill patients shifted from public institutions to community care settings, the functions traditionally associated with public mental hospitals remained but were now more dispersed among varying community agencies and different levels of government. Severely disabled patients still required medical and psychiatric care, housing, psychosocial and educational services, a program of activities, assistance in attaining welfare benefits, and supervision of their medication and daily routines. The strategic task of integrating these functions outside of institutions is a formidable one, and there is persistent evidence of failure in meeting these needs in even the most rudimentary ways (Torrey 1988; Mechanic 1989).

A Note on Cross-National Experience

Even in the United States deinstitutionalization proceeded differently among the states, depending on the structure of their mental health systems, social and economic conditions, the power base of interested constituencies, and the strength of the mental health reform movement. Comparative analysis is extremely difficult with nations that vary greatly in their economic and political systems, and in the structure of their health care and welfare services. Some analysts examine deinstitutionalization in the context of the rise of the welfare state and the way "in which group interests were aggregated, represented and mediated," and its specific urban manifestations (Dear & Wolch 1987). However, few studies garner data from localities in more than one or two countries.

Information and new technical approaches diffuse rapidly throughout the world and, thus, ideas about deinstitutionalization and the value of neuroleptic drugs were widely available in the developed countries by the late 1950s. Moreover, experience in community living for the mentally impaired has long existed as in Gheel (Belgium) and other communities. In contrast, ideologies, leadership, political participation, social control, and the organization of health and welfare are not specific only to nation, but also to locality. In England, a source of many of the social psychiatric ideas about community care, the population of mental hospitals began to fall around 1954 with the introduction of reserpine and chlorpromazine, ideas about therapeutic communities, and change in administrative practices (Brown et al 1966, Wing & Brown 1970). Despite much experimentation with alternatives and rehabilitation approaches, deinstitutionalization in Britain never developed the momentum seen in the United States. Many reasons may account for the contrast including the fact that British psychiatry is a hospital-based consulting specialty; the focus of interest in Britain is on therapeutic hospital alternatives; a cultural environment supports incremental change; and a different social history affects the management of the impaired elderly.

Canada followed a course similar to that of the United States, although deinstitutionalization occurred later and to a smaller extent. In Ontario, for example, patients in provincial asylums increased until 1960 to a peak of almost 19,507 but by 1976 was 5,030 (Dear & Wolch 1987). Deinstitutionalization in Australia has accelerated in recent years, influenced by American programs (Hoult 1987).

Despite these commonalities, deinstitutionalization has not been universal. In much of Europe, where a medically oriented, hospital-based psychiatry is dominant, the treatment of serious mental illness remains substantially centered in hospitals. In Austria, for example, there is extremely strong resistance to community-based care and little deinstitutionalization. In Japan, private psychiatric hospitals are growing rapidly and are replacing informal sources of care (Ikegami 1980). Deinstitutionalization must be seen in relation to a nation's values and in the historical context of its political, economic, social, and health and welfare institutions.

In recent years much attention has focussed on deinstitutionalization in Italy, and particularly in Trieste, which closed its mental hospital. This movement, based on the ideology of Franco Basaglia, a Venetian psychiatrist, viewed hospitalization as psychiatric repression and deinstitutionalization as one element of a class struggle. As in the United States in the 1960s, hospitalization is viewed as a cause of illness and disability. The dilemmas of mental illness are explained in the light of struggles among interests over power and control of social institutions (Lowell 1985). Good data arc difficult to obtain, and there is much controversy and conflicting views about the changes that have spread throughout Italy. There is indication of significant transfer of patients to other institutions, no longer called hospitals. As in the United States, the evaluation of the consequences of change depend very much on appraisals of local situations in a context of large variability.

IMPACT OF DEINSTITUTIONALIZATION AND FUTURE NEEDS

The long-term care patients who had been resident in mental hospitals prior to deinstitutionalization, if still surviving, are now relatively elderly and are not a major focus of the controversy that rages around the issue of de-institutionalization. Indeed, long-term studies of the course of schizophrenia in the United States and abroad demonstrate persuasively that with time the most severe symptoms abate and schizophrenic patients can make reasonable adjustments to the community (Harding et al 1987a, b, Bleuler 1978, Ciompi 1980). Older patients in the United States released from mental hospitals were relocated in nursing homes, sheltered care facilities, and families. Some were demented patients who had been kept in mental hospitals because of a lack of alternative institutional settings. Others were elderly patients whose psychotic symptoms had substantially abated but who retained social disabilities due to their long confinements.

The deinstitutionalization debate confuses this population at more advanced ages who were relocated from public hospitals to other settings during the decades of rapid deinstitutionalization with new cohorts of seriously mentally ill patients who are now part of an entirely different system of care (Mechanic 1987). It is this younger population of patients with psychoses and personality disorders, socialized in different cultural and treatment contexts, who are often difficult to manage and who frighten the community. These younger patients often resist the idea that they are mentally ill, are uncooperative with treatment, abuse alcohol and drugs, and generally live an unconventional style of life (Schwartz & Goldfinger 1981, Sheets et al 1982, Pepper & Ryglewicz 1982). Much of the debate, however it is framed, really focusses on this new and growing population of severely mentally ill youth and young adults. The problem is exacerbated by demographic trends that result in large subgroups in the population at ages of high risk for occurrence of schizophrenia and substance abuse (Mechanic 1987).

In the United States, the problems have also become more visible and acute with the contraction of public programs during the 1980s. Recall that the large waves of deinstitutionalization occurred with the expansion of social welfare activities in the late 1960s and 1970s, particularly Medicaid, SSI and SSDI, housing programs, and food stamps. These programs provided the subsistence base essential for relocating patients to the community. This subsistence base was not maintained relative to the growing numbers of seriously mentally ill persons, and in many instances it substantially shrank. Federal and state governments faced with budget deficits tightened eligibility, benefits, and reimbursement in the Medicaid program so that by the 1980s, only two fifths of the poor were covered (Curtis 1986). The Social Security Administration (SSA) faced with growing disability rolls was directed by Congress to review the eligibility of disability recipients. Vast numbers of the disabled mentally ill lost their benefits, although many were subsequently reinstated by the courts (Osterweis et al 1987). Government subsidy of housing also underwent a contraction in the 1980s, making low income housing in many cities extraordinarily difficult to obtain and contributing to the growing numbers of the homeless. In short, the enabling factors that made significant deinstitutionalization possible greatly eroded in the aftermath.

The cutbacks in social programs particularly affected the seriously mentally ill. Although some evidence suggested that on occasion the SSA specifically targeted the mentally ill for disability review, the vulnerability of this population was probably due more to their relative youth. As a general economic strategy, the SSA was more motivated to excise from the disability rolls younger persons who were likely to draw benefits for many years than those at older ages. As in the case of other welfare entitlements, aggressive advocacy on behalf of the mentally ill over a period of years resulted in reinstatements to the disability rolls of significant numbers of persons. In respect to other benefits such as housing, the mentally ill have been particularly vulnerable because they typically lack bureaucratic skills to gain eligibility, and administrators who run these generic programs have little appreciation of their special needs. In addition, the mentally ill suffer considerable stigma and discrimination relative to other eligible competing groups such as the poor elderly. In recent years, mental health programs have become more aggressive in helping the mentally ill attain eligibility for Medicaid, SSI, and housing benefits, but in an environment of shrinking resources.

Homelessness and Deinstitutionalization

Estimates of the numbers of the homeless range widely (US Department of Housing and Urban Development 1984, US General Accounting Office 1985, Institute of Medicine 1988), and it is difficult to know precisely the size of this changing population. Analysts also differ in their definitions of homelessness, making comparability among estimates difficult. Estimates of the homeless range from two hundred thousand to more than two million (Institute of Medicine 1988). There is broad agreement, however, that the homeless population has been growing. A significant proportion of the homeless suffer from mental impairments. There are no extensive studies using rigorous standardized psychiatric tools, but most of the smaller studies suggest that between a quarter and a half of the homeless have significant psychiatric symptoms (Bassuk 1984a, b, Lamb 1984, Rossi et al 1987). For example, one in four of the Chicago homeless reported having been in a mental hospital for stays of over 48 hours. Nearly half exhibited levels of depression that suggested a need for clinical attention (Rossi et al 1987). The proportion of homeless that acknowledge a history of psychiatric hospitalization ranges from 11 to 33%, across studies (Institute of Medicine 1988, p. 52).

Opponents of deinstitutionalization have used estimates of the homeless mentally ill to discredit current mental health practices, arguing that deinstitutionalization causes homelessness (Appelbaum 1987, Wyatt & De-Renzo 1986). Others associate homelessness mainly with poverty, the diminishing supply of low-cost housing in many areas, and the inability of low-income persons to afford available housing (Rossi & Wright 1987). No one contests that many of the homeless have profound medical and psychiatric needs, but the impact of deinstitutionalization is quite another issue. While homelessness stems from the unavailability of housing and is exacerbated by the symptoms, vulnerability, and stigma of the mentally ill, its link specifically to deinstitutionalization is less clear. Studies demonstrating that substantial numbers of the homeless have psychiatric symptoms, or have a history of psychiatric treatment, are not sufficiently precise to identify persons who would have had illnesses or disabilities sufficient to require long-term hospitalization under policies prevailing prior to deinstitutionalization. Putting some of the mentally ill homeless into institutions would obviously reduce the homeless population but would not address the basic causes of homelessness. Thus, the entire debate generates far more heat than light. There is little evidence to support the contention that deinstitutionalization is the primary cause of homelessness; it is one of many interacting causes (Rossi & Wright 1987, Mechanic 1987).

In contrast, homelessness and inappropriate housing options pose extraordinary problems for the effective administration of mental health services. Housing problems are a major impediment to effective care and contribute to episodic hospitalization. Many public mental health authorities view housing deficiencies as their most serious programmatic shortcoming and report that only a fraction of the needed housing appropriate for their patients is available (Aiken et al 1986). The lack of suitable housing remains a major barrier in many mental health systems to releasing from mental hospitals patients who are judged to be legally and clinically ready for discharge. Mentally ill persons require a range of housing options depending on their assets and vulnerabilities ranging from highly supervised residential units to independent living. But a reasonable range of options is unavailable in most communities (Randolph et al 1989). A major demonstration effort is now underway in nine large cities to develop mental health authorities that have the capacity to develop and manage housing options for the seriously mentally ill (Aiken et al 1986).

ALTERNATIVES TO MENTAL HOSPITALIZATION

A large number of studies have documented that alternatives to hospitalization, whatever the specific programmatic features, attain better results by a number of outcome criteria as compared to traditional hospital care. Kiesler and Sibulkin (1987), for example, identified 14 experimental studies, most with random assignment, comparing hospital treatment to some alternative care arrangement. They conclude that alternative care is more effective than hospitalization across a wide range of patient populations and treatment strategies.

Documenting that a particular pattern of care is effective is only one aspect of developing a viable system of care. The larger challenge is developing financial and organizational arrangements assuring that such care could be made available to a widely dispersed population. The basic task is a difficult one, and the existing fragmentation of responsibility and financing poses large barriers to coordinating the needed services. Three initiatives intended to deal with these issues include case-management, financing arrangements based on capitation, and the development of public mental health authorities.

Case Management

Case-management is the device most commonly advocated to deal with the inefficient coordination of services needed by the chronic mentally ill. Case-management usually refers to a process of integrating the elements of a client's total care, filling in gaps by either providing services directly or arranging for necessary services, and insuring that the client receives essential entitlements. There is, however, little consistency in the conceptions of case-management or in its implementation. Even within the more limited legislative context of Medicaid programs and demonstrations, definitions of case-management are characterized by a lack of clarity and consistency (Spitz 1987). Case-management roles vary from therapeutic care to tasks solely concerned with garnering entitlements and coordination. Those who perform these roles vary enormously in training, position, salary and career structures, authority, and control over resources. They often find themselves in conflict between treatment goals and cost-containment pressures from the agencies that employ them (Dill 1987). The gaps between the rhetoric and realities of case-management are large.

In one of the few systematic studies examining a particular case-management strategy, 417 chronically mentally ill were randomized into experimental and control groups. The control group had access to all services other than case-management, while experimental patients were assigned to a unit staffed by eight experienced case-managers and a supervisor (Franklin et al 1987). During the study, case-managers spent about half their time providing nonclinical services to patients and two-fifths of their time brokering services. The follow-up at 12 months found that the patients in the experimental group received more services, were admitted to inpatient care more frequently, and were more costly to manage. There were some tendencies in favor of the experimental group on quality of life measures, but they were small and not statistically significant (Franklin et at 1987). This study suggests the importance of clarity in defining case-management models and the necessity for their careful evaluation.

Case management is a function that can be examined on its own terms or viewed as an approach embedded within a larger service strategy. How case management fits within the goals and operational approaches of an agency may affect its performance on critical indicators. In Wisconsin's Training in Community Living (TCL) Program, case management teams are used for aggressive community-based care organized within a well-articulated system of services (Stein & Diamond 1985). The effectiveness of the TCL program has been demonstrated and has now been widely replicated (Stein & Test 1985). Case-management teams are so significant a component of this program as to be inseparable from the larger system of care. Case management is a function and not a total service. Its evaluation must be understood within the context of a particular system of care.

Capitation as a Financing Strategy

Capitation is a predetermined payment for a specified set of services for individuals over a defined time period. It has been used extensively to pay general practitioners in Europe and in HMOs in the United States. The basic idea is that the provider receives the identical prepaid reimbursement per person regardless of levels of utilization. Capitation disconnects the link between services and fees for service, and modifies the incentives affecting provider behavior. One theory is that capitation allows the clinician to provide services on the basis of need independent of fee considerations. The evidence indicates, however, that capitation mechanisms in contrast to fee-for-service approaches result in a lower intensity of services. Capitation in mental health has been applied in two ways: mainstreaming the mentally ill into HMOs and by developing mental health HMOs (Mechanic & Aiken 1989).

In the case of mainstreaming, mental patients supported by public programs such as Medicaid are enrolled in existing HMOs that take responsibility for providing an expanded range of mental health services for these enrollees. The single largest demonstration of mainstreaming the mentally ill in Minnesota was terminated because of operational problems (Christianson et al 1989), and we have relatively little direct data on treatment outcomes using this approach. Research, in general, on the performance of HMOs with chronic patients suggests the need for caution in mainstreaming (Schlesinger 1986). In addition, HMOs provide a much lower intensity of mental health care than is evident in fee-for-service practice (Wells et at 1986). The data necessary to link intensity of care with outcomes remain undeveloped.

The idea of capitation in general medical care is one based on sharing risk across a population. It is assumed that some will need care and others not, with one group balancing the other. In contrast, most of the chronically mentally ill require fairly intensive services, making the risk-sharing concept less pertinent. Those developing mental health HMOs, however, seek to use capitation as a strategy to consolidate financing, focus responsibility, and reduce services fragmentation. By capitating chronic mental patients, they anticipate greater flexibility in managing care than is now possible with categorical funding streams, and they hope to aggregate sufficient resources to develop new needed services. Also, by linking capitation to care for specific chronic patients, they hope to ensure that these typically neglected patients receive appropriate attention.

The effectiveness of using capitation as a strategy to consolidate resources and to focus attention on the care of a neglected group remains unclear. Major efforts have been undertaken in a variety of localities including Rochester, New York (Babigian & Marshall 1989) and Rhode Island (Mauch 1989), and others are in the process of development. Existing experience suggests that developing a viable capitation approach requires much planning and very careful implementation, and there are many unanticipated difficulties (Mechanic & Aiken 1989). Yet, it constitutes one of the more exciting potentials to develop managed care for the chronic mentally ill within our unwieldy health care system.

Mental Health Authorities

The mental health authority, like capitation, represents an effort to focus authority, capacity, and responsibility in caring for the chronic mental patient in the community. Various groups seek a new public or nonprofit entity to take charge, given the fragmentation of responsibility and lack of coordination among community mental health and welfare agencies. Such an organization is seen as having the authority and resources to direct care for public patients by developing its own services or by contracting with other community entities. Authorities would receive federal, state, and local funds for mental health services and have more discretion in their use than is characteristic of many existing categorical programs. Some regions have developed mental health boards or other broad agencies with the authority to receive mental health funds from diverse sources and to make allocations for care with more discretion than many categorical programs allow. With the support of the Robert Wood Johnson Foundation and the US Department of Housing and Urban Development, efforts are now underway in nine cities to develop public authorities with greater clout and a capacity for increased flexibility (Aiken et al 1986). The promise of this strategy will be assessed through an extensive evaluation directed by Howard Goldman at the University of Maryland School of Medicine.

CHALLENGES OF DEINSTITUTIONALIZATION AS PUBLIC POLICY

The notion of returning to a state hospital-centered mental health system would be unrealistic today, even if such a course was seen as desirable.

Thirty-five years of deinstitutionalization and the growth of a broad range of services have resulted in a decentralized, pluralistic mental health sector funded by a diversity of public and private programs. Thus, a monolithic hospital-based system is an impractical model from both an organizational and a political standpoint. Especially in this era of government deficits, it would be prohibitively expensive to upgrade and expand hospital facilities to the point where they could provide a decent living environment and continuous appropriate treatment to large numbers of patients. A well-planned, treatment-oriented, hospital-based system is not inconceivable, but without substantial reinvestment, state mental hospitals would quickly degenerate into the human warehouses of the past. Moreover, a policy of long-term institutionalization is inconsistent with the principle of care in the least restrictive setting that now stands as accepted legal doctrine in our society and is the conditioned expectation of persons who receive mental health services. Finally, the idea of a hospital-based system is inconsistent with a large body of research showing that alternatives to hospitalization improve function and quality of life relative to hospital-based care (Kiesler & Sibulkin 1987).

The impulse for reinstitutionalization reflects a longstanding tendency within the mental health field toward vacillation between hospital and community alternatives (Rochefort 1988). These debates typically neglect the complex nature and variety of mental disorders and the full spectrum of service programs required (Grob 1987b). The present challenge of deinstitutionalization as public policy is to avoid this cyclical trend by ensuring that community and hospital sectors come to play complementary roles in an integrated system, providing patients with care suited to their distinctive needs and capabilities. Necessary reforms in mental health financing and service delivery have already been described. We conclude by noting some of the larger social policy issues.

Deinstitutionalization is one of a group of social initiatives of the 1960s that began with great expectations but resulted in a neoconservative backlash against government interventionism. For many of these initiatives, including deinstitutionalization, a distorted public image has taken hold that exaggerates the dimensions of failure while ignoring positive accomplishments (Schwarz 1988). Even in a more balanced assessment, however, the reality of disappointing performance is plain and underscores the difficulty of translating reformist policy design into effective programmatic action. This has come to be known in the policy sciences literature as the implementation problem (Bardach 1977, Williams 1980).

Implementation difficulties have undermined the deinstitutionalization effort from its inception and are evident in such basic disjunctions as the neglected relationship between community mental health centers and state hospitals. Coordination processes of this nature, like those essential to the creation of a comprehensive sociomedical support system for chronically mentally ill persons in the community, represent the classic implementation challenge. They require the long-term cooperation of multiple service bureaucracies and levels of government. What makes the task so hard—and what promises to test case management, special mental health authorities, and other current approaches in the mental health system—are overlapping issues of territoriality, resource supply, technical capability, and conflicting organizational objectives and styles (Dill & Rochefort 1989). In attempting to overcome these obstacles, mental health professionals and administrators confront the powerful force of tradition and an American human services apparatus built around the concept of dispersed responsibility.

Uncertainty about control and accountability in mental health care at the level of service delivery is matched by persistent ambivalence on these questions within government as a whole. Here, again, problems experienced by the mental health sphere reflect broader social policy dynamics of our federal political order.

The provision of public mental health services began as a local responsibility in the colonial era. With the spread of public mental hospitals in the 1800s, the task then shifted to the states. The Community Mental Health Centers Act of 1963 staked out a national interest in mental health care, one consciously designed to bypass the state role which was viewed as too tradition-bound for the necessary reforms. Roughly 30 years later, the Reagan administration's Alcohol, Drug Abuse, and Mental Health block grant decentralized administrative responsibility for this community mental health program to state officials. At the same time, however, the national government continues to seek to provide leadership—and a set of common priorities—in mental health policy through its ongoing work to bring psychiatric services in general hospitals into Medicare's prospective payment system, and through legislation to provide funding for such purposes as state mental health planning (Public Law 99–660) and services for the homeless mentally ill (Public Law 100-77) (Levine & Haggard 1989). It also exerts a massive indirect influence on mental health policy through general entitlement programs and the administrative regulations that govern these. A tangled, unresolved intergovernmental relationship results that makes it exceedingly difficult to develop rational or even coherent policy.

The low standing of mental health issues on the national social agenda poses another impediment to needed improvement of the mental health system. Except for brief interludes in American history, the mentally ill have not captured the serious attention of elected officials, who generally have little interest or knowledge relating to mental illness. The rule, instead, has been neglect and a failure to appreciate the scope, severity, and degree of dysfunction and suffering associated with mental disorder. Chronically starved for resources and outside of public consciousness, the mental health sector persists as a kind of poor relation to other social commitments and without integration into the modern welfare state. It is significant that a recent comprehensive evaluation of the US social welfare system sponsored by the Ford Foundation did not even identify the mentally ill as a population of concern (Ford Foundation 1989).

Several factors account for this tendency toward exclusion. The expansion of social programs in the United States has followed a pattern of interest-group liberalism in which well-organized and visible clientele groups receive the most benefits (Lowi 1979). Lacking a mass membership and the resources this could provide, lobbying organizations for the mentally ill are a weak political force. The stigma of mental illness also limits the degree to which the general public is inclined to identify with this population. Further, mental health advocates have encouraged the separation of mental health and other social programs by stressing the unique plight of the mentally ill rather than the problems shared in common with other needy groups. The mental health constituency itself has been bitterly divided between diagnostic categories, advocates for children and adults, emphasis on varying priorities such as prevention versus care, and on medical-legal issues such as civil commitment policy. These divisions embody neither good strategy nor sound policy analysis, however. In recent years the emergence of the National Alliance for the Mentally Ill (NAMI) offers better prospects for effective interest group representation, but mental health advocacy continues to be fragmented and weak.

It is difficult to understand mental health policy outside of the large constellation of health and welfare entitlements whose gaps in coverage affect a variety of socially disadvantaged groups—the high prevalence of un-insurance for health needs and the lack of adequate affordable housing are just two examples. The severely mentally ill are multiply disadvantaged by poverty, disability, lack of housing and employment opportunities, and persistent social stigma. Public mental health care responsive to the needs of a de-institutionalized system requires coverage of this population within the entitlement structures on which their subsistence and welfare depend. This will require eliminating eligibility restrictions that discriminate against the mentally ill, and repairing the social "safety net" to make it truly comprehensive and reliable. Deinstitutionalization remains an unfulfilled promise. Having initiated policies that keep sick and disabled patients in the community, we require a framework of protections and supports to make the rhetoric of deinstitutionalization less a dream and more a reality.

Literature Cited

Aiken, L. H., Somers, S. A., Shore, M. F. 1986. Private foundations in health affairs. A case study of the development of a national initiative for the chronically mentally ill. *Am Psychol.* 41:1290–95

Appelbaum, P. 1987. Crazy in the streets. *Commentary* 83:34–39

Babigian, H. M., Marshall, P. 1989. Rochester: A comprehensive capitation experiment. See Mechanic & Aiken 1989

Bardach, E. 1977. *The Implementation Game.* Cambridge, Mass: MIT Press

Bassuk, E. L. 1984a. The homeless problem. *Sci. Am.* 251:40–45

Bassuk, E. L., Rubin, L., Lauriat, A. 1984b. Is homelessness a mental health problem? *Am. J. Psychiatry.* 141:1546–49

Belknap, I. 1956. *Human Problems of a State Mental Hospital.* New York: McGraw-Hill

Bleuler, M. 1978. *The Schizophrenic Disorders: Long-Term Patient and Family Studies.* Transl. S. M. Clements. New Haven: Yale Univ. Press

Bockoven, J. S. 1972. *Moral Treatment in Community Mental Health.* New York: Springer-Verlag

Brooks, A. D. 1974. *Law Psychiatry and the Mental Health System.* Boston: Little, Brown

Brown, G. W., Bone, M., Dalison, B., Wing, J. K. 1966. *Schizophrenia and Social Care.* London: Oxford Univ. Press

Brown, P. 1985. *The Transfer of Care: Psychiatric Deinstitutionalization and Its Aftermath.* London: Routledge & Kegan Paul

Cameron, J. M. 1978. Ideology and policy termination: Restructuring California's mental health system. *Public Policy* 4:533–70

Christianson, J. B., Lurie, N., Finch, M., Moscovice, I. 1989. Mainstreaming the mentally ill into HMOs. See Mechanic & Aiken 1989, pp. 19-28.

Ciompi, L. 1980. Natural history of schizophrenia in the long term. *Br. J. Psychiatry* 136:413–20

Connery, R. H., et al. 1968. *The Politics of Mental Health.* New York: Columbia Univ. Press

Curtis, R. 1986. The role of state governments in assuring access to care. *Inquiry* 23:277–85

Dear, M., Wolch, J. 1987. *Landscapes of Despair: From Deinstitutionalization to Homelessness.* Princeton, NJ: Princeton Univ Press

DeLong, G. 1979. Independent living: From social movement to analytic paradigm. *Arch. Phys. Med. Rehabil.* 60:435–46

Dill, A. E. P. 1987. Issues in case management for the chronically mentally ill. See Mechanic 1987, pp. 61-70

Dill, A. E. P., Rochefort, D. A. 1989. Coordination, continuity, and centralized control: A policy perspective on service strategies for the chronically mentally ill. *J. Soc. Issues* 45:145–59

Dowell, D. A., Ciarlo, J. A. 1989. An evaluative overview of the community mental health centers program. See Rochefort 1989, pp. 195-236

Ennis, B. J. 1972. *Prisoners of Psychiatry: Mental Patients, Psychiatrists, and the Law.* New York: Harcourt Brace Jovanovich

Foley, H. A. 1975. *Community Mental Health Legislation: The Formative Process.* Lexington, Mass: Heath

Foley, H. A., Sharfstein, S. S. 1983. *Madness and Government: Who Cares for the Mentally Ill?* Washington, DC. Am. Psychiatr. Press

Ford Foundation. 1989. *The Common Good: Social Welfare and the American Future.* New York: Ford Found.

Franklin, J. L., Solovitz, B., Mason, M., Clemons, J. R., Miller, G. E. 1987. An evaluation of case management. *Am. J. Public Health* 77:674–78

Goffman, E. 1961. *Asylums: Essays on the Social Situation of Mental Patients and Other Inmates.* Garden City, NY: Doubleday (Anchor)

Gralnick, A. 1985. Build a better hospital: Deinstitutionalization has failed. *Hosp. Comm. Psychiatry* 36:738–41

Greene, S., Witkin, M. J., Fell, A., Manderscheid, R. W. 1986. State and county mental hospitals, United States, 1982–83 and 1983–84, with trend analyses from 1973–74 to 1983–84. *Mental Health Statist. Note No. 176.* Rockville, Md: NIMH

Grob, G. N. 1987a. Mental health policy in post-World War II America. See Mechanic 1987, pp. 15-32

Grob, G. N. 1987b. The forging of mental health policy in America: World War II to New Frontier *J. Hist. Med. Allied Sci.* 42: 410–46

Gronfein, W. 1985a. Incentives and intentions in mental health policy: A comparison of the Medicaid and community mental health programs *J. Health Soc. Behav.* 26:192–206

Gronfein, W. 1985b. Psychotropic drugs and the origins of deinstitutionalization. *Soc. Probl.* 32:437–53

Harding, C. M., Brooks, G. W., Ashikaga, T., Strauss, J. S., Breier, A. 1987a. The

Vermont longitudinal study of persons with severe mental illness: I. Methodology, study sample, and overall status. *Am. J. Psychiatry* 144:718–26

Harding, C. M., Brooks, G. W., Ashikaga, T., Strauss, J. S., Breier, A. 1987b. The Vermont longitudinal study of persons with severe mental illness: II. Long-term outcome of subjects who retrospectively met DSM-III criteria for schizophrenia. *Am. J. Psychiatry* 144:727–35

Hoult, J. 1987. Replicating the Mendota Model in Australia. *Mental Health Care & Soc. Pol.* 38:565

Ikegami, N. 1980. Growth of psychiatric beds in Japan. *Soc. Sci. Med.* 14A:561–70

Institute of Medicine. 1988. *Homelessness, Health, and Human Needs.* Washington, DC: Natl. Acad. Press

Kennedy, J. F. 1963. Special message to the Congress on mental illness and mental retardation. *Public Papers of the Presidents of the United States: John F. Kennedy, 1963.* Washington, DC: GPO

Kiesler, C. A., Sibulkin, A. E. 1987. *Mental Hospitalization: Myths and Facts about a National Crisis.* Newbury Park, Calif: Sage

Klerman, G. L. 1982. The psychiatric revolution of the past twenty-five years. In *Deviance and Mental Illness,* ed. W. R. Gove, pp. 177-98. Beverly Hills, Calif: Sage

Lamb, H. R. 1979. The new asylums in the community. *Arch. Gen. Psychiatry* 36:129–34

Lamb, H. R., ed. 1984. *The homeless mentally ill: A task force report of the American Psychiatric Association.* Washington, DC: Am. Psychiatr. Assoc.

Lerman, P. 1982. *Deinstitutionalization and the Welfare State.* New Brunswick, NJ: Rutgers Univ. Press

Lerman, P. 1985. Deinstitutionalization and welfare policies. *Ann. Am. Acad. Polit. Soc. Sci.* 479:132–55

Levine, I. S., Haggard, L, K. 1989. Homelessness as a public mental health problem. See Rochefort 1989, pp. 293-310

Linn, M. W., Stein, S. 1989. Nursing homes as community mental health facilities. See Rochefort, 1989, pp. 267-92

Lovell, A. M. 1985. From confinement to community: The radical transformation of an Italian mental hospital. In *Mental Health Care and Social Policy,* ed. P. Brown, pp. 375-86. Boston: Routledge & Kegan Paul

Lowi, T. J. 1979. *The End of Liberalism.* New York: W. W. Norton. 2nd ed.

Lutterman, T., Mazade, N. A., Wurster, C. R., Glover, R. W. 1987. State mental health agency revenues and expenditures for mental health services: Trends from 1981 to 1985. In *Mental Health, United States, 1987,* ed R. W. Manderscheid, S. A. Bar-

rett, NIMH, pp. 158-86. Washington, DC: GPO

Manderscheid, R. W., Witkin, M. J., Rosenstein, M. J., Millazzo-Sayre, L. J., Bethel, H.E., et al. 1985. Specialty mental health services: System and patient characteristics—United States. In *Mental Health, United States, 1985,* ed, C. A. Taube, S. A. Barrett, NIMH, pp. 7-69. Washington, DC: GPO

Mauch, D. 1989. Rhode Island: An early effort at managed care. See Mechanic & Aiken 1989, pp. 55-64

Mechanic, D. 1987a. Correcting misconceptions in mental health policy: Strategies for improved care of the seriously mentally ill. *Milbank Mem. Fund Q.* 65:203–30

Mechanic, D. 1987b. *New Directions for Mental Health Services, Improving Mental Health Services: What the Social Sciences Can Tell Us.* San Francisco: Jossey-Bass

Mechanic, D. 1989. *Mental Health and Social Policy.* Englewood Cliffs, NJ: Prentice-Hall. 3rd ed.

Mechanic, D., Aiken, L. H., eds. 1989. *Paying for Services: Promises and Pitfalls of Capitation.* San Francisco: Jossey-Bass

Miller, K. S. 1976. *Managing Madness: The Case Against Civil Commitment.* New York: Free Press

Morrissey, J. P. 1982. Deinstitutionalizing the mentally ill: Process, outcomes, and new directions. In *Deviance and Mental Illness,* ed W. R. Gove, pp. 147–76. Beverly Hills, Calif: Sage

Morrissey, J. P. 1989. The changing role of the public mental hospital. See Rochefort 1989, pp. 311–38

Moynihan, D. P. 1989. Letter to the editor. *New York Times,* May 22

National Center for Health Statistics, 1988. 1987 Summary: National Hospital Discharge Survey. *Advance Data From Vital and Health Statistics, No. 159.* DHHS Publ. No. (PHS) 88–1250. Public Health Service, Hyattsville, Md.

National Institute of Mental Health, 1989. Unpublished data from Division of Biometry and Applied Sciences

Newsweek. 1986. Abandoned. Jan. 6, pp. 14–19

New York Times. 1987. A record prison census. May 17

Osterweis, M., Kleinman, A., Mechanic, D. 1987. *Pain and Disability: Clinical, Behavioral and Public Policy Perspectives.* Washington, DC: Natl. Acad. Press

Pepper, B., Ryglewicz, H., eds. 1982. *The Young Adult Chronic Patient* New Directions for Mental Health Services No. 14. San Francisco: Jossey-Bass

Randolph, F. L., Zipple, A. M., Rowan, C.

A. et al., 1989. *A survey of selected community residential programs for people with psychiatric disabilities*. Community Residential Rehabil. Proj. Cent. Psychiatr. Rehabil. Boston Univ.

Rich, R. F. 1986. Change and stability in mental health policy: The impact of two transformations. *Am. Behav. Sci.* 30:111–42

Rochefort, D. A. 1989. *Handbook on Mental Health Policy in the United States*. Westport, Conn.: Greenwood

Rochefort, D. A. 1988. Policymaking cycles in mental health: Critical examination of a conceptual model. *J. Health Polit. Policy Law* 13:129–52

Rochefort, D. A. 1987. The political context of mental health care. See Mechanic 1987, pp. 93–105

Rochefort, D. A. 1984. Origins of the 'Third Psychiatric Revolution': The Community Mental Health Centers Act of 1963. *J. Health Polit. Policy Law* 9:1–30

Rossi, P., Wright, J. D. 1987. The determinants of homelessness. *Health Affairs* 6:19–32

Rossi, P. H., Wright, J. D., Fisher, G. A., Willis, G. 1987. The urban homeless: Estimating composition and size. *Science* 235:1336–41

Rothman, D. J. 1980. *Conscience and Convenience: The Asylum and Its Alternatives in Progressive America*. Boston: Little, Brown

Scheerenberger, R. C. 1983. *A History of Mental Retardation*. Baltimore: Brookes

Schlesinger, M. 1986. On the limits of expanding health care reform: chronic care in prepaid settings. *Milbank Mem. Fund Q.* 64:189–215

Schwartz, S., Goldfinger, S. 1981. The new chronic patient: clinical characteristics of an emerging subgroup. *Hosp. Comm. Psychiatry* 32:470–74

Schwarz, J. E. 1988. *America's Hidden Success*. New York: W. W. Norton, Rev. ed.

Scull, A. 1984. *Decarceration: Community Treatment and the Deviant—A Radical View*. New Brunswick, NJ: Rutgers Univ. Press. 2nd ed.

Segal, S. P., Kotler, P. 1989. Community residential care. See Rochefort 1989, pp. 237–65

Sheets, J., Prevost, J., Reihmank, J. 1982. Young adult chronic patients: Three hypothesized subgroups. *Hosp. Comm. Psychiatry* 33:197–202

Spitz, B. 1987. A national survey of medicaid case-management programs. *Health Affairs* 6:61–70

Stein, L., Diamond, R. J. 1985. A program for difficult-to-treat patients. See Stein & Test 1985, pp. 29–39

Stein L., Test, M. A., eds. 1985. *The Training in Community Living Model: A Decade of Experience*. San Francisco: Jossey-Bass

Sykes, G. M. 1978. *Criminology*. New York: Harcourt Brace Jovanovich

Taube, C. A. 1978. State trends in resident patients—state and county mental hospital inpatient services 1967–1973. *Mental Health Statistical Note No. 113*. Rockville, Md: NIMH

Thompson, J. W., Bass, R. D., Witkin, M. J. 1982. Fifty years of psychiatric services: 1940–1990. *Hosp. Comm. Psychiatry* 33: 711–17

Torrey, E. F. 1988. *Nowhere to Go: The Tragic Odyssey of the Homeless Mentally Ill*. New York: Harper & Row

Tyor, P. L., Bell, L. V. 1984. *Caring for the Retarded in America: A History*. Westport, Conn: Greenwood

US Bureau of the Census. 1975. *Historical Statistics of the United States, Colonial Times to 1970, Bicentennial Edition, Part 2*. Washington, DC: GPO

US Bureau of the Census. 1987. *Statistical Abstract of the United States: 1988*. Washington, DC: GPO 108th ed.

US Dept. of Housing and Urban Development (HUD). 1984. *A Report to the Secretary on the Homeless and Emergency Shelters*. Washington, DC: Office of Policy Dev. Res.

US General Accounting Office. 1985. *Homelessness: A Complex Problem and the Federal Response*. Washington, DC: GAO

Wells, K. B., Manning, W. G. Jr., Benjamin, B. 1986. Use of outpatient mental health service in HMO and fee-for-service plans: Results from a randomized controlled trial. *Health Serv. Res.* 21:453–74

Williams, W. 1980. *The Implementation Perspective*. Berkeley: Univ. Calif. Press

Wing, J. K., Brown, G. W. 1970. *Institutionalism and Schizophrenia: A Comparative Study of Three Mental Hospitals, 1960–1968*. Cambridge: Cambridge Univ. Press

Witkin, M. J., Atay, J. E., Fell, A. S., Manderscheid, R. W. 1987. Specialty mental health system characteristics. In *Mental Health, United States, 1987*, ed. R. W. Manderscheid, S. A. Barrett. NIMH 14–58. Washington, DC: GPO

Wyatt, R., J., DeRenzo, E. G. 1986. Scienceless to homeless. *Science* 234:1309

Annu. Rev. Sociol. 1990. 16:329–51

EPISTEMOLOGY AND SOCIOHISTORICAL INQUIRY

John R. Hall

Department of Sociology, University of California-Davis, Davis, California 95616

KEY WORDS: espistemology, positivism, structuralism, hermeneutics, postmodernism

Abstract

In sociohistorical inquiry, no epistemology prevails as a widely accepted account of knowledge. Positivism yet retains its defenders. As alternatives, both structuralist and hermeneutic challenges to science are undermined as foundations of knowledge by their own accounts, yielding the postmodern loss of certitude. Conventionalism, rationalism, and realism have been proposed as "local epistemologies" under the new conditions, and on a broader level, pragmatic and transcendental theories of communication substitute for epistemology classically conceived. As yet, these contending developments do not resolve the crisis of sociohistorical knowledge.

INTRODUCTION

Whether or not there exists a platform from which to begin: That is the question that prefigures any effort to write about epistemology—the problem of knowledge and its basis. If there is no such platform, then I must begin without one, either building one without resort to presuppositions, or claiming that such an activity is unnecessary or impossible. On the other hand, it has not yet been disproved that such a platform exists (or might be established), and if I could begin in a way that led me to such a platform, that platform might inform us of the basis upon which I had begun, and whether that beginning depended on the platform itself.

Historians and sociologists face broadly shared epistemological problems,

329

0360-0572/90/0815-0329$02.00

here designated as those of sociohistorical inquiry. Mostly we leave to philosophers the problem of accounting how we do what we do. Nevertheless, we orient our efforts on the basis of assumptions about the valid practices of creating knowledge and assessing its truth. Not that the assumptions are universally shared: To the contrary, the hallmark of present-day social inquiry is the absence of wide agreement about its philosophical grounding. But the various philosophical positions do not simply align with particular methodologies or substantive theories of society. There are those who try to ground Marxism in assumptions of historicism that undermine any claims of generalizability, while others seek to establish a theoretical Marxism. As an epistemological presupposition, methodological individualism may undergird both a theory of rational actors and antitheoretical historicism. Thus, the present controversy over epistemology cannot be reduced to a conflict of theories or methods; at the least it bears discussion in terms that do not derive from any effort to establish a basis for a particular theoretical approach. However, given the extensive discourses relevant to social inquiry, a thorough review is out of the question; all I attempt here is a broad-gauged survey that arbitrarily uses certain work to mark the general terrain of debate.

The classic problems of epistemology have attracted the efforts of giants on whose shoulders we stand (or fall). Recently, however, rapid unfoldings in philosophy are matched by other arguments formulated within previously disconnected realms. Literary theory, psychology, the sociologies of knowledge and of science, anthropology, feminist theory, deconstruction, hermeneutics, language analysis—this is but a surface list of the approaches that now gain currency in the consideration of problems that once were effectively contained within debates about the empirical world, logic, concept formation, correspondence theories, and a philosophy of cognition. Epistemology of the social sciences is no longer a field in any narrow sense of the term. Better to say that the field has been replaced by "social epistemology" (Fuller 1988). Those who would confront epistemological problems these days must be willing to entertain discourse from any quarter. Whether or not social inquiry will ever be consolidated under some comprehensive warrant—logical or social—remains to be seen. Perhaps a broader syntax simply will establish the differential locations of diverse knowledge forms. But meanwhile, the problem of epistemology implodes: no single logic, no experience, no cognition offers a point of departure from the epistemological circle. I have no basis on which to present this discourse, yet I do so anyway. It is fashionable in some quarters to leave the matter at that, hanging. But let us push on: You are reading some words and can read more, and you may make some sense (or nonsense) out of them, no matter what your presuppositions. The wonder of discourse is that it may engage more than one reader, even those who do not share its outlook. Perhaps there can be knowledge without knowledge of how knowledge is. But that is a question for epistemology, and not for this survey of epistemological discourses.

Matters would be clearer if we knew whether there was a social world to be known (and what it was like), independently of knowing how to know about it. If we knew that world to have some coherence of objects, events, and processes in its actuality, that is, independently of our knowledge about it, we would at least know whether our task was to gain valid knowledge about what exists, or to gain knowledge that, even if it did not explain reality, nevertheless might serve some purpose—pragmatic, critical, revolutionary—or other. Issues of epistemology thus become bound up with issues of ontology in a way that ties a Gordian knot. We seem blocked from comprehending the nature of the social world (if it has any coherent nature) unless we have an epistemological path, yet an epistemological path may depend upon an ontology of both the knower and that to be known. Of course the distinction between epistemology and ontology may be meaningful only in the absence of a solution, but until the Gordian knot is cut, the distinction attests to the complexity of the problem. Indeed, it is emblematic of a series of logical conundrums that mark the abyss of epistemology.

To my knowledge, no one has cut the knot, but there has been no lack of recent efforts. By now the old faiths of positivism and empiricism are widely discredited. The problem facing the defenders of science has been one of offering a new account of its basis, one that takes into consideration the critiques. If, on the other hand, objective knowledge is regarded as an impossibility, an array of alternative projects would establish the epistemological basis of relativity as the condition of knowledge, without lapsing into solipsism, subjectivism, or nihilism. Yet even relativity has been relativized; that is, in postmodern veins of thought, any theory of relative knowledge still amounts to a claim to found knowledge, define it, and authorize certain approaches to attaining it. Perhaps the postmodern thrust can be described most generically as the project of unfounding general knowledge—scientific or other. What, then, remains? Nothing, and yet everything. No form of discourse is established; yet shorn of privileging claims, a series of proposals have been set forth to offer, as it were, the foundations of foundationlessness, for example, in research programs, in realism, in pragmatism, and in critical theory. Surveying this complex array of discourses clarifies the (difficult) circumstances under which students of sociohistorical inquiry now carry on.

POSITIVE SCIENCE AND ITS DISCONTENTS

The outlook for positivism no longer is positive. By the 1960s it was increasingly difficult to find a philosopher who would take on the designation of positivist or defend a positivist position (Adorno et al 1976). For most, the "dispute" today no longer is about positivism; it is about "postpositivism" (Alexander 1982). Indeed, continued discussion of positivism might be taken as the beating of a dead Trojan horse if it weren't that positivism persists as a popular worldview among practitioners of science (Miller 1987). Moreover, positivism remains important to the extent that attacks on it have defined the parameters of current debate (Halfpenny 1982).

It may be, as Halfpenny suggests, that many sociologists share emancipatory and critical values which arguably lie at the Comtean core of positivism as a philosophy of knowledge. But as Halfpenny details, the uses of knowledge became subordinated to the basis of knowledge in the incarnations of positivism since Comte, especially J. S. Mill's inductive approach, the logical positivism of the Vienna circle and Carl Hempel, logical empiricism, and the falsificationist strategy championed by Karl Popper. These approaches (and the sociohistorical methods based upon them) all seek to establish science as a form of true knowledge subject to validation, that depends neither on metaphysical, ontological, or other unfounded assumptions, nor on mere opinion of investigators. Such efforts to establish an objective basis of empirical knowledge have been beset by a multitude of problems (Suppe 1977, Halfpenny 1982). Purely in the realm of logic, positivists themselves have identified a labyrinth of dead ends, such as the intractable problem of establishing a "law," the issue of how to distinguish a causal relation from a merely accidental or spurious correlation, or how to distinguish the hypothesis being tested from untested assumptions. The problems are magnified when a statistical or probabilistic approach is substituted for a deterministic one. Especially telling, in the end, is the difficulty in differentiating science from pseudoscience (Wallis 1985).

Tilting toward the empirical and away from the logical facet of positivism creates new problems as it solves others. The question arises of how the world is known, and the answer depends on a theory of sense data that raises problems of fallible subjective observation and judgment—particularly acute for social research (Shweder 1980, Phillips 1973, Faust 1984). The pursuit of empirical observation also raises the difficult problem of whether there can be a shared and theory-neutral observation language. The possibility of establishing such a language is challenged in the first instance by the "later" Wittgenstein's account of language emphasizing the absence of meaning independent of usage in context (Wittgenstein 1968). It is further thrown into doubt by Richard Rorty's (1979) exploration of the idea of correspondence, which would require a context-free language of scientific terms (if one could be established) that could "mirror" reality.

Quite apart from the problems of cognition and language internal to logical positivism, there is the classic *Methodenstreit*—the debate about natural vs social inquiry, and a set of contextual problems: arguments about the ideology, history, and sociology of science. Whether the enterprise of studying science itself has any epistemological basis is at best a moot point that does not easily offer an edge to anyone interested in defending science. Thomas Kuhn (1962) may not initially have been particularly interested in challenging the epistemic foundations of science, but neither did his account—showing normal science ignoring disconfirming evidence that awaited revolutionary paradigm shifts—accord with the positivist idea that science could claim an integrity of logic, procedure, and evidence. Kuhn's basic argument has been elaborated and extended by historical and sociological studies that counter Robert Merton's normative view by showing how broad historical forces as well as everyday activity, organization, socialization, funding, competition, communication, and other extrinsic factors derail the actual practice of science from any neat and tidy epistemological formula (Bourdieu 1975, Brannigan 1981, Barnes & Edge 1982, Collins 1983, Barnes 1985, Latour & Woolgar 1986, Latour 1987, Wuthnow 1989, Clark & Gerson 1990). A parallel set of charges focuses on value orientations. Especially in sociohistorical inquiry, science in the technical sense is a commitment that arguably serves some interests, not others—a point made most strongly by critical theorists and feminists (Habermas 1973: 263–64, Bleier 1986, Smith 1987, Agger 1989). On their debunking of science as ideology, together with research on the social practice of science, whatever foundation positivism might claim in theory, it lacks in practice; what counts as scientific knowledge depends partly on factors extrinsic to the assessment of ideas and their validity.

These problems hardly distinguish sociohistorical inquiry from the natural sciences, where the philosophical crisis of knowledge is equally acute. However, a further difficulty specific to sociohistorical analysis turns on the relation of would-be scientists to the objects of their inquiry—societies of knowing and acting subjects. To reckon the basic faultline of epistemology, we cannot and need not consider the manifold specific controversies: for example, the issue of the historicity and secular development of social phenomena and in turn, the reflexivity of social knowledge; behavioral vs *verstehende* knowledge; the question of methodological individualism vs holism or organicism; the status of social rules or norms as explanations. What if the general claims about cultural historicity are true? Positivism thereby fails, first, on the ontological grounds that the social world lacks the patterned coherence of the natural world, and second, because an essential premise—the unity of scientific method—is difficult to sustain if idiosyncratic meaning is taken as an explanation of action.

Whatever detractors may conclude about the logical and ontological difficulties of positivistic social science, it retains adherents. Gellner (1985) offers an impassioned defense of positivism as a special realm of discourse where no assertion can be privileged, set against the Hegelianist alternative in which privileged discourses of holism and realism establish a realm ruled by dogma that cannot be subjected to disproof. Bryant (1985: 181–82) chides critics of positivism for defining it so narrowly as to ignore the positivist origins of contemporary realist epistemologies (discussed below) and to miss the fundamental importance of "reason and observation" as the basis for sociological knowledge. But despite the rhetorical defense of positivism, there are few direct responses to the critiques. Instead, even those who would seek a foundation for scientific knowledge look elsewhere, while other voices decry the possibility altogether and seek alternative ways of accounting for sociohistorical knowledge. The postpositivist alternatives can only be considered in light of the postmodern condition that emerges from acceptance of the relativity of knowledge.

EPISTEMOLOGICAL PROJECTS OF RELATIONAL KNOWLEDGE

Even if sociologists and historians of science have argued its social relativity, acceptance of relativity does not signal the end of epistemology. Instead, it has fostered points of departure that do not depend on a foundation in analytic philosophy. In the absence of a foundation, various arguments are made against epistemology (or more narrowly, "method") in any privileging form (e.g. Gadamer 1975, Feyerabend 1978). But even these arguments, and especially the variety of studies that locate knowledge as a social and linguistic accomplishment, in turn elevate sociological theories about knowledge to the status of ontologically grounded social epistemologies. Such theories have tended toward one of two points of departure: the knowing subject or the structures of symbols by which things are known. What remains as a question of debate is what basis either relativistic epistemology could offer for obtaining knowledge about the social world. It is this question that frames the postmodern turn.

Structuralist Epistemologies

If scientific knowledge were to take a positivist form, its concepts and language-use rules would transcend any cultural matrix of meaning. Put differently, scientific knowledge could not be predicated upon ways of knowing that take their form independently of science as an activity. Thus, the centrality of language and logic in the classical attempts to found science. With the structuralist turn, scientific discourse itself is viewed as an institutionalized pattern. Suggestions that science is ordered by more fundamental cultural, cognitive, or social patterns—extrinsic to science—tend to undermine its special claims of knowledge: Science becomes one among many symbol structures, universes of discourse, or language games. The rationalist solution to this problem amounts to an idealism that eschews any empirical investigation so as to establish a theoretical discourse uncontaminated by the naively observed world. In Marxist thought, Althusser & Balibar (1970) offered the most thorough-going structuralist attempt at rationalism (mercilessly satirized from a Marxist historiographic viewpoint by E. P. Thompson 1978). The effort by Hindess & Hirst (1975) to translate Althusser's approach into an empiricist-free sociological theory, by the authors' own admission (Hindess & Hirst 1977), foundered on the historicity of the referents of Marxist theory, specifically, the confounding of "mode of production" by actual social formations.

The alternative to an idealist structuralism is an empirical and historicized one. Lévi-Strauss (1966) offers one basis for this solution by exploring the ways in which classification systems operate. The "savage mind" is no less complex than the scientific one; instead, each operates according to an underlying logic of classification that gives rise to particular forms of knowledge, and not others. A parallel structuralist problematic is established in linguistics—by the semiotic theory originating with Saussure (reviewed by Eagleton 1983: ch. 3), which suggests that signs take on their significance systemically, in ways that have structural patterns independent of the things to be signified or the individuals using the signs. Clearly, however, the most influential approach—seminal for diverse contemporary thinkers—has been Wittgenstein's quasistructuralist theory of group communication. In Wittgenstein's "language games," meaning is established not by its relation to other signs, as in semiotics, but contextually, within particular social groups and their usages. It may well be, with Bloor (1983), that Wittgenstein's vision of language requires the subvention of sociology to study the structural properties of the language games. Hazelrigg (1989a:241) argues that Wittgenstein's approach cannot offer an account of language outside of itself. Nor is there any ready standard for evaluating conflicting claims that each "make sense" on the level of ordinary language and rhetoric. The approach thus lacks (and indeed does not assert) any special foundation for its claims, and it can offer little solace to those who seek firm knowledge.

Essentially the same problem haunts the epistemological solutions of Lévi-Strauss, semioticians, and other structuralists: It is revealing to confront the structure of scientific knowledge independently of the knower, yet this view cannot be taken itself as other than mythological; it offers no escape from its own account, in which all accounts seem culturally tinged. Structuralist approaches thus can render no basis for validation of the general claim of relativism or specific structuralist findings. Yet even if this "poststructuralist" criticism is taken, a profound hyperrelativism substitutes for scientific knowledge. The self-subsuming character of structural approaches notwithstanding, unless a way of knowing can be established that escapes their frame, the language of science is not simply a description language, it is the product of cultural, cognitive and social structures of discourse extrinsic to the logic of scientific inquiry.

Knowledge and the Knowing Subject

The alternative is to begin with the relativity of the subject who would know. Here, entirely different problems surface. In the late nineteenth century, it was the neo-Kantian question of how values shape inquiry that initiated the German *Methodenstreit,* or conflict over methods. The solution of Max Weber demanded both causal and meaningful adequacy of explanations, and it distinguished sociohistorical inquiry from the physical sciences on the basis of an interpretive interest in phenomena of cultural significance. Cultural significance is, of course, a matter of valuation, and Weber resisted the idea that values could be justified scientifically. Yet what if, as Heinrich Rickert tried to assert, certain values could be identified as universal, such that individuals would not differ in estimations of their cultural significance? Guy Oakes (1988) argues that this would be the only basis for an objective social science. But Rickert's theory of values fails, Oakes contends, and Weber is unable to solve the problem of scientific objectivity. Weber sought to maintain a delicate balance, recognizing the distinctive nature of social inquiry, yet salvaging arguably scientific approaches to concept formation, interpretation, and explanation. Given this commitment on Weber's part, the directions of neo-Weberian sociology will hinge on careful assessment of Oakes' argument. Here, it will be important to consider Guenther Roth's (1976; Roth & Schluchter 1979) explication of Weber's analytic strategy and Bryan Green's (1988) depiction of Weber's argumentation as casuistic, for these discussions suggest that Weber tackled the problem of values at another level as well as the foundational one, i. e. in discourse. Whatever the resolution of the value controversy, Weber's epistemology stands at the Archimedean point of sociological concept formation. Rejecting the natural-science correspondence approach to sociological concepts, Weber instead promoted the use of ideal-type constructs as a basis of rigorous sociological analysis (Burger 1976), an approach that holds promise today for a postpositivist synthesis (Hekman 1983b).

Weber's specific solution also raises a more general problem: the common referents of a sociological concept (e.g. class, revolution, action) may have a different analogical relation to each other and to the concept than is the case in the natural sciences (Stinchcombe 1978). Possibly, the project of social scientific concept formation depends on embracing a theory of metaphor and perspectivity (Ricoeur 1977, Brown 1977, Rothbart 1984). In a somewhat different vein traced through Winch (1958) back to Wittgenstein, for Turner

(1980), sociological explanation is a comparative exercise in exploring translations between assertions about social rules and practices in diverse settings. Translation, in turn, becomes a key element in Paul Roth's (1987) argument for methodological pluralism in the social sciences. Yet Levine (1985; cf Fuller 1988: ch. 6) has suggested that conceptual and explanatory ambiguities are grounded in the ambiguities of social life and its normative practices. Clear conceptualization thus paradoxically depends upon the capacity to encompass ambiguity.

The more radical subjectivist turn is to reject the scientific project of causal explanation and accept the relativity of meaning, yet establish relativism as the basis of a different epistemological project than that of science. The major channels of thought have developed through hermeneutics and phenomenology, often tied to the problems of historiography. Contemporary hermeneuticists, after Gadamer (1975), trace back through Heidegger to Wilhelm Dilthey (1976), who attempted a history founded in subjective temporality and biography. Dilthey thus offers a counterpoint to Althusser's structuralist antihistory (Hall 1980). His complex approach was historicist in its avoidance of explanation by reference to general laws, yet, like Ranke, Dilthey held out the hope of identifying the objective spirit of history (Makkreel 1975). Mostly, historical sociology today has abandoned the hermeneutic program, seeking instead to clarify the logical and ontological bases for historical inquiry in ways that parallel wider epistemological debates (Martin 1977, Atkinson 1978, Skocpol & Somers 1980, Skocpol 1984, Tilly 1981, 1984, Ragan & Zaret 1983, Hall 1988). But there is a countercurrent: Interpretive historians develop a theory of action and meaning that explores explanatory plots through narrative and cultural history (Hall 1990). For this approach, it becomes important to ask both about historical time and the difference between historical narrative and fiction, and about the status of historical narratives that conflict with one another (Burke 1984, 1969, Stone 1979, Hall 1980, Veyne 1984, Carr 1985, Danto 1985, Mink 1987, Ricoeur 1984, 1985, 1988, Alker 1987).

In a way different from the new narrative program in historiography, hermeneutics offers counterpoint to science by positing the realm of meaning as irreducible to causal explanation. Interpretation attends instead to "local knowledge" (Geertz 1973). Yet the same issues that obtain for scientific knowledge—of truth and objectivity—confront hermeneutics. Emilio Betti (1984; cf Bleicher 1982) would search for objectivity in interpretation, on the basis of methodological principles. This project, it would seem, moves him back toward Weber's problem of values considered by Oakes: even if an objective methodology could be established in the absence of universal values, estimations of cultural significance, and thereby interpretations, would differ in ways that could not be resolved by resort to rules of knowledge production and validation. By contrast, for Gadamer, honestly confronting the conditions of interpretation in social life cannot support any privileging of interpretive claims: Dilthey's hope of an objective history must be wrong, for truth is relational, and the project of reconstructing history thus impossible. More generally, given the occasioned and episodic pursuit of understanding, there is neither reason nor basis to formalize hermeneutic method, and no basis of definitive interpretation. Whatever the capacities of science to control natural phenomena, in the social realm, both science as activity and the rest of life are conditioned by efforts at mutualities of understanding that shift in the currents of biography and history and values, such that, however precious, truth can be no more than relative (Gadamer 1975; Bleicher 1982: ch. 4: Weinsheimer 1985: 134, 137, 164; Rodi 1985).

The phenomenological development paralleling hermeneutics moved from Edmund Husserl's attempt to resolve the crisis of science through a transcendental phenomenology. By now it is widely agreed that Husserl's work, while fertile and provocative, has not served as the foundation that he sought to establish. Yet Alfred Schutz took Husserl as a point of departure for challenging Weber's use of ideal types, on the basis that such types objectify actors' intentions in a way that eclipses their salience as a basis of sociological explanation (Hall 1981). Despite vigorous critiques of both Husserl and Schutz (Adorno 1983, Hindess 1977, Hazelrigg 1989a), from this lifeworld phenomenology emerged both a quasihermeneutic approach to fieldwork (Wolff 1976; Hall 1977) and an ethnomethodological discussion of scientific versus "mundane" epistemology (Pollner 1987). The phenomenological and ethnomethodological moves claim an epistemology of the subject whereby knowledge—scientific or otherwise—becomes a social accomplishment (Douglas 1970). The turn to the knowing subject also spawns efforts to disestablish the social analyst's voice in favor of a life-history approach (McCall & Wittner 1990), and it has triggered important points of debate for feminist sociologists (Collins 1986, Grant 1987, Haraway 1988). Anthropologists similarly seek to contend with the asymmetric assumptions that yield unreflexive accounts of "other" social actors (Sahlins 1985, Clifford 1988).

In these approaches, the task of knowledge amounts to understanding the ways in which actors—sociologists or others—make the world meaningful in their own terms, prior to others' categorization of their lifeworlds. Thoroughgoing subjectivism thus pushes past the cultural science of Weber and the idiographic historicism of Dilthey to a terrain peopled with knowing and understanding subjects, where truth is relative and the conflict of intepretations prevails. In this realm, not only the utterances and interactions of individuals, but the cultural products of social action—from normative catalogues to cityscapes—become texts, such that the reading of a text is not only a first-order social activity, but also a second-order sociological activity (Brown 1987). The task of reading texts turns on either a structuralist and semiotic epistemology or subjectivist hermeneutics. Yet either approach affirms an optimistic relativity: Even if science does not equal truth, and truth does not exhaust significant understanding, a cardinal point of faith holds that the account of relativity itself offers a possibility for proceeding with the project of relative knowledge. Hermeneutics and semiotics each would offer a foundation for relativism, whereby, at the least, myth or plot could be placed within intelligible structures and movements of meaning. Put differently, even if the quest for scientific knowledge seemed doomed, it still might be possible to make sense of things.

The Postmodern Turn

Relativism seems forever to ravage itself, in the end rendering its own knowledge and understandings problematic. Such is the postmodern turn. Even so, at least one observer, Jean-François Lyotard, argues that the supposed postmodern crisis of science represents more a phase of the modernist assault on knowledge, rather than any fundamental break. It seems that modernism has its triumphant scientific mode and its questioning, interpretive, humanistic mode; in some sense, postmodernism is marked by the collapse of the distinction between scientific and humanistic thought. Thus, Lyotard will differentiate the modern use of "metadiscourse" to legitimate science versus a postmodern "incredulity toward metanarratives" (1984: xxiii–iv, 79). Whence the incredulity? If postmodern thought often is described as "post-structuralist" (Eagleton 1983: ch. 4), it is (*a*) because it originates in part in critiques of the abstracted, ahistorical character of structuralist thought, which fails to address the problem of situated meaning and action (Bourdieu 1977), and (*b*) because it continues the investigation of the text as a problematic. Yet the postmodern target is not only structuralism, but the subjective relativism of philosophical hermeneutics as well. Incredulity turns upon the fabrication of the textual world. In the postmodern terrain, critical analysis is turned from the texts of fiction to the texts of knowledge: indeed, whether the texts are "fictions" or "knowledge" is a distinction of convention accomplished in the texts themselves.

Certain important points can be sighted in the panorama of postmodern texts. First, even if Foucault sometimes depended on modernist (structuralist, totalizing) categories of analysis, he (1970, 1972) originally envisioned a method that could not yet be fully described, perhaps should not be codified. This very pastiche lends to his analysis a postmodern flavor (cf Poster 1987, Hoy 1988, D'Amico 1989). For Foucault, genealogy reveals "an historical ontology of ourselves in relation to truth through which we constitute ourselves as subjects of knowledge" (Foucault, in Dreyfus & Rabinow 1983:

237). The "archeology of knowledge" may not establish a science that transcends this constituting phenomenon, but it unmasks the way the social world obtains its coherence through the power of disciplines, scientific or otherwise. Whether Foucault is substantively correct in this or that example may be controversial, but for Foucault the controversy can be taken as demonstration of the world that he describes, where the gaze of discipline and the "technologies of the self" guard the boundaries of civilization from the abyss of the uncategorized world (Foucault 1988). Epistemology is unmasked as a moment of power, Western science as a cultural practice of discipline.

Second, the content of knowledge no longer can be said to stand independently of its communication. Instead, the epistemological concerns with legitimating knowledge become blurred with issues of rhetoric and poetics. Foundational to these decenterings of the scientific text is Austin's (1975) speech-act theory: words do not just reflect or describe the world; they also perform. Narrative no longer can be seen simply as a (good or bad) methodological tool of humanistic historians like Paul Veyne. Instead, literary theories of narrator, story, performance, and audience (Maclean 1988) shift the problem of narrative from one of reflecting "what really happened," to demonstrating how narrative sustains a textual world. In history (Cohen 1986; cf White 1978, 1987), writing is said to sustain a sense of "aboutness" that transcends the events about which narratives are written. Economists are less disposed to trouble themselves over critics of a discipline that is much narrower than its potential subject matter, and even if this hubris seems patently self-serving, McCloskey's (1985) excavation of the rhetoric which advances economics as science likely falls on deaf ears. But elsewhere, social scientists (Nelson et al 1987) are taking seriously the principle that ideas and findings do not issue forth independently of distinctive forms of argumentation; the style of persuasion embodies theoretical position (Green 1988). In anthropology, under the collapse of the distinction between native and anthropological storytellers, "the very right to write—to write ethnography—seems at risk" (Geertz 1988: 133).

Third, with Derrida (1978), any effort to systematically describe the ideas of Foucault, deconstruction, rhetoric, relativism, the general problem of epistemology, or the social world and its processes (etc) would itself be an act of violence. Indeed, structure and coherence in texts and in analysis of them can only be achieved on the basis of linguistic feats that mask the contradictions and ellipses of text and world. As Margolis has put it, "Deconstruction demonstrates that, in any [our own] historical setting, it is always possible to construe any established schemata for analyzing and interpreting familiar phenomena as more restrictive, more distorting, more inadequate than another that can be generated, now, by submitting the one or ones in question to the process of supplementation" (1985: 105, brackets in original).

In this restless and relentless text turning from text, we reach "the end of philosophy," a prospect from which epistemology can escape no more than other texts. A new task seems to replace it: creating vision by destroying knowledge.

In the postmodern turn, then, the clear lenses through which to explain or simply interpret the world become irretrievably clouded; then, shattered into myriad crystals, they remain available for us to pick up, polish and peer through, telling others what we see through the lens that fixes our gaze. Is this supposedly postmodern condition anything new? There is good reason to doubt whether we really have moved past modernist skepticism in our predicament, even if the embrace of the predicament creates an acceptance of pastiche and collage that creates new kinds of discourse. Defenders of epistemology might argue that nothing really has changed, yet in epistemology, the saying of the postmodern performs its tasks, leaving it to others to found knowledge or forget it. What of the logical retort—that the critiques themselves must claim truth, in order that their accounts of the morass be sustained? Even this classic conundrum seems to lose its force when contradiction itself no longer can be devalued.

UP FROM POSTMODERNISM?

We are left as actors making meaning by use of structured symbols in communication with others in an institutionalized world. Indeed, this position informed certain philosophies of science even before the collapse of the positivist consensus, and broadly speaking, it represents the assumption of all discourse of knowledge since the publication of Kuhn's *The Structure of Scientific Revolutions*. Yet once the social condition of knowledge is acknowledged, what account can be offered of science and of sociohistorical inquiry? In the wake of deconstruction, rhetoric, poetics, and Foucault's archeology and genealogy, those who write about the problem at all will know that their own texts only with difficulty escape treatment solely as texts, rather than for what they say. As Geertz (1988: 138) remarks, ". . . the burden of authorship seems suddenly heavier." But the clamor of texts, I suspect, has only begun. Basically, two broad lines of discourse are developing. First, with Rorty (1979: 361, 321), if the collapse of the effort to "mirror" the world by conceptual representation or correspondence amounts to the end of epistemology as a general theory of knowledge, then "objectivity" becomes redefined as involving "conformity to the norms for justification" of knowledge or "agreed-upon practices of inquiry." Under these conditions, epistemology becomes local, specific to the particular issue being investigated (cf Lyotard 1984: 54). Second, there is the broader question of relationships among different epistemologies and alternative kinds of knowledge.

Epistemologies

What, then, of local epistemologies? The central problem concerns reconciling objectivism and relativism (Bernstein 1983), science and relativism (Alexander 1990), or objectivism and subjectivism (Collins 1989), yet a myriad of alternatives present themselves. It seems, as Halfpenny (1982) asserted, that the ways out of positivism lead in one of two directions—either toward a scientific realism that (for positivists) amounts to a metaphysic about the world, or toward a "conventionalism" that depends on shared assumptions of investigators. In either case, the boundaries of positivism are exceeded by the solution. Rationalism—abandoning the quest for absolute truth in favor of reasonable belief—offers a vehicle in either direction, and it has been the subject of efforts to constitute "internal" normative standards of science directed to truth as a goal (Toulmin 1972, Newton-Smith 1981, Foley 1987) and theories about the significance of discursive rhetoric, argumentation, and persuasion (Willard 1983, Schrag 1986). Whatever the contributions of refurbished rationalism, it seems that realism and conventionalism will continue to be debated on their promise for clarifying sociohistorical inquiry.

Conventionalism holds out the promise of shortcircuiting logical problems altogether, by the fiat of looking to the actual practices of scientists as ongoing exercises in claiming and disclaiming the legitimacy of knowledge and proper procedures for evaluating it. Science becomes something of an intellectual wrestling match. This approach, which emerged even as logical positivism reached its internal crisis, developed further support in the wake of social and historical studies of science. Polanyi (1967), following Nagel, recognized in the 1960s that science could not depend on a philosophical foundation; instead, he argued, it depended upon the "self-coordination" of informed scientists who adjust their research to the results of others, and on "mutual authority" in which scientists "Keep watch over each other." On the claim that scientists don't do what they are supposed to do anyway, constructivists can ask after what they do when they succeed. The sociohistorical critique of logical positivism is thereby turned to the advantage of science, for example, in the work of Lakatos (1971: 99). By backing off from strict "naive" experimental falsification and attending to the ways scientists develop the "hard core" of a pattern of ideas that generates further ideas and subsumes anomalies, Lakatos could advocate a methodology of historical research programs "which can be evaluated in terms of progressive and degenerating problemshifts." This approach gains credence among some sociologists (e.g. Wagner & Berger 1985, 1986; Kiser & Hechter 1988, but cf Turner 1990), for it provides an account of science without making specific assumptions about reality or the methodologies of research, thus salvaging objective knowledge by containing subjectivity within the battles over research agendas. In parallel ways, Bourdieu (1975) asks us to explore the social conditions under which scientists are motivated to search for truth, instead of pursuing other agendas such as prestige: Meja & Stehr (1988) assert that the problem of relativity should be recast by casting the sociology of knowledge in the role of "an interlocutor for epistemological discourse." Conventionalism need not be arbitrary, for the conventions of science can be scrutinized pragmatically in terms of their sources and their consequences.

The alternative, realist, turn away from positivism is marked in the first instance by the emergent position of Karl Popper (1979, 1983), who with other postpositivists, recognizes the theory-ridden nature of observation, yet has sought to posit a "world 3" of objective knowledge in a way that ducks the problems unmasked in the social and historical studies of science. Coupled with a metaphysical "critical" (rather than naive) realist belief in a world that exists independently of our knowledge, Popper posited an "evolutionary epistemology." Others, like Donald Campbell (1988) and David Papineau (1978), try to resolve the special problems of the social sciences within this sort of framework. Campbell would subsume the hermeneutic problem within scientific analysis of interpretive adequacy, while Papineau seeks to move from the level of meaning to that of objective reasons. Such efforts have their sociological roots in the "analytical realism" of Talcott Parsons (1937), and they may face the same issue as does Parsons' approach, namely, whether the realist conceptualization eclipses meaningful action by reducing it to variable characteristics (Hall 1984a,b).

Still within the broad domain of realism, Papineau's attempt to salvage science is countered by the alternative rationalist approach developed, for example, by Bhaskar (1975), Keat & Urry (1982), and Sylvan & Glassner (1985). Although they are concerned with the overall coherence of theory, Sylvan & Glassner nevertheless seek to avoid the idealist and antiempiricist difficulties in the structuralist rationalism of Althusser (discussed above) by proposing alternatives to statistical analysis. Their realism also rejects the purported subjectivism of symbolic interactionism and ethnomethodology, arguing that action occurs within existing frameworks subject to multiple interpretations, and that actors' interpretations do not constitute "in themselves explanations of why those arrangements operate as they do" (1985: 6). Similarly, Robert Wuthnow (1987: 65) distinguishes between the subjective meanings that may be important for understanding social action and the "cultural constructions" on which such meanings are "contingent."

The central problem for a realist epistemology of social inquiry would be to conceptualize what is real in a way that aligns on the one hand with metaphysicalist assumptions of reality, and on the other, with the complexities entailed by social definitions of reality, whether everyday or scientific. This problem seems largely ignored by Miller (1987), despite his interest in encompassing the social sciences within realism. But the attempt at a solution has been sketched in a philosophical vein by Outhwaite (1987), who proposes reconciling realism with the insights of hermeneutics and the emancipatory interest of critical theory. In a more rhetorical way, Christopher Lloyd (1986) argues for the reality of social structures. Both Outhwaite and Lloyd hinge key parts of their arguments for realism on the structuration theory of Anthony Giddens (1984), as a way of overcoming the subject-structure and understanding-explanation disjunctures.

Whatever may be concluded about Giddens' theory as ontology, there is a fundamental problem with much of the discussion about realism: It has an abstract and unreal air about it (cf O'Neill 1986). The work of Michel De Certeau (1984), among others, suggests the ceaseless reformulation of life at the borderlands of the unfolding everyday world, outside the ontology of its description by realists, ungrasped by the ways it can be known at one remove through social science epistemology, methods, and concept formation. Even if realism is granted as a *metaphysical* truth, the practical benefits seem few: Realists disagree with each other about the reality that supposedly is there and knowable. This problem is serious enough in the natural sciences, and it is compounded in sociohistorical inquiry by the symbolic and meaningful aspects of social reality (for a dialectical and materialist approach to the problem, for example, see Sayers 1985). Thus, it would seem that realists still are forced back to conceptualizations of reality in which they must confront anew the neo-Kantian problem of epistemology and the Parsonian problem of the relationship of disciplines (discussed by Outhwaite 1987). Accepting realism metaphysically does not entail recognizing the reality or character thereof described by any particular concept (e.g. "social class," or "status group"); thus, practically speaking, it remains for metaphysical realism to offer the social ontology that it would claim to warrant (cf Spencer 1982, Layder 1985, Feyerabend 1988). Absent such an ontology, realism becomes the conventionalism of likeminded scientists.

Pragmatic and Ideal Theories of Communication

Beyond the "agreed-upon practices of inquiry" that I have called "local epistemologies," there is the larger question about the possibilities of discourse when the kinds of knowledge drawn upon are diverse. Here, the post-Wittgensteinian debate among Gadamer, Habermas and Apel, and Lyotard poses the fundamental puzzle. As I already have indicated, the work of Bourdieu and others suggests the limitations of structuralism without action, as fundamentally ahistorical and unreflexive. If Wittgenstein's theory of language games is taken as a general model of scientific discourse, for

Habermas, the structuralist problem reappears in it—on the level of knowledge—as a problem of incommensurability and relativity. Whatever the validity of knowledge within a particular language game, the problem of translation between self-contained language games eluded Wittgenstein, and in this respect, Habermas regards Gadamer's characterization of "porous" language games as offering a route out of the relativism he finds in Wittgenstein's position (Habermas 1988: 130ff, Hekman 1983a). Yet in turn, Gadamer's relativization of values cannot support the project that Habermas wishes to advance, namely, the establishment of a rational universal structure of discourse that accords a place for, and mediation between, the transcendentally established kinds of "knowledge-constitutive interests" directed to technical control," "mutual understanding," and "emancipation from seemingly 'natural' constraint" (Habermas 1971: 311). It is this project that occasions both Habermas's theory of communicative action based on a social ontology of the modern situation (1984; 1987) and his colleague Karl-Otto Apel's (1984) effort to reformulate the explanation-understanding debate on a "transcendental-pragmatic" basis that contributes to the project of emancipation. For neither Habermas nor Apel is the Enlightenment dead. It continues through the containment of science and technical knowledge within human interests, in the decolonization of the system-subordinated lifeworld.

Here, despite Habermas's denial that he is a foundationalist (1984: xli; 1987: 400), postmodern, postfoundationalist philosophers part company with Habermas and Apel, proclaiming them modernists who maintain the faith of a "metanarrative" (Lyotard 1984). For Rorty (1979: 379ff) the attempt to create a transcendental standpoint is misguided. Gadamer regards the search for absolutes as "totally absurd" (q. in Hekman 1983a: 222). Calvin Schrag (1986: 61, 100) questions whether Habermas's "ideal speech situation" is indeed transcultural, and Schrag seeks an alternative basis for discourse in a reformulation of the explanation-understanding debate and a deconstruction that retrieves "communicative praxis." A reinvigorated pragmatism provides Rochberg-Halton (1986), Margolis (1986), and Antonio (1989) with what they regard as an alternative, nonfoundationalist path to critical discourse. Lyotard (1984: 65, 74) is most emphatic: Habermas rightly seeks to transcend the systems philosophy of Niklas Luhmann, but in the attempt, wishfully seeks a unity of experience that links the realms of knowledge. For Lyotard (1984: 63-64), this "seems neither possible, nor even prudent," and he embraces a more anarchistic pragmatics. For him, modern science is infused with (grand) narrative as a tool of legitimation, even as the cogency of this legitimation erodes from within. In the collapse of the modernist legitimation of knowledge, science is acknowledged as a language game in which rules cannot be the basis for the suppression of ideas, and legitimation does not come through a metanarrative account of it, but piecemeal, in language-game "moves." These are "played in the pragmatics of knowledge" that leaps past what is conventionally settled knowledge to search out "instabilities": "It is producing not the known, but the unknown" (Lyotard 1984: 39–41, 60). Thus, Lyotard seeks to salvage the language-game model from structuralism by a Gadameresque solution, while Habermas links such a solution to a project that may be seen as an attempt to solve Rickert's value quandary (Oakes 1988) with communication as an objective value.

The disagreements notwithstanding, the protagonists share much of an outlook, and their ideas sweep away old issues and generate a new problematic. Whatever the status of Habermas's quest for a new grand narrative of legitimation in communication, like Rorty, Habermas disavows the project of establishing a basis for his knowledge epistemologically: "The theory of communicative action that I have since put forward [i.e., after writing *On the Logic of the Social Sciences*] is not a continuation of methodology by other means" (Habermas 1988: xiv). Both Habermas and Lyotard recognize the established institutional arrangements of technical knowledge production as power-based impediments to the production of nonconforming ideas and ideas which take other forms than science, institutionally defined. Yet Habermas's theory of communicative action posits a utopian speech situation in a way that ironically offers little counsel to the inhabitants of bureaucratically institutionalized spheres of life today, including those where the production of scientific knowledge transpires on a large scale. Lyotard, too, is in his own way utopian: strong on showing the "terror" of modernist science, he can only posit the asystemicity of normatively liberated scientists and an information-accessing public as the basis of "a politics that would respect both the desire for justice and the desire for the unknown" (1984: 67). Even if Lyotard does not project a value-consensus, still, he advocates an ideal—of non-authoritarian communication.

Yet communication as a value offers insufficient grounds for anchoring sociohistorical inquiry. The world is too much upon us to think that we can afford the luxury of knowledge for its own sake (Hazelrigg 1989a,b). The old master legitimations of inquiry are gone. Nor can practicing sociologists easily alter the institutional matrix in which inquiry is conducted: Whatever the vision of inquiry and communication, confronting the legitimations of institutionalized knowledge will be a matter of ongoing praxis, not of tidy intellectual solution. Nor will those struggles, even in the degree to which they succeed, resolve the questions of what is to be studied, and why. Thus, we are forced back to the realm of values, to the selection of projects of inquiry that bear cultural significance. Yet no calculus seems capable of rescuing inquiry from the multiplicity of values that animate it. Even if, in the end, we assume emergent "local epistemologies" based either on research programs or realist ontology as language games that orient inquiry for clusters of practicing researchers, the de facto absence of a world calculus of cultural significance assures that social inquiry will be manifold in its forms of discourse for the foreseeable future. Must we then succumb to incommensurate language games that crosscheck the possibility of communication, say, between a hermeneuticist and a functionalist and a positivist? Or can a new form of discourse be established where scientific communication proceeds admidst the diversity of values, ideologies, and language games of knowledge? Karl-Otto Apel (1984) has worked hard to resolve the explanation-*Verstehende* problem, yet his solution seems more ontological than epistemological. That is, he tries to assert the cogency of each kind of inquiry, not the working relations between them. That latter task, for Schrag (1986), involves rhetoric and persuasion. Richard Rorty (1979: 317) has suggested that it is a hermeneutic task, ". . . of the informed dilettante, the polypragmatic, Socratic intermediary between various discourses. In his [*sic*] salon, so to speak, hermetic thinkers are charmed out of their self-enclosed practices. Disagreements between disciplines and discourses are compromised or transcended in the course of the conversation." Such a conversation offers at least the hope of communication. But it cannot proceed unselfcritically; instead, the hermeneutics of conversation must itself be the object of reflexive deconstruction and clarification. Nor can these activities be regarded as philosophical problems, in the traditional sense. Instead, they require further inquiry into the practicing conducts of local epistemologies and their points of value contact and logical convergence/divergence. As James Rule (1988) well demonstrates, by closely considering a wide range of theories concerning civil violence, the positivist assessment of falsifiable theories may inform such an inquiry, with or without foundations. Rule's study in social theory may not salvage positivism foundationally, but it underscores the fact that sociohistorical knowledge will continue to be produced by a variety of means which neither deny nor capitulate to the crisis of knowledge. Even if epistemology as metanarrative is dead, and whether through a persisting positivist agenda or other critical approaches, we can still hope to clarify the shared or incommensurate ontological assumptions, the forms of discourse, concepts, and theories by which we carry on a collective conversation about the social world.

ACKNOWLEDGMENTS

I wish to thank Charles Tilly and Kai Erikson for their encouragement and suggestions. I have benefitted, in the composition of this essay, from an ongoing conversation with Michele Lipner and Jim Scott, and from the comments of J. Kenneth Benson.

Literature Cited

Adorno, T. 1983 [1956]. *Against Epistemology*. Cambridge: MIT Press

Adorno, T. W., Albert, H., Dahrendorf, R., Habermas, J., Pilot, H., Popper, K. R. 1976 [1969]. *The Positivist Dispute in German Sociology*. New York: Harper & Row

Agger, B. 1989. *Socio(onto)logy: A Disciplinary Reading*. Urbana: Univ. Ill. Press

Alexander, J. C. 1982. *Theoretical Logic in Sociology*, Vol. I. *Positivism, Presuppositions, and Current Controversies*. Berkeley: Univ. Calif. Press

Alexander, J. C. 1990. General theory in the postpositivism mode: the "epistemological dilemma" and the search for present reason. See Seidman & Wagner

Alker, H. R. Jr. 1987. Fairy tales, tragedies and world histories: towards interpretive story grammars as possibilist world models. *Behaviormetrika:* 21:1–28

Althusser, L., Balibar, E. 1970 [1968]. *Reading Capital*. London: NLB

Antonio, R. 1989. The normative foundations of emancipatory theory: evolutionary versus pragmatic perspectives. *Am. J. Sociol.* 94:721–48

Apel, K.-O. 1984 [1979]. *Understanding and Explanation: A Transcendental-Pragmatic Perspective*. Cambridge: MIT Press

Atkinson, R. F. 1978. *Knowledge and Explanation in History*. Ithaca, NY: Cornell Univ. Press

Austin, J. L. 1975. *How to Do Things with Words*. New York: Oxford Univ. Press. 2nd ed

Barnes, B. 1985. *About Science*. New York: Basil Blackwell

Barnes, B., Edge, D., eds. 1982. *Science in Context*. Cambridge: MIT Press

Becker, H. S., McCall, M., eds. 1990. *Symbolic Interactionism and Cultural Studies*. Chicago: Univ. Chicago Press

Bernstein, R. J. 1983. *Beyond Objectivism and Relativism: Science, Hermeneutics and Praxis*. Univ. Penn. Press

Betti, E. 1984 [1967]. The epistemological problem of understanding as an aspect of the general problem of knowing. In *Hermeneutics: Questions and Prospects,* ed. G. Shapiro, A. Sica, pp. 25–53. Amherst: Univ. Mass. Press

Bhaskar, R. 1975. *A Realist Theory of Science*. Leeds, England: Leeds Books

Bleicher, J. 1982. *The Hermeneutic Imagination: Outline of a Positive Critique of Scientism and Sociology*. Boston: Routledge & Kegan Paul

Bleier, R., ed. 1986. *Feminist Approaches to Science*. New York: Pergamon

Bloor, D. 1983. *Wittgenstein: A Social Theory of Knowledge*. New: York Columbia Univ. Press

Bourdieu, P. 1975. The specificity of the scientific field and the social conditions of the progress of reason. *Soc. Sci. Inf.* 14(4):19–47

Bourdieu, P. 1977 [1972]. *Outline of a Theory of Practice*. New York: Cambridge Univ. Press

Brannigan, A. 1981. *The Social Basis of Scientific Discoveries*. New York: Cambridge Univ. Press

Brown, R. H. 1977. *A Poetic for Sociology: Toward a Logic of Discovery for the Human Sciences*. Cambridge: Cambridge Univ. Press

Brown, R. H. 1987. *Society as Text*. Chicago: Univ. Chicago Press

Bryant, C. G. A. 1985. *Positivism in Social Theory and Research*. New York: St. Martin's Press

Burger, T. 1976. *Max Weber's Theory of Concept Formation: History, Laws, and Ideal Types*. Durham, NC: Duke Univ. Press

Burke, K. 1969 [1950]. *A Rhetoric of Motives*. Berkeley: Univ. Calif. Press

Burke, K. 1984 [1937]. *Attitudes Toward History*. Berkeley: Univ. Calif. Press

Campbell, D. T. 1988. *Methodology and Epistemology for Social Science*. Chicago: Univ. Chicago Press

Carr, D. 1985. Life and the narrator's art. See Silverman & Ihde 1985, pp. 108–21

Certeau, M. de. 1984 [1974]. *The Practice of Everyday Life*. Berkeley: Univ. Calif. Press

Clark, A., Gerson, E. 1990. Symbolic interactionism in social studies of science. See Becker & McCall 1990

Clifford, J. 1988. *The Predicament of Culture*. Cambridge: Harvard Univ. Press

Cohen, S. 1986. *Historical Culture*. Berkeley: Univ. Calif. Press

Collins, H. M. 1983. The sociology of scientific knowledge: studies of contemporary science. *Annu. Rev. Sociol.* 9:265–85

Collins, P. H. 1986. Learning from the outsider within: the sociological significance of black feminist thought. *Soc. Prob.* 33:514–32

Collins, R. 1989. Sociology: proscience or antiscience? *Am. Sociol. Rev.* 54:124–39

D'Amico, R. 1989. *Historicism and Knowledge*. New York: Routledge

Danto, A. C. 1985. *Narration and Knowledge*. New York: Columbia Univ. Press

Derrida, J. 1978 [1967]. *Writing and Difference*. Chicago: Univ. Chicago Press

Dilthey, W. 1976. *Selected Writings,* ed. and transl. H.P. Rickman. New York: Cambridge Univ. Press

Douglas, J., ed. 1970. *Understanding Everyday Life*. Chicago: Aldine

Dreyfus, H. L., Rabinow, P. 1983. *Michael Foucault: Beyond Structuralism and Hermeneutics*. Chicago: Univ. Chicago Press. 2nd ed.

Eagleton, T. 1983. *Literary Theory*. Minneapolis: Univ. Minn. Press

Faust, D. 1984. *The Limits of Scientific Reasoning*. Minneapolis: Univ. Minn. Press

Feyerabend, P. 1978. *Science in a Free Society*. London: NLB

Feyerabend, P. 1988. Knowledge and the role of theories. *Philos. Soc. Sci.* 18:157–78

Foley, R. 1987. *The Theory of Epistemic Rationality*. Cambridge: Harvard Univ. Press

Foucault, M. 1970 [1966]. *The Order of Things*. New York: Random House

Foucault, M. 1972 [1969]. *The Archeology of Knowledge*. London: Tavistock

Foucault, M. 1988. The political technology of individuals. In *Technologies of the Self*, ed. L. H. Martin, H. Gutman, P. H. Hutton, pp. 145–62. Amherst: Univ. Mass. Press

Fuller, S. 1988. *Social Epistemology*. Bloomington: Indiana Univ. Press

Gadamer, H.-G. 1975. *Truth and Method*. New York: Seabury Press

Geertz, C. 1973. Thick description: toward an interpretive theory of culture. In *The Interpretation of Cultures*. pp. 3–30. New York: Basic

Geertz, C. 1988. *Works and Lives: The Anthropologist as Author*. Stanford: Stanford Univ. Press

Gellner, E. 1985. *Relativism and the Social Sciences*. New York: Cambridge Univ. Press

Giddens, A. 1984. *The Constitution of Society*. Berkeley: Univ. Calif. Press

Grant, J. 1987. I feel therefore I am: a critique of female experience as the basis for a feminist epistemology. *Women Polit.* 7:99–114

Green, B. S. 1988. *Literary Methods and Sociological Theory*. Chicago: Univ. Chicago Press

Habermas, J. 1971 [1968]. *Knowledge and Human Interests*. Boston: Beacon

Habermas, J. 1973. *Theory and Practice*. Boston: Beacon

Habermas, J. 1984 [1981]. *The Theory of Communicative Action*, Vo. 1. *Reason and the Rationalization of Society*. Boston: Beacon

Habermas, J. 1987 [1981]. *The Theory of Communicative Action*. Vol. 2. *Lifeworld and System: A Critique of Functionalist Reason*. Boston: Beacon

Habermas, J. 1988 [1967]. *On the Logic of the Social Sciences*. Cambridge: MIT Press

Halfpenny, P. 1982. *Positivism and Sociology: Explaining Social Life*. London: Allen & Unwin

Hall, J. R. 1977. Alfred Schutz, his critics, and applied phenomenology. *Cult. Hermeneut.* 4:265–79

Hall, J. R. 1980. The time of history and the history of times. *Hist. Theory* 19:113–31

Hall, J. R. 1981. Max Weber's methodological strategy and comparative lifeworld phenomenology. *Hum. Stud.* 4:153–65

Hall, J. R. 1984a. Temporality, social action, and the problem of quantification in historical analysis. *Hist. Methods* 17:206–18

Hall, J. R. 1984b. The problem of epistemology in the social action perspective. In *Sociological Theory 1984*. ed. R. Collins: 253–89

Hall, J. R. 1988. *Where history and sociology meet: modes of discourse and analytic strategies*. Pres. Ann. Meet. Am. Sociol. Assoc., Atlanta

Hall, J. R. 1990. Social interaction, culture, and historical studies. See Becker & McCall 1990

Haraway, D. 1988. Situated knowledges: the science question in feminism and the privilege of partial perspective. *Fem. Stud.* 14:575–99

Hazelrigg, L. 1989a. *Social Science and the Challenge of Relativism*. Vol. I. *A Wilderness of Mirrors*. Tallahassee: Fla. State Univ. Press

Hazelrigg, L. 1989b. *Social Science and the Challenge of Relativism*. Vol. II. *Claims of Knowledge: On the Labor of Making Found Worlds*. Tallahassee: Fla. State Univ. Press

Hekman, S. J. 1983a. From epistemology to ontology: Gadamer's hermeneutics and Wittgensteinian social science. *Hum. Stud.* 6:205–24

Hekman, S. J. 1983b. *Weber, the Ideal Type, and Contemporary Social Theory*. Notre Dame, Ind: Univ. Notre Dame Press

Hindess, B. 1977. *Philosophy and Methodology in the Social Sciences*. Atlantic Highlands, NJ: Humanities Press

Hindess, B., Hirst, P. Q. 1975. *Pre-Capitalist Modes of Production*. London: Routledge & Kegan Paul

Hindess, B., Hirst, P. Q. 1977. *Mode of Production and Social Formation*. London: Routledge & Kegan Paul

Hoy, D. C. 1988. Foucault: modern or postmodern? In *After Foucault*, ed. J. Arac, pp. 12–41, New Brunswick, NJ: Rutgers Univ. Press

Keat, R., Urry, J. 1982. *Social Theory as Science*. Boston: Routledge & Kegan Paul. 2nd ed.

Kiser, E., Hechter, M. 1988. *Beyond inductivism and historicism: toward a theory-driven methodology for comparative-historical* sociology. Pap. pres. Ann. Meet. Am. Sociol. Assoc., Atlanta

Kuhn, T. 1962. *The Structure of Scientific Revolutions*. Chicago: Univ. Chicago Press

Lakatos, I. 1971. History of science and its rational reconstructions. *Boston Stud. Philos. Sci.* 8:91–136

Latour, B. 1987. *Science in Action: How to Follow Scientists and Engineers through Society*. Cambridge: Harvard Univ. Press

Latour, B., Woolgar, S. 1986. *Laboratory Life: The Construction of Scientific Facts*. Princeton, NJ: Princeton Univ. Press

Layder, D. 1985. Beyond empiricism? The promise of realism. *Philos. Soc. Sci.* 15:255–74

Levine, D. N. 1985. *The Flight From Ambiguity*. Chicago: Univ. Chicago Press

Lévi-Strauss, C. 1966 [1962]. *The Savage Mind*. London: Weidenfeld & Nicholson

Lloyd, C. 1986. *Explanation in Social History*. New York: Basil Blackwell

Lyotard, J.-F. 1984 [1979]. *The Postmodern Condition: A Report on Knowledge*. Minneapolis: Univ. Min. Press

Maclean, M. 1988. *Narrative as Performance*. London: Routledge

Makkreel, R. A. 1975. *Dilthey: Philosopher of the Human Studies*. Princeton, NJ: Princeton Univ. Press

Margolis, J. 1985. Deconstruction; or the mystery of the mystery of the text. See Silverman & Ihde 1985, pp. 138–51

Margolis, J. 1986. *Pragmatism without Foundations: Reconciling Realism and Relativism*. New York: Basil Blackwell

Martin, R. 1977. *Historical Explanation*. Ithaca, NY: Cornell Univ. Press

McCall, M., Wittner, J. 1990. The good news about life history. See Becker & McCall 1990

McCloskey, D. 1985. *The Rhetoric of Economics*. Madison: Univ. Wis. Press

Meja, V., Stehr, N. 1988. Social Science, epistemology, and the problem of relativism. *Soc. Epistemol.* 2:263–71

Miller, R. W. 1987. *Fact and Method: Explanation, Confirmation and Reality in the Natural and the Social Sciences*. Princeton: Princeton Univ. Press

Mink, L. O. 1987. *Historical Understanding*. Ithaca, NY: Cornell Univ. Press

Nelson, J. S., Megill, A., McCloskey, D., eds. 1987. *The Rhetoric of the Human Sciences*. Madison: Univ. Wis. Press

Newton-Smith, W. H. 1981. *The Rationality of Science*. Boston: Routledge & Kegan Paul

Oakes, G. 1988. *Weber and Rickert: Concept Formation in the Cultural Sciences*. Cambridge: MIT Press

O'Neill, J. 1986. A realist model of knowledge: with a phenomenological deconstruction of its model of man. *Philos. Soc. Sci.* 16:1–19

Outhwaite, W. 1987. *New Philosophies of Social Science: Realism, Hermeneutics, Critical theory*. New York: St. Martin's

Papineau, D. 1978. *For Science in the Social Sciences*. New York: St. Martin's

Parsons, T. 1937. *The Structure of Social Action*. New York: Free Press

Phillips, D. L. 1973. *Abandoning Method*. San Francisco: Jossey-Bass

Polanyi, M. 1967. Knowing and being. Reprinted 1969 in *Knowing and Being: Essays by Michael Polanyi*, ed. M. Grene, pp. 123–37. Chicago: Univ. Chicago Press

Pollner, M. 1987. *Mundane Reason*. New York: Cambridge Univ. Press

Popper, K. R. 1979 [1972]. *Objective Knowledge: An Evolutionary Approach*. Oxford: Clarendon. Rev. ed

Popper, K. R. 1983. *Realism and the Aim of Science*. Totowa, NJ: Rowman & Littlefield

Poster, M. 1987. Foucault, post-structuralism, and the mode of information. In *The Aims of Representation: Subject/Text/History*, ed. M. Krieger, pp. 107–30. New York: Columbia Univ. Press

Ragin, C., Zaret, D. 1983. Theory and method in comparative research: two strategies. *Soc. Forces* 61:731–54

Ricoeur, P. 1977. *The Rule of Metaphor*. Toronto: Univ. Toronto Press

Ricoeur, P. 1984, 1985, 1988. *Time and Narrative*. 3 Vols. Chicago: Univ. Chicago Press

Rochberg-Halton, E. 1986. *Meaning and Modernity*. Chicago: Univ. Chicago Press

Rodi, F. 1985. Hermeneutics and the meaning of life: a critique of Gadamer's interpretation of Dilthey. See Silverman & Ihde 1985, pp. 82–90

Rorty, R. 1979. *Philosophy and the Mirror of Nature*. Princeton, NJ: Princeton Univ. Press

Roth, G. 1976. History and sociology in the work of Max Weber. *Br. J. Sociol.* 27:306–18

Roth, G., Schluchter, W. 1979. *Max Weber's Vision of History: Ethics and Methods*. Berkeley: Univ. Calif. Press

Roth, P. A. 1987. *Meaning and Method in the Social Sciences*. Ithaca, NY: Cornell Univ. Press

Rothbart, D. 1984. The semantics of metaphor and the structure of science. *Philos. Sci.* 51:595–615

Rule, J. B. 1988. *Theories of Civil Violence*. Berkeley: Univ. Calif. Press

Sahlins, M. 1985. *Islands of History*. Chicago: Univ. Chicago Press

Sayers, S. 1985. *Reality and Reason*. New York: Basil Blackwell

Schrag, C. O. 1986. *Communicative Praxis and the Space of Subjectivity*. Bloomington: Ind. Univ. Press

Seidman, S., Wagner, D. G., eds. 1990. *Postpositivism and Modern Theory*. New York: Basil Blackwell

Shweder, R. A., ed. 1980. *Fallible Judgment in Behavioral Research. New Directions for Methodology of Social and Behavioral Science*, Vol. 4. San Francisco: Jossey Bass

Silverman, H. J., Ihde, D., eds. 1985. *Hermeneutics & Deconstruction*. Albany: State Univ. New York Press

Skocpol, T. 1984. Emerging agendas and recurrent strategies in historical sociology. In *Vision and Method in Historical Sociology*, ed. T. Skocpol, pp. 356–91. Cambridge: Cambridge Univ. Press

Skocpol, T., Somers, M. 1980. The uses of comparative history in macrosocial inquiry. *Comp. Stud. Soc. Hist.* 22:174–97

Smith, D. E. 1987. Women's perspective as a radical critique of sociology. In *Feminism and Methodology*, ed. S. Harding, pp. 84–96. Bloomington: Indiana Univ. Press

Spencer, M. E. 1982. The ontologies of social science. *Philos. Soc. Sci.* 12:121–41

Stinchcombe, A. L. 1978. *Theoretical Methods in Social History*. New York: Academic

Stone, L. 1979. The revival of narrative: reflections on a new old history. *Past & Present* 85 (Nov.): 3–24

Suppe, F. 1977. Afterword. In *The Structure of Scientific Theories*, ed. F. Suppe. pp. 617–730. Urbana: Univ. Ill. Press

Sylvan, D., Glassner, B. 1985. *A Rationalist Methodology for the Social Sciences*. New York: Basil Blackwell

Thompson, E. P. 1978. *'The Poverty of Theory' and Other Essays*. New York: Monthly Rev.

Tilly, C. 1981. *As Sociology Meets History*. New York: Academic

Tilly, C. 1984. *Big Structures, Large Processes, Huge Comparisions*. New York: Sage

Toulmin, S. 1972. *Human Understanding*. Vol. I: *The Collective Use and Evolution of Concepts*. Princeton, NJ: Princeton Univ. Press

Turner, S. P. 1980. *Sociological Explanation as Translation*. New York: Cambridge Univ. Press

Turner, S. P. 1990. The strange life and hard times of the concept of general theory in sociology: a short history of hope. See Seidman & Wagner 1990

Veyne, P. 1984 [1971]. *Writing History*. Middletown, Conn: Wesleyan Univ. Press

Wagner, D. G., Berger, J. 1985. Do sociological theories grow? *Am. J. Sociol.* 90:697–728

Wagner, D. G., Berger, J. 1986. Programs, theory, and metatheory. *Am. J. Sociol.* 92:168–82

Wallis, R. 1985. Science and pseudo-science. *Soc. Sci. Inf.* 24:585–601

Weinsheimer, J. C. 1985. *Gadamer's Hermeneutics: A Reading of Truth and Method*. New Haven: Yale Univ. Press

White, H. 1978. *Tropics of Discourse*. Baltimore: Johns Hopkins Univ. Press

White, H. 1987. *The Content of the Form: Narrative Discourse and Historical Representation*. Baltimore: Johns Hopkins Univ. Press

Willard, C. A. 1983. *Argumentation and the Social Grounds of Knowledge*. Tuscaloosa: Univ. Ala. Press

Winch, P. 1958. *The Idea of a Social Science and its Relation to Philosophy*. New York: Humanities

Wittgenstein, L. 1968 [1953]. *Philosophical Investigations*. New York: Macmillan

Wolff, K. H. 1976. *Surrender and Catch*. Boston: Reidel

Wuthnow, R. 1987. *Meaning and Moral Order*. Berkeley: Univ. Calif. Press

Wuthnow, R. 1989. *Communities of Discourse: Ideology and Social Structure in the Reformation, the Enlightenment, and European Socialism*. Cambridge: Harvard Univ. Press

Annu. Rev. Sociol. 1990. 16:353–77

PEASANTS AND PROLETARIANS

B. R. Roberts

Department of Sociology, University of Texas at Austin, Austin, Texas 78712

KEY WORDS: peasant, proletarian, class, development, work

Abstract

Peasants and proletarians are key actors in the social changes that produced the modern world. The concepts identify different forms of demographic behavior, social organization and political action. The peasant is locally oriented and defensive politically, yet has contributed to revolutionary change. The proletarian looks to association beyond locality and is the basis of modern class politics, but the political impact of the proletariat has varied with time and place. There are many types of peasantry and many types of proletariat. The categories serve usefully in comparative and historical analysis, but the variations in types and in the social and political context in which they act need to be specified. The orientations to action and the life chances that both categories describe need to be modified to take account of current social and economic changes. In many parts of the world, the peasant disappears in face of the modernization of agriculture or survives by combining agricultural work with nonagricultural work or migration. The proletarian also retreats in face of the decline of full-time wage employment in the cities, and the increasing importance of independent and part-time employment. Other forms of identity, based on gender or generation, or community-based ones, such as religion or ethnicity, are reinforced as a basis of political action, particularly in face of the growing significance of the state, not the employer, in determining the life chances of different social groups.

INTRODUCTION

The terms *peasant* and *proletarian* are key concepts in the literature on social change and modernization. Peasants, farming a small amount of land directly

0360-0572/90/0815-0353$02.00

with the aid of household labor and mainly for their own consumption, have been the enduring basis of agricultural production throughout the ages (Wolf 1966, Shanin 1987: 2–9). The proletarian is equally old; from Roman times, at least, there has been a place for those who—following Tilly's definition (1984:1)—work for wages with little or no control over the means of production. The shift in the balance of population from predominantly peasant to predominantly proletarian is one of the major social changes of the modern era, marking the transition from agriculturally based, mainly subsistence-oriented economies to those in which industry and services predominate and the majority of people depend on the market for selling their labor and for their consumption. Proletarianization, it can be argued, is the most significant process in the making of the contemporary world: It is at the heart of modern class formation; it is associated with fundamental changes in demographic processes and with restructuring of family relationships.

For the social sciences of developed countries, the terms *peasant* and *proletarian* have mainly had a historical significance, conjuring images of two worlds that have disappeared: one, in which most people made their living from the land in small and scattered settlements, and the other, a world that destroyed the first, in which men and women crowded into cities, powering the factories and furnaces, and working in the mines of the Industrial Revolution. By the census of 1891, 74% of the population of England and Wales was urban (Lawton 1978: Table 3.2). Over 80% of its economically active population were wage-earners, and even in agriculture, in which some 12% worked, the proletariat made up approximately 70% of the total (*Census of England and Wales,* 1893: Table 5). Urbanization and proletarianization were slower in continental Europe, but there, as in the United States, by 1930 agriculture and independent production provided a livelihood for only a minority of the population.

In developing countries, in contrast, peasant and proletarian, and the transition from the one type to the other, have a clear contemporary relevance. As of 1980, 65.4% of the economically active population of the developing countries of Africa, Asia, and Latin America worked in agriculture, compared to 12.7% in the developed world (International Labour Office 1986: 116). From the available census tables brought together by the International Labour Office, a reasonable estimate is that three quarters of those working in agriculture are peasants (self-employed or family workers); the proletariat is only a small majority (58%) even in the nonagricultural sectors (ILO 1988; Table 2A).

The transition from peasant to proletarian is neither final nor unequivocal. The trend toward full-time wage labor as the near-universal means of subsistence appears to be ending. Debates over the informal economy and over the increase in nonstandard forms of employment reflect a world-wide trend toward deproletarianization (Portes et al 1989). Though these trends may be the temporary result of economic cycles, there is the equally strong possibility that they reflect structural changes in the world economy in terms of its integration and technological base.

Proletarianization and its countertrends are broad changes and difficult to define precisely. They need to be reviewed with caution and with a degree of skepticism. Though sociological theory sharply distinguishes between peasant and proletarian in terms of class position and collective action, there is a particularly acute tension in this field of research between the concepts and the reality which they seek to approximate. There are many types of peasant and many varieties of proletariat, depending on the particular form of agricultural production and land tenure, and on the nature of industrialization. Historical and national contexts, particularly state formation, also make for differences in the experiences and organization of peasants and proletarians. The elusiveness of the concepts raises the possibility, as Somers (1989) suggests with reference to the proletariat, that more is obscured than illuminated. The tension between broad but suggestive concepts and the varieties of experience has, however, generated a particularly rich set of research findings.

THE NATURE OF THE PEASANTRY

Though the term *peasant* is often used descriptively to refer to the rural peoples of preindustrial Europe or those of contemporary developing countries, it is the subject of considerable theoretical debate as how best to interpret peasant acceptance or resistance to change. From marxist perspectives, peasant economies are seen as persisting and adaptable units of production, because they fulfill a subordinate role to dominant modes such as captialism, providing, for instance, cheap seasonal labor to capitalist enterprises (Wolpe 1972, Meillassoux 1975). Decision-making approaches to change in peasant society, in contrast, emphasize the individual and culturally specific calculation of alternatives that offer maximal return in face of scarce resources (Salisbury 1970, Popkin 1979). Durkheimian perspectives give priority to the moral economies of peasant communities and their defensiveness or conservatism based both on perceptions of the dangers arising from individual competition over limited resources and on strong communal institutions (Foster 1967, Scott 1976). There are also regional differences in the nature of the peasantry, depending on factors such as the importance of a landlord class, the degree of peasant involvement in market economies, the prevalence or absence of private property in land or animals, or the type of production—whether, for instance, based on livestock or crops. These contrasts in cultural ecology when combined with the differences in theoretical perspective make generalization about the peasantry a risky but interesting exercise. In the discussion that follows, I focus on the broad issue of whether there is anything special about peasant culture that makes their behavior intractably different from that of other classes. My material is drawn mainly from the Latin American and European peasantries, and my account would need to be modified for other regions, such as, for instance, subsaharan Africa.[1]

The 'classness' of the peasantry—the material and cultural basis on which appeals to common interest are grounded—is the key to understanding what is sometimes called the peasant problem—their role in resisting social and economic change. It is also the key to understanding their role in producing it: Peasant rebellions have been frequent throughout recorded history, and many of the major revolutions of the twentieth century have been peasant-based. Teodor Shanin (1972) labels them an awkward class, indicating that peasants do not fit easily into bi-polar class models of haves and have-nots. The class basis of the peasantry contains, in an irresolvable tension, both the individual interests and strategies of peasant households, and their common interests in defending themselves against powerful outsiders and using the community as an insurance against misfortune.

In a series of studies at the turn of the century, the Russian agricultural economist, A. V. Chayanov, developed a theory of peasant economy (1966) which stressed the peculiar economic rationale of the peasantry. Basically, Chayanov sees the peasant farm as being primarily oriented to secure the subsistence needs of its members. Decisions over crops or the amount of land to farm are determined by the number of mouths to feed and by the available number of household workers. The peasant, from this perspective, seeks not to maximize income or profit, but to ensure that all family members are adequately fed and employed. Chayanov's analysis is generated by and applied to the specific conditions of the Russian peasant village, in which among other special factors there were few alternative employment possibilities. This limits, as Hilton (1975) points out in his review of the medieval English peasantry, the general applicability of the theory.

Though Chayanov concentrates on optimizing strategies, his emphasis on the household and village gives his analysis certain similarities to that of Polanyi (1957). Polanyi stresses the importance of substantive rationalities in economic behavior against those who argue for the universality of formal or

---

[1]In contrast to the Latin American or European peasantries, those of Africa have been less involved in a cash economy, are less socially and economically differentiated, and have shorter histories of subjection to a bureaucratic state (Hart 1987, Bernstein & Campbell 1985). In the case of the Ujamaa movement in Kenya, the peasant farming community could be presented as the basis for a new society in a way that would be quite unrealistic in Latin America (Hyden 1980).

market rationalities.[2] Peasant economic behavior has a powerful substantive rationality arising from the priority given to maintaining the household and community. Peasants are, consequently, less susceptible to market forces and, thereby, less likely to fall victim to the external pressures, both market and political, that turn a few into successful commercial farmers and the majority into laborers. Ensuring their survival from one year to the next means that peasants must be conservative in their farming practices, sowing those crops or rearing those animals that minimize risks rather than maximize gains.

Other analysts have concentrated on the social and political institutions that make peasants an awkward class. Researchers working on very different historical periods and in different parts of the world portray peasants as living on the margins of subsistence, in which their survival depends on the web of family and communal relationships (Dalton 1967, Shanin 1987). The basic unit is the household, characterized by a division of labor among male and female, young and old. The household needs to call on the aid of others in times of emergency or when its own labor resources are insufficient, as, for example, in harvest periods. Institutionalized practices of exchange and redistribution are reported as common features of peasant communities. Access to communal resources, whether land or hunting and gathering rights—the communal grid which Thompson (1976:342–347) describes for eighteenth century rural England—is vital for those households that do not have access to sufficient land.

It would be a mistake to infer from the reports of communitarian practices and ideologies that peasant villages are socially and economically homogencous. The other aspect of peasant communities is that they are riven by factionalism and internal conflicts. In addition to the tensions produced by the presence of a local landowning class, differences in family size and in the fortunes of inheritance and farming result in peasant communities often internally differentiated between strata of rich, middle, and poor peasants (Long & Roberts 1978).

The precarious subsistence equilibrium of peasant society results in fluctuations in population size with disasters such as famine and plague. Over time, stability is based on high fertility and high mortality. The former, as Coale (1986) points out, is needed to counteract the latter, since otherwise communities would literally die out. The population balance produced by the high fertility/high mortality regime is, it has been argued, partly the result of the characteristics of the peasant household economy (Laslett 1979: 94, Tilly

---

[2]Halperin (1988) provides a careful account of these controversies in economic anthropology, showing the difficulties produced for analysis by too rigid a separation of the formal and the substantive. The substantive refers to the institutionalized practices arising out of the ways in which particular groups adapt to their environment.

1978:22). The main mechanism of control is marriage. Couples could not marry until there were openings for the new household unit in the social structure, usually through inheritance. Those unable to find a place would move away, join other households as live-in servants or laborers, or remain as unmarried members of the household of parent or sibling.

Inheritance patterns affected these outcomes. Where land was divided among the children, more opportunities were created, at least initially, to establish new households. This process resulted in the predominance of nuclear families, with only a few extended ones (Berkner 1976). Ultimately, however, the iron logic of finite resources would impose its control as inadequate resources would force households to break-up and move away. Even without community constraints, the negative consequences of population growth for living standards, as measured, for instance, by the rising price of food, would tend to restore population balance through rising mortality or declining marriage rates (Wrigley 1983).

Tight supervision of reproductive and other behavior by the peasant household and community is an ideal typical construct. It applies best to those areas of Europe where land resources were limited and there were few alternative means to gain an income. The demographic behavior of the preindustrial European peasantry is, in any event, unusual in comparative perspective: because of late marriage and high levels of celibacy, fertility was only moderately high. Outside Europe, in Asia, for example, men and women have always married early; their very high levels of fertility were offset by equally high levels of mortality (Coale 1986). In contemporary developing countries, reductions in mortality, brought about by modern medicine and health care, have been dramatic when compared to events in Europe in the eighteenth and nineteenth centuries. In some developing countries, this decline in mortality has been counterbalanced by sharp declines in fertility, though the overall tendency has been a fairly slow decline or, as in the case of China, a fluctuating pattern of fertility decline. The demographic transition to a regime of low fertility and low mortality is consequently slower, and population growth much higher, than Watkins (1986) describes for Europe during the nineteenth century.

The Peasant in a Changing World System

These internal processes take place within the context of a wider society, so that a defining characteristic of peasant society is that it is a part society (Kroeber 1948: 284). Peasants look to themselves and to their needs as much as they can, but they are closely linked to wider institutions, such as urban markets and the state. Because the peasant is not only an economic agent but is also responsible for a household and its continuity, s/he must maintain a balance between external demands and internal needs, including those investments in time or resources needed to maintain the community.

Peasants provide the food to feed the cities, are subject to taxes, and share, if marginally, in the dominant culture of the metropolis. The demands of the outside world, including market opportunities, and the power of outsiders to control peasant production is, as Wolf (1955, 1966: 13–17) argues, a major dynamic of peasant society, resulting in many types of peasantries. Brenner (1985) uses a similar argument to analyze the different outcomes for economic development of the agrarian class structures of Europe in the early modern period. Brenner emphasizes the changes in the relations between lords and peasants that resulted in such seeming paradoxes as the association of peasant freedom with backwardness in France, and the constraints on peasant rights that resulted in economic development in England.

Peasant society is not, then, traditional society in the sense that it maintained an unchanged culture from time immemorial. As various researchers have shown, "traditional" rituals are often of recent invention, and their practices are linked to new types of external demand on peasant villages, such as when labor migrants to mines or plantations finance *fiestas* (which had not previously existed) in their home villages (Mallon 1984, Long & Roberts 1984, Hobsbawm & Ranger 1983).

In his later work, Wolf (1982) puts the case more generally, linking the various types of peasant organization found outside the developed world to the evolution of an integrated world system. He argues that the internal processes of peasant communities, including their conservatism, their occasional rebelliousness, and, finally, their disintegration need to be understood in terms of the expansion of the European states from the fifteenth century onwards.

The impact of colonialism and the expansion of mining production and plantation agriculture changed the agrarian structures of the world outside Europe. The subsistence base of peasant communities was directly or indirectly destroyed, market systems disrupted, and labor migration generalized as a necessary supplement to peasant agriculture. In contrast to what happened in western Europe, where most proletarians were rural until the mid-nineteenth century, in developing countries agricultural modernization and industrial development have not led, in any clear way, to the creation of a substantial *rural* proletariat. In countries, such as Indonesia and Peru, the rural population has instead become caught in semi-proletarian, semi-peasant positions (Geertz 1963, Laite 1981).

In Latin America, the peasant populations exist on land that is rarely adequate to survival, and so they diversify their economies through off-farm employment, commerce, and craft activities. As in the case of Levine's (1977) cottage weavers, setting up a new household is a means of survival, allowing, for example, a man to migrate for work, while the woman attends to the small plot of land and to the community obligations that provide a safety net for the household.

These Latin American peasantries have a markedly different situation from their counterparts in seventeenth and eighteenth century Europe. They live and work in a context in which, because of modern technological change and improvements in communications, rural-urban differences have been eroded. The peasant has access to the media, and to urban markets and consumer goods, while beset by more external intervention than in the past, whether by private entrepreneurs or by state and international agencies. Faced with inadequate land resources, and price competition from large-scale farming at home and abroad, the monetary costs of peasant farming increase through the generalized use of inputs such as hybrid seeds, fertilizer, and insecticide. These processes mean that there are few 'true' peasants left, in terms of households that survive mainly by the produce of their land. Figueroa (1984) shows how even remote villages in the Peruvian Andes buy most of their foodstuffs on the market, obtaining the cash for their purchases mainly from migrant labor. A similar situation is reported by Adelman et al (1988) for Oaxaca in Mexico, where the incomes of almost all families depend on remittances from national and international migration and where the highest standards of consumption are among those with little or no land because they have the highest number of outmigrants.

The peasantries of contemporary developing countries differ from one another as a result of their varying histories of incorporation into the world system and because of differences in farming systems. Research indicates that peasants are not doomed to extinction in face of the spread of capitalism. Various commentators have pointed to the flexibility of the peasant enterprise—its 'fungibility' to use Lipton's (1984) term—and its capacity to find niches for itself in the new economic order (Goodman & Redclift 1981). Repeasantization has been reported in certain areas of the developing world, such as northeast Brazil, in which large-scale commercial agriculture has ceased to be profitable, leaving the land to be farmed by families that previously had provided the wage labor for the plantations. Also, peasant farmers continue to open up the agricultural frontiers of many parts of the world, clearing the land, although, as in Brazil, they often are then displaced by large-scale commercial enterprises which buy or force them out while using them as convenient and cheap wage labor (Foweraker 1981). The continuing functionality of the peasant for capitalist farming, mainly as a source of cheap labor, is one of the main arguments in De Janvry's (1981) account of agrarian change and the failure of land reform in Latin America.

In some areas, peasants have accommodated to market pressures, and they, rather than large-scale commercial farmers, contribute the bulk of modern agricultural production. Chang (1989) describes how land reform in South Korea has created a land-owing peasantry which is increasingly producing and marketing vegetables and fruits in place of grains, while using the rice crop for self-consumption. The growth of large cities stimulated by South Korea's export-oriented industrialization has enabled the South Korean peasantry to become farmers, producing for the market and using the market to guide their production decisions. They still make use, however, of communal institutions, both in production and in marketing. Chang (1989) claims they evidence little of the factionalism and differentiation reported in modern Latin American peasant communities. This peasant success story is based on two factors that have weakened large-scale capitalist farming. The first is the decision of the new South Korean state to eliminate large-landholdings, many of which were in Japanese hands or in the hands of collaborators with the Japanese colonial regime. The second is the labor-intensive character of Korean agriculture, based on irrigated rice fields and market-gardens, that is unsuited to mechanization. Additionally, rural wage labor is in decreasing supply because of rural-urban migration; the proportion of family labor is thus rising.

Peasants and Politics

Throughout history, peasants have formed the basis of a decentralized political order. Peasants are incorporated into the wider society through subsumption: members of the household through the head of household, heads of households through village elders or richer peasants, and these in turn through the 'great houses' of the local nobility or landowners (Laslett 1979). Even where peasants are dominated by governments with a long centralist tradition, as in the case of the Latin American republics, the state controls the peasantry through many intermediaries. From this perspective, Laslett's (1979:21) description of the political structure of seventeenth century rural England is similar to Parsons' (1936) account of the Mexican rural municipality of Mitla, or to De la Peña's (1988) account of the contemporary power structure of rural Mexico.

Because of their apparent economic conservatism and political localism, peasants are often viewed by outsiders, both academic and nonacademic, as constituting a problem for political and economic modernization. In Barrington Moore's (1966) scholarly analysis, the resolution of this peasant problem is one of the keys to whether political regimes take on a democratic or authoritarian cast. The gradual elimination of the peasantry through market forces and their transformation into rural or urban laborers, and the emergence of a substantial middling stratum of farmers and urban merchants—the path taken by England—inhibits the concentration of power and favors democracy. In contrast, where the commercial development of agriculture occurs through subordinating peasants to large landowners—the path taken in Germany—and these dominate rural society and agricultural production, a more authoritarian form of government is likely to emerge. The landowners support a strong central state that ensures their dominion over the countryside, and this state takes on an authoritarian cast in the absence of an extensive and independently based middling stratum of urban and rural capitalists.

There are exceptions to this description of peasant political subsumption and to the role of a landed class in promoting authoritarianism, particularly because the bourgeoisie is just as likely to be authoritarian when the balance of forces permits, as Stephens (1989) points out in his review which is generally supportive to the Moore thesis. Peasant communities also differ considerably in their relationships with their masters, whether landowners or the state. Malefakis (1970) argues that peasant political responses in rural Spain before the civil war varied greatly according to region, for both historical and economic reasons. Conservative forces received support from the staunchly catholic Castilian peasants, who farmed their own land in villages in which social and economic differentiation was not marked. The anarchists were strong in Andalusia among the communities of landless farm laborers. There, a strong moral sense of community reinforced antagonism to the oppression of absentee landowners and a state whose main representatives, the Guardia Civil, were outsiders. Socialism received most rural support in Extremadura where farm laborers were less predominant, and tenant farmers and sharecroppers proportionately more important. Malefakis (1970: 129) comments that this occupational differentiation made the socialists a more moderate and more organized force in the rural politics of southern Spain than were the anarchists.

Peasants have never been passive recipients of changes from above, and they continue to be important social actors in transformations at the national level. There is no single convincing explanation for peasant political movements, and attempts to provide one, while generating useful debate, are not mutually exclusive. Paige (1975) emphasizes the interaction of economic factors based on the sources of income of the agricultural classes in terms of the distinction between capital, wages, and land. While recognizing the contribution that such factors make, Skocpol (1979: 112–157) emphasizes the institutional and organizational conditions that foster or inhibit peasant insurrection, especially the breakdown of a centralized state. Scott (1976) emphasizes the defensive nature of peasant rebellion in Southeast Asia, seeking its roots in the peasant moral economy. Peasants react bitterly to changes in a traditional order that they view as legitimate when, even in the presence of widespread poverty, it provides a stable basis for subsistence. In Southeast Asia, the perceived threats to subsistence and the challenge to authority came from the insecurities generated by fluctuations in the world economy and by practices such as unvarying taxes, which signalled to peasants a lack of reciprocity in the relations with powerful outsiders (Scott 1976: 32–58). In contrast, Popkin (1979: 32–35), covering much the same geographical area as Scott, looks for his explanation to the calculus of relative economic advantage that leads peasants to see both individual and group gain in rebellion. Other analyses such as that of Paige (1983), who points to the similarities between peasant rebellion in Vietnam and Guatemala, have emphasized the importance of the class conflict between landowners and landless in producing peasant rebellion.

On balance, however, the literature on this topic does not provide unequivocal support for any one position: What factors are foremost depends on the particular national and international conjuncture, and the ways in which that conjuncture weakens the power and legitimacy of elites, making opportunities appear more attainable and grievances sharper, while breaking down the barriers to intervillage communication (Tutino 1986: 362–371). This is the case for the Mexican Revolution which was a product of regionally diverse types of peasant and nonpeasant rebellion. Many of the peasants that rebelled did so for moral economy considerations; but they and their leaders were also influenced by the new opportunities for economic gain brought by the rapid but uneven capitalist development of the previous 30 years. Finally, class conflict and especially its ideologies were present, to some degree, in all the major regions of rebellion (Knight 1986, Tutino 1986, Brading 1984).

THE NATURE OF THE PROLETARIAT

In Marx's account, the proletarian is the social and economic antithesis of the peasant. Where the peasant is tied to the land and to locality, the proletarian is free of both. Survival for the proletarian depends on selling his or her labor on the market since the proletarian controls no property which will provide even a meager subsistence. The independent urban craftsman of the preindustrial period had, in these respects, more in common with the peasant farmer than with the wage-worker. In both the first two cases, property was the basis for the enterprise, family labor was essential to its functioning, and the household, through its head, had some control over the pace and extent of work to be done. In the proletarian household, the tie between property, family, and enterprise is broken, weakening family bonds, at least in theory, promoting greater geographical mobility, and forcing people to work at the dictate of those for whom the survival of the household is of no consequence.

The proletarian, then, is a concept decidedly on the modern side of the traditional/modern divide. The peasant is particularistic, the proletarian is universalistic; the peasant looks to family, community, and locality, while the proletarian looks to association on an international scale. In the marxist literature, the proletariat is the progressive class which, while tactically allying with the peasantry to achieve revolution, must provide the leadership and be the basis for the transition to socialism and communism. These expectations give the proletariat a more determined role in history than the peasantry. *Proletarian* is both a term of analysis and a theory of political change.

The analysis of the proletariat and of its historical role is complicated by ambiguities over membership. The proletariat has two separable and essential characteristics: wage-earning and lack of control over the means of production. Tilly (1984: 14) stresses the importance of recognizing that both these variables are continuous, not discrete, creating many degrees and types of proletarian. Wage workers, especially those in households with other income earners, can vary in their dependence on wage earning because of the possibilities of obtaining their subsistence from other sources such as exchanges with others, self-resourcing, and state-provided welfare.

Workers also possess different degrees of control over the work process, depending on skills and the division of labor. Loss of control is produced not only by employment in large-scale organizations in which machines dictate the pace of work.[3] Citing the expression used by a handloom weaver, Cottereau (1986: 120) argues that nineteenth-century French industrialization, powered by small-scale and profitable enterprises, reduced various types of worker to machines—craftsmen and domestic outworkers as well as factory workers. The European countries differed in the scale of their industrialization and in the importance of the different industrial sectors such as textiles, metals, or chemicals; these differences created many types of working-class. Other categories of wage-earners apart from manual workers can also be included within the proletariat. Office workers can be proletarianized, as a long tradition of Marxist research has noted (Abercrombie & Urry 1983: 49–66). Many self-employed workers can be more 'proletarian' than certain types of skilled workers in a factory. Thus, the domestic worker in contemporary Lima, Peru, who receives material to make into dresses and is paid by the piece has little control over production and is, to all intents and purposes, a dependent wage-earner—a 'disguised' proletarian (MacEwen-Scott 1979).

Proletarianization in Historical Perspective

The change from a world mainly inhabited by peasants to one mainly inhabited by proletarians occurred in Europe between the sixteenth and twentieth centuries. Tilly (1984: 36) estimates that in 1500 proletarians composed

---

[3]Marx (1974:506) describes the change as the move from the formal to the real subsumption of labor by capital. In this process modern manufacture, in which the worker's craft skills are still needed and give some control over production, is replaced by large-scale industry in which the worker becomes merely an appendage to the machine: he or she becomes deskilled.

30% of Europe's population, by 1800 67%, and by 1900 70%. The demographic components of this proletarianization are important fields of research, and similar work needs to be done on the contemporary trends in developing countries. Tilly (1978, 1984) argues that the relative contributions of natural increase, net migration between countries, and social mobility (the lifetime move from peasant to proletarian) are crucial elements in working-class formation, affecting class homogeneity and the nature of class traditions.

We noted above that peasant demographic regimes are likely to result in population balance. Proletarianization, in contrast, is likely to have changed the pattern in Europe. The readiness of the proletarian to marry and establish a new household depended on wage opportunities, tying fertility to the dynamic of capitalism, its economic cycles and capacity to create work. The eighteenth and nineteenth centuries were periods in which, first in England and later in other parts of Europe, production rose fast enough to break the vicious circle of population growth that resulted in declines in real wages and rises in food costs with subsequent declines in natural increase (Wrigley 1983). In his analysis of demographic trends in four English villages, Levine (1984) argues that in the first period of cottage industry, the labor of family members, including children, provided a reasonable income and was an incentive to marriage. In his comparisons of farmers and weavers, he shows how weavers married earlier and had, on average, more children. When proletarianization increased in one of the farming communities as a result of dairy farming, fertility increased as the increasing numbers of farm laborers married earlier.

The possible differences in the reproductive patterns of peasants and proletarians, combined with the rapid numerical growth of the proletariat and the likely negative net effects of the outmigration of proletarians to the new world make it likely that the origins of the proletariat are mainly to be found among the proletariat themselves.[4] According to Tilly's (1984: 36) figures, the majority of proletarians were rural throughout the period so that even by 1900 they outnumbered urban proletarians by a ratio of 5 to 3.

The urbanization of Europe in the nineteenth century owed much to migration, but mainly, it seems, to the migration of proletarians. Peasants were the last to leave the land. The formation of the European proletariat was not, then, based on people fresh from the fields. The factory workers of the early twentieth century had old proletarian roots and called on old working-class traditions. By the end of the nineteenth century, urban populations, particularly in Britain, were beginning to grow mainly through their own natural increase, and the new cohorts that entered the expanding industrial occupa-

---

[4]Tilly (1984:36) estimates that the proletariat grew from 17 million in 1500 to 200 million in 1900, whereas the nonproletarian component of the European population grew from 39 million to 85 million in these years.

tions were urban-born. The 'traditional' urban working-class of Britain was created at this time in which generations succeeded each other in the same cities and urban neighborhoods and in which there appears to have been a marked 'inheritance' of working-class occupations from father to son and mother to daughter (Roberts 1978).

This continuity in working-class formation does not appear to be the case for one of the major developing countries of the early twentieth century—Russia. Trotsky (1977:33) comments: "the reservoir from which the Russian working class formed itself was not the craft-guild, but agriculture, not the city, but the country." It is the freshness and youth of this proletariat to which Trotsky (1977:55) attributes their revolutionary zeal. The proletariat of contemporary developing countries is also more heterogeneous and has less of a proletarian tradition than seems to have been the case in nineteenth century Europe. Findings for Mexico and in Argentina in the 1960s, and for South Korea in the 1970s show that even the industrial proletariat of cities are migrants from villages and small towns, many of whom are of peasant origin (Deyo 1986, Muñoz et al 1982, Marshall, 1978).

These differences in proletarianization between developing societies today and Europe in the 'long' nineteenth century have their demographic components. Because of the substantial fall in mortality and the high rates of fertility, the general rate of population increase is much higher in developing societies, and the capacity of their agrarian structures to absorb this increase, whether in agriculture, crafts, or commerce, is undoubtedly much less. The rural economies of developing societies have been distorted by the uneven modernization described above. Cities not only attract rural migrants because of the growth of employment, they also become places of refuge as a result of rural collapse, places in which petty commerce and personal services are the channels by which urban wealth trickles down to the poor. Net outmigration of proletarians to other countries, which absorbed a substantial part of European population growth, is proportionately less important in contemporary developing societies, despite high rates of international migration from countries such as Mexico (Massey 1988).

Household and Class Formation

The urban households of preindustrial Europe seem to have maintained a domestic organization akin to that of rural households; wealth or poverty had more impact on that organization than did urban or rural residence. The richer households, whether in city or countryside, were the largest, containing nonfamily members; the urban and rural poor had the smallest households (Laslett 1979). Nor did the change from agricultural to industrial or service work necessarily produce changes in household organization. In domestic industry and the first factories, women could, for example, work as members of a household team in much the same way as they did in agriculture. Urban craftsmen and tradesmen made extensive use of family labor in much the same way as did peasant farmers. Likewise, the self-employed and small-scale employers of the urban informal economy in developing countries today have a household organization and use income generating and consumption strategies similar to those of their peasant contemporaries.

The varieties of proletarian experience in nineteenth century Europe affected family organization, changing the relationship between work, home, and community. The Lyon silk weaving neighborhoods had a close association of home, work, and community, but the separation of these spheres is likely to have been greater in mining townships, and pronounced in the new industrial suburbs of Paris. In general, proletarianization seems to have been an important variable in accounting for the changes in the domestic economy and in the roles of different family members. Tilly & Scott (1978:77–79) argue that it is proletarianization, rather than urbanization or industrialization, that has had the most profound effect on the role of women. The increasing prevalence of wage work results in the substitution of a family wage economy for the older family economy in which husband and wife's productive contribution was essential and inseparable (Scott & Tilly 1978: 105). In the family wage economy, married women are less likely to engage in productive work, attending instead to domestic chores and the care of children. The female contribution to the wage economy is made by their unmarried daughters. In the family wage economy, the contribution of all adult household members remains important to family welfare, but roles specialize and overlap less with each other as husbands work away from home, and wives concentrate on domestic chores and on caring for children who will be educated and trained to work outside the household. In this situation, individual strategies of survival and betterment acquire greater salience, accentuating individuality within the family. The link between property, enterprise (whether farm or urban business), and subsistence is broken, permitting adult children and wives greater independence in making consumption choices, creating the possibility of intrahousehold tensions, and resulting in a diversity of household types including female-headed single parent households, single person households, and households of unrelated adults.

Class Formation and Politics

For Marx, the proletariat represents the force of political change. Unconstrained by property, the proletarian has literally nothing to lose. As a class they, unlike the peasantry, are not caught in the contradictions of self-exploitation. Thus, they have no special interests, and even those of family and locality are attenuated. They act as a universal class, joining together as workers in opposition to the bourgeoisie, the owners of capital, to overthrow the regime of private property.

These postulates can be interpreted to suggest a unilinear relation between class position, as determined by the relations of production, and class action. This argument has, possibly, occasioned more debate and stimulated more empirical research than any other in the literature on working-class formation (Przeworski 1985: 47–97). A major critique from within the marxist tradition is that of E. P. Thompson (1963, 1978) in his writings on the making of the English working-class. He emphasizes that the working class is not simply the product of the economic structures created by capitalism, but creates itself culturally and politically through shared historical experiences of economic exploitation.

A more radical qualification of the argument has come from recognizing that proletarianization gives rise to different types of working class and to different patterns of working-class politics, depending on national patterns of industrialization, urbanization, and state formation (Katznelson & Zolberg 1986). Just as proletarianization was not uniform in Europe or the United States, neither were its consequences uniform for class formation and collective action. Singelmann (1978) analyzes the early numerical importance of an industrial proletariat in Europe, and its variation from country to country. He cites the lesser weight of the proletariat in the United States as one of the factors explaining the reduced salience of class-based politics there. Arguing against those who would see an unequivocal link between class position and class action, Katznelson (1986) analyzes the diverse social and political consequences of proletarianization. He identifies four components of proletarianization, each of which can vary over time and between countries, and which result in different types of working-class formation and working-class politics. The first is the economic structure provided by the spread of capitalism, such as the type of industrialization; the second is the way of life associated with industrialization and urbanization, seen in the degree of concentration of workers in urban neighborhoods and the separation of work and residence; third are the dispositions of workers to see themselves as workers with collective interests different from those of employers or nonworkers, mediated by factors such as ethnicity or religion; and fourth are the types of collective action mediated by the nature of the state, whether democratic or authoritarian. The main conclusion of the various articles of the Katznelson & Zolberg (1986) collection is that there is no normal working-class experience in Europe or the United States. As Zolberg (1986) puts it, all the cases are exceptions—the major characteristic of proletarianization is the diversity of working classes and working-class action.

THE PROLETARIAN IN THE MODERN WORLD

Proletarianization remains an issue in class and political analysis in both developed and developing societies. Wallerstein (1983) uses his world-system perspective to elaborate a research agenda for understanding the trajectory of the world working class, the complexity of workers movements, their anti-systematic nature, and the differences between these movements in core and periphery. The issues in the developed world are those of postindustrial society, in which manual wage workers in the secondary sector—the classic proletariat—are now a small fraction of the employed population. Though wage earners predominate, they work in service enterprises and are, in the majority, nonmanual workers. The significance of the increase in nonmanual employment was, to be sure, recognized by Marx ([1894] 1959:299–300). He recognized that the office clerks of his day had a status, income, and proximity to their bosses that made it unlikely they would see themselves as having a common interest with manual workers, but Marx argued that they too would be subject to declining wages. However, Marx and later marxists, with exceptions such as Wright (1985), discussed below, underestimate the significance of occupational upgrading: the rise in real wages brought by capitalism, and the increasing proportions of jobs for highly skilled and relatively autonomous workers to which modern service employment has given rise.

In the developed world, proletarianization appeared until recently to be an irreversible trend, and the major issues in debate concerned the deskilling of white collar work and the consequent proletarianization of the middle class (Abercrombie & Urry 1983). Compared to their status in earlier times, clerical and sales occupations have become relatively less skilled and less well paid (Abercrombie & Urry 1983:53 54, Tilly & Scott 1978:183). Yet the differentials in pay and status between manual and nonmanual work remain, and a certain degree of occupational upgrading has occurred. Wright & Martin (1987) produce data for the United States contradicting Braverman's (1974) thesis and Wright's earlier hypotheses (Wright & Singelmann 1982), postulating the deskilling of labor under capitalism, showing how in the period 1970–1980, an upward grading of jobs appears to have occurred in all sectors of the American economy.

Wright has also sought to accommodate the marxist concern with the polarization of proletariat and bourgeoisie to the realities of contemporary economic trends—in which there has been a substantial increase in both developed and developing countries in white collar work of a professional, technical, and managerial kind. Thus he uses the notion of intermediate classes in capitalist society to denote the contradictory class pressures to which nonmanual occupations are exposed, subject as they are to capital while enjoying the privileges of a closer proximity to the centers of control than do manual workers (Wright 1978). Subsequently, Wright (1985) has examined the factors that place these intermediate classes either on the side of capital or on the side of labor, expanding the notion of exploitation beyond the capital-labor relation to include the zero-sum advantages accruing from expertise and bureaucratic position, as a means of identifying the class position of white collar workers.

The contemporary developing world would appear to be closer to nineteenth century Europe, since many of these countries still have a majority of their population in peasant types of agriculture, and in them industrialization has begun on a significant scale only in the last 50 years. The contrast with nineteenth century Europe is, however, misleading. Developing countries cannot repeat the historical experience of Europe, as if they lived in a world operating within its own time warp. They are part of an integrated world economy in which they use the same technology and produce and consume the same goods as does the developed world, but on a more limited scale. Proletarianization is, consequently, affected by the logic of uneven and combined development, mixing at one and the same time the growth of highly modern sectors of employment and the persistence of apparently archaic forms such as domestic outwork and industrial sweatshops.

Even the archaic forms, present in the substantial growth of informal employment, are often modern in their products and technology, and these forms are closely related, as Benaria & Roldan (1987) show, to the sophisticated sectors of the economy, including multinational enterprises. In developing countries, the classic proletariat—full-time manual workers in manufacturing and construction—is a small proportion of even the nonagricultural population and seems destined to remain so. In Latin America, this proletariat attained its highest point in 1960 when it represented 26.2% of the nonagricultural population; by 1980 it had declined to 23.6% (De Oliveira & Roberts 1989). In contrast, informal workers (self-employed, family workers, and domestic servants) made up 28.7% by 1980, and they are an increasing component of the urban economically active population (Portes 1985, Portes et al 1989). The professional, technical, and managerial classes formed 15.9% of total nonagricultural employment by 1980, and other white-collar workers a further 19%, totalling nearly 35%. This is a substantial proportion in comparison with the 12% that white collar occupations contributed to nonagricultural occupations in England in 1891, when it was already highly industrialized and urbanized (Census of England and Wales 1891: Table 5).

The small size of the industrial proletariat, and their privileged position with respect to peasants or the urban casually employed, has been used to explain the populist character of democratic regimes and their instability. Indeed the weakness of both fundamental classes—bourgeoisie and proletariat—in Latin America leads Touraine (1987) to argue that it is the absence of true social actors in the region that limits the possibilities of economic development and political modernization.[5]

The industrial proletariat of the developing world is dispersed among a large variety of economic sectors, and in small as much as large-scale enterprises. Job mobility between formal and informal sectors is high, as are turnover rates in large plants which can reach over 100% in a year (Escobar 1986). High turnover was, however, also the experience of the German working-class in the late nineteenth century, with fluctuation rates of between 70 and 80% for the unskilled and 40 and 50% for the skilled (Kocka 1986:369). Perhaps more significant in differentiating industrialization in the developing world from that of the developed world or from late nineteenth century Europe is the new industrial division of labor in which many developing countries assemble industrial products for export (Fröbel et al 1980). This occurs because that industrialization often brings an uneven balance of skilled and unskilled jobs in manufacturing. Indeed, almost a majority of the new jobs in manufacturing in developing countries are low-paid and held by women (Standing 1989).

The recent trends that most call proletarianization into question are the growth in both developed and developing countries of what the International Labour Office calls nonstandard forms of work (Marshall 1987, Standing 1988). Two labor force trends are pertinent here. The first is the decline of the rates of participation among both men and women, mainly as a result of education in the younger age cohorts and, to somewhat lesser extent, earlier retirement in the older cohorts. The second trend is the proportionate growth, again in both developed and developing world, of self-employment, of part-time and casual employment, and of female employment. Though these trends may reflect cyclical forces, there is the suggestion that they are produced by structural changes in the world economy: the integration of capital-intensive production on a world scale, and the growth of more flexible forms of production partly as a result of communications technology (Portes & Sassen-Koob 1987). Evidence from the United States suggests that the recent growth of self-employment there is due partly to changes within industries in their production strategies, and partly to the increasing importance of sectors, such as business or professional services, in which self-employment is more prevalent (Steinmetz & Wright 1989).

Under these conditions, variables such as gender and age become as

[5]Bergquist (1986), in contrast, emphasizes the crucial role that all workers, including small-scale producers or semi-proletarians, have played in shaping the history of various Latin American countries. He concentrates on workers in the export sector and emphasizes variables in the specific political economy of the export sector in each country that lead to militancy or cooptation at different periods.

significant an indicator of income and lifestyle as does occupation. Thus, in Wright's analysis of income distribution among the various classes in the United States, the difference accounted for by gender is as great as that accounted for by the difference between middle and working classes, though these differences occur within classes also (Wright 1985). In a series of case studies in Brazilian factories Humphrey (1987) demonstrates how gender actively shapes the work process, with women carrying out jobs as skilled as those of their male counterparts, but under different classifications that are paid less. It is not the technical requirements of work, but the ways in which both men and women view each other's place, both in and outside of work, that determine the rewards such as pay and job security that one gets from employment. Age, too, is important in both developed and underdeveloped countries, but in different ways. In developing countries, the young worker usually earns the most, and wages decline systematically after about age 40, a transition that is often associated with moving from manual work in large-scale enterprises to casual and self employment.

Both age and gender must be understood in the context of the household and its cycles. Indeed the household is as much a key to the analysis of the proletariat as it is to the peasant. The period in which class position could be identified with the male wage earner—a common practice in both Marxist and non-marxist analysis of class—was, at most, a limited one and confined to the developed world. In the interwar years, the real rise in wages for most workers made a reality of the family wage—a wage, earned by the 'breadwinner' sufficient to maintain the whole family. This was the period when the proportion declined of married women who worked for a wage (Tilly & Scott 1978: 197). Before and after the Second World War, though for different reasons, the family wage economy has depended on more than one earner: before, because of low wages and need for children or wife to supplement a husband's income; after, because rising standards of consumption (some of them forced by changes in the environment, necessitating greater expenditures on transport, utilities, housing, etc) and women's own desire to have an independent work career have also had the result that most families have more than one wage-earner.

The modern basis of a family wage economy among the working class is more heterogeneous than that of the nineteenth century. The combinations vary from country to country, and between developed and developing world, but are likely to include casual and part-time work, self-employment, and state unemployment benefits, as well as stable full-time work. The proportions of the nonstandard forms of work are growing, but the way in which they combine within households, dividing or uniting the working class in terms of income, lifestyle, and politics varies according to the specific history of state formation and to the place of a country within the world economy (Pahl 1984, 1989, Mingione 1987, Roberts, 1989).

CONCLUSION

Despite the caveats introduced by research and theoretical argument, the contrast between peasants and proletarians remains suggestive. The peasantry survives in the context of limited resources, which must be managed through locally based relationships. The direct control that a peasant exercises over subsistence is constrained not only by natural events and the strategies of powerful outsiders, but ultimately, because there are only a limited number of positions to fill in peasant society, by land of which there is only so much to subdivide among the potential claimants. Proletarians have their labor as their basic resource, and locality is, if anything, a limitation on their strategies for survival. These differences in the significance of family, locality, and work entail differences between peasant and proletarian in demographic processes, in family relationships, and in politics.

They also have a more general analytic significance. The terms refer, after all, not only to categories of people, but also to ways of surviving and bettering oneself and one's family. Each strategy has its strengths and weaknesses in the contemporary world. Peasant strategies tend to be locally focussed and to involve a careful manipulation of family and community resources. Peasant strategies can be found in cities, in community-based urban social movements, not only among newly arrived rural migrants. Because it is localized and fragmented, peasant resistance benefits from the 'weapons of the weak' and is often hard to break (Scott 1985), but its capacity to change conditions of work for the better is often limited by its parochial nature.

Proletarian strategies are likely to involve a higher degree of spatial mobility, of association with others outside the family or community, and an emphasis on individual or group as against family social mobility. Proletarians are the basis of effective trade union movements, but their resistance in the face of harshly coercive governments is likely to be less enduring than that of peasants. The relative presence of proletarian traditions and strategies as against peasant ones is a useful variable in comparative political research, as Walton (1988) demonstrates in his analysis of the types and incidence of recent urban protest in Latin America.

The debate over proletarianization continues, then, to be relevant to understanding social relations and class formation, but it must take account of factors additional to the contrast between wage-work and peasant household production. In the contemporary world, occupation, and the skills and experiences associated with it, may be a less relevant source of identity than in the immediate past. Unemployment, casual work and declining economic participation rates suggest that capitalism, after creating the proletariat as an ubiquitous category, is no longer based on generalizing full-time wage work in either developed or developing countries. In this situation, both state and community may become the more relevant variables in class formation. The state, whether directly by providing welfare and regulating work, or indirectly by overseeing the deregulation of work and throwing welfare back to the community, defines the interests around which classes form.

The community, in its caring capacity, must often replace the market and the state as the basis for the survival of many categories of people—the old, the infirm, the poor (Friedmann 1989). The revival of interest in the peasant community in some parts of the world is, in part, based on the contemporary failure of both state and capitalism to cater for needs of the rural population. Forms of identity such as gender, generation, religion, or ethnicity, rather than those based on economic relations, also become as, if not more, salient to class formation, than does work.

Combining the proletarianization variables—wage-work and degree of control—with those to do with state and identity is a formidable but necessary challenge for research on class formation. One recent attempt to bring these variables together is through the informal/formal dichotomy, based, mainly, on whether the employment or economic activity is regulated by the state (Portes et al 1989). The conditions of formal employment for the workers, whether in rural or urban areas, depend on the state, either positively through the enforcement of labor rights or negatively through coercion and support for employer rights. The conditions of informal employment are less directly affected by state policies and depend on community resources such as those of the household and of personal networks. There are difficulties in using the formal/informal dichotomy: The variable is a continuous rather than a discrete one; and the significance of informality varies widely from country to country. Yet, as Portes (1985) shows, incorporating the distinction provides new insights into the changing basis of stratification in many parts of the world.

A somewhat different approach focuses on social relations and considers work in all its forms, not just paid work (Pahl 1989). Work obtains its significance from the different types of social relation in which it is embedded—those generated by different forms of employment, by gender, by generation, or by exchange. Pahl (1989) points out that new inequalities in the distribution of work, and the class interests they generate, are often hidden by the focus on paid work. For instance, the decline in paid employment among certain categories of a population may result in a heavier burden for those doing other forms of work such as domestic work.

These issues may seem a far cry from the classic debate over peasant and proletarian, but the research focus remains the same. Conditions of work are crucial variables in explaining social behavior, whether in terms of household roles, voting preferences, or collective action.

Literature Cited

Abercrombie, N., Urry, J. 1983. *Capital, Labour and the Middle Classes*. London: Allen & Unwin

Adelman, I., Taylor, J. E., Vogel, S. 1988. Life in a Mexican village: A SAM perspective. *J. Dev. Stud.* 25:5–24

Benaria, L., Roldan, M. 1987. *The Crossroads of Class and Gender*. Chicago: Univ. Chicago Press

Bergquist, C. W. 1986. *Labor in Latin America: Comparative Essays on Chile, Argentina, Venezuela, and Colombia*. Stanford, Calif: Stanford Univ. Press

Berkner, L. K. 1976. Inheritance, land tenure and peasant family structure: a German regional comparison. See Goody et al 1976, pp. 71–95

Bernstein, H., Campbell, J., eds. 1985. *Contradictions of Accumulation in Africa: Studies in Economy and State*. Beverly Hills: Sage

Brading, D. A. ed. 1984. *Caudillo and Peasant in the Mexican Revolution*. Cambridge: Cambridge Univ. Press

Braverman, H. 1974. *Labor and Monopoly Capital*. New York: Monthly Rev.

Brenner, R. 1985. Agrarian class structure and economic development in pre-industrial Europe. In *The Brenner Debate: Agrarian Class Structure and Economic Development in Pre-industrial Europe*, ed. T. H. Aston, C. Philpin, pp. 10–63. Cambridge: Cambridge Univ. Press

Census of England and Wales. 1891. Vol III. 1893. London: HMSO

Chang, Y. 1989. Peasants go to town: the rise of commercial farming in Korea. *Hum. Organ.* 48:236–51

Chayanov, A. V. 1966. *The Theory of the Peasant Economy*. (Trans. and ed. D. B. Thorner, B. Kerblay, R. E. F. Smith). Homewood, Ill: Irwin

Coale, A. J. 1986. The decline of fertility in Europe since the eighteenth century as a chapter in demographic history. See Coale & Watkins 1986, pp. 1–30

Coale, A. J., Watkins, S. M. eds. 1986. *The Decline of Fertility in Europe*. Princeton: Princeton Univ. Press

Cottereau, A. 1986. The distinctiveness of working-class cultures in France, 1848–1900. See Katznelson & Zolberg 1986, p. 111–54

Dalton, G., ed., 1967. *Tribal and Peasant Economies*. Austin: Univ. Texas Press

De Janvry, A. 1981. *The Agrarian Question and Reformism in Latin America*. Baltimore: Johns Hopkins Univ. Press

De la Pena, G. 1988. Local and regional power in Mexico. *Texas Papers on Mexico, No. 88-01*. Austin: Univ. Tex.

De Oliveira, O., Roberts, B. R. 1989. Los antecedentes de la crisis urbana: urbanizacion y transformacion ocupacional en America Latina, 1940–1980. In *Crisis Urbano en el Cono Sur*, ed. M. Lombardi, D. Veiga, pp. 23–80. Montevideo, Uruguay: Ediciones Banda Azul

Deyo, F. C. 1986. Industrialization and the structuring of Asian Labor movements: the "gang of four." In *Confrontation, Class Consciousness, and the Labor Process*, ed. M. Hanagan, C. Stephenson, pp. 167–198. New York: Greenwood

Escobar, A. 1986. *Con el Sudor de tu Frente: Mercado de Trabajo y Clase Obrera en Guadalajara*. Guadalajara, Mexico: El Colegio de Jalisco

Figueroa, A. 1984. *Capitalist Development and the Peasant Economy in Peru*. Cambridge: Cambridge Univ. Press

Foster, G. M. 1967. *Tzintzuntzan: Mexican Peasants in a Changing World*. Boston: Little Brown

Foweraker, J. 1981. *The Struggle for Land*. Cambridge: Cambridge Univ. Press

Friedmann, J. 1989. The dialectic of reason. *Int. J. Urban Reg. Res.* 13:220–36

Fröbel, F., Heinrichs, J., Kreye, O. 1980. *The New International Division of Labor*. Cambridge: Cambridge Univ. Press

Geertz, C. 1963. *Agricultural Involution*. Berkeley: Univ. California Press

Goodman, D., Redclift, M. 1981. *From Peasant to Proletarian*. Oxford: Basil Blackwell

Goody, J. R., Thirsk, J., Thompson, E. P., eds. 1976. *Family and Inheritance: Rural Society in Western Europe, 1200–1800*. Cambridge: Cambridge Univ. Press

Halperin, R. H. 1988. *Economies Across Cultures*. New York: St. Martin's

Hart, K. 1987. Rural-urban migration in West Africa. In *Migrants, Workers and the Social Order*, ed. J. Eades, pp. 65–81. London: Tavistock

Hyden, G. 1980. *Beyond Ujamaa in Tanzania: Underdevelopment and an Uncaptured Peasantry*. Berkeley: Univ. California Press

Hilton, R. H. 1975. *The English Peasantry in the Later Middle Ages*. Oxford: Oxford Univ. Press

Hobsbawm, E., Ranger, T. O. 1983. *The Invention of Tradition*. Cambridge: Cambridge Univ. Press

Humphrey, J. 1987. *Gender and Work in the Third World*. London: Tavistock

Hyden, G. 1980. *Beyond Ujamaa in Tanzania: Underdevelopment and an Uncaptured Peasantry*. Berkeley: Univ. Calif. Press.

International Labour Office (ILO). 1986. *Economically Active Population: Estimates and*

Projects 1950–2025, Vol 5. Geneva: Int. Labor. Organ. (ILO)

International Labour Office. 1988. *Year Book of Labour Statistics.* Geneva: ILO

Katznelson, I. 1986. Working-class formation: constructing cases and comparisons. See Katznelson & Zolberg 1986, pp 3–41

Katznelson, I., Zolberg, A. R. 1986. *Working-Class Formation: Nineteenth-Century Patterns in Western Europe and the United States.* Princeton: Princeton Univ. Press

Knight, A. J. 1986. *The Mexican Revolution.* 2 vols. Cambridge: Cambridge Univ. Press

Kocka, J. 1986. Problems of working-class formation in Germany. See Katznelson & Zolberg 1986, pp. 279–351

Kroeber, A. L. 1948. *Anthropology.* New York: Harcourt & Brace

Laite, A. J. 1981. *Industrial Development and Migrant Labour.* Manchester: Manchester Univ. Press.

Laslett, P. 1979. *The World We Have Lost.* London: Methuen

Lawton, R., ed., 1978. *The Census and Social Structure.* London: Frank Cass

Levine, D. C. 1977. *Family Formation in an Age of Nascent Capitalism.* New York: Academic

Levine, D. C. ed. 1984. *Proletarianization and Family History.* Orlando: Academic

Levine, D. C. 1984. Production, reproduction, and the proletarian family in England, 1500–1851. See Levine 1984, pp. 87–127

Lipton, M. 1984. Family, fungibility and formality: rural advantages of informality. In *Human Resources, Employment and Development,* ed. S. Amin, pp. 189–242. London: Macmillan

Long, N. E., Roberts, B. R., eds., 1978. *Peasant Cooperation and Capitalist Development in Central Peru.* Austin: Univ. Tex. Press for the Inst. Latin Am. Stud.

Long, N. E., Roberts, B. R. 1984. *Miners, Peasants and Entrepreneurs.* Cambridge: Cambridge Univ. Press

MacEwen-Scott, A. 1979. Who are the self-employed? In *Casual Work and Poverty in Third World Cities,* ed. R. Bromley, C. Gerry, pp. 105–29. Chichester: Wiley

Malefakis, E. E. 1970. *Agrarian Reform and Peasant Revolution in Spain.* New Haven: Yale Univ. Press

Mallon, F. E. 1983. *The Defense of Community in the Peru's Central Highlands.* Princeton: Princeton Univ. Press

Marshall, A. 1978. *El Mercado de Trabajo en el Capitalismo Periferico.* Santiago de Chile: PISPAL

Marshall, A. 1987. Non-standard employment practices in Latin America. *Discuss. Pap. OP/06/1987.* Geneva: International Inst. Lab. Stud.

Marx, K. [1867] 1974. *Capital.* Vol I. London: Dent, Everyman's

Marx, K. [1894] 1959. *Capital.* Vol III. London: Lawrence Wishart

Massey, D. S. 1988. Economic development and international migration in comparative perspective. *Popul. Dev. Rev.* 14:383–413

Meillassoux, C. 1975. *Femmes, Greniers e Capitaux.* Paris: Francois Maspero

Mingione, E. 1987. Urban survival strategies, family structure and informal practices. In *The Capitalist City: Global Restructuring and Community Politics,* ed. M. P. Smith, J. R. Feagin, pp. 297–322. Oxford: Blackwell

Moore, B. 1966. *The Social Origins of Dictatorship and Democracy.* Boston: Beacon

Muñoz, H., De Oliveira, O., Stern, C. 1982. *Mexico City: Industrialization, Migration and the Labour Force, 1930–1970. Selected Studies on the Dynamics, Patterns and Consequences of Migration, I, No. 46.* Paris: Unesco

Pahl, R. E. 1984. *Divisions of Labour.* Oxford: Blackwell

Pahl, R. E. 1989. From 'informal economy' to 'forms of work'. In *Industrial Societies: Crisis and Division in Western Capitalism and State Socialism,* ed. R. Scase, pp. 90–119. London: Unwin Hyman

Paige, J. 1975. *Agrarian Revolution: Peasant Movements and Export Agriculture in the Underdeveloped World.* New York: Free

Paige, J. 1983. Social theory and peasant revolution in Vietnam and Guatemala. *Theory Soc.* 12:699–737

Parsons, E. W. 1936. *Mitla, Town of the Souls.* Chicago: Univ. Chicago Press

Polanyi, K. 1957. The economy as instituted process. In *Trade and Market in the Early Empires,* ed. K. Polanyi, C. M. Arensberg, H. W. Pearson, pp. 243–270. Glencoe, Ill: Free

Popkin, S. L. 1979. *The Rational Peasant: the Political Economy of Rural Society in Vietnam.* Berkeley: Univ. California Press

Portes, A. 1985. Latin American class structures. *Lat. Am. Res. Rev.* 20:7–39

Portes, A., Sassen-Koob, S. 1987. Making it underground. *Am. J. Sociol.* 93:30–61

Portes, A., Castells, M., Benton, L., eds. 1989. *The Informal Economy.* Baltimore: Johns Hopkins Univ. Press

Przeworski, A. 1985. *Capitalism and Social Democracy.* Cambridge: Cambridge Univ. Press

Roberts, B. R. 1978. Agrarian organization and urban development. In *Manchester and Sao Paulo,* ed. J. D. Wirth, R. L. Jones, pp. 77–105. Stanford: Stanford Univ. Press

Roberts, B. R. 1989. The other working class:

uncommitted labor in Britain, Spain and Mexico. In *Cross-national Research in Sociology*, ed. M. L. Kohn, pp. 352–72. Newbury Park, Calif: Sage

Salisbury, R. F. 1970. *Vunamami: Economic Transformation in a Traditional Society.* Berkeley: Univ. Calif. Press

Scott, J. C. 1976. *The Moral Economy of the Peasant: Rebellion and Subsistence in Southeast Asia.* New Haven & London: Yale Univ. Press

Scott, J. C. 1985. *Weapons of the Weak: Everyday Forms of Peasant Resistance.* New Haven: Yale Univ. Press

Shanin, T. 1972. *The Awkward Class.* Oxford: Oxford Univ. Press

Shanin, T., ed., 1987. *Peasants and Peasant Societies.* Oxford: Blackwell. 2nd ed.

Singelmann, J. 1978. *From Agriculture to Services: the Transformation of Industrial Employment.* Beverly Hills: Sage

Skocpol, T. 1979. *States and Social Revolutions: a Comparative Analysis of France, Russia and China.* Cambridge: Cambridge Univ. Press

Somers, M. J. 1989. Workers of the world, compare! *Contemp. Sociol.* 18:325–329

Standing, G. 1988. European unemployment, insecurity and flexibility: a social dividend solution. *World Employment Programme Labour Market Analysis Working Paper, No. 23.* Geneva: ILO

Standing, G. 1989. Global feminisation through flexible labour. *World Employment Prog. Lab. Market Analysis Work. Pap.* No. 31. Geneva: ILO

Steinmetz, G., Wright, E. O. 1989. The fall and rise of the petty bourgeoisie; changing patterns of self-employment in the post-war United States. *Am. J. Sociol.* 94:973–1018

Stephens, J. D. 1989. Democratic transition and breakdown in Western Europe, 1870–1939: a test of the Moore thesis. *Am. J. Sociol.* 94:1019–77

Thompson, E. P. 1963. *The Making of the English Working Class.* New York: Vintage

Thompson, E. P. 1976. The grid of inheritance: a comment. See Goody et al 1976, pp. 328–60

Thompson, E. P. 1978. *The Poverty of Theory and Other Essays.* London: Merlin

Tilly, C. 1978. The historical study of vital processes. In *Historical Studies of Chang-ing Fertility*, ed. C. Tilly, pp. 3–56. Princeton: Princeton Univ. Press

Tilly, C. 1984. Demographic origins of the European proletariat. See Levine 1984, pp. 1–85

Tilly, L., Scott, J. 1978. *Women, Work, and Family.* New York: Holt, Rinehart & Winston

Touraine, A. 1987. *Actores Sociales y Sistemas Politicos en America Latina.* Santiago de Chile: Prealc

Trotsky, L. 1977. (First published in England, 1932–1933). *The History of the Russian Revolution.* London: Pluto

Tutino, J. 1986. *From Insurrection to Revolution in Mexico.* Princeton: Princeton Univ. Press

Wallerstein, I. ed. 1983. *Labor in the World Social Structure.* Beverly Hills, Calif: Sage

Walton, J. 1988. Debt, protest, and the state in Latin America. In *Power and Protest: Contemporary Social Movements in Latin America*, ed. S. Eckstein, pp. 299–328. Berkeley: Univ. Calif. Press

Watkins, S. C. 1986. Conclusion. See Coale & Watkins 1987, pp. 420–49

Wolf, E. R. 1955. Types of Latin American peasantry: a preliminary discussion. *Am. Anthro.* 57:452–71

Wolf, E. R. 1966. *Peasants.* Englewood Cliffs, NJ: Prentice-Hall

Wolf, E. R. 1982. *Europe and the People without History.* Berkeley: Univ. Calif. Press

Wolpe, H. 1972. Capitalism and cheap labour-power in South Africa: from segregation to apartheid. *Econ. Soc.* 1:425–56

Wright, E. O. 1978. *Class, Crisis and the State.* London: New Left Books

Wright, E. O. 1985. *Classes.* London: New Left Books

Wright, E. O., Martin, B., 1987. The transformation of the American class structure. *Am. J. Scoiol.* 93:1–29

Wright, E. O., Singelmann, J. 1982. Proletarianisation in the changing American class structure. *Am. J. Sociol.* 88 (Suppl) 176–209

Wrigley, E. A. 1983. The growth of population in eighteenth-century England: a conundrum resolved. *Past Present* 98:121–50

Zolberg, A. R. 1986. How many exceptionalisms? See Katznelson & Zolberg 1986, pp. 397–455

Annu. Rev. Sociol. 1990. 16:379–403

DIVORCE AND THE AMERICAN FAMILY

Frank F. Furstenberg, Jr.

Department of Sociology, University of Pennsylvania, Philadelphia, Pennsylvania 19104

KEY WORDS: stepfamily, single parent, divorce, father's remarriage, kinship

Abstract

This paper reviews the cultural, demographic, economic, and social sources that have produced a transformation in the institution of marriage over the past century. It describes trends in marriage and remarriage that have altered the life course of children in families. The consequences of growing levels of marital instability for children are described. Particular attention is devoted to the changing parenting system and alterations in the kinship system of children whose parents divorced and remarried. Some problems in interpreting the effects of divorce on children are identified. The paper concludes with a discussion of public policy issues related to divorce and remarriage.

INTRODUCTION: SOURCES OF MARITAL INSTABILITY

Americans have always had a higher propensity to divorce than do Europeans and people of North Atlantic countries. A century ago, when voluntary dissolution was still uncommon, divorce rates in the country were unusually high by European standards (Good 1963). This trend has continued throughout the twentieth century. In the 1930s, the incidence of divorce was ten times higher in the United States than in Britain or Canada and four to five times the rate in Scandinavia (Carter & Glick 1976). These relative differences have narrowed during the past 50 years, but the United States still has the highest rate of marital instability among developed nations, by a considerable margin, (Davis 1985, Lye 1988).

379

0360-0572/90/0815-0379$02.00

It is not obvious why divorce is a more popular solution to marital discontent in this country than elsewhere. Many scholars who have studied the matter believe that divorce is an inevitable byproduct of a marriage system that puts a high premium on voluntary choice and that values emotional satisfaction above all (Goode 1956, Bohannon 1970). Even before the industrial revolution, Americans were unusually willing to give young people a high amount of discretion in mate selection. Broader kinship concerns figured little into marriage decisions, and parents exercised minimal control either in the timing of marriage or in children's choice of a partner (Rothman 1987). Partly for these reasons, Americans married much earlier than Europeans, a fact which may have contributed to the instability of unions.

Apart from the limited degree of control exercised by the kinship network on married couples, Americans have long regarded marriage as a central locus for emotional gratification (Degler 1980). From the 1930s and onward, a central focus of family sociology was the study and measurement of marital compatibility (Lasch 1977). This professional preoccupation seemed to capture the growing concern of Americans with the personal benefits of marriage, companionship and intimacy. The historical movement from a "contractual marriage," founded on instrumental exchange, to a "companionate marriage," supported by mutual interests and emotional exchange, was first noted by Ernest Burgess (1948) and heralded by a host of family scholars, who believed that the institution of marriage was evolving into a more personally rewarding arrangement.

The more that marriage was touted for its personal benefits, the less stability was valued for its own sake (Swidler 1980). As emotional gratification became the sine qua non of marriage, divorce became an indispensable element in the institution of matrimony, permitting couples to rectify poor choices (Goode 1956). Gradually, the standard shifted from one which required couples to remain married even if they were not in love to one which virtually demanded divorce unless they remained in love.

These shifting cultural standards, no doubt, also reflected a change in the economic basis of marriage (Huber & Spitze 1988). The gender-based division of labor that created a strong interdependency between men and women began to disintegrate in the latter half of the twentieth century. Married women steadily increased their participation in the labor force (Ross & Sawhill 1975, Bianchi & Spain 1986). The increase has been most spectacular among those with younger children, who previously were totally reliant on the economic support of their spouses. The quest for a better standard of living partially brought about these changes. More recently, women have insisted on a large role in the market place as a source of power and independence (Sorensen & McLanahan 1987). Though difficult to demonstrate empirically, it is probably the case that women have also entered and remained in the labor force as an insurance policy against the increasingly likely prospect of having to support themselves and their children (Cherlin 1988, Huber & Spitze 1988).

This shift in cultural norms and social roles has been described in economic terms by Becker (1981) as the reduction of gender-specific capital within marriage. In the past, specialization of tasks within the family fostered exchange, encouraging women to trade domestic labor, principally childcare, for men's greater earning capacity outside the home. During the second half of the twentieth century, this bartering system has disintegrated as women entered the job market and domestic services could be more easily purchased outside the home. Declining fertility rates and the diminished value of domestic labor have depreciated the value of full-time motherhood. At the same time, the growth of a service-based economy has expanded the opportunities for women in the labor force, further eroding the claim of male superiority in the work force (Fuchs 1983).

While women have indisputably increased their involvement in the labor market, it is not as clear whether men have responded by expanding their involvement in domestic activities (Bernard 1981, Huber & Spitze 1988, Goode 1982, Lamb 1987). Evidence suggests that men are more actively involved in parenthood, but it is still an open question whether they are assuming a larger share of household tasks (Presser 1990, Thompson & Walker 1989). Egalitarian marriage—in which partners more or less equally share economic and domestic tasks—may be more difficult to achieve, or it may take time to modify longstanding patterns of behavior (Ross & Sawhill 1975). Undoubtedly, the current high rates of divorce reflect the present state of role conflict and ambiguity within our marriage system—the unwillingness of women to settle for an unfair share of family tasks and the reluctance of men to give up the advantages that they traditionally enjoyed when they contributed most or all of the household income (Becker et al 1977).

In a very real sense, then, the causes of the high rate of marital instability are "over determined" by a confluence of cultural, economic, and political change, any one of which might have brought about a significant revision of the institution of marriage. In combination, they have profoundly shaken the commitment to lifelong marriage. These trends have occurred in all Western nations (Davis 1985), but they have been most dramatic in the United States because of a preexisting tendency toward a voluntaristic form of marriage. There seems little reason to predict that the currently high levels of divorce in the United States or the growing rates of divorce in other Western nations will subside in the near future (Lesthaege & Meekers 1986). Divorce has become an intrinsic part of the family system.

Recent Trends in Divorce and Remarriage

For the past hundred years, the rate of divorce (divorces per 1000 *marriages* until 1920; after 1920, divorces per 1000 *married women*) has risen more than ten-fold (Cherlin 1981). As an indicator of marital instability, it must be said that divorce rates have certain limitations. A century ago, formal divorce was difficult to obtain and undoubtedly dissolution resulting from desertion was undercounted. Today, divorce rates have leveled off but the rising numbers of informal marriages formed by cohabitation go unrecorded. Moreover, when the incidence of marriage drops, as it has in the past decade, the divorce rate necessarily will probably fall at least temporarily. This happens because fewer couples in the early stages of marriage (those at highest risk of divorce) are in the pool of married persons. Divorce rates also can be affected by changes in the age composition of the marriage population or the duration of marriages.

Recently, demographers have calculated a more precise measure of marital stability—the proportion of a given marriage cohort that voluntarily ends their union by a fixed time interval. A century ago, fewer than one in ten marriages were ended by divorce (after 40 years). By mid-century, slightly under a third of all marriages contracted would end in divorce (Preston & McDonald 1979, Cherlin 1981). Today, if projections prove to be correct, at least half of all those marrying will divorce. Many experts think that the rate of voluntary dissolution is actually much higher than that because a number of couples who separate may never bother to obtain a divorce. Disputing the claims of some demographers that divorce is leveling off, if not declining (Norton & Moorman 1986), Castro-Martin and Bumpass (1989) estimate that close to two thirds of all first marriages contracted in the 1980s will end in separation or divorce.

Marital disruption, of course, is not randomly distributed. The risk of dissolution in first marriages is far higher for younger couples than those marrying after their early twenties. Similarly high school dropouts have twice the rate of marital breakup as those with at least some college. And the rate of disruption is about 50% higher among blacks (net of socio-economic status) (Carter & Glick 1976, Sweet & Bumpass 1987, Castro-Martin & Bumpass 1989).

Second marriages have a higher risk of divorce than do first marriages (McCarthy 1978, Weed 1980). Cherlin (1978), among others, has argued that this risk can be traced to the strains on remarriage involving children (cf Bohannon 1985). The ambiguity of stepfamily roles jeopardizes the formation of strong marital bonds (White & Booth 1985). Cherlin's hypothesis of "incomplete institutionalization" has been the subject of some debate as researchers have begun to probe the link between stepfamily life and divorce. Some researchers have argued that second marriages are more prone to divorce principally because those who enter second marriages include individuals who are willing to leave an unhappy relationship or who are more vulnerable to marital instability (Halliday 1980, Furstenberg & Spanier 1984). Castro-Martin & Bumpass (1989) discovered that virtually all the risk associated with second marriages could be explained by compositional differences. In other words, remarriers constitute a different risk pool than first marriages because of lack of education and because they married prematurely the first time.

Children and Divorce

The growing instability of marriages has altered the course of childhood during the past century; the change has been most sharply experienced in the past several decades as divorce has become a common event in children's lives. At the turn of the century, general mortality rates were still quite high. Even though voluntary disruption was rare, children had a substantial risk of losing a parent through death. Uhlenberg (1983) has estimated that about a quarter of all children lost one or both parents by age 15. The added risk of divorce and desertion is difficult to estimate, but perhaps as many as a third of all children spent time in a single parent family by their mid-teens.

The overall rate of marital instability due to death and divorce probably declined by mid-century. Less than a tenth of all children witnessed the death of a parent by their mid-teens. The incidence of separation and divorce was correspondingly greater, but it still had not reached epidemic proportions. While it is difficult to arrive at a precise estimate, it seems unlikely that more than a quarter of all children born in the 1940s and 1950s spent time in a single parent family—a decline in the numbers of those experiencing disruption, compared to numbers from the beginning of the century. The world of childhood changed after the mid-1960s when both the incidence of divorce and out-of-wedlock childbearing soared. Several demographers have attempted to calculate the odds of a child born today spending time in a single parent family by their mid-teens. Their estimates range widely depending on their projections of the future and the data source. Hofferth (1985), for example, figured that close to three fourths of all children either would be born to a single parent or would lose a parent to divorce. Bumpass (1984) and Glick (1984) in separate estimates arrive at a lower figure—about three out of five. Recently Bumpass & Sweet (1989) calculated that 44% of children will live in a single parent household by age 16.

The odds of growing up in a single-parent family or, at least spending some time in one, are significantly greater for blacks. Three fifths of all black children are born to single mothers, most of whom will remain unmarried for at least a few years (US Bureau of the Census 1989b, Furstenberg 1987). Rates of marital instability are also much higher for blacks (Sweet & Bumpass 1987). Extrapolating from current figures, fewer than one black child in five born in the 1980s will spend their entire childhood living with both of their biological parents.

For most children, black and white alike, living in a single-parent household is a transitional status. Marriages dissolve, but most unmarried and formerly married parents enter or re-enter marriage. This means that most children of single parents in time acquire a stepparent. The average length of time in a single-parent household is about six years, but it is likely to be much shorter for children who encounter divorce at an early age (Bumpass 1984). About a quarter of all children born in the late 1960s could be expected to acquire a stepparent before reaching the age of 18 (Furstenberg et al 1983). That figure might be slightly higher for children born today. Many children who enter stepfamilies in early life will see the breakup of those unions before they reach the age of 18. The National Survey of Children disclosed that more than a third of all children whose parents remarried had already witnessed a second divorce by the early teens. Overall, it seems likely that close to 15% of *all* children will go through at least two family disruptions by late adolescence. This estimate includes only recorded marriages. If cohabitational unions were included, the figure would be significantly larger.

Since the middle of this century, then, family life has become considerably less stable and predictable. Half or more of all children will spend some time living in a single-parent family. At least a quarter will enter a stepfamily, and about half of these children will see the breakup of this new family unit before the end of their teens. Rates of family flux are particularly high for black children. The following section traces some of the consequences of marital instability for adults, children, and society at large.

Divorce Consequences

The most obvious effect of divorce is that it typically brings about a sudden reconfiguration of the family. The transition from a two-parent household to a single-parent household disrupts the parenting system and usually reduces the economic support available to children. Custody and economic support legally are separate issues, but in fact they are inextricably related.

Custody Practices

Until the end of the nineteenth century, men were generally awarded custody of their children following a divorce (Halem 1980, Weitzman 1981). But as divorce became more common, children generally remained with their mothers. Specialized roles within the family led courts to favor maternal custody. Possibly, too, as children became less of an economic asset and more of a responsibility, men were less eager to maintain their rights. Recently, custody dispositions have been reconsidered in light of the changing roles of women and the recognition that bonds between noncustodial fathers and their children have become extremely tenuous. In the late 1960s and 1970s, the "divorce revolution" brought about a demand for joint custody (Weitzman 1985)—the sharing of parental responsibility for the child.

Even in states such as California, which promoted joint custody, most women continued to maintain principal responsibility for childcare. In the most systematic investigation of how joint custody actually operates, Albiston, Mnookin & Maccoby (1990) have followed a sample of California families from the time of separation for several years. They show that even among couples who are awarded joint custody of their children, women assume a greater measure of childcare over time while men often diminish their contact. Their study confirms the impression of many previous studies that custody arrangements frequently are revised following divorce (Spanier & Furstenberg 1984, Furstenberg 1987). Joint physical custody is an especially unstable arrangement, but sole custody is often informally renegotiated as well. Older children are especially likely to shift residence, often going to live with their fathers for a time during adolescence. About twice as many children in one-parent families lived with their fathers at 15 to 17 as children under the age of two (13.1 vs. 6.5%) in 1980 (Sweet & Bumpass 1987).

The enthusiasm over joint physical custody waned during the 1980s. For a brief time, it was viewed as a panacea for maintaining parental responsibilities in the wake of divorce. Most studies have shown that only a small minority of formerly married parents are willing and able to adopt this arrangement (Emery 1988). It is still an open question whether children benefit if they divide their time between two households. It also remains to be seen whether joint legal custody (as opposed to joint physical custody) is a useful device for maintaining parental collaboration and reenforcing the role of the parent who does not have physical custody.

The Economic Consequences of Marital Instability

Divorce typically is a transitional family status. Eventually, nearly three fourths of all men and about three fifths of all women reenter marriage (Spanier & Furstenberg, 1987). But the interval between unions has been growing as remarriage rates have slowed during the past decade (Cherlin forthcoming). Men remarry more quickly than women in large measure due to the greater availability of marriage partners. Males typically marry women of younger ages whereas women generally face a more restricted marriage pool. This differential rate of remarriage contributes to the significant economic disadvantage that formerly married women experience, especially those with children.

Abundant evidence shows that the economic effects of marriage are quite divergent for men and women. Males generally leave marriage with much greater earning capacity (Kahn & Kamerman 1988, Duncan & Hoffman 1985). Moreover, they typically do not bear a fair share of child support when children remain in the mother's custody. Since almost 90% of women retain physical custody of the children, most females are severely disadvantaged by divorce.

Varying estimates of the size of this disadvantage have been calculated (Weitzman 1985, Weiss 1979, Duncan & Hoffman 1985, Peterson 1989). Using longitudinal data from the Panel on Income Dynamics, Duncan & Hoffman (1985) show that men actually improve their economic status following a divorce, doing about as well as men in intact families. In contrast, women experience a significant drop in income, which lasts for several years. Gradually, most women recover, that is, return to the income level prior to divorce, though they do much less well than women in stably married families. Most of the recovery occurs as a result of remarriage. Women who remain unmarried continue to experience a sizable economic loss despite the fact that they greatly increase their participation in the labor market. One present study suggests that over time, women who remain divorced improve their position in the labor market substantially (Peterson 1989).

Alimony and child support are potentially important mechanisms for redressing the imbalances created by divorce. The changing economic status of women and the movement to no-fault divorce may have reduced the claim for alimony (Weitzman 1985). Data collected by the Census Bureau shows a sharp decline in the past decade in alimony payments. More surprising is the persistent pattern of low child support provided by noncustodial fathers to their children. In 1985, 61% of single women living with children under 21 had child support agreements; the remainder had no award. Of those who had a legal award and were entitled to support, just half were receiving their full payments (US Bureau of the Census 1989a). In other words, fewer than one custodial mother in four was receiving regular and full child support. The prevalence of child support agreements has remained relatively stable over the past seven years despite strenuous efforts to increase compliance. Moreover, the actual amount of payments, adjusted for inflation, has declined.

Interpretation of these trends is complicated by changes in the composition of the pool of custodial mothers. More women today are never married, lowering, evidently, the level of support awards (because paternity was not established) and the compliance. Moreover, more separated and divorced women are working now than in the late 1970s; this fact may lead courts to reduce court-ordered child support. Still, nearly half of all separated and divorced women were unable to obtain awards despite a desire to do so. Many of these women are not earning sufficient incomes to provide adequate support to their children. In 1985, 26% of divorced mothers, 47% of separated mothers; and 58% of never married mothers were living in poverty. Women who received child support payments had substantially lower rates of poverty though it is not clear whether or how much income transfers per se accounted for the reduction of poverty (US Bureau of the Census 1989a).

Nevertheless, lack of adequate child support places great economic strain on women who often suffer the twin disadvantages of low earnings capacity and poor marriage prospects (Ellwood 1988).

Formerly married black women and their children are especially vulnerable to all these sources of poverty. They have limited earnings capacity, face bleak prospects of remarriage, and receive less help from noncustodial fathers than do previously married white women. In 1986, black separated women between the ages of 15 and 44 were 28% more likely to be living below the poverty line than were white separated women (52 vs. 40.5%), and black divorced women were more than twice as likely to be poor—61.3 vs 25.2% (US Bureau of the Census 1988).

The income figures cited above provide only a rough measure of the economic consequences of divorce. Studies of the process of divorce reveal that downward mobility has many far-reaching effects on family life (Newman 1988). Divorce often requires the sale of the family home and unsettling residential changes. Mothers may be forced to increase work hours, change childcare arrangements, and rely more heavily on the domestic contributions of children (Weiss 1979). These changes are not always unwelcome or wholly negative, but they usually are stressful for parents and children. McLanahan (1988) has speculated that the indirect effects of rapid economic decline frequently contribute to the adverse consequences of divorce for children. Several studies have examined the economic ramifications of divorce for the adjustment of women and children in single-parent households (Brandwein et al 1974, Weiss 1975, Arendell 1986, Peterson 1989). In an excellent summary of the economic effects of divorce, Garfinkel & McLanahan conclude:

> According to official government data, about half of all children and mothers in families headed by women suffer from the most extreme form of economic insecurity—poverty. No other major demographic group is so poor, and none stays poor longer . . . Even mother-only familes who are not poor are subject to economic insecurity and other forms of instability . . . In view of the instabilities confronting such families, it is not surprising that family members suffer disproportionately from mental health problems and use a disproportionate share of community mental health services. (1986:167–68)

The Declining Involvement of Fathers

One reason why noncustodial fathers contribute so little child support is that most sharply reduce their involvement in childrearing after divorce. Whether they discontinue child support because they reduce contact or vice versa is the subject of some debate (Seltzer et al 1989). The sources of disengagement are not well understood. Some fathers are pushed out of the family, but most seem to retreat from paternal responsibility when they no longer reside with their children. Elsewhere Cherlin and I have argued that many men view marriage and childcare as an inseparable role-set (Furstenberg & Cherlin, forthcoming). Accordingly, men often sever ties with their children in the course of establishing distance from their former wives. Remarriage by either former partner usually hastens this process of disengagement. Geographical mobility, increased economic demands, and new family responsibilities, which often accompany remarriage, may erode the tenuous bonds between noncustodial fathers and their children.

Table 1 reports on data from the second wave of The National Survey of Children, an ongoing study of a representative sample of children who have been followed over time. In 1981 over 400 children between the ages of 11 and 16, who had experienced marital disruption, were asked to provide information on their current relations with their noncustodial parent (Furstenberg & Nord 1985). All indicators suggest a strikingly low level of contact, especially among the children who have not lived with their fathers for ten or more years. Few of these children have regular contact with their noncustodial parent; indeed, most have not seen him in the past year or have ever visited his

Table 1   Children's relations with their outside biological parents by duration since separation and gender of parent (percentages, U.S. children aged 11–16, 1981)

Relation items	Duration since separation (in years)			Total of outside fathers	Total of outside mothers
	< 2	2–9	10+		
When child last saw outside parent					
1–30 days ago	74	53	28	40	64
31–365 days ago	24	15	19	18	29
1–4 years ago	2	12	5	7	4
5+ years ago	—	20	49	35	3
		$p < .01$[a]			$p < .01$[b]
In a Typical Month:					
Number of times child sees outside parent					
Never	31	55	74	64	42
1–3 days	20	21	13	16	39
4+ days	49	25	13	20	18
Mean number of days	7.4	2.0	2.2	2.5	4.5
		$p < .01$			$p < .05$
Number of times child sleeps over at outside parent's					
Never	60	71	89	80	42
1–3 days	22	19	7	12	40
4+ days	18	10	5	8	18
Mean number of days	1.6	0.8	0.5	0.7	2.9
		$p < .01$			$p < .01$

Table 1 *(continued)*

Relation items	Duration since separation (in years)			Total of outside fathers	Total of outside mothers
	< 2	2–9	10+		
Child talks with outside parent on telephone					
Never		41	70	55	18
1–3 times	48	28	17	23	39
4+ times	46	31	13	22	43
Mean number of times	8.1	4.3	1.8	3.1	4.1
		$p < .01$			$p < .01$
Child receives a letter from the outside parent					
Never	92	92	93	93	65
1+ times	8	8	7	8	35
Mean number of times	0.1	0.2	0.1	0.1	0.8
		$p > .01$			$p < .01$
Child spends a week or more at a time at the outside parent's	28	31	16	22	57
		$p < .01$			$p < .01$
Child thinks outside parent's home is					
Like own home	35	27	18	22	74
Like someone else's home	23	28	13	19	16
Child was never in it	42	44	69	58	10
		$p < .01$			$p < .01$
Child has a place to keep things at the outside parent's	14	25	14	18	56
		$p < .01$			$p < .01$
Unweighted N^c	(25)	(131)	(239)	(395)	(28)

(Note: Restricted to children living with one biological parent and whose other biological parent is presumed alive.) Length-of-separation figures are calculated only when outside parent is the biological father.

[a] Represents significant chi-squares comparing outside biological parents with varying degrees of duration since separation.

[b] Represents significant chi-squares comparing outside father and outside mother.

[c] Ns vary slightly by question because of nonresponses.

home. Contact occurs more frequently when the noncustodial parent is the child's mother, but residence with the father is uncommon, especially among younger children.

A more recent study by Seltzer & Bianchi (1988) provides essentially the same picture of low contact between noncustodial fathers and their children. Of course, studies of children in families with joint-custody show a distinctly different pattern of contact, but as reported earlier, such arrangements are uncommon even in localities that mandate joint legal custody. The shift in the legal system emphasizing the desirability of joint legal custody and the strong pressure toward strengthening child support may help bring about a greater level of involvement of noncustodial parents (i.e. fathers) following divorce. As yet, this trend is only incipient if it is taking place at all.

Even when the noncustodial parent maintains regular contact, many families adopt a pattern that is best described as "parallel parenting." Parents consult infrequently, often communicate through the child, and rarely are visible to one another. The imperatives of emotional divorce (Bohannon 1970) and the high priority given to privacy among separate family units, especially after remarriage, probably contribute to this style of postmarital parenting. This pattern has the desirable consequence of reducing conflict between parents, but it creates two distinct family worlds for the child. Little research has been done on how children manage to integrate the sometimes conflicting cultures of active participation in two separate family systems (Johnson 1988). There is even much work to be done on how children manage the routines of family life when their parents live apart. Most investigators have assumed that this form of the family imposes psychological as well as economic hardships on children (Clingempeel & Reppucci 1982, Emery 1988).

Measuring the Impact of Divorce on Children

Long before divorce became common, social commentators worried about the children of "broken" families and whether family instability would impair their functioning in later life (Lichtenberger 1931). Much of the debate about divorce was based on the prevailing assumption that the nuclear family is the best—and some would say the only—fitting environment for raising children. While the notion that children can thrive only when they grow up in stable two-parent families persists, the complexity of contemporary family arrangements has forced social scientists to rethink the family conditions that are most congenial to effective socialization. Scholars have begun to explore how and why children seem to succeed when they are raised in adverse circumstances (Garmezy & Rutter 1983). There is growing interest in why the experience of siblings varies so greatly within families of all types (Plomin 1989). These questions go beyond the scope of this chapter, but when the effects of divorce on children are considered, it is important to remember that early family experience, and certainly the form of the family of origin, seems to account for only a modest portion of the variation in adult performance.

Nonetheless, there is virtual agreement among researchers that children are better off when raised by parents whose relationship is stable, warm, and mutually supportive. Family researchers have shown far more interest in how the disintegration of marital bonds adversely affects the socialization process and the well-being of children than why or how a happy marriage confers advantage to them. Most of what we know is based on how socialization is disrupted when marriages break up rather than why children benefit from stable family relations (Dornbusch 1989).

Over the years, researchers have produced literally hundreds of studies comparing children in two-parent and single-parent families. Just in the past several years, a number of volumes have been produced with fresh studies, and quite a few excellent research reviews have appeared summarizing and synthesizing recent empirical findings (Emery 1988, Hetherington & Arasteh 1988, Chase-Lansdale & Hetherington 1989). No attempt is made here to carry out a further review. Instead, I extract some important themes that seem to have emerged, many of which are still open to disagreement, and I point out some key questions that deserve further attention in future studies.

Age-Effects

Much of the research has been built upon the preoccupation of developmentalists with the notion that divorce affects children differently according to their age when it occurs (Longfellow 1979, Emery 1988). Much of the research on age effects can be traced to Wallerstein & Kelly's (1980) influential clinical study, *Surviving the Breakup,* showing that children of different ages organized the experience of divorce quite differently depending on their cognitive capacities and differing understandings of the social world. Since the publication of their book, numerous studies that have looked for systematic age differences in the response to marital disruption and for patterns of long-term adjustment that can be traced to the age of the child when their parents split up.

Sadly, the yield from these studies has not been as great as one might hope. In large measure, the age of the child at the time of divorce is often confounded with other temporal effects such as the interval since separation, current age, and even period effects (Emery 1988). Few studies have followed children of varying ages (divorce cohorts) over time, looking for systematic variations in age and interval since separation. Obviously, this strategy requires a longitudinal design with a large sample.

One study that attempted to sort out age and stage effects did discover some modest support for the prevailing belief that younger children experience more enduring effects of divorce (Allison & Furstenberg 1989). Yet, existing evidence is neither strong enough or consistent enough to draw a firm conclusion that marital disruption is hardest on children in their tender years, much less to explain why this is so if it were true. Do younger children have more difficulty managing the disappearance of a parent? Are the concomitant effects of divorce (e.g. economic strain, postmarital conflict or loss of child support from the noncustodial parent) more likely to appear with the dissolution of briefer marriages—marriages that typically end when children are young? Or, are individuals who divorce more quickly less capable or committed parents? Until these questions are addressed, we will not have secure knowledge about the impact of divorce timing in children's lives for their subsequent adjustment.

Researchers do seem to agree that divorce effects are most evident immediately at the time of separation. Hetherington et al (1982) carefully documented the process of deterioration of parenting in a small sample of middle-class families around the time of divorce, and its restoration in the year or two after separation occurred. However, the process of recovery seems to be different for boys and girls, suggesting the possibility that gender mediates a child's response to divorce.

Gender Effects

Among others, Hetherington (1987) has shown that young boys display more behavioral disturbance immediately following marital dissolution and continue to exhibit more symptoms of maladjustment several years after divorce. It has been argued by some developmentally oriented researchers that males may generally be more vulnerable to stressful events. Boys may react by exhibiting aggressive or "acting out" responses that elicit punitive responses by frustrated parents, thus initiating a "coercive cycle." Some investigators have argued that gender effects can be traced to custody arrangements which isolate boys from their fathers (Herzog and Sudia 1973, Wallerstein & Kelly 1980, Zaslow 1987).

While gender-specific responses to divorce are entirely plausible, most studies reporting such findings have one or another methodological limitation. Many studies lack an adequate comparison group of children in intact families. Others look at behaviors at only one point in time, leaving open the question of whether gender differences appeared before or after the divorce. Still others select a limited set of indicators that may be more sensitive to areas of dysfunction in one gender or the other. The hazards of divorce may not be greater for boys than for girls—only different. Boys "act out" in response to divorce, while girls exhibit less socially visible forms of maladjustment.

Possibly, too, boys and girls have characteristic ways of responding to conflict that are manifested at different stages in the divorce process. Boys, for example, may respond more quickly (or perhaps more openly) to marital conflict than do girls. Impairments to girls may emerge more gradually or may be temporarily masked by greater short-term coping ability. Possibly, too, the recovery time from the stressful effects of divorce may vary by gender. Hetherington's study, for example, suggests that boys may take longer to adjust to family transitions. It remains to be seen, then, whether gender differences in the response to divorce are transitory or permanent.

The recent discovery reported by several investigators that girls may only exhibit certain effects of divorce in late adolescence or early adulthood complicates the picture even further (McLanahan & Bumpass 1988). In two separate extensive reviews of existing literature on sex differences, Zaslow (1987) and Chase-Lansdale & Hetherington (1989) both conclude that girls may experience greater distress when their mothers enter remarriage. More generally, they speculate the possibility of a "sleeper effect" for adolescent girls who have experienced marital disruption. Girls not living with their biological fathers may encounter more problems in managing sexuality and adjusting to heterosexual relations. Recently, Wallerstein & Blakeslee (1989) in a follow-up of a small sample of children from divorced families also cited evidence of a "sleeper effect." In contrast to the males in their study, females encountered particularly severe problems in establishing emotional commitments in early adulthood. The notion that divorce can have latent effects that only emerge in later life is an intriguing hypothesis that points to the need for longitudinal research that traces the life course of children of divorce from early childhood to adulthood.

The Long-Term Effects of Divorce

Virtually all investigators believe that divorce is usually an extremely stressful event for children and that many react by displaying symptoms of distress—anxiety, acting out, diminished performance in school, and problems at home. In time, these symptoms abate for many children. A relatively small number of children remain impaired as adults, though most adults who experience divorce in childhood regard divorce as a turning point in their lives. But recently more evidence is surfacing to suggest that the long-term effects of marital disruption may have been underestimated (Glenn & Kramer 1985; McLanahan 1988). The evidence for adverse long-term effects of divorce seems to be especially conspicuous in two areas: educational attainment and family formation. There is a growing body of literature that points to consistent differences in the amount of schooling achieved by children who grew up in intact and non-intact families (Hetherington et al 1982, Krein & Beller 1988). Of course, part of this difference can be attributed to preexisting differences in couples who are stably and unstably married. Even after controlling for a number of prior differences (race, socioeconomic status, religion, among others), Krein & Beller (1988) report moderately large differences in the educational attainment among children who did and did not grow up with both biological parents. Marital disruption has been associated with school problems, grade failure, higher dropout, lower attendance, and completion of college leading to a reduction of occupational attainment and income in later life. It is also likely that children from disrupted families attend inferior schools and may receive less economic support for advanced education. It remains to be seen how much of the difference in educational attainment can be traced to psychological or economic differences resulting from divorce.

Adverse effects in later life relating to the timing and stability of marriage are also impressively consistent. In a series of studies, Glenn & Kramer (1985) have shown that children with a history of divorce display a number of different attitudes about marriage and marital stability. Unstable family life in childhood has also been linked to earlier timing of sexual activity, higher levels of premarital pregnancy, earlier marriage, and less marital stability (McLanahan & Bumpass 1988, McLanahan 1988). Most studies report sharper differences for whites than blacks. Paralleling the findings on educational attainment, prior controls seems to account for only a limited portion of the differences between children who grew up in intact and non-intact families.

Some of the disadvantage associated with divorce may well be spurious. Statistical controls eliminate only a portion of the preexisting differences. Unquestionably, some portion of the differences might be accounted for by selective factors that distinguish the parents who remain married from those who divorce. But it seems unlikely that selective factors alone would explain all of the long-term effects of divorce. Children of divorce are far more likely to grow up in poverty or with limited economic resources and hence to live in less desirable neighborhoods, attend poor-quality schools, receive less help when they encounter problems, and have more limited contacts for gaining access to desirable higher education and good jobs. If only because divorce affects the child's economic status, it is likely to shape certain features of the life course.

Most family authorities also assume that family dynamics differ in families with solo parents. Single parents have greater problems supervising their children (Dornbusch et al 1985). Given the likelihood that they will reside in less favorable neighborhoods, the problems of monitoring children may be greater than those required by parents in families with two parents. Thus, solo parents may have less capacity to shield their children from negative peer influences, which in any event are probably more omnipresent in the social environments of single-parent families (Steinberg 1987). Again, we lack a good estimate of the size of the effect associated with the diminished capacity of parental supervision, but the studies cited above suggest its importance as a potential mediating mechanism.

There is far less convincing, but equally intriguing, evidence on other mechanisms that might mediate the impact of divorce on children. For example, some researchers have contended that children are less likely to develop strong emotional ties with their parents in maritally disrupted families. There is little or no evidence that children develop weaker ties with their residential parent if they live in a single-parent family. However, they do have far weaker bonds with their nonresidential parent (Furstenberg 1988, Peterson

& Zill 1986). Some studies show that strong bonds to the noncustodial parent reduce the adverse affects of divorce, but other evidence fails to confirm this hypothesis (Peterson & Zill 1986, also, see Mechanic & Hansell 1989). Clearly, further evidence on the conditions that promote and sustain meaningful ties with parents outside the home and the consequences of such ties for the well-being of children is needed before we can draw any firm conclusions about whether and how much emotional relations with the noncustodial parent buffer children from the potentially adverse effects of divorce.

The Effects of Remarriage on Children

Disentangling the effects of divorce from the effects of remarriage is an extraordinarily difficult task. Many studies that have examined divorce effects have simply ignored remarriage; conversely, studies of remarriage frequently do not examine the preexisting adjustment to divorce among either parents or children. As happens in divorce, entrance to remarriage perturbs an existing family system (Bernard 1956, Messinger 1984, Hetherington 1989). And even more than divorce, it may divide the interests of parents and children. Evidence suggests that parents benefit psychologically and economically from durable remarriages (Pasley & Ihinger-Tallman, 1988). Several studies have shown that remarriage restores women's economic status to a level equivalent to what it would have been had they remained stably married (Jacobs & Furstenberg, 1986, Duncan & Hoffman 1985).

The benefits of remarriage for children are less clear cut. Certainly, children profit from the improved economic status of their residential parent. On the other hand, remarriage of the residential parents may actually result in a reduction of child support and visitation from the nonresidential parent. Nonetheless, it is safe to assume that on balance remarriage removes many children from severe economic disadvantage and mitigates many of the indirect costs associated with downward social mobility.

The psychological effects of remarriage are less easily calculated. The literature on the experience of children in stepfamilies has grown enormously, but it has produced little consensus on the consequences of remarriage for children's long-term adjustment. In recent years, several books and articles have attempted to review and synthesize the diverse findings (Ihinger-Tallman & Pasley 1987, Hetherington 1989). The same sorts of methodological issues plague the interpretation of remarriage effects as researchers face in investigating the impact of divorce on children. Few longitudinal studies have been carried out tracing children's transition from one marriage to the next. With rare exceptions, researchers have relied on comparisons of children in divorced and remarried families; they have not examined children's changing functioning as they move from a single-parent to a stepparent household.

A few small-scale studies have followed children into remarriage (Cling-empeel et al 1984, Hetherington 1989). As happens with divorce, remarriage may affect children differently depending on their gender and age at the time of the event. In contrast to divorce, several studies have shown that remarriage creates more problems for girls than for boys (Zaslow 1987, Chase-Lansdale & Hetherington 1989). But one analysis of the National Survey of Children was unable to find a strong gender effect among children in remarried households, though some slight evidence indicated that remarriage may pose greater adjustment problems for girls (Allison & Furstenberg 1989).

There is widespread agreement that stepfamilies have distinctive features that alter family processes (Bohannon 1985, Johnson 1988). Displaying affection and managing sexual attractions between stepparents and children or stepsiblings, exercising authority and discipline over a spouse's children, forming a common family culture among two subfamilies, and relating to outside nonbiological kin are but a few examples of issues for stepfamilies that set them apart from nuclear family forms (Beer 1988). Add to these, the common dilemma that children in stepfamilies are often managing relations with two sets of parents and stepparents. Cherlin (1978), who describes remarriage as an "incomplete institution," contends that the rules of family life are less clearly defined in remarried than in nuclear families. He argues that the weak institutionalization of family norms after remarriage strains marital ties and elevates the level of intergenerational conflict. As I have already reported, the evidence showing that remarriages are more stressful than first unions is equivocal at most.

The ambiguity of family norms may help explain why bonds between stepparents and their children are weaker and sometimes fraught with conflict. Few children come to view their stepparents as indistinguishable from a biological parent, and few parents treat their stepchildren in ways identical to those with their biological offspring. Consequently it is not surprising that ties to stepparents are described as less close than ties to biological parents, and relations in stepfamilies are generally somewhat less harmonious and gratifying (Ferri 1984, Furstenberg 1988). White & Booth (1985) show that parents in stepfamilies are far more likely than parents in first marriages to report difficulties in childrearing. They concur with Cherlin that remarriage often disrupts the parenting system within the family, creating problems for children.

While studies on the long-term effects of remarriage on children are sparse, there is little evidence to suggest that remarriage enhances the psychological well-being of children even when it improves their economic circumstances (Ferri 1984). For example, children in remarriages seem to display the same inclination toward early family formation as do children of divorce—they commence sexual relations earlier than children in nuclear families, are more likely to leave home earlier (Goldscheider & Goldscheider 1988), cohabit more often, marry at a younger age, and begin having children sooner (McLanahan & Bumpass 1988, McLanahan & Book 1989). Whether these results can be traced to lingering effects of divorce or to experiences of residing in stepfamilies has not been resolved by empirical investigation.

These aggregate contrasts conceal a great deal of variability within stepfamilies. A substantial minority of children manage to form close and important ties with their stepparents. The likelihood of establishing such ties, not surprisingly, is related to the age of the child at the time that he or she enters a stepfamily, but it is clear that even adolescents and young adults are able to form strong bonds with their stepparents. Curiously, at least one study shows that contact with and positive bonds to the nonresidential parent is unrelated to a child's likelihood of establishing strong bonds to a stepparent (Furstenberg 1988).

An intriguing area for further sociological investigation is the alteration of kinship relations which comes about when remarriage occurs (Bohannon 1970, Johnson 1988). Divorce typically truncates relations between children and their noncustodial kin, creating a matrilineal tilt in the structure of kin contacts (Cherlin & Furstenberg 1986). To some extent, remarriage, especially when it occurs early in the child's life, restores the bilateral balance that characterizes the American kinship system (Schneider 1980). Elsewhere, I have speculated that remarriage widens the child's kinship network and that children who have more than two parents may accordingly benefit from a larger pool of kin (Furstenberg 1981, Johnson et al 1988). However, it is unclear just how deep the kinship ties extend when they are created by marriage. Step-grandparents are, in effect, grandparents in-law and, they may take on the special character of affinal ties.

Our kinship system is generally permissive, giving individuals great latitude to construct meaningful relations from a wide pool of potential kin (Schneider 1980). But we also make important distinctions between "real" relatives, that is consanguineous relatives, and relatives acquired by marriage. An important topic for further investigation is the persistence of ties between children and their steprelations in later life. For example, virtually nothing is known about the social support extended to stepparents as children move into adulthood or about the inheritance patterns established in stepfamilies. The examination of intergenerational relations within nuclear and stepfamilies in later life would enrich our understanding of the structural and cultural differences among different family forms and the consequences of divorce and remarriage for the functioning of our kinship system.

Divorce, Remarriage, and Public Policy

Concern continues to mount over the effects of divorce and remarriage on the vitality of the family and the preparation of children for adult roles. Worried observers fear that high rates of marital disruption may be a primary source of rising rates of problem behavior among adolescents and young adults. Certainly, some evidence suggests that childhood divorce elevates the risk of academic failure and jeopardizes educational and occupational attainment. The process of family formation may also be altered when divorce occurs, raising the probability of marital disruption in the next generation. Awareness of the costs of divorce to children may be reducing the relatively benign view that some social scientists had about the long-term consequences of divorce (Garfinkel & McLanahan 1986, Wallerstein & Blakeslee 1989). Still, it is possible to overstate the effects of divorce on family and children's functioning. Claims that rising divorce rates can explain the rise of youthful problem behavior in the 1970s, the growth of more permissive sexual norms, or changes in patterns of family formation over the past two decades have not been well documented. It seems unlikely that these social trends have been greatly shaped by the rising prevalence of divorce (Furstenberg & Condron 1988, Zill & Rogers 1988).

Nonetheless, few social scientists would argue that marital disruption is a trivial or inconsequential event. The evidence strongly suggests otherwise. Moreover, even if the consequences of divorce proved to be modest, family dissolution is regarded by children at the time and later in adulthood as a powerful influence on their course of their lives. As we have seen, divorce typically reduces the family's economic resources, it stresses the parent-child relationship, it alters and sometimes destroys the parenting system, and it reshapes kinship ties.

In the introductory section of this chapter, I argued that the pattern of divorce and remarriage has become an intrinsic feature of the Western marriage system. Despite the leveling off of divorce rates, a majority of marriages contracted today will end in divorce (unless rates were to drop much lower). Still, we have not adapted our public policies to take account of the fact that most children will experience some time living in a single-parent family and that a significant minority will enter stepfamilies. Can the dislocating effects associated with divorce be mitigated by governmental initiatives designed to reduce the costs of divorce for family members?

Large efforts were mounted over the past two decades to reform the legal system, first to reduce conflict at the time of divorce through so-called no-fault divorce procedures and later to redistribute postmarital responsibilities by establishing the notion of joint custody. While assessments of these reforms are still underway, it is probably not too early to conclude that neither legal change achieved a dramatic improvement in the functioning of families after divorce. Changing legal procedures may have helped to establish and purvey new standards for families undergoing the process of divorce. Parents may be more aware of their obligation to manage their conflicts and more sensitive to the need to maintain joint responsibilities following divorce. But the evidence suggests that a high proportion of parents are unable to manage the divorce in a way that protects the child's economic and emotional interests. Marital separation often still brings about a partial collapse of the parental system or worse.

Some have argued that ambiguities regarding postmarital rights and responsibilities encourage conflict (Mnookin & Kornhauser 1979). Recently, there have been efforts to promulgate a clearer definition of the rights and obligations of parents after divorce. Some states, for example, have promoted the concept of joint legal custody to establish a general standard for parents. Whether this will result in greater collaboration among parents after divorce remains to be seen. It seems that still clearer normative standards regulating postmarital ties are required. Perhaps it is necessary for couples entering marriage or upon the birth of their first child to make explicit provisions for allocating rights and responsibilities between parents in the event that their relationship dissolves. The standardization of custody arrangements may in fact establish a de facto expectation that provides a fixed guideline unless parents mutually agree to alter it.

The recent national campaign to enforce stricter standards of child support by the noncustodial parents also reflects the trend toward establishing unambiguous standards for divorcing couples. The recently enacted Family Support Act of 1988 mandates states to standardize levels of child support based on a fixed proportion of the father's earnings. Collection procedures are also being made routine by garnisheeing wages much as taxes are deducted from earnings. These procedures were thought to be extraordinary only a few years ago but now are being instituted throughout the country. Several ongoing studies designed to evaluate the impact of child support enforcement should tell us whether they improve the economic situation of children or change the level of involvement of the noncustodial parent in childrearing.

The legal changes in custody and child enforcement signal a profound shift in our posture toward divorce. The first holds that parents should be free to negotiate their own private arrangements when marriage breaks up; the second attempts to regulate the outcome ensuring that the competing interests of various parties—parents and their children—are protected.

The current system has broken down in part because private bargaining has not worked well to ensure the security of children. In part, this has occurred because nonresidential parents (specifically fathers) have not been constrained to maintain responsibilities for child support after divorce. The recent efforts to redress the economic ill-effects of divorce for women and children after divorce have shifted the balance between private and public regulation of postmarital relations.

The role of stepparents and steprelationships are treated ambiguously within the law. David Chambers (1989) argues that stepparents are effectively regarded as legal non-entities. The legal status of stepparents is a symptom of their anomalous status. Though we have a system of conjugal succession where fathers effectively engage in a system of child swapping, we continue to count blood ties as the basis of enduring bonds. The law provides a convenient barometer for expressing (and therefore measuring) shifts in our current rules of marriage and kinship. Child support enforcement clearly establishes the responsibilities of the biological parents, but it leaves open the question of whether remarried parents should have lasting obligations to their stepchildren.

Marital disruption and remarriage inevitably invites social scrutiny of the family by exposing certain structural weaknesses and contradictions within our kinship system; no longer is it possible to assume the stability of the conjugal unit or even that childbearing will be regulated by marriage. Not much thought or public attention has been given to whether it is possible to strengthen the institution of marriage or parental arrangements that are the functional equivalent of marriage. Difficult as it is to define provisions for dealing with the consequences of divorce, it is even more difficult to invent ways of rejuvenating commitment to marriage or promoting the stability of existing family units. Consideration of this should ultimately push us in the direction of cross-national comparisons—a much underutilized method of inquiry.

Direct research on the consequences of policy changes on the function of the family also remains a relatively underdeveloped area of family research. The recent Family Support Act of 1988 provides an unusual opportunity to observe legislative experimentation on a grand scale. Will current legal and political efforts designed to improve the functioning of families after divorce affect the well-being of children from maritally disrupted families? Surely, this is one of the most interesting empirical questions facing the next generation of researchers interested in the sociology of divorce.

Literature Cited

Albiston, C. R., Maccoby, E. E., Mnookin, R. H. 1990. Joint legal custody. *Stanford Law Policy Rev.* 1: Forthcoming.

Allison, P., Furstenberg, F. F. Jr. 1989. How marital dissolution affects children: Variations by age and sex. *Dev. Psychol.* 25:4:540–49

Arendell, T. 1986. *Mothers and Divorce.* Berkeley: Univ. Calif. Press

Becker, G. S., Landes, E. M., Michael, R. T. 1977. An economic analysis of marital instability. *J. Polit. Econ.* 85:141–187

Becker, H. 1981. *A Treatise on the Family.* Cambridge, Mass: Havard Univ. Press

Beer, W. R. Ed. 1988. *Relative Strangers.* Totowa, NJ: Rowman & Littlefield

Bernard, J. 1956. *Remarriage.* New York: Dryden

Bernard, J. 1981. The good provider role: Its rise and fall. *Am. Psychol.* 36:1:1–12

Bianchi, S., Spain, D. 1986. *American Women in Transition.* New York: Russell Sage Found.

Bohannon, P. ed. 1970. *Divorce and After: An Analysis of the Emotional and Social Problems of Divorce.* Garden City, NY: Anchor

Bohannon, P. 1985. *All the Happy Families.* New York: McGraw-Hill

Brandwein, R. A., Brown, C. A., Fox, E. M. 1974. Women and children last: The social situation of divorced mothers and their families. *J. Marriage Fam.* 36:498–514

Bumpass, L. 1984. Children and marital disruption: A replication and update. *Demography* 21:71–82

Bumpass, L. L., Sweet, J. A. 1989. Children's experience in single-parent families: Implications of cohabitation and marital transitions. *Fam. Plan. Perspect.* 6:256–60

Burgess, E. W. 1948. The family in a changing society. *Am. J. Sociol.* 53:417–21

Carter, H., Glick, P. C. 1976. *Marriage and Divorce: A Social and Economic Study.* Cambridge, Mass: Harvard Univ. Press

Castro-Martin, T., Bumpass, L. 1989. Recent trends and differentials in marital disruption. *Demography* 26:37–51

Chambers, D. 1989. Stepparents, biological parents, and the law's perceptions of "family" after divorce. In *Divorce Reform at the Crossroads,* ed. S. D. Sugarman, H. H. Kay. Cambridge, Mass: Harvard Univ. Press. In press

Chase-Lansdale, P. L., Hetherington, M. 1989. The impact of divorce on life-span development: Short and longterm effects. In *Life-Span Behavior and Development.* In press

Cherlin, A. J. 1978. Remarriage as an incomplete institution. *Am. J. Sociol.* 84:634–50

Cherlin, A. J. 1981. *Marriage, Divorce, Remarriage.* Cambridge, Mass: Harvard Univ. Press

Cherlin, A. J., Furstenberg, F. F. Jr. 1986. *The New American Grandparent.* New York: Basic

Cherlin, A. J. 1988. The weakening link between marriage and the care of children. *Fam. Planning Perspect.* 20:6:302–6

Cherlin, A. J. 1990. *Marriage, Divorce, Remarriage.* Cambridge: Harvard Univ. Press. Rev. ed. In preparation

Clingempeel, W. G., Reppucci, N. D. 1982. Joint custody after divorce: Major issues and goals for research. *Psychol. Bull.* 91:102–27

Clingempeel, W. G., Brand, C., Sevoli, R. 1984. Stepparent-stepchild relationships in stepmother and stepfather families: A multimethod study. *Fam. Relat.* 33:465–73

Davis, K., ed. 1985. *Contemporary Marriage.* New York: Russell Sage Found.

Degler, C. N. 1980. *At Odds.* New York: Oxford Univ. Press

Dornbusch, S. M. 1989. The sociology of adolescence. *Annu. Rev. Sociol.* 15:233–59

Dornbusch, S. M., Carlsmith, J. M., Bushwall, S. J., Ritter, P. L., Leiderman, H., et al. 1985. Single parents, extended households, and the control of adolescents. *Child Dev.* 56:326–41

Duncan, G. J., Hoffman, S. D. 1985. A reconsideration of the economic consequences of marital dissolution. *Demography* 22:4:485–97

Ellwood, D. 1988. *Poor Support: Poverty in the American Family.* New York: Basic

Emery, R. E. 1988. *Marriage, Divorce, and Children's Adjustment.* Beverly Hills: Sage

Ferri, E. 1984. *Stepchildren: A National Study.* Windsor, Berkshire: Nfer-Nelson

Fuchs, V. R. 1983. *How We Live.* Cambridge, Mass: Harvard Univ. Press

Furstenberg, F. F. Jr. 1981. Implicating the family: Teenage parenthood and kinship involvement. In *Teenage Pregnancy in a Family Context: Implications for Policy,* ed. T. Ooms, pp. 131–64. Philadelphia: Temple Univ. Press

Furstenberg, F. F. Jr. 1987. Race differences in teenage sexuality, pregnancy, and adolescent childbearing. *Milbank Q.* 65:Suppl. 2:381–403

Furstenberg, F. F. Jr. 1988. Child care after divorce and remarriage. In *The Impact of Divorce, Single Parenting and Stepparenting on Children,* ed. E. M. Hetherington, J. Arasteh, pp. 245–61. Hillsdale, NJ: Erlbaum

Furstenberg, F. F. Jr., Cherlin, A. J. 1990. *Divided Families.* Cambridge: Harvard Univ. Press. Forthcoming

Furstenberg, F. F. Jr, Condran, G. A. 1988. Family change and adolescent well-being: A reexamination of family trends. In *The Changing American Family and Public Policy,* ed. A. J. Cherlin, pp. 117–55

Furstenberg, F. F. Jr., Nord, C. W. 1985. Parenting apart: patterns of childbearing after marital disruption. *J. Marriage Fam.* 47:4:893–905

Furstenberg, F. F. Jr., Nord, C. W., Peterson, J. L., Zill, N. 1983. The life course of children and divorce: marital disruption and parental conflict. *Am. Sociol. Rev.* 48:5:656–68

Furstenberg, F. F. Jr., Spanier, G. B. 1984. *Recycling the Family.* Beverly Hills: Sage

Garfinkel, L., McLanahan, S. 1986. *Single Mothers and Their Children.* Washington, DC: Urban Inst. Press

Garmezy, N., Rutter, M. 1983. *Stress, Coping and Development in Children.* New York: McGraw-Hill

Glenn, N. D., Kramer, K. B. 1985. The psychological well-being of adult children of divorce. *J. Marriage Family* 47:905–12

Glick, P. C. 1984. Marriage, divorce, and living arrangements: Prospective changes. *J. Fam. Iss.* 5:1:7–26

Goldscheider, F. K., Goldscheider, C. 1988. Leaving home and family structure: Nestleaving expectations in step- and single parent families. Pres. Ann. Meet. Popul. Assoc. Am. New Orleans. April 1988

Goode, W. J. 1956. *Women in Divorce.* New York: Free Press

Goode, W. J. 1963. *World Revolution and Family Patterns.* New York: Free Press

Goode, W. J. 1982. Why men resist. In *Rethinking the Family: Some Feminist Questions,* ed. B. Thorne, M. Yalom, pp. 131–50. New York: Longman

Halem, L. C. 1980. *Divorce Reform.* New York: Free Press

Halliday, T. C. 1980. Remarriage: The more complete institution. *Am. J. Sociol.* 86:630–35

Herzog, E., Sudia, C. E. 1973. Children in fatherless families. In *Child Development and Social Policy,* ed. B. M. Caldwell, H. N. Ricciuti. Chicago: Univ. Chicago Press

Hetherington, E. M., Cox, M., Cox, R. 1982. Effects of divorce on parents and children. In *Nontraditional Families,* ed. M. E. Lamb, pp. 233–88. Hillsdale, NJ: Erlbaum

Hetherington, E. M., Camara, K. A., Featherman, D. L. 1982. Achievement and intellectual functioning of children in one parent households. In *Assessing Achievement,* ed. J. Spence. San Francisco: Freeman

Hetherington, E. M. 1987. Family relations six years after divorce. In *Remarriage and Stepparenting Today: Current Research and Theory,* eds. K. Pasley, M. Ihinger-Tallman, pp. 185–205. New York: Guilford

Hetherington, E. M., Arasteh, J. eds. 1988. *The Impact of Divorce, Single Parenting and Stepparenting on Children.* Hillsdale, NJ: Erlbaum

Hetherington, E. M. 1989. Coping with family transitions: Winners, losers, and survivors. *Child Dev.* In press

Hofferth, S. L. 1985. Updating children's life course. *J. Marriage Fam.* 47:1:93–115

Huber, J., Spitze, G. 1988. Trends in family sociology. In *Handbook of Sociology,* ed. N. J. Smelser, pp. 425–48. Beverly Hills, Calif: Sage

Ihinger-Tallman, M., Pasley, K. 1987. *Remarriage.* Beverly Hills: Sage

Jacobs, J., Furstenberg, F. F. Jr. 1986. Changing places: Conjugal careers and women's marital mobility. *Soc. Forc.* 64:3:711–32

Johnson, C. L. 1988. *Ex Familia.* New Brunswick: Rutgers Univ. Press

Johnson, C., Schmidt, C., Klee, L. 1988. Conceptions of parentage and kinship among children of divorce. *Am. Anthropol.* 90:24–32

Kahn, A. J., Kamerman, S. B. eds. 1988. *Child Support: From Debt Collection to Social Policy.* Beverly Hills, Calif: Sage

Krein, S. F., Beller, A. H. 1988. Educational attainment of children from single-parent families: Differences by exposure, gender, and race. *Demography* 25:2:221–34

Lamb, M. E. ed. 1987. *The Father's Role: Applied Perspectives.* New York: Wiley

Lasch, C. 1977. *Haven in a Heartless World.* New York: Basic

Lesthaege, R., Meekers, D. 1986. Value changes and the dimensions of familism in the European community. *Eur. J. Popul.* 2:225–68

Lichtenberger, J. P. 1931. *Divorce: A Social Interpretation.* New York: McGraw-Hill

Longfellow, C. 1979. Divorce in context: Its impact on children. In *Divorce and Separation: Context, Causes and Consequences,* ed. G. Levinger, O. C. Moles, pp. 287–306. New York: Basic

Lye, D. N. 1988. *The rise of divorce in fifteen countries: A comparative study of changes in economic opportunities and family values.* PhD thesis. Univ. Penn., Philadelphia

McCarthy, J. F. 1978. A comparison of the probability of dissolution of first and second marriages. *Demography* 15:345–59

McLanahan, S. 1988. Family structure and dependency: Early transitions to female household headship. *Demography* 25:1–16

McLanahan, S., Bumpass, L. 1988. Intergenerational consequences of family disruption. *Am. J. Sociol.* 94:130–52

McLanahan, S., Booth, K. 1989. Mother-only families: Problems, prospects, and politics. *J. Marriage Fam.* 51:3:557–580

Mechanic, D., Hansell, S. 1989. Divorce, family conflict, and adolescents' well-being. *J. Health Soc. Behav.* 30:(March): 105–116

Messinger, L. 1984. *Remarriage: A Family Affair.* New York: Plenum

Mnookin, R. H., Kornhauser, L. 1979. Bargaining in the shadow of the law: The case of divorce. *Yale Law J.* 88:950–997

Newman, K. 1988. *Falling from Grace: The Experience of Downward Mobility in the American Middle Class.* New York: Free

Norton, A. J., Moorman, J. E. 1986. *Marriage and divorce patterns of U.S. women in the 1980s.* Pres. Meet. Popul. Assoc. Am. San Francisco, April 1986

Pasley, K., Ihinger-Tallman, M. eds. 1988. *Remarriage and Stepparenting Today: Current Research and Theory.* New York: Guilford

Peterson, J. L., Zill, N. 1986. Marital disruption, parent-child relationship and behavior problems in children. *J. Marriage Fam.* 48:295–307

Peterson, R. R. 1989. *Women, Work, & Divorce.* Albany: State Univ. New York Press

Plomin, R. 1989. Environment and genes: Determinants of behavior. *Am. Psychol.* 44:2:105–11

Presser, H. B. 1990. Can we make time for our children? The economy, work schedules, and child care. *Demography,* November 1989. In press

Preston, S., McDonald, J. 1979. The incidence of divorce within cohorts of American marriages contracted since the Civil War. *Demography* 16:1:1–26

Ross, H. L. & Sawhill, I. V. 1975. *Time of Transition: The Growth of Families Headed by Women.* Washington, DC: Urban Inst. Press

Rothman, E. K. 1987. *Hands and Hearts.* Cambridge, Mass: Harvard Univ. Press

Schneider, D. M. 1980. *American Kinship.* Chicago: Univ. Chicago Press. 2nd ed.

Seltzer, J. A., Bianchi, S. M. 1988. Children's contact with absent parents. *J. Marriage Fam.* 50:663–77

Seltzer, J. A., Schaeffer, N. C., Charng, H. 1989. Family ties after divorce: The relationship between visiting and paying child support. *J. Marriage Fam.* 51: 4:1013–32

Sorensen, A., McLanahan, S. 1987. Married women's economic dependency, 1940–1980. *Am. J. Sociol.* 93:3:659–87

Spanier, G., Furstenberg, F. F. Jr. 1987. Remarriage and reconstituted families. In *Handbook of Marriage and the Family,* ed. M. B. Sussman, S. K. Steinmetz, pp. 419–34. New York: Plenum

Steinberg, L. 1987. Single parents, stepparents and the susceptibility of adolescents to antisocial peer pressure. *Child Dev.* 58:269–75

Sweet, J. A., Bumpass, L. L. 1987. *American Families and Households.* New York: Russell Sage Found.

Swidler, A. 1980. Love and adulthood in American culture. In *Themes of Work and Love in Adulthood,* ed. N. J. Smelser, E. H. Erikson. Cambridge, Mass: Harvard Univ. Press

Thompson, L., Walker, A. 1989. Gender in families: Women and men in marriage, work and parenthood. *J. Marriage Fam.* 51:4:845–71

Uhlenberg, P. 1983. Death and the family. In *The American Family in Social-Historical Perspective,* ed. M. Gordon, pp. 169–78. New York: St. Martin's

US Bureau of the Census. 1988. Current Population Reports, Series P-60, No. 160, Poverty in the United States: 1986. Washington, DC: US Gov. Printing Off.

US Bureau of the Census. 1989a. Current Population Reports, Series P-23, No. 154, Child Support and Alimony: 1985. (Suppl. Rep). Washington, DC: U.S. Government Printing Office

US Bureau of the Census. 1989b. Current Population Reports, Series P-23, No. 162., Studies in Marriage and the Family. Washington, DC: US Government Printing Office

Wallerstein, J. S., Kelly, J. B. 1980. *Surviving the Breakup.* New York: Basic

Wallerstein, J. S., Blakeslee, S. 1989. *Second Changes: Men, Women and Children a Decade After Divorce.* New York: Ticknor & Fields

Weed, J. A. 1980. National estimates of marriage dissolution and survivorships: United States. *Vital and Health Statistics:* Series 3, *Analytic Statistics: No. 19. DHHS Publication No. (PHS) 81-1403.* Hyattsville, Md: Nat. Cent. Health Statist.

Weiss, R. S. 1975. *Marital Separation.* New York: Basic

Weiss, R. S. 1979. *Going It Alone.* New York: Basic

Weitzman, L. 1981. *The Marriage Contract.* New York: Free

Weitzman, L. 1985. *The Divorce Revolution.* New York: Free

White, L., Booth, A. 1985. The quality and stability of remarriages: The role of stepchildren. *Am. Sociol. Rev.* 50:689–98

Zaslow, M. J. 1987. *Sex differences in children's response to parental divorce.* Pres. Symp. on Sex Differences in Children's Responses to Psychosocial Stress, Woods Hole, Mass.

Zill, N., Rogers, C. C. 1988. Recent trends in the well-being of children in the United States and their implications for public policy. In *The Changing American Family and Public Policy,* ed. A. J. Cherlin, pp. 31–115. Washington, DC: Urban Inst. Press

Annu. Rev. Sociol. 1990. 16:405–33

CHOICES, DECISIONS, AND PROBLEM-SOLVING

Irving Tallman and Louis N. Gray

Department of Sociology. Washington State University, Pullman, Washington 99164

KEY WORDS: choices, decisions, problem-solving

Abstract

Theory and research on choice and decision-making behavior is reviewed with the intent of identifying the core elements of these behavioral processes. Two distinct theoretical perspectives—"subjective/cognitive" and "behaviorist"—are critically examined and evaluated within the framework of their contribution to sociological theory. We then explore lacunae and ambiguities in the research and theory in the field. Definitional distinctions are drawn between the concepts of choice, decision-making, and problem-solving. Finally, we make a preliminary attempt to synthesize the work in this field, to identify core elements and suggest that the moment of choice can be considered as a microcosm of the social and behavioral forces affecting a given action at both the individual and collective level.

INTRODUCTION

In his introduction to the volume on *The Microfoundations of Macrosociology,* Michael Hechter (1983:4) refers to the aphorism (attributed to Deusenberry 1960:233) that "economics is all about how people make choices and sociology is all about why they don't have any choices to make." Many of us steeped in the sociological tradition will find the statement intuitively appealing. Ours is a discipline concerned with explaining social order. Our key concepts—norms, roles, social structure—all focus on how individual choices are constrained and controlled by socialization and by historical,

405

0360-0572/90/0815-0405$02.00

structural, or cultural forces. Yet, any science committed to explaining human behavior cannot (or, at least, should not) be content with eliminating one fundamental aspect of the behavioral equation. If we are to understand how "macro" forces operate we should know the conditions under which they affect or fail to affect individual choices and, therefore, individual actions. Consequently we should understand the impact of individual decisions (made for personal gain or by agents of a collective) on institutions and social-historical events.

Consider the decision of a CEO of a large corporation to resist installing costly pollution control devices in company plants and by so doing to risk public disapproval and perhaps the health of his/her own children and grand-children; or consider the decision of a potential voter not to vote in a national election. In the one case the single decision may have sizeable consequences for the earth's future; in the other case, such decisions taken in aggregate can have profound effects on the nation's political and socioeconomic climate. Indeed, aggregated decisions of the latter type contribute to the weighting of choices by the CEO. What values are brought to bear in making these decisions? How do the actors estimate the consequences of their choices? What factors in their life histories, or in the history of their social worlds, brought them to the point of decision?

The moment of choice may be conceived of as a microcosm within which all the forces that affect human and social behavior combine to influence the course of collective or individual action. It is therefore desirable to see if these forces can be distilled into the essential elements needed to explain human choice. This review suggests that such a distillation is possible and, indeed, has been underway in a number of social science disciplines, including sociology.

In this review, we explore various attempts to answer the question of why an individual in a given situation chooses one course of action over another. In so doing, we seek to identify core elements that constitute choice and decision processes. Our central focus is on individual choice and decision behavior. The processes we shall identify are not isomorphic with group decision processes. A review of the latter is beyond the scope of this paper. However, at the end of the chapter we briefly consider how individual choice behavior may impinge on collective decisions.

We begin the search for the basic elements of individual choice and decision-making by reviewing some of the more prominent theories and models in the field. We selectively draw from the extensive body of empirical research bearing on these theories and identify those studies that tend to either support or refute these theories. We also consider some theoretical lacunae and conceptual ambiguities and, in the process, draw definitional distinctions between the concepts of choice, decision-making, and problem-solving. We conclude by examining the contribution of theory and research in choice behavior to sociology.

THEORIES OF CHOICE AND DECISION-MAKING

The commonly used distinction between descriptive (empirically focused, predictive) theories and prescriptive (normative) theories is not easily made when considering theories of choice and decision-making. Indeed, this seems to be one of the few areas of scientific inquiry where it is difficult to separate the two types of theory. (See March 1978 and Einhorn & Hogarth 1981 for detailed discussions of this interrelationship). Our concern in this review is with descriptive theory, but like those before us, we are unable to avoid giving serious consideration to various normative theories.

Despite various intellectual cross-currents and some areas of heated debate, certain paths of development are discernable and some seminal contributions stand out. Remarkably, these developmental paths and contributions follow two distinct, virtually independent traditions. These traditions, which we label objective/behaviorist and subjective/cognitive, employ virtually the same variables to explain the same types of behaviors; yet rarely do their practitioners refer to each other's work. Although these traditions are most clearly identified with developments in psychology, they attract a wide array of social scientists including sociologists, economists, political scientists, and statisticians. The lack of communication between these perspectives is surprising because, as we shall see, it is possible to consider them as complementary rather than opposing.

The two perspectives share three necessary assumptions. First, if choice is to be possible, the actor must have the opportunity to take or refrain from taking an action. Second, under conditions in which choices have consequences that are relevant to an actor's values and/or well being, the actor will choose those actions that s/he expects (or hopes) will result in desired outcomes. And third, the consequences of choices are rarely certain. Thus, actors live in a probabilistic world, and their choices represent guesses that a given course of action (or nonaction) will produce a given result.

Perhaps because of the third assumption, early choice and decision theory was closely linked to theories of probability and chance. The initial studies of choice, dating back to the sixteenth century, were concerned with the outcome of gambles; these studies defined probabilities as the ratio of the number of favorable outcomes to the total number of equally possible outcomes (Raiffa 1968). Subsequent investigations began to explore the empirical utility of this conception of probability, noting considerable variation. Finally, in the early nineteenth century Denis Poisson "formally defined probability as a limit of a long-run relative frequency" (Raiffa 1968:274). From about this period forward probabilities began to be seen in two ways: in objective terms (i.e. the actual odds or probabilities associated with possible outcomes of a gamble) and in subjective terms (i.e. the actor's degree of belief that a particular outcome will occur). Since the subjective perspective has had the most profound influence on sociology, we consider it first.

The Subjectivist/Cognitive Approach

As early as the eighteenth century, scholars noted that human choices did not necessarily reflect objective probabilities. It was James Bernoulli in 1738 (Raiffa 1968) who initially demonstrated how and why this might occur. Bernoulli's contribution was twofold: First, he defined probability in subjective terms, as an actor's "degree of confidence" that a given outcome or event will occur; second, he introduced the idea that choices are not based simply on the objective value of an outcome, but also on its subjective value (utility). He noted, for example, that the subjective value of money does not increase proportionately to its objective amount. If one has little money additional units are highly valued, but the more money one has or expects to gain, the less value (utility) is placed on additional units. In this sense utility is a concave function of the amount of money an actor has or can expect. The closer to zero that amount is, the greater the value attached to gaining or losing a unit of money. Thus, the difference between $200 and $100 has greater subjective value than the difference between $1200 and $1100.

In the twentieth century, utility theory became the predominant perspective in the study of choice and decision-making. It also became essentially a prescriptive or normative theory. The intent was to develop models that helped individuals and collectivities to make choices that allowed them to maximize their utilities; i.e. to make rational choices (Elster 1986, Harsanyi 1977/1986). The emphasis on rational, normative models reached its height with the introduction of game theory.

GAME THEORY   The publication of the 1947 edition of Von Neumann & Morgenstern's *Theory of Games and Economic Behavior* provided a careful and elegant axiomization of utility theory in relation to probability theory (Luce & Raiffa 1957:chapter 2, and Marschak 1964). Game theory was concerned with developing strategies for maximizing utilities in situations involving conflicts of interests. Game theorists provided formal solutions to problems calling for either defeating, cooperating with, or compromising with an opponent (see Rappaport 1960). The theories were designed to assist people, organizations, businesses, and societies to behave rationally, that is, to find the right means for attaining desired ends. Choices and decisions were considered sequentially and were put to the service of short- and long-range contingent planning. Choices were represented as nodes in game decision trees. Utilities were also conceptualized in series form and could be scaled and averaged (Marschak 1964). Thus, game theory provided a more precise specification of the temporal dimensions involved in choice and decision-making behavior.

The game theoretical perspective was adapted by a number of sociologists to account for: (a) choice and bargaining behavior (Bartos 1966, 1972; (b) social stratification and satisfaction with stratification systems (Boudon 1986); (c) social conflict (Bernard 1954) and coalition formation (Vanacke & Ackoff 1957).

The enormous literature on the "Prisoner's Dilemma" represents another, essentially normative, offshoot of game theory (e.g. Axelrod 1984, Harsanyi 1977, Rappaport & Chammah 1965). The Prisoner's Dilemma Game involves two players each of whom has two choices, to cooperate or to defect. Each must make the choice without knowing what the other will do. For each player defection offers the best possible payoff if the other player chooses to cooperate. If both defect they fare worse than if they both cooperate. The Prisoner's Dilemma identifies essential elements in the conflict between individual benefit and collective good (Olson 1965). It fostered investigations into topics such as the "Free Rider" phenomenon in which an actor may contribute nothing but still experience the benefits of a public good. The following situations suggested by Parfit (1986:36) serve as examples of the type of conflicts implicit in the prisoner dilemma game.

Commuters: Each goes faster if he drives, but if all drive each goes slower than if all take buses.

Soldiers: Each will be safer if he turns and runs, but if all do, more will be killed than if none do.

Fisherman: When the sea is overfished, it can be better for each if he tries to catch more. Worse for each if all do.

Peasants: When land is overcrowded, it can be better for each if he has more children, worse for each if all do.

Generally, but not always, it is shown that in the short run actors' benefit from noncooperative or self-serving choices; in the long run, cooperative solutions seem to be more beneficial (Axelrod 1984).

With the exception of the prisoner's dilemma research, interest in game theory has declined considerably in the past few decades. Despite its mathematical elegance, precision, and scope, it proved to have serious limitations when considered as an empirical theory (Allais & Hagen 1979). Two of the theory's key postulates—the substitute principle (if A is preferred to B, then an even chance to get A or C is preferred to an even chance to get B or C), and the principle of invariance (the preference order between options does not change with different presentations of the choice situation)—have been challenged on empirical grounds (Kahneman & Tversky 1984). To illustrate the weakness of these postulates Kahneman & Tversky provide the following example. They posed two problems to college undergraduates:

Problem 1 (N = 152 subjects): Imagine that the US is preparing for the outbreak of an unusual Asian disease, which is expected to kill 600 people. Two alternative programs to combat the disease have been proposed. The accepted scientific estimate of the consequences of the programs are as follows:

If program A is adopted, 200 people will be saved (72%)*;

If Program B is adopted, there is a one third probability that 600 people will be saved (28%).

Which of the two programs would you favor?

Problem 2 (N = 155 different subjects) . . . If program C is adopted 400 people will die (22%). If program D is adopted, there is a one third probability that nobody will die and a two thirds probability that 600 people will die (78%).

(*: numbers in parentheses indicate the percentage of respondents choosing a particular program).

Objectively, program A is equivalent to program C, and program B is equivalent to program D. The majority of respondents heavily favor risk aversion in choosing A over B when the issue is framed in terms of possible benefits, and they tend to adopt the risky alternative, D over C, when the issue is framed in costs or losses. Since A and C are equivalent, and in one problem A is chosen and in the other D rather than C is chosen, neither the substitute or the invariance principle holds.

Another fundamental problem with the game theory perspective is the amount of information the theory required for any actor to make a "rational" choice. Game theory assumes that all possible outcomes and the variables that control outcomes can be specified (Luce & Raiffa 1957). Rarely do actors have such complete knowledge. Most choice situations occur under conditions of risk or uncertainty. Employing the generally accepted convention, we use the term "risk" to refer to known outcome probabilities and "uncertainty" to refer to probabilities that are unknown (Elster 1986, Knight 1957, Lopes 1987). Risk situations raise questions about an actor's ability to accurately interpret probabilities. Efforts to include risk in utility theory have given rise to the development of the concept of "expected utility." Expected utility is defined as the utility of an outcome weighted by the probability of that outcome occurring (Elster 1986:5). Under conditions of uncertainty there is virtually no assurance that the game theory or rational choice assumptions can be met (Harsanyi 1977/1986).

SUBJECTIVE EXPECTED UTILITY (SEU)   The efforts of game theorists to formalize utility theory have been continued and extended by scholars interested in developing formal decision models by applying principles of subjective expected utility theory (SEU). This perspective has attracted a considerable number of sociologists, perhaps because it has tended to be less normative than the other approaches (see, for example, Blalock & Wilkin 1979, Camilleri et al 1972, Ford & Zelditch 1988). These decision models are consistent with earlier utility theories in that they maintain the underlying premise that actors combine subjective values and probabilities in determining utilities and select that alternative which they believe offers the best expected utility.

A critical assumption adapted by this group of investigators is that behavior is purposive and goal directed (Blalock & Wilken 1979, Coleman 1973, 1986). It is also assumed that an actor's goals and goal hierarchies are relatively stable (Blalock & Wilken 1979:45, Camilleri et al 1972:31). Thus, for Blalock & Wilken (1979:37–55) expected utility is equivalent to the anticipated level of goal fulfillment for a given alternative.

A sizeable body of research has been generated within this framework and the SEU model has been used successfully to predict choices in a variety of two and three choice situations (e.g. Camilleri & Conner 1976, Lindenberg 1980, 1981, Ofshe & Ofshe 1970, Siegel et al 1964).

SEU has also been used to assess the relative power of actors in a relationship and consequently to predict which actor is most likely to submit and which to dominate (Tedeschi et al 1973, Zelditch et al 1983, Ford & Zelditch 1988). Ford & Zelditch employed SEU to derive the "Law of Anticipated Reactions" which holds essentially that if A has a structural power advantage (i.e. is in a position to reward or punish) over B, and B is aware of A's preferences, B is inclined to comply with A's preferences even if A does not make overt use of his/her power advantage. Using a Bavelas wheel communication network with the central person in a position to impose negative sanctions, Ford & Zelditch report that subjects who were most likely to believe that the powerful person would impose negative sanctions were least likely to take advantage of opportunities to change the structure so that it would be more equitable.

It follows from the SEU perspective that actors make choices to maximize expected utilities. To achieve this end, they must know as much as possible about the outcomes associated with alternative courses of action. Such knowledge is attained through predecision information searches. One of the key purposes of such searches is to reduce the level of uncertainty concerning the possible outcomes. The formal model most frequently used to describe how this process is (or should be) undertaken is Bayes' Theorem. This theorem, derivable from probability theory, designates the inferences rational actors would make given the information they have available. It is not necessary to develop the formulation here. Rather, we shall simply describe its basic premises. A rational choice is defined as one which maximizes expected gain.

To calculate expected gain, the decision-maker must specify the probability that each alternative is the right one. The theory is intended to calculate the chances that a given alternative is in fact the right choice. Thus (H1) represents the hypothesis that alternative 1 is the right choice and p(H1) is the actor's assessment of the probability that H1 is true. Similar definitions obtain for H2 and p(H2). H1 is considered mutually exclusive of H2. The basic theorem can be depicted as follows:

$$\frac{p(H1 \mid D)}{p(H2 \mid D)} = \frac{p(D \mid H1)}{p(D \mid H2)} \frac{p(H1)}{p(H2)}$$

Presumably p(H1) and p(H2) depend upon data gathered up to the decision point. As each new datum is observed, the probabilities are revised according to the formulation. The left side of the equation is a ratio of the probabilities of H1 vs H2 given that datum D has been observed. The right side of the equation can be separated into two ratios. One is the ratio of probabilities of H1 to H2 prior to D and is called the *prior odds ratio*. The rest of the expression is a ratio of the likelihood of observing D given that H1 compared to H2 is true. This is, not surprisingly, called the *likelihood ratio*. In effect, the theorem says that the prior odds ratio times the likelihood ratio for the new datum gives the new (posterior) odds ratio. In this way, it is assumed that repeated information search develops more accurate probability estimates of the alternative choices available to an actor.

The Bayesian model gained enormous popularity in the 1960s. It was thought that, despite a noted tendency toward conservative estimates (Edwards 1968), the Bayesian analysis reflected the human information processor with considerable accuracy (Peterson & Beach 1967). More recently, however, serious questions have been raised as to how well the model predicts the way humans go about making probability estimates (Eddy 1982, Einhorn 1980, Slovic et al 1977). Writing in 1977, Slovic et al suggest that, "a psychological Rip Van Winkle who dozed off after reading Peterson and Beach would be startled by the widespread change of attitude exemplified by statements such as, 'In his evaluation of evidence, man is apparently not a conservative Bayesian; he is not Bayesian at all. . . .' " (The inner quotation is from Kahneman & Tversky 1972).

The Bayesian formulation has been criticized on two grounds. First, the observed data generally are not sufficiently reliable or valid to make either the prior odds ratio or the likelihood ratio effective indicators for estimating future events. Second, there is growing evidence that human beings do not identify and process data in Bayesian terms (see Slovic et al 1977 for a review of the research challenging the utility of Bayes' Theorem).

In the wake of criticisms of Bayesian thinking, investigators began examining how actors actually assess probabilities. Recognizing the problems of organizing information in an environment of almost infinite stimuli, a number of cognitive psychologists began examining the principles people seem to employ when making probability estimates. These "heuristics" not only provide useful ways for people to incorporate information (see Marcus & Zajonc 1985 for a review of this research), they also frequently produce biased and distorted estimates of the real probabilities associated with given outcomes (Nisbett & Ross 1980, Tversky & Kahneman 1982, Thaler 1983).

Tversky & Kahneman (1982) propose three primary heuristic/biases: representativeness (the tendency to rely on stereotypes to predict outcomes), availability (the tendency to consider events that come easily to mind as occurring more frequently than they actually do), and anchoring (the tendency to use some arbitrary starting point or experience as an anchor for probability estimates). These heuristics/biases are discussed in detail elsewhere (see, for example, Heimer 1988) so we do not do so here. It is important to note, however, that there is a considerable body of research suggesting the validity of these concepts (see as examples Kahneman et al 1982, Abelson & Levi 1985).

CRITIQUE OF SUBJECTIVE EXPECTED UTILITY   The criticisms leveled against Bayesian analysis seem to hold for most subjective expected utility (SEU) "rational choice" models. The requirement of perfect or near perfect knowledge of means, probabilities, and outcomes attached to alternatives, the assumption that actors are goal directed, and the overall inference that choices are made on a calculative basis often did not mesh with the observations of investigators.

The failure to specify the component elements that make up utilities or expected utilities also contributed to a growing body of criticism. Utility is usually defined as any preference that can be represented numerically in some kind of ordered manner (Luce & Raiffa 1957), and preference is inferred from the actor's choice. Thus, Luce & Raiffa (1957:50) offer the following postulate: "*Of two alternatives which give rise to outcomes, a player will choose the one which yields the more preferred outcome, or more precisely, in terms of the utility function he will attempt to maximize expected utility*" (italics in the original). There are two primary problems with this formulation: One lies in the operationalization of utility as preference, the other in the failure to specify the differential effects of costs and benefits.

Without additional definition, the preference/utility equivalence and its linkage to choice behavior violate the assumption that the options available to the actor must "connect" him or her to the outcomes. Sen (1973/1986) argues that, without establishing the logical property of connectedness, preference cannot be inferred from the fact that a choice has been made; that is, choosing option "a" over option "b" is not sufficient to logically link that choice to a specific preference. If a patient in a doctor's waiting room absent-mindedly picks up a magazine from an available stack on a table, the inference that the magazine was preferred to other magazines is hardly justified. Nor can one infer that the person is indifferent in the sense that the preferences have equal utility. The patient could just as well have picked up an ornament or a ball if it were available. Under such conditions the inference that the choice was based on a preferential ordering cannot be justified.

The second problem with the definition of utility is that the definition ignores or glosses over the complexities involved in balancing costs against benefits. There is a growing body of evidence that costs and benefits (or losses and gains) do not have the same psychological meaning for actors (see Lopes 1987 for a more complete discussion of this issue). Nor do they seem to evoke the same behavioral responses. For example, in the Asian disease problem used earlier, it can be seen that decision-makers are more likely to be risk-seeking when options are posed in terms of avoiding losses, and to be risk-avoiding when faced with choosing between possible benefits (Tversky & Kahneman 1981). In their experimental study on the differential effects of contingent costs and rewards on choice behavior, Gray & Tallman (1987) concluded from their data that cost is a more direct factor than rewards in determining choices. Regardless of the validity of such conclusions, the point is that the definition of utility used by SEU models does not allow for testing hypotheses about the differential weighting of costs and benefits.

The most influential critique of rational choice models is provided by Herbert Simon. The essence of Simon's position is that human limitations make it impossible for people to make meaningful probability estimates and engage in extensive information processing necessary to make a truly rational choice. Rather, actors tend to function in a restricted or "bounded" area of rationality (Simon 1979). Moreover, instead of maximizing outcomes they generally "satisfice," that is, accept the first alternative that is "good enough" to meet their needs or desires (Simon 1955). Subsequent research provided considerable support for the satisficing notion (See Cyert & March 1963, primarily with regard to business decisions; Janis & Mann 1977:26–29 for data pertaining to organizations and a variety of interpersonal choices; and Schwartz 1970, Simmons et al 1977:241–250, and Etzioni 1988:95ff for moral decisions).

James March (1978) suggests that Simon's conception of "bounded rationality" can be reinterpreted as evidence of various types of human intelligence. For example, he suggests that bounded rationality represents a way for the intelligent human to simplify the decision problem in the face of impossible numbers of alternatives and excessive information. March also questions the need for the assumption that goals must be considered as exogenous and stable or even relevant to all choice situations. Since events change rapidly, goals are likely also to be constantly changing. Thus, intelligent behavior may not always require the clear specification of goals. "We choose preferences and actions jointly in part to discover—or construct—new preferences" (p. 596). In sum, March suggests that the decision-maker can be viewed as an intelligent actor capable of balancing internal needs and external demands in an ongoing process involving multiple desires and changing events which almost simultaneously value and devalue the same outcome. Evidence in support of March's perspective of the fluid, continuous nature of the decision process comes mainly from the field of organization research (Hickson 1987, Starbuck 1983, Weick 1976).

Etzioni (1988) has mounted a related attack on the expected utility/rational choice perspective. He is primarily concerned with the assumption that choice is entirely motivated by self-interest. Etzioni holds that self-interest is only part of the force that drives people to act; they are also motivated by moral considerations. Moral considerations, Etzioni argues, do not require taking into account alternative courses of action and do not require any form of cognitive mediation. "The *imperative quality* of a moral act is reflected in that persons who act morally sense that they must, that they are in fact obligated, duty bound" (1988, p. 42). Thus, moral acts do not involve choices but are driven by some inner compulsion or value. Evidence for this position comes from research on kidney donors who, if they agree to be a donor, tend to do so immediately and without deliberation (Simmons et al 1977), and from experimental studies of altruistic behavior (Latane & Darley 1970). Research on altruism is examined below.

The focus of subjective utility theory is primarily on how actors assess or can be taught to assess what happens in their environment. We turn now to considerations of how the environment affects human choices.

The Behaviorist Approach

Behaviorist theories are based on fewer assumptions than are needed to build subjectivist/cognitive theories. Tracing their roots to John Watson, behaviorists seek to develop parsimonious explanations of overt behavior and avoid, as much as possible, assumptions about actors' mental activities. Thus, instead of the concept of utility, behaviorists focus on the effects of rewards and punishments, and instead of subjective probabilities, they are concerned with objective probabilities in the form of events that directly influence behavioral responses (reinforcement schedules and contingent probabilities).

Both classical and operant conditioning are relevant to our discussion. Classical conditioning results from the pairing of an unconditioned stimulus with some neutral stimulus. For example, the presence of a mother (neutral stimulus) with food (unconditioned stimulus) for her child creates a warm satisfying feeling in the child. The mother's presence becomes a conditioned stimulus that is associated with a feeling of warmth and satisfaction. This process can link a series of conditioned stimuli in a chain-like fashion so that the child associates many of the mother's activities and values with positive feelings. These activities and values are eventually internalized so that the child essentially rewards him or herself for behaving in ways that were previously rewarded by his/her environment (Aronfreed 1969, Scott 1971). This chain process is also associated with punishment and is linked to learned inhibitions. Such inhibitions are often reinforced by internalized fears and anxieties. In a classic study, Estes & Skinner (1941) created a conditioned emotional response (CER) by shocking an animal independent of its behavior but paired with other environmental stimuli. The effect was that the animal evidenced anxiety and avoidance behavior when confronted with the stimuli. In the same way a child who is frightened by the sounds of a thunderstorm while eating oatmeal may become anxious and subsequently refuse to eat oatmeal.

Operant conditioning refers to learning that takes place when an actor is rewarded or punished for a given action. A child who is periodically rewarded for expressing a given belief will tend to persist in expressing that belief. Similarly, children who are frequently punished if they lie will learn to inhibit this behavior and may internalize an intense dislike for liars (Aronfreed 1969).

The frequency and consistency of the rewards and punishments (reinforcement schedules) in response to a given act have been shown to have a direct effect on the persistence with which the act will be emitted as well as the time it takes for it to be extinguished (Blackman 1974:Ch. 5). Such reinforcement schedules affect the choices actors make. Behaviorists would predict that an actor in a known situation will make choices proportionate to the rate at which those choices have been reinforced. This proportionate relationship between choices and reinforcement schedules is formally expressed in Herrnstein's "matching law," the prevailing model in behaviorist choice theory today (Baum 1974, 1979, Gray & von Broembsen 1976, Hamblin 1977, 1979, Herrnstein 1961, 1970). In its simplest form the model holds that,

$$A_1/A_2 = R_1/R_2,$$

where, if we adapt the convention of using the subscript "i" to indicate any given choice, A_i indicates the frequency of choice of alternative i and R_i indicates the frequency of reinforcement of alternative i. The equation describes a situation in which an actor learns through experience both the types of behaviors that result in rewards or costs and the relative frequencies associated with a particular type of behavior in a particular situation. This can occur only if the actor has had a sufficient number of repeated experiences with the same types of variable reinforcement schedules that his/her responses are virtually automatic. Research on the matching law shows that, rather than maximizing payoffs, choices are proportional to the degree to which the actor was rewarded or punished (Baum & Rachlin 1969, Rachlin et al 1986).

Closely associated with the matching law as defined by Herrnstein is Estes' (1950, 1959) conception of probability matching. With probability matching the actor tends to learn and match the probability schedules through which he/she is reinforced. For example, if a child repeatedly finds that a jar on the counter contains cookies three out of four times it is opened and the jar on the back porch contains cookies one out of four times, probability matching predicts that the child will tend to go to the counter 75% of the time and the back porch 25% of the time (assuming both jars are equally accessible). Essentially what is learned and acted upon are the objective probabilities attached to each alternative. Unfortunately, the matching law in its various forms does not provide a formulation that allows for considering costs and benefits at the same time. This is a serious limitation since most real life choices involve both costs and benefits.

In general, however, a consistent body of empirical evidence supports the notion that preferences, tastes, and attitudes can be learned by means of classical and operant conditioning (see Aronfreed 1969, Bandura 1969, Logue 1986: esp. Ch. 7). This, of course, is not the only way such learning takes place. Other mechanisms such as modeling, imitation, identification, and vicarious learning also play critical roles in learning preferences (Bandura 1977, 1986). Moreover, the context within which the learning takes place and the distribution of power and dependency plays a critical role in the process of establishing preferences and values (Gecas 1981, Tallman et al 1983). Within any context, however, the effects of reinforcement schedules are embedded in each of the mechanisms described above. Thus, Bandura, (1986:239) stressing the importance of learning through interaction notes, "Positive incentives affirm that if individuals do certain things, they are entitled to specified rewards and privileges. In the case of negative sanctions, censurable conduct carries punishment costs."

Sociologists, who tend to be vitally concerned with the transmission of values, norms, and cultural beliefs have in general shown little interest in behaviorism. Indeed, at times, there have been open expressions of hostility toward the perspective and its adherents (see Wentworth 1980:42 for a particularly virulent expression of the latter position). There are notable exceptions of course. Homans (1974) and Emerson (1972) employed principles of operant conditioning to establish the antecedent to social exchange theory. Burgess & Akers (1966) employed a behaviorist approach to account for the development of criminal behavior, Gray and his colleagues (Gray et al

1982) and Molm (1981, 1987, Molm & Wiggins 1979) used behaviorist principles to explain power relationships and Hamblin (1977, 1979) has used the principles to account for and demonstrate processes of learning among elementary school children.

The Social Contexts of Choice and Decisionmaking

The sociological contribution to the study of choice and decision-making has tended to center around the ways in which choices are constrained and controlled, usually by reference to social institutions. Sociologists have relied on the concept of socialization to explain how such institutions are able to influence individual choice and action. It is through the process of socialization that children learn the opportunities and constraints associated with being members of families and parts of larger social systems.

It seems reasonable to infer, along with the life-course theorists, that any social action occurs at the confluence of at least three temporal or developmental streams: a given period of historical time, a point in social time (i.e. a point in the development of the relevant organizations or institutions), and a particular phase of personal development (Elder 1974, 1981, Hareven 1978, 1982).

Thus an adolescent deciding whether to get a job or go to college makes that decision at the intersect of these three developmental periods. At the historical level he or she is influenced by the special cultural and structural conditions that exist at that time (i.e. do the prevailing values support education for someone in the individual's social strata?) Is it a period of stability or change? Is it a period of growth or retention? At the social level, the stage of the family life cycle is relevant. Is the child the oldest or the youngest? Can the family support the child in college, given other family obligations? How independent is the child from the family? What are the effects of previous family members experience in college? What is the special role the child plays in the family? Finally the adolescent's own life experiences in school, with friends, and with jobs are relevant as are the skills and abilities s/he has acquired.

This confluence of three developmental processes may vary in salience at different times and for people in different social positions. Our point is simply that no choice can take place free of constraints of the historical events, situational demands, and individual capacity.

Much of this cumulative influence on an actor's choices need not be brought to bear in the form of conscious calculations. Options are eliminated because, within an actor's milieu, they have never occurred in his/her experience, or they are morally repugnant, or they are not considered accessible. Other behavioral patterns are so much a part of the "generalized other" and what collectivists have come to call "institutional thinking" that they may be perceived as non-optional. They represent "the sum total of 'what everybody knows' about a social world" (Berger & Luckman 1967:65, see also Douglas 1986). Much of the effect of this institutional thinking can be considered "habit" as Dewey (1910) and Mead (1934) use the term.

There is still another area of perceived non-optional behavior that is relevant for our purposes. Goode (1972, 1986) suggests that people in all on-going social systems live in some degree in a "force-threat" environment. "When the force-threat is strong and predictable enough, people can come to view it as normal even when unjust, and in any event as unwise to be challenged" (Goode 1986:47). Thus we can infer that actors accept, internalize, and act in accordance with a set of maxims, beliefs, moral values, attributions, and interpretations of reality, not only because they have learned these (and not other) knowledge systems but also because their perception that adopting alternative courses of actions has a high probability of leading to costly outcomes.

LACUNAE AND AMBIGUITIES

The current state of theory and research on choice and decision-making suffers from three general problems. First, the perspectives are ambiguous and inconsistent with regard to the critical dimension of time. Second, the lack of communication between behaviorists and subjective utility theorists has resulted in the failure to consider the conditions in which one or the other perspective is more appropriate. Finally, the literature tends to confound the concepts of choice, decisionmaking, and problem-solving.

Time

Time has rarely been treated in a systematic way by choice and decision investigators. Behaviorists who rely on interval reinforcement methods use time in the form of the delay between the animal's action and its reinforcement as a critical aspect of the learning process. For this group, probability is considered to vary inversely with delay (Rachlin et al 1986). In a similar way, varying contingent delay patterns with greater or lesser benefits are used to teach animals to defer gratifications (Logue 1986:104–111, Logue et al 1984, Mazur & Logue 1978). Investigators have focused on time pressures as a factor affecting the quality of decisions and information search (Janis & Mann 1977, Tallman et al 1974). In general, it appears that time pressures force actors to simplify their decision tasks and to make more cautious decisions (Abelson & Levi 1985:282, Wright 1974). Under time pressure there is a tendency to overweight negative information (Wright 1974). Janis & Mann (1977:59–64) find that under severe time pressures or other high stress conditions actors become what they term "hypervigilent"; in essence they become transfixed and do not use the limited time available for optimal processing of alternatives.

The amount of time it takes for human beings to process information has also been assessed. Here time depends, in part, on the structural and cultural context within which a decision is made, and on the actor's information processing capacity. With regard to the contextual issue, research suggests that choices vary in terms of how a task is framed (Tversky & Kahneman 1981). A related body of research indicates that prior or preparatory experiences tend to prime the decision-maker to deal with some issues and not others (Higgins et al 1985). For example, in kidney donor research (Simmons et al 1977) described earlier, it was noted that donors appear to make their decisions virtually instantaneously. One possible explanation for this finding is that donors framed the issue in the light of prior experience with emotionally laden or morally salient situations. If the situation is framed in moral terms, there is little information that requires processing; one either behaves morally or immorally. Moral choices are similar in this respect to situations that evoke high levels of emotion. Affect arrousal tends to result in immediate responses (see review of relevant research in Zajonc 1980).

> One of the clearest statements concerning temporal aspects of human information processing is provided by Simon (1979:96). He maintains, the evidence is overwhelming that the system is basically serial in its operation: that it can process only a few symbols at a time and that the symbols being processed must be held in special, limited memory structures whose content can be changed rapidly. The most striking limits on subjects' capacities to employ efficient strategies arise from the very small capacity of the short-term memory structure (four chunks) and from the relatively long time (five seconds) required to transfer a chunk of information from short-term to long-term memory. (Quoted in Etzioni, 1988)

Despite its force and clarity, the premise of the above statement is arguable. Evidence, primarily from emergency or crisis research, suggests that under some conditions actors process considerable information with remarkable rapidity. Janis & Mann (1977:65) note the speed with which persons respond to warnings of immediate danger and indicate that a considerable amount of relevant information is processed in seconds by imagining different alternative actions. They further suggest that such information is processed rapidly primarily because it takes the form of visual images that flash through the actor's mind (pp. 65–67).

Behaviorist and subjectivist alike consider time a valuable resource that is beneficial to save and costly to expend. Careful analysis of the various ways in which time affects the choice or decision process has yet to be undertaken.

Behaviorist and Subjectivist: Cognitive Commonalities and Differences

One consistent, and often ignored, difference between the subjectivist/cognitive and behaviorist research paradigms is that the former is designed to assess subjects' responses to a single event (or at most a small series of events), whereas the latter exposes subjects to an initial learning period that results in an asymptotic (stable) behavioral pattern. Choices that occur at asymptote provide the essential data for testing behavioral hypotheses.

An important implication of the matching law discussed earlier is that over repeated trials an organism's choice of a given alternative tends to be proportional to the rate at which the alternative is reinforced (Herrnstein 1961, 1970, Gray & Tallman, 1984, 1986, 1987, Stafford et al 1986). In the behaviorist experiments the actor learns experientially both the types of behaviors that result in rewards or costs and the frequency with which a particular behavior is reinforced in a particular situation. The real life situations that most approximate these behaviorist experiments involve everyday routine choices such as selecting a breakfast food or a route to drive to work.

On the other hand, decisions such as whether to get married, which of two job offers to accept, whether to invest in a new stock issue, how to avoid a deadly disease, or whether to make a preemptive strike against a potential enemy are hardly routine. These are the general form of the kinds of issues posed in subjectivist/cognitive research. In each of these situations decision-makers cannot fall back on a set of experiences that permit prediction with any degree of confidence as to the probabilities associated with a given choice. They are forced to rely on subjectively generated estimates of those probabilities. Nor is trial and error learning feasible in such situations. Few of us have had sufficient experience with marriage to estimate the consequences of a subsequent marriage. Even if one has been "fortunate" enough to have had several prior experiences, such experiences can only be applied inferentially by establishing parallels or by abstracting a set of principles that can be transferred to the new situation. The same is true of vicarious learning by means of observation. The large combinations of endogenous and exogenous variables affecting the marital relationship plus the longitudinal nature of the marriage commitment make the level of uncertainty as to outcomes extremely high. The best one can do in such nonroutine situations is to make educated guesses, i.e. make subjective probability estimates.

In assessing such estimates it is necessary to identify clearly the decision-maker's objectives. Given the range and diversity of potential outcomes some must be more salient than others. What is the desired outcome of a marriage— to live together for a lifetime, to be happy, to provide an environment for raising children, to improve one's status in the community? The best way to determine the salient outcomes is in terms of the desires or goals of the decision-maker. Thus, the assumption that actors are goal seekers, unnecessary for classic or operant conditioning theories of choice, becomes necessary when considering choices in nonroutine situations.

Whether it is necessary to assume that these goals are stable or only relatively so is less clear. Decisions are often made on a tentative and incremental basis in which actors initially do not fully absorb the impact but become committed to a sequence of events from which they can only extricate themselves at great cost (Janis & Mann 1977). The process of "falling in love" typifies this stepwise involvement in which initial decisions change the cost-benefit ratio in a way that changes the actors' perception of available options. It is rare, for example, that a young couple who go out on a date can anticipate the sequence of events that eventuate in a decision to get married. Simmons et al (1977) make a similar point about some kidney donors who in the process of taking preliminary actions, such as submitting to initial medical tests, find themselves increasingly committed to becoming a donor.

Berkeley & Humphreys (1982) are among the few investigators who have addressed the issue of goal ambiguity directly. They employ techniques for decomposing the relative goals (values) associated with a complex outcome. The method which is called Multiattribute Utility Theory (MAUT) examines the consequences of an "act-event" by breaking it down into "part-worths." The example they provide pertains to evaluating the consequences of building a rapid transit system. They suggest this would be done by decomposing the outcomes into categories such as travel time, user comfort, vehicle construction cost, and so forth. Trade-offs are then assessed and an axiomized composition rule is applied that weights the part-worths in accord with the trade-off ratios. Berkeley & Humphrey's approach is normative; their intent is to help decision-makers better understand what they are about and what they want (see Slovic et al 1977 for a critique of MAUT). Nevertheless, in their decomposition of outcomes, they demonstrate the complexities involved in identifying some goals and the multiple and sometimes confusing perceptions actors have about their goals.

The failure of subjectivists and behaviorists to communicate with one another (combined perhaps with the tendency of adherents of both perspectives to consider their orientation as sufficient for all explanations) has resulted in some resistance to considering the complementarity of the two positions. Behaviorists have provided a viable framework for explaining choices that are made in day-to-day routine situations, whereas the subjectivists explain choices under novel, or at least nonroutine, conditions. As a result, both the theories and the experimental paradigms employed tend to be linked to different social conditions. Similarly, the assumption that humans are goal seekers, while not necessary for behaviorist research, is essential when explaining responses in many nonroutine situations.

Distinguishing Between Choice, Decisions, and Problem-Solving

Closely linked to the failure to stipulate clearly the conditional differences underlying behaviorist and subjectivist theories is the confounding of the concepts of choice and decisionmaking. Only Etzioni (1988:150) appears to have addressed this issue. He notes, "The term *choice* should be used to encompass the sorting out of options, whether conscious or nonconscious. Deliberate choices are to be referred to as *decisions*" (italics in original). This distinction not only identifies different sets of behaviors, it is implicit in much of the literature. Behaviorists tend to use the term "choice" almost exclusively. Cognitive/subjectivists are less consistent in their use of the terms, but when they focus on issues that imply deliberation, such as information processing, or when judgment comes into play, the term "decision" tends to be applied much more frequently. In our view, communication between scholars would be enhanced if the term "choice" were restricted to selecting between routine options such as which route to take to work, whereas "decisions" would be used for nonroutine situations under conditions of risk or uncertainty, such as whether or not to get married. As noted above, choices may be either conscious or unconscious; decisions on the other hand, because they are deliberative and require some level of deduction, are always conscious.

The current state of definitional ambiguity is compounded when we consider problem-solving. A problem is generally defined as a barrier to attaining some desired goal under conditions of uncertainty as to: (*a*) the appropriate means for overcoming the barrier, and (*b*) the outcome of using any given means (Agre 1982, Bourne et al 1971:9, Hattiangadi 1978). By definition, then, problems are nonroutine events. Thus, if a problem is to be solved it requires some type of nonroutine mental or physical activity that successfully removes, circumvents, or overcomes the goal-impeding barrier (Agre 1982, Tallman 1988). Problem-solving is a process that involves, at a minimum, three stages—recognition, selection from among alternative course of action and an evaluation of outcomes. It is a process that is driven by decisions, but it is not synonymous with decisions. For example, making a decision to get married may or may not involve problem-solving. If, for normative or other reasons, the person's goal is to get married and s/he has a willing partner, and if there is no other obstacle to goal attainment, the decision will not involve the person in the problem-solving process. On the other hand, an actor's decision to find someone to marry, or to attempt to convince a friend or partner to marry, is the initial step in a problem-solving process.

Our reading of the literature suggests that the concepts of decision-making and problem-solving have frequently been used interchangeably. Game theory, for example, seems more a problem-solving theory than a decision theory. Consider Shubik's (1964:8) definition of game theory: "a method for the study of decision making in situations of conflict," and later Shubik says, "The individual must consider how to achieve as much as possible, taking into account that there are others whose goals differ from his own" (p. 9). What is depicted by Shubik under the rubric of conflict is essentially a set of interpersonal obstacles to goal attainment, i.e. a problem. Similarly, Janis & Mann's (1977) "Conflict Decision Theory" comes closer to approximating problem-solving than decision-making. They suggest some challenge or disruption of an on-going state of affairs as essential to initiating responses. "Until a person is challenged by some disturbing information or event that calls his attention to a real loss . . . he will retain an attitude of complacency" (p. 172). Challenges call for mobilizing forces to change a state of affairs. This activity seems more reasonably to fall under the category of problem-solving. Many of Janis & Mann's findings better inform problem-solving issues than decision-making. For example, their discussion of "defensive avoidance" provides numerous examples of how an actor's desire for group approval results in the failure to recognize key obstacles for achieving desired goals (pp. 129–130).

Is the distinction between decisions and problem-solving necessary? Clearly Janis & Mann's insights are of value whether termed decision-making or problem-solving. Nevertheless, failure to distinguish between the concepts inhibits the development of adequate theories of choice, decision-making or problem-solving. For example, the last three of Berkeley & Humphreys' (1982) seven types of uncertainty in decisions—"procedural uncertainty," "uncertainty about how the decision maker will feel and wish to act in the future," and "uncertainty about one's agency"—are better understood as relevant to problem-solving. Each of these types of uncertainty pertain to assessing the competence or potential of the actor to deal with events leading to goal attainment. In fact, Berkeley & Humphrey tend to use the phrase "decision problem" virtually interchangeably with "decision." The clarity gained by considering the two concepts separately is peprhaps most evident in their criticism of Tversky & Kahneman's work. Berkeley & Humphrey suggest that the Asian disease question referred to earlier in the paper is not complete because it fails to consider the uncertainty associated with human agency. Such complexities are best understood by recognizing that Tversky & Kahneman's question poses more than a situation calling for a decision, it poses a problem—how best to deal with the losses associated with the disease.

Problem-solving differs from decision-making in that the former always implies a process driven by a related series of decisions. These include, at a minimum, (a) the decision as to whether to commit oneself to attempt to solve the problem, (b) the decision to search for problem solutions, (c) the decision to take a particular course of action, (d) the evaluation of the outcome and the decision as to whether to stop the process, continue with the same effort, or search for alternative avenues for solving the problem.

We have not discussed, in any detail, factors influencing individual differences in decision-making and problem-solving styles. An adequate discussion of this literature would require a separate review. Suffice it to say here that these differences can be attributed to social learning as well as genetic factors. A variety of structural and cultural conditions have been shown to affect problem-solving styles. Thus, structural conditions linked to personal family experiences, social class, and levels of societal development have been shown to affect people's tolerance of ambiguity, tolerance of conflict, and readiness to take risks, all factors that can be linked to problem-solving effectiveness (Tallman et al 1983). In a similar way, communication networks and power relationships are linked to the problem-solving abilities of individual family members (Tallman & Miller 1974).

TOWARD A SYNTHESIS

All theories of choice and decision-making, stripped of qualifying conditions, are concerned with the interaction of three kinds of variables: benefits (rewards, gains, resources, satisfactions, costs foregone), costs (losses, punishments, investments, resource expenditures, and rewards foregone), and probabilities (objective or subjective). Even though utility theorists do not always specify the exact relationship between costs and benefits, they are implicitly incorporated in virtually all conceptions of utility (see, as examples, Camilleri et al 1972, and Blalock & Wilken 1979). Similarly, the avoidance of costs and the seeking of benefits as prime decision motives are implicit in the work of most cognitively oriented theorists, including symbolic interactionists (see, as examples, Rose 1962: Ch. 1, Gecas 1981, Stryker 1980: Ch. 3).

The above statement has not gone unchallenged. The essence of the challenge is that not all choice behavior is motivated by self-interest, and therefore cost/benefit analysis is sometimes inappropriate. It is a premise deeply rooted in sociology. No less a figure than Auguste Comte, who coined the term altruism, believed that some aspects of social behavior are motivated by an unselfish desire to live for others (Batson 1987:67). Like Comte, Etzioni (1988:esp. Ch. 1) has maintained that humans have two forces operating on choice processes, one a desire for self benefit and the other a moral commitment. Moral commitments produce nondeliberated, instantaneous responses (p. 42). Etzioni claims, "the majority of choices involve little information processing or none at all but they draw largely and exclusively on affective involvements and moral commitments" (p. 95). But Etzioni, while criticizing utility theory for its failure to provide an explanation for the development of preferences, provides no such explanation for the genesis of moral commitments. The wide range of individual and cultural differences in belief systems implies that moral commitments are learned

(Rokeach 1973). If such commitments are learned, they are subject to basic learning principles, i.e. beliefs that are punished tend to be extinguished and those that are rewarded tend to be retained.[1]

Etzioni also claims that moral commitments represent nonchoices for actors; he states that they are "obligated, duty bound" to act in a moral way (p. 42). Although this statement may reflect some actor's subjective responses, most students of behavior accept the premise that, in choice situations, actors have at least two options—to act or not to act (Wheelis 1969). Given these options, we must ask what moral persons would do or feel in a situation calling for action if they did not act? The likely response is that they would feel guilt or shame, either of which is a painful experience, and one to be avoided.

In a careful review of the literature on prosocial and altruistic motivation, Batson (1987:82) concludes that the best possibility for building a theory of altruism would be to base the theory on conditions for developing empathic responses in people. Empathy enables an actor to experience vicariously the pain or suffering of another. Once again, the underlying motive is to avoid personal anguish. Thus, it could be argued that empathic people seek to assist others in trouble to relieve their own empathy-generated discomfort.

The problem of building an adequate choice theory, then, is not to rid ourselves of the three variables central to all such theories, but to understand better how they relate to each other and how they are affected by, and function within, social and cultural parameters. To achieve this goal, there is a need to meld or integrate the behaviorist subjective/cognitive, and collectivist approaches. Behaviorist research provides a basis for explaining the development of that part of our emotional responses and moral development that is learned. Thus "spontaneous," nondeliberative actions as well as daily routine habitual behavior can best be understood within this framework. Moreover, in accounting for the development of these behaviors, assumptions concerning the actor as a goal-directed being are unnecessary. The assumption of goal direction becomes necessary only when actors are put in nonroutine situations in which the outcomes are uncertain. Such situations call for deliberation, information search, and subjective probability estimates—all of which are put

---

[1]Through the learning process we call socialization, people internalize values and norms so that they punish themselves through guilt and self-derogation when they violate these beliefs and reward themselves when their behavior is consonant with their beliefs (Aronfreed 1969, Scott 1971). This makes it possible, under certain conditions, for people to display considerable resistance to changing beliefs even under the threat of punishment. Nevertheless, as the brainwashing and conversion literature suggest, people are amenable to changing belief systems when they find them no longer beneficial, or when they are subject to conditions of severe isolation combined with severe levels of threat if they continue to maintain their beliefs and the possibility of rewards if they change them (Lifton 1963, see Gecas 1981 and Zurcher & Snow 1981 for a review of more recent literature).

to the use of assessing the costs and benefits of alternative options for obtaining a desired outcome. Viewed in this way behaviorists and subjectivists are not competing perspectives but are complimentary, each dealing with different choice conditions.

A sociological theory of choice should incorporate choices made under routine and nonroutine conditions, employ both objective and subjective probabilities, consider the relationship between costs and rewards as independent and differentially weighted variables, and account for single event choices, repeated choices, and choices designed to set in motion a sequence of events involving subsequent choices.

Beginning efforts have been made to produce the kind of synthesis suggested above. Gray & Tallman (1984, 1986, 1987) building on the work of Lindenberg (1980, 1981) have developed the Satisfaction Balance Model which, while incorporating probability matching, is sufficiently flexible to account for repeated as well as single choice situations. One form of the model is:

$$\frac{b}{1-b} = \left(\frac{R1 \; V1 \; (1 \; - \; R2) \; C2}{R2 \; V2 \; (1 \; - \; R1) \; C1}\right)^{.5},$$

where b is the probability of a given choice or decision, $1-b$ is the probability of the alternative choice(s), R_i is the probability of a reward or benefit occurring with the i'th choice, $1-R_i$ is the probability of the cost (punishment) occurring with the i'th choice, V_i is the magnitude of the benefit and C_i is the magnitude of the cost accruing with the i'th choice. The model conceives of the three key components (probability, benefits, and costs) as interactive. At the same time each of the components for each option considered can be weighted separately. The model has been compared favorably with Lindenberg's model (Gray & Tallman 1984, 1986) and several behavioral models (Gray et al 1986). It has also predicted deterrent effects and homicide rates (Stafford et al 1986). Though the S-B Model is sufficiently flexible to integrate the three variables and to differentially weight their magnitudes, it does not provide us with a theory that accounts for how people arrive at the magnitudes or the weightings.

The most ambitious and comprehensive attempt to explain both probability weightings and magnitudes is Kahneman & Tversky's (1979) Prospect Theory. Briefly summarized, the theory focuses on two functions, probability weighting and valuation. The probability weighting function indicates that actors generally overweight small probabilities and underweight large ones. They also suggest a general tendency (except at the extremes) for conservatism or slightly underweighting probabilities. The value function, in the region of gains, tends to be concave; that is each additional unit of a benefit has less and less value as the gain increases. This is in accord with Bernoulli's original conception of utility. As noted earlier, this suggests a tendency to avoid risks and prefer certainty in gain situations. When losses are considered, however, each unit of loss below a reference point has less impact on the negative value. The function for losses is convex and suggests that the dominant tendency in risk situations is to avoid the certain loss and to be risk-seeking in attempting to avoid the loss.

There are considerable data to support these essential premises of Prospect Theory (for a review of criticisms of the theory see Abelson & Levi 1985). Unfortunately the theory tells us nothing of how actors place value on different goods and relationships, or on different types of costs. For example, what is more important to an actor: a raise in salary or a high-status job? What is more aversive: the loss of a job or the loss of a lover? The answer to such questions may vary by culture and subculture and by the resources an actor controls in each of these value domains. Nevertheless, we seem bereft of theory for adequately weighting the magnitudes of costs and benefits in given situations. Emerson (1987) addresses the need for such a theory, calling for recognition that things have relative, rather than absolute value, and suggesting that a thing's worth is best understood in terms of what is given up to get it. Like Etzioni (1988) and Simmons et al (1977), Emerson considers the expression of values to be instantaneous. However, he accepts the premise that conditioning experiences are a primary source for developing an individual's value hierarchy. Emerson's theory is preliminary and incomplete, but it is suggestive of the type of theory that can inform students of choice and decision making.

The growing body of theory and research on distributive justice (Berger et al 1972, Cook & Hegtvedt 1983, Jasso 1980, 1987, 1988) is also helpful in gaining a better understanding of the weighting of costs and benefits. Recent research suggesting different conditions affecting norms of equality and equity (Meeker & Elliot 1987, Jasso 1988) can contribute to developing a better understanding of antecedent conditions influencing the magnitudes of costs and benefits in choice situations.

These are bits and pieces, but they seem to be converging. A theory of value may evolve that is articulated precisely enough to enable students of choice to specify more clearly the magnitudes attached to costs and benefits and to better understand when and how goal-seeking and goal-altering behaviors affect the choice process.

We are left with the final question of how the three critical variables assist sociologists in understanding the linkages between individual choice and macro social behavior. There is little debate about the importance of these variables at the macro level. Cost avoidance, benefit seeking, and probability estimates are essential elements of all large-scale organizations. The assumption that nations, corporations, and governments are focused on survival and the accumulation and control of resources is rarely questioned. Less well articulated are the mechanisms through which collectivities act to protect themselves against external and internal threats and to obtain the resources they seek. What is lacking, in Coleman's (1988) terms, is identifying the "engine of action." This engine is driven by human fuel, and human beings regardless of their social position are rarely simple automotons. The spark that ignites the engine is human choice.

The major emphasis of sociological theory and research has been on explaining how such choices are constrained and channeled—by ideologies and belief systems, by the distribution of wealth and other resources, by patterns of industrialization and urbanization, by the rate of technological change, by the distribution and access to political and economic power, by patterns of stratification, by the use and manipulation of the media, by ethnic and race relations, and so forth. But in the last analysis human beings, however constrained and whether serving as agents for collectivities or acting in their own interests, make the choices and decisions that propel events and alter structural conditions and belief systems. It is these decisions that determine crime rates, divorce rates, create mobs and political demonstrations, force changes in political systems, cause depressions and revolutions, and so forth.

There is no shortage of efforts to try to develop theoretical bridges between micro and macro phenomenon (Blalock & Wilkin 1979, Coleman 1986, 1988, Heckter 1983). It seems to us, however, that these efforts do not focus sufficient attention on questions of human motivation. Without an explanation of what drives people to act or not to act, the micro-macro linkage is incomplete. To return to our previous metaphor, without a theory of motivation, we cannot explain what sparks the "engine of action." In this review, we have concluded that this spark is manifest in the desire of people to seek benefits, avoid costs, and figure out their chances of successfully achieving these ends. It is a relatively simple formula and as such has been attacked by sociologists as being "atomistic" (Coleman 1988). But being atomistic is not necessarily bad. Identifying and combining basic elements to explain how phenomena form and change has proved to be a useful strategy for many sciences.

We began by suggesting that the moment of choice may be considered the microcosm which brings together all of the social forces that propel and channel social action. We have also suggested that these forces can be understood as the interplay of three variable domains—costs, benefits, and probabilities. This kind of a model may grossly oversimplify reality. Alternatively, it is possible that in our desire to explain interesting things like wars, revolutions, the growth and decline of political economies, changing crime and divorce rates, and so forth, we may overlook the forces and conditions that constitute the atom of human interactions—the choice that occurs at a given moment and that can set entire systems of action and interaction in motion.

ACKNOWLEDGMENTS

We wish to express our deep appreciation to our colleagues Viktor Gecas, Marilyn Ihinger-Tallman, Lisa McIntyre, Robert Meier, Gene Rosa, James Short, Jr., and Charles Tittle for their thorough, careful, and insightful comments on an earlier draft of this paper. We are also grateful for the generous help provided by the anonymous reviewer.

Literature Cited

Abelson, R. P., Levi, A. 1985. Decision making and decision theory. In *Handbook of Social Psychology,* ed. G. Lindzey, E. Aronson 3:231–309. New York: Random House.

Agre, G. P. 1982. The concept of problem. *Educ. Studies* 13:121–41

Allais, M., Hagen, O. eds. 1979. *Expected Utility Hypotheses and the Allais Paradox.* Hingham, Mass: D. Reidel

Aronfreed, J. 1969. The concept of internalization. In *Handbook of Socialization Theory and Research,* ed. D. A. Goslin, pp. 263–323. Chicago: Rand McNally

Axelrod, R. 1984. *The Evolution of Cooperation.* New York: Basic

Bandura, A. 1969. Social learning theory of identificatory processes. In *Handbook of Socialization and Research,* ed. D. A. Goslin, pp. 213–62. Chicago: Rand McNally

Bandura, A. 1977. *Social Learning Theory.* Englewood Cliffs, NJ: Prentice Hall

Bandura, A. 1986. *Social Foundations of Thought and Action: A Social Cognitive Theory.* Englewood Cliffs, NJ: Prentice Hall

Bartos, O. J. 1966. Concession making in experimental negotiations. In *Sociological Theories in Progress,* ed. J. Berger, M. Zelditch, B. Anderson, 1:3–28. Boston: Houghton Mifflin

Bartos, O. J. 1972. Foundations of a rational-empirical model of negotiation. In *Sociological Theories in Progress,* ed. J. Berger, M. Zelditch, B. Anderson, 2:3–20. Boston: Houghton Mifflin

Batson, C. D. 1987. Prosocial motivation: Is it ever truly altruistic? In *Advances in Experimental Social Psychology,* ed. L. Berkowitz, 20:65–122. San Diego: Academic

Baum, W. M. 1974. On two types of deviation from the matching law: bias and undermatching. *J. Exp. Anal. Behav.* 22:231–42

Baum, W. M. 1979. Matching, undermatching and overmatching in studies of choice. *J. Exp. Anal. Behav.* 32:269–81

Berger, J., Zelditch, M., Anderson, B. eds.

1972. *Sociological Theories in Progress.* Boston: Houghton Mifflin

Berger, P. L., Luckman, T. 1967. *The Social Construction of Reality* Garden City, NY: Anchor

Berkeley, D. Humphreys, P. C. 1982. Structuring decision problems and the "Bias Heuristic". *Acta Psychol.* 50:201–52

Bernard, J. 1954. The theory of games of strategy as modern sociology of conflict. *Am. J. Sociol.* 59:411–36

Blackman, D. 1974. *Operant Conditioning: An Experimental Analysis of Behavior* London: Methuen

Blalock, H. M., Wilkin, P. H. 1979. *Intergroup Processes.* New York: Free

Boudon, R. 1986. The logic of relative frustration. In *Rational Choice,* ed. J. Elster, pp. 171–96. New York: New York Univ. Press

Bourne, L. E., Ekstrand, B. R., Dominowski, R. L. 1971. *The Psychology of Thinking.* Englewood Cliffs, NJ: Prentice Hall

Burgess, R. L., Akers, R. L. 1966. A differential association—reinforcement theory of criminal behavior. *Soc. Probl.* 14:128–47

Camilleri, S. F., Berger, J., Conner, T. L. 1972. A formal theory of decision making. In *Sociological Theories in Progress,* ed. J. Berger, M. Zelditch, B. Anderson, 2:21–37. Boston: Houghton Mifflin

Camilleri, S. F., Conner, T. L. 1976. Decision making and social influence: a revised model and further experimental evidence. *Sociometry* 39:30–38

Coleman, J. S. 1973. *The Mathematics of Collective Action.* Chicago: Aldine

Coleman, J. S. 1986. Social theory, social research, and a theory of action. *Am. J. Sociol.* 91:1309–35

Coleman, J. S. 1988. Social capital in the creation of human capital. *Am. J. Sociol.* 94:95–120

Cook, K. S., Hegtvedt, K. 1983. Distributive justice, equity and equality. *Annu. Rev. Sociol.* 9:217–41

Cyert, R. M., March, J. G. 1963. *A Behavioral Theory of the Firm.* Englewood Cliffs, NJ: Prentice Hall

Dewey, J. 1910. *How We Think*. New York: D. C. Heath

Douglas, M. 1986. *How Institutions Think*. Syracuse: Syracuse Univ. Press

Deusenberry, J. 1960. Comment in universities-national bureau committee for economic research. *Demographic and Economic Change in Developed Countries*, pp. 231–34. Princeton, NJ: Princeton Univ. Press

Eddy, D. M. 1982. Probabilistic reasoning in clinical medicine: problems and opportunities. In *Judgment Under Uncertainty: Heuristics and Biases*, ed. D. Kahneman, P. Slovic, A. Tversky, pp. 249–67. Cambridge: Cambridge Univ. Press

Edwards, W. 1968/1982. Conservatism in human information processing. In *Judgment Under Uncertainty: Heuristics and Biases*, ed. D. Kahneman, P. Slovic, A. Tversky, pp. 249–67. Cambridge: Cambridge Univ. Press originally in *Formal Representations of Human Judgement*, ed. B. Kleinmuntz, New York: Wiley

Einhorn, H. J., Hogarth, R. M. 1981. Behavioral decision theory: processes of judgment and choice, 32:53–88 *Annu. Rev. Psychol.*

Einhorn, H. J. 1980. Learning from experience and suboptimal rules in decision making. In *Cognitive Processes in Choice and Decision Behavior*, ed. T. S. Wallstein, pp. 195–222. Hillsdale, NJ: Lawrence Erlbaum

Elder, G. 1974. *Children of the Great Depression*. Chicago: Univ. Chicago Press

Elder, G. 1981. Social history and life experience. In *Present and Past in Middle Life*, ed. D. Eichorn et al, pp. 3–31. New York: Academic

Elster, J. 1986. Introduction. In *Rational Choice*, ed. J. Elster, pp. 1–33. New York: New York Univ. Press

Emerson, R. 1972. Exchange theory, Parts I and II. In *Sociological Theories in Progress*, ed. J. Berger, M. Zelditch, B. Anderson, pp. 2:38–87 Boston: Houghton Mifflin

Emerson, R. 1987. Toward a theory of value in social exchange. In *Social Exchange Theory*, ed. K. Cook, pp. 11–45. Newbury Park, Calif: Sage

Estes, W. K. 1950. Toward a statistical theory of learning. *Psychol. Rev.* 57:94–107

Estes, W. K. 1959. Component and pattern models with markovian interpretations. In *Studies in Mathematical Learning Theory*, ed. R. R. Bush, W. K. Estes, pp. 9–52. Stanford: Stanford Univ. Press

Estes, W. K., Skinner, B. F. 1941. Some quantitative properties of anxiety. *J. Exp. Psychol.* 29:512–23

Etzioni, A. 1988. *The Moral Dimension: Toward a New Economics*. New York: Free

Ford, J., Zelditch, M. 1988. A test of the law of anticipated reactions. *Soc. Psychol. Q.* 51:164–71

Gecas, V. 1981. The contexts of socialization. In *Social Psychology: Sociological Perspectives*, ed. M. Rosenberg, R. H. Turner, pp. 165–99. New York: Basic

Gecas, V. 1982. The self concept. *Annu. Rev. Sociol.* 8:1–33

Goode, W. J. 1972. The place of force in human society. *Am. Sociol. Rev.* 37:507–19

Goode, W. J. 1986. Individual choice and the social order. In *The Social Fabric: Dimensions and Issues*, ed. J. Short, pp. 39–62. Beverly Hills: Sage

Gray, L. N., von Broembsen, M. H. 1976. On the generalization of the law of effect: social psychological measurement of group structures and processes. *Sociometry* 39:175–83

Gray, L. N., Griffith, W. I., Sullivan, M. J., von Broembsen, M. H. 1982. Social matching over multiple reinforcement domains: an explanation of local exchange imbalance. *Soc. Forces* 61:156–82

Gray, L. N., Stafford, M., Tallman, I. 1986. Rewards and punishments in complex human choices. Ninth symposium on quantitative analysis of behavior. Harvard Univ. June 6, 7. Cambridge, Mass.

Gray, L. N., Tallman, I. 1984. A satisfaction balance model of decision making and choice behavior. *Soc. Psych. Q.* 47:146–59

Gray, L. N., Tallman, I. 1986. Predicting choices in asymptotic decisions: a comparison of two models. *Soc. Psych. Q.* 49:201–6

Gray, L. N., Tallman, I. 1987. Theories of choice: contingent reward and punishment applications. *Soc. Psych. Q.* 50:16–23

Hamblin, R. L. 1977. Behavior and reinforcement. A generalization of the matching law. In *Behavioral Theory in Sociology*, ed. R. L. Hamblin, R. Kunkel, pp. 252–80. New Brunswick, NJ: Transaction

Hamblin, R. L. 1979. Behavioral choice and social reinforcement: step function versus matching. *Soc. Forces* 57:1141–56

Hareven, T. 1978. Introduction: the historical study of the life course. In *Transitions: The Family and the Life Course in Historical Perspective*, ed. T. Hareven, pp. 1–16. New York: Academic

Hareven, T. 1982. *Family Time and Industrial Time*. Cambridge: Cambridge Univ. Press

Harsanyi, J. 1977/1986. Advances in understanding rational behavior. In *Rational Choice*, ed. J. Elster, pp. 82–105. New York: New York Univ. Press. Previously publ. in *Foundation Problems in the Special Sciences*, ed. R. E. Butts, F. Hintikka. (Dordrecht 1977)

Hattiangadi, J. N. 1978. The structure of problems (Part 1). *Philos. Soc. Sci.* 8:345–65

Hechter, M. 1983. Introduction. In *The Microfoundations of Macrosociology*, ed. M. Hechter, pp. 3–15. Philadelphia: Temple Univ. Press

Heimer, C. A. 1988. Social structure, psychology, and the estimation of risk. *Annu. Rev. Sociol.* 14:491–519

Herrnstein, R. J. 1961. Relative and absolute strength of response as a function of frequency of reinforcement. *J. Exp. Analy. Behav.* 4:267–72

Herrnstein, R. J. 1970. On the law of effect. *J. Exp. Anal. Behav.* 4:267–72

Hickson, D. J. 1987. Decision making at the top of organizations. In *Annu. Rev. Sociol.* 13:165–92

Higgins, E. T., Bargh, J., Lombardi, W. 1985. The nature of priming effects on categorization. *J. Exp. Psychol: Learning, Memory and Cognition* 11:59–69

Homans, G. C. 1974. *Social Behavior: Its Elementary Forms*. New York: Harcourt Brace Jovanovich

Janis, I. L., Mann, L. 1977. *Decision Making: A Psychological Analysis of Conflict Choice and Commitment*. New York: Free

Jasso, G. 1980. A new theory of distributive justice *Am. Sociol. Rev.* 83:1398–1419

Jasso, G. 1987. Choosing a good: models based on the theory of the distributive justice force. *Adv. Group Proc: Theory Res.* 4:67–108

Jasso, G. 1988. Distributive justice effects of employment and earnings on marital cohesiveness: An empirical test of theoretical predictions. In *Status Generalization: New Theory and Research*, ed. M. Webster, M. Foschi, pp. 123–62. Palo Alto, Calif: Stanford Univ.

Kahneman, D., Tversky, A. 1972. Subjective probability: a judgment of representativeness. *Cognitive Psychol.* 3:430–54

Kahneman, D., Slovic, P., Tversky, A. 1982. *Judgement Under Uncertainty: Heuristics and Biases*. Cambridge: Cambridge Univ. Press

Kahneman, D., Tversky, A. 1979. Prospect theory: an analysis of decision under risk. *Econometrica* 47:263–91

Kahneman, D., Tversky, A. 1984. Choices, values and frames. *Am. Psychol.* 39:341–50

Knight, F. H. 1957. *Risk, Uncertainty, and Profit*. London Sch. Econ. Polit. Sci. *Econ. Polit. Sci.* #16. New York: Kelley

Latane, B., Darley, J. M. 1970. The unresponsive bystander: why doesn't he help? New York: Appleton

Lifton, R. J. 1963. *Thought Reform and the Psychology of Totalism: A Study of Brainwashing in China*. New York: Norton

Lindenberg, S. 1980. Marginal utility and restraints of gain maximization: the discrimination model of rational, repetitive choice. *J. Math. Sociol.* 7:289–316

Lindenberg, S. 1981. Rational, repetitive choice: the discrimination model versus the Camilleri-Berger Model. *Soc. Psychol. Q* 44:312–30

Logue, A. W. 1986. *The Psychology of Eating and Drinking*. New York: Freeman

Logue, A. W., Rodriguez, M. L., Pena-Correal, J. W., Mauro, B. C. 1984. Choice in a self-control paradigm: quantification of experience-based differences. *J. Exp. Anal. Behav.* 41:53–67

Lopes, L. L. 1987. Between hope and fear: the psychology of risk. In *Advances in Experimental Psychology*, ed. L. Berkowitz, 20:255–95

Luce, R. D., Raiffa, H. 1957. *Games and Decisions*. New York: Wiley

March, J. G. 1978. Bounded rationality, ambiguity, and the engineering of choice. *Bell J. Econ. Manage. Sci.* 9:587–608

Marcus, H., Zajonc, R. B. 1985. The cognitive perspective in social psychology. In *The Handbook of Social Psychology*, ed. G. Lindzey, E. Aronson, pp. 137–230. New York: Random House

Marschak, J. 1984. Scaling of utilities and probability. In *Game Theory and Related Approaches to Social Behavior*, ed. M. Shubik, pp. 151–82. New York: Wiley

Mazur, J. E., Logue, A. W. 1978. Choice in a self-control paradigm: effects of a fading procedure. *J. Exp. Anal. Behav.* 30:11–17

Mead, G. H. 1934. *Mind, Self, and Society*. Chicago: Univ. Chicago Press

Meeker, B. F., Elliott, G. C. 1987. Counting the costs: equity and the allocation of group products. *Soc. Psychol. Q* 50:7–15

Molm, L. D. 1981. Power use in the dyad: The effects of structure, knowledge and interaction history. *Soc. Psychol. Q.*

Molm, L. D. 1987. Linking power structure and power use. In *Social Exchange Theory*, ed. K. S. Cook, pp. 101–29. Newbury Park, Calif: Sage

Molm, L. D., Wiggins, J. A. 1979. A behavioral analysis of social exchange in the dyad. *Soc. Forces* 57:1157–79

Nisbett, R. E., Ross, L. 1980. *Human Inferences: Strategies and Shortcomings of Social Judgment*. Englewood Cliffs, NJ: Prentice Hall

Ofshe, L., Ofshe, R. 1970. *Utility and Choice in Social Interaction*. Englewood Cliffs, NJ: Prentice Hall

Olson, M. 1965. *The Logic of Collective Action*. Cambridge: Harvard Univ. Press

Parfit, D. 1986. Prudence, morality, and the prisoner's dilemma. In *Rational Choice*, ed. J. Elster, pp. 34–59. New York: New York Univ.

Peterson, C. R., Beach, L. R. 1967. Man as an intuitive statistician. *Psychol. Bull.* 68:29–46

Rachlin, H. 1970. *Introduction to Modern Behaviorism*. San Francisco: Freeman

Rachlin, H., Logue, A. W., Gibbon, J., Frankel, M. 1986. Cognition and behavior in studies of choice. *Psychol. Rev.* 93:33–45

Raiffa, H. 1968. *Decision Analysis: Introductory Lectures on Choices Under Uncertainty*. Reading, Mass: Addison-Wesley

Rappaport, A., Chammah, A. 1965. *Prisoner's Dilemma*. Ann Arbor: Univ. Michigan

Rappoport, A. 1960. *Fights, Games and Debates*. Ann Arbor: Univ. Michigan

Rokeach, M. 1973. *The Nature of Human Values*. New York: Free Press

Schwartz, S. H. 1970. Moral decision making and behavior. In *Altruism and Helping Behavior*, ed. J. R. Macaulay, L. Berkowitz, pp. 121–45. New York: Academic

Schwartz, S. H. 1984. Internalized values as motivators of altruism. In *Development and Maintenance of Prosocial Behavior*, ed. E. Staub, D. Bar-Tel, J. Karylowsky, J. Reykowski, pp. 229–55. New York: Plenum

Scott, J. F. 1971. *Internalization of Norms*. Englewood Cliffs, NJ: Prentice Hall

Sen, A. 1986. Behavior and the concept of preference. In *Rational Choice*, ed. J. Elster, pp. 60–81. New York: New York Univ. Press

Shubik, M. 1964. Game theory and the study of social behavior: an introductory exposition. In *Game Theory and Related Approaches to Social Behavior*, ed. M. Shubik, pp. 3–77. New York: Wiley

Siegel, S., Siegel, A. E., Andrews, J. M. 1964. *Choice, Strategy and Utility*. New York: McGraw Hill

Simmons, R., Klein, S. D., Simmons, R. L. 1977. *Gift of Life: The Social and Psychological Impact of Organ Transplantation*. New York: Wiley

Simon, H. 1955. A behavioral model of rational choice. *Q. J. Econ.* 63:129–38

Simon, H. 1957. *Models of Man*. New York: Wiley

Simon, H. 1979. Rational decision making in business organizations. *Am. Econ. Rev.* 69:493–513

Slovic, P., Fischoff, B., Lichtenstein, S. 1977. Behavioral decision theory. *Annu. Rev. Psychol.* 28:1–39

Stafford, M. C., Gray, L. N., Menke, B. A., Ward, D. A. 1986. Modeling the deterrent effects of punishment. *Soc. Psychol. Q* 49:338–47

Starbuck, W. H. 1983. Organizations as action generators. *Am. Sociol. Rev.* 48:91–102

Stryker, S. 1980. *Symbolic Interactionism: A Social Structural Version*. Menlo Park, Calif: Benjamin/Cummings

Tallman, I. 1980. Problem solving in families: a revisionist view. In *Social Stress and Family Development*, ed. D. M. Klein, J. Aldous, pp. 102–28. New York: Guilford

Tallman, I. 1988. Problem-solving in families: A revisionist view. In *Social Stress and Family Development*, ed. J. Aldous, D. Klein. New York: Guilford

Tallman, I., Klein, D., Cohen, R., Ihinger, M., Marotz, R., Torsiello, P., Trost, K. 1974. *A Taxonomy of Group Problems and Implications for a Theory of Group Problem Solving*. Techn. Rep. 3. Minneapolis: Minn. Family Study Cent.

Tallman, I., Marotz-Baden, R., Pindas, P. 1983. *Adolescent Socialization in Cross-Cultural Perspective*. New York: Academic

Tallman, I., Miller, L. 1974. Class differences in family problem solving: the effects of verbal ability, hierarchical structure, and role expectations. *Sociometry* 37:13–37

Tedeschi, J. T., Schlenker, B. R., Bonoma, T. V. 1973. *Conflict, Power and Game: The Experimental Study of Interpersonal Relations*. Chicago: Aldine

Thaler, R. H. 1983. Illusions and mirages in public policy. In *The Public Interest* 73:60–74

Tversky, A., Kahneman, D. 1981. The framing of decisions and the psychology of choice. *Science* 211:453–58

Tversky, A., Kahneman, D. 1982. Judgments under uncertainty: Heuristics and biases. In *Judgment Under Uncertainty: Heuristics and Biases*, ed. D. Kahneman, P. Slovic, A. Tversky, pp. 3–20. Cambridge: Cambridge Univ. Press

Vanacke, W. E., Ackoff, A. 1957. An experimental study of coalitions in the triad. *Am. Sociol. Rev.* 22:406–14

Weick, K. E. 1976. Educational organizations as loosely coupled systems. *Admin. Sci. Q.* 21:1–18

Wentworth, W. M. 1980. *Context and understanding: An Inquiry into Socialization Theory*. New York: Elsevier

Wheelis, A. 1969. How people change. *Commentary* 47:56–66

Wright, P. 1974. The harassed decision maker: time pressures, distractions and the use of evidence. *J. Appl. Psychol.* 59:555–61

Zajonc, R. B. 1980. Feeling and thinking: preferences need no inferences. *Am. Psychol.* 35:151–75

Zelditch, M., Harris, W., Thomas, G. M., Walker, H. A. 1983. Decisions, nondecisions, and metadecisions. In *Research in Social Movements, Conflicts, and Change*, 5:1–32. Greenwich, Conn: JAI

Zurcher, L. A., Snow, D. A. Collective behavior: social movements. In *Social Psychology: Sociological Perspectives*, ed. M. Rosenberg, R. H. Turner, pp. 447–82. New York: Basic

Annu. Rev. Sociol. 1990. 16:435–63

NETWORK DATA AND MEASUREMENT

Peter V. Marsden

Department of Sociology, Harvard University, Cambridge, Massachusetts 02138

KEY WORDS: network, data, survey, measurement

Abstract

Data on social networks may be gathered for all ties linking elements of a closed population ("complete" network data) or for the sets of ties surrounding sampled individual units ("egocentric" network data). Network data have been obtained via surveys and questionnaires, archives, observation, diaries, electronic traces, and experiments. Most methodological research on data quality concerns surveys and questionnaires. The question of the accuracy with which informants can provide data on their network ties is nontrivial, but survey methods can make some claim to reliability. Unresolved issues include whether to measure perceived social ties or actual exchanges, how to treat temporal elements in the definition of relationships, and whether to seek accurate descriptions or reliable indicators. Continued research on data quality is needed; beyond improved samples and further investigation of the informant accuracy/reliability issue, this should cover common indices of network structure, address the consequences of sampling portions of a network, and examine the robustness of indicators of network structure and position to both random and nonrandom errors of measurement.

INTRODUCTION

Progress in the study of social networks has been rapid over the past two decades. The network approach, developed out of analytical insights from social anthropology and methodological leads from sociometry (Shulman 1976, Wellman 1983) conceives of social structure as patterns of specifiable relations joining social units—including both individual actors and collectives

435

such as organizations and nation-states. Moving away from the use of the concept of a social network as a sensitizing metaphor and toward its development as a research tool, the approach seeks to describe social structure in terms of networks and to interpret the behavior of actors in light of their varying positions within social structure. Emphasis is on constraints placed by social structure on individual action and the differential opportunities—known variously as social resources, social capital, or social support—to which actors have access.

This chapter reviews methods that have been used to gather social network data, and what is known about issues of data quality and measurement in social network studies. Much work has gone into developing methods for the analysis of such data (see, for example, Burt 1980, Marsden & Laumann 1984, Pappi 1987, Freeman et al 1989), and computer software supporting such analyses is now available (e.g. Rice & Richards 1985, Freeman & McEvoy 1987, Burt 1989). As the approach turns toward applied studies focused on substantive problems, however, questions having to do with data collection and data quality have assumed increased importance.

There is an extensive earlier literature on sociometric measurement, summarized in Lindzey & Byrne (1968) and Mouton et al (1955). Much of this material remains relevant, although the contemporary network approach stresses actual social ties and exchanges more than the social psychological constructs such as affect and interpersonal attractiveness with which sociometry was concerned. Holland & Leinhardt (1973) reviewed approaches to sociometric measurement and assessed their implications for certain models of social structure. More recently, substantial work on network measurement has been done by those studying social support (House & Kahn 1985) and family and personal relationships (Huston & Robins 1982, Milardo 1983, 1989). Bernard et al (1984) give a general discussion of the problem of informant accuracy for retrospective data which is pertinent to many network measurement issues.

The next section briefly highlights some general issues bearing on network measurement. I then cover questions of study design and review different sources of social network data, before turning to questions of data quality for individual data elements. These include measures that enumerate ties as well as those describing their properties and the characteristics of other units ("alters") involved in them. Recent work on indices or measures built from measurements on individual ties is next summarized. The chapter concludes with a discussion of general themes and needed work.

CONCEPTUAL QUESTIONS

Network analysts commonly write about social structure conceived as patterns of specific or concrete social relations as if the issue of what constitutes a social relation were self-evident. Sound conceptualization must precede measurement, however, and not all studies are precise about their theoretical definitions of social ties or the relationship to be established between concepts and measures. I discuss some important unresolved issues here; those taking different positions on these will draw different conclusions about the quality of network measurement from many of the methodological studies to be reviewed.

A central question is that of whether one seeks to measure actually existing social relations, or social relations as perceived by actors involved in them, sometimes called "cognitive" networks. Many network analysts take an objectivist or behavioral position in keeping with the view that networks are external constraints on action over which an individual actor can exercise at best limited control. Clearly, though, the appropriate concepts and measurements should differ, according to the dependent variables to be interpreted in light of the network data. Accurate knowledge of actually existing ties is arguably important to the study, for example, of certain diffusion processes (e.g. Klovdahl 1985) while perceived ties might be more appropriate for studying social influences on attitudes or opinions.

A second concern is with temporal elements in the definition of social ties. Radical microsociological approaches to the study of social interaction (Collins 1988, ch. 11) focus on events such as utterances that occur in very short time frames. To write of social structure as "a persisting order or pattern of relationships among some units of sociological analysis" (Laumann & Knoke 1986, p. 84) presumes some means of abstracting from these empirical acts to relationships or ties. Measurements could refer to episodic and transient, even momentary, transactions between pairs of actors in particular behavioral events, or to routinized, recurrent configurations of transactions that involve interdependence and/or mutual orientation on the part of the actors (Huston & Robins 1982).

A focus on routinized ties, typical of many network studies, has led to charges of static bias. Attempts to move toward dynamic studies raise difficult questions of defining, conceptually and operationally, when relationships start, change, and end (Doreian 1988). Legal criteria such as marriage or incumbency in formally defined positions (like corporate directorships) sometimes suffice to do this. In many other cases it is difficult to define the initiation or termination of social ties apart from operational procedures. While friendship, for example, can be defined theoretically as a bond involving both freedom and intimacy (Wiseman 1986), in practice the term is used to cover a wide variety of links (Fischer 1982a), few of which have well-defined starting and ending points.

A final theme has to do with the relationship sought between concepts and measures: does the researcher seek to obtain precise *descriptions* of the social ties that compose a network, or *indicators* which reflect either differences between individual units in network positions or differences across networks in structural properties? If description is the goal, then concerns about accuracy are paramount in the evaluation of measures. Analysts seeking indicators should instead evaluate measures in terms of the traditional validity-reliability framework and be concerned with the robustness of analytic methods to errors in measurement.

NETWORK STUDY DESIGNS

Levels of Analysis

Network studies focus on several levels of analysis, and indeed the network approach is viewed as one promising strategy for cross-level analysis. The broadest concern is with comparing entire social structures—e.g. work groups, organizations, communities—to one another. This often requires complete network data on all social ties linking elements of a population to one another. Complete enumeration of a closed population is essential for analytic techniques that make use of information about compound or indirect ties linking actors; examples include many techniques for studying centrality (Freeman 1979) and some kinds of positional analysis (Winship & Mandel 1983). At a minimum, one kind of social tie is measured, but data on several types are often sought.

Some methods can produce analyses of properties of total social structures based on data obtained by enumerating all ties linking a sample of units to one another. Such a design is suitable for estimating certain structural properties (see the discussion below of network sampling), or for techniques such as blockmodel analysis for identifying roles and positions based on relaxations of structural equivalence concepts (e.g. Arabie et al 1978).

A second concern is at the level of individual actors. Here, analysts may seek to explain differences across actors in social position, or to link such differences to variations in outcomes (e.g. well-being). This can be accomplished with measures of social position derived from analyses of complete network data, but a different design is often used. Variously known as egocentric, personal, or survey network data, this method samples individual units, or stars, and enumerates the local networks surrounding them. This design does not yield an overall description of the social structure of a population unless units are redefined as generalized social positions such as occupational or ethnic groups (Laumann 1973). On the other hand, this approach gives representative samples of the social environments surrounding particular elements and is compatible with conventional statistical methods of generalization to large populations.

Network studies occasionally focus on levels of analysis intermediate between the individual and the population. Most often these are dyads, but triads and even larger subsets are also studied. Such levels are usually studied by using the set of, e.g., dyads obtained in either complete or egocentric network data; note that the latter tend to be biased toward the inclusion of comparatively close ties. It is in principle possible to sample dyads or triads directly, but this is seldom if ever done.

Boundary Specification

For both complete and egocentric network data, the researcher faces the problem of specifying boundaries on the set of units to be included in a network. This in some ways parallels the general problem of defining the population to which research results are to be generalized. It is of special importance in network studies, however, since analyses focus explicitly on interdependencies among the particular units studied. Omission of pertinent elements or arbitrary delineation of boundaries can lead to misleading or artifactual results (Barnes 1979).

Laumann et al (1983) review boundary specification strategies for complete networks. They distinguish between realist approaches based on the sub-jective perceptions of actors and nominalist approaches taking an observer's standpoint, and they contrast three procedural tactics for defining boundaries. Tactics based on attributes of units rely on membership criteria set by formal organizations such as schools (Coleman 1961) and work organizations (Kapferer 1969) or occupancy of specific social positions deemed pertinent by researchers for membership in, e.g., professional communities (Coleman et al 1966), or elites (Useem 1979). Social relations may also be used to delimit boundaries, as in snowball sampling procedures (Erickson 1978). Participa-tion in a set of events, such as publication in scientific journals (Breiger 1976) or Congressional testimony (Laumann & Knoke 1988),[1] can also be used as a criterion delimiting a set of mutually relevant actors.

For egocentric network data, the boundary specification problem is that of operationally determining which other units are to be regarded as part of a given unit's network. Usually, such data refer to a subset of the direct contacts of a focal unit—the "first-order zone," in Barnes's (1969) terminology. In principle, one could collect data on elements in the second-order zone—those linked to the focal unit by one intermediary—or even more distal units. Strong pragmatic pressures tend to restrict attention to direct contacts, however, and little is known about the amount of distortion such restrictions introduce. With the typical survey methods for gathering data, boundaries for egocentric network data are set via one or more name generator queries (Burt 1984) that elicit the names of elements with which a unit is in direct contact.

A related issue is that of specifying the kind(s) of ties to be measured. Most often researchers try to tap contents entailing positive affect, supportive

---

[1]Laumann & Knoke used this in combination with four other boundary specification criteria.

exchanges, coordination and the like; conflictual links are occasionally included as well. Efforts at empirical typology for types of interpersonal relations (Burt 1983c, 1990) suggest that they vary along dimensions of tie strength, frequency of contact, and role relationships (a contrast of kinship versus workplace contact).

Network Sampling

Sampling considerations arise in several connections in network studies. At the population or total network level of analysis, sampling of units is generally not an issue: a complete enumeration, sometimes called a "dense" or "saturation" sample, is often sought. The comparatively few studies contrasting entire networks with one another [e.g. Knoke & Rogers (1979) on interorganizational networks; Laumann & Knoke (1988) on national policy domains] usually select networks to study on a purposive or convenience basis.

Conventional random sampling procedures can be used to gather egocentric network data and generalize results about the networks surrounding units to a large population. The use of such data to address questions at other levels of analysis is more involved. For example, the sample of dyads from this design is clustered within individuals and typically skewed toward relatively close ties.

A literature on network sampling has also developed, focusing on the estimation of properties of a complete network based on data collected from a subset of the units composing it. Reviewed in Frank (1981), this work has in large part focused on the problem of estimating overall network density (Granovetter 1976, Morgan & Rytina 1977, Erickson et al 1981, Erickson & Nosanchuk 1983) or the density of contact between subgroups (Beniger 1976).

Network notions are also used to design sampling methods for studies having other concerns. Sudman (1985, 1988a) is concerned with social networks as part of multiplicity sampling procedures for locating rare individuals. McPherson (1982) and Spaeth (1985) describe hypernetwork sampling methods that use reports of the organizational affiliations of survey respondents to generate probability-proportional-to-size samples of voluntary and work organizations.

SOURCES OF NETWORK DATA

Researchers have been imaginative in obtaining data on social ties from diverse sources. Surveys and questionnaires soliciting self-reports, however, are the predominant research method used. Archival sources are also used extensively. Other methods include diaries, electronic traces, observation, informants, and experiments.

Surveys and Questionnaires

Self-reports of the presence or absence of social ties are the most common method used to gather network data. Most often such data are obtained with single-item questions that ask a respondent to enumerate those individuals with whom he or she (or an organization for which he or she is an agent) has direct ties of a specified kind. In studies of delimited populations, respondents can be asked to recognize their contacts from a listing, but often only unaided recall methods are practical. Holland & Leinhardt (1973) listed different formats that have been used in collecting such data: dichotomous indicators of the presence or absence of a given type of relationship, which may or may not fix the number of links per respondent; scales or ranks differentiating ties in terms of intensity; or paired comparisons of the strength of different relationships.

Techniques for collecting egocentric network data have been studied somewhat more systematically. The typical procedure used (Burt 1984) is to determine membership in a respondent's network via one or more name generators and then to obtain additional data via name interpreter items. Name interpreters are of three kinds: (a) reports on attributes of persons or alters enumerated (e.g. age, education, race/ethnicity); (b) reports on properties of the tie between respondent and alter (e.g. frequency of contact, duration of acquaintance, intensity); and (c) reports on the intensity of ties between pairs of alters, which can be used to measure the structure of the egocentric network (e.g. in terms of density).

Initial studies of networks in mass populations used affective and/or role relation (friend, coworker, neighbor) criteria as name generators, and many placed an upper limit on network size, presumably for reasons of practicality. The 1966 Detroit Area Study (Laumann 1973), among the first such studies, asked its white male respondents to enumerate their three "best friends." Wellman's (1979) study of a Toronto district asked about up to six "persons outside your home that you feel closest to." Holland & Leinhardt's (1973) discussion criticized the practice of fixing network size by design because it can distort descriptions of both local and global structure, and most succeeding instruments allow network size to vary across respondents.

McAllister & Fischer (1978) sought data on a broader segment of the social worlds surrounding respondents than that provided by affective name generators. Their method uses multiple name generators, most of which refer to specific social exchanges; these vary in intensity from sociability and discussion of hobbies to confiding about personal problems and borrowing large sums of money. Names of adult members of respondents' households are elicited, and others "important to you" can be added. No definite upper limit is placed on overall network size, though only the first eight names cited in response to individual name generators were recorded by McAllister & Fischer. To limit interview time, which ranged between 20 and 30 minutes for one version of this instrument (Fischer 1982b), some name interpreter items were asked for only a subsample of names.

Burt (1984, 1985) coordinated the development of the network items that appeared in the 1985 General Social Survey (GSS). These data had to be gathered in a short (15 minute) amount of interview time, so a single, relatively intense name generator was used, requesting those persons with whom a respondent had "discussed matters important to you within the past six months." No upper limit on network size was specified, but name interpreter data were collected on only the first five names given.

Numerous instruments for gathering egocentric network data have been developed by those studying social support (see House & Kahn 1985). These range from simple measures referring to relationships with a confidant (Dean & Taussig 1986) to lengthy questionnaires seeking to measure both the availability of social support and a respondent's satisfaction with it. Many of these instruments omit name interpreter data on network structure.

A few examples will convey the variety of approaches used to collect data on social support networks; Tardy (1985) and Pearson (1986) compare some of these instruments. Kahn & Antonucci (1980) describe procedures for identifying convoys providing social support, using both affective and role-relation name generators and a concentric circle diagram for listing network members in relation to a respondent. Barrera's (1980, 1981) Arizona Social Support Interview Schedule includes two name generators for each of six support functions (material aid, physical assistance, intimate interaction, guidance, feedback, and social participation). The Norbeck Social Support Questionnaire (Norbeck et al 1981) enumerates alters "who provide personal support for you or who are important to you now." Flaherty et al (1983) describe the Social Support Network Inventory, which uses an affective name generator. Sarason et al (1983) generate names for their Social Support Questionnaire on the basis of specific supportive behaviors. The Social Network Inventory, developed by Daugherty et al (1988), generates names by a frequency of contact criterion and includes measures of whether alters know one another.

Wellman (1981), among others, has noted that most instruments for network measurement seek to elicit supportive ties and ignore difficult, disruptive, or conflictual connections. This may be of special importance in the study of effects of social support, where some studies suggest that the absence of unsupportive ties is more crucial than the presence of supportive ones (Barrera 1981, Rook 1984). Questions eliciting negative or conflictual ties raise clear sensitivity problems, but some efforts have been made. An instrument used in a community survey by Leffler et al (1986; see also Gillespie et al 1985) included questions requesting names of people who are "overly demanding," "most likely to let you down," and who "make you angry or upset." Respondents gave 68% of the names possible (they were limited to three names per question). Less than 10% of the respondents named no one. The Barrera (1980) and Daugherty et al (1988) instruments also include items measuring negative aspects of social ties.

Recent methodological studies have compared the sets of alters elicited by some of these different instruments. Van Sonderen et al (1989) compare personal networks obtained using affective, specific exchange, and role-relation name generators. They find that specific exchange questions yield a larger number of alters, who tend to be more weakly tied to the respondent than those given in response to the other types of questions. Overlap in the sets of names given across methods was appreciable but incomplete: 46% of the alters from the exchange method were also obtained with the affective approach; 73% of the latter were included in the exchange network. These results are compatible with those reported by Hoffmeyer-Zlotnik (1989) in a comparison of a specific exchange instrument to the GSS "important matters" name generator. The exchange instrument gave roughly 8 alters per respondent in comparison to 2.6 for the GSS question.

There are instruments for measuring properties of personal networks other than the name generator/name interpreter sequence. Lin & Dumin (1986) present an instrument for measuring network range on the basis of contacts with categories of people. Hoffmeyer-Zlotnik (1989) discusses a related global instrument. Laumann's subjective distance scale (Laumann & Senter 1976) provides data on desired relations to social categories (occupations or ethnoreligious groups, for example).

Surveys and questionnaires have also been used in the study of interorganizational relations, through interviewing one or more informants as agents of an organization of interest. Rogers (1974) used six items to measure the intensity of interorganizational relations for public agencies. Galaskiewicz (1979) developed questions about transfers of information, money, and support for a variety of community organizations, measuring both inflows and outflows of each type of resource. The questionnaire for Knoke & Wood's (1981) study of ties among voluntary associations drew on both of these sources. Laumann & Knoke (1988) asked representatives of organizations identified as elements of national policy domains questions about communication, resource transfers, and joint activities. Van de Ven & Ferry (1980) developed indicators of numerous aspects of dyadic interorganizational relationships, such as domain similarity, resource dependence, communication, and formalization (see also Morrissey et al 1982).

When surveys and questionnaires are used to study interorganizational relationships, problems of respondent selection arise due to specialization within organizations. Most studies select only one agent to report on an organization's ties to all other organizations, but it is plausible to expect that the quality of such reports might be better for those kinds of relations that involve the informant's own activities. To date there is little research on the quality of reports on networks by organizational agents, or on how reports by multiple agents might best be combined into organization-level measures.

Archives

As will be seen below, the quality of network data obtained by surveys and questionnaires is far from perfect, and gathering such data often requires substantial research budgets. Archival sources of various kinds are inexpensive, and advantageous for studying social networks in the past or in which units are otherwise inaccessible.

Interlocking directorate studies (e.g. Mintz & Schwartz 1985, Burt 1983a) are probably the most common use of archival data. Information about relationships between banks or corporations is assembled from records giving the names of persons who sit on the boards of directors of major corporations; organizations having one or more directors in common are said to be related (Breiger 1974). The same general approach has been used to study relationships between organizations in the nineteenth-century US women's movement (Rosenthal et al 1985).

A notable literature in the sociology of science relies on archives of citations in efforts to identify specialty groups. Cocitation studies create a relation between two scientists when their work is cited by the same authors (Lievrouw et al 1987, White & McCann 1988).

Archives are also used in the study of international and interurban networks. Snyder & Kick (1979) seek to identify positions in the world system based on records of trading, military incursions, treaties, and diplomatic exchanges. Breiger (1981) and Nemeth & Smith (1985) use more extensive information on trading patterns. Duncan & Siverson (1982) study formal and informal alliances between European powers over a period of a century. Ross (1987) analyzes interurban links of dominance or control, defined using records giving the locations of administrative headquarters and production facilities of multiestablishment firms.

Only a limited methodological literature exists on archival network data. Particularly valuable here would be triangulation studies that show how indirect measures of ties, like cocitations or shared affiliations, correspond to more direct indicators of interaction (e.g. Lievrouw et al 1987, Baker 1987, Burt et al 1980a).

Other Data Sources

Other methods of assembling network data have been used less often. The social anthropologists who were early contributors to development of the network orientation tended to rely on observational methods of data collection (e.g. Mitchell 1969, Boissevain 1974). These certainly have the advantage of increased naturalness and may yield greater descriptive accuracy. They are, however, very time-consuming and more or less restricted to relatively small-scale studies. Data can also be provided by informants other than the investigator or individuals involved in the network under study. Burt et al (1980b) illustrate one such use of informants.

Certain methods can be used in small or special populations only, either because they require unusual cooperation from subjects or the presence of special recording equipment. Participants in some studies have agreed to keep diaries of their contacts over a period of time (Wheeler & Nezlek 1977, Conrath et al 1983, Milardo 1982). Recently developed interactive communications media (Rogers 1987) can gather network data unobtrusively. Higgins et al (1985) studied an intraorganizational network using data assembled by a traffic data analyzer for telephone calls. Rice (1982) analyzed data recorded by a computer-conferencing system.

A few studies have collected data via experiments. The best known of these were conducted via the "small-world" technique, in which subjects (starters) are asked to forward a packet of information to a person they do not know (target) via personal acquaintances (Travers & Milgram 1969; Lin et al 1978). A variation on this is the "reverse small world" technique of Killworth & Bernard (1978). This generates names in a subject's network by asking about the personal contacts he or she would use to contact a large and diverse number of (often hypothetical) targets.

ENUMERATING NETWORKS AND THE INFORMANT ACCURACY ISSUE

Most methodological research on network measurement has focused on data obtained through surveys and questionnaires. This work assumes that researchers seek to measure social ties that have an objective existence, beyond respondent cognitions. The accuracy or reliability of self-reported information about a respondent's network ties can be assessed in several ways: through comparing responses to an observed or otherwise known standard; through interviews with alters cited; or through over-time studies which measure the stability of responses to network items. Use of multiple indicators—comparing the alters mentioned in response to different name generators, for example—is problematic for assessing reliability, because of the common assumption that, rather than being realizations of a common underlying link, different kinds of relationships may exhibit different patterns (Laumann & Knoke 1986).

Comparing Survey Responses to a Known Standard

A series of studies reported by Bernard, Killworth, and Sailer (BKS; see Killworth & Bernard 1976, Bernard & Killworth 1977, Bernard et al 1981,

1982) have occasioned the greatest amount of discussion in this area. These studies focus on the descriptive accuracy with which respondents can recall communication over a definite period of time. For several relatively small populations, they compare data on social ties obtained via questionnaires or similar methods to behavioral records obtained via diaries, monitoring of radio communication, observers, or electronic monitoring. While the two sets of measurements are not independent of one another, neither is their correspondence especially close. Hence, Bernard et al (1981, p. 15) conclude that "people do not know, with any acceptable accuracy, to whom they talk over any given period of time."

Other similarly designed studies yield results consistent with BKS. Milardo (1989) elicited social networks from married couples using an instrument like that of McAllister & Fischer (1978) and compared them to reports of voluntary social activities of more than five minutes duration obtained in telephone interviews conducted every other day for two weeks. An average of 25% of the persons named in either source were named in both.

Several critics have commented on the BKS studies (Hammer 1980, Burt & Bittner 1981, Richards 1985). It is claimed that the studies deal with special populations or unusual forms of communication, but there is no particular reason to think that the specific populations or kinds of contact studied would produce the low correspondence observed. Others point to the fact that respondents are involved in other social networks besides the groups studied, and that therefore they were asked to recall relatively trivial communication events; it is perhaps not surprising, then, that they cannot recall these events very well.

Those concerned with the reliability, as distinct from the descriptive accuracy, of recall data (Hammer, 1980) note that the correlation between responses and observations is relatively high by the standards of social science data—0.8 in one of the studies reported (Killworth & Bernard 1976). One argument for viewing the correspondence against a standard of reliability rather than accuracy is that time-sampling and other problems of recording the observational data make it problematic to take them as an exact standard, but this does not apply to all of the BKS studies.

Richards (1985) argues that using self-reports to gather network data necessarily presumes some interpretive or subjective viewpoint, and that the use of observational data as a standard of accuracy is thus inappropriate. Many investigators do, however, use self-reported data to measure actual communication links, and the BKS findings are pertinent to them.

The BKS studies have stimulated a healthy skepticism about taking self-reported network data from surveys and questionnaires at face value, and it is difficult to take issue with their view that either the quality of such data must be improved or procedures used for analysis must be shown to be robust to errors in measurement. The central BKS conclusion (quoted above) was stated somewhat negatively, but the work has stimulated constructive suggestions as attention has shifted from the gap between recall and observation to understanding how the two measurements are related. The main theme here is that there are systematic rather than random discrepancies between self-reported and observed network data. For example, Hammer (1985) shows that reciprocated reports are substantially more likely to match observed interactions than are unreciprocated reports. It appears that self-reports tend to yield data on typical network ties, even when respondents are asked about a definite period of time. This result should comfort those who seek to measure routinized ties as distinct from time-bound transactions.

An especially promising line of research has been pursued by Freeman & Romney (1987, Freeman et al 1987). Drawing on principles of cognitive psychology, they argue that informant errors will be biased toward the routine, typical structure. In their research, they compare respondent reports of persons present at specific events to actual attendance records. The reports tend to include those who generally do attend but did not on the specific day about which respondents were questioned; they tend to omit irregular attenders who were present that day. The implication for network measurement is that people are incapable of reporting accurately on transactions that take place within highly specific time frames, but are able to recall and report their typical social relations. To date, however, this has not been demonstrated for actual social network data in a design comparable to that of the BKS studies.

A related line of work focuses on systematic differences in accuracy among informants. Romney & Weller (1984) reanalyze much of the BKS data, showing that the more reliable informants—defined as those for whom the correspondence between reports and overall observed interaction frequencies is high—give reports that are highly associated with each other. This is linked to a more general model for discovering unknown cultural knowledge, by Romney et al (1986). This approach, however, transforms the problem from one of measuring the accuracy with which individuals report their own network ties to one of the accuracy with which they report overall participation levels for elements of the network (see also Hildum 1986).

Sudman (1985, 1988a) explores the accuracy problem in a different way. He defines work groups, associations, neighborhoods, and kinship units as networks and studies three different interview methods for measuring their size: unaided recall, recognition based on a list of members, and direct estimation of size, with respondents rather than analysts performing aggregation. Recognition methods yield substantially larger estimates of size than do recall methods. For several groups studied, it appeared that the quality of recall declined for less proximate ties, e.g. for distal kin or for more geographically extensive definitions of neighbors (Sudman 1988a). Somewhat surprising was the finding that direct estimation of network size gave much the same mean as recognition, though with appreciably higher variability. Question-order effects were also apparent: more accurate numerical estimates were obtained when respondents were asked first about their close ties instead of about their acquaintances.

Hammer's (1984) research also compared recall and recognition methods. Consistent with Sudman's results on biases in recall, she found that alters named by recall methods tend to be frequent, intense, and recent contacts. There was no tendency for respondents in her study to cite relationships of long duration, however.

Reciprocation of Survey Responses

The strategy pursued by BKS for studying network measurement is viable only in relatively small groups whose communication can be readily monitored. In large or open populations it is more difficult to obtain a behavioral standard for assessing accuracy; one alternative method is to presume that mutually acknowledged ties are genuinely present and to see how often citations are reciprocated. In a study of high school students asked to name same-sex alters with whom they "go around most often" (Alexander & Campbell 1964), about 60% of respondents were named among the first three listings by their first-cited alters. The Coleman et al (1966) study of physicians reports a 37% rate of reciprocation for doctors seen most often socially, but substantially lower rates for discussions of cases or therapy (26%) and advice about questions of therapy (13%). Laumann (1969) interviewed some of the "best friends" cited by respondents in a mass survey and found that 43.2% of them named the respondent among his three best male friends. Pappi & Wolf (1984) replicated Laumann's study in a West German community, reporting similar findings. Shulman (1976) reported a 36.2% rate of reciprocation for naming of the six closest intimates, and showed that reciprocation declined steadily for alters less close to the respondent. Hammer (1984) reported reciprocal naming for 86% of the "close" ties mentioned by respondents in her studies, also finding that reciprocity was lower for less intense relationships.

At least two studies in the social support area have gathered reciprocation data. Barrera et al (1985) questioned 36 pairs of subjects and alters about six types of support. For support provided to subjects by alters, rates of reciprocation ranged from 69.4% for "intimate interaction" to 97.4% for "physical assistance"; similar results were obtained for support to alters from subjects. Antonucci & Israel (1986) studied 497 dyads and found that 84% of the alters independently named the respondent. Reciprocation was lower for specific forms of support, between 49% and 60%. It was higher for close kin and substantially lower for "friends."

One study of reciprocation (Conrath et al 1983) compared questionnaire responses to diary entries, for communication events. Reciprocity was found to be substantially higher for the diaries.[2]

It is difficult to judge whether these rates of reciprocation are high or low; failure to reciprocate could be the result of inaccuracy or unreliability in the data or of genuine asymmetry in the relationships under study. Conceptions of friendship or closeness that vary between respondents and alters, and the affective component of such citations, suggest that there will be some asymmetry in designations of best friends or intimates. Differences between respondents and alters in network size or overall level of interaction will generate other asymmetries. For example, the most frequent contact of a respondent with a low rate of interaction may report accurately and still not reciprocate the citation, especially if the study design limits the number of citations, as it does in many of these studies. These definitional and design considerations are less problematic for the social support studies, which may help to account for the generally higher reciprocity levels reported there. Clearly, also, rates of reciprocation are affected by network density, higher rates being observed in high-density settings, as illustrated by the contrasting results presented by Deseran & Black (1981) and Williams (1981) for reports of interaction in decision making activities by rural influentials identified by positional/reputational methods.

Overall, rates of reciprocation are high enough to suggest that self-reports reflect more than mere respondent perceptions. At the same time, it is difficult to claim on the basis of this evidence that these measures are free of error.

Test-Retest Studies

There is an inherent problem in interpreting the results of over-time studies of network measures, since it is not presumed that properties of networks are unchanging traits. Unreliability in reports is thus mixed together with genuine turnover. Still, it is plausible that instruments eliciting routinized, relatively intense relationships should exhibit appreciable test-retest associations, at least for short time intervals, since the rate of change in such ties is presumably low. Over-time studies have been conducted for a variety of instruments and time intervals. Here I concentrate on the levels of turnover in specific alters, rather than on the stability of measures of network properties. Two general themes appear: there is an appreciable level of stability, and it is higher for more intense relationships.

Shulman (1976) compares networks of intimates obtained one year apart.

---

[2]A subsequent study (Higgins et al 1985) evaluated recording biases in telephone diaries by comparing entries to electronic records maintained by a traffic data analyzer system. Diaries tended to understate the frequency of communications, and to omit short, incoming, and extraorganizational contacts.

Exactly the same alters were named by 28.8% of his respondents; 19.2% changed a majority of alters, and there was complete turnover for 2.2%. Barrera (1980) conducted a test-retest study with a two-or-more-day interval. He reports the alters named on both occasions as a percentage of those named on either one. For specific kinds of social support, these range from 48% (for material aid within the past month) to 73% (for typical sources of material aid). When all six forms of support were studied jointly, there was 74% stability in the "past month" citations and 80% in the "typical" citations.

Two recent studies examine the stability of citations for different instruments for collecting egocentric network data. Broese van Groenau et al (1989) examine networks elicited on the basis of role relations, affective criteria, and specific exchanges; interviews were separated by about 4 weeks. Overlap was measured as the average percentage of alters named in common on the two occasions relative to network size. For role-generated networks, this was 88%; it was lower for the affective approach (78%) and the exchange approach (74%). There was more turnover in larger networks. For the affective approach, overlap was notably higher for the "first-degree network" (94%) than for "friends" (69%) or "others" (58%). Over 50% overlap was reported for all but 2 of 20 specific exchanges studied; it was about 70% for discussion of personal problems.

Hoffmeyer-Zlotnik (1989) studied an instrument using eight specific exchanges to enumerate names (modelled on that of McAllister & Fischer 1978) and the GSS "important matters" instrument, with a three-week interval between administrations. Of the alters named in the first wave 63% were also named on the second for the specific exchange instrument; but only 45% of the wave 1 "important matters" alters were named in wave 2.[3] Effects of ordinal position were apparent for the GSS instrument; there was greater stability in the naming of alters cited first or second in wave 1 than for those cited later.

QUALITY OF NAME INTERPRETER ITEMS

The question of how well data collection methods can identify social contacts is perhaps the most central one for network measurement. Other data obtained by instruments for egocentric network data have important uses in building measures of network structure or in multiplicity sampling, though, so it is of interest to know about the quality of respondent reports on attributes of alters or properties of their relationships to alters, given that they are correctly

---

[3]Unlike the original GSS version (Burt 1985), the instrument used in Hoffmeyer-Zlotnik's study prohibited the naming of spouses or live-in partners as alters; however, he reports that 90% of respondents, if permitted, would have named these on both waves.

enumerated. There are few if any data that bear on the accuracy of respondent reports about relationships between pairs of alters.

Reports on Attributes of Alters Cited

There is a substantial body of work on the correspondence of responses given by husbands and wives. Much of this has been done by demographic researchers interested in the use of proxy responses in studies concerned with fertility and fertility control. In some cases both spouses are asked to report on objective couple or household characteristics; in others they are asked to give proxy reports on each other's attributes or attitudes; in still others analysts examine the extent of correspondence between reports of their own attitudes or characteristics. Proxy reports are of greatest interest to those with interests in network measurement; the general theme here is that observable features such as demographic characteristics can be reported with substantially greater accuracy than attitudes.

Anderson & Silver (1987) studied recent emigrant couples from the Soviet Union to the United States, finding high correspondence between reports for objective items other than family income. Studying the discrepancies found, they point to variations between husbands and wives in understandings of terms such as household used in questions and to differences in time frames assumed by respondents for retrospective questions. Coombs & Cheng (1981) report 80% agreement between husbands and wives on current use of contraception, and that couples who agree on use had fewer children in succeeding years. Koenig et al (1984) report a similar level of agreement for Indian couples, but focus attention on factors affecting it—including age, education, interview conditions, and differences in the status of men and women; they also list a large number of studies that have examined husband-wife concordance in reports on contraceptive use.

Williams & Thomson (1985) examined the correspondence between a respondent's desired family size and a proxy report of this by his or her spouse. The correlations between actual and proxy reports were about 0.6, relatively high for attitudinal data. Williams & Thomson found little evidence that proxy reports were contaminated by projection of one's own expectations or desires; they note that reports of family size may not be representative of proxy reports in general.

Other studies deal with close ties, but not couples, and they generally find that projection does play a part in responses to questions asking for proxy reports of attitudes. Wilcox & Udry (1986) studied perceptions of sexual attitudes and behavior by adolescents matched to best same-sex friends. They compared respondent perceptions of the friend's attitudes and behavior to the friend's own reports, with special attention to the degree to which perceptions reflect the respondent's own characteristics. Perceived attitudes of the friend were strongly influenced by the respondent's attitudes and bore almost no resemblance to the friend's attitudes. Perceived coital status of the friend was related to the friend's report of coital status, but independently influenced by the respondent's own coital status.

Such results are generally consistent with studies of pairs of close friends conducted by Laumann (1969) and Pappi & Wolf (1984). These find extremely high rates of agreement between respondent proxy reports of the sociodemographic characteristics of alters such as age, education, and occupational prestige and the direct reports from alters. Reports of political party preference, however, are problematic. First, many respondents refuse on grounds of knowledge limitations. In addition, the reports that are given reflect projections of respondent preferences onto their friends.

Sudman (1988b) examined informant reports of disabilities of relatives, cancer patients in their households, Vietnam era veterans among relatives, missing children in the household of a relative, neighbor, or coworker, and crime victimization of relatives, coworkers or friends. In many of these studies, reasonable accuracy levels were found: reports were good for disabilities and cancer patients, but quite poor for Vietnam veterans by more distant kin such as aunts and uncles; victimization outside the household was also poorly reported.

Reports on Properties of Relationships

Several researchers have studied the correspondence between respondents and alters on descriptions of the relationship between them. Here, agreement rather than accuracy is the standard used. Respondent reports are often in concordance with alter reports, particularly for close ties and reasonably general types of interaction.

Shulman (1976) reported agreements of between 55% and 72% on five kinds of exchange; agreement was less common for less close ties, however, and there was a tendency for both parties to claim that they gave more than they received. Hammer (1984) found very high concordance on frequency of contact, duration, kinship, and intensity of relationship.

Studies of couples also provide some information here. Clark & Wallin (1964) studied reports on frequency of intercourse by married couples, finding correlations of about 0.6; discrepancies appeared higher in dissatisfied couples. Christensen et al (1983) conducted research on dyadic interaction for both married and dating couples, finding agreement to be higher on objective and specific, rather than diffuse, items; happier couples had higher concordance than unhappy ones.

A study by Card (1978) suggests some of the limits to what may be expected of respondents. She reports low correlations between husbands' and wives' responses to questions about the extent to which they talk about ten topics. With one exception, correlations were lower than 0.46, and were negative for the topic of "relatives" in both samples examined.

RECENT DEVELOPMENTS FOR BASIC INDICES AND MEASURES

Network data are generally of less interest as individual items than as components of measures that characterize a complete network, a unit's location within a network, or a property of a dyad. Authors including Mitchell (1969), Shulman (1976), and Mitchell & Trickett (1980) have reviewed different types of measures, and much of the work on network models and analysis of network data can be viewed as part of a research program to develop social structural measures (Marsden & Laumann 1984). I concentrate here on basic indices or measures which have been developed recently, or for which recent empirical work on measurement has been done. This has used diverse designs and techniques, including test-retest studies, examination of correlations of multiple items or measures, and simulations. I omit discussion of measurement issues related to identification of network subgroups (cliques, social positions), on the grounds that this topic is sufficiently involved to merit separate treatment (see Burt 1980, 1988, Faust & Romney 1985).

Network Size

A basic indicator of interest is network size—the number of direct ties involving individual units. This is used variously to measure integration, popularity, or range. Mouton et al (1955) summarize the early evidence on this measure; it has reasonably high stability over short periods of time. This is one feature that the BKS research suggests is reliably measured by the observations and the self-reports they studied (Bernard et al 1982), though the self-reports tended to understate network size. Barrera (1980) gives 2-day test-retest correlations of 0.88 for both the number of persons recently providing social support and the number who "typically" provide such support; the correlation is only 0.54 for the size of the "conflicted" network, however. Fischer et al (1986) report a 1-week test-retest correlation of 0.91 for family and friendship network size. Sarason et al (1987) give 3–4 week test-retest correlations of about 0.85 for network size for a short form of their Social Support Questionnaire. Broese van Groenau et al (1989) report 4-week test-retest correlations for network size that are above 0.8; the correlations are somewhat higher for a role-relation name generator than for affective or specific exchange generators.

Network Density

Network density—the mean strength of connections among units in a network, or (for dichotomous measurements) the proportion of links present relative to those possible—is probably the most common index of network structure. Little systematic empirical work on its measurement has been done, however, aside from the material on network sampling reviewed earlier. Friedkin (1981) shows, using simulations, that density is a problematic index of structural cohesion if a network has subgroups, and that comparisons of density measures across networks that differ in size can likewise be misleading.

Centrality and Centralization

Perhaps the greatest amount of recent work has been done on the measurement of centrality in networks. Freeman (1979) presents an important conceptual review of centrality measures for dichotomous network data; "degree-based" measures (in essence, network size) focus on levels of communication activity; "betweenness" measures stress control or the capacity to interrupt communication; and "closeness" measures reflect freedom from the control of others. Gould (1987) extends Freeman's betweenness measures to nonsymmetric data. Stephenson & Zelen (1989) give a related centrality measure based on information; unlike the measures described by Freeman, this makes use of all direct and indirect ties between pairs of units.[4]

Other work on centrality measures is based on Bonacich's (1972) measure, which does not assume dichotomous measurement of ties; Knoke & Burt (1983) note that such "prominence" measures, unlike Freeman's centrality measures, weight ties by the centrality or prominence of the affiliated units. Mizruchi et al (1986) extend the Bonacich measure in several ways, distinguishing between hub locations which have high scores due to large network size and bridge locations which are close to a small number of other highly central units. They also discuss techniques for partitioning change in centrality over time.[5] Bonacich (1987) generalizes the measure by allowing indirect ties to lower, rather than raise, a unit's centrality. This enables his measure to reproduce experimental results obtained under conditions of negative connections among exchange relations (Cook et al, 1983).

The Bonacich measure is often used in efforts to index the relative power of units within a network. Mizruchi & Bunting (1981) study results obtained with this measure using several different rules for coding data on corporate interlocks, finding that sensitivity to directionality and differential tie strength gives a closer correspondence to historical accounts. Mariolis & Jones (1982) find very high reliability and stability coefficients for centrality measures based on data on interlocking directorates collected at two-year intervals; these were slightly lower for measures that coded directionality. Bolland (1988) compares the three Freeman measures and the Bonacich measure for

---

[4]That is, this measure considers more than minimum-distance or "geodesic" paths.
[5]Tam (1989) provides an alternative method of disaggregating centrality scores.

one network, finding that the betweenness measure is least redundant with the others—all are positively correlated—and that the extent of redundancy increases when random perturbations are added to the data.

Centrality measures themselves focus on the relative positions of units within a network, but Freeman (1979) shows that there is a corresponding network-level measure of *centralization* for each centrality measure. Centralization measures reflect the variability in centrality scores among units (see also Snijders, 1983).

Tie Strength

Several authors have studied multiple measures of properties of individual dyads in an effort to obtain indices of tie strength. In the literatures on personal relationships and social support there are various multiple-item indices. For example, Lund (1985) gives scales for love, commitment, and investments in close personal relationships. Cramer (1986) studies the Relationship Inventory, a 69-item instrument concerning a single tie, finding factors of empathy, congruence, and level of and unconditionality of regard.

Network studies are often concerned with measuring numerous social relationships, however, and it is difficult to expect respondents to complete long batteries of items about each of numerous ties. Some studies have examined the correlations among name interpreter items such as closeness, frequency, and duration. Marsden & Campbell (1984) found in a study of best-friend ties that measures of closeness or intensity were the best indicators of an unobserved tie strength concept, in the sense that they were not contaminated by other measures. Duration tended to overstate the strength of kinship connections, and frequency exaggerated the strength of ties to coworkers and neighbors; frequency was quite weakly associated with both closeness and duration. Mitchell (1987) obtained many similar results in a study of strong ties among homeless women. Recent work by Wegener (1989) on contacts activated in the course of job searches, however, isolates aspects of tie strength that he labels intimacy, formality, and leisure. Closeness, duration, and frequency are all positively related to an "intimacy" focus which appears to be the most consequential property of social ties for explaining the outcomes of the searches studied.

Network Range

Burt (1983b) defines the concept of network range as the extent to which a unit's network links it to diverse other units. Range can be measured by network size or, inversely, by network density—less dense networks having higher range, by Granovetter's (1973) argument. Other measures include indices of diversity in the characteristics of alter units, and Burt's (1983b) measures sensitive to the positional similarity of alter units to one another and to the strength of links between the focal unit and alters. Campbell et al (1986) examine the associations between different range measures. They find that different measures of range are only weakly correlated and suggest that size, density, and diversity are empirically distinct aspects of range.

DISCUSSION

Social networks have been measured in many ways, and the available research indicates that these can make some claim to being reliable, though certainly imperfect, measures. Some important issues are yet to be systematically studied, but network analysts are much more conscious of the limitations of their data than a decade ago.

Some conclusions about data gathered by surveys and questionnaires seem appropriate in light of what is known. It is generally agreed that designs should not constrain network size to be identical for all units. Recognition methods, when feasible, will provide more complete coverage of networks than recall methods, and recall will be biased toward inclusion of stronger links. Respondents do appear capable of reporting on their local networks in general terms but are probably unable to give useful data on detailed discussion topics or the exact timing of interactions. Name interpreter data on observable features of alters are of high quality, while those on attitudes or internal states are generally poor; data on broad features of relationships like duration or frequency are of moderate to high quality. Most network data appear to be of better quality for close and strong ties than for distal and weak ones.

The research that leads to these conclusions also points to various problems with extant network data, and two responses to such difficulties seem useful. One is to improve the quality of measures for individual data elements. In large part this involves sound practice of the survey research craft (e.g. Converse & Presser, 1986): ensuring that meaning is shared between respondent, interviewer, and investigator; asking questions about which respondents are in fact knowledgeable; avoiding both excessively diffuse and excessively minute items; thoroughly pretesting instruments, and the like. The development of the GSS network items (Burt, 1984) gives one model.

The main alternative is to develop measures that are robust to errors in individual items. This approach would assume that an analyst seeks indices contrasting structures and positions, rather than exact descriptions of networks. Notable improvements in reliability of attitude constructs, for example, are gained by forming multiple-item scales in which individual item idiosyncrasies and fluctuations tend to cancel one another out.

This approach has not been systematically explored for measures of network properties. It appears most promising for indices that involve addition of individual elements; network size is of this type, and appears to have high reliability even with flawed measures. Network density has not been studied as much, but involves a similar sort of aggregation. Likewise, measures of network composition—average levels of attributes for units that are part of a network—are additive and should improve over the reliability of individual items. Other common network indices are nonadditive, and for these the way in which combining measures affects reliability is not well understood. For example, BKS studies on triads (Killworth & Bernard, 1979) and on clique-finding algorithms (Bernard et al, 1980) found less correspondence between recalled and behavioral data than at the level of dyads. These and other network techniques—centrality analysis, for example—involve concatenation and multiplication of data elements instead of addition, and this may amplify rather than dampen the impact of errors in measurement. There are also some indications that errors are nonrandom, and the development of robust measures should take this into account.

One standard by which the utility of current measures could be judged is that of construct validity—do available measures perform as they should according to extant theory? In some areas, such as social support, definite construct validity criteria are available. This is not as plain for other applications, though certainly some propositions are available, like that linking network range to greater accessibility of information. With others who have studied measurement problems of this sort (e.g. Huston & Robins, 1982; Bernard et al, 1981), I would agree that specification of what we require of measures must precede their evaluation. Whether a general-purpose "network instrument," suitable for the study of topics as diverse as social support and interpersonal diffusion, can be developed is very much open; different batteries of questions may be needed for researching core networks that affirm identity and more extensive ones that provide access to resources.

Several research needs are prominent. To begin, it should be noted that most methodological research reviewed in this chapter is based on convenience or highly clustered samples, and/or special populations. There are no obvious reasons to think that the studies are invalid because of this, but at the same time it is quite difficult to know how far the results of such studies reported above—percentages or test-retest correlations, for example—might be generalized. Improved sampling methods for methodological studies of network data are essential if we are to become confident about the levels of accuracy or reliability for network items.

Certainly more studies that pursue understanding of how different measures of network links correspond are necessary; among other things, these would assist in isolating nonrandom biases. The Freeman et al (1987) line of work has comforted many who were troubled by the conclusions of BKS, but it needs to be replicated and applied to the particular problem of measuring network ties. Over-time studies have been largely restricted to network size and turnover in individual links; they should be broadened to include often-used measures such as density and centrality.

A set of problems is particularly pertinent to the egocentric network strategy. It is clear here that the actual ties surrounding a respondent are being sampled, but little is known about the consequences of this. Are there, for example, substantial losses in the validity or reliability of measures based on network data when studies restrict attention to the direct ties surrounding units? How well do relatively efficient single items such as the GSS name generator represent networks investigated through more intensive methods? Are the measures of structural properties based on data as diverse as those provided by the GSS instrument and the reverse small-world technique well correlated, even if there is little overlap in the specific sets of alters elicited (Bernard et al, 1987)? Some of these issues might be addressed by studying a bounded group, but gathering data using egocentric network methods; this would, among other things, allow the reliability of respondent reports on network structure (links between alters) to be assessed.

Clearly, robustness studies of measures are necessary, in that surveys and questionnaires are likely to remain as primary modes of gathering network data. Parallel to BKS, they could examine results obtained for a given technique on multiple measures of a network. Simulation studies that assess the effects of different kinds and levels of observation error on particular indices and measures could also yield important insights.

ACKNOWLEDGMENTS

I am indebted to Steven Andrews and Priscilla Preston for research assistance in the preparation of this chapter. For helpful comments I am grateful to Steven Andrews, Ronald S. Burt, Karen E. Campbell, David Knoke, Mary Ellen Marsden, Joel Podolny, W. Richard Scott, and Thomas Schøtt.

Literature Cited

Alexander, C. N., Campbell, E. Q. 1964. Peer influences on adolescent educational aspirations and attainments. *Am. Sociol. Rev.* 29:568–75

Anderson, B. A., Silver, B. D. 1987. The validity of survey responses: insights from interviews of married couples in a survey of Soviet emigrants. *Soc. Forc.* 66:537–54

Antonucci, T. C., Israel, B. 1986. Veridicality of social support: A comparison of principal and network members' responses. *J. Consulting Clin. Psychol.* 54:432–37

Antonucci, T. C., Knipscheer, C. P. M. 1989. *Social network research: methodological questions and substantive issues.* Lisse, the Netherlands: Swets & Zeitlinger. In press

Arabie, P., Boorman, S. A., Levitt, P. R. 1978. Constructing blockmodels: how and why. *J. Math. Psychol.* 12:21–63

Baker, W. E. 1987. Do corporations really do business with the investment bankers who sit on their boards? Pres. Sunbelt Soc. Network Conf. VII, Clearwater Beach, Fla.

Barnes, J. A. 1969. Networks and political process. See Mitchell 1969, pp. 51–76

Barnes, J. A. 1979. Network analysis: orienting notion, rigorous technique, or substantive field of study? In *Perspectives on Social Network Analysis,* ed. P. W. Holland, S. Leinhardt, pp. 403–23. New York: Academic

Barrera, M. 1980. A method for the assessment of social support networks in community survey research. *Connections* 3(3):8–13

Barrera, M. 1981. Social support in the adjustment of pregnant adolescents: assessment issues. See Gottlieb 1981, pp. 69–96

Barrera, M., Baca, L. M., Christiansen, J., Stohl, M. 1985. Informant corroboration of social support network data. *Connections* 8:9–13

Beniger, J. 1976. Sampling social networks: the subgroup approach. *Proc. Bus. Econ. Stat. Sec.* pp. 226–31. Washington, DC: Am. Stat. Assoc.

Bernard, H. R., Killworth, P. D. 1977. Informant accuracy in social network data II. *Hum. Commun. Res.* 4:3–18

Bernard, H. R., Killworth, P., Kronenfeld, D., Sailer, L. 1984. The problem of informant accuracy: The validity of retrospective data. *Annu. Rev. Anthropol.* 13:495–517

Bernard, H. R., Killworth, P. D., Sailer, L. 1980. Informant accuracy in social network data IV: A comparison of clique-level structure in behavioral and cognitive network data. *Soc. Networks* 2:191–218

Bernard, H. R., Killworth, P. D., Sailer, L. 1981. Summary of research on informant accuracy in network data, and on the reverse small world problem. *Connections* 4(2):11–25

Bernard, H. R., Killworth, P. D., Sailer, L. 1982. Informant accuracy in social network data V. An experimental attempt to predict actual communication from recall data. *Soc. Sci. Res.* 11:30–66

Bernard, H. R., Shelley, G. A., Killworth, P. 1987. How much of a network does the GSS and RSW dredge up? *Soc. Networks* 9:49–61

Boissevain, J. F. 1974. *Friends of Friends.* Oxford, UK: Blackwell

Bolland, J. M. 1988. Sorting out centrality: An analysis of the performance of four centrality models in real and simulated networks. *Soc. Networks* 10:233–53

Bonacich, P. 1972. Technique for analyzing overlapping memberships. In *Sociological Methodology 1972*, ed. H. L. Costner, pp. 176–85. San Francisco: Jossey-Bass

Bonacich, P. 1987. Power and centrality: A family of measures. *Am. J. Sociol.* 92: 1170–82

Breiger, R. L. 1974. The duality of persons and groups. *Soc. Forc.* 53:181–90

Breiger, R. L. 1976. Career attributes and network structure: A blockmodel study of a biomedical research specialty. *Am. Sociol. Rev.* 41:117–35

Breiger, R. L. 1981. Structures of economic interdependence among nations. In *Continuities in Structural Inquiry*, ed. P. M. Blau, R. K. Merton, pp. 353–80. Beverly Hills: Sage

Broese van Groenau, M., van Sonderen, E., Ormel, J. 1989. Test-retest reliability of personal network delineation. See Antonucci & Knipscheer 1989. In press

Burt, R. S. 1980. Models of network structure. *Annu. Rev. Sociol.* 6:79–141

Burt, R. S. 1983a. *Corporate Profits and Cooptation: Networks of Market Constraints and Directorate Ties in the American Economy.* New York: Academic

Burt, R. S. 1983b. Range. See Burt & Minor 1983, pp. 176–94

Burt, R. S. 1983c. Distinguishing relational contents. See Burt & Minor 1983, pp. 35–74

Burt, R. S. 1984. Network items and the General Social Survey. *Soc. Networks* 6: 293–339

Burt, R. S. 1985. General social survey network items. *Connections* 8:119–23

Burt, R. S. 1988. Some properties of structural equivalence measures derived from sociometric choice data. *Soc. Networks* 10: 1–28

Burt, R. S. 1989. *STRUCTURE: A General Purpose Network Analysis Program.* Version 4.1. New York: Res. Prog. Structural Analy. Columbia Univ.

Burt, R. S. 1990. Kinds of relations in American discussion networks. In *Structures of Power and Constraint: Papers in Honor of Peter M. Blau*, ed. C. Calhoun, M. W. Meyer, W. R. Scott, New York: Cambridge Univ. Press. In press

Burt, R. S., Bittner, W. M. 1981. A note on inferences regarding network subgroups. *Soc. Networks* 3:71–88

Burt, R. S., Christman, K. P., Kilburn, H. C. 1980a. Testing a structural theory of corporate cooptation: Interorganizational directorate ties as a strategy for avoiding market constraints on profits. *Am. Sociol. Rev.* 45:821–41

Burt, R. S., Lieben, K. L., Fischer, M. G. 1980b. Network power structures from informant perceptions. *Hum. Organ*, 39:121–33

Burt, R. S., Minor, M. J., eds. 1983. *Applied Network Analysis: A Methodological Introduction.* Beverly Hills: Sage

Campbell, K. E., Marsden, P. V., Hurlbert, J. S. 1986. Social resources and socioeconomic status. *Soc. Networks* 8:97–117

Card, J. J. 1978. The correspondence of data gathered from husband and wife: implications for family planning studies. *Soc. Biol.* 25:196–204

Christensen, A., Sullaway, M., King, C. E. 1983. Systematic error in behavioral reports of dyadic interaction: egocentric bias and content effects. *Behav. Assess.* 5:129–40

Clark, A. L., Wallin, P. 1964. The accuracy of husbands' and wives' reports of the frequency of marital coitus. *Popul. Stud.* 18:165–73

Coleman, J. S. 1961. *The Adolescent Society.* New York: Free

Coleman, J. S., Katz, E., Menzel, H. 1966. *Medical Innovation: A Diffusion Study.* Indianapolis: Bobbs-Merrill

Collins, R. 1988. *Theoretical Sociology.* New York: Harcourt Brace Jovanovich

Conrath, D. W., Higgins, C. A., McClean, R. J. 1983. A comparison of the reliability of questionnaire versus diary data. *Soc. Networks* 5:315–23

Converse, J. M., Presser, S. 1986. *Survey Questions: Handcrafting the Standardized Questionnaire.* Beverly Hills: Sage

Cook, K. S., Emerson, R. M., Gillmore, M. R., Yamagishi, T. 1983. The distribution of power in exchange networks: theory and experimental results. *Am. J. Sociol.* 89:275–305

Coombs, L. C., Cheng, M-C. 1981. Do husbands and wives agree? fertility attitudes and later behavior. *Pop. Envir.* 4:109–27

Cramer, D. 1986. An item factor analysis of the original relationship inventory. *J. Soc. Pers. Relat.* 3:121–7

Daugherty, S. R., Salloway, J. C., Nuzzarello, L. 1988. A questionnaire for the measurement of social networks and social support. *Connections* 11(2):20–25

Dean, A., Taussig, M. 1986. Measuring intimate support: the family and confidant relationships. In *Social Support, Life Events, and Depression,* ed. N. Lin, A. Dean, W. Ensel, pp. 117–28. New York: Academic

Deseran, F. A., Black, L. 1981. Problems with using self-reports in network analysis: some empirical findings in rural counties. *Rural Sociol.* 46:310–8

Doreian, P. 1988. Mapping networks through time. Pres. MASO Conf. on Network Anal. Utrecht, The Netherlands

Duncan, G. T., Siverson, R. M. 1982. Flexibility of alliance partner choice in a multipolar system. *Int. Stud. Q.* 26:511–38

Erickson, B. 1978. Some problems of inference from chain data. In *Sociological Methodology 1979,* ed. K. F. Schuessler, pp. 276–302. San Francisco: Jossey-Bass

Erickson, B., Nosanchuk, T. A., Lee, E. 1981. Network sampling in practice: some second steps. *Soc. Networks* 3:127–36

Erickson, B., Nosanchuk, T. A. 1983. Applied network sampling. *Soc. Networks* 5:367–82

Faust, K., Romney, A. K. 1985. Does STRUCTURE find structure? A critique of Burt's use of distance as a measure of

structural equivalence. *Soc. Networks* 7:77–103

Fischer, C. S. 1982a. What do we mean by "Friend"? An inductive study. *Soc. Networks* 3:287–306

Fischer, C. S. 1982b. *To Dwell Among Friends: Personal Networks in Town and City.* Chicago: Univ. Chicago Press

Fischer, J. L., Sollie, D. L., Morrow, K. B. 1986. Social networks in male and female adolescents. *J. Adolescent Res.* 6:1–14

Flaherty, J. A., Gavaria, F. M., Pathak, D. S. 1983. The measurement of social support: the social support network inventory. *Comprehensive Psychiatry* 24:521–9

Frank, O. 1981. A survey of statistical methods for graph analysis. In *Sociological Methodology 1981,* ed. S. Leinhardt, pp. 110–55. San Francisco: Jossey-Bass

Freeman, L. C. 1979. Centrality in social networks. conceptual clarification. *Soc. Networks* 1:215–39

Freeman, L. C., McEvoy, B. 1987. *UCINET: A Microcomputer Package for Network Analysis.* Irvine, Calif: Sch. Soc. Sci., Univ. Calif.

Freeman, L. C., Romney, A. K. 1987. Words, deeds and social structure: A preliminary study of the reliability of informants. *Hum. Organ.* 46:330–34

Freeman, L. C., Romney, A. K., Freeman, S. C. 1987. Cognitive structure and informant accuracy. *Am. Anthropol.* 89:310–25

Freeman, L. C., Romney, A. K., White, D. R., eds. 1989. *Research Methods in Social Network Analysis.* Fairfax, Va: George Mason Univ. Press

Friedkin, N. 1981. The development of structure in random networks: an analysis of the effects of increasing network density on five measures of structure. *Soc. Networks* 3:41–52

Galaskiewicz, J. 1979. *Exchange Networks and Community Politics.* Beverly Hills: Sage

Gillespie, D. L., Krannich, R. S., Leffler, A. 1985. The missing cell: amiability, hostility, and gender differentiation in rural community networks. *Soc. Sci. J.* 22:17–30

Gottlieb, B. H., ed. 1981. *Social Networks and Social Support.* Beverly Hills: Sage

Gould, R. 1987. Measures of betweenness in non-symmetric networks. *Soc. Networks* 9:277–82

Granovetter, M. 1973. The strength of weak ties. *Am. J. Sociol.* 78:1360–80

Granovetter, M. 1976. Network sampling: some first steps. *Am. J. Sociol.* 83:1287–1303

Hammer, M. 1980. Some comments on the validity of network data. *Connections* 3(1):13–15

Hammer, M. 1984. Explorations into the

meaning of social network interview data. *Soc. Networks* 6:341–71

Hammer, M. 1985. Implications of behavioral and cognitive reciprocity in social network data. *Soc. Networks* 7:189–201

Higgins, C. A., McClean, R. J., Conrath, D. W. 1985. The accuracy and biases of diary communication data. *Soc. Networks* 7:173–87

Hildum, D. C. 1986. "Competence" and "performance" in network structure. *Soc. Networks* 8:79–95

Hoffmeyer-Zlotnik, J. H. P. 1989. The Mannheim comparative network research. Pres. Sunbelt Social Network Conf. IX, Tampa

Holland, P. W., Leinhardt, S. 1973. The structural implications of measurement error in sociometry. *J. Math. Sociol.* 3:85–111

House, J., Kahn, R. L. 1985. Measures and concepts of social support. In *Social Support and Health*, ed. S. Cohen and S. L. Syme, pp. 83–108. New York: Academic

Huston, T. L., Robins, E. 1982. Conceptual and methodological issues in studying close relationships. *J. Marriage Fam.* 44:901–25

Kahn, R. L., Antonucci, T. C. 1980. Convoys over the life course: attachment, roles and social support. *Life-Span Dev. Behav.* 3:253–86

Kapferer, B. 1969. Norms and the manipulation of relationships in a work context. See Mitchell 1969, pp. 181–244

Killworth, P. D., Bernard, H. R. 1976. Informant accuracy in social network data. *Hum. Organ.* 35:269–86

Killworth, P. D., Bernard, H.R. 1978. The reverse small-world experiment. *Soc. Networks* 1:159–92

Killworth, P. D., Bernard, H. R. 1979. Informant accuracy in social network data III: A comparison of triadic structure in behavioral and cognitive data. *Soc. Networks* 2:19–46

Klovdahl, A. 1985. Social networks and the spread of infectious disease: the AIDS example. *Soc. Sci. Med.* 21:1203–16

Knoke, D., Burt, R. S. 1983. Prominence. See Burt & Minor 1983, pp. 195–222

Knoke, D., Rogers, D. 1979. A blockmodel study of interorganizational relations. *Sociol. Soc. Res.* 64:28–52

Knoke, D., Wood, J. 1981. *Organized for Action: Commitment in Voluntary Associations.* New Brunswick: Rutgers Univ. Press

Koenig, M. A., Simmons, G. B., Misra, B. D. 1984. Husband-wife inconsistencies in contraceptive use reports. *Pop. Stud.* 38:281–98

Laumann, E. O. 1969. Friends of urban men: an assessment of accuracy in reporting their socioeconomic attributes, mutual choice, and attitude agreement. *Sociometry* 32:54–69

Laumann, E. O. 1973. *Bonds of Pluralism: The Form and Substance of Urban Social Networks.* New York: Wiley Intersci.

Laumann, E. O., Knoke, D. 1986. Social Network Theory. In *Approaches to Social Theory*, ed. S. Lindenberg, J. S. Coleman, S. Nowak, pp. 83–104. New York: Russell Sage Found.

Laumann, E. O., Knoke, D. 1988. *The Organizational State: Social Choice in National Policy Domains.* Madison, Wis: Univ. Wisc. Press

Laumann, E. O., Marsden, P. V., Prensky, D. 1983. The boundary specification problem in network analysis. See Burt & Minor 1983, pp. 18–34

Laumann, E. O., Senter, R. 1976. Subjective social distance, occupational stratification, and forms of status and class consciousness: a cross-national replication and extension. *Am. J. Sociol.* 81:1304–38

Leffler, A., Krannich, R. S., Gillespie, D. L. 1986. Contact, support and friction: three faces of networks in community life. *Sociol. Perspect.* 29:337–55

Lievrouw, L., Rogers, E. M., Lowe, C. U., Nadel, E. 1987. Triangulation as a research strategy for identifying invisible colleges among biomedical scientists. *Soc. Networks* 9:217–48

Lin, N., Dayton, P. W., Greenwald, P. 1978. Analyzing the instrumental use of relations in the context of social structure. *Sociol. Meth. Res.* 7:149–66

Lin, N., Dumin, M. 1986. Access to occupations through social ties. *Soc. Networks* 8:365–85

Lindzey, G., Byrne, D. 1968. Measurement of social choice and interpersonal attractiveness. In *Handbook of Social Psychology*, ed. G. Lindzey, E. Aronson, pp. 452–525. Reading, Mass: Addison-Wesley. 2nd ed.

Lund, M. 1985. The development of investment and commitment scales for predicting continuity of personal relationships. *J. Soc. Pers. Relat.* 2:3–23

Mariolis, P., Jones, M. H. 1982. Centrality in corporate networks: reliability and stability. *Admin. Sci. Q.* 27:571–84

Marsden, P. V., Campbell, K. E. 1984. Measuring tie strength. *Soc. Forc.* 63:482–501

Marsden, P. V., Laumann, E. O. 1984. Mathematical ideas in social structural analysis. *J. Math. Sociol.* 10:271–94

McAllister, L., Fischer, C. S. 1978. A procedure for surveying personal networks. *Sociol. Methods Res.* 7:131–48

McPherson, J. M. 1982. Hypernetwork sampling: duality and differentiation among voluntary organizations. *Soc. Networks* 3:225–49

Milardo, R. M. 1982. Friendship networks in

developing relationships: converging and diverging social environments. *Soc. Psychol. Q.* 45:162–72

Milardo, R. M., 1983. Social networks and pair relationships: a review of substantive and measurement issues. *Sociol. Soc. Res.* 68:1–18

Milardo, R. M. 1989. Theoretical and methodological issues in the identification of the social networks of spouses. *J. Marriage Fam.* 51:165–74

Mintz, B., Schwartz, M. 1985. *The Power Structure of American Business.* Chicago: Univ. Chicago Press

Mitchell, J. C. 1969. The concept and use of social networks. In *Social Networks in Urban Situations*, ed. J. C. Mitchell, pp. 1–50. Manchester, UK: Manchester Univ. Press

Mitchell, J. C. 1987. The components of strong ties among homeless women. *Soc. Networks* 9:37–47

Mitchell, R. E., Trickett, E. J. 1980. Task force report: social networks as mediators of social support: an analysis of the effects and determinants of social networks. *Commun. Mental Health J.* 16:27–44

Mizruchi, M. S., Bunting, D. 1981. Influence in corporate networks: an examination of four measures. *Admin. Sci. Q.* 26:475–89

Mizruchi, M. S., Mariolis, P., Schwartz, M., Mintz, B. 1986. Techniques for disaggregating centrality scores in social networks. In *Sociological Methodology 1986*, ed. N. B. Tuma, pp. 26–48. Washington, DC: American Sociol. Assoc.

Morgan, D. L., Rytina, S. 1977. Comment on "Network Sampling: Some First Steps" by Mark Granovetter. *Am. J. Sociol.* 83:722–27

Morrissey, J. P., Hall, R. H., Lindsey, M. L. 1982. *Interorganizational Relations: A Sourcebook of Measures for Mental Health Programs.* Dep. Health Hum. Serv. Pub. No. (ADM)82–1187. Washington, DC: USGPO

Mouton, J. S., Blake, R. R., Fruchter, B. 1955. The reliability of sociometric responses. *Sociometry* 18:7–48

Nemeth, R. J., Smith, D. A. 1985. International trade and world-system structure: a multiple-network analysis. *Review* 8:517–60

Norbeck, J. S., Lindsey, A. M., Carrieri, V. L. 1981. The development of an instrument to measure social support. *Nursing Res.* 30:264–69

Pappi, F. U., ed. 1987. *Methoden der Netzwerkanalyse.* Munich: Oldenbourg (In German).

Pappi, F. U., Wolf, G. 1984. Wahrnehmung und Realitaet sozialer Netzwerke: Zuverlaessigkeit und Gueltigkeit der Angabe ue-

ber beste Freunde im Interview. In *Soziale Realitaet im Interview,* ed. H. Meulemann, K.-H., Reuband, pp. 281–300. Frankfurt: Campus (In German)

Pearson, J. E. 1986. The definition and measurement of social support. *J. Counsel. Devel.* 64:390–95

Rice, R. E. 1982. Communication networking in computer-conferencing systems: a longitudinal study of group roles and system structure. In *Communication Yearbook 6,* ed. M. Burgoon, pp. 925–44. Beverly Hills: Sage

Rice, R. E., Richards, W. D. 1985. An overview of network analysis methods and programs. In *Progress in Communication Sciences,* vol. VI, ed. B. Dervin, M. J. Voigt, pp. 105–65. Norwood, NJ: Ablex

Richards, W. D. 1985. Data, models, and assumptions in network analysis. In *Organizational Communication: Traditional Themes and New Directions,* ed. R. D. McPhee, P. K. Tompkins, pp. 108–28. Beverly Hills: Sage

Rogers, D. L. 1974. Towards a scale of interorganizational relations among public agencies. *Sociol. Soc. Res.* 59:61–70

Rogers, E. 1987. Progress, problems and prospects for network research: investigating relationships in the age of electronic communication technologies. *Soc. Networks* 9:285–310

Romney, A. K., Weller, S. C. 1984. Predicting informant accuracy from patterns of recall among individuals. *Soc. Networks* 6:59–77

Romney, A. K., Weller, S.C., Batchelder, W. H. 1986. Culture as consensus: a theory of culture and informant accuracy. *Am. Anthropol.* 88:313–38

Rook, K. S. 1984. The negative side of social interaction: impact on psychological well-being. *J. Personality Soc. Psychol.* 46:1097–1108

Rosenthal, N., Fingrutd, M., Ethier, M., Karant, R., McDonald, D. 1985. Social movements and network analysis: a case study of nineteenth-century women's reform in New York State. *Am. J. Sociol.* 90:1022–54

Ross, C. O. 1987. Organizational dimensions of metropolitan dominance: prominence in the network of corporate control, 1955–1975. *Am. Sociol. Rev.* 52:258–67

Sarason, I. G., Levine, H. M., Basham, R. B., Sarason, B. R. 1983. Assessing social support: the social support questionnaire. *J. Personality Soc. Psychol.* 44:127–39

Sarason, I. G., Sarason, B. R., Shearin, E. N., Pierce, G. R. 1987. A brief measure of social support: practical and theoretical implications. *J. Soc. Personal Relat.* 4:497–510

Shulman, N. 1976. Network analysis: a new addition to an old bag of tricks. *Acta Sociologica* 19:307–23

Snijders, T. 1983. The degree variance: an index of graph heterogeneity. *Soc. Networks* 3:163–74

Snyder, D., Kick, E. L. 1979. Structural position in the world system and economic growth, 1955–1970: a multiple-network analysis of transnational interactions. *Am. J. Sociol.* 84:1096–1126

Spaeth, J. L. 1985. Multiplicity samples of organizational hierarchies. Pres. Am. Assoc. Public Opinion Res. McAfee, NJ

Stephenson, K., M. Zelen. 1989. Rethinking centrality: methods and examples. *Soc. Networks* 11:1–37

Sudman, S. 1985. Experiments in the measurement of the size of social networks. *Soc. Networks* 7:127–51

Sudman, S. 1988a. Experiments in measuring neighbor and relative social networks. *Soc. Networks* 10:93–108

Sudman, S., 1988b. The use of networks to identify rare populations. Pres. Sunbelt Soc. Network Conf. VIII, San Diego

Tam, T. 1989. Demarcating the boundaries between self and the social: the anatomy of centrality in social networks. *Soc. Networks* 11:387–401

Tardy, C. H., 1985. Social support measurement. *Am. J. Community Psychol.* 13:187–202

Travers, J., Milgram, S. 1969. An experimental study of the small world problem. *Sociometry* 32:425–43

Useem, M. 1979. The social organization of the American business elite. *Am. Sociol. Rev.* 44:553–72

Van de Ven, A. H., Ferry, D. L. 1980. *Measuring and Assessing Organizations.* New York: Wiley

Van Sonderen, E., Ormel, J., Brilman, E., van den Heuvall, C. v. L. 1989. Personal network delineation: a comparison of the "Exchange", "Affective", and "Role Relation" Approaches. See Antonucci & Knipscheer, 1989. In press

Wegener, B. 1989. Mobility and the structure and sex composition of social ties. Pres. Int. Sociol. Assoc. Res. Commun. 28. Utrecht, The Netherlands

Wellman, B. 1979. The community question: the intimate networks of East Yorkers. *Am. J. Sociol.* 84:1201–31

Wellman, B. 1981. Applying network analysis to the study of support. See Gottlieb 1981, pp. 171–200

Wellman, B. 1983. Network analysis: some basic principles. *Sociol. Theory* 1:155–99

Wheeler, L., Nezlek, J. 1977. Sex differences in social participation. *J. Personality Soc. Psychol.* 10:742–54

White, D. R., McCann, H. G. 1988. Cites and fights: material entailment analysis of the eighteenth-century chemical revolution. In *Social Structures: A Network Approach*, ed. B. Wellman, S. D., Berkowitz, pp. 380–400. New York: Cambridge Univ. Press

Wilcox, S., Udry, J. R. 1986. Autism and accuracy in adolescent perceptions of friends' sexual attitudes and behavior. *J. Appl. Soc. Psychol.* 4:361–74

Williams, A. S. 1981. Commentary: problems with using self reports in network analysis. *Rural Sociol.* 46:514–7

Williams, R., Thomson, E. 1985. Can spouses be trusted? a look at husband/wife proxy reports. *Demography* 22:115–23

Winship, C., Mandel, M. 1983. Roles and positions: a critique and extension of the blockmodeling approach. In *Sociological Methodology 1983–1984*, ed. S. Leinhardt, pp. 314–44. San Francisco: Jossey Bass

Wiseman, J. P. 1986. Friendship: bonds and binds in a voluntary relationship. *J. Soc. Personal Relat.* 3:191–211

Annu. Rev. Sociol. 1990. 16:465-90
Copyright © 1990 by Annual Reviews Inc. All rights reserved

ECONOMIC RESTRUCTURING AND THE AMERICAN CITY

Saskia Sassen

Urban Planning, Columbia University, New York, NY 10027

KEY WORDS: urban restructuring, services, earnings, minorities

Abstract

Transformations in the composition and locational patterns of the economy have assumed specific forms in cities and in the urban hierarchy. The new service-dominated urbanization, particularly evident in major cities, has distinct consequences for a range of social conditions. Here we focus especially on the characteristics of today's leading industries, the producer services, disproportionately concentrated in major cities; the impact of restructuring on the earnings distribution generally and in major cities in particular; and the impact of urban restructuring on minorities, a population increasingly concentrated in large cities.

INTRODUCTION

Research on economic restructuring and on cities has recently begun to merge into a new type of urban analysis. Examining cities in the context of economic restructuring introduces a number of variables not usually part of the main strands in urban sociology. The emphasis on space and markets characterizing human ecology is also important in studies on economic restructuring, but the assumptions about their function and meaning are quite different. Similarly, the extremely broad range of topics covered by urban sociologists, from the impact of size on behavior to poverty, can be of great use to studies on urban economic restructuring, even through the analytical frameworks are fun-

465

0360-0572/90/0815-0465$02.00

damentally diverse. These conceptual issues have been addressed in several recent publications (Frisbie & Kasarda 1988, Hawley 1984, Gottdiener & Feagin 1988, Jaret 1983, Zukin 1980).

The main themes in studies on economic restructuring and cities are central to sociology. The decline of manufacturing and the shift to services raise questions about changes in the economic base of cities and the impact of these changes on earnings and employment distribution. They also raise the possibility of changes in the urban hierarchy, and a new form of service-based urbanization. These major themes are at the heart of current debates and establish both a conceptual and an empirical connection between the two subjects at hand—economic restructuring and the cities. They serve to organize the discussion of the literature.

Since the study of economic restructuring is an immensely broad field as is that of cities, it may be helpful to specify that this review is limited to: (a) studies explicitly concerned with economic restructuring and cities from a sociological perspective; (b) studies on economic restructuring that may not have at their center an analysis of cities but which clearly are contributing to urban sociology; (c) studies focused on cities that may not be explicitly concerned with economic restructuring but are in fact contributing knowledge to our understanding of this subject as it plays itself out in cities.

Equal attention does not go to all the processes usually thought of as constituting economic restructuring. The shift to services and the spatial redistribution of manufacturing have received considerable attention throughout the 1970s and that attention continues today (Browning & Singelmann 1980, Bluestone & Harrison 1982, Sawyers & Tabb 1987, Glickman 1983, Perry & Watkins 1977). The impact of the shift to services on the earnings and occupational distribution, on the other hand, is at the center of current debates and hence deserves more attention (Harrison & Bluestone 1988, Lawrence 1984, Garofalo & Fogarty 1979, Evans & Timberlake 1980, Fiala 1983, Nelson & Lorence 1985, Silver 1984, Sheets et al 1987). Finally, the location patterns of the new leading industries, the producer services, and their impact on urban economies and the urban hierarchy are a new subject which has begun to command great attention (Stanback & Noyelle 1982, Friedmann 1986, Castells 1989, Sassen 1990).

The urban manifestations of these processes of restructuring are especially evident in large cities, also the focus of much of the sociological literature on current urban change. Among the processes of urban change central to this literature (and which this review discusses in the second half) are the following: First, the acceleration in the already disproportionate concentration of the poor, blacks, and Hispanics in large cities, along with rapid decline and suburbanization of the low skill jobs traditionally held by significant segments of these populations (Kasarda 1985, Peterson 1985, McGeary & Lynn 1988). Second, and in this context of large cities, several studies have posited the expansion and consolidation of distinct social forms, such as an underclass (Wilson 1987, Ricketts & Sawhill 1988), an informal economy (Portes et al 1989, Sassen 1989) and the renewed growth of immigrant communities with strong entrepreneurial elements (Light & Bonacich 1988, Wilson & Portes 1980). Third, major transformations in housing are particularly evident in large cities, notably the simultaneous expansion of poverty areas with severely decaying housing stocks and of newly gentrified areas in what were often once poverty areas. These developments have in some cases been linked to economic restructuring through the growth of poverty associated with the loss of manufacturing jobs and the growth of advanced services and high-income workers (Smith & Williams 1986, Hopper & Hamberg 1986, Marcuse 1986). But such developments are also linked to a variety of other processes, among them reductions in federal support for housing, escalating prices of housing, and changes in financing (Hartman 1986) as well as the social relations that characterize housing markets (Appelbaum & Gilderbloom 1986).[1]

ECONOMIC RESTRUCTURING

The notion of economic restructuring contains a quantitative dimension, typified by the loss of manufacturing jobs and the growth of services; a spatial dimension, most commonly associated with the geographic redistribution of manufacturing jobs at the national and international scale; and a qualitative one, suggested by the greater incidence of both low-wage, low-skill jobs and high-level professional jobs in service industries, a decline in wages and unionization rates in manufacturing jobs, and a feminization of the job supply.

Sectoral and Spatial Shifts

Total US manufacturing employment declined by 10% between 1979 and 1985, from 21 million to 18.9 million jobs. During this same period, service employment increased by 8.8%, adding a total of 7.8 million jobs. At the national level, the decline of manufacturing employment is a fairly recent development. Throughout the 1960s and 1970s total employment in this sector kept growing. From 1960 to 1970 it grew by 15.2% and from 1970 to 1979 by 8.7%.

---

[1]This review does not focus on studies that have analyzed the current transformation of urban space in the context of culture, notably Sennett's (1990) theoretical study on the organization of urban space in terms of exposure and shelter, and Zukin's (1989) on the particular cultural forms through which inner-cities can be opened to high-income gentrification.

But these figures mask the onset of a spatial redistribution of manufacturing jobs. According to Bureau of Labor Statistics, from 1979 to 1985 the midwest lost over a million jobs, the northeast lost 800,000, the south lost 231,000 and the west gained 53,500, for a total national loss of 2.1 million jobs (Sawyers & Tabb 1987, Perry & Watkins 1977, Glickman & Glasmeier 1989, Bluestone & Harrison 1982).[2] In the midwest these losses affected both urban and rural areas, small and large cities; only a few booming suburban towns escaped these trends (Markusen 1987).[3] Using data from the Bureau of Labor Statistics, Hill & Negrey (1987) found that in the Great Lakes States, which concentrate the key northern industrial complex, manufacturing employment had already declined by 3.4% from 1970 to 1979 and fell by 16.4% from 1979 to 1985. The loss was even more severe in the Lakefront cities which on the aggregate already registered zero growth in the decade of the 1960s, a 36.5% loss from 1970 to 1979, and a 25.4% loss from 1979 to 1985. Correspondingly, the share of all manufacturing employment in the Great Lakes States fell from 47.9% of all US manufacturing jobs in 1960 to 39.7% in 1979, and to 35.9% by 1985. By the mid-1980s plant closings and manufacturing job losses also had increased in many communities of states with overall employment growth—California, Florida, and Texas (Markusen et al 1986). And the Massachusetts growth boom of the early 1980s has been followed by 250 plant closings and the elimination of 90,000 manufacturing jobs from 1984 to 1988 (see also Norton & Rees 1979).

The debate in the early 1980s centered on whether changes in manufacturing employment levels represented a cyclical downturn (Lawrence 1983, Klein 1983) or a more basic transformation (Bluestone & Harrison 1982, Harrison & Bluestone 1988, Magaziner & Reich 1982). Lawrence (1983) and Klein (1983) argue that notwithstanding the apparent divergence of manufacturing employment from overall growth since the late 1970s, manufacturing growth and GNP growth remain very closely related over this period. We now have very detailed analyses at the local level, and it has become evident

---

[2]There has long been disparity in regional growth rates. In the 1950s and early 1960s deindustrialization was centered in New England and Appalachia and in the 1970s in the Middle Atlantic states. What distinguishes the 1980s is the acuteness of the regional disparity in growth rates and the magnitude of the losses.

[3]It has been argued that manufacturing simply suburbanized. But intrametropolitan movement of plants only accounted for a small share of job losses in midwestern cities, so that even suburban areas did not have significant growth. In the 1980s Chicago suburban growth did not reverse the absolute decline in areawide employment. As a whole the midwestern region had 1.2 million displaced workers from 1981 to 1985, the highest of any of the nine census subregions. According to a special BLS study of displaced workers, only 65% of this group had found new jobs, a level far lower than the reemployment rate of 74% in New England (Glickman & Glasmeier 1989).

that the losses are such that they cannot be fully explained in cyclical terms.[4] This is further suggested by highly disparate recovery rates by industry and region (LeGrande 1985, Hill & Negrey 1987). Regression results show a sharp break in the manufacturing/GNP relationship beginning in the late 1970s. US direct foreign investment in off-shore manufacturing facilities grew immensely over the decade of the 1970s indicating that an increasing number of US manufacturing jobs are now abroad (Bluestone & Harrison 1982, Sassen 1988, Hill 1989, Rodwin & Sazanami 1989).[5] Bergman & Goldstein (1983) show that many of the observed metropolitan growth differentials are more easily interpreted as structural than as cyclical.

The decline of manufacturing and the shift to services as the leading growth sector in major cities invites an examination of the locational patterns of the major new service industries. The industrial recomposition in the economic base of cities is not simply a function of the general shift from a manufacturing to a service economy. Thus, while all cities contain a core of service industries, location quotients for different size SMSAs clearly show the largest ones to have a disproportionate concentration of certain types of service industries, such as financial and advanced corporate services, and the smaller ones greater concentrations of manufacturing. In a classification of the 140 largest SMSAs for 1976 in the United States, Stanback & Noyelle (1982: 20–26) found a distinct relation between size and functional specialization. Of the 16 largest SMSAs (population over 2 million), 12 were centers for the production and export of producer and distributive services and the other four were government and educational centers. Of these twelve, four were global centers and the remaining eight, regional. Furthermore, control-

---

[4]Parallel trends are evident in other highly industrialized countries. One of the most acute examples is probably the United Kingdom with a 25% decline in manufacturing jobs from 1978 to 1985; London alone lost 0.8 million manufacturing jobs. Finally there is now a similar trend in Japan with plant closings in basic industry and development of off-shore manufacturing in consumer durables, including auto parts (Rodwin & Sazanami 1989). Tokyo has lost 0.2 million manufacturing jobs from 1975 to 1985, and several of its traditional manufacturing areas are in severe decline (Sassen 1990).

[5]There have been massive realignments in international investment over the last three decades (Sassen 1988). The decade of the 1970s saw the enormous development of such industrial production sites in select areas of Southeast Asia and the Caribbean basin. In the case of the United States, the average annual growth rate of direct foreign investment was 11.7% for developed countries from 1950–1966 and 6.3% in developing countries; from 1966–1977 these rates were respectively, 10.7% and 9.7% and from 1973–1980, 11.8% and 14.2%. (These figues exclude petroleum). The estimated world stock of foreign direct investment tripled from 1960 to 1983, going from $66 billion in 1960 to $213 billion in 1973 and reaching over $549 billion by 1984. The large-scale increases in direct foreign investment in a multiplicity of Third World locations during the 1970s, central to the internationalization of production, were followed by a subsequent phase of large increases in financial flows in the 1980s on a scale that dwarfed the magnitudes of the earlier phase.

ling for type of service export, the authors found a direct relation between size and type of service export. The larger the SMSA, the greater the weight of producer services compared with distributive services. It should be noted that the larger SMSAs were once predominantly centers for the production and export of manufacturing.[6]

On the other hand, the group of smaller SMSAs (population under one million) had the highest single concentration of "production centers," mostly in manufacturing. Indeed, the authors found that comparing the location quotient of manufacturing in the smaller SMSAs for 1976 with 1959, the importance of manufacturing had increased. This was sharpest in SMSAs with populations under 0.25 million where the manufacturing quotient went from 92.8 in 1959 to 113.0 in 1976 (see also Markusen 1987, Glickman & Glasmeier 1989, Moriarty 1986). In contrast, in the largest SMSAs this quotient went from 99.0 in 1959 to 90.5 in 1976. In terms of employment the share of manufacturing rises as the size of the SMSA declines. On the other hand, the share of the "corporate headquarters" complex declines with size, ranging from 20% in the largest SMSAs to 8.7% in the smallest. While this 1976 information is somewhat dated, the more recent information discussed here points to a strengthening of these patterns.[7]

Furthermore, in the 1970s the share of services as final output (e.g. consumer services) actually declined relative to the production of services as intermediate outputs, that is, producer and distributive services (Denison 1979, Ginzberg & Vojta 1981, Myers 1980, Singelmann 1978, Stanback & Noyelle 1982). This shift from final to intermediate services is another indicator of restructuring. National trends in the United States show that total

[6]Daniels (1985) tested several of the hypotheses on locational patterns of services using data for the European Economic Community, covering 1973–1979. The evidence supported the hypothesis that consumer services are more evenly distributed than producer services, and that they lack a strong contrast between central and peripheral locations. Producer services were found to be highly concentrated in central places with gradually reduced representation in the less central places. The evidence points to a strong relationship between central regions and relative specialization in producer services. See Also Form (1954) on the determination of land use patterns.

[7]The interaction between growth and decline trends is well illustrated by the case of New York City, the leading center for producer services. Manhattan already had a disproportionate concentration of finance, insurance, and real estate (FIRE) jobs 30 years ago. Using the industrial distribution of the New York Metropolitan Region as the base (100), Hoover & Vernon (1962) calculated Manhattan's "specialization index" (location quotient) for finance, insurance and real estate in the New York Metropolitan Region at 169 in 1956. Harris (1988) shows that by 1980 it had increased to 195, an uncommonly high quotient. Manhattan accounts for 90% of all FIRE employment in New York City and 64.3% of business services. The "rest of the core," consisting largely of the rest of New York City and one New Jersey county, suffered declines in the finance quotient. A second pronounced trend that emerges is the decline in manufacturing in the rest of the core, with the specialization index reduced from 121 in 1956 to 86 in 1980.

employment increased by 15% from 1977 to 1981 and by 8.3% from 1981 to 1985, but that total employment in producer services for those same periods increased by 24% and 22% respectively.[8] Second, producer services have emerged as a key sector in major cities. Jobs in financial and real estate (FIRE), business, and legal services and the communications group employed 26.4% of all private sector workers in New York City in 1985, 20.3% in Chicago, and 17.8% in Los Angeles, compared with 15% for the United States as a whole (Sassen 1990). A third trend is that the national employment share of producer services in major cities is at least a third higher and often twice as large as the share of these cities in total national employment. But the degree of concentration as measured by locational quotients is declining, signalling growth of such services in nonmajor cities as well.

The Leading Industries: Producer Services

The concentration of producer services in major cities is in part explained by the characteristics of production of these services. Producer services, unlike other types of services, do not follow residential patterns and are not as dependent on proximity to buyers as are consumer services. Hence, concentration of production in suitable locations and export, domestically and abroad, are feasible.[9] Production of these services benefits from proximity to a wide array of specialized firms, sellers of key inputs or necessities for joint production of certain service offerings.[9] Another kind of agglomeration economy consists in the amenities and lifestyles that large urban centers can offer the high income personnel employed in the producer services.

Whether the production of these services is internalized by a firm or bought on the market depends on a number of factors. The available evidence shows that the freestanding producer services industry is growing fast and accounts for a rising share of the GNP. Thus we know that a large share of these inputs are bought rather than produced internally. In what has become a classic study

[8]Considerable disparity between the level of overall national employment growth and growth in producer services is evident in several major industrialized countries. For example, total national employment in Japan grew by 5% from 1977 to 1985, but the FIRE sector grew by 27% from 1975–1985; in the UK total employment grew by 5% from 1978–1985, while FIRE increased by 44% (Sassen 1990).

[9]These general trends hold in varying degree for the various branches in the producer services industries. The 1983 *U.S. National Study on Trade in the Services* notes that some industries lend themselves more readily to transborder trade and others to investment trade. Advertising and accounting for example have tended to establish a multiplicity of domestic and foreign branch offices because of the importance of dealing directly with clients. Management consulting, engineering, or architectural firms on the other hand have not tended to set up branches and affiliates but have kept all functions in centralized locations. Furthermore, these locational patterns are also affected by the existence of regulatory restrictions, especially when foreign locations or international trade are involved.

of the services industry, Stigler (1951) posited that the growing size of markets would increase both specialization and the realization of economies of scale on the production of such services. Stanback et al (1981) note that Stigler failed to see that specialization preceded the possibility of realizing economies of scale. The increasing specialization of service functions that arose first within the large firm indicated to entrepreneurs that there was a market for these services, creating conditions for separating these functions. From this came the development of a specialized producer services industry. Greenfield (1966) argues that specialization is the key factor pushing toward externalization. Eventually, a large demand reduces the price of such producer services and extends the market of such services to firms that otherwise would have been unable to buy them. This in turn further expands the specialized services industry. The specialization of inputs explains why there is a freestanding market for such services that can support a large number of small firms. The standardization of outputs explains why it can be freestanding market.

These industries are clearly overrepresented in major cities, notwithstanding relative declines in their shares over the last decade. The levels of overrepresentation and growth tend to vary considerably among industries. Thus New York City with 3.7% of all US employment in 1985 accounted for 11% of US employment in banking and 9% in legal services, but only 5.2% in insurance. On the other hand, Boston and Chicago have a greater share of insurance than of the other major producer services or of national employment in producer services.

Organizing this information in terms of location quotients underlines the extent to which major cities have an overrepresentation of most of these producer services, though there is considerable variation in the degrees and type of industry.[10] New York City is the premier banking center in the country, with a location quotient of 2.8 over the last decade, reaching 3.0 in 1985. Boston is a major insurance center, with location quotients of 3.2 in 1977 and 2.7 in 1985. It is also the city with the second highest LQ in banking, going from 1.8 in 1977 up to 2 in 1985. The magnitude of these quotients clearly describes a market that extends significantly beyond average overrepresentation to reveal a highly specialized spatial organization of an industry.[11]

---

[10]These are employment-based quotients, using the overall share of producer services in national employment as the base (1.0).

[11]The figures for Los Angeles are underestimates of the extent of concentration because they cover the whole county, which in this case corresponds far less closely to the city than is the case of other counties, e.g. Cook County for Chicago. The massive industrial complex and active harbor are central to the growth of producer services in the Los Angeles area, but will tend to create a demand for different types of services from that engendered by Los Angeles's expanding financial activities.

Table 1 US: Location Quotients of Selected Producer Services Industries 1977–1985

	Total Employment	Banking (SIC 60–62, 67)	Insurance (63 & 64)	Real estate (65)	Business services (73)	Legal services (81)
New York City						
1977	2,714,385	2.81	1.54	2.42	2.00	2.27
1981	2,941,325	2.98	1.55	2.19	2.00	2.21
1985	3,018,000	3.04	1.40	2.18	1.72	2.36
Detroit (Wayne County)						
1977	797,342	1.22	0.66	0.51	0.92	0.91
1981	739,866	1.02	0.70	0.53	0.84	1.07
1985	698,986	0.93	0.95	0.47	0.99	1.03
Chicago (Cook County)						
1977	2,189,598	1.22	1.55	1.25	1.38	1.18
1981	2,247,119	1.40	1.51	1.29	1.33	1.34
1985	2,187,992	1.41	1.51	1.22	1.41	1.42
Boston (Suffolk County)						
1977	382,546	1.84	3.20	1.25	1.85	2.52
1981	452,189	1.81	3.12	1.25	1.74	2.62
1985	486,045	2.08	2.68	1.75	1.55	2.86
Houston (Harris County)						
1977	925,257	0.92	0.84	1.43	1.83	1.01
1981	1,256,765	0.63	0.93	1.20	1.65	0.95
1985	1,215,870	1.13	0.79	1.60	1.38	1.14
Los Angeles (LA County)						
1977	2,647,263	1.12	1.00	1.12	1.48	1.26
1981	3,173,460	1.16	0.93	1.33	1.41	1.29
1985	3,345,520	1.09	0.87	1.18	1.28	1.34

Sources: County Business Patterns, issues for Illinois, Michigan, Mass. New York, California, and Texas, in 1977, 1981, and 1985, U.S. Bureau of Census.

These patterns along with those found by Stanback & Noyelle (1982) regarding concentration of producer services in large urban areas and manufacturing in small urban areas raise the possibility of a transformation in the urban system or hierarchy.[12] Thus, it is not enough to know that New York City has the highest Location Quotient for producer services. We also need to ask whether there are significant differences among these cities in the composition and market orientation of their industries. We need to know whether Boston is as specialized in international banking and finance as New York and Los Angeles, and if so whether it is the same type of international finance. Secondly, the absolute weight of transactions is going to diverge dramatically given the much smaller employment base of Boston—under half a million, compared with 3 million each in New York and Los Angeles, and 2.1 million in Chicago. Houston has overrepresentation in certain business services but underrepresentation in two such key industries as banking and insurance. This fact is quite surprising given that it is a major hub in the Southwest, an area that has seen much growth over the last decade. It is evident that the sectors where Houston is overrepresented are linked to the oil industry and the real estate boom that came about with the large domestic migration of people and firms to the South and Southwest of the United States in the 1970s (Feagin 1985). On the other hand, the underrepresentation in banking and insurance indicates the extent to which firms in Houston and the Southwest generally use the large banks and insurance companies of the Northeast (Sassen 1990). Detroit, once the premier manufacturing city of the country, has unexpectedly low representation of real estate services, an indication of its acute manufacturing losses (Hill 1989). Given that Detroit is still the home of major car manufacturers, it has significant underrepresentation in business services, legal services, real estate, and insurance. The very low relative representation of banking in Detroit, only slightly above the national norm, indicates that to a large extent this may be consumer banking. This situation is reminiscent of the one in Britain where once major manufacturing centers now have an underrepresentation of producer services (Daniels 1985). What is the connection between the high incidence of business services in Los Angeles and its vast and dynamic industrial sector (Cohen & Zysman 1987, Soja et al 1983)? The incidence of producer services in Chicago probably follows a more expected pattern, somewhere between the acute overrepresentation of some producer services in New York, Los Angeles, and Boston and marked

---

[12]Intersecting with this question is another one concerning the type of urban system formed by the leading finance and business centers in the world economy today. New forms of interdependence among these cities, with a strong world market orientation, in some ways disconnect these cities from their national context and strengthen their interdependence, a sort of Hanseatic league at the global level (Sassen 1990: 310). In his major new book, *The Informational City,* Castells (1989) posits the emergence of a "space of flows" whose logic supercedes that of the nation, region, and city. See also Smith (1988), Timberlake (1985).

underrepresentation in Houston and Detroit. Chicago is the financial, marketing, and insurance center for the once powerful agroindustrial complex in the Midwest (Markusen 1987). The Chicago case raises two questions: The first is the extent to which the composition of the producer services is quite different from that in New York or Los Angeles because it is directly related to the servicing of the agroindustrial base of the region. Second, to what extent has the decline of the agroindustrial complex and the growth of the futures market reoriented Chicago to the world market and to finance (Sassen 1990)?[13]

The massive concentration of advanced service industries in major cities should, conceivably, push them as close as any economy has yet come to the post industrial model of a new social order, with the overall effect of raising the quality of life and the quality of jobs for large segments of the workforce and population. Yet we know from many studies that this has only partly taken place. The second half of this review examines central aspects of the social order in service-dominated urban economies.

SOCIAL IMPACT OF RESTRUCTURING

Earnings

A major question arising from the sectoral shift concerns the earnings distribution in a service-dominated economy and more generally the income structure. There is a growing body of studies on the occupational and earnings distribution in services. These studies find that services produce a larger share of low-wage jobs than does manufacturing, though the latter may increasingly be approaching parity with services; secondly, several major service industries also produce a larger share of jobs in the highest paid occupations (Stanback & Noyelle 1982, Harrison & Bluestone 1988, Sheets et al 1987, Nelson & Lorence 1985, Hirsch 1982, Maume 1983, Silver 1984).[14] Much attention has been paid to the importance of manufacturing in reducing income inequality in the 1950s and 1960s (Stanback 1979, Blumberg 1980, Haworth et al 1978, Hirsch 1982, Garofalo & Fogarty 1979). Central reasons typically identified for this effect are the greater productivity and higher levels

---

[13]New York's is a producer services sector catering to a world market. It is heavily internationalized, servicing or making transactions at the axis between a firm and the international market. Chicago's sector would seem to be much less so. Chicago's large export-oriented firms were typically highly integrated with extensive internal production of the necessary services. Now we may be seeing the beginnings of a free-standing producer services industry fed by the growth of foreign investment in the region and of the futures market.

[14]Using census data and the 1976 Survey on Income and Education, Stanback et al (1981) showed that there is a high incidence of the next-to-lowest earning class in all services, except distributive services and public administration. Almost half of all workers in the producer services are in the two highest earnings classes; but only 2.8% are in the middle earnings class, compared with half of all construction and manufacturing workers.

of unionization found in manufacturing. These studies tend to cover a period largely characterized by such conditions. But the organization of jobs has also undergone pronounced transformation in manufacturing. In what is at this point the most detailed analysis of occupational and industry data, Harrison & Bluestone (1988) found that earnings in manufacturing have declined in many industries and occupations. Glickman & Glasmeier (1989) found that a majority of manufacturing jobs in the sunbelt are low-wage, and Sassen (1989) found growth of sweatshops and homework in several industry branches in New York and Los Angeles (see also Portes & Sassen-Koob 1987, Fernandez-Kelly & Garcia 1989).

There is now a considerable body of studies with a strong theoretical bent (Scott & Storper 1986, Lipietz 1988, Hill 1989, Massey 1984, Sassen 1988) which argues that the declining centrality of mass production in national growth and the shift to services as the leading economic sector have contributed to the demise of a broader set of arrangements. In the postwar period, the economy functioned according to a dynamic which transmitted the benefits accruing to the core manufacturing industries on to more peripheral sectors of the economy. The benefits of price and market stability and increases in productivity could be transferred to a secondary set of firms, including suppliers and subcontractors, but also to less directly related industries. Although there was still a vast array of firms and workers that did not benefit from the shadow effect, their number was probably at a minimum in the post-war period. By the early 1980s the wage setting power of leading manufacturing industries, and this shadow effect, had eroded significantly.[15]

[15]The numbers of workers who are not employed full-time and year-round have increased. (But see Deuterman & Brown 1978) Part-time work rose from 15% in 1955, to 22% in 1977 and 24% in 1986. Over the last few years the government has implemented a number of decisions which promote the growing use of part-time and temporary workers (US Congressional Budget Office 1987). Circular A-76 by the Office of Management and Budget ordered all agencies to raise their use of private firms for service work unless the agency could demonstrate that it could do it more economically in-house. The result has been a growing subcontracting out of such services as food preparation, building maintenance, warehousing, and data processing. They involve types of jobs that can be organized in terms of part-time or temporary work hours, and, being labor intensive, can cut costs significantly by reducing wages. In 1984 the government implemented a two-tiered wage system in the United States Postal Service, one of the largest employers among government agencies. The purpose was to create more flexible work schedules. The second tier paid wages 25% below the previous standard. In 1985 the government implemented a regulation authorizing the employment of temporary workers at all levels for up to four years and in fact urging agencies to do so "whenever possible." This represented a severe erosion of the contractual arrangement regulating the Civil Service guarantee of permanent employment after a probationary period. Finally, in 1986 the government implemented regulations that make it easier for companies to use homeworkers. This is reminiscent of the privatization of these types of services in London, where many of these jobs went from being full-time, year-round regulated government jobs with fringe benefits, to part-time or temporary jobs in subcontracting firms with no fringe benefits and lacking the regulatory protection of the state.

The importance of this combination of processes for the expansion of a middle class and the generally rising wages should conceivably be evident in a comparison of earnings and income data for the post-War period with the last two decades. Yet different analysts have produced different results, often due to methodological or definitional differences.[16] One can identify broadly three strands in the literature: those that show no increase in earnings and/or income inequality; those that show an increase and explain it mostly in terms of demographic shifts; and those that find an often significant increase in earnings and/or income and explain it mostly in terms of economic restructuring, including prominently the intrasectoral reorganization of work.

The evidence showing inequality is substantive. Blumberg (1980) found increases in the degree of equality in the earnings distribution up to 1963. Inflation-adjusted average weekly wages peaked in 1973, stagnated over the next few years, and fell in the decade of the 1980s.[17] Harrison & Bluestone (1988) using CPS data show that the index of inequality grew 18% from 1975 to 1986. Other studies found the same trend (Bell & Freeman 1987, OECD 1985: 90–91). The data show a clear increase in low-wage, full-time, year-round jobs since the late 1970s and a less pronounced increase in high income jobs compared with the decade from 1963 to 1973 when 9 out of 10 new jobs were in the middle earnings group and high paying jobs actually lost share. After 1973 only one in two new jobs was in the middle earnings category.[18]

Central to the literature on the earning distribution has been the demography vs structure debate. Several analysts maintain that increases in earnings

---

[16]E.g. differences in procedures for deflating for inflation, for measuring wages and earnings, for categorizing worker's earnings (by occupation, median or average earnings, or by occupation within industry), for measuring inequality, and others.

[17]Inflation adjusted average weekly wages of workers increased from $67 to almost $92 in 1965 and declined slightly to $89 in 1979. BLS data shows that from 1947 to 1957 real spendable earnings grew over twenty percent; from 1957 to 1967 by thirteen percent, and from 1967 to 1977 by three percent (Blumberg, 1980: 71).

[18]It should be noted that notwithstanding an increase in multiple-earner families several studies found the family income distribution has also become more unequal. Using CPS data on family income, Blumberg (1980) found that family income adjusted for inflation increased by 33% from 1948 to 1958; by 42% from 1958–1968; by 9% from 1968 to 1978. Median family income kept growing throughout the postwar period but stagnated after 1973. By 1984, the Gini coefficient, the inequality measure used by the Bureau of the Census, stood at its highest since the end of World War II. The increase in inequality began sharply in 1980, after slight increases in the 1970s. A report prepared by the staff of the House Ways and Means Committee and released in July 1989, found that from 1979 to 1987 the bottom fifth of the population had a decline of 8% in private income and the top fifth, an increase of 16% in private income. Adjusting income for inflation and family size, the bottom fifth of the income distribution suffered a 1% decline from 1973 to 1979 and a 10% decline from 1979 to 1987; for the top fifth, there was an increase of 7% from 1973 to 1979 and a 16% increase from 1979 to 1987. It should be noted that 1979 and 1987 were both years of prosperity and low unemployment.

inequality are a function of demographic shifts, notably the growing participation of women in the labor force and the large number of young workers representing the baby boom generation—two types of workers that traditionally earn less than white adult males (Levy 1987, Lawrence 1984). Harrison & Bluestone (1988: Chapter 5) analyzed the data, controlling for various demographic factors as well as the shift to services, and found that within each group, e.g. white women, young workers, white adult men, and so on, there has been an increase in earnings inequality.[19] They found that the sectoral shift accounted for one fifth of the increase in inequality, but most of the rest of the growth in inequality occurred *within* industries so that, as with demographic groups, there is a growth in inequality in the earnings distribution within industries. (See their appendix Table A.2 for 18 demographic, sectoral, and regional factors.) The authors explain the increased inequality in the earnings distribution in terms of the restructuring of wages and work hours (Chapters 2 & 3).

There are several detailed analyses of the social impact of service growth in major metropolitan areas (Sheets et al 1987, Bergman & Goldstein 1983, Fainstein et al 1986, Maume 1983, Ross & Trachte 1983, Hawley et al 1978, Hirsch 1982, Nelson & Lorence 1985, Stanback & Noyelle 1982, Silver 1984). Using the 1980 Census PUMS file, Sheets et al (1987) found that from 1970 to 1980 several service industries had a significant effect on the growth of what they label *underemployment* and define as employment paying below poverty-level wages in the 100 largest metropolitan areas. The strongest effect was associated with the growth of producer services and retail trade. The highest relative contribution resulted from what the authors call "corporate services" (FIRE, business services, legal services, membership organizations and professional services) such that a 1% increase in employment in these services was found to result in a 0.37% increase in full-time, year-round low-wage jobs; a 1% increase in distributive services, in a 0.32% increase in such jobs. In contrast, a 1% increase in personal services was found to result in a 0.13% increase in such jobs, explained by the high incidence of part-time jobs in this industry. The retail industry had the highest effect on the creation of part-time, year-round, low-wage jobs, such that a 1% increase in retail was found to result in a 0.88% increase in such jobs.

But what about the impact of services on the expansion of high income jobs? Nelson & Lorence (1985) examined this question using census data on the 125 largest such areas.[20] In order to establish why male earnings are more

---

[19]Bradbury (1986), comparing 1973 and 1984 data, found a substantial decline in the share of income going to middle income families (defined as families with income between $20,000 and $50,000) from 53% in 1973 to 47.9% in 1984. Of the 5.1% decline, 4.3% lost income and the rest gained income. She also tested the demographic explanations and found these to account for only four tenths of 1% of the 5.1% change. Gottschalk & Danziger found a sharp increase in the rate of poverty since 1979 due to declines in transfer payments and growing wage inequality.

unequal in metropolises with high levels of service-sector employment, they measured the ratio of median earnings over the 5th percentile to identify the difference in earnings between the least affluent and the median metropolitan male earners, and the ratio at the 95th percentile to establish the gap between median and affluent earners.[21] Overall, they found that inequality in the 125 areas appeared to be due to greater earnings disparity between the highest and the median earners than between the median and lowest earners (Nelson & Lorence 1985:115). Furthermore they found that the strongest effect came from the producer services and that the next strongest was far weaker (social services in 1970 and personal services in 1980).[22]

Housing

The occupational and sectoral transformation, particularly in large cities with once large manufacturing sectors and now growing producer services, has contributed to simultaneous deterioration of some areas and high income rehabilitation of others, especially in central areas of large cities. The rapid increase in housing demand by the growing numbers of high-income workers has raised the profitability of the market for expensive housing, while growing unemployment among low-income workers has further depressed the lower end of the housing market.[23] Forced displacement affected about 2.5

[20]Two clarifications on this study. The 125 became 124 by 1980 with the merging of Dallas and Fort Worth. They focused only on men to facilitate comparability with other and previous research on individual earnings dispersion in metropolitan areas which has been largely restricted to male earnings.

[21]A larger ratio between the upper end and the median indicates that the more affluent have a greater economic advantage over median earners than do high earners in another metropolitan area. They disaggregated service employment into four major groups, following Singelmann & Browning (1978, 1980), and included a number of control variables (race, age, education, unemployment).

[22]The authors regressed the various income and percentile measures on the other four service sectors and select control variables and found that the producer services sector had the most substantial relationship to overall inequality of the four service sectors and were more highly related to inequality than most of the control variables associated with the traditional explanations of inequality.

[23]There were sharp increases in homeownership in the decades after WWII from 44% in 1940 to 66% in 1980, along with a sharp decrease in substandard housing conditions (Bratt et al 1986; see also Weiss 1987). In 1983, for the first time in 20 years the homeownership rate fell, though very slightly from 65.6% to 64.6% (US Bureau of the Census 1984a). The 10 year goal established in the 1968 Housing Act of producing 26 million units, 6 million of which were to have been subsidized, has not been achieved. 17.6 million were built, with only 210,000 publicly owned (US Bureau of the Census 1984b: p. 662, table 1328). Housing costs now represent a growing proportion of disposable family income for both renters and homeowners. For renters median gross rent as a percentage of median income rose from 22% to 29% from 1973 to 1983 (US Bureau of the Census 1983e). A growing share of these renters pays over half of their income in rent. Among lower income households the median rent-to-income ratio was 50% and above.

million people a year in the 1970s for varied reasons—gentrification, undermaintenance, formal eviction, arson, rent increases, mortgage foreclosures, conversions of low to high income housing, etc. (LeGates & Hartman 1981) (US Congress 1982). Most cities now have a growing population of homeless that includes not only deinstitutionalized mental patients and derelicts but families and employed low-wage workers. Informed estimates put the number at 2 million, mostly in large cities. Increasingly former homeowners are also present among the homeless due to eviction for mortgage delinquency. Evictions are higher today than at any time since the 1930s. Minorities face far more severe housing problems than do whites on all standard measures (affordability, physical inadequacy, overcrowding, homeownership rates) (Feins & Bratt 1983, US HUD 1979: p. 665). In 1978–1979, official rates of poverty and doubling-up rates began to grow after long-term declines. According to Bratt et al (1986), the severity of the twin recessions of 1979 and 1982 and the particularly high and protracted unemployment rates, in addition to the Reagan administration's drastic budget cuts pushed a growing number of people into marginal housing and even homelessness. The fact that the 1983 upturn and often high growth rates in many of the large cities did not reduce this condition, and that it actually increased, points to a structural transformation, according to some analysts (Hopper & Hamberg 1986: 24–25). "Housing today reproduces and perpetuates the other economic and social divisions in society" (Achtenberg & Marcuse 1983: 207).

Much of the debate on housing centers on policy aspects. The most critical authors (Bratt et al 1986, Smith & Williams 1986, Hopper & Hamberg 1986, Marcuse 1986) maintain there is a housing crisis and that it can be understood in the context of the broader economic transformation and with reference to the actions and interests of the principal actors involved (financial institutions; developers, owners and managers of real estate; government at all levels). Other analysts reject the notion of a crisis in housing or see it as existing only among a very limited and disadvantaged sector of the population and that the market overall functions well in providing the nation with housing (Downs 1980; US Dep. HUD 1982).

MINORITIES AND THE URBAN TRANSFORMATION

The consequences of the various processes discussed thus far have become particularly evident in the largest cities, partly because they had large manufacturing sectors, and partly because they had disproportionate concentrations of low-income blacks, and eventually Hispanics, likely to be employed in manufacturing. As has been widely recognized, in the 1970s and 1980s our large cities became poorer, blacker, and more Hispanic (see

Peterson 1985; see Bane & Jargowsky 1988; McLanahan 1985). From 1969 to 1979, the share of black families in cities with populations over 0.5 million increased sharply while that of white families dropped. From 1979 to 1986 the most pronounced change was the increase in the share of Hispanic and Asian families. In 1969, 75.8% of families in cities with over half a million population were white; by 1979 this figure was down to 68.6%. The percentage of black families went from 22.7% in 1969 to 27.5% in 1979 and 26.1% in 1986. Hispanics, for whom there is no figure for 1969, increased from 11.7% in 1979 to 16.3% in 1986. Both black and white families in large metropolitan areas have higher median incomes than those in nonmetropolitan areas. Yet within these areas a strong difference exists for both whites and blacks between cities and suburbs. There has been a relative decline in city median family income from 1969 to 1976. After 1979, white city families maintained their relative standing while black families' median income declined further and their poverty rate increased significantly (Drennan 1988).[24] In 1986, the poverty rate was 10.8% for white families in cities and 5.6% in suburbs, and for blacks respectively 29% and 19.4%. In non metropolitan areas whites had a poverty rate of 12.6% and blacks 36.8%.

The most detailed information on urban poverty comes from the 1980 census. Using census data for the 100 largest cities in the United States and a measure for concentrated poverty tracts developed by Ricketts & Sawhill (1988), Mincey (1988) found that 73% of all such tracts with a majority of blacks were in the 50 largest metropolitan areas of the U.S. This share rises to 83% for the 100 largest areas. The highest level of concentration was among Hispanics, with 95% of such tracts in the 50 largest cities; for whites the share was under 50%. Clearly, black and Hispanic poverty is disproportionately concentrated in the largest cities. Furthermore, Mincey (1988) found that non-minority poor were more likely to gain access to housing in nonpoverty and nonextreme poverty tracts than were minorities. Finally, poor Hispanic whites are less concentrated in extreme poverty tracts than are blacks and nonwhite Hispanics, which leads Mincey to posit that racial differentials in access to housing among the poor may be more important to explain the high concentration of minority poor than are ethnic differentials (Mincey 1988: 5, see also Massey 1981).

In sum, the concentration of poor in large cities has increased, and median family income is lower in large cities than in their suburbs. Controlling for race we can see increasing differentials between whites and blacks as of 1969, with the urban poverty rate of blacks reaching a level triple that of whites in

[24]The 1969 median income of white families in cities was 84.5% of those in suburbs of large metropolitan areas; by 1979 this had fallen to 78.5% and 77.9% by 1986. That of blacks stood at 85.5% in 1969, 71.9% in 1979 and 65.6% by 1979.

1986; median income of black families in the cities has lost ground relative to that of blacks in the suburbs and to whites generally, and the concentration of blacks in large cities has increased while that of whites has decreased[25].

The growing urbanization of poor blacks and Hispanics has occurred at a time of pronounced transformations in the occupational distribution in major cities (Kasarda 1988, Orfield 1985). Using the 1980 census PUMS file, Kasarda (1988) found that large northern and northeastern cities all had severe losses in clerical and sales occupations and in blue collar occupations, and they all had gains in managerial, professional, technical, and administrative support occupations. The suburban rings had gains in these occupational groups, but they also gained blue-collar jobs. This left cities with net job losses ranging from 46,480 in Boston to 104,860 in Detroit and net gains in suburban rings from 97,060 in Cleveland to 489,080 in New York.[26] The share of job holders with a high school degree or less declined sharply while that of job holders with some college or a college degree increased sharply. At the same time it is important to note that about half of all job holders in major cities in 1980 had only a high school degree or less. This was the case for half or more of all job holders in New York City, Baltimore, Chicago, Cleveland, Detroit, St. Louis, Philadelphia (Kasarda 1988). Thus, the rates of change do not necessarily mean that a vast majority of all jobs in cities are now held by individuals with advanced educations. In fact, 10% of black male job holders in these cities had only a high school degree or less; but among black males not working, 80% had no high school degree. For all regions of the United States, the share of black males of working age without a high school degree has increased sharply over the last 20 years in both central cities and suburban rings of metropolitan regions. From about a fifth in cities in 1969, the proportion increased to almost half by 1987, ranging from a low of 44% in the Northeast to a high of 60.8% in the West. The figures for suburbs are considerably lower but still reveal a sharp increase, and they are far higher than those for whites, going from about a sixth in 1969 to well over a third by

[25]In the 1970s black migration into large cities subsided and there was in fact a net outmigration to the suburbs; but in the 1980s this outmigration also declined, and there was little movement in either direction. Births accounted for most of the increase in the urban black population (Hauser 1981). Wilson points out that this would mean that for the first time in the twentieth century "the ranks of central city blacks are no longer being replenished by poor migrants" (Wilson 1985; p 14). Lieberson (1980) found that the cessation of immigration benefitted European and Asian immigrants. This should presumably also occur with the black urban population. Census data (Hauser 1981) indicate that blacks migrating from nonmetropolitan areas in the South were going predominantly to the large cities in the South such as Atlanta and Houston, where we are seeing the formation of larger inner city ghettoes that resemble the northern ghettoes. This will further add to the disproportionate concentration of poor blacks in large cities who are particularly vulnerable to the changes brought about by restructuring.

[26]Blue collar jobs did grow in particular industries in cities: notably in producer services in New York and Chicago and in the public sector.

1987, from a "low" of 30.8% in the Northeast to a high of 41.3% in the Midwest.[27]

Wilson (1985, 1987) finds that various types of social dislocation have acquired catastrophic dimensions in the inner areas of large cities and have further widened the gap between the poor and the growing successful black middle class. Since the mid-1960s the share of black births outside marriage has doubled, from one quarter to over half by 1980; the number of black families headed by women has doubled, as have black crime rates and joblessness. While only one in nine persons was black in the United States, one in every two persons arrested for murder and non-negligent manslaughter was black and 44% of the murder victims were black (see also Samson 1987). These conditions are all disproportionately concentrated in what Wilson describes as the underclass, "a heterogenous grouping of inner city families and individuals who are outside the mainstream of the American occupational system" (1985: 133).

This severe deterioration for a significant share of the black population concentrated in cities occurred at a time when major antidiscrimination legislation was in place and the growth of a strong black middle class emerged, partly through increasing access to well-paying public sector jobs. Wilson argues that while discrimination will explain part of that deterioration, one must bring into account the structural transformation of the economic base in the large cities where disadvantaged blacks are concentrated.[28]

A key debate centers on the weight of spatial factors in the rise of joblessness among urban blacks (Freeman & Holzer 1986, Ellwood 1986, Hughes 1987, Leonard 1986, Orfield 1985, Kasarda 1985). Some emphasize that the suburbanization of blue-collar and other low-skill jobs has worked to the economic disadvantage of blacks who remain residentially constrained to inner-city housing (Kasarda 1985, Farley 1987).[29] Ellwood (1986) presents

[27]Kasarda found that about three fourths of those blacks who lacked a high school degree and who commuted to suburban jobs did so by private vehicle presumably because public transportation was unavailable or too cumbersome. This fact suggests that it could be very difficult for blacks with low levels of education, who will tend to be poor, to gain access to suburban jobs.

[28]This is clearly a highly complex and difficult issue with a wide range of theoretical and empirical lines of inquiry. Wilson (1985, 1987) argues that present day discrimination cannot be seen as the main culprit for this severe deterioration, but that it is rather the legacy of historic discrimination in combination with contemporary social and economic forces. Lieberson (1980) found that the large and prolonged influx of Southern black migrants was a central factor in producing economic disadvantages in the large ghettoes of the Northeastern cities.

[29]Farley (1987) found that black unemployment is higher relative to whites where jobs are most suburbanized and the black population is least so. Price & Mills (1985) found that blacks earn 19% less than whites due to poorer qualifications and 15% less due to discrimination, and an additional 6% less due to concentration in central cities. Vrooman and Greenfield (1980) found that 40% of the black-white racial earning gap could be closed by the suburbanization of central city black labor. And Strazheim (1980) found a positive wage gradient from city to suburb employment among lesser educated blacks in contrast to whites.

strong evidence that race, not spatial factors (differential proximity to jobs), is the key variable explaining employment differentials.

In these same large cities, many of the new immigrants have made disproportionate "gains" into declining manufacturing industries (Tienda et al 1984), and typically they show much lower joblessness than blacks. One key difference is the centrality of the immigrant community to the well-being of immigrants. The immigrant community can be thought of as a mechanism that transforms whatever its people have into resources: their labor power becomes entrepreneurship in a coethnic's enterprise, their cultural or language segregation becomes a captive market for ethnic entrepreneurs and a vehicle for the recirculation of earnings, extended households offer flexibility in the allocation of members to the labor market, and so on (Sassen 1988). There is a vast literature on this subject. (Light & Bonacich 1988, Wilson & Portes 1980, Waldinger 1985, to name but a few.) This has meant many things, from job generation in the immigrant community to the possibility of surviving—through household income pooling—on extremely low-wage jobs in declining manufacturing industries.

A recent development in immigrant communities in large cities, which contrasts sharply with the growth of an underclass in black neighborhoods in these same cities, is the expansion of an informal economy (Portes et al 1989, Sassen 1989, Stepick 1989). The informal economy is defined as the production and distribution of (mostly) licit goods and services outside the regulatory apparatus covering zoning, tax, health and safety, minimum wage laws, and other types of standards in a context where such activities are usually regulated.

Because the informal economy in the United States is perhaps most evident in immigrant communities, there has been a tendency to explain its expansion as resulting from the large influx of Third World immigrants and their propensity to replicate survival strategies typical of home countries. Not unrelated is the notion that the availability of a large supply of cheap immigrant workers facilitates the survival of backward sectors of the economy in that it contributes to lower the costs of social reproduction and production. Both of these views posit or imply that if there is an informal sector in advanced industrialized countries, the sources are to be found in Third World immigration and in backward sectors of the economy. Explaining the expansion of informal arrangements as a Third World import or a remnant of an earlier phase of industrialization resolves the tension between this fact and prevailing conceptions of advanced industrialized economies (see Portes & Sassen-Koob 1987).

An important question for theory and policy is whether the formation and expansion of informal work in advanced economies is the result of conditions created by these economies. Rather than assume that Third World immigration is causing informalization, we need a critical examination of the role it may or may not play in this process. Immigrants, insofar as they tend to form communities, may be in a favorable position to seize the opportunities represented by informalization. But the opportunities are not necessarily created by immigrants. They may well be a structured outcome of current trends in advanced industrial economies. Several studies attempt an analytic differentiation of immigration, informalization, and characteristics of the current phase of advanced industrialized economies in order to establish the differential impact of (a) immigration and (b) conditions in the economy at large on the formation and expansion of informal sectors (Castells & Portes 1989, Fernandez-Kelly & Garcia 1989, Stepick 1989, Sassen 1989).[30]

The sectoral and occupational transformation in large cities and the associated expansion of low- and high-income strata have brought about (a) a proliferation of small firms engaged in the production and retail of both highly priced and very cheap products for firms and for final consumers a partial concentration of such small firms in major cities due to the critical mass of both high- and low-income residents and commuters in cities and, further, the need for small firms to be close to suppliers and buyers. These growth trends contain inducements toward the informalization of a whole range of activities. In contrast, standardized mass production is not conducive to informal work arrangements.

In sum, one particular instance of the increased inequality associated with urban restructuring is the disengagement of significant sectors of the minority population from mainstream economic and social institutions. This is happening either through what amounts to expulsion (the case of extreme poverty and long-term unemployment) or through a downgraded form of participation (the case of informal work).

CONCLUSION: OLD QUESTIONS IN NEW CONTEXTS

The growth of service employment in cities and the evidence on the associated growth of inequality have also raised questions about how fundamental a change this shift entails. Several of these questions stand out. One concerns the nature of service-based urban economies and another the relation of

---

[30]These studies are to be distinguished from studies that aim at overall estimates of the underground economy based on aggregate figures for the supply and circulation of money (Gutmann 1979). As categories for analysis, the underground economy and the informal economy overlap only partly. Studies on the underground economy have sought to measure all income not registered in official figures, including income derived from illicit activities such as drug dealing.

structure and agency, specifically the place of urban politics at a time when economic forces are increasingly global yet social costs are local.

Regarding the first, there are the beginnings of a theory on the service-based economy. There are elements for a theoretical framework in such work as Stanback & Noyelle (1982), and theoretical models of service-based urbanization in Castells (1989), Friedmann (1986) and Sassen (1990) (see also Blau 1980). Some of the best and most illuminating work on service-based economies has focused on Third World cities (Timberlake 1985, Evans & Timberlake 1980, Fiala 1983, Kentor 1981, London 1987). Issues raised in this literature are of interest to us here as are broader discussions on models of economic development (Jaffe 1985, Delacroix & Ragin 1981).

On the second issue, the place of urban politics given global economic forces and the withdrawal of federal resources from local governments, several general conclusions can be drawn from the literature. First, notwithstanding the diversity of forms that economic restructuring has assumed in specific localities and the range of policy responses, many studies show that larger, translocal economic forces have more weight than local policies in shaping urban economies in the current period (Castells 1989, Feagin 1985, Hill 1989). Furthermore, much of this literature shows that national policies can have a very strong impact on local policies, and today these are mostly more influential in shaping cities than are local policies (Parkinson et al 1988, Fainstein et al 1986). Finally, much of this literature also shows that national policies have not escaped the influence and constraints of economic restructuring and the global forces that are part of it (Scott & Storper 1986, Sassen 1988).

A central question for theory and research is what spheres of local development can be objectively and ideologically relocalized (Marris 1987, Pickvance 1988, Castells 1983, Baldassare & Protash 1982, Plotkin 1987, Savitch 1988). The globalization of the economy and its detrimental effects on urban politics is increasingly also presented as an ideology that robs cities even of the notion that local politics matter. Under certain conditions local governments or local initiatives can resist the tendencies of economic restructuring and of national political objectives. Examples include the citizens coalitions fighting the "growth machines" described by Logan and Molotch (1987), the municipalities run by leftist governments in France described by Preteceille (1988), and several cities in the United States and in the United Kingdom described by Clavel (1986) which resisted the overall tendencies of economic restructuring through the implementation of progressive or mainstream agendas for economic growth.

Literature Cited.

Achtenberg, E. P., Marcuse, P. 1983. Towards the decommodification of housing: A political analysis and a progressive program. In *America's Housing Crisis: What is to be Done?* ed. C. Hartman. Boston: Routledge & Kegan Paul

Appelbaum, R. P., Gilderbloom, J. I. 1986. Supply-side economics and rents: Are rental housing markets truly competitive? See Bratt et al 1986

Baldassare, M., Protash, W. 1982. Growth controls, population growth and community satisfaction. *Am. Sociol. Rev.* 47:339–46

Bane, M. J., Jargowsky, P. A. 1988. Urban poverty areas: Basic questions concerning prevalance, growth and dynamics. In *Urban Change and Poverty*, ed. M. G. H. McGeary, L. E. Lynn Jr. Washington, DC: Natl. Acad. Press

Bell, L., Freeman, R. B. 1987. The facts about rising industrial wage dispersion in the U.S. *Proc. Ind. Relat. Res. Assoc.* May

Bergman, E., Goldstein, H. 1983. Dynamics and structural change in metropolitan economies. *Am. Plan. Assoc. J.* Summer:263–79

Blau, P. M. 1980. Implications of growth in services for social structure. *Soc. Sci. Q.* 61:3–21

Bluestone, B., Harrison, B. 1982. *The Deindustrialization of America.* New York: Basic Books

Blumberg, P. 1980. *Inequality in an Age of Decline.* New York: Oxford Univ. Press

Bradbury, K. L. 1986. The shrinking middle class. *N. Engl. Econ. Rev.,* Sept.-Oct.

Bratt, R. G., Hartman, C., Meyerson, A. 1986. *Critical Perspectives in Housing.* Philadelphia: Temple University Press

Browning, H., Singelmann, J. 1980. Industrial transformation and occupational change in the U.S., 1960–70. *Soc. Forces* 59:246–64

Browning, H., Singelmann, J. 1978. The transformation of the U.S. Labor Foree: the interaction of industry and occupation. *Polit. Soc.* 8:481–509

Castells, M. 1989. *The Informational City.* London: Blackwell

Castells, M. 1983. *The City and the Grassroots: A Cross-Cultural Theory of Urban Social Movements.* Berkeley: Univ. Calif. Press

Castells, M., Portes, A. 1989. World underneath: The origins dynamics, and effects of the informal economy. See Portes et al 1989, pp. 11–37

Clavel, P. 1986. *The Progressive City.* New Brunswick: Rutgers Univ. Press

Cohen, S., Zysman, J. 1987. *Manufacturing Matters.* New York: Basic Books

Daniels, P. W. 1985. *Service Industries.* London: Methuen

Delacroix, J., Ragin, C. 1981. Structural blockage: A cross-national study of economic dependency, state efficacy and underdevelopment. *Am. J. Sociol.* 86:1311–47

Denison, E. 1979. *Accounting for Slower Economic Growth: The U.S. of the 1970s.* Washington, DC: Brookings Inst.

Deutermann, W. V. Jr., Brown, S. C. 1978. Voluntary part-time workers: A growing part of the labor force. *Mon. Labor Rev.* 101:3–10

Drennan, M. P. 1988. *Deconstruction of the New York Economy.* Prepared for a Meeting of the Dual City Work. Group, SSRC Comm. New York City, June 11–13

Downs, A. 1980. *Rental Housing in the 1980s.* Washington, DC: Brookings Inst.

Edel, M., Sclar, E. D., Luria, D. 1984. *Shaky Palaces.* New York: Columbia Univ. Press

Ellwood, D. T. 1986. The spatial mismatch hypothesis: Are there teenage jobs missing in the ghetto? See Freeman & Holzer 1986

Evans, P., Timberlake, M. 1980. Dependency, inequality and the growth of the tertiary: A comparative analysis of less developed countries. *Am. Sociol. Rev.* 45:531–52

Fainstein, S., Fainstein, N., Hill, R. C., Judd, D., Smith, M. P. 1986. *Restructuring the City: The Political Economy of Urban Redevelopment.* New York: Longman Revis. ed.

Farley, J. E. 1987. Disproportionate Black and Hispanic Unemployment in U.S. Metropolitan Areas. *Am. J. Econ. Sociol.* 46(2):129–50

Feagin, J. R. 1985. The global context of metropolitan growth: Houston and the oil industry. *Am. J. Sociol.* 90:1204–30

Feins, J. D., Bratt, R. G. 1983. Barred in Boston: Racial discrimination in housing. *J. Am. Plan. Assoc.* 49:Summer:344–55

Fernandez-Kelly, M. P., Garcia, A. 1989. Informalization at the core: Hispanic women, homework, and the advanced capitalist state. See Portes et al 1989, pp. 247–64

Fiala, R. 1983. Inequality and the service sector in less developed countries: A reanalysis and re-specification. *Am. Sociol. Rev.* 48:421–28

Form, W. 1954. The place of social structure in the determination of land use. *Soc. Forces* 32:317–23

Freeman, R. B., Holzer, H. J., eds. 1986. The black youth employment crisis: summary of findings. In *The Black Youth Employment Crisis,* Chicago, IL: The Univ. Chicago Press

Friedmann, J. 1986. The world city hypothesis. *Dev. Change* 17:69–83

Frisbie, P., Kasarda, J. 1988. Spatial processes. In *Handbook of Sociology*, ed. N. Smelser. Newbury Park, CA: Sage

Garofalo, G., Fogarty, M. S. 1979. Urban income distribution and the urban hierarchy-inequality hypothesis. *Rev. Econ. Stat.* 61:381–88

Ginzberg, E., Vojta, G. 1981. The service sector of the U.S. economy. *Sci. Am.* 244:48–55

Glickman, N. J. 1983. International trade, capital mobility and economic growth: Some implications for American cities and regions in the 1980s. In *Transition to the 21st Century: Prospects and Policies for Economic and Urban-Regional Transformation*. ed. D. Hicks, N. Glickman. Greenwich, Conn:JAI Press

Glickman, N. J., Glasmeier, A. K. 1989. The international economy and the American South. See Rodwin & Sazanami 1989, pp. 60–80

Gottdiener, M., Feagin, J. R. 1988. The paradigm shift in urban sociology. *Urban Aff. Q.* 24:163–87

Greenfield, H. I. 1966. *Manpower and the Growth of Producer Services*. New York: Columbia Univ. Press

Gutmann, P. M. 1979. Statistical illusions, mistaken policies. *Challenge* 22:5–13

Harris, R. 1988. *Home and Work in New York Since 1950*. Paper prepared for the Workshop for the Dual City, Comm. New York City, Soc. Sci. Res. Counc., New York, Feb. 26–27

Harrison, B., Bluestone, B. 1988. *The Great U-Turn*. New York: Basic Books

Hartman, C. 1986. Housing policies under the Reagan administration. See Bratt et al 1986

Hauser, P. M. 1981. The Census of 1980. *Sci. Am.* 245:53

Hawley, A. 1984. Human ecological and Marxian theories. *Am. J. Sociol.* 89(4):904–17

Hawley, C. T., Long, J., Rasmussen, D. W. 1978. Income distribution, city, size and urban growth. *Urban Stud.* 15:1–7

Hill, R. C. 1989. Comparing transnational production systems: The case of the automobile industry in the United States and Japan. *Int. J. Urban Reg. Res.* 13(3):462

Hill, R. C., Negrey, C. 1987. Deindustrialization in the Great Lakes. *Urban Aff. Q.* 22(4):580–97

Hirsch, B. 1982. Income distribution, city size and urban growth: A re-examination. *Urban Stud.* 19:71–74

Hoover, E., Vernon, R. 1962. *Anatomy of a Metropolis*. New York: Anchor

Hopper, K., Hamberg, J. 1986. The making of America's homeless: From skid row to new poor, 1945–1984. See Bratt et al 1986

Hughes, M. A. 1987. Moving up and moving out: Confusing ends and means about ghetto dispersal. *Urban Stud.* 24:503–17

Jaffe, D. 1985. Export dependence and economic growth: A reformulation and respecification. *Soc. Forces* 64:102–18

Jaret, C. 1983. Recent neo-Marxist urban analysis. *Annu. Rev. Sociol.* 9:499–525

Kasarda, J. D. 1985. Urban change and minority opportunities. See Peterson 1985

Kasarda, J. D. 1988. Jobs, migration, and emerging urban mismatches. In *Urban Changes and Poverty*, ed. M. G. H. McGeary, L. E. Lynn Jr. Washington DC: Natl. Acad. Press

Kentor, J. 1981. Structural determination of peripheral urbanization: The effects of international dependence. *Am. Sociol. Rev.* 46:201–11

Klein, L. 1983. Identifying the effects of structural change. In *Industrial Change and Public Policy: A Symp. Sponsored by the Fed. Reserve Bank of Kansas City*, Aug. 1–21

Lawrence, R. Z. 1983. Changes in U.S. industrial structure: The role of global forces, secular trends and transitory cycles. In *Industrial Change and Public Policy: A Symp. Sponsored by the Fed. Reserve Bank of Kansas City*, Aug. 29–79

Lawrence, R. Z. 1984. Sectoral shifts and the size of the middle class. *Brookings Rev.* 3(1)

LeGates, R., Hartman, C. 1981. Displacement. *Clearinghouse Rev.* 15: 207–49

LeGrande, L. 1985. *Jobs and the Economic Recovery: How Have Industries, Regions, and Workers Fared?* Washington, DC: Congress. Res. Serv., Library Congr.

Leonard, J. S. 1986. Comment on David Ellwood's: The spatial mismatch hypothesis. See Freeman & Holzer 1986

Levy, F. 1987. *Dollars and Dreams: The Changing American Income Distribution*. New York: Sage Found.

Lieberson, S. 1980. A Piece of the Pie: Blacks and White Immigrants Since 1880. Univ. Calif. Press

Light, I., Bonacich, E. 1988. *Immigrant Enterprise*. Berkeley, CA: Univ. Calif. Press

Lipietz, A. 1988. New tendencies in the international division of labor: Regimes of accumulation and modes of regulation. See Scott & Storper 1988

Logan, J. R., Molotch, H. 1987. *Urban Fortunes: The Political Economy of Place*. Berkeley: Univ. Calif.

London, B. 1987. Structural determinants of third world urban change: An ecological and political economic analysis. *Am. Sociol. Rev.* 52:28–43

Magaziner, I., Reich, R. 1982. *Minding America's Business.* New York: Harcourt Brace Jovanovich

Marcuse, P. 1986. Abandonment, gentrification, and displacement: the linkages in New York City. See Smith & Williams 1986

Markusen, A. 1987. *Region Building: The Politics and Economics of Territory.* Totowa, NJ: Rowman & Allenheld.

Markusen, A., Hall, P., Glasmeier, A. 1986. *High Tech America: The What, How, Where and Why of the Sunrise Industries.* London/Boston: Allen & Unwin

Marris, P. 1987. *Meaning and Action: Community Planning and Conceptions of Change.* London: Routledge & Kegan Paul

Massey, D. S. 1984. *Spatial Divisions of Labor.* London: Macmillan

Massey, D. S. 1981. Dimensions of the new immigration to the United States and the prospects for assimilation. *Annu. Rev. Sociol.* 7:57–85

Maume, D. S. 1983. Metropolitan hierarchy and income distribution: A comparison of explanations. *Urban Aff. Q.* 18:413–29

McLanahan, S. 1985. Family structure and the reproduction of poverty. *Am. J. Sociol.* 90:873–901

Meyer, D. R. 1986. The world system of cities: Relations between international and financial metropolises and South American cities. *Soc. Forces* 64:553–81

Meyer, S. J. 1980. GNP: Perspectives on Services. Conservation of Human Resources Project: Columbia Univ.

Mincey, R. B. 1988. *Industrial restructuring, dynamic events and the racial composition of concentrated poverty.* Paper prepared for the SSRC, Comm. Urban Underclass, New York, Sept. 21–23

Moriarty, B. 1986. Hierarchies of cities and the spatial temporal distribution of manufacturing. In *Technology, Regions, and Policy,* ed. J. Rees. New York: Praeger

Nelson, J. I., Lorence, J. 1985. Employment in service activities and inequality in metropolitan areas. *Urban Aff. Q.* 21(1):106–25

Norton, R. D., Rees, J. 1979. The product cycle and the spatial decentralization of American manufacturing. *Reg. Stud.* 13: 141–51

OECD. 1985 *OECD Environmental Outlook.* Paris: OECD

Orfield, G. 1985. Ghettoization and its alternatives. See Peterson 1985, pp.

Parkinson, M., Foley, B., Judd, D. 1988. *Regenerating the Cities: The UK Crisis and the U.S. Experience.* Manchester: Manchester Univ. Press

Perry, D., Watkins, A. 1977. *The Rise of Sunbelt Cities.* Beverly Hills, CA: Sage

Peterson, P. E. 1985. *The New Urban Reality.* Washington, DC: Brookings Instit.

Pickvance, C. G. 1988. *The Failure of control and the success of structural reform: An interpretation of recent attempts to restructure local government in Britain.* Paper presented at the Int. Sociol. Assoc., RC 21 Conf. Trends and Challenges of Urban Restructuring, Rio de Janeiro, Brazil, Sept.

Plotkin, S. 1987. *Keep Out: The Struggle for Land Use Control.* Berkeley: Univ. Calif. Press

Portes, A., Castells, M., Benton, L., eds. 1989. *The Informal Economy: Studies in Advanced and Less Developed Countries.* Baltimore: Johns Hopkins Univ. Press

Portes, A., Sassen-Koob, S. 1987. Making it underground: Comparative material on the informal sector in Western Market Economies. *Am. J. Sociol.* 93:30–61

Preteceille, E. 1988. Decentralization in France: New citizenship of restructuring hegemony? *Eur. J. Polit. Res.* 16:409–24

Ricketts, E. R., Sawhill, I. V. 1988. Defining and measuring the underclass. *J. Policy Anal. Manage.* 7(2):316–25

Rodwin, L., Sazanami, H. 1989. *Deindustrialization and Regional Economic Transformation: The Experience of the United States.* Winchester, MA: Unwin Hyman

Ross, R., Trachte, K. 1983. Global cities and global classes: The peripheralization of labor in New York City. *Review* 6 3:393–431

Sampson, R. J. 1987. Urban Black violence: The effect of male joblessness and family disruption. *Am. J. Sociol.* 93:348–82

Sassen, S. 1988. *The Mobility of Labor and Capital.* Cambridge: Cambridge Univ. Press

Sassen, S. 1989. New York City's informal economy. In *The Informal Sector: Theoretical and Methodological Issues,* ed. A. Portes, M. Castells, L. Benton, pp. 60–77. Baltimore: Johns Hopkins University

Sassen, S. 1990. *The Global City: New York London Tokyo.* Princeton, NJ: Princeton Univ. Press

Savitch, H. 1988. *Post-Industrial Cities.* Princeton: Princeton Univ. Press

Sawyers, L., Tabb, W., eds. 1987. *Sunbelt/Snowbelt: Urban Development and Regional Restructuring.* New York: Oxford Univ. Press

Sennett, R. 1990. *The Conscience of the Eye.* New York: Knopf

Sheets, R. G., Nord, S., Phelps, J. J. 1987. *The Impact of Service Industries on Un-*

deremployment in Metropolitan Economies. Lexington, MA: Heath & Co.

Silver, H. 1984. *Regional shifts, deindustrialization and metropolitan income inequality.* Presented at the Annu. Meet. Am. Sociol. Assoc., San Antonio, Texas

Singelmann, N. J. 1978. *From Agriculture to Services: The Transformation of Industrial Employment.* Beverly Hills, CA: Sage

Smith, M. P. 1988. *City, State and Market: The Political Economy of Urban Society.* New York: Basil Blackwell

Smith, N., Williams, P. 1986. *Gentrification of the City.* Boston: Allen & Unwin

Soja, E., Morales, R., Wolff, G. 1983. Urban restructuring: An analysis of social and spatial change in Los Angeles. *Econ. Geogr.* 59(2):195–230

Stanback, T. M. Jr., Noyelle, T. J. 1982. *Cities in Transition: Changing Job Structures in Atlanta, Denver, Buffalo, Phoenix, Columbus (Ohio), Nashville, Charlotte.* Totowa, NJ: Allenheld, Osmun

Stanback, T. M. Jr., Bearse, P. J., Noyelle, T. J., Karasek, R. 1981. *Services: The New Economy.* NJ: Allenheld, Osmun

Stepick, A. 1989. Miami's two informal sectors. In *The Informal Economy,* ed. A. Portes, M. Castells, X. Benton. Baltimore, Md: Johns Hopkins Univ. Press, pp. 111–31

Stigler, G. 1951. The division of labor is limited by the extent of the market. *J. Polit. Econ.* 58(3):185–93

Strazheim, M. 1980. Discrimination and the spatial characteristics of the urban labor market for black workers. *J. Urban Econ.* 7(1):119–40

Tienda, M., Jensen, L., Bach, R. L. 1984. Immigration, gender and the process of occupational change in the United States, 1970–1980. *Women Migr. Int. Migr. Rev.* 18(4):1021–44

Timberlake, M. ed. 1985. *Urbanization in the World Economy.* Orlando: Academic

US Bureau of the Census. 1983. *Annual Housing Survey.* Part C. Financial Characteristics of the housing inventory, U.S. and regions. Ser. H150–183. Washington, DC: GPO

US Bureau of the Census. 1984a. Press release CB–84–86. April 30

US Bureau of the Census. 1984b. *Statistical abstract of the United States: 1984.* Washington, DC: GPO

US Congress. House. Subcomm. Housing Comm. Dev. 1982. Hearings, June 24

US. Depart. HUD. 1982. *The President's National Urban Policy Report.* Washington, DC: US GPO

US Depart. HUD. 1979. *Measuring racial discrimination in American housing markets: the housing market practices survey.* Washington, DC: GPO

Vrooman, J., Greenfield, S. 1980. Are blacks making it in the suburbs. *J. Urban Econ.* 7: 155–67

Waldinger, R. 1985. Immigration and industrial change in the New York City apparel industry. In *Hispanics in the US Economy,* ed. G. J. Borjas, M. Tienda. Orlando: Academic

Weiss, M. A. 1987. *The Rise of the Community Builders: The American Real Estate Industry and Urban Land Planning.* New York: Columbia Univ. Press

Wilson, K. L., Portes, A. 1980. Immigrant enclaves: An analysis of labor market experiences of Cubans in Miami. *Am. J. Sociol.* 86:295–319

Wilson, W. J. 1985. The urban underclass in advanced industrial societies. See Petersen 1985

Wilson, W. J. 1987. *The Truly Disadvantaged: The Inner City, the Underclass, and Public Policy.* Chicago: Univ. Chicago Press

Zukin, S. 1989. *Loft Living.* New Brunswick, NJ: Rutgers Univ. Press

Zukin, S. 1980. A decade of the new urban sociology. *Theory Soc.* 9:575–602

Annu. Rev. Sociol. 1990. 16:491–519

THE RISKS OF REPRODUCTIVE IMPAIRMENT IN THE LATER YEARS OF CHILDBEARING

Joseph A. McFalls, Jr.

Sociology Department, Villanova University, Villanova, Pennsylvania 19085

KEY WORDS: reproductive impairment, delayed childbearing, age, infertility, subfecundity

Abstract

A notable feature of the present baby bust in the United States is that substantial proportions of women are delaying much of their childbearing until relatively late in their reproductive lives. One concern about this delayed childbearing is that many women may end up either childless or with fewer children than they desire, owing to reproductive impairment. This paper reviews evidence concerning the decline of reproductive ability with age. The findings can be distilled into two main facts. First, the proportion of women with low reproductive ability increases steadily from age 15 to age 50. Second, this rise is moderate until the mid-30s when it begins to increase more sharply. While the current consensus is that most healthy women in their late thirties have a good prospect of giving birth to a healthy infant, a substantial minority of postponers will end up childless or with fewer children than they desire, due to reproductive impairment as well as to social causes.

INTRODUCTION

American women averaged more than seven children until the early decades of the nineteenth century. Average family size declined gradually after then, interrupted only by the baby boom following World War II. It reached an all time low of 1.74 children in 1976 (as measured by the total fertility rate which tells how many children the average woman would have throughout her

491

0360-0572/90/0815-0491$02.00

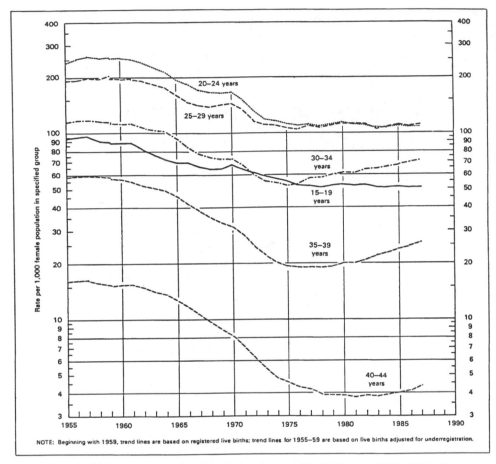

Figure 1   Birth rates by age of mother: United States, 1953–87 (Source: NCHS 1989b: 3)

life if she reproduced according to the age-specific rate schedule of a given year). The rate has remained within about a tenth of a point of this level ever since (National Center for Health Statistics (NCHS) 1989b). This baby bust came about because of dramatic cuts in childbearing at all ages. These cuts can be seen clearly in Figure 1 which presents age-specific birth rates for US women from the peak baby boom years of the mid-1950s thru 1987.

One notable feature of the present baby bust is the fact that substantial proportions of women have delayed much of their childbearing until relatively late in their reproductive lives, a practice that usually leads to lower completed fertility, all other things being equal. This practice can also be discerned in Figure 1. The birth rate for women aged 30–34 in 1987 was 71.3 per thousand, fully 36% higher than it was in 1975 when the trend began. The rate for women aged 35–39 increased 34% over roughly the same period. Because of these rate increases and the relatively large number of women in these baby-boom age categories, mothers aged 30 and over accounted for 27% of all births in 1987, the highest fraction since 1961 (NCHS 1989b).

One facet of this delayed childbearing trend is that the initiation of childbearing has been pushed later and later into the reproductive period. The first birth rates for women under 30 have declined or increased very little in recent years, while rates for women aged 30 to 44 have increased dramatically. For example, between the early 1970s and 1987 the first birth rate declined by 33% among women aged 20–24, but increased 162% for those aged 30–34, 205% for those aged 35–39, and 133% for those aged 40–44 (NCHS 1989b, Ventura 1989).[1]

But the delayed childbearing trend is not confined to older women having a first child. Second and third order birth rates for women aged 30–44 have also increased considerably in recent years. For example, between 1975 and 1987, the second and third order birth rates for women aged 35–39 rose 160% and 72%, respectively (NCHS 1989b).

The reasons for this pattern of delayed childbearing, which is common in European countries as well (Toulemon 1988), are wide ranging and complex. The desire of increasing numbers of women to pursue education and to establish themselves in careers before embarking on motherhood is probably the most important reason (Ventura 1982, 1989, Bloom & Trussell 1984). Deferred marriage also plays a role, as many more women now postpone the event until sizeable parts of their reproductive lives have elapsed. Another factor is the high divorce rate among American couples. Given the common knowledge that about 50% of recent first marriages are projected to end in divorce (Jones et al 1988), many couples undoubtedly delay childbearing until they are certain their marriages are stable. Other factors that account for the upswing in delayed childbearing include economic problems confronting the jumbo-sized baby boom cohorts involved, the availability of legal abortion and effective contraceptives which make postponement decisions more feasible, and a host of basic changes in the family institution and in the relations between men and women within and outside of marriage (Levy & Michel 1985). Whatever the reasons for the upswing, there are no signs that American women will revert to early childbearing patterns anytime soon (Baldwin & Nord 1984).

One concern about delayed childbearing is that many women (and couples) might end up either unintentionally childless or with fewer children than desired. An indication that this is happening is the fact that relatively large

---

[1]For the sake of perspective it is important to keep in mind that most births (73%) and the vast majority of first births (84%) occur to women under age 30 (NCHS 1989b).

proportions of women in the older age groups were still childless in recent years compared with the proportions in the 1970s.[2] For example, 42% of women aged 25–29 in 1988 had never given birth, compared to 31% in 1976 and 24% in 1970; for women aged 30–34, the proportions were 25%, compared to 16% and 12%, respectively. When queried, large proportions of these older childless women say they expect to have children eventually—e.g. more than half (51%) of those aged 30–34 in 1988 said this. But judging from past and current delayed childbearing trends, demographers believe that a large fraction of these women are unlikely to become mothers despite their intentions (US Bureau of the Census 1989, Baldwin & Nord 1984). Indeed, Bloom (1982) estimated that as many as 25% of white women and 20% of black women in various cohorts born since 1950 could finish their reproductive careers either intentionally or unintentionally childless. The proportion childless among cohorts at or near the end of their reproductive careers is already rising. For example, approximately 15% of women 40 to 44 years old in 1988 will complete their childbearing years childless, a proportion about 50% higher than in 1976 (US Bureau of the Census 1989). Thus, the concern that delayed childbearing may cause much unintentional childlessness (and fewer children than desired) is well founded (Bloom & Trussell 1984).

DAVIS BLAKE INTERMEDIATE VARIABLES

How can delayed childbearing result in unintended childlessness or fewer children than desired? The framework for answering this question is contained in a classic article by Davis & Blake (1956). They point out that social factors like the decision to delay childbearing can affect completed fertility only through a set of *intermediate* variables (IVS). These twelve variables can be arranged into three groups as follows (see McFalls & McFalls 1984:42):

Intermediate Variables
I. Fecundity variables
      1. Involuntary abstinence due to coital inability
      2. Conceptive failure (infertility, sterility)
      3. Fetal mortality from involuntary causes (pregnancy loss)
II. Mate exposure variables
    A. Those governing the formation and dissolution of sexual unions (i.e. marriage, consensual unions, etc) in the reproductive period
      4. Age of entry into sexual unions

---

[2]It is worth noting that this current phenomenon of delayed childbearing in the United States is not unprecedented. The proportions of women still childless at ages 25–29 and 30–34 are similar to those experienced by American women during the first half of the twentieth century. Thus the current proportions are only relatively large compared to proportions childless during the 1960s and early 1970s which were unusually low (cf Baldwin & Nord 1984).

     5. Proportion never entering sexual unions
     6. Amount of reproductive period spent after or between sexual unions
       a. When unions are broken by divorce, separation, or desertion
       b. When unions are broken by death of spouse
  B. Those governing the exposure to intercourse within unions
     7. Voluntary abstinence
     8. Involuntary abstinence due to reasons other than coital inability (unavoidable temporary separations)
     9. Coital frequency (excluding periods of abstinence)
III. Birth control variables
    10. Use or nonuse of contraception
    11. Fecundity or infecundity, as affected by voluntary causes (sterilization, medical treatment, etc)
    12. Fetal mortality from voluntary causes (induced abortion)

From an inspection of these twelve variables it is clear how each can contribute to childlessness or fewer children than desired. The prevalence of the fecundity variables (Intermediate variable-1, IV-2, IV-3) increases with age, and the longer the decision to have children is delayed, the greater the risk of lower fecundity and even infecundity. Postponers face the prospect of trying to achieve their desired fertility during their later years of childbearing when fecundity is lower owing to normal aging and to the possibility of accumulated subfecundity from causes such as disease.

Mate exposure variables governing the formation and dissolution of unions are influential because most childbearing is done by married women. The decision to postpone childbearing can lead to a decision to postpone entry into marriage (or a long-term sexual union) (IV-4), and one of the iron laws of demography is that this age of entry into sexual unions is inversely related to completed fertility. Moreover, marriage postponers do not have total control over their age at marriage. Sophisticated studies (see Goldman et al 1984) indicate that white women under age 25 are the only female age group that is in a good position to find a mate. After age 25 marriage prospects plummet. By ages 30 to 34, for instance, there are two college-educated women available for every suitable never-married man. The situation for black women is similar, but somewhat worse. Because of these marriage market problems, many women may end up marrying much later than they plan, some at, say, age 37 rather than at age 32. Hence there are substantially fewer years to have children than they had originally intended. Other postponers will never succeed in finding a mate and will never enter a sexual union (IV-5).

Similarly for already married postponers, the proper marital circumstances may not exist during the planned childbearing period. For example, many married women, who in their 20s plan to have their children in their 30s, are no longer married in their 30s due to divorce, separation, or death of the spouse (IV-6). Divorce, the most important of these disruption sources, is concentrated in early adulthood (52% of husbands and 61% of wives who divorced in 1986 were under the age of 35) (NCHS 1989a). This fact, coupled with the projection that between one half and two thirds of recent and current marriages are disrupted (Martin & Bumpass 1989, Preston 1983, NCHS 1987, Davis 1983), means that a sizeable portion of delayed childbearing never takes place because of marital disruption.

One indicator of the influence of this first set of mate exposure variables on the actualization of delayed childbearing plans is the growing proportion of women in their late twenties and early thirties who are unmarried. In 1987, for example, about one third of 25–29-year-old white women and more than one half of nonwhite women were unmarried,[3] more than twice the proportions observed in the early 1960s when baby boom women married unusually early. Of women aged 40–44 23% also were unmarried in 1987 (US Bureau of the Census 1988.) But the impact of this rapid growth in the population of unmarried women on the actualization of delayed childbearing plans has been softened to some extent by the increased rate of childbearing by older unmarried women in recent years. Between 1975 and 1986 the overall birthrates for unmarried women aged 30–34 and 35–39 rose 50% and 34%, respectively. First-birth rates also shot up between 1980 and 1986, 47% for unmarried women aged 30–34, and 80% for those aged 35–39. The presumption is that many of these older women are deliberately choosing to become single mothers despite the norm against unwed motherhood (Ventura 1989).

The second set of mate exposure intermediate variables are those that govern exposure to intercourse within sexual unions or marriages. Voluntary abstinence (IV-7) increases with age, and coital frequency (IV-9) decreases with age (Bachrach & Horn 1988, NCHS 1987, James 1979). [Among married women, for instance, the percent having intercourse more than once a week falls from 56% to 42% for women aged 20–24 and 35–39, respectively (NCHS 1987).] Both these phenomena—voluntary abstinence and low coital frequency—are prejudicial to childbearing once the delay period has elapsed. Again, marriages that are sexually vibrant when the decision to delay childbearing is made can turn sexually lukewarm or even moribund by the time the planned childbearing period occurs. Low coital frequency is sometimes the result of inhibited sexual desire (ISD) or asexuality, both of which increase with age. Though good prevalence data are unavailable, some experts estimate that as many as 20% of the population have such desire problems as well as a variety of other sexual disorders (Frank et al 1978,

---

[3]More than half of 25–29 year old nonwhite women were unmarried in 1987. However, since more than half of all births to nonwhites are to unmarried women, these mate exposure variables have far less influence on the actualization of their delayed childbearing plans.

Ende et al 1984). Involuntary abstinence due to reasons other than coital inability (IV-8) may also unexpectedly interfere with delayed childbearing. Reasons for such involuntary abstinence include institutionalization and other forms of temporary separation such as in the case of spouses with jobs in different regions.

There is always a fraction of women who postpone childbearing who just never get around to having children (Poston & Kramer 1980, Rindfuss & Bumpass 1976). For some, the same forces such as career demands that initially led them to delay childbearing do not let up and may cause them reluctantly to forego children in the end. For others, the desired circumstances such as being married do not exist during the planned childbearing period. For still others, fears of pregnancy and delivery problems (such as spontaneous abortion or long bedridden periods), birth defects, infant mortality, and maternal mortality—all of which increase with age—cause attempts to have children to be halfhearted, or they result in the reluctant cancellation of childbearing plans altogether (Baldwin & Nord 1984, Ventura 1989, Fonteyn & Isada 1988, Rochat et al 1988, Naeye 1983). In this category those sexually active usually turn to the birth control variables (IV-10, IV-11, IV-12) to retard or terminate childbearing. Certainly, these actions are voluntary. Yet these are women who wanted children in the past and would still like to have them under better circumstances. Since the actual circumstances often are out of their control, these frustrated childbearing plans also have an involuntary or at least unintentional element. Of course, there are other women who, because of changed priorities, forgo planned late childbearing without regret. They too may use birth control to accomplish this objective (Fortney 1987).

Childlessness or having fewer children than desired is often the result of the operation of more than one of these intermediate variables, as in the case of an individual who delays marriage and uses contraception as well. Making matters more complicated still, the intermediate variables interact with each other. Subfecundity, for instance, can reduce the amount of the reproductive period spent after or between unions (McFalls & McFalls 1984); and premarital sex can lead to subfecundity (Bachrach & Horn 1988).

The main focus of this paper is on the fecundity intermediate variables. The purpose is to assess the impact of fecundity variables on the ability of postponers to have the children they desire in their later years of childbearing. Nevertheless, scarce space has been devoted to the above discussion of all the intermediate variables for two reasons. The first reason is to draw attention to the many ways that childlessness or having fewer children than desired can occur among childbearing postponers, and to provide perspective for the following criticism. In evaluating the risk of these outcomes among postponers, the social sciences pay relatively too much attention to the fecundity factors and too little to mate exposure and birth control factors. However, women are not just concerned about the fecundity risks, they are concerned about all the intermediate variable risks (US Congress Off. Technology Assessment 1988). (Indeed, their concerns are broader yet, encompassing age-related risks concerning birth defects, infant mortality, and maternal mortality). Thus, the salient research question is: For any given age at postponement and length of postponement, what is the probability that the average women will achieve specified childbearing goals? The answer to that question would permit, for instance, a 25-year-old woman to know her rough probability of having two healthy children if she postponed the start of childbearing to age 33. Certainly, the study of fecundity risks contributes to the assessment of the overall risks, but it is important to consider the other intermediate variable risks as well.

The second reason for discussing all twelve intermediate variables is to help the reader understand the complexity of the issue under review. To evaluate the impact of fecundity on delayed childbearing, researchers must screen out the effects of the other nine variables which, of course, is difficult to do. It is even more difficult to screen out the effects of the other eleven variables when only a single fecundity variable like infertility is under study. No study discussed in this review was able to control these other variables completely, and much of the criticism of this literature involves biases introduced by failing to rule out the effects of these other variables.

FECUNDITY AND SUBFECUNDITY

Terminology

Fecundity is used here to mean reproductive ability as opposed to *fertility* which denotes actual childbearing. *Subfecundity* refers to an *abnormally* diminished capacity to reproduce. *Infecundity* is the total inability to reproduce both currently and in the future. Infecundity may develop in an individual who in the past was fecund and perhaps even had children. A *subfecundity factor* refers to a cause of subfecundity, such as disease or psychic stress.

Fecundity diminishes through impairment of any of the biological aspects of reproduction—coitus, conception, and the carrying of a conceptus to a live birth. *Coital inability* is defined as the inability to perform normal heterosexual intercourse. It afflicts both men and women, especially the former, and can be chronic or temporary. *Infertility* is defined as the diminished ability to conceive or to bring about conception. Thus, infertility refers here only to conceptive difficulties, although the term has been used elsewhere to cover pregnancy loss and even coital problems. Another term for infertility is conceptive failure. *Sterility* is the complete inability to conceive or bring about conception; it is simply the lowest point on the infertility continuum. Infertility is an important cause of diminished fecundity in both men and women and, like coital inability, can be chronic or temporary. Finally, *pregnancy loss* refers to the involuntary termination of a pregnancy before a live birth. It includes spontaneous abortion (miscarriage), late fetal death, and stillbirth, but not induced abortion or neonatal mortality (death in the first 4 weeks of life). Although primarily a form of female reproductive impairment, some pregnancy loss may be due to defective sperm.

The terms above were defined not simply because most sociologists are unfamiliar with them, but because there is tremendous confusion about them in the literature even among scholars who do fecundity research. Indeed, a major criticism of this literature is that several of these terms are defined differently within the same discipline as well as among different disciplines. In the medical literature, for example, fertility is defined as the ability to reproduce, and fecundity refers to actual childbearing. And some demographers treat coital frequency (a Davis-Blake mate exposure variable) as a component of fecundity.

Probably the most common definitional problem centers on the term *infertility*. Some authors use this term to include both conceptive failure and pregnancy loss. Others use infertility to mean coital inability and conceptive failure. A third group uses the term to refer to women who have no liveborn children, regardless of the reasons. Finally, other authors use the term to mean only conceptive failure.

This lack of agreement on definitions leads in part to another problem in this literature, the habit of some authors of using different definitions of a term without warning in the same publication. It also paves the way for a similar problem, authors using different definitions of the same terms in different publications which often have a sequential nature. For example, one author defined infertility as "the reduced ability to conceive and bear a live child" in one article, but in a second expanded article published within a year of the first, this definition referred to infecundity, and infertility denoted only problems in "the capacity to conceive." This problem of definitional ambiguity leads to an even more troublesome problem, the tendency of some authors to use terms with different meanings synonymously in the same publication, equating, for instance, fecundity with fecundability (the probability of conceiving in a given month), or infecundity with infertility.

There is no need to cite actual articles as representative of each of the above usages. At this stage there are no right or wrong definitions. But there should be. Definitional homogeneity is essential to good science and scholarship. Terms are not just names. They help determine, among other things, the nature of the questions asked, the categories of answers, the analytical schemes, and the comparability of results. A universally agreed upon specification of fecundity terms would eliminate, for example, the debate in this literature concerning whether a woman is infecund or infertile if she does not conceive within twelve months of unprotected intercourse. It would also minimize the noncomparability of fecundity data that has plagued major American fertility surveys over the last 50 years by eliminating the problem of changing definitions. The National Survey of Family Growth, presently the major fertility survey in the United States and one conducted periodically (1973, 1976, 1982, 1988) by the National Center for Health Statistics, has succeeded in using consistent definitions in its publications since 1980. But its definitions are not universally used by others, and there is no assurance that some future US government or other major survey will adopt them. Thus, there is a genuine need for fecundity researchers to agree upon terminology and then regulate usage via the publication review process.

One advantage of the definition system advocated above is that it is fully compatible with the Davis Blake intermediate variable framework. It reduces fecundity to its basic components—coitus, conception, and gestation—and eschews the use of complex variables such as "the ability to conceive plus the ability to carry the pregnancy to a successful conclusion." Separate components can always be spliced together if necessary, but complex variables often cannot be disaggregated. Wherever possible, this article uses its own terminology to discuss the literature. Where conversion is not possible, terminological differences are noted. Also this article follows the demographic convention of attributing all reproductive impairment solely to the woman even though it is often a male problem or a joint one. (Leridon 1977, Potter & Bongaarts 1983).

Population Fecundity

A population's fecundity is the average fecundity of its individual members. Individual fecundity varies widely. Some women are unable to have children throughout their reproductive lives. Others are superfecund, giving birth to more than 30 children. Pearl (1939), for instance, described one woman who had 32 children by age 40. Thus, individual fecundity varies from zero to more than 30 children. Maximum population fecundity falls somewhere between these extremes. It is impossible to calculate actual population fecundity, but by splicing together the highest age-specific fertility rates on record and considering other hypothetical models, most authorities (see Hansluwka 1975, Peterson 1975) estimate maximum population fecundity to be about 15 children per woman. In other words, a population of women who engage in regular sexual intercourse from menarche to menopause without using any form of birth control would, under the most favorable reproductive circumstances, average about 15 children per woman.

Fecundity, of course, varies by age. The exact age pattern is unknown, but its general features are apparent. Fecundity is relatively low in the years just after menarche and before menopause, and reaches a broad peak between ages 18 and 30 (Gindoff & Jewelewicz 1986, Sherris & Fox 1983). Thus, a woman's fecundity declines during the second half of her reproductive period as a natural result of the aging of the reproductive system (Mastroianni & Paulsen 1986, Minaker & Rowe 1986).

This lower fecundity due to normal aging must be distinguished from subfecundity which refers to reproductive capacity *below normal for a given age*. A population is subfecund to the extent that it is biologically incapable of achieving the roughly estimated average of 15 children per woman (Leridon 1977, Potter & Bongaarts 1983). No population enjoys completely favorable reproductive circumstances. Some causes of subfecundity—genetic, disease, nutritional, environmental, or psychopathological—are present in all real populations, and hence all are subfecund according to this definition. It is their relative ability to achieve this standard of maximum fecundity, however, that is pertinent and of demographic significance.

Like fecundity, subfecundity varies by age. Subfecundity factors accumulate with time, and as a group exert an ever-increasing downward pull on fecundity. Reviews of these subfecundity factors are available (cf US Congress, Office of Technology Assessment 1988, Sherris & Fox 1983, McFalls 1979a), but more research is needed concerning their identity and power to reduce fecundity.

In a sense, fecundity and life expectancy are analogous concepts. Both have a genetically determined population maximum, about 15 children per woman for the former and about 85 years for the latter (cf Fries 1980). Both have two limiting forces, (*a*) normal aging, and (*b*) negative environmental forces (subfecundity and premature mortality, respectively). Normal aging affects fecundity and life expectancy in a similar pattern—both increase at the outset, hit a peak, and then decline to zero. Subfecundity factors can lower fecundity below what is maximal for a given age; and premature mortality factors can do the same to life expectancy. Thus, when women delay childbearing until their 30s and 40s, they confront lower fecundity because of two forces—normal aging and subfecundity factors.

This paper reviews evidence concerning the decline of fecundity with age. There is no systematic attempt here, however, to separate the effects on fecundity of normal aging and subfecundity factors. That task is simply too complex for a literature review of this nature. However, some studies based on historical societies come close to estimating the impact on fecundity of age alone, and these findings are noted.

AGE PATTERN OF FECUNDITY

National Survey of Family Growth

Data on the prevalence of reproductive impairment in the United States come mainly from the major US fertility surveys of the past several decades. These surveys were not designed to differentiate between the effects of normal aging and subfecundity, and they cannot do so. They are only able to roughly categorize women into two groups, those who are able to produce children at variously defined "normal" rates and those who cannot. The latter women are labeled "fecundity impaired" in the most recent of these surveys, and that term is used here. Note that "fecundity impaired" is not synonymous with "subfecund" as defined above. The former is a broader term containing, among other things, some effects of normal aging.

Impaired fecundity is surprisingly common in developed countries such as the United States. Indeed, even though most major US fertility surveys of the past several decades have tended to omit fecundity-impaired women, they still found high rates of impaired fecundity (variously defined) among their respondents. About one third of the married white couples of reproductive age surveyed in the 1941 Indianapolis Study (Whelpton & Kiser 1946–1958) and in the 1955 and 1960 Growth of American Families Studies (Freedman et al 1959, Whelpton et al 1966) were categorized as fecundity impaired.

The best study of the current level of fecundity impairment in the United States is that of Mosher & Pratt (1987 and Mosher 1985). The estimates of fecundity impairment used in this study were based on findings obtained from the 1982 National Survey of Family Growth (Cycle 3). Mosher & Pratt found that about 4.5 million women had impaired fecundity in that year, or about 8.4% of the 54.1 million women aged 15–44. The percent of women with impaired fecundity increased with age although there were two nonsignificant decreases in the percents between adjacent five-year groups, as can be seen below:

Table 1 Percentage of women with impaired fecundity

Age	All women	Nonsterilized women
15–44 years	8.4	11.3
15–19	2.1	2.1
20–24	6.4	6.7
25–29	10.6	12.5
30–34	9.3	14.8
35–39	13.0	27.9
40–44	11.0	28.2

However, this came about because of large increases in surgical steriliza-tion with age. Once the numbers of surgically sterilized women were re-moved, the expected continuous increase of impaired fecundity with age emerged.

Other authors (e.g. Henshaw & Orr 1987, McFalls & McFalls 1984) have separated and recombined various NSFG fecundity components to arrive at different though similar prevalence data. McFalls & McFalls (1984), for instance, classify as fecundity impaired those women who were sterilized for noncontraceptive reasons. The rationale is that such women do have a di-minished capacity to reproduce. Indeed, the vast majority are infecund, being totally unable to reproduce both presently and in the future. The fact that this condition was caused by medical surgery rather than by some natural process is of little import. The key factor is that these sterilizations are almost always due to involuntary pathological factors such as disease. Thus, the real cause of the sterility is the pathological factor, not the intermediate medical solution. Moreover, about one out of eight of these individuals knew they were already subfecund prior to the sterilizing operation and doubtless others who did not know were also. Chronic pelvic inflammatory disease, for example, is an important cause of subfecundity. It is also a serious health problem in other ways, and its resolution sometimes requires surgical procedures that result in sterility. But this sterility is often redundant because of the preexisting fecundity impairment.

Table 2 displays the percentage distribution by fecundity status and age of the NSFG women in 1982, counting the surgically sterilized for noncon-traceptive reasons as fecundity impaired. Altogether, some 16.2% of all US couples with wives aged 15–44 were classified as fecundity impaired. Removing the contraceptively sterile from the pool of women and collapsing various categories in Table 2 yields the following data in Table 3.

In sum, it is clear from the data that fecundity impairment increases significantly with age (and roughly doubles after age 35) among individuals who have not truncated their fecundity via contraceptive sterilization. It should be noted that these data are somewhat more relevant to childbearing postponers than is data for the whole population because postponers include no women who sterilize themselves for contraceptive reasons.

Mosher & Pratt (1987) also provide NSFG data on the relationship between impaired fecundity and age for childless women. These data show an increas-ing risk of impairment with age (plus some unavoidable selection effects) for women who, probably for the most part, were postponing the initiation of childbearing. The percentages of various groups of childless women with impaired fecundity by age are as follows (see Table 4).

Nevertheless, it is not possible using NSFG data to compute fecundity impairment proportions by age just for women who are postponing childbear-

Table 2 Percentage distribution by fecundity status and age: United States, 1982

Age	Number of women (in 1,000s)	Total	Total fecund (%)	Surgically sterilized for contraceptive reasons (%)	Surgically sterilized for non-contraceptive reasons (%)	Fecundity impaired			
						Nonsurgically sterile (%)	Other problems (%)	Long birth intervals (%)	Total fecundity impaired (%)
15–44	54,099	100.0	66.3	17.5	7.8	1.7	5.6	1.1	16.2
15–19	9,521	100.0	97.9	0.0	0.0	0.5	1.6	0.0	2.1
20–24	10,629	100.0	89.3	3.7	0.6	0.9	5.3	0.2	7.0
25–29	10,263	100.0	73.6	12.1	3.7	1.5	8.0	1.0	14.3
30–34	9,381	100.0	53.8	26.8	10.1	1.7	6.6	1.1	19.4
35–39	7,893	100.0	33.4	35.2	18.4	3.1	7.3	2.5	31.4
40–44	6,412	100.0	27.8	39.4	21.8	3.0	4.9	3.1	32.8

Source: Constructed from Mosher & Pratt (1987:22) The "Other problems" category consists of women for whom it is difficult but perhaps not impossible to conceive and/or carry a pregnancy to term.
(Note: See McFalls & McFalls (1984:24) for the same table using 1976 data. The definition of fecundity impairment used above and in McFalls & McFalls (1984) is different than that used in official NSFG publications.)

Table 3 Percentage distribution by fecundity status

Age	Total Women	Fecund	Fecundity Impaired
15–44	100.0	80.4	19.6
15–19	100.0	97.9	2.1
20–24	100.0	92.7	7.3
25–29	100.0	83.7	16.3
30–34	100.0	73.5	26.5
35–39	100.0	51.5	48.5
40–44	100.0	45.9	54.1

Table 4 Childless women with impaired fecundity

Age	Total Women	Fecund	Fecundity Impaired
15–44	100.0	94.7	5.3
15–24	100.0	96.9	3.1
25–34	100.0	88.8	11.2
35–44	100.0	85.0	15.0

ing. The Mosher & Pratt data for childless women (above) provide one approximation, but "childlessness" is not a perfect proxy for "postponing childbearing." Some childless women are not postponers because they do not want children or are infecund. The proportion of childless women who are fecundity-impaired rises with age in part because more fecund women select themselves out of the childless category by having children.

The NSFG is an extraordinarily valuable study with respect to information about fecundity and a host of other fertility and health related variables. Moreover, it gets better with every cycle, and researchers are looking forward to the results of Cycle IV which was fielded in 1988. Nevertheless, the NSFG is not an ideal vehicle for studying the prevalence and age pattern of fecundity impairment. Its drawbacks include, but are not limited to, the following problems (cf Menken et al 1986, Menken & Larsen 1986, Menken 1985, McFalls & McFalls 1984, Mosher & Pratt 1987). One problem is that the basic fecundity categories are not pure, owing to misreporting and inadvertent misclassification. Inherent biases lead to both underestimation and over-estimation of the number of women in the impaired fecundity category. Underestimation results primarily because the NSFG is based on a household survey that must rely on the accuracy of respondents' reports, and there are a number of reasons to question this accuracy. First, there is a stigma associated with impaired fecundity, and some women undoubtedly conceal it during

NSFG interviews (Miall 1986). Second, many of the causes of fecundity impairment are asymptomatic, making it difficult for some women to know and thus report about their impairment. Third, fecundity impairment is obscured by contraception and sterilization (both contraceptive and noncontraceptive), which results in the misclassification of some fecundity-impaired women.

Overestimation of the number of fecundity-impaired women results from the same study-design limitations. Overreporting of fecundity impairment may come about because the NSFG's operational criterion, i.e. "having difficulty in conceiving or delivering a baby," is in part subjective. Fecundity impairment may also be overestimated because of the reluctance of some women to report induced abortions, a practice that results in (false) long birth intervals, one criteria of impairment.

The exclusion of the contraceptively sterile from the pool of women and, hence, from the fecund/fecundity-impaired breakdowns, also introduces biases. Fecundity-impaired women, especially those for whom pregnancy is problematic or hazardous, may be drawn toward sterilization. Conversely, highly fecund women may flock to sterilization as a safe haven against unwanted childbearing. The latter is undoubtedly the stronger of these two forces, making the pool of women not contraceptively sterilized self-selected for fecundity impairment. But this self-selection process is attenuated by the present trend toward delayed childbearing.

In sum, there are a number of selectivity and reporting errors leading to over- and underestimation of the number of women in each fecundity category. How strong these biases are is unknown. The fact that they are countervailing does limit their effect on the various fecundity category proportions, but their net effect could still be sizeable. Cycle IV of the NSFG promises to reduce some of these sources of error. It is to be hoped that future cycles will ask a set of specific questions about delayed childbearing as well.

Historical Population Data

Recognizing the fact that it is difficult to study fecundity and its age pattern in contemporary developed societies like the United States, Menken, Trussell, and Larsen turned their attention to historical societies where the nonfecundity Davis-Blake variables like contraception, abortion, and surgical sterilization were less a confounding problem (cf Menken 1985, Menken & Larsen 1986, Menken et al 1986). This line of research has been well summarized in a 1986 article (Menken et al 1986) which forms the basis of the discussion here.

Studies of fecundity in historical societies generally have three things in common. First, they focus only on married women, thus minimizing the effect on fertility of some mate exposure variables. Second, societies are chosen in which little or no family limitation is practiced, thus controlling away most birth control variables. Finally, these studies use marital fertility as an indicator of fecundity. That is, the decline in the marital birth rate with age is used as a proxy for the decline in fecundity with age.

An early oft-cited example of this historical work is an article by Henry (1961) which identified such historical populations. Menken and her associates plotted the level of fertility against age for ten of these populations, the ones with the best age reporting. They found that the age patterns of fertility decline are roughly parallel even though the overall level of fertility of these populations varies. Taking the same ten populations, Menken & Larsen (1986) calculated an average age pattern using the average rate for women aged 20–24 as a base. The fertility rates for the other age groups declined by the following proportions (Table 5):

Table 5 Decline in fertility by age group

Age	Percent decline from average rate of women aged 20–24
25–29	6
30–34	14
35–39	31
40–44	64
45–49	95

The inference is that fecundity falls at about the same rate.

However, the fertility rate of women is not a perfect indicator of fecundity. As Menken and her associates (1986) pointed out, marital rates are also inversely related to the age of spouses and to marital duration. Fertility rates typically fall as marital duration lengthens, owing to increases in reproductive impairment associated with childbearing and to the action of a nonfecundity Davis-Blake variable—decreases in coital frequency (Wood & Weinstein 1988). But Menken and associates downplayed the importance of spousal age and marital duration (to a lesser extent) by pointing to a study by Mineau & Trussell (1982) which separated the effects of wife's age, husband's age, and marital duration by estimating a multiplicative model.

The Mineau-Trussell model was applied to geneological data for married Mormon women born between 1840 and 1859. Estimates of these effects are displayed in Table 6, where the base is the estimated value when both the wife and husband are age 20–24 and in the initial five years of marriage. This table can be read like the example to be discussed after Table 6.

Table 6   Effects of variables on fertility

Age	Effects of wife's age	Effects of husband's age	Years of marriage	Effect of duration of marriage
15–19	0.96	.90	0–4	1.00
20–24	1.00	1.00	5–9	.89
25–29	1.03	.99	10–14	.81
30–34	.99	1.04	15–19	.79
35–39	.90	.97		
40–44	.62	.83		
45–49	.14	.82		
50–54	—	.73		
55–59	—	.48		

A hypothetical woman aged 40–44 married less than five years to a husband aged 20–24 would have a fertility rate 62% as great as a comparable woman aged 20–24. Thus, the effect of the women's age was isolated from the other two factors. The grid shows that the fertility rate declined hardly at all for women until their late thirties. The drop off for men was much slower, but the decline due to marital duration was sizeable. Thus, Menken and her associates concluded that the fecundity pattern by age of couples is a function primarily of the aging of women and of marital duration.

Menken and her associates also narrowed their focus and examined indicators of the pattern of fecundity by age of women who delayed childbearing in historical populations (Menken & Larsen 1986). To do this they gathered data from seven historical populations where late marriage was common, where little or no deliberate fertility control was practiced, and where parity distributions by age at marriage were calculable. The percentages of married women who were childless, who had one child, and who had two or more children can be averaged by age at marriage for the seven populations. These average percentages are presented in Table 7 below.

Table 7   Percentage of married women childless and with children by age at marriage

Age at marriage	Percent childless	Percent with 1 child	Percent with two children or more	Total
20–24	6	5	89	100
25–29	9	7	84	100
30–34	15	11	74	100
35–39	30	20	50	100
40–44	64	19	17	100

The increase in the percentages in the first three columns is relatively modest until the age reaches the mid-thirties when the increase begins accelerating. Women who married between age 30 and 34, for example, had about a 15% risk of ending up childless; the risk doubled for those marrying in the next segment and doubled again in the next. Only 50% of the women who married between age 35 and 39 had more than one child. Given the reported near-absence of deliberate fertility control, Menken and associates attribute these inabilities to have children largely to the decline of fecundity due to aging alone.

Like the NSFG, these often ingenious historical studies are not flawless vehicles for studying the prevalence and age pattern of fecundity impairment among current US women (Wilson et al 1988). The most obvious drawback is that these populations, whether taken singly or averaged together, are not representative of the US population, either biologically or behaviorally. Populations such as the Hutterites and the Mormons and, indeed, all societies where a large majority of individuals are the descendants of many generations of high fertility ancestors, probably have higher population fecundity than do societies like the United States where widespread birth control and, hence, low fertility make it possible for low fecundity individuals to contribute proportionally more offspring to succeeding generations than their number would otherwise yield (Tietze 1957, Ericksen et al 1979, McFalls 1979a). There is also the concern that the less fecund in historical societies, who are often less healthy, due to such conditions as tuberculosis, syphilis, and alcoholism, have higher rates of death prior to and during the childbearing years, and lower rates of marriage. Thus, those married survivors, especially those who reach age 50, would be selected for fecundity. Differences in behavioral factors such as premarital sexuality, multiple sexual partners and the resultant sexually transmitted diseases, the proportion marrying, age at marriage, contraception, abortion, coital frequency, and breastfeeding are also sources of noncomparability, and these are an issue because their effects cannot be entirely extricated from proxy measures of fecundity such as the marital fertility rate.

The latter problem calls to mind a more general drawback. Historical studies, much more so than current fertility surveys like the NSFG, must rely on proxy variables with their inherent problems rather than on detailed information on the elements and causes of reproductive impairment itself. This in turn contributes to another problem, the tendency to attribute too much of the age pattern of fecundity to the effects of normal aging and too little to environmental causes of subfecundity such as disease. Moreover, the fact that some of the conclusions from historical studies, though invariably relevant and insightful, come from a single, relatively small, and highly select group is grounds for caution. Finally, modern medical advances in the treatment of fecundity problems introduce some noncomparability in fecundity category proportions (Aral & Cates 1983, Hirsch & Mosher 1987).

In short, demographic findings from historical societies, though extremely valuable, are not fully applicable to today's societies. This is true not only with respect to fecundity in the United States but to such other issues as the character of demographic transition in developing societies.

COMPONENTS OF LOW FECUNDITY

The section above presented data from different sources showing that fecundity declines significantly with age, beginning sometime during the midthirties. This decline comes about because the components of low fecundity—coital inability, conceptive failure, and pregnancy loss—all increase with age.

Coital Inability

Coital inability is the stepchild of fecundity research. Little if anything has been written about it in the demographic literature, though its effects have sometimes been lumped together with conceptive failure under the rubric of "infertility," in part because of the difficulty of separating the two (Hendershot 1984). Another reason for this situation is that, despite the fact that more than four decades have elapsed since Kinsey's pathbreaking study on human sexuality, sexual behavior in the United States continues to be a subject with many unknowns. Accurate statistics on sexual dysfunction are unavailable, and the studies that exist are fraught with methodological problems and points of noncomparability. They often are based on individuals and couples seeking help at general medical clinics or from sex therapists (Katchadourian 1989).

Despite this lack of representative quantitative data, sex researchers contend that sexual dysfunction is rife in the United States. For instance, Masters & Johnson (1970) estimated—conservatively, they said—that half of US couples experience sexual dysfunction sometime during their lives. This view has been corroborated by the work of many other sex researchers including Ende et al (1984) and Frank et al (1978). Frank and his associates found that among white, well-educated, and happily married US couples, a startling 40% of men and 63% of women reported sexual dysfunction.

Not all of this dysfunction compromises fecundity (though it all can affect coital frequency): Only three types do—vaginismus, male and female dyspareunia, and impotence—and only the last may have demographic significance (McFalls 1979b). Again, there are no accurate statistics available for the prevalence of impotence. In the Frank et al (1978) study group, 7% of men had difficulty getting an erection and 9% had difficulty maintaining it. Twelve percent of men in Ende et al's (1948) general clinic population had similar difficulties.

There are no impotence prevalence figures by age for any population. All that is possible is to estimate prevalence by piecing together data from surveys such as the Kinsey (1948) study. McFalls (1979b) did this for nontransient impotence and concluded that prevalence rose from about 1% for men in their 20s to about 4% for those in their 40s. The prevalence of relative impotence must be added to these figures.

Impotence could thus have a small though nontrivial impact on the fertility of childbearing postponers. And so too could the other forms of sexual dysfunction chronicled by Frank and others. But, if so, it is curious that these factors do not seem to be reflected in survey statistics on coital frequency. The NSFG, for example, found that 99% of white and black currently married women aged 35–44 had intercourse within the last three months (NCHS 1987). Where are the women who are married to these impotent men? And where are the women whose marriages suffer from one of the other far more common forms of intercourse-inhibiting sexual disorders? Miall (1986) contends that such disorders and the voluntary childlessness that can result are stigmatizing, and this may lead to overreporting of sexual activity in surveys. She notes in particular that fecund women are particularly active in protecting their husbands from this stigma. Research is needed to spell out the relationship between sexual dysfunction and fecundity and fertility.

Conceptive Failure

There are only a handful of studies concerning the impact of age on a man's ability to impregnate (e.g. Schwartz et al 1983, Nieschlag & Michel 1986, Anderson 1975, Mineau & Trussell 1982). Nevertheless, it is generally agreed that conceptive ability in men does not begin to fall appreciably until after age 40. As a result, most studies focus primarily on infertility and sterility in women.

Data about the female age pattern of infertility come from a variety of sources including the NSFG and historical studies. These sources contain the selection and other methodological problems already discussed.

The NSFG defines infertility as the inability to conceive after one or more years of unprotected intercourse. There is a thoughtful debate in the literature about the efficacy of defining a woman who cannot conceive within just one year as infertile (cf Menken et al 1986, Trussell & Wilson 1985), but NSFG analysts defend the definition as a screening device for physicians and stress that it is an all-inclusive estimate of infertility, not just a measure of serious infertility or sterility. In any event, the NSFG classified about 2.4 million married women as infertile in 1982 or about 8.5% of those in which the wife was 15–44 years of age. The percentages of married nonsterilized women who were infertile by age are given below (Table 8). The proportion that were infertile rises moderately until the mid-30s and then increases more sharply (Mosher & Pratt 1987, Mosher 1987).

Table 8 Percentages of
married nonsterile women
who were infertile by age

Age	Percent infertile
15–19	2
20–24	7
25–29	13
30–34	15
35–39	28

Much attention has been given to an article by Schwartz & Mayaux (1982) suggesting that the risk of infertility (defined as not conceiving in 12 months) increases sharply as early as age 30 (see figures below) (cf also De Cherney & Berkowitz 1982). However, this study contains serious methodological flaws that lead to overestimates of infertility, and it has been challenged by critics, most notably John Bongaarts. Bongaarts (1982a,b) argued that infertility rates are much lower than those reported in the Schwartz & Mayaux study. Using 1976 NSFG data (which are also based on the 12-month criteria for infertility), he estimated the proportions in the middle column of Table 9 below. Moreover, Bongaarts contended that allowing women more than twelve months to conceive lowers these proportions even more. Using data from appropriate historical societies, he calculated the longer term infertility proportions in column three of Table 9 below:

Table 9 Estimates of proportion of women infertile, by age

Approximate age group	Schwartz & Mayaux	Bongaarts (1976 NSFG)	Bongaarts (Historical Population)
20–24	27	7	4
25–29	26	11	6
30–34	39	16	9
35–39	44	23	20

The Bongaart estimates are also consistent with estimates of the proportions of women who were sterile and/or infecund based on studies of historical societies provided by Trussell & Wilson (1985) and Menken & Larsen (1986). These estimates from historical studies, because of their designs, may approximate the impact of aging alone on conceptive ability.

In sum, the prevailing consensus is that infertility does rise with age, but only moderately before age 35.

Pregnancy Loss

The exact amount of pregnancy loss is unknown since there are no uniform reporting standards. However, using new highly sensitive tests, experts now conclude that 31% of all "implanting" embryos and 75% of all fertilized eggs never yield a live baby (Wilcox et al 1988). But only about 25% of women are aware of ever having had a spontaneous abortion or a stillbirth (Mosher & Pratt 1987). The 1982 NSFG found that about 17% of pregnancies known to women without special means of detection, and which were not terminated by induced abortion, ended as pregnancy loss (Mosher 1988), a figure that compares well with other survey data (cf Leridon 1977).

The risk of pregnancy loss rises markedly with the mother's age (Fonteyn & Isada 1988, Gindoff & Jewelewicz 1986, Resnick 1986, Kiely et al 1986, Virro & Shewchuk 1984, Forman et al 1984, Daniels & Weingarten 1979, Nortman 1974). This relationship can be seen in the data below. The first two columns come from the NSFG, after dropping induced abortion from the denominators (Ventura et al 1988) and the Columbia-Presbyterian Medical Center (CPMC) respectively (Warburton et al 1986).

The third column is an estimate of the age pattern of pregnancy loss based on the average pattern found in nine studies and conservatively adjusted to reflect the true overall prevalence of such mortality (Wood & Weinstein 1988). Incidentally, Wood & Weinstein argue that pregnancy loss is by far the most potent cause of fecundity change due to normal aging between ages 25 and 40 (see Table 10).

Table 10 Risk of pregnancy loss rises with age

Age	NSFG	CPMC	Weinstein/ Wood
15–19	21.1%	9.9%	29%
20–24	12.8	9.5	28
25–29	16.2	10.0	30
30–34	20.3	11.7	35
35–39	26.6	17.7	43
40–44	—	33.8	55
40 and over	26.7	—	—

Data on the relationship between age and perinatal mortality specifically is available from the Collaborative Perinatal Project (cf McFalls 1976). The following analysis of the outcome of 44,386 pregnancies is provided by Naeye (1983) and shown in Table 11.

Table 11 Relationship between age and perinatal mortality

Age	Perinatal Mortality rates number/1000 births	Neonatal deaths/ 1000 births	Stillbirths/1000 births
18–19	25	14	11
20–30	29	14	15
31–34	44	18	26
35–39	45	17	28
40–50	69	18	51

Similar findings are reported by Lehmann & Chism (1987).

Pregnancy loss rates rise with age in part because the frequency of chromosomal abnormalities increase with age (Gindoff & Jewelewicz 1986). But there is also an increase with age in the loss of genetically normal embryos, which is due to such maternal factors as uterine dysfunction (Fonteyn & Isada 1988). However, not all of the observed increase in pregnancy loss with age is due to age itself. Evidence from the best research studies strongly indicates that many of the adverse pregnancy outcomes that increase with age reflect other circumstances associated with late childbearing (Mansfield 1986, Fonteyn & Isada 1988, Spellacy et al 1986, Kirz et al 1985, Yasin & Beydoun 1988, Erickson & Elliott 1988, Fortney et al 1982). Such circumstances include preexisting diseases and other subfecundity factors, altered medical management, high parity, poverty, and race, to mention just a few. Hence, the predominantly middle class women who postpone childbearing, tend to be highly motivated, and seek the best medical care, should have relatively less pregnancy loss with advancing age than would the population as a whole.

It is also noteworthy that men may contribute to pregnancy loss attributed to women via, for example, genetically defective sperm, and that this contribution probably increases with paternal age (Hook 1986, Nortman 1974, Daniels & Weingarten 1979).

CONCLUSIONS

The findings assembled in this article can be distilled into two main facts. First, the proportion of women with low fecundity and infecundity increases steadily from age 15 to age 50, the age by which the vast majority of women have reached menopause. Second, this rise is moderate until the mid-30s when it begins to increase more sharply. These two facts are generally supported by results from both the NSFG and the historical studies (Mosher 1988). Nevertheless, the exact slope of the decline in fecundity with age among US women remains unknown (Hendershot et al 1982).

The fact that low fecundity and its three components—coital inability, conceptive failure, and pregnancy loss—all escalate around age 35 does not mean that most postponers have bleak prospects of having children beyond that age. The medical literature is increasingly optimistic about medicine's ability to thwart or circumvent the effects on fecundity of both aging and subfecundity factors (US Congress (OTA) 1988, Gindoff & Jewelewicz 1986), and the current consensus is that most healthy women in their late thirties have good prospects of giving birth to healthy infants and remaining well themselves (*Harvard Medical School Health Letter* 1985).

What the age-related data on low fecundity do mean, however, is that a substantial minority of postponers end up childless or with fewer children than they desired, as a result of reproductive impairment. This is true actually even for those who do not wait until age 35 or after to begin childbearing. As Menken and her associates (1976) conclude, evidence (from their seven-population study discussed above) indicates that the risk of being unable to bear a child seems to increase from about 6% at ages 20 to 24 to about 16% at ages 30 to 34. While these authors characterize this risk as not "great," nonetheless it does suggest that about 10% of previously fecund postponers become involuntarily childless due to infecundity. For those who delay childbearing until ages 35–39, the risk of involuntary childlessness rises to about 30%, thus about one in four postponers who are fecund at ages 20–24 becomes childless due to postponing childbearing. These outcomes generally apply to women who either abstain from sex or participate in a monogamous relationship before childbearing. Since many postponers in the United States do otherwise, the proportions ending up childless could be higher yet.

But the impact of low-fecundity is not limited to causing involuntary childlessness. Other postponers, although able to have at least one child, are unable to have the number they desire. The Menken & Larsen (1986) data set speaks directly to this point as well. It indicates that only 74% and 50%, respectively, of those who begin childbearing between ages 30–34 and 35–39, are able to have more than one child, as a result of infecundity. The fact that second and third order birth rates for women aged 30–34 and 35–39 all rose considerably during the 1980s (NCHS 1989b) indicates that this inability of many women to have second and third children is a serious individual and social problem.

One researcher sums the fecundity-impairment risks to delayed childbearing:

> I think the literature suggests that if a woman has never had gonorrhea, chlamydia, cervical infections or PID, has never used an IUD, is monogamous, and her husband's sperm count is normal, her risk in waiting till the *early* 30's is not large. However, if she waits until she is 35 or later, or she has had any of the above conditions, her risk may be larger than she realizes, particularly if she wants two children. (W. D. Mosher, personal communication)

Moreover, it is important to return to a theme struck in the introduction to this paper, that is, that low fecundity is only one of the forces that threaten the fertility of those who postpone childbearing. The other intermediate variables pose serious risks as well. And all of these risks interact with one another, sometimes in synergistic ways. This interaction is illustrated by the following excerpt from a case study (McFalls research in progress) of a former postponer who is done childbearing:

> I got married when I was 25. . . . During my late 20s I put off having children, not to any particular time, I just didn't want to have kids then. I had jobs but it wasn't that I had a great career going or anything; I just wanted to be free to do other things. . . . When I was 34 I decided it was time to have kids. I didn't feel then that my biological clock was running out or anything, although that may have been somewhere in the back of my mind. I was just ready for kids. I had no problem getting pregnant the first time, and I had my first child when I was 35. . . . I wanted two children so I tried again. . . . I had a miscarriage when I was 37 when I was about three months pregnant. That was an awful experience, and I was a little leary of getting pregnant again. But we wanted another child a lot, so we tried again. Didn't get pregnant after more than a year of trying. My doctor said I was probably okay. My husband got checked out and he was fine, so we kept trying and we had our second child when I was 39. . . . We enjoyed our first two kids so much we tried for a third. But I had another miscarriage at 40 and decided to call it quits. I couldn't hack a third miscarriage, and I was afraid that a third baby might not come out right.

This woman clearly had fecundity problems. But she probably could have had the third child if she had kept trying, especially if she had availed herself of the high-tech medical assistance that is now available to some of such women. The third child was prevented by contraception, but the remote cause was low fecundity. In any standard analysis the forgone child would be credited to contraception, but it is clear from her case history that it was the combination of the two forces.

In short, women who postpone childbearing run many risks of ending up childless or with fewer children than desired. At present the total risk is incalculable, but it is clearly substantial. Some authors have opined that this risk is worth it, given the liberating options opened up by delayed childbearing. Others have suggested that women must carefully assess the risks, costs, and benefits of the alternative choices (e.g. US Congress, Office of Technology Assessment 1988). That certainly would be rational and praiseworthy behavior.

But it is uncertain just how many women (and men) make this kind of rational, costs/benefits assessment of their reproductive plans. It may be that many, like the woman in the case history above, just put off childbearing to the indefinite future without any real sense of the magnitude of the risks involved. More research is obviously needed in this area. But the fact that the aforementioned gap between expected and actual childbearing continues to open up at the cohort level indicates that a sizeable minority of women are losing this game of reproductive roulette.

ACKNOWLEDGMENTS

The author is grateful to William Mosher and Judith Blake for their extremely helpful suggestions and comments. This work was partially supported by Villanova University.

Literature Cited

Anderson, B. A. 1975. Male age and fertility results from Ireland prior to 1911. *Popul. Index* 41:561–67

Aral, S. O., Cates, W. 1975. The increasing concern with infertility. Why now? *J. Am. Med. Assoc.* 250:2327–31

Bachrach, C. A., Horn, M. C. 1988. Sexual activity among U.S. women of reproductive age. *Am. J. Public Health* 78:320–21

Baldwin, W. H., Nord, C. W. 1984. Delayed Childbearing in the U.S.: Facts and fictions. *Popul. Bull.* 39(4):1–44

Bloom, D. E. 1982. What's happening to the age at first birth in the United States? A study of recent cohorts. *Demography* 19:351–70

Bloom, D. E., Trussell, J. 1984. What are the determinants of delayed childbearing and permanent childlessness in the United States. *Demography* 21:591–611

Bongaarts, J. 1982a. Infertility after age 30: A false alarm. *Fam. Plann. Perspect.* 14:75–78

Bongaarts, J. 1982b. Not so unresolved: A reply. *Fam. Plann. Perspect.* 14:289–90

Bongaarts, J., Potter, R. G. 1983. *Fertility, Biology, and Behavior.* New York: Academic

Daniels, P., Weingarten, K. 1979. A new look at the medical risks in late childbearing. *Wom. Health* 4:5–36

Davis, K. 1983. The future of marriage. *Bull. Am. Acad. Arts Sci.* 36:15–48

Davis, K., Blake, J. 1956. Social structure and fertility: An analytic framework. *Econ. Dev. Culture Change* 4:211–35

DeCherney, A. H., Berkowitz, G. S. 1982. Female fecundity and age. *N. Engl. J. Med.* 306:424–26

Ende, J., Rockwell, S., Glasgow, M. 1984. The sexual history in general medicine practice. *Arch. Int. Med.* 144:558–61

Ericksen, J., Ericksen, E., Hostetler, J., Huntington, G. 1979. Fertility patterns and trends among the Old Order Amish. *Popul. Stud.* 33:255–76

Erickson, D., Elliot, B. 1988. Pregnancy risk in women over 35. *Minn. Med.* 71:433–36

Fonteyn, V. J., Isada, N. B. 1988. Nongenetic implications of childbearing after age thirty-five. *Obstet. Gynecol. Surv.* 43:709–20

Forman, M. R., Meirik, O., Berendes, H. W. 1984. Delayed childbearing in Sweden. *J. Am. Med. Assoc.* 252:3135–39

Fortney, J. A. 1987. Contraception for American women 40 and over. *Fam. Plann. Perspect.* 19:32–34

Fortney, J. A., Higgins, J. E., Diaz-Infante, A., Batar, I. 1982. Childbearing after age 35: Its effect on early perinatal outcomes. *J. Biosoc. Sci.* 14:69–80

Frank, E., Anderson, C., Rubinstein, D. 1978. Frequency of sexual dysfunction in normal couples. *N. Engl. J. Med.* 299:111–15

Freedman, R., Whelpton, P., Campbell, A. 1959. *Family Planning, Sterility, and Population Growth.* Princeton: Princeton Univ. Press, 515 pp.

Fries, J. 1980. Aging, natural death, and the compression of morbidity. *N. Engl. J. Med.* 303:130–35

Gindoff, P. R., Jewelewicz, R. 1986. Reproductive potential in the older woman. *Fertil. Steril.* 46:989–1001

Goldman, N., Westoff, C., Hammerslough, C. 1984. Demography of the marriage market in the United States. *Popul. Index* 50:5–25

Hansluwka, H. 1975. Health, population, and socio-economic development. In *Population Growth and Economic Development is the Third World,* ed. L. Tabah. Liege, Belgium: Ordina. 816 pp.

Harvard Medical School Health Letter 1985. Pregnancy: Age and outcome. X (12):1–3

Hendershot, G. E. 1984. Maternal age and overdue conceptions. *Am. J. Public Health* 74:35–38

Hendershot, G. E., Mosher, W. D., Pratt, W. F. 1982. Infertility and age: An unresolved issue. *Fam. Plann. Perspect.* 14:287–89

Henry, L. 1961. Some data on natural fertility. *Eug. Q.* 8:81–91

Henshaw, S. K., Orr, M. T. 1987. The need and unmet need for infertility services in the U.S. *Fam. Plann. Perspect.* 19:180–86

Hirsch, M. B., Mosher, W. D. 1987. Characteristics of infertile women in the U.S. and their use of infertility services. *Fertil. Steril.* 47:618–25

Hook, E. B. 1986. Paternal age and effects on chromosomal and specific locus mutations. See Mastroianni & Paulsen 1986, pp. 117–45

James, W. H. 1979. The causes of the decline in fecundability with age. *Soc. Biol.* 26:330–34

Jones, B. J., Gallagher, B. J., McFalls, J. A. 1988. *Social Problems.* New York: McGraw Hill. 568 pp.

Katchadourian, H. A. 1989. *Fundamentals of Human Sexuality.* Fort Worth: Holt, Rinehart & Winston. 747 pp.

Kiely, J., Paneth, N., Susser, M. 1986. An assessment of the effects of maternal age and parity in different components of perinatal mortality. *Am. J. Epidemiol.* 123:444–54

Kinsey, A. C., Pomeroy, W. B., Martin, C. E. 1948. *Sexual Behavior in the Human Male.* Philadelphia: Saunders

Kirz, D. S., Dorchester, W., Freeman, R. K. 1985. Advance maternal age: The mature gravida. *Am. J. Obstet. Gynecol.* 152:7–12

Lehmann, D. K., Chism, J. 1987. Pregnancy outcome in medically complicated and uncomplicated patients aged 40 years or older. *Am. J. Obstet. Gynecol.* 157:738–42

Leridon, H. 1977. *Human Fertility: The Basic Components.* Chicago: Univ. Chicago Press

Levy, F., Michel, R. 1985. Are baby boomers selfish? *Am. Demog.* April: 38–41

Mansfield, P. K. 1986. Re-evaluating the medical risks of late childbearing. *Wom. Health* 11:37–60

Martin, T. C., Bumpass, L. L. 1989. Recent trends in marital disruption. *Demography* 26:37–51

Masters, W., Johnson, V. 1970. *Human Sexual Inadequacy.* Boston: Little Brown. 467 pp.

Mastroianni, L., Paulsen, C. A. 1986. *Aging, Reproduction, and the Climacteric.* New York: Plenum. 316 pp.

McFalls, J. A. 1976. Social science and the Collaborative Perinatal Project. *Rev. Public Data Use* 4:34–47

McFalls, J. A. 1979a. Frustrated fertility: A population paradox. *Popul. Bull.* 34 (2):1–44

McFalls, J. A. 1979b. *Psychopathology and Subfecundity.* New York: Academic. 264 pp.

McFalls, J. A., McFalls, M. H. 1984. *Disease and Fertility.* New York: Academic. 595 pp.

Menken, J. L. 1985. Age and fertility: How late can you wait? *Demography* 22:469–84

Menken, J. L., Larsen, U. 1986. Fertility rates and aging. See Mastroianni & Paulsen 1986, pp. 147–66

Menken, J. L., Trussell, J., Larsen, U. 1986. Age and infertility. *Science* 233:1389–94

Miall, C. E. 1986. The stigma of involuntary childlessness. *Soc. Prob.* 33:268–82

Minaker, K. L., Rowe, J. W. 1986. Methodological issues in clinical research on the aging reproductive system. See Mastroianni & Paulsen 1986, pp. 35–44

Mineau, G., Trussell, J. 1982. A specification of marital fertility by parents' age, age at marriage and marital duration. *Demography* 19:335–50

Mosher, W. D. 1985. Reproductive impairments in the United States, 1965–1982. *Demography* 22:415–30

Mosher, W. D. 1987. Infertility: Why business is booming. *Am. Demography* July:42–43

Mosher, W. D. 1988. Fertility and family planning in the United States: Insights from the National Survey of Family Growth. *Fam. Plann. Perspect.* 20:207–17

Mosher, W. D., Pratt, W. F. 1982. Reproductive impairments among married couples: United States. *Vit. Health Stat.* Series 23, No. 11. National Center for Health Statistics, Public Health Service. Washington: US Government Printing Office (USGPO)

Mosher, W. D., Pratt, W. F. 1987. Fecundity, infertility, and reproductive health in the United States, 1982. *Vit. Health Stat.* Series 23, No. 14. National Center for Health Statistics, US Public Health Service. Washington: USGPO

Naeye, R. L. 1983. Maternal age, obstetric complications, and the outcome of pregnancy. *Obstet. Gynecol.* 61:210–16

National Center for Health Statistics, (Bachrach, C. A., Horn, M. C.) 1987. Married and unmarried couples, United States, 1982. *Vit. Health Stat.* Series 23, No. 15. US Public Health Service. Washington: USGPO

National Center for Health Statistics. 1989a. Advance report of final divorce statistics, 1986. *Mon. Vit. Stat. Rep.* 38 (2) (suppl.)

National Center for Health Statistics 1989b. Advance report of final natality statistics, 1987. *Mon. Vit. Stat. Rep.* 36 (3) (suppl.)

Nieschlag, E., Michel, E. 1986. Reproductive functions in grandfathers. See Mastroianni & Paulsen 1986, pp. 59–71

Nortman, D. 1974. Parental age as a factor in pregnancy outcome and child development. *Rep. Popul./Fam. Plann.* 16:1–52

Pearl, R. 1939. *The Natural History of Population.* New York: Oxford Univ. Press

Petersen, W. 1975. *Population.* New York: Macmillan. 784 pp.

Poston, D., Kramer, K. 1980. Patterns of voluntary and involuntary childlessness in the United States, 1955–1973. *Texas Popul. Res. Ctr. Pap.* Ser. 3

Preston, S. 1983. Estimation of certain measures in family demography based upon generalized stable population relations. Pres. IUSSP Conf. on Family Demography, New York

Resnick, R. 1986. Age-related changes in gestation and pregnancy outcome. See Mastroianni & Paulsen 1986, pp. 167–75

Rindfuss, R. R., Bumpass, L. L. 1976. How old is too old? Age and the sociology of fertility. *Fam. Plann. Perspect.* 8:226–30

Rochat, R. W., Koonin, L. M., Atrash, H. K., Jewett, J. F. 1988. Maternal mortality in the United States: Report from the Maternal Mortality Collaborative. *Obstet. Gynecol.* 72:91–97

Schwartz, D., Mayaux, M. J. 1982. Female fecundity as a function of age. *N. Engl. J. Med.* 307:404–06

Schwartz, D., Mayaux, M. J., Spira, A., Moscato, M. L., Jouannet, P., et al. 1983. Semen characteristics as a function of age in 833 fertile men. *Fertil. Steril.* 39:530–35

Sherris, J. D., Fox, G. 1983. Infertility and sexually transmitted disease: A public health challenge. *Popul. Rep.* Series L, 4, 114–51

Spellacy, W. N., Miller, S. J., Winegar, A. 1986. Pregnancy after 40 years of age. *Obstet. Gynecol.* 68:452–54

Tietze, C. 1957. Reproductive span and rate of reproduction among Hutterite women. *Fertil. Steril.* 8:89–97

Toulemon, L. 1988. Historical overview of fertility and age. *Maturitas* (Suppl.) 1:5–14

Trussell, J., Wilson, C. 1985. Sterility in a population with natural fertility. *Popul. Stud.* 39:269–86

US Bureau of the Census. 1988. Marital Status and Living Arrangements, March 1987. *Curr. Popul. Rep.* Series P-20, no. 423. Washington: U.S. Department of Commerce

US Bureau of the Census. 1989. Fertility of American women: June 1988. *Curr. Popul. Rep.* Series P-20, No. 436. Washington: US Dep. Commerce

US Congress, Office of Technology Assessment 1988. *Infertility: Medical and Social Choices* (OTA-BA-358). Washington DC: USGPO

Ventura, S. 1982. Trends in first births to older mothers, 1970–79 National Center for Health Statistics. *Mon. Vit. Stat. Rep.* 31 (2): Supp. 2

Ventura, S. J. 1989. Trends and variations in first births to older women, 1979–86. National Center for Health Statistics. *Vit. Health Stat.* 21 (47)

Ventura, S. J., Taffel, S. M., Mosher, W. D. 1988. Estimates of pregnancies and pregnancy rates for the United States, 1976–85. *Am. J. Public Health* 78:506–11

Virro, M. R., Shewchuk, A. B. 1984. Pregnancy outcome in 242 conceptions after artificial insemination with donor sperm and effects of maternal age on the prognosis for successful pregnancy. *Am. J. Obstet. Gynecol.* 148:518–24

Warburton, D., Kline, J., Stein, Z., Strobino, B. 1986. Cytogenic abnormalities in spontaneous abortions of recognized conceptions. In *Perinatal Genetics: Diagnosis and Treatment,* ed. I. H. Porter, A. Wiley, pp. 133–51. New York: Academic

Whelpton, P. K., Kiser, C. 1946–1958. *Social and Psychological Factors Affecting Fertility.* New York: Milbank Memorial Fund. (1946, 1950, 1952, 1954, 1958)

Whelpton, P. K., Campbell, A. A., Patterson, J. E. 1966. *Fertility and Family Planning in the United States.* Princeton: Princeton Univ. Press. 443 pp.

Wilcox, A. J., Weinberg, C. R., O'Connor, J. F., Baird, D. D. et al. 1988. Incidence of early loss of pregnancy. *N. Engl. J. Med.* 319:189–94

Wilson, C., Oeppen, J., Pardoe, M. 1988. What is natural fertility? The modeling of a concept. *Popul. Index* 54:4–20

Wood, J. W., Weinstein, M. 1988. A model of age-specific fecundability. *Popul. Stud.* 42:85–113

Yasin, S. Y., Beydoun, S. N. 1988. Pregnancy outcome at greater than or equal to 20 weeks' gestation in women in their 40s: A case control study. *J. Reprod. Med.* 33:209–13

SUBJECT INDEX

CUMULATIVE INDEXES

Contributing Authors, Volumes 1–16

CHAPTER TITLES, VOLUMES 1–16

DIFFERENTIATION AND STRATIFICATION

ANNUAL REVIEWS INC.

A NONPROFIT SCIENTIFIC PUBLISHER

 4139 El Camino Way
P.O. Box 10139
Palo Alto, CA 94303-0897 • USA

ORDER FORM

ORDER TOLL FREE
1-800-523-8635
(except California)

Annual Reviews Inc. publications may be ordered directly from our office; through booksellers
and subscription agents, worldwide; and through participating professional societies. Prices
subject to change without notice. ARI Federal I.D. #94-1156476

- **Individuals:** Prepayment required on new accounts by check or money order (in U.S. dollars,
  check drawn on U.S. bank) or charge to credit card—American Express, VISA, MasterCard.
- **Institutional buyers:** Please include purchase order.
- **Students:** $10.00 discount from retail price, per volume. Prepayment required. Proof of student
  status must be provided (photocopy of student I.D. or signature of department secretary is
  acceptable). Students must send orders direct to Annual Reviews. Orders received through
  bookstores and institutions requesting student rates will be returned. You may order at the
  Student Rate for a maximum of 3 years.
- **Professional Society Members:** Members of professional societies that have a contractual
  arrangement with Annual Reviews may order books through their society at a reduced rate. Check
  with your society for information.
- **Toll Free Telephone orders:** Call 1-800-523-8635 (except from California) for orders paid by
  credit card or purchase order and customer service calls only. California customers and all other
  business calls use 415-493-4400 (not toll free). Hours: 8:00 AM to 4:00 PM, Monday-Friday,
  Pacific Time. **Written confirmation** is required on purchase orders from universities before
  shipment.
- **FAX: 415-855-9815 Telex: 910-290-0275**

Regular orders: Please list below the volumes you wish to order by volume number.
Standing orders: New volume in the series will be sent to you automatically each year upon
publication. Cancellation may be made at any time. Please indicate volume number to begin
standing order.
Prepublication orders: Volumes not yet published will be shipped in month and year indicated.
California orders: Add applicable sales tax.
Postage paid (4th class bookrate/surface mail) **by Annual Reviews Inc.** Airmail postage or UPS,
extra.

ANNUAL REVIEWS SERIES		Prices Postpaid per volume USA & Canada/elsewhere	Regular Order Please send:	Standing Order Begin with:
Annual Review of **ANTHROPOLOGY**			Vol. number	Vol. number
Vols. 1-16	(1972-1987)	$31.00/$35.00		
Vols. 17-18	(1988-1989)	$35.00/$39.00		
Vol. 19	(avail. Oct. 1990)	$39.00/$43.00	Vol(s). _____	Vol. _____
Annual Review of **ASTRONOMY AND ASTROPHYSICS**				
Vols. 1, 4-14, 16-20	(1963, 1966-1976, 1978-1982)	$31.00/$35.00		
Vols. 21-27	(1983-1989)	$47.00/$51.00		
Vol. 28	(avail. Sept. 1990)	$51.00/$55.00	Vol(s). _____	Vol. _____
Annual Review of **BIOCHEMISTRY**				
Vols. 30-34, 36-56	(1961-1965, 1967-1987)	$33.00/$37.00		
Vols. 57-58	(1988-1989)	$35.00/$39.00		
Vol. 59	(avail. July 1990)	$39.00/$44.00	Vol(s). _____	Vol. _____
Annual Review of **BIOPHYSICS AND BIOPHYSICAL CHEMISTRY**				
Vols. 1-11	(1972-1982)	$31.00/$35.00		
Vols. 12-18	(1983-1989)	$49.00/$53.00		
Vol. 19	(avail. June 1990)	$53.00/$57.00	Vol(s). _____	Vol. _____
Annual Review of **CELL BIOLOGY**				
Vols. 1-3	(1985-1987)	$31.00/$35.00		
Vols. 4-5	(1988-1989)	$35.00/$39.00		
Vol. 6	(avail. Nov. 1990)	$39.00/$43.00	Vol(s). _____	Vol. _____

ANNUAL REVIEWS SERIES	Prices Postpaid per volume USA & Canada/elsewhere	Regular Order Please send:	Standing Order Begin with:
		Vol. number	Vol. number

Annual Review of COMPUTER SCIENCE
Vols. 1-2	(1986-1987)...............$39.00/$43.00		
Vols. 3-4	(1988, 1989-1990)...........$45.00/$49.00	Vol(s). _____	Vol. _____

Annual Review of EARTH AND PLANETARY SCIENCES
Vols. 1-10	(1973-1982)...............$31.00/$35.00		
Vols. 11-17	(1983-1989)...............$49.00/$53.00		
Vol. 18	(avail. May 1990)...........$53.00/$57.00	Vol(s). _____	Vol. _____

Annual Review of ECOLOGY AND SYSTEMATICS
Vols. 2-18	(1971-1987)...............$31.00/$35.00		
Vols. 19-20	(1988-1989)...............$34.00/$38.00		
Vol. 21	(avail. Nov. 1990)...........$38.00/$42.00	Vol(s). _____	Vol. _____

Annual Review of ENERGY
Vols. 1-7	(1976-1982)...............$31.00/$35.00		
Vols. 8-14	(1983-1989)...............$58.00/$62.00		
Vol. 15	(avail. Oct. 1990)...........$62.00/$66.00	Vol(s). _____	Vol. _____

Annual Review of ENTOMOLOGY
Vols. 10-16, 18	(1965-1971, 1973)		
20-32	(1975-1987)...............$31.00/$35.00		
Vols. 33-34	(1988-1989)...............$34.00/$38.00		
Vol. 35	(avail. Jan. 1990)...........$38.00/$42.00	Vol(s). _____	Vol. _____

Annual Review of FLUID MECHANICS
Vols. 2-4, 7-19	(1970-1972, 1975-1987).......$32.00/$36.00		
Vols. 20-21	(1988-1989)...............$34.00/$38.00		
Vol. 22	(avail. Jan. 1990)...........$38.00/$42.00	Vol(s). _____	Vol. _____

Annual Review of GENETICS
Vols. 1-21	(1967-1987)...............$31.00/$35.00		
Vols. 22-23	(1988-1989)...............$34.00/$38.00		
Vol. 24	(avail. Dec. 1990)...........$38.00/$42.00	Vol(s). _____	Vol. _____

Annual Review of IMMUNOLOGY
Vols. 1-5	(1983-1987)...............$31.00/$35.00		
Vols. 6-7	(1988-1989)...............$34.00/$38.00		
Vol. 8	(avail. April 1990)...........$38.00/$42.00	Vol(s). _____	Vol. _____

Annual Review of MATERIALS SCIENCE
Vols. 1, 3-12	(1971, 1973-1982)...........$31.00/$35.00		
Vols. 13-19	(1983-1989)...............$66.00/$70.00		
Vol. 20	(avail. Aug. 1990)...........$70.00/$74.00	Vol(s). _____	Vol. _____

Annual Review of MEDICINE
Vols. 9, 11-15	(1958, 1960-1964)		
17-38	(1966-1987)...............$31.00/$35.00		
Vols. 39-40	(1988-1989)...............$34.00/$38.00		
Vol. 41	(avail. April 1990)...........$38.00/$42.00	Vol(s). _____	Vol. _____